THE UNION
IT MUST AND
SHALL BE
PRESERVED

JEWELRY *in* AMERICA

1600-1900

Frontispiece: Bracelet, yellow gold and diamonds, Tiffany & Co., 1865, designed by Major General Joshua L. Chamberlain (1828-1914) of Brunswick, Maine, for his wife on the occasion of their tenth anniversary and engraved inside the band 'Fannie C. Chamberlain / Dec. 7th 1865'. Enamelled in the flag colours of the United States and bordered with chased military cording. The bracelet bears a red Maltese cross on a white ground, the insignia of the 5th Corps Army of the Potomac which included the 20th Regiment, Maine Volunteers, commanded by Chamberlain. The arms of the cross are outlined with sixty-four small faceted diamonds and there is a solitaire diamond in the centre. On the opposite side is the design of Chamberlain's shoulder bar, two silver stars on a bright blue field, indicating his rank as Major General. The red and blue enamelling is applied to a guilloche ground. The band of the bracelet is formed of twenty-four struts in the shape of hour glasses which family tradition explains were symbolic of the weary hours of each day that he was away from his wife while he was engaged in battles, the names of which are engraved on the struts, beginning with Antietam and ending with the surrender at Appomattox Court House. Guard chain added later. 2 9/16in.x 2 5/8 x 11/16in. Gift of Chamberlain's granddaughter Eleanor Wyllys Allen. Bowdoin College Library.

JEWELRY *in* AMERICA

1600-1900

MARTHA GANDY FALES

ANTIQUE COLLECTORS' CLUB

ISBN 1 85149 223 2

British Library Cataloguing-in-Publication Data
A catalogue record for this book is available from the British Library

Printed in England
by the Antique Collectors' Club Ltd., Woodbridge, Suffolk
on Consort Royal Art paper
supplied by the Donside Paper Company, Aberdeen, Scotland

CONTENTS

Cameo portrait of George Washington, c.1800, signed by Teresa Talani who was born and trained in Rome, worked in Naples. Based on the Houdon life mask of Washington in the guise of a classical hero. Courtesy of D.S. Lavender Ltd., London.

CONTENTS continued

Gold and enamelled bracelet set with a miniature portrait of Samuel Blatchley Webb (see page 162). Photograph by John Giammatteo. The Webb-Deane-Stevens Museum.

Flower jewelry by Marcus & Co. (see page 394). Photograph by David Behl, New York. Private Collection.

Acknowledgements

My debt to those who aided in the preparation of this book is obvious in the length of the list that follows here.

Among the most rewarding public collections and the most helpful staff in New England, I thank particularly Paula B. Richter, Joan Parks Whitlow, Nancy Heyward, Kathy Flynn, H.A. Crosby Forbes, and Mary Silver Smith of the Peabody Essex Museum in Salem, Massachusetts; Jeannine Falino, Janis L. Staggs, Diana Larsen, Lauren D. Whitley, Yvonne J. Markowitz, Karen Otis and Mary Sluskonis of the Museum of Fine Arts, Boston; Susan Sinclair at the Isabella Stewart Gardner Museum in Boston; Anne E. Bentley and Christopher Steele of the Massachusetts Historical Society; Richard Nylander and Jane C. Nylander, Ann Clifford and Anne M. Donaghy of the Society for the Preservation of New England Antiquities; Sally R. Freitag, Sue Meyer and Lyn Voyda at the Worcester Art Museum; Bette Copeland and Erik C. Jorgensen at the Pejepscot Historical Society in Brunswick, Maine; and Robert F. Trent, Christine Bobish and Elizabeth Blakelock of the Connecticut Historical Society in Hartford, Connecticut.

In New York, Frances Gruber Safford, Eileen Sullivan and Deanna Cross of the Metropolitan Museum of Art greatly facilitated my requests, as did Deborah Dependahl Waters and Marguerite Lavin at the Museum of the City of New York. In addition, Deborah's doctoral dissertation on the precious metals trade shed light on the Philadelphia jewelers of the early nineteenth century and provided references to other pertinent materials. At the New-York Historical Society, I was assisted by Christine I. Oaklander and Jim Francis. At Tiffany & Company, Patricia L. Russo and Annamarie V. Sandecki generously lent their support. Ulysses G. Dietz and Margaret C. DiSalio of the Newark Art Museum provided long-distance support as did David Cassedy and Robert A. Harman at the Historical Society of Pennsylvania in Philadelphia.

At the Winterthur Museum in Wilmington, Delaware, I am grateful to Donald L. Fennimore, Eleanor Mc. D. Thompson and Karol A. Schmiegel, and further wish to acknowledge the important role played by the Winterthur Program in Early American Culture. Without the training I received there, learning the discipline of research and studying a very broad range of decorative arts in many different media, I would never have had the courage to undertake this book. The wide network of Winterthur graduates forty years later provided unexpected far-reaching benefits.

At the Smithsonian Institution, Shelley J. Foote, Kathryn Henderson and Felicia G. Pickering offered assistance. Christine Meadows and Karen Van Epps Peters at Mount Vernon in Virginia facilitated my study and further use of the significant collection of the Washington family jewelry, as did Kathaleen Betts at the Society of Cincinnati Headquarters in Washington, D.C.

At Colonial Williamsburg in Virginia, Beatrix T. Rumford, Carolyn J. Weekley,

Catherine H. Grosfils, Graham Hood, and John D. Davis amiably assisted; and The Museum of Early Southern Decorative Arts in Winston-Salem, North Carolina made their research sources available through Mrs. Whaley M. Batson, Bradford L. Rauschenberg, Rosemary N. Estes, Martha Rowe and Paula Locklair.

The Charleston Museum in South Carolina possesses an outstanding collection of American owned jewelry. Christopher T. Loeblein, Curator of History, kindly invited me to serve as Guest Curator of an exhibition of *Jewelry in Charleston: Two Centuries of Adornment,* thereby offering me the opportunity to study the collection and objects on loan in greater depth. He and his staff were tireless in providing information requested.

In New Orleans, Jessie Poesch armed me with introductions to a cadre of willing and able contributors including J. Burton Harter and Deena Bedigan at the Louisiana State Museum, H. Parrott Bacot at Louisiana State University Museum of Art, John W. Keefe at the New Orleans Museum of Art, and Judith H. Bonner at the Historic New Orleans Collection.

In Chicago, assistance was extended by Anndora Morginson and Lieschen A. Potuznik at the Art Institute of Chicago and by Gayle Strege and Susan Samek at the Chicago Historical Society. In California I was befriended by Edgar W. Morse and Michael Weller who generously shared the fruits of their own research.

The many individuals, whether collectors, curators or purveyors of pertinent information, who took their time to permit study and photography deserve special credit for their contributions as well:

Carol Aiken, Joan Bailey, David Beasley, Phyllis Berdos, Lynda Best, Lynn Blair, Stephen L. Bolin-Davis, Richard C. Borges, David C. Boyle, Joanna C. Britto, Marie T. Capps, Carolyn K. Carr, James W. Cheevers, Edwin A. Churchill, Jean L. Collier, Wendy A. Cooper, John Curtis, Philip N. Cronenwett, Nan A. Cumming, F. James Dallett, Suzanne Decker, Caroline Demaree, Lisa Denisevich, Dona Mary Dirham, Kristine Douglas, John H. Dryfhout, Richard Edgcumbe, Doris D. Fanelli, Daphne Farago, Dawn Ferguson, Nancy Finlay, Jeffrey Fitch, Holly Hurd Forsyth, Carl Francis, Jim and Donna-Belle Garvin, M.J. Gibbs, Charles Gilday, Charles A. Hammond, Mason Hammond, M.K. Harwood, Rebecca Haskell, Sinclair Hitchings, Neil W. Horstman, William N. Hosley, Jr., Kate Johnson, William R. Johnston, Pamela D. King, Tamatha Kuenz, Maria LaLima, Lee Langston-Harrison, Charles Langton, Ann LeVeque, Ruth Levin, David Revere McFadden, Pamela D. McTigue, Janet Mavec, Shannon Morse, Mrs. M.B. Mumford, Brenda Otto, Nicole Pelto, Jane C. Perham, Jennifer Presti, Penny Proddow, AnnMarie F. Price, Jules D. Prown, Susan Roberts-Manganelli, Diana Royce, Taria Sammons, Helen Sanger, Henry H. Schnabel, Jr., Dorothy Schwartz, Sarah J. Sibbald, Mary P. Smith, J. Peter Spang, Beth Ann Spyrison, Peggy M. Timlin, Robert C. Vose, Jr., Roberta Waddell, Suzanne Warner, William Waters, Joyce W. Wellford, Kendall F. Wiggin, Stephen A. Wilbur, John H. Wright, Philip Sea, Mark Zurolo

Others preferring anonymity are equally deserving of credit for their generosity even though their names cannot be included here.

Auction houses here and abroad played an important part in the learning process, with their published catalogues containing a trove of information, and their helpful suggestions. Especially supportive were Gloria Lieberman at Skinner's in Boston; Jeanne Sloane and her assistants at Christie's; and Wendell D. Garrett, Elisabeth D. Garrett, Melanie Brownrout and Julie Liepold at Sotheby's. Others in the trade who cheerfully shared their knowledge included Edith Weber, Andrew Nelson, Judith A. Keating, Geraldine Wolf, Neil Letson, and Roland B. Hammond in the United States, and David Callaghan of Hancock's, and Geoffrey Munn of Wartski in London.

Booksellers, largely through their detailed catalogues, led me to significant sources, books that formed the basic bibliography, as well as the random scarce items that explained the business of the jeweler. John and Marjorie Sinkankus of Peri Lithon Books, Joslin Hall, Peter L. Masi, Timothy Trace Booksellers, and F.M. O'Brien were especially helpful. I commend highly the United States Public Library system and its interlibrary loan program which allowed me to read books and microfilm that would otherwise have cost me dearly to utilise. The entire run of United States Patent Office Records from 1790-1900 was made available to me on microfilm by the University of Maine in Orono. Runs of city directories and newspapers on microfilm were sent to me from a legion of libraries throughout the country. My special thanks for their ingenuity and persistance go to Virginia Hopcroft, Brian Damien and Cynthia Arnold, research librarians at Curtis Memorial Library in Brunswick, Maine. The libraries of Bowdoin College have proved rich indeed and yielded a wealth of background materials. My thanks go especially to Dianne M. Gutscher and Susan B. Ravdin in Special Collections, and the staff in charge of the microfilm machines.

The Magazine *Antiques* which extends from 1922 to the present deserves special praise for their contributions over the years. Allison Eckhardt Ledes, editor, has been most helpful, publishing several of my articles on eighteenth and nineteenth century jewelry in America, which in turn brought forth letters and information from a number of readers. One respondent deserves special thanks: William A. Lanford, who inherited the design/account book of his great-great-great grandfather Henry W. Clapp, a New York jeweler in partnership with James Palmer from 1829-1833. This unusual survival, with its drawings of the gem-set jewelry they were producing and notations concerning which jewelers in their employ did the work, provided an amazingly detailed picture of diamond jewelry being produced in this country during those years. I am grateful to him for making a photographic copy of the book available for study purposes as well as for publication.

Through their research, lectures and publications, English jewelry historians have been exceedingly helpful. Judy Rudoe, Shirley Bury, Charlotte Gere, Hugh Tait, Vivienne Becker, Peter Hinks, Diana Scarisbrick deserve special mention. The Society of Jewellery Historians based in London, through its extensive programmes and scholarly publications, has been especially useful and enjoyable. The Society of Jewelry Historians USA in New York has provided a clearing house for information and activities for its members. My gratitude is also extended to Joseph and Ruth Sataloff who created the annual Antique Jewelry and Gemstone Course at the University of Maine in Orono. This series of lectures and workshops attracts people from all over the United States and other countries who bring their knowledge and enthusiasm to the programme.

Janet Zapata has been a constant source of encouragement and substantive assistance, selflessly passing on to me the discoveries of her own research and recommending other sources of information. Elenita C. Chickering, whose special expertise concerns Arthur J. Stone and the Arts & Crafts movement, has cheered me on, as has Katharine Watson Nyhus, Director of the Bowdoin College Museum of Art, who has kept an eye out for my interests. Peter L. Theriault spent days photographing objects from a variety of sources. Nancy C. Fales got me through my days of research in New York City, providing just the right combination of work and conviviality.

At the Antique Collectors' Club, Diana Steel and Primrose Elliott in England and Dan Farrell in New York have made the process of publishing the book as painless as possible in a most reassuring way.

As always, my biggest debt belongs to Dean who hoped I had finished writing books years ago. His interest in minerals and gems proved very enlightening to me. His love of travel got me to the places I needed to go to study jewelry. Most of all I thank him for his love and continuing defence of the English language which he maintains with a fierce sense of humour.

Colour Plate 1. In his pastel portrait of Mrs. Gawen Brown, John Singleton Copley of Boston eliminated the Countess of Coventry's elaborate head dress, fancy girandole earrings and her second necklace, while retaining the triple strand of pearls and her pose. This suggests that Copley's subjects were able to select the type and amount of finery that suited their own taste. Height 17½in., width 14½in. Bayou Bend Collection of Museum of Fine Arts, Houston, Texas.

Plate 1. Engraved portrait of Maria, Countess of Coventry, by Thomas Fry, 1761. This English print provided a model for American painter John Singleton Copley to use for his portrait of Mrs. Gawen Brown of Boston in 1763.

PREFACE

Jewelry, one of the first and most important forms of art, has long been considered one of the most enlightening sources of information about ancient civilizations. It informs the beholder of basic beliefs, customs, trade patterns and artistic creativity. What is useful for our study of ancient societies surely is useful for our knowledge of our own country. Countless books on the subject of American houses, furnishings and the fine arts of the nation appear each year. However, little has been said about jewelry owned by Americans, the very possessions that they prized most highly.

There are several explanations for this conspicuous absence. For one, jewelry passed down from one generation to the next is often kept locked away where it is hoped it will be safe. Over the years the materials used in its fabrication have become dull or tarnished, the foil used to back gems may have begun to disintegrate, and the stones themselves may have lost their sparkle because they have not been cleaned for years. When the safe box is opened, diamonds may look like paste and silver may look like base metal. Either the box is shut again or the jewelry is carted off to the jeweler to be remade or sold.

Jewelry is a very vulnerable possession. Until the modern era, jewelry was available to a relatively small proportion of the population. It was the object of greatest interest to the thief or plunderer. In times of war, it was often sacrificed for the cause or seized by invaders. At the time of the American Revolution, much of the valuable jewelry owned in the colonies was taken out of the country by fleeing Tories. During the Civil War, there were great losses, not only of old family jewelry, but also of recently purchased gems. Union Lieutenant Thomas J. Myers of Boston wrote to his wife from his camp near Camden, South Carolina, on 26 February 1865, 'Tell Sallie I am saving a pearl bracelet and earrings for her'. These pieces of jewelry were part of a set that was confiscated from the daughters of the man who had presided over the convention of the South Carolina secession. Another soldier got the matching necklace and breast pin.[1]

Jewelry is one of the most demanding and complex of all the arts to study. It is made of an endless variety of materials, genuine and imitative, and requires specialized knowledge of gems and minerals. Jewelry is also the most international of arts in both substance and form, and cuts across national boundaries. In order to present a balanced and realistic picture of the jewelry used in America, imported jewelry is discussed simultaneously with the jewelry that was made there. Not only does this give a more accurate picture, but it also allows a better understanding of American preference and production.

The role of the jeweler is an important part of the total picture. In the past there has been confusion concerning who was a gold- or silversmith and who was a jeweler. Americans often called themselves by both names and indeed often performed both functions, especially in regions that could barely support a single craftsman. Often the jeweler could make silver spoons and the silversmith could set a jewel in a gold ring. However, even in the seventeenth century, both goldsmiths and jewelers appeared in their separate roles in the largest towns. Both augmented their own production with imports of foreign goods, primarily English goods until after the Revolution. With increased American production, a distinction was made between manufacturing jewelers and retail jewelers. By the middle of the nineteenth century, a further distinction was made for wholesale jewelers. By that time, too, there were many who performed specialist jobs such as assaying, casting, repoussé, finishing and engraving. Both handmade and factory productions are considered in this study.

Locating examples of antique jewelry owned by Americans, as well as the documentary information regarding its history, has been a veritable treasure hunt no less exciting than archaeological expeditions. Museums, historical societies and private collections throughout the country have been mined for appropriate information and illustrations, most of which have never been published before. Information has been gleaned from a wide range of sources, including advertisements, accounts, letters, newspapers, contemporary literature, fashion and trade magazines, designs, patent records and auction catalogues. Original boxes bearing the imprint of the jeweler who sold the objects and marks of makers on pieces of jewelry have been particularly useful. An attempt has been made to tell the story from the viewpoint of those living at the time the jewelry was made and used.

Pictures of Americans wearing jewelry have been especially illuminating and illustrate not only what was worn but how it was worn. The question arises as to whether the sitters actually owned the jewelry that appears in their paintings. The answer is yes, most of the time. Early American portraiture is distinguished by its realism and accuracy. Furthermore, enough jewelry has been handed down to the present day together with the portraits themselves to illustrate the faithfulness of the rendition.

The paintings of John Singleton Copley, whose many portraits have been identified, collated and studied in great detail, reveal that he copied the strings of pearls that festooned the hair and necks of his American sitters from the popular English copperplate engravings in circulation in the mid-eighteenth century (Colour Plate 1 and Plate 1). However, as he gained confidence, he no longer relied so heavily on these pictures. Additionally, some of the jewelry in the prints was minimized or eliminated, indicating that the sitters were able to choose how much and what kind of jewelry they would like to have in their portraits. Copley appears to have had strings of artificial pearls and flowered aigrettes on hand in his studio for his sitters to use if they desired. The same ornaments appear again and again in his early paintings. However, looking at all his portraits, it becomes evident that the jewelry that appears only once in his paintings was probably the property of the sitter. Copley enjoyed the challenge of correctly representing different kinds of textures and materials. His success in making clear what the jewelry was made of is another indication of the greatness of his painting and an added bonus for the jewelry historian.

In the Colonial period, Americans were usually portrayed in their daytime clothing. Showy elaborate jewelry was considered inappropriate unless worn in the evening or on state occasions. In the late eighteenth and nineteenth century, this custom gradually changed so that elaborate accessories such as jewelry were frequently included in portraits. Portraits sometimes disclose local attitudes toward types of jewelry and the manner of wearing it. For example, in nineteenth century Louisiana, women liked to be portrayed wearing their gold or silver spectacles, apparently considering them desirable ornaments.

A word must be said concerning the American spelling of jewelry and jeweler. During the colonial period the preferred spelling followed the English practice of doubling the final consonant. With independence the spelling in this country gradually changed from jewellery and jeweller to jewelry and jeweler. The English spelling of these words is retained when original sources are being quoted.

The purpose of this book is to identify, document and illustrate the most prevalent forms of jewelry owned and worn in the United States from 1600 to 1900, whether it was made here or imported at the time. The jewelry is discussed in chronological order to clarify technological and stylistic changes. Wherever appropriate, the history and significance of these precious objects is told in the words of contemporary owners and observers. A discussion of the role played by individual jewelers accompanies each of the four major divisions.

This is the first book to be devoted to the subject and, while an effort has been made to be comprehensive but selective, there will no doubt be omissions and misplaced emphases. Many significant examples of American jewelry still lie hidden in secret places, unrecognized, unidentified and unappreciated. When these objects were purchased, they represented something very precious – a special relationship, a milestone, an expression of love, or even a tangible form of one's deepest thoughts and attitude toward life. It is hoped that this book will light the way to an understanding of what was considered important to our ancestors, illuminating another important facet of our country's history.

Martha Gandy Fales
1995

Portrait of Elizabeth Eggington, 1664 (see page 21). Gift of Walter H. Clark, Wadsworth Atheneum, Hartford, Conn.

PART I

COLONIAL JEWELRY 1600–1775

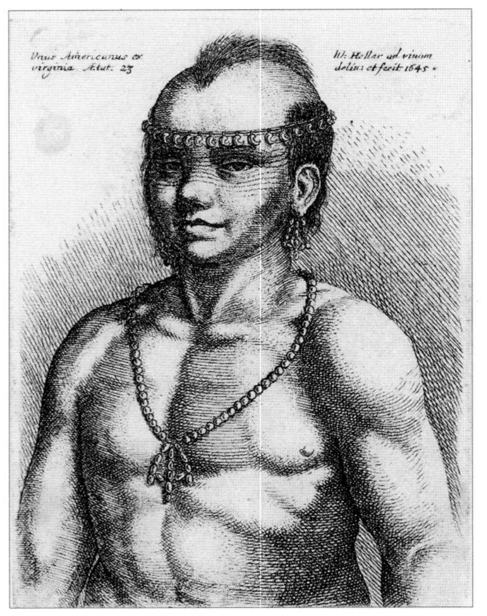

Plate 2. Etching of a Virginian native, drawn from life by Wenceslaus Hollar (1607-1677) and published in Antwerp in 1645. The twenty-three year old man wears a necklace and earrings of round and elliptical pearls with tripartite pendants of a distinct design. He also wears a bandeau of small animal claws and has tattoo marks around his eyes. Length 4⅛in., width 3⅛in. Massachusetts Historical Society.

Early Colonial

Man's exploration of new realms has forever been motivated by the hope of finding something of value (Colour Plate 2). In the golden age of exploration of the fifteenth century, European ships probed the world seeking overseas routes to the fabulous Indies described several centuries earlier by Marco Polo. The Spanish and Portuguese met with great success in South and Central America where the Maya, Mixtec and Inca had found gold beyond belief. It is little wonder that the reports coming back from these successful expeditions inspired the English, Dutch and French to search for areas to exploit and colonize themselves.

Before the Europeans came to this area, the natives still lived in a primitive state of civilization. Like all paleolithic and neolithic human beings, these indigenous people adorned themselves with objects they found, such as shells, teeth, small bones, pebbles, fossils and feathers (Plate 2).

Investigations of the Mound Builders in the Eastern Woodlands reveal a greater development than that of the Indians living in subsistence areas along the coast where initial contact was made with the Europeans. Because the Indians were migrating people, there was continuous cultural contact between native groups. This resulted in an exchange of materials used for jewelry such as seashells from both the Atlantic and Pacific Oceans, turquoise and copper.

Few accurate representations exist of Indians of the early colonial period. Most helpful are the drawings of Jacques Le Moyne in Florida in 1564 and those of John

---

Colour Plate 2. Contrasting the differences in costume and ornamentation between people of the old and the new world, this engraving is taken from a watercolour by Jacques le Moyne, authorized staff artist of the second expedition of René de Laudonnière which arrived in Florida in June 1564. It was engraved by Theodore de Bry for his book America *published in Germany c.1590-1595. Laudonnière is shown with chief Athore. Length 13⅛in., width 9⁷⁄₁₆in. Massachusetts Historical Society.*

Colour Plate 3. Group of pendants, featuring Christian symbolism, buried in the 16th century with Indians who had been converted by the Spanish at St. Catherine's Mission on the south-eastern coast of the Carolinas. Length (cross) about 7in. Photograph by Bill Ballenberg. National Geographic Society.

Plate 3. Part of a gold ring, c.1620-1650, found in an archaeological dig at Flowerdew Hundred, in Hopewell, Virginia. The English ring is stamped with a strong chevron pattern. Flowerdew Hundred Foundation.

White in Virginia between 1585 and 1590, which were engraved and printed by Theodore de Bry in 1590. In these pictures the Florida Indians wore conical headdresses, feathers, double earbobs, and elaborate tattoos. They had necklaces, wristlets, and anklets made of beads. The Virginia Indians likewise wore beads along with their tattoos and bone earplugs. Indian women wore double rings in their ears and noses.

With the arrival of Europeans on the eastern coast of North America, Indian adornment quickly began to change in the areas of contact. Along the Carolina coast, sixteenth century Spaniards brought rings, crosses and medals bearing symbols of their Catholic faith which the natives prized highly enough to have buried with them (Colour Plate 3). Quantities of glass trade beads made in Venice and Amsterdam were brought by the explorers and colonists to placate and to barter. These were soon turned into articles of jewelry by the Indians.

Contrast this pictorial information with the report circulated in England in 1605: 'I tell thee, gold is more plentiful there than copper is with us...Why, man, all their dripping pans and their chamber pots are pure gold...and for rubies and diamonds they go forth on holidays and gather 'em by the seashore to hang on their children's coats.'[1] Such was the propaganda urging Englishmen to settle in America so that they too could enjoy the same wealth of gold and jewels found by the Spanish in Central and South America.

As a result, the response was amazingly successful. A jeweler, two refiners and two goldsmiths joined the other would-be settlers who came to Virginia in 1608 on the *Phoenix*. Their disillusionment must have been enormous. Captain John Smith reported that these men never had a chance to exercise their craft because there were no precious metals or jewels except for the paltry pearls that were found in the abundant oysters. Smith blamed the backers of the Virginia Company for being concerned only with immediate profit in 'sending us so many Refiners, Gold-smiths, Iewellers, Lapidaries, Stone-cutters,...with all their appurtenances but materialls...'[2] As the American colonies burgeoned, these craftsmen continued to arrive and, in due course, through trade, the necessary materials became available here.

The first jewelry owned by the settlers was brought with them from the old world (Plate 3). Jewelry could be worn or even sewn into the seams or pockets of clothing and so was much more portable than sacks of coins; being of greater value per ounce, jewelry provided a better form of negotiable wealth in an uncertain country.

In 1628 Walt Bagnall, the first settler on Richmond Island off Cape Elizabeth in Maine, brought with him a gold ring (Colour Plate 4) as well as some coins. These he hid in an earthenware jar and buried in the ground for safekeeping. English-made, the betrothal ring was engraved inside 'United hearts death only partes'. It is similar in basic design to the ring given by Mary, Queen of Scots, to Lord Darnley at the time of their engagement in 1565. The oval bezel on Bagnall's ring is engraved with the initials G V divided by a shaft with a lover's knot at the base and a pretty looped border.[3]

A gold ring that was worn by Barbara Ilsley when she came from England to Newbury, Massachusetts, in 1638 is still owned by a descendant. It had a true-lover's knot under the central stone with a small stone on either side.

Seals set in rings provided early Americans with a means of establishing their identity through symbolic emblems, devices and initials which they used to mark their legal documents and correspondence. Signet rings can be seen in portraits of

1. George Chapman and John Marston, *Eastward Ho*, 1605 cited in *The Magazine Antiques*, May 1978, p. 1033.
2. *The Travels, Adventures and Observations of Captain John Smith*, from the London edition of 1629, I, 169. *Capt. John Smith, Advertisements: or The Pathway to Experience to Erect a Plantation* (Ivor Noël Hume, *Here Lies Virginia*, p. 212).
3. In 1631 Bagnall was killed by the Indians with whom he had been trading. It was not until 1855 that farmers ploughed up the earthenware jar containing the ring and coins dating from 1568 and 1625. Maine Historical Society Library published account.

Plate 4. Portrait of John Leverett (1616-1679) by unidentified artist, probably painted in England when Leverett was there from 1655 to 1662. Born in Boston, England, John Leverett migrated to Massachusetts in 1633 where he served as Governor of the Colony from 1673 to 1679. His gold signet ring (Colour Plate 5) is shown in his portrait. He wears the ring on the little finger of his left hand. The cornelian setting is engraved with the same heraldic design featured in the upper right corner of the portrait and includes three leverets (young hares), a rebus of the Governor's surname. In addition, Leverett wears a large belt buckle and an ornamented sword. Oil on canvas, 43½in. x 35in. Peabody Essex Museum, Salem, Massachusetts.

colonists such as John Leverett (1616-1679) who came to Massachusetts in 1633. He distinguished himself in matters mercantile and military, becoming Deputy Governor of the Colony during King Philip's War and Governor from 1673 until his death in 1679. Both his portrait (Plate 4) and the ring (Colour Plate 5) were acquired in England, probably during his sojourn there from 1655 to 1662. This signet ring was engraved on cornelian with the same heraldic display seen in the upper right section of his portrait. The armorial motif was a rebus of the Governor's surname, a leveret being a hare in its first year.[4]

Captain John Freake, when he died in 1675, had 'His own Signet [ring] and Sett of Gould Buttons'.[5] His portrait at the Worcester Art Museum reveals that, like Leverett, he also wore his ring on his little finger, as did Edward Winslow whose portrait of 1651 is at Pilgrim Hall in Plymouth, Massachusetts.

4. There was a skull on the seal above the helmet crest and mantling. The same arms appear on Leverett's tomb in King's Chapel, Boston.

5. John Marshall Phillips, *American Silver*, p. 26.

Colour Plate 4. Gold signet ring (two views), made in England, late 16th century, which was buried on Richmond Island, on the coast of Maine near Portland, probably by Walt Bagnall who was killed by Indians in 1631. The ring had been placed in a jug with twenty-one gold pieces (the earliest dated 1602) and thirty-one silver coins (the earliest dated 1564) and the latest was struck in 1625. This trove was dug up by a plough in 1855. The ring is engraved on the bezel with the initials G V with a cord passing between, a tie at the tip and a lover's knot below. Inside the band is engraved 'United [conjoined hearts] death only partes'. Diameter ⅞in. Maine Historical Society.

Colour Plate 6. Portrait of Mrs. John Freake and daughter Mary, c.1671-1674, painted by an unidentified American artist. Mrs. Freake is adorned with a double strand of pearls, a four-strand bracelet made of jet or glass beads, and a gold ring on her thumb, probably her wedding ring. Height 42½ in., width 36¾in. Gift of Mr. and Mrs. Albert W. Rice. Worcester Art Museum.

Colour Plate 5. Gold signet ring set with cornelian engraved with the arms of Governor John Leverett, probably purchased in England in the mid-17th century. Both ring and coat of arms can be seen in the portrait of Leverett (Plate 4.) Diameter 1in. Seal ⅝in. x ⅝in. Photograph by Mark Sexton. Peabody Essex Museum, Salem, Massachusetts.

Rings bearing the family arms were often bequeathed from father to son. Charles Frost of Kittery, one of Maine's wealthier residents in 1724, left his eldest son and namesake his seal ring, as well as his best plate hilted sword, his silver tobacco box, and his best plate hatband. To his son John he left his other plate hat band and plate hilted sword. To son Simon he gave his watch, silver seal and silver-hilted scimitar. Youngest son Eliot got all his father's gold rings other than his seal rings. The gifts provide an idea of what the well dressed seventeenth century gentleman might have worn in colonial America.[6]

Ornaments for men, as early portraits and inventories suggest, consisted largely of rings, big fancy buttons, buckles, watches, gold-headed canes and silver-hilted swords. Until the Renaissance the wearing of jewelry had been the prerogative of nobility and wealthy men. By the end of the seventeenth century, women were beginning to outshine untitled men.

Captain Freake's wife Elizabeth (Colour Plate 6) was portrayed in the 1670s wearing a gold ring on her thumb, a two-strand necklace of pearls, and a four-strand bracelet of black beads, possibly made of jet. 'Jett' was included on the list of rates for products

Colour Plate 7. A rich gem-set pendant, an elaborate gold and pearl necklace, a tear drop pearl suspended from the knot of her hood, and a ring all add elegance to the portrait of Elizabeth Eggington, 1664, and testify to the fact that hers was a family of wealth. The pendant with dangling pearls is set with a painted miniature perhaps of her father Jeremiah Cotton, son of the Puritan Divine John Cotton, who came from England to Boston, Massachusetts, in 1633. Elizabeth was born in 1656 and died in 1664, the year her portrait was painted by an unidentified artist in the Boston area. Height 36¼in., width 29½in. Gift of Walter H. Clark, Wadsworth Atheneum, Hartford, Conn.

imported and exported to the Colonies that the House of Parliament established in 1660. Other jewelry listed included beads made of amber, bone, box, coral, crystal, glass, wood, and jasper; bracelets or necklaces 'Red or of glass'; ivory; and watches.[7]

Amber necklaces were owned by a number of seventeenth century American women like Elizabeth Tatham of New Jersey, whose inventory of 1700 included an amber necklace as well as ivory and tortoise combs.[8] Mrs. Mary Anderson of Accomack County, Virginia, owned two amber necklaces.[9] This light resinous material had long been invested with therapeutic qualities and, as late as the nineteenth century, was burned to cleanse the air for the sick. In Boston in 1711, an amber necklace was stolen from the wife of Captain John Bonner.[10] One early amber necklace had cylindrical beads turned in such a way that when strung they resembled the spool turnings on seventeenth century furniture.[11]

There was, in general, an intrinsically utilitarian aspect to much of the jewelry worn in the British colonies in the seventeenth century, no doubt brought about by the simplicity of life in the new world as well as the effects of the Reformation and the Civil War in England. In addition, old world governments had passed sumptuary laws in an effort to regulate the kind and amount of jewelry that could be worn by nobles and the rising middle class.

Nevertheless, the variety and value of jewelry owned by the more affluent colonists continued to increase with each generation. Puritan John Cotton's grand-daughter Elizabeth Eggington (Colour Plate 7) was portrayed in 1664 wearing an intricately tiered gold necklace with pendant pearls, a ring on her right hand, a fan in her left hand and, most importantly, a rich, enamelled gold brooch, set with a miniature portrait (possibly of her father) ringed by what appear to be rubies or garnets and hung with baroque pearls. By the mid-seventeenth century, English jewelers and their patrons favoured the use of miniature portraits in the tradition of Nicholas Hilliard and Hans Holbein. Pendants like Elizabeth's were derived from late Renaissance jewelry designs popularized by engravers whose prints carried the style throughout Europe.

6. *Maine Wills*, p. 259.
7. Dow, *Every Day Life*, pp. 246-257.
8. Lois Given, 'The Great and Stately Palace,' *The Pennsylvania Magazine of History and Biography*, July 1959, *LXXXIII*, p. 269.
9. *Virginia Wills &c. 1692-1715*, p. 330, 8 Dec. 1703, Museum of Early Decorative Art, Winston-Salem, N.C.
10. *Boston N-L*, 5-12 Mar. 1710/11, cited by Dow, *Every Day*, p. 68.
11. The necklace was given by the Reverend John Smith to his wife Mary Cleveland in the 18th century. Colonial Dames, Boston.

As Elizabeth Eggington's portrait suggests, jewelry set with precious stones was owned in America during the seventeenth century. Diamond rings were occasionally listed in the inventories of estates of well-to-do men and women throughout the Colonies. Anne Hibbins of Boston owned a diamond ring which was listed in her inventory of 1652. A diamond ring and mourning ring valued at £3 were listed in the inventory of Robert Richbell in 1682.[12] In Lower Norfolk County, Virginia, a wealthy planter was recorded as owning at the time of his death a sapphire set in gold, a diamond ring with several sparks, and a silver-set beryl, as well as lesser rings set with blue, yellow and green stones, and an amber necklace.[13] Both Edmund Custis of Virginia and his sister Tabitha inherited diamond rings from their father in 1702. Tabitha also received gold lockets (one of which was engraved with her name and the date 1687), a silver crucifix and a pearl necklace.[14]

Dutch colonists had a particular fondness for diamond jewelry. 'They sparkle in rings, lockets, earrings, chains and pendants of various descriptions' reported one chronicler.[15] In New York in 1682 Mrs. Jacob de Lange owned a significant amount of diamond jewelry:

> one gold boat, wherein thirteen diamonds & one white coral chain,
> one pair gold stucks or pendants each with ten diamonds
> two diamond rings
> one gold ring or hoop bound round with diamonds.[16]

In 1693 in New York, widow Christina Cappoens bequeathed a gold rose-cut diamond ring to her daughter Maria and a gold finger ring set with a diamond to her grand-daughter Sara Molenaer. The local goldsmith who made the appraisal, Jacobus van der Spiegel, valued the rose-cut diamond ring at £5 and 'the gold ear pendant and jewels weighing '2 oz. good' at £5 per ounce, £10.'[17]

Madam Sarah Knight, travelling to New York in 1704, contrasted the Dutch residents there with what she considered were the more fashionably dressed English colonists, noting that the Dutch women 'especially the middling sort,...go loose, wear French muches, which are like a cap and a head band in one, leaving their ears bare, which are set out with jewels of a large size and many in number; and their fingers hooped with rings, some with large stones in them of many colors, as were their pendants in their ears, which you should see very old women wear as well as young'.[18]

The Puritan ethic undoubtedly led to greater restraint. Many New Englanders were content with a gold, silver, or enamelled ring, and silver or gold buttons and buckles. Others like Mrs. Ursula Cutt[s] of Portsmouth, New Hampshire, owned agate pendants, a seed pearl necklace, four gold rings and twelve dozen silver and gold breast buttons which she kept in her chest of drawers in 1694.[19] By the end of the century, Mrs. Samuel Shrimpton of Boston possessed a diamond girdle buckle as well as three diamond rings, a pearl necklace, a gold locket and watch chain.[20]

Seventeenth century jewelry in America ranged from latten and gilt brass rings like those that have been found at the earliest sites of settlement in Plymouth, Massachusetts, and in Virginia, to diamond and pearl jewelry known to us today primarily through documentary evidence and early portraits. Most, but not all of it, was brought from the old world. By the latter part of the seventeenth century American-made jewelry began to make its presence known.

12. Anne Hibbins, 1652, *Suffolk County Probate Records,* iv. 51; Robert Richbell, 1682, *v.* 59.
13. Cited by Elizabeth McClellan, *Historic Dress in America 1607-1800*, p. 72, 110.
14. Accomack County, *Virginia Wills &c. 1692-1715,* p. 287a, 26 Mar. 1702, MESDA.
15. Edward Warwick and Henry Pitz, *Early American Costume*, p. 164.
16. Cited by McClellan, pp. 133-34.
17. Cited by Phillips, p. 38.
18. *Antiques*, Nov. 1973, p. 877.
19. Ibid., July 1970, p. 58.
20. Lillian B. Miller, 'The Puritan Portrait' in *Seventeenth Century New England*, pp. 177-178.

Plate 5. Mourning ring, gold, made in 1693 in Boston, by Jeremiah Dummer (1645-1718) in memory of James Lloyd who died on 21 August 1693. Barbed diagonal chasing and a convex outer surface give the ring the appearance of a wreath. Traces of black enamel remain in the chased areas. Marked inside band with the goldsmith's initials ID in a rectangle. Diameter ¾in. Courtesy, Winterthur Museum.

MOURNING, LOVE AND FANCY PIECES

Mourning

Today the concept of mourning jewelry is thought by some to be morbid. In the colonial period, however, death was ever present. In the best of circumstances life expectancy averaged about half what it is today. It is little wonder that people spent a great deal of time thinking about death. Mourning jewelry provided a tangible link to the souls who had gone before and served as a constant reminder to the wearer of the fragility of their own human mortality. The ring was a symbol of eternity and that comforted them.

As was the custom in the Middle Ages, rings were made for presentation to close relatives and friends at funerals. This tradition was given momentum in England by the execution of Charles I in 1649. Royalists showed their loyalty by wearing rings and pendants bearing enamelled miniature portraits of their respected leader.[1] At first, the decedent's own jewels were distributed at funerals but, as the practice grew, jewelry was made especially for the purpose of presentation. Often rings were provided by the will of the deceased and the costs charged to the estate. Mrs. Jane Kind who died in 1705 gave by will

> to the wives of Mr. Increase Mather, Mr. Cotton Mather and the wife of Stephen French jun., of Weymouth and to Sarah Knight, to each of them a Ring of Twenty Shillings value...I give unto my Grandaughter Mary Harrison and my two Great Grandaughters Sarah Guille & Katherine Guille to each of them Three a Ring of Twenty Shillings value...

Probate Court records show payment by the executors of her estate to goldsmith John Dixwell of Boston 'for Rings given in the dec'd's will [£]13..1..6.'[2]

Mourning rings are the earliest marked pieces of jewelry made by American goldsmiths and jewelers. It may seem unusual that so many early mourning rings were marked by American makers when most jewelry of the colonial period was unmarked. However, in this matter they were simply following the requirements of the craft in their mother land. According to the regulations of the goldsmiths' guild in England during this period, mourning rings were the only items of jewelry that were required to be marked.[3]

The earliest known example of a marked mourning ring in America was made by Jeremiah Dummer, the first American-born and American-trained goldsmith (Plate 5). Made for the funeral of James Lloyd in 1693, its solid gold band was flat on the inside and rounded on the outside. A simple diaper pattern was chased around the sides and accentuated with black enamel, which gave the ring the appearance of a braided wreath. Inside the memorial was engraved 'Iames Lloyd. Obyt.21. Augt 1693'.

1. Vivienne Becker, *Antique & 20th Century Jewellery*, p. 84.
2. Biggs, Hummel and Lanier, Some Sidelights on Early Boston Silver and Silversmiths, *Winterthur Newsletter*, 24 Oct. 1958, p. 7.
3. Rolt, *A New Dictionary of Trade & Commerce*, section on 'Goldsmith'.

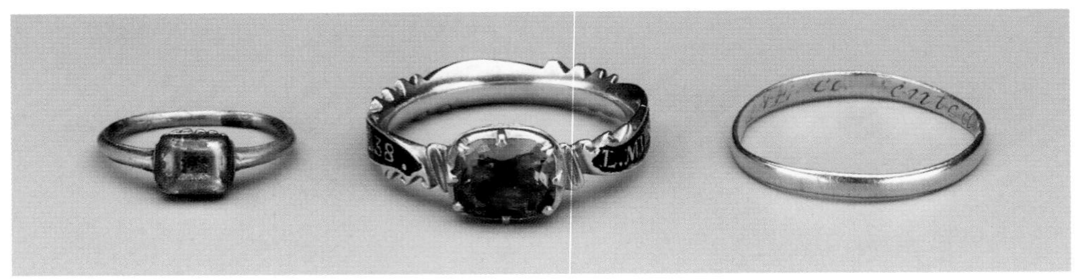

Colour Plate 8. Three gold rings attributed to Paul Revere (1735-1818) of Boston. Mourning ring (centre), 1768, set with faceted amethyst, in memory of Lucretia Murray for whom Revere had made silver. Diameter ½in. Bequest of Maxim Karolik. Plain gold wedding ring (right), c.1773, inscribed inside '[L]ive Co[n]tented' was owned by Revere's wife Rachel Walker. Diameter ¹¹⁄₁₆in. (The ring has been enlarged for a subsequent owner.) Gift of Mrs. Henry B. Chapin and Edward H.R. Revere. Also owned by Mrs. Revere was the rectangular crystal and cypher ring (left). Diameter ½in. Pauline Thayer Revere Collection. Courtesy, Museum of Fine Arts, Boston.

The following year Dummer's colleague, John Coney, made a gold ring (Plate 6, upper left) embossed with a death's head, sadly it seems, for his own wife Sarah who had died on 17 April 1694. Coney's inventory, taken at the time of his death in 1722, included jeweler's tools such as ring swages, as well as numerous tools used in fashioning silver objects.[4]

Judge Samuel Sewall was among the most frequent recipients of funeral rings. In his diary Sewall listed the fifty-seven rings he received between 1687 and 1725. If he was not able to attend the service, he noted the *memento mori* that he had missed. That these rings were made in large numbers can be verified by John Coney's charges to Peter Sergeant for making thirty gold rings in three different weights for one funeral. Obviously not all the bereaved were created equal.[5] At one funeral in Boston in 1738, two hundred gold rings costing more than a pound each were given away.[6]

Periodically, the Massachusetts General Court attempted to restrict the amount that could be spent on funerals and gifts, but the custom not only continued, it flourished. In 1758 one Salem minister, Dr. Samuel Buxton, was able to leave his heirs a quart

4. Hermann Frederick Clarke, *John Coney, Silversmith (1655-1722),* between pp. 12 and 13.
5. Curwen Family Mss., Library, Peabody Essex Museum, Salem, Mass.
6. Alice Morse Earle, *Two Centuries of Costume in America,* II, 655.

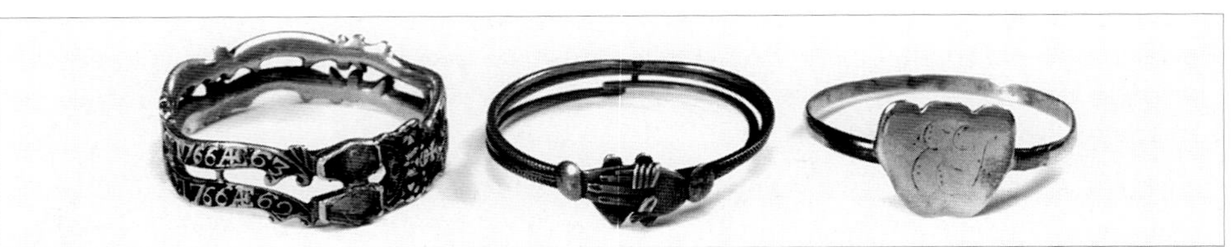

Plate 6. Left. Group of colonial Massachusetts mourning rings made for funerals in Salem and one in Boston. The earliest (upper left) was made by John Coney in memory of his wife Sarah who died in Boston in 1694. It was decorated with a Death's head as was the ring (upper right) memorializing Nathaniel Ropes of Salem by David Northey in 1752. Two rings (centre row) were made for William Pickman's funeral in 1735. One was set with a square stone and the other with a rectangular stone over a paper skeleton. The ring (lower left) made in memory of Timothy Orne of Salem in 1767 was embellished with openwork around three stones. William Hunt, Jr., was remembered in 1769 by a ring (lower right) with a central stone cut in the shape of a coffin and set over the image of a full-length skeleton, and flanked by small stones. Photograph by Mark Sexton. Peabody Essex Museum, Salem, Massachusetts.

Plate 7. Above. Double coffin ring, gold with two bands and two bezels set with crystals over paper skeletons. The gold bands are enamelled and bear the legends 'Zephaniah Leonard OB: 23 April AC. 1766 AE 63' and 'Hannah Leonard OB: 23 April AC. 1766 AE 69'. The unusual circumstance of a couple dying on the same date remains unexplained. Gold heart and hand rings, one engraved EF for Elizabeth Fish. Diameter ¾in. (both) Photograph by David Bohl. Courtesy of Society for the Preservation of New England Antiquities, Boston, Massachusetts.

Colour Plate 9. Two heart-shaped gold lockets and a small clasp set with a plait of hair and a gold twist cypher under faceted quartz. The larger locket is dated 1704 and the smaller one 1706. Boston, early 18th century. The clasp is marked EW in rectangle on tongue for Edward Webb (1666-1718) who worked as a jeweler and goldsmith in Boston c.1690-1715. Length ⅝in. (clasp), 13⁄16in. and 15⁄16in. (rings). Photograph by Peter J. Theriault. Private Collection.

tankard that he had filled with mourning rings. Thomas Barton, the town's apothecary, bequeathed to his wife all the gold memorial rings he had received 'save what may be made use of for my own funeral'.[7] Dorcas Cutts of York in the District of Maine was one of the few it seems who was 'sensible of ye Vanity of Splendid & pompous Funerals' when she willed that no rings be given at her funeral in 1758. If anything remained of her estate she wanted it given to the poor.[8]

Richard Conyers, the Boston goldsmith, owned a ring swage that was used to emboss the band with a winged-skull design popular during the colonial period.[9] Jacob Hurd of Boston and David Northey of Salem made variations of the same design in rings fashioned in 1740 and 1752 (Plate 6, upper right). As late as 1765 Boston jeweler Daniel Parker advertised that he had imported and for sale death-head ring swages. The same motif could be enamelled on mourning rings instead of being embossed or engraved.[10] A gold ring enamelled with a death's head and owned by the first Edward Norris in this country was shown to the Reverend William Bentley of Salem in 1798.[11]

Symbols of death were also incorporated into the design of these early mourning rings by mounting a clear stone, crystal or glass, over a tiny piece of paper bearing a skull or even a full-length skeleton. In the sixteenth century these macabre motifs had been executed in carved ivory or enamel in high relief. When the skeleton was used, the stone was often faceted in the shape of a coffin, carrying on the Renaissance reliquary tradition. The earliest recorded American coffin-style ring was made in 1719 in memory of the wife of President Holyoke of Harvard. It was described as having a sarcophagus on the top supported by two skeletons in black enamel around the ring, with their heads touching the coffin and their feet meeting at the bottom.[12]

Both square and coffin shaped stones were used in rings made for the funeral of William Pickman of Salem in 1735 (Plate 6, centre row).[13] Engraved inside or enamelled on the outside of these rings was the name of the deceased, date of death and age. Black enamel was usually used but white was also appropriate for mourning in the case of women. Jeweler Charles Dutens advertised in *The New-York Gazette Revived* on 3 June 1751, that he had mourning rings for sale that were 'fine white & black...with Death Heads and Skeletons to put under'.[14]

One of the most unusual of these rings (Plate 7, left) was set with two coffins and two bands conjoined. It was made for the double funeral of Zephaniah and Hannah Leonard who died on the same day in 1766, aged sixty-three and sixty. This ring was given to the eldest daughter of the eldest son in each succeeding generation. While

7. Martha Gandy Fales, 'The Early American Way of Death,' Essex Institute *Historical Collections, C* (Apr. 1964), 75-84.
8. *Maine Wills*, p. 838. Probated 3 Aug. 1758.
9. Phillips, pp. 14-16.
10. *Boston Gazette*, 28 Oct. 1765.
11. *The Diary of William Bentley, II*, 253.
12. George Rea Curwen, *Funeral Customs*, p. 12.
13. 'A Mourning Ring, with a stone in the Form of a Coffin' was lost by its careless custodian in the Broad-Way in New York, according to the advertisement placed in the local newspaper by its finder in 1768. Gottesman, *The Arts and Crafts in New York, 1726-76*, p. 78, *The N-Y Mercury*, 4 Jan. 1768.
14. Gottesman, 1726-76, p. 70.

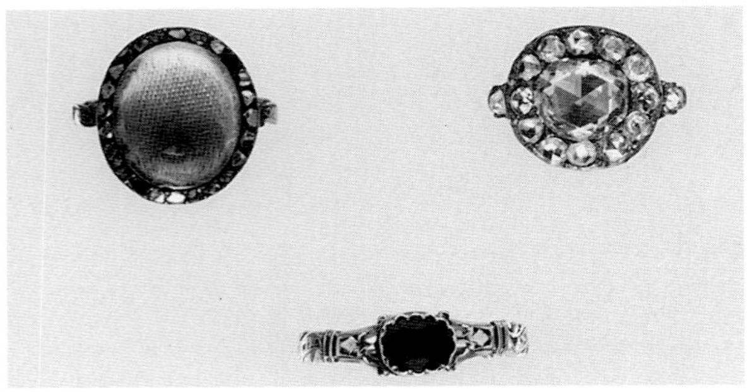

Plate 9. (Below). Memorial ring for Ann Minot 'OB 17 JAN 1758 AE 29 Y 7M', probably English. Garnet set in gold scroll ring. Marked EH. Diameter ⅞in. (Above right). Diamond ring presented to Judith Crommelin by Samuel Verplank of New York at the time of their wedding in 1760. Probably Dutch. Diameter ¾in. (hoop), width 9/16 in. (bezel). Gift of Mrs. Bayard Verplank. (Above left). Ring, made in memory of Col. Peter Schuyler of New Jersey, enamelled inscription on wavy band OB: 7 MAR: 1762. AE: 53. Gold set with pastes, hinged locket in back to contain hair under glass, probably New York. Diameter ¾in. Gift of Mrs. J. Amory Haskell. Metropolitan Museum of Art.

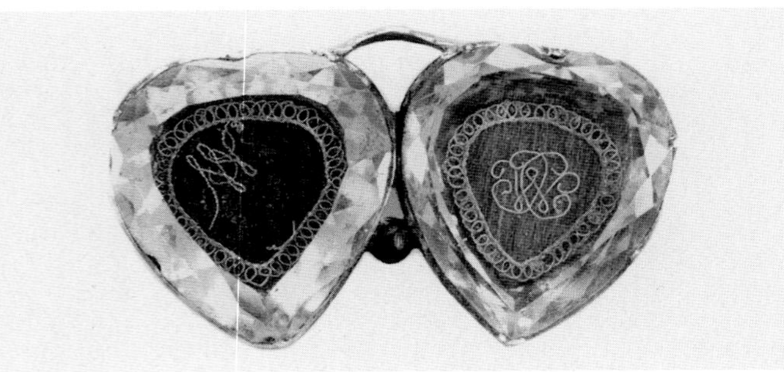

Plate 10. Crystal and cypher, double heart slide, formed by joining two memorial pendants containing the hair of Jonathan Belcher, Governor of Massachusetts, and his wife Elizabeth. Engraving on the back of each notes that Elizabeth's hair was cut off on 6 October 1736 when she was fifty-one years old and her husband's on 8 January 1737 when he was fifty-seven. At Mrs. Belcher's funeral in Boston in 1736 more than 1,000 pairs of black gloves were given away. Photograph by David Bohl, Boston. Massachusetts Historical Society.

most of the extant coffin rings that have survived were made of gold, some were made of lesser materials. An interesting example found in the dirt cellar of an old house in Exeter, New Hampshire, was made of silver with a carved turtle shell band riveted to the shank. It was made in 1773.

In New York during the mid-eighteenth century, simple gold bands with two or three parallel grooves filled in with black enamel seemed to have enjoyed a regional preference. Examples made in 1742 by Adrian Bancker and as late as 1768 by Myer Myers are known.[15]

Concurrently fashionable throughout the colonial capitals were the cast gold rings with undulating scrolled borders enamelled with black or white. This style can be seen in a few of the jewelers' trade cards and advertisements of the period. Derived from French rococo designs of the early eighteenth century, these rings were popular in America from about 1740 to 1770. Such rings could be further enhanced by the addition of coloured stone settings. One of the prettiest American examples (Plate 8) was composed of open-work scrolls set with a central oval amethyst with clear pastes set on each side. The memorial was enamelled in black in the name of Jane Borland who died in 1749 at the age of forty-two.

Less macabre and more fashionable, the stone-set scrolled rings emphasized the close relationship between the design of jewelry and that of other decorative arts of the period (Colour Plate 8). Paul Revere is believed to have made a ring set with an amethyst in memory of Lucretia Murray who died in 1768 and for whom he had previously made silverware. The back of the ring's bezel was rayed and the scrolled sections of the ring had nicely articulated terminal furls.[16]

While most mourning rings made for Americans probably were produced in that country for expediency's sake, some people preferred to take the time and order them from London. When Andrew Faneuil died in Boston in 1737, his nephew Peter wrote to his London agent requesting him to 'procure the handsomest Rings you can to be made and Engraven with the Following Inscription Viz *A Faneuil...Ob. 13 Feb:^{y} 1737 AEt 66'*. Seventeen months later Faneuil wrote that he had received the four rings and was very pleased with them.[17] Ann Minot's funeral ring, set with garnets in 1758, bore the maker's mark of Edward Holmes, a London goldworker of the mid-eighteenth century (Plate 9, below).

When Andrew Pepperrell died in 1751, his father Sir William wanted several close

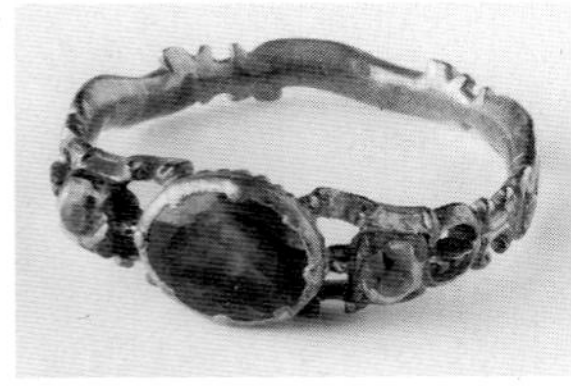

Plate 8. Gold ring with open-work setting, oval amethyst, flanked by small pastes. Enamelled in black with the inscription 'J. Borland / OB: 22 June/ 1749. AE 42', for Jane Borland, wife of Francis Borland of New England. Height 15/16 in., width 13/16 in. Courtesy, Winterthur Museum.

15. Peter J. Bohan, *American Gold*, p. 43.
16. Kathryn C. Buhler, *American Silver 1655-1825 in the Museum of Fine Arts Boston, II*, 410.
17. Peter Faneuil, Letter Book, New England Historic Genealogical Society, to Samuel and William Baker, 27 Feb. 1737, 27 July 1738.

Plate 11. Gold heart-shaped slide with faceted crystal over gold wire cypher CW (or MC upside down) on fine dark plaiting within rose-coloured foil with gold wire loops forming the border. Engraved on back 'Sep 19 1721 ER'. Length 5/8in. Gift of Mrs. George L. Batchelder, Jr. 1964 by exchange. Museum of Fine Arts, Boston.

Plate 12. Silver heart pendant with elaborate engraving and the name of Susanna Dennett, possibly Connecticut, c.1759-1775. Private Collection.

friends in England to have memorial rings, worth four guineas each, made in his only son's name. One of the recipients wrote to thank Sir William and said that his wife had added, at her own expense, some diamonds to the ring noting that this was not an unusual thing to do where they lived.[18]

Heart-shaped pendants were a more personal and less common form of American mourning jewelry than were the somewhat mass-produced funeral rings. It is possible that the 'Hair Locket set with Gold' listed in James Lloyd's inventory taken in Boston in 1693 was such a pendant. Several New England examples (Colour Plate 9) have survived and resemble their English counterparts.[19] They had a faceted heart-shaped crystal held in a two-part setting, the lower half of which had a scalloped edge that was crimped around the upper half. Inside on a silk background was a tightly woven fabric or plait of hair on which was laid an enamelled skull and crossbones as well as initials or cyphers formed of finely twisted gold wire. The border was also made of gold wire laid in loops around the edges conforming to the heart shape. Engraved on the back of one was 'Obiit the 10th Feby 1704'. The intricacy of design and the craftsmanship were impressive. A simpler example (Colour Plate 9, smaller locket) had only the looped border laid on a background of unplaited light brown hair, but on the back below the inscription was engraved a sunken-eyed skull. The date in its memorial inscription was 1706.

In another example, two heart lockets were conjoined to form a slide, preserving the hair of Governor and Mrs. Jonathan Belcher of Massachusetts (Plate 10). When Mrs. Belcher died in 1736, a thousand pairs of gloves were distributed to mourners.[20] A remarkably well preserved, deep oval crystal and cypher jewel, made as a slide to be worn on a ribbon, was engraved on the back 'Sep 19, 1721 ER' (Plate 11). Crystal and cypher jewelry was not only used for mourning, but was also used for tokens of love. The necklace clasp made by Edward Webb of Boston in the first quarter of the eighteenth century had a faceted crystal set in a deep octagonal setting that resembled the top of a contemporary pepper box (Colour Plate 9). Beneath was a tiny cypher of gold twisted wire laid on a plaited dark background. The clasp was engraved 'IL to SB'.[21]

A country cousin of the heart-shaped mourning pendant several generations removed was popular in Connecticut (Plate 12).One example in silver commemorated birth as well as death. Engraved on the obverse around a central spray of flowers it proclaimed Susanna Dennett's birth on 13 October 1759. On the reverse was a shapely funeral urn with a skull and crossbones and on its base the announcement of M.B.'s death on 24 October 1775. The edges were decorated with bright-cutting and the suspension loop was an integral part of the pendant.

18. William B. Weeden, *Economic and Social History of New England, II,* 699 citing Parsons, *Pepperrell,* 238.
19. See Becker, *Antique and 20th C. J.,* pp. 85-88.
20. Earle, II, 655.
21. The clasp was made prior to 1718, the year of Webb's death.

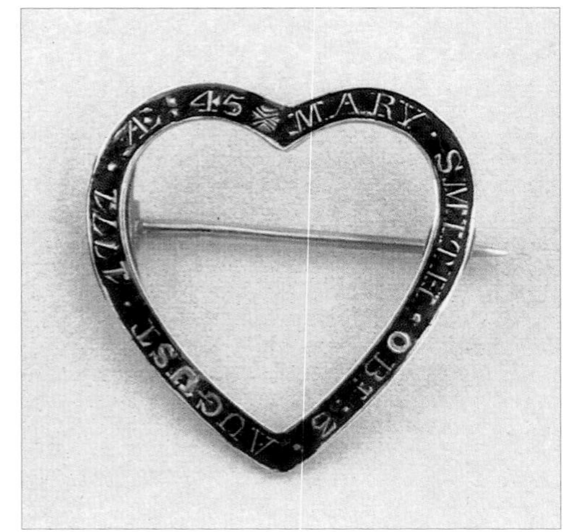

Colour Plate 10. Open, heart-shaped gold brooch with black enamel, inscribed 'Mary Smith, Obt. 3/ August 1771 / AET 45'. Charleston, S.C. Length ⅞in. Photograph by Leland Cook by courtesy of The Magazine Antiques. *The Charleston Museum, Charleston, S.C.*

An open-heart mourning brooch, enamelled in black in memory of Mary Smith of Charleston, South Carolina, who died in 1771, was another of the rarer colonial forms of *memento mori* (Colour Plate 10). Its design was French in origin and indicated the extent of the Huguenot influence in Charleston.

By the end of the colonial period, a great variety of mourning jewelry was offered, among which were mourning buckles. As soon as the news of the death of King George II reached Charleston, South Carolina, in 1760, John Paul Grimke advertised 'Mourning swords, buckles, necklaces, rings with or without diamond, and other articles used on such occasions'. The mourning buckle, whether rectangular or octagonal in shape, was panelled with conforming crystals beneath which were the obituary inscriptions in gold wire over hair.[22]

Love

Heart-in-hand rings were designed with a pair of clasped right hands or with the two hands actually moulded to form the bezel. Made in silver as well as gold, these rings were sometimes fashioned like a twin or gimmel ring (from the Latin *gemelli* meaning twins) with the hands on separate hoops fastened together. Each half could be worn separately by the two betrothed until the marriage took place. After the wedding, the two halves were joined together and worn by the wife. Fede rings (from the Italian *mani in fede)* were known in Roman times and were associated with contractual agreements. They were revived in Europe in the twelfth century and continued to be made in the eighteenth century as a token of love.

American jewelers often made rings with a heart between the hands or set on a third hoop so that when the hands clasped they covered the heart (Plate 13). For this reason, in colonial America, the fede ring was called a heart-in-hand or heart-and-hand ring. John Butler advertised 'Heart and Hand rings' as early as 1758 in Boston.[23] Daniel Parker, goldsmith, advertised in the *Boston Gazette* on 28 October 1765, that he had for sale, among other jeweler's tools, heart-in-hand ring swages.

Colonial printers used the heart-and-hand design as a tailpiece ornament.[24] The motif was a popular one with folk artists, the symbolism of which was explained in numerous early emblem books.

An interesting variation on heart-and-hand rings occurred in a Massachusetts ring made of three gold hoops, the central one having two tiny hearts and gadroon-like ridging. On the wrist of each hand a white paste was set in silver (see Plate 7, centre).[25]

Similar forms of endearment were the posy or motto rings that were engraved with sentimental inscriptions and given to loved ones. An early example dating from about 1650 to 1675 was recently excavated at Flowerdew Hundred, Virginia and bore the

22. S. Bury, *Sentimental Jewellery*, p. 23.
23. Dow, *Arts & Crafts*, p. 42.
24. Elizabeth C. Reilly, *A Dictionary of Colonial American Printers' Ornaments and Illustrations* , p. 61.
25. Colonial Dames, Boston 1965 #4, gift of Penelope Noyes.

Colour Plate 11. Above left. Martha Custis Washington's gold wedding ring, with seven diamonds set in silver mounts in a rosette and one on each shoulder, probably made in England about the time of her first marriage in 1749 to Daniel Parke Custis. A gold locket containing a lock of hair was added to the rayed back of the bezel. Diameter 13/16in. The Mount Vernon Ladies' Association, Mount Vernon, Virginia.

Colour Plate 12. Above right. Flowerpot ring, English, c.1740-60, similar to rings sold by American jewelers in the mid-18th century, set with diamonds, rubies and an emerald. Diameter about ¾in., height about ½in. (bezel). Photograph by Dennis Griggs. Private Collection.

sentiment, 'Time Shall tell, I love the[e] w[ell]'. The thumb rings owned by Edmund Custis of Virginia in 1703 had the following posies:

> I like my Choice to[o] well to Change
> as God decreed so we agreed
> Amantium in amoris redente gratia est.[26]

Francis Richardson, one of Philadelphia's earliest goldsmiths, received a request for a gold ring in 1705 from a woman 'who desires it may be handsomely made & have this posie – Remember the Giver'.[27] Among the posies engraved on rings by Richardson's son Joseph in the 1730s and 1740s were 'I Pray Love well & Ever not the Gift but the Giver' and 'Within this sphere moves all thats dear'. Other commonplace sentiments expressed on these rings were 'When this u see rem[ember] me' and 'The love is true I bear to you'.[28]

26. Accomack Co., *Virginia, Wills &c. 1692-1715*, p. 336a, 1 Feb. 1703/4.
27. Downs Memorial Manuscript Collection, 53.165.59, Winterthur Museum.
28. Martha G. Fales, *Joseph Richardson and Family, Philadelphia Silversmiths*, pp. 9, 59, 143, 268, 291, 298.

Plate 13. Silver ring fashioned with two hands clasping a crowned heart, commonly called heart and hand rings. Engraved inside 'Hearts united live Contented', an obvious token of love. New England, mid-18th century. Diameter ⅞in. Gift of Miss Alice Norton Dike and Miss Elizabeth Anderson Dike. Pair of cypher and quartz cuff links, English or American, mid-18th century. The twisted wire cypher is laid on black fabric, backed with red foil beneath faceted quartz. Benjamin Swan of Boston, who died in 1813, is said to have owned these cuff links. Diameter ¾in. Gift of Miss Amy Sacker, Courtesy Museum of Fine Arts, Boston.

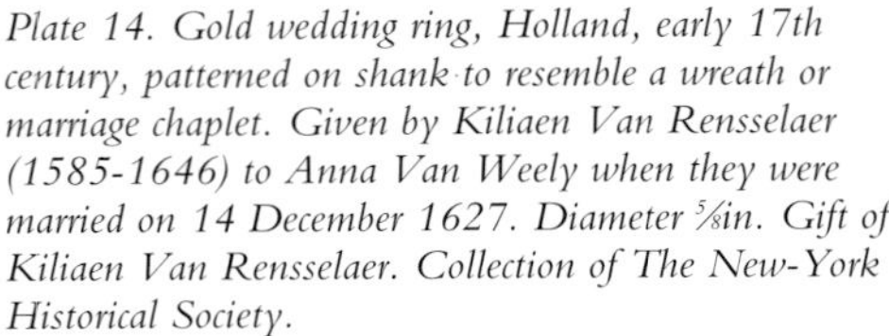

Plate 14. Gold wedding ring, Holland, early 17th century, patterned on shank to resemble a wreath or marriage chaplet. Given by Kiliaen Van Rensselaer (1585-1646) to Anna Van Weely when they were married on 14 December 1627. Diameter ⅞in. Gift of Kiliaen Van Rensselaer. Collection of The New-York Historical Society.

Wedding rings of course represent the ultimate token of love in jewelry. London's famous lexicographer Samuel Johnson jocularly defined a ring as 'a circular instrument placed upon the noses of hogs and the fingers of women to restrain them and bring them into subjection'. From ancient Roman times, wedding rings and betrothal or engagement rings could be one and the same thing. These rings were customarily worn on the left hand. It may be that the mid-seventeenth century Puritan rebellion against the religious customs and the trappings of the Catholic Church caused true Puritans to disdain the use of wedding rings. Samuel Butler's *Hudibras* made light of the matter:

Others were for abolishing
That tool of matrimony, a ring
With which the unsanctified bridegroom
Is marry'd only to a thumb.[29]

As the Butler verse also implies, in the time of George I in England, the wedding ring was sometimes worn on the thumb.

Wedding rings were by no means universally worn or necessarily a part of the marriage ceremony in colonial America. Portraits of colonial wives reveal that many apparently wore no rings although they were wealthy enough to have a painting of themselves. Those who did have rings wore them on either hand or any finger they fitted.

Kiliaen Van Rensselaer (1585-1646), one of the first settlers in New York, was married to Anna Van Weely on 14 December 1627. Her gold wedding ring (Plate 14) was probably made in Holland and brought with them to New Amsterdam.[30] Wedding rings were sometimes recycled and given to next-generation brides. Massachusetts Judge Samuel Sewall wrote of visiting his daughter-in-law and giving her his wife's wedding ring. He told her that he hoped she would wear it with the same nobility as its first owner had done.[31] It is interesting to note that Anne Hibbins' gold wedding ring was valued at 16 shillings in 1656, twice the value of her diamond ring.[32]

Among the earliest typical plain gold bands that can be documented as American-made wedding rings was one made for Deborah Lyde who married Captain Francis Brinley of Massachusetts on 13 April 1718. The nuptial date was inscribed inside the band where the maker, John Edwards of Boston, also placed his mark.[33] The plain gold wedding ring (see Colour Plate 8) that Paul Revere is believed to have made for his wife Rachel Walker in 1773 is engraved with the posy '[L]ive Co[n]tented'. Revere was probably also the maker of her stone-set ring (Colour Plate 8, left) about the same time. The gold band had a closed-back setting that was rayed. A rectangular crystal was set over a twisted wire design similar to those in heart-shaped pendants.

George Christopher Dorwig, jeweler and goldsmith, advertised in the *Pennsylvania Gazette* on 1 August 1765, that he made 'most curious Wedding-rings of an entire

29. Cited by George Frederick Kunz, *Rings for the Finger*, p. 222.
30. It was given by Kiliaen Van Rensselaer V, the 15th Patroon and 13th Lord of the Manor, to The New-York Historical Society. *N-Y Historical Quarterly Bulletin*, Jan. 1945, p. 23.
31. *The Diary of Samuel Sewall, 1674-1729*, edited by M. Halsey Thomas, 2 vols., II, 871.
32. McClellan, p. 110.
33. This ring was lent by a descendant to the exhibition of 'Masterpieces of New England Silver' held at the Yale University Art Gallery in 1939.

new Invention...' George Smithson advertised in the *South Carolina Gazette* on 3 April 1775, that he could provide 'Wedding Rings on the shortest Notice' for those upon whom the Revolution forced urgency.

The use of diamond wedding rings on the part of European royalty appears to have been established by the end of the fifteenth century.[34] Nevertheless, the addition of diamonds to wedding rings was still not common in eighteenth century America. Judith Crommelin's lovely sparkling wedding ring (Plate 9) probably came from Amsterdam to New York for her 1760 marriage to Samuel Verplank. Set in silver, as colourless gems were traditionally set prior to the nineteenth century, and with a gold closed-back mounting, the ring had a large and deep central diamond, faceted in a Dutch rose cut, weighing about two carats, rimmed with diamonds, and flanked by two side diamonds. For centuries, Amsterdam had been one of the important gem-cutting centres of the world.[35]

Martha Washington's diamond wedding ring (Colour Plate 11) was similar to Judith Verplank's, with a central diamond surrounded by six smaller stones and one small stone on each shoulder. The back of the bezel was rayed and to it was later added a rose gold locket to hold a swatch of hair under a crystal. It is likely that this ring was made for her first marriage to Daniel Parke Custis in 1749 and that the locket was added to receive a lock of hair from George Washington, her second husband.[36]

Fancy Pieces

One of the most exquisite varieties of mid-eighteenth century gem-set jewelry was fashioned to look like a miniature vase of flowers, with multicoloured stones for blossoms. While the ring illustrated in Colour Plate 12 has no American history of ownership, it is similar to rings known to have been owned in colonial America. Called *giardinetti* rings today, from the Italian for 'little gardens', they were known in colonial times, in England as well as in America, as flower pot rings. George Wickes, the London goldsmith, recorded two flower pot rings in his extant ledgers, one purchased in 1740.[37] An excellent description was provided in a New York advertisement of 1765: 'one [ring] set in the Form of a Flower-pot, the Middle a Diamond, two Sparks, three Rubies above, and an Emerald and a Topaz on each Side'.[38] Another example three years earlier was made entirely of diamonds: 'one Diamond Ring with seven diamonds, 3 *[sic]* large and four small, one Diamond in most the Shape of a Flower Pot'.[39]

It is not surprising that jewelry would be fashioned like a vase of flowers in an era when Robert Furber's flower prints, the *Twelve Months of Flowers* first issued in London in 1730, were enjoying great popularity in England and America and when flower pots were carved for overmantels and finials on furniture. The settings of flower pot rings had individual closed backs and spaces between the branches and flower heads, with little furls on the collets to give a leaf-like appearance to each. The coloured stones had gold or gilt collets and the colourless stones, silver collets. Usually the pot itself was formed entirely of metal but occasionally the more opulent examples had a diamond faceted to fit the general shape of the vase.

Floral spray brooches were also very desirable, romantic gifts in jewelry in the mid-eighteenth century. It was in these charming floral displays that the jeweler's art was best displayed. Some gem-set floral sprays were made to be sewn on dresses. When

34. Kunz, *Rings*, p. 234.
35. Both Mrs. Crommelin's ring and her wedding dress were given to the Metropolitan Museum of Art.
36. Fales, 'The jewelry [at Mount Vernon]', *Antiques*, Feb. 1989, pp. 512-13.
37. Elaine Barr, *George Wickes*, p. 82.
38. 20 May 1765, *The N-Y Mercury*, Gottesman, 1726-76, p. 55.
39. 8 Feb. 1762, *The N-Y Mercury*, Gottesman 1726-76, p. 62.

Plate 15. Reverse of the floral spray brooch illustrated in Colour Plate 13. The Charleston Museum, Charleston, S.C.

Colour Plate 13. Floral spray brooch, Charleston, S.C., c.1750-1760, originally owned by Eliza Lucas Pinckney (1722-1793). Set with twenty-two diamonds, five almandite garnets, five emeralds, three rubies, a pink and a yellow sapphire and one amethyst. Possibly made by John Paul Grimke who advertised in 1741 that he had imported the same kinds of gems for his jewelry work. Mounted in silver which may have been gold washed at the time. Length 1⅞in. Photograph by Terry Richardson. The Charleston Museum, Charleston, S.C.

the dresses went out of fashion, the spray could have been removed, broken up and reset in the latest style. This practice added considerably to their present rarity.

Large ornamental floral sprays called stomachers were worn on the front of the bodice filling a triangular shape extending from under the décolletage to the waistline. These could be made in sections so that they could be separated into two or three different parts to be worn individually. Such elaborate jewelry was more suitable to old world courts than new world colonists. However, occasional references in American newspapers and inventories confirm that stomachers were known there.

'One Set of Woman's Breast Jewels for a Stomacher set in Silver wash'd with Gold, consisting of six different Pieces, the Uppermost and Largest with a large Chrystal Stone in the Middle, set round with small Stones of different Colours, the lowermost or Girdle Hook being set round with Emeralds and Pearl' was advertised as stolen in New York in 1741.[40] In 1770 Martha Washington purchased a parure, albeit set with pastes, consisting of a necklace, earrings, sprig, hair combs, with pins and buttons for the stomacher.[41]

Smaller spray brooches were known and worn by colonial women. Mrs. Charles

40. Gottesman, 1726-1776, p. 40.
41. Fitzpatrick, *Writings of Washington*, 3:23.

Colour Plate 14. A floral aigrette adorns the hair of Elizabeth Boush of Norfolk, Virginia, who wears a flower corsage and holds a swag of pink and white roses in her hands. Students at schools for young ladies were sometimes taught how to make 'flowers for the head'. Her portrait was painted by John Durand in 1769 when she was sixteen. Height 30in., width 25½in. Colonial Williamsburg Foundation.

Pinckney of Charleston, South Carolina, owned a lovely flower spray (Colour Plate 13 and Plate 15) set with twenty-two rose-cut diamonds, five emeralds, three rubies, a pink and a yellow sapphire, five almandite garnets and an amethyst.[42] The larger central flower with a yellow centre and diamond petals is set with two smaller flowers above, and multicoloured buds and leaves. While there is a naturalistic design to the brooch, it is more fanciful than faithful in its approach.

Although Charleston imported most of its manufactured goods from England in the mid-eighteenth century, this brooch was probably made by a local jeweler. John Paul Grimke (1713-1791) came to Charleston, South Carolina, from London about 1740, and established himself as a jeweler at the sign of the Hand and Ring in Elliott Street, announcing that he 'makes and mends all sorts of Jeweller's Work after the newest Fashion, and at reasonable Rates'. He augmented his business over the next twenty-five years by doing goldsmith's work and importing silver and jewelry from London. Among the loose stones he imported that he could set in jewelry for his customers were 'Brilliant and Rose [cut] Diamonds, Rubies, Emeralds, Saphirs, Jacints, Topaz's, Amethists, Turky Stones [turquoise], Garnets...'[43] The same varieties of precious stones appear in Eliza Pinckney's brooch. That Grimke was a working jeweler and not just an importer can be verified by the fact that when he was planning a trip to England in 1752 he told his customers that 'What loose diamonds and other stones he has on hand, will be work'd up' before he departed and that he would give them boxes for the jewelry at no extra charge.[44]

Spray pins could be worn in many ways. As hair ornaments, they were called *aigrettes,* or in American parlance, egrets, denoting the derivation of the term from the egret plume. These could be made of small gemstones, or enamelled, or made out of ornamented cloth, wire and horsehair. Colonial women were often portrayed with the latter type of floral spray in their hair apparently provided by the artist in many cases as a conventional form of stylish dress. Since they were made of somewhat flimsy materials, fabric aigrettes were discarded when they became worn and few mid-eighteenth century examples survive today.

It has been suggested that the flowers in the aigrette worn in the 1769 portrait of Elizabeth Boush (Colour Plate 14) may have been made by her when she was at E. Gardner's school in Norfolk, Virginia, where the schoolmistress advertised instruction in making artificial flowers along with other handiwork.[45]

---

42. Fales, 'Jewelry in Charleston,' *Antiques,* Dec. 1990, pp. 1216-27
43. *South Carolina Gazette,* Charleston, 1 Aug. 1740 and 12 Sept. 1741. The same stones were specified again in the *Gazette* on 23 Oct. 1751. Similar stones and design were described in Colman and Garrick's *Clandestine Marriage,* by a wealthy bride: 'I have a bouquet to come home tomorrow, made up of diamonds and rubies and emeralds and topazes, and amethysts...jewels of all colours, green, red, blue, yellow, intermixt...the prettiest thing you ever saw in your life.' Quoted by Joan Evans, *A History of Jewellery 1100-1970,* p. 156.
44. Ibid., 10 Aug. 1752.
45. Letter to author from Betty Ring, Houston Texas, 17 July 1986. Other advertisements for girls' schools at the time mentioned 'flowers for the head' as being among the things the students would learn to make.

GARNETS

Garlands of glittering garnets were quite the fashion in mid-eighteenth century jewelry. Ruby-coloured pyrope from mines in Bohemia made its way to jewelers in England and America where the stones were set in the same floral designs that were fashionable for diamond jewelry of the period.[1] Except for the fact that they are not rare, garnets are gems that have very desirable characteristics. They are beautiful and durable, have a wide range of colour, often resembling the finest rubies, and in some cases can out-sparkle a diamond. Whole sets of garnets were advertised in colonial newspapers, as were individual necklaces, earrings, brooches, rings, bracelets, and lockets. Jeweler John Paul Grimke boasted that, 'the greatest variety of neat garnet work that ever was seen in any shop in the province at any one time' was available in his Charleston shop.[2]

Grimke could well have made the gold pendant brooch set with garnets and a miniature portrait of a member of the Gibbes or Shoolbred family (Colour Plate 15) The miniature was signed by Mary Roberts of Charleston, one of the first women artists in America, who died in 1761.[3] The garnets were set in closed-back collets with little furls of gold to give a naturalistic effect to the tendrils and buds. Garnets encircled the miniature frame of Joseph Hewes, signer of the Declaration of Independence from North Carolina. Painted by Charles Willson Peale in 1776, the likeness was set as a brooch and was sent to Hewes' fiancée shortly before his tragic death (Colour Plate 16).

Mrs. Barnard Elliott of Charleston was portrayed wearing a garnet necklace and a pair of bracelets with garnet-set medallion clasps (Colour Plate 17). Her necklet was formed of closely fitted openwork rosettes and foliate designs. Suspended from the centre was a bowknot above an ovoid pendant. An English necklet of the same period and style is in the Victoria & Albert Museum, London.[4]

Martha Washington's necklace (Colour Plate 18) originally looked very much like Mrs. Elliott's before it was lengthened. A necklace had been ordered from England by George Washington for his bride in 1759, along with a garnet aigrette. These came from the London shop of Susanna Passavant. The following year he ordered a pair of '3 dropt Garnet Earings' from another London jeweler whose surname was Grymes (Colour Plate 18).[5] The style of the earrings known today as girandole had a bowknot suspended from a rosette top, and supported three pear-shaped pendants. Simpler garnet earrings without the intermediary bowknot and with a single pendant were advertised by Christopher Hughes as 'top and drop' in Baltimore in 1776.[6] Parts of these pieces were interchangeable so that the bowknot and pendants could be suspended either from the necklace or the rosette top of the earring.

Garnet jewelry was also ordered for Martha's nine-year-old daughter Patsy in 1764. Due to the nonimportation agreement, the necklace, earrings, and hoop ring did not arrive until 1768. When Patsy was sixteen, the London firm of Gurdon & Son was requested to provide her with a garnet comb for her hair, made to match the set she already had from them. To this were added more garnets: hair pins and a pair of garnet shoe buckles. While all of this jewelry was London-made, a pair of garnet earrings was also purchased by George Washington from James Craig, a jeweler in

1. Hugh Tait, ed., *The Art of the Jeweller, I,* 22; *II,* Plate 7 and Figs. 7, 40-44.
2. *SC Gaz.*, 25 Aug. 1764.
3. Fales, *Antiques,* Dec. 1990, pp. 1217-18.
4. Bury, *Jewellery Gallery Summary Catalogue,* pp. 109, 103, 108. *Antiques,* 1990, 1216-18. In New England, Alice Hooper appears to be wearing garnet jewelry in her portrait by Copley. Jules D. Prown, *John Singleton Copley, I,* #117.
5. Fales, *Antiques,* Feb. 1989, pp. 512-13.
6. Dunlap's *Maryland Gazette or the Baltimore General Advertiser,* 27 August. 1776.

Colour Plate 17. Mrs. Barnard Elliott (1715-1774) of Charleston wore a floral necklet and a pair of bracelets set with garnets in her portrait taken about 1766 by Jeremiah Theus (1716-1774). Her garnet jewelry may have been imported from England, but Charleston jeweler John Paul Grimke advertised that he could make a variety of jewels with garnets he imported. A floral aigrette made of artificial blossoms decorated Mrs. Elliott's head and she had fancy buttons sewn on her bodice. Height 50in., width 40½in. Gibbes Museum of Art, Carolina Art Association Collection, Charleston, S.C.

Colour Plate 15. The miniature portrait of a member of the Gibbes or Shoolbred family was set in a frame with a border of garnets each mounted in gold with leafy furls. The portrait was signed by Mary Roberts (d.1761), one of the first women to paint miniatures in America. The frame could have been made in Charleston by someone like John Paul Grimke who advertised his own garnet jewelry in 1764. Watercolour on ivory. Length 1¾in. Gibbes Museum of Art, Carolina Art Association Collection, Charleston, S.C.

Colour Plate 16. Garnets formed the border of the frame for the miniature painting of Joseph Hewes (1730-1779) painted by Charles Willson Peale (1741-1827) in Maryland in 1776. Length 1¼in., width 1½in. From collection of the United States Naval Academy Museum, Annapolis, Maryland.

Colour Plate 18. Group of Washington garnet jewelry. Martha Washington was partial to garnet jewelry, some of which was ordered from London by her illustrious husband George in 1759: a necklace and an aigrette from Susanna Passavant. A pair of 'three dropt Garnet Earings' purchased from a London jeweler named Grymes may have been these shown here, with a cluster top, a girandole section featuring a bowknot, and terminating in a detachable tear drop pendant (right). The garnets were mounted in silver, originally gold washed, and backed with foil, c.1760. Gurdon & Son provided garnet earrings for Martha's daughter Patsy, c.1764-1768. Mrs. Washington also had a garnet-set hoop ring that was ordered from Benjamin Gurdon & Son. Small garnet pins in the form of a crescent or a flower spray could be worn in the hair. Length 1⅛in. (crescent pin). Mount Vernon Ladies' Association, Mount Vernon, Virginia.

Williamsburg, Virginia, in 1766.[7] When Patsy died in 1773, it is likely that Martha Washington made occasional use of the jewelry she had intended for her daughter.

Much of this garnet jewelry is preserved at Mount Vernon (Colour Plate 18). Some of it has been reworked. Martha Washington's necklace was originally designed with close-coupled clusters encircling the neck and a pendant cluster that could be attached to the central rosette. Some time in the nineteenth century, probably about 1825, the clusters were separated by two rows of chains to make a festoon necklace that was more fashionable. The crescent-shaped pin and the spray pin complement the design of the necklace. The spray probably originally included a bird, mounted on a wire so that it trembled, filling the space between the central scrolls of garnets.[8]

While the Washington garnet jewelry apparently did not include bracelets, they too were popular in the mid-eighteenth century. Bracelets mounted with garnets and pearls were made by John Hector of Charleston in 1774. His competitor Philip Tidyman advertised a lost garnet bracelet that had a gold enamelled locket attached to it.[9]

Rings were by far the most widely used form of garnet jewelry. Several pretty garnet rings were described by New York jeweler Otto de Parisen. One had a heart-shaped garnet, 'very long', in the middle with two Bristol stones on each side. Another had four garnets 'set across' with a white stone in the middle, and a third had an octagonal-cut garnet with a spark on each side.[10] Garnet hoop rings, fancy double-hearted and single-hearted rings, garnet and diamond twisted rings, and rings set with mocha agate and garnet clusters, all were offered to New York customers by jeweler John Mecom in 1763.[11] A 'twist shank ring with a heart, garnet' was noted in a Baltimore advertisement of 1776 by Christopher Hughes.[12] Garnets were also used in mourning rings. A garnet rimmed ring, with a representation of an urn or tombstone and a head above it, was lost in New York in 1780 and was worth a guinea for its return.[13] The ring made in memory of Ann Minot was set with an oval faceted garnet (see Plate 9).

A delicate, scrolled ring in the rococo taste adorned the hand of Mrs. John Winthrop, painted by Copley in 1773.[14] With its tiny asymmetrical flourish, the ring appears to be set with garnets and is worn by Mrs. Winthrop with a multiple-strand of pearls.

Buckles for shoes, knees, stocks, and shirts set with garnets were offered in New York. London-made garnet fancy and plain gold shirt buckles were offered for sale by James Gautier in New York's *Royal Gazette* on 7 November 1778.[15]

---

7. George Washington Invoices & Letters 1755-1766, Mt.V., Va., pp. 11, 28, 59; GW Ledger A, 1750-1752 (GW Papers, Library of Congress); *The Writings of GW from the Original Manuscript Sources, 1745-1799,* ed. John C. Fitzpatrick, II, 418-19, III, 23, 91, 93. See also Fales 'The jewelry [at Mount Vernon]', *Antiques,* Feb. 1989, pp. 512-17.
8. Tait, *Jewelry 7,000 Years,* p. 186. Garnet aigrettes were available in the the Williamsburg, Virginia, shop of Catherine Rathell who ordered '3 Garnet Sprigs from 9 to 12 / a ps' from her London agent in 1771. F.N. Mason, *John Norton & Sons,* p. 212.
9. *S.C.&Am.Gen.Gaz.,* 16 Dec. 1774; *S.C. Gaz.,* 9 March 1765.
10. *The N-Y Mercury,* 20 May 1765, Gottesman 1726-76, p. 55.
11. *The N-Y Mercury,* 23 May 1763. Gottesman 1726-76, pp. 70-71.
12. Dunlap's, *Md. Gaz. & Balto. Advtr, 27 Aug. 1776.*
13. *The N-Y Gaz. & The Wkly. Mercury,* 29 May 1780. Gottesman 1777-99, p. 87.
14. Prown #327, Metropolitan Museum of Art.
15. Bennett & Dixon, Jewellers, Goldsmiths, and Lapidaries from London, *The N-Y Gaz. etc,* 26 Aug. 1771, Gottesman 1726-76; Gottesman 1777-99, p. 86. See also Copley portrait of Alice Hooper (Prown #117).

Plate 16. Below. A necklace of artificial pearls, owned in the mid-18th century by Abigail Smith Adams, was tied around her neck with a wide ribbon fashioned into a bow at the back. Smithsonian Institution.

Plate 17. Left. Princess Ann, mezzotint portrait by Isaac Becket, c.1683, used by the young Bostonian artist John Singleton Copley for the pose of Mrs. Mann in 1753 (Colour Plate 21). Both women hold strings of pearls to be fastened around their necks with silk ribbons. Height 13 1/16in., width 9 7/8in. Gift of Waldron P. Belknap. Courtesy, Winterthur Museum.

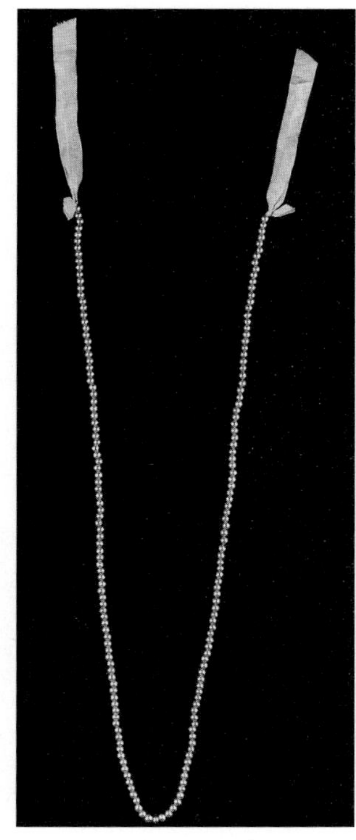

Pearls

Pocahontas, the Indian girl who married John Rolfe in seventeenth century Virginia, had a father with a treasure house full of pearls, according to Captain John Smith's description. These fresh-water pearls were made into jewelry by the Indians (see Plate 2). Quantities of such pearls have been found in American burial mounds. However, the most beautiful pearls came from the depths of the Pacific and Indian Oceans and, along with pearls from the Persian Gulf, were brought to this country through trade and migration. Pearls, like coral, amber, and jet, are organic substances widely used in jewelry. Their warm, shimmering lustre has never gone out of fashion.

Seventeenth century pearl jewelry with American histories of ownership is a rarity. Pearls are very fragile and are easily damaged. Nevertheless, pearls – real or artificial – can be seen in the earliest surviving portraits of colonial women. This visual evidence indicates that necklaces were often made of single strands of medium-sized pearls such as can be seen in the portrait of Elizabeth Paddy Wensley (Colour Plate 19). Mrs. Wensley also wore pear-shaped pendant pearl earrings, the sort that continued to be in fashion for another hundred years.[1] Also popular were multiple strands of smaller pearls. Elizabeth Eggington's interlaced pearl and gold necklace (see Colour Plate 7) was undoubtedly more elaborate than most, while Mrs. John Winthrop's was more typical.[2]

The pearls worn by Abigail Adams in her pastel portrait (Colour Plate 20) may well be the same pearls that have survived with a family tradition of belonging to her (Plate 16). These pearls are artificial, so-called French pearls, made of hollow glass beads. The interior of the bead was coated with a substance to produce a nacreous appearance, and the exterior was treated with acid to give the surface an iridescent appearance. Because they were very light in weight they were sometimes filled with wax, although this is not the case with Abigail Adams' pearls. Hers still have the

1. Mrs. Patteshall of Boston, whose portrait is attributed to Thomas Smith and dated about 1679, wore a similar pearl necklace and earrings. Mrs. James Otis was depicted by Copley in 1758 with a pearl necklace indistinguishable from Mrs. Patteshall's, and Dorothy Murray wore the same kind of pendant pearl earrings as Mrs. Patteshall's in her Copley portrait of 1759-61 (Prown #55 and #96).
2. Portrait of Mrs. John Winthrop by Copley, 1773, at MMA.

Colour Plate 19. Mrs. Elizabeth Paddy Wensley, Massachusetts, c.1665, wears a pearl necklace around her neck and pear-shaped pearl earrings in her portrait by an anonymous American artist. Two stone-set rings appear on the third finger of her left hand. There appears to be some sort of ornamentation above her earrings, possibly pieces of beaded galloon. Height 41in., width 33½in. Courtesy of the Pilgrim Society, Plymouth, Massachusetts.

Colour Plate 20. Below. A triple round of pearls (perhaps those seen in Plate 16) fastened at the back with a wide ribbon provide a simple graceful addition to the portrait of Abigail Smith Adams (1744-1818), painted in pastel by Benjamin Blyth in 1766. Abigail was married in 1764 to John Adams of Braintree, Massachusetts, future President of the United States. Height 23in., width 17½in. Photograph by David Bohl, Boston. Massachusetts Historical Society.

Colour Plate 21. Portrait of Mrs. Joseph Mann, painted by John Singleton Copley, Boston, 1753. A similar string of artificial pearls was owned by young Abigail Adams. Mrs. Mann's pose was based on an English engraving of Princess Ann (Plate 17). Height 36in., width 28¼in. Gift of Frederick and Holbrook Metcalf. Museum of Fine Arts, Boston.

Colour Plate 22. Above left. Mrs. Gavin Lawson's display of pearls and pendants confirms the variety of jewelry to be found in the colonies in the mid-18th century. Her portrait was painted by John Hesselius in Virginia in 1770 when she was twenty years old. Height 49¾in., width 39in. Colonial Williamsburg Foundation.

Colour Plate 23. Above right. Cluster earrings complement the pearl necklace set with plump oval mother-of-pearl bosses strung between rows of round pearls, tied at the back of the neck with an ivory satin ribbon. The round pearls may have been artificial. This portrait of Mary Oxnard Watts of Falmouth, Maine, was painted in 1765 by John Singleton Copley of Boston. Height 30in., width 25in. Vose Galleries of Boston.

Colour Plate 24. A necklace made of mother-of-pearl ovals, set with pastes was backed with a black velvet ribbon for contrast and the comfort of Mrs. Isaac Winslow of Boston, seen in this detail of the portrait of Mr. and Mrs. Winslow by John Singleton Copley in 1774. A similar necklace can be seen in Colour Plate 25. Length 40¼in., width 48¾in. M. and M. Karolik Collection of Eighteenth Century American Arts. Courtesy, Museum of Fine Arts, Boston.

Plate 18. Girandole earrings and rows of pearls for a necklace were worn by Rhoda Cranston of Massachusetts in her portrait painted by John Singleton Copley about 1757. Height 57½in., width 48in. Photograph by Edwin S. Roseberry. Bayley Art Museum of the University of Virginia.

ribbon by which they were fastened around the neck in the mid-eighteenth century fashion. One of Copley's earliest portraits showed Mrs. Joseph Mann in 1753 (Colour Plate 21) holding a similar string of pearls by the ribbons as though she were just about to put them on.[3]

Colonial women were sometimes portrayed wearing pearls that may or may not have belonged to them, but that mimic the fashion as seen in popular prints of London pace-setters. John Singleton Copley apparently had both prints and strands of pearls in his studio to be used as decorative props, according to the taste of his sitter. Using a print as a guide, his American subject could select the jewelry she would wear, omitting anything that was too elaborate or unpleasing. Many women were shown with strings of pearls in their hair, around their sleeves, across one shoulder and around the bodice. It is doubtful that Mrs. Gawen Brown actually owned the three-strand necklace of pearls she wore in her 1763 portrait (Colour Plate 1), since it has been conclusively proven that Copley copied Mrs. Brown's pose, dress, and necklace from a 1761 engraving (Plate 1) of Maria, Countess of Coventry. It is interesting to note that the artist omitted the Countess' second dark-beaded necklace, the elaborate headdress and the earrings.[4]

In other portraits, it is apparent that the jewelry depicted was actually owned by the sitter. Rhoda Cranston's ears were fairly burdened by her distinctive girandole pearl earrings suspended from three big round pearls. (Plate 18).[5] Girandole earrings consisted of three pear-shaped drops, suspended from a bow or a large central gem. These were still the height of fashion in the mid-eighteenth century, although they had originated more than a hundred years earlier.

Elsewhere in the colonies, Mary Bonticou Lathrop of New York wore a five-strand choker of small pearls.[6] In Virginia, Mrs. Gavin Lawson had a most unusual multiple-strand pearl necklace with pear-shaped pearls suspended from the middle of the three

3. Prown #20.
4. Ibid., #108-09.
5. Griselda Oliver wore a simpler version with three pear-shaped pearls suspended from a central ring (Prown #82, Deerfield Academy).
6. See portrait by John Durand, c.1770, *American Naive Painting of the 18th and 19th Centuries, 111 Masterpieces from the Collection of Edgar William and Bernice Chrysler Garbisch* (New York, 1969), Plate 16.
7. MESDA, May 1987, 89.
8. Prown #133, Gilcrease.
9. Ibid., #202.
10. Ibid., #159, painted in 1765.

Plate 19. Mrs. George Purdie of Smithfield, Virginia, wears a necklace made of what appear to be freshwater pearls with a pendant surprisingly like the necklace worn by the native of Virginia depicted by William Hollar in 1645 (see Plate 2). Her portrait was painted by John Durand c.1760-65. Height 31in., width 26in. Museum of Early Southern Decorative Art.

lower strands, amply filling her décolletage (Colour Plate 22). Mrs. George Purdie owned a shell and pearl necklace (Plate 19) similar to one worn by a Virginian Indian in the seventeenth century (Plate 2).[7]

Another fashion in pearl necklaces was a strand of large pearls flanked by two strands of smaller pearls on each side. Both Mrs. John Apthorp[8] and Mrs. Robert Hooper[9] were portrayed by Copley in the 1760s wearing these. Several of Copley's sitters wore necklaces consisting of a central row of large mother-of-pearl ovals, and outer strands of small round pearls. With such a necklace Mrs. Edward Watts wore cluster pearl earrings made of large and small pearls (Colour Plate 23)[10].

Mrs. Isaac Winslow of Boston wore a necklace in 1774 made of mother-of-pearl ovals surrounded by either pyrites or pastes and backed by a velvet ribbon (Colour Plate 24). Her jewelry was carefully painted by Copley to show the light blue and pink reflections characteristic of the shell's opalescence. The necklace was quite similar to one that was once owned by Lady Bernard, wife of Massachusetts Governor Sir Francis Bernard (Colour Plate 25). Lady Bernard's necklace was made of mother-of-pearl ovals set in silver and bordered with circles of nicely faceted pastes. It was given by her, along with a pair of earrings, to Mrs. M. Nichols when the Bernards left the country at the time of the Revolutionary War.

A member of the Salisbury family of Worcester owned a pair of earrings (Plate 20) made of mother-of-pearl

Plate 20. Mother-of-pearl earrings with iron pyrites forming clusters between shells, English, c.1750. The pearl from the nautilus shell is called 'coque de perle' and is usually formed in a perfect oval suitable for use in matching earrings. Similar to the Bernard necklace (Colour Plate 25), owned by a member of the Salisbury family in Worcester, Massachusetts, mid-18th century, English. Photograph by Stephen Briggs. Bequest of Stephen Salisbury III Estate. Worcester Art Museum.

Colour Plate 25. This necklace set in silver with pastes surrounding bosses of mother-of-pearl (coque de perle) *and of English origin was owned by Lady Bernard, wife of Sir Francis Bernard, Governor of Massachusetts from 1760 to 1669. In 1768, when they left Massachusetts, Lady Bernard gave the necklace (and matching earrings which do not survive) to her friend Mrs. M. Nichols. The necklace passed to Mrs. Thomas Lamb whose descendants presented it to the Massachusetts Historical Society in 1973. Length 16 9/16 in. (overall). Gift of Rosamund Lamb and Aimee Lamb. Massachusetts Historical Society.*

bosses enhanced by pyrites. A similar pair of earrings set with *coques de perle* and framed by iron pyrites is in the Hull-Grundy Collection at the British Museum. They were made in England in the mid-eighteenth century. *Coque de perle* is a central whorl of the convex outer shell of the nautilus.[11] 'Coc de pearl' earrings with drops were imported from England and offered for sale in 1772 by Timothy Berrett in Philadelphia.[12]

A more elaborate example of this type of pearl jewelry is the necklace seen in the portrait of sixteen-year-old Elizabeth Boush of Virginia painted by John Durand in 1769 (see Colour Plate 14). It had an attached pendant in the centre, a pear-shaped drop suspended from a bow, and complementary cluster earrings.[13]

11. Tait, I, 29, #148.
12. *Pa. Packet,* 30 Nov. 1772.
13. M.J. Gibbs, 'Precious Artifacts: Women's Jewelry in the Chesapeake, 1750-1799', Journal of Early Southern Decorative Arts, MESDA, May 1987, pp. 90-92.

Colour Plate 26. This resplendent lady was portrayed by John Durand (working about 1766 to 1782 in New York, Connecticut and Virginia). He was noted for his details of dress. The unidentified sitter wears a necklace and earrings apparently set with red pastes. An unusual series of three knots of diamond-like pastes (similar to corsage ornaments) separates the necklace from its tear-drop pendant. The long delicate chain is probably made of black glass beads. It connects to an additional pendant set with a miniature portrait and is a type of ornament that appears in 17th century Dutch portraiture. Height 29½in., width 21½ in. Private Collection.

Diamonds and Pastes

Diamonds

By the middle of the eighteenth century, diamonds were becoming increasingly available to the American colonists. Expanding trade brought these precious stones in ever greater quantities from India and Brazil to Europe and eventually to the Colonies. In addition, the lapidary was developing new ways of enhancing the natural assets of diamonds.

Diamonds crystallize from carbon into the shape of an octahedron, the silhouette of which we call diamond shaped. These most brilliant and durable gems were worn in classical times in their uncut rough or slightly polished state. Lapidaries in India discovered that diamonds lend themselves to cleavage. By splitting a single crystal

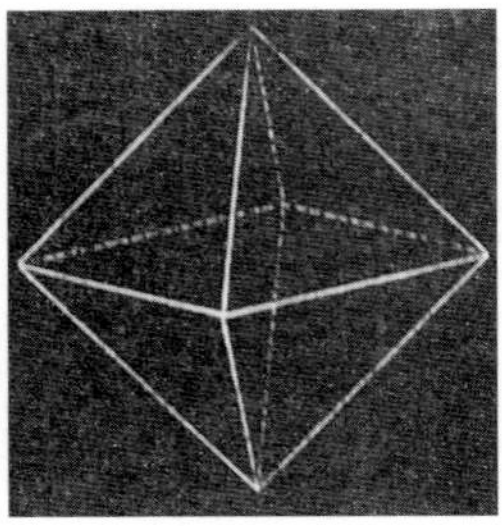

A

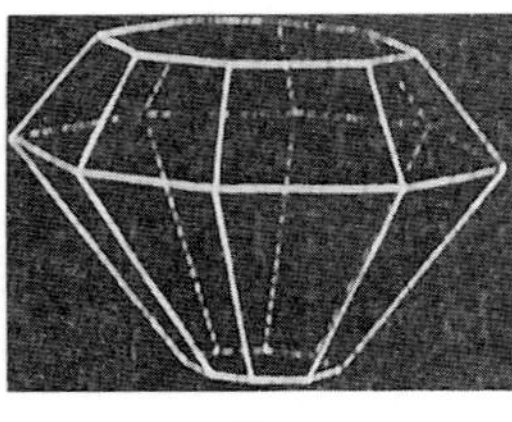

B

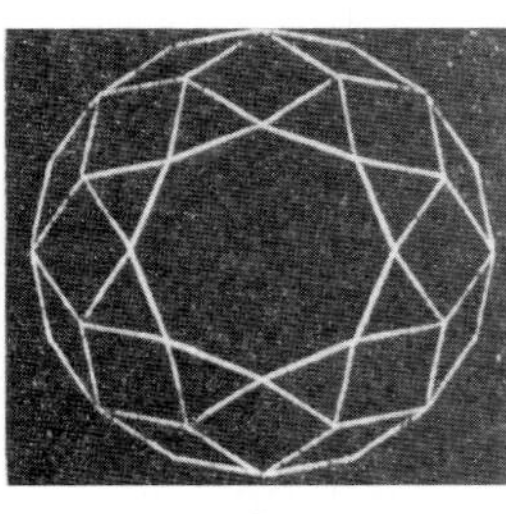

C

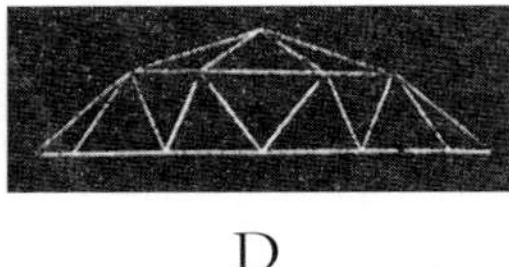

D

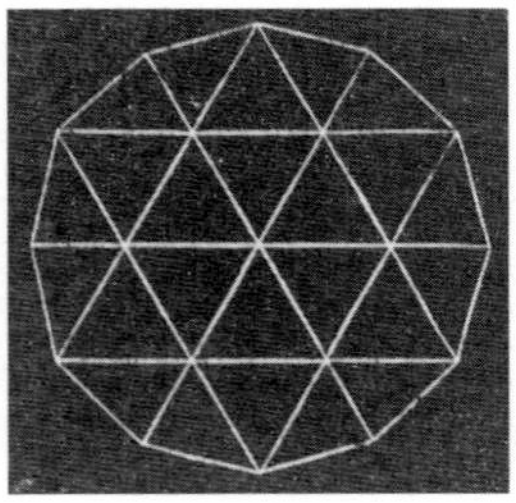

E

along its widest point, two gems could be made from one and brilliance could be increased. Removing the natural points of the crystal produced the table cut (Plate 21). This cut was introduced early in the fifteenth century and continued to be popular until the introduction of the rose cut in the mid-seventeenth century. The earliest diamond jewelry owned in America would therefore have been made of gems in their original octahedral shape or table cut.

The rose-cut diamond, fashionable in the latter part of the seventeenth century, was cut with a flat base and usually had two horizontal rows of facets rising to a point on top. The standard rose cut developed by the Dutch and seen in the diamond wedding ring of Judith Crommelin (Plate 9) had six facets meeting at the top point and eighteen cross facets below. Early in the eighteenth century, the rose cut was surpassed in beauty by the brilliant cut with fifty-six or fifty-eight facets of different sizes and shapes which maximized the diamond's natural qualities of refraction and reflection. It is little wonder, given its clarity, sparkle and durability, that during the colonial period the diamond was the most sought after gem for jewelry, as it still is today.

While Louis XIV and other crowned heads of Europe vied to obtain the largest, most important diamonds, Americans were fortunate to have any sort of jewelry made of this most precious gem. In addition to diamond rings and an occasional pendant owned in seventeenth century America and discussed earlier (see page 22), there were in the eighteenth century increasing numbers of diamond wedding rings like Martha Washington's (see Colour Plate 11) and brooches like Mrs. Pinckney's (Colour Plate 13) with diamonds among other precious stones. However, due to the value of diamonds both here and abroad, many examples were inevitably broken up to be sold or reset and so are lost to us today. Furthermore, many of the wealthy Tories who possessed significant diamond jewelry took it with them when they fled the country at the time of the Revolution, thereby depleting further the supply of surviving examples of American-owned diamond jewelry. Another factor affecting our knowledge of this type of jewelry is that diamonds were more suitable for evening or formal occasions, and therefore were rarely, if ever, seen in colonial portraits of Americans in everyday poses and clothes.

The Reverend George Whitefield spoke out during his visit to Boston in 1740 against 'jewels, patches and gay apparel commonly worn by the female sex'.[1] Much of the diamond jewelry owned in New England consisted of rings and earrings, with less frequent mention of anything more elaborate.[2] Boston jewelers of the mid-eighteenth century, such as Daniel Parker and Daniel Boyer (see page 65), offered modest selections of diamond rings in their shops. Even Sir William Pepperrell, hero of the battle at Louisburg, with all his wealth and large amount of silver, bequeathed only one diamond ring to his granddaughter Mary Pepperrell Sparhawk when he died in 1759.[3]

Philadelphians of the 1750s, in spite of the number of Quakers among them, could find diamond rings for sale in several shops. John Leacock imported jewelry from London and supplied 'large rose diamond sparks for middle stones for rings' as well as small ones for side stones.[4] Austin Machon, a jeweler from London, made and sold all

Plate 21. Illustrations of early cuts of diamonds from Louis Dieulafait's Diamonds and Precious Stones, *New York, 1874. a. Regular octahedron in a natural state. b. With a pyramid removed from the top and the bottom. c. Brilliant cut. d. Semi-brilliant. e. Holland rose cut.*

sorts of diamond rings and earrings. Theodore Carbin had very neat brilliant and rose diamonds to set in rings. Goldsmith and jeweler, Edmund Milne, promised his customers imported London-made fancy diamond rings, diamond and garnet rings, and twisted wire topaz rings with brilliant diamonds. He also had brilliant and rose diamonds as yet unset.[5]

From newspaper advertisements it becomes evident that in New York and Charleston, South Carolina, residents were more desirous of diamond jewelry than were Boston Puritans and Philadelphia Quakers. In New York, the diamond rings were more elaborate. Fancy rings, rose rings and rings designed in the shape of a vase of flowers set entirely with diamonds could all be had there. Jeweler Otto de Parisen had a ring set with a heart-shaped diamond surrounded with sparks.

Diamond earrings occurred more frequently in advertisements. Mrs. Rebecca Hays was robbed of her diamond earrings with drops in 1767. Charles Oliver Bruff illustrated a girandole style of diamond earring with three pendant drops in his advertisement in May 1772 (Plate 22). Earrings consisting of three pear-shaped drops suspended from a bow had been in fashion for more than a century and continued in favour in the eighteenth century. In 1763 Bruff hired a jeweler from London who understood diamond work and went to great expense to send to London for diamonds, in the hope that he would meet with encouragement from ladies and gentlemen. Toward this end he promised to 'study to use them well'.[6]

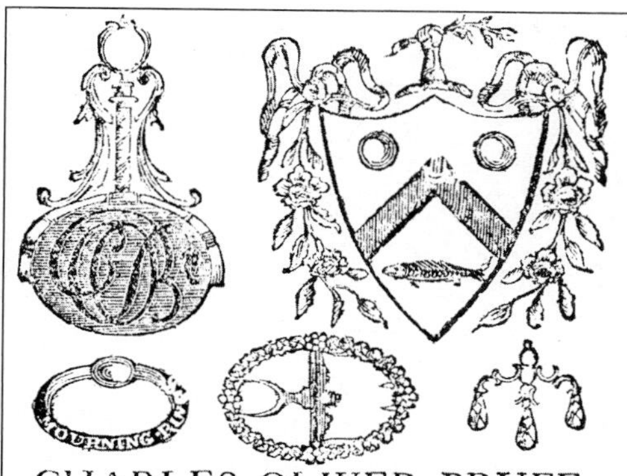

CHARLES OLIVER BRUFF,
GOLDSMITH and JEWELLER,
At the ſign of the tea-pot, tankard, and ear-ring, between Maiden-Lane and Crown-Street, next door to Doctor Kemmeneau, near the Fly-Market;

WHERE he makes and mends any kind of diamond or enamell'd work in the jewellery way: Alſo all manner of ſtone buckles, ſtone rings, ear-rings and broaches, ſolitaires, hair jewels, lockets, enamell'd ſleeve buttons, mourning rings of all ſorts, trinkets for ladies, rings and lockets, plain or enamelled; gold necklaces and ſtones of all ſorts: Likewiſe makes and mends all ſorts of ſilver-ſmiths work; Alſo ladies fans neatly mended. He gives the higheſt price for old gold, ſilver and jewels; buys rough coral, handſome pebble, and blank cornelian, fit for ſeal ſtones: He has fitted a Lapidary mill up, where he cuts all ſorts ſtones. He wants immediately a lapidary, jeweller, and an apprentice boy; none need apply but what can be well recommended: Where he engraves all ſorts of arms, creſts, cyphers, heads and fancies, in the neateſt manner and greateſt expedition, with the heads of Lord Chatham, Shakeſpeare, Milton, Newton, Pope, Homer, Socrates, Hannibal, Marc Anthony, Cæſar, Plato, Jupiter, Apollo, Neptune, Mars, Cleopatria, Diana, Flora, Venus, Marcelania, Maſons arms, with all emblems of Liberty; Cupid fancies, hearts and dores neatly engraved for ladies trinkets; Likewiſe ſilver and ſteel ſeals: He alſo plaits hair in the neateſt manner. N. B. Takes likeneſſes off in hair as natural as poſſible, as to the form of viſages, works hair in ſprigs, birds, figures, cyphers, creſts and cupid fancies. He has for ſale, beſt curls for whiſtles and bell; likewiſe cleans watches 2s. china dial plates fitted in at 6s. each, glaſſes fitted in at [illegible] each, and other repairs in proportion.

Plate 22. Charles Oliver Bruff (1735-1817) advertised in the New-York Gazette and the Weekly Mercury *in 1774 all kinds of jewelry, illustrating the types of rings, earrings, buckles and seal fobs his customers could purchase, including diamond work.*

Other forms of diamond jewelry offered in New York included cluster and knot rings, brooches, lockets, aigrettes and buckles. A diamond girdle buckle, with some thirty diamonds in it, was reported stolen in New York in 1762.[7]

Charleston's John Paul Grimke was one of the first jewelers in America to offer much in the way of diamond work. That he made, as well as imported, diamond jewelry, and actually owned a diamond scale in 1741, is an indication of the seriousness of his work along these lines. Periodically over the next twenty-five years, Grimke advertised a new shipment of rose-cut and brilliant-cut diamonds which he could set to order. In the 1750s, he had not only loose diamonds for setting, but English-made 'very rich' diamond rings and earrings. By the 1760s, he was also importing such London-made temptations as diamond necklaces, earrings, egrets and bosom hearts, as well as buckles and finger rings.

Another jeweler from London working in Charleston in the early 1750s, Philip Tidyman, by contrast, offered only diamond rings, although he said he could make and mend all sorts of diamond work. Diamond hoop rings were popular with Tidyman's customers and he kept several of these in stock.[8] Jeweler John Hector sold his Carolina patrons 'beautiful Brilliants and Rose Diamonds of different sizes' that he had ready for setting on demand. He pointed out that 'every piece of work that he offers to the Publick is entirely begun and finished in this place'.[9]

Christopher Hughes of Baltimore offered fashionable diamond rings for both men

1. Weeden, *II*, 536.
2. A 'fine brilliant diamond ring' was advertised in the *Boston Evening Post*, 20 Feb. 1738.
3. *Maine Wills*, p. 848.
4. *Pa. Gaz.*, 25 Jan. 1759. See also *Pa. Journal & Wkly. Advtr.*, 26 July 1750, for diamond rings sold by Joseph Redmond from the shop of Peter David, silversmith.
5. *Pa. Journal & Wkly Advtr.*, 27 Sept. 1759; 1 June 1758; 17 Dec. 1763.
6. *The N-Y Mercury*, 20 May 1765; 3 Jan. 1763.
7. Ibid., 8 Feb. 1762.
8. *SC Gaz.*, 12 Sept. 1741; 3 Dec. 1750; 19 Oct. 1765; 3 Mar. 1751; 7 May 1753; 8 Oct. 1763; 11 Aug. 1766.
9. *S.C. & Am. Gen. Gaz.*, 16 Dec. 1774.

Colour Plate 27. Unidentified young woman of the Claypoole family, attributed to James Claypoole, Jr., Philadelphia, c.1767. Her necklace, slightly heart-shaped pendant and triple-drop earrings appear to be made of paste or quartz. A similar necklace appears in a portrait of Rebecca Doz by the same artist. Height 20¹⁄₁₆in., width 16in. Private Collection.

and women in 1773 and, when his shop was broken into a few years later, he lost several rings set with rose-cut diamonds flanking a single central coloured gem of emerald or topaz.[10]

The evidence is clear. Diamond jewelry was owned and made in the colonies. Some of it, no doubt, resides in family vaults unrecognized, unappreciated, and unfortunately separated from the documentation that could identify it. Perhaps the certain knowledge of its existence will help to bring this diamond jewelry to light.

Pastes

With the high value placed on diamonds, it was inevitable that attempts would be made to imitate them. Glass, of course, was an early substitute because of its transparency. The glass used by Italian jewelers during the Renaissance period was highly refractive and suggested the diamond's quality of brilliance. Glass imitations of diamonds are called pastes, possibly derived from the Italian word *pasta*.

Glass capable of being cut into gem-like forms was brought to new levels in the eighteenth century, especially by a jeweler from Strasbourg working in Paris, Georges Frédéric Strass (1701-1773).[11] Building upon George Ravenscroft's discovery of flint glass in England about 1675, and the invention of lead glass about 1681, Strass developed in the 1730s a kind of lead glass that was not only transparent and highly refractive, but could also be faceted and set just like diamonds and other precious gems.

At the time paste was not considered merely a fake, but enjoyed popularity on its own merit. Wickes and Netherton, fashionable goldsmiths and jewelers in London, made no apologies when they announced on their trade card in 1750 that they sold 'False Stonework in Aigrettes, Earrings, Buckles, etc.'.[12] Today paste is prized for its rarity, since much of it was discarded because it was not 'real'. Given the lack of examples of diamond jewelry of the early and mid-eighteenth century, paste jewelry

10. *The Md. Journal & Balto. Advtr.*, 20 Aug. 1773; *Dunlap's Md. Gaz. or the Balt. Gen. Advtr.*, 27 Aug. 1776.
11. M.D.S. Lewis, *Antique Paste Jewellery*.
12. Barr, p. 70.

Colour Plate 28. A heart-shaped paste brooch is seen in the portrait of Mrs. Eunice Huntington Devotion painted by Winthrop Chandler, Connecticut, in 1772. Height 52½in., width 37in. Lyman Allyn Museum.

Detail of brooch

presents a picture of the next best thing. The same kind of craftsmanship was extended to settings for paste as was given to jewelry made of true gems.

Paste was most practical for functional jewelry like buckles and buttons. Paste buckles first became fashionable in England and France in the 1730s. A man of the world was described in 1753:

> His buckles, like diamonds, must glitter and shine
> Should they cost fifty pounds they would not be too fine.[13]

Paste buckles were widely advertised in the 1760s in colonial cities. A fine example fashioned in the delicate airy rococo style of the 1760s and owned in Boston might be

13. Quoted from *Monsieur à la Mode* by G. Bernard Hughes, *Small Antique Silverware* , p. 179.

Plate 23. Pair of paste shoe buckles, English, mid-18th century, with variously faceted stones. Museum of Fine Arts, Boston.

the sort described at the time as 'Ladies rose or knot Buckles' (Plate 23).[14] The curvilinear outlines were made up of flowers and bows, set with pastes of varying sizes and shapes, held in silver collets carefully hammered to conform to the shape of the stones.

The technical skill required in the setting of pastes was equal to, if not greater than, that needed by the diamond setters. Pastes, though often rose cut, could be more freely faceted and shaped to suit the sizes and forms of the designs and, since wastage was not a great concern, could be more closely fitted than could the more expensive diamonds. Air-tight closed-back settings were used for the early pastes which were backed with thin pieces of shiny metal foil. It was also customary for eighteenth century paste, as well as many early diamonds, to have a dot of pitch-like paint applied to the culet of each stone. Looking carefully at the buckles in Plate 23, one can see these black spots.

Rings are the most widespread survivors of paste-set colonial jewelry. American mourning rings were set with pastes foiled to imitate amethysts or topaz, as well as diamonds. When Colonel Peter Schuyler of New Jersey died in 1762, his gold memorial ring was set with a large oval glass surrounded by numerous tiny pastes (Plate 9). The back of the setting was hinged to form a locket to contain a plait of hair.

The range of paste jewelry can be seen in the 1763 advertisement of Edmund Milne of Philadelphia who had imported from London paste shoe, knee, and stock buckles, paste-set bracelets, stay hooks and girdle buckles, single and three-drop paste earrings (Colour Plate 27), paste necklaces and paste brooches.[15] Brooches followed the same rococo designs as gem-set brooches and were especially pretty as floral sprays. One little silver spray pin (Plate 69) was set with brilliant-cut pastes in the form of three branches interspersed with flowers, all springing from a circle of stones. The terminal settings were finished off with irregular furls, giving the piece a delightful asymmetry and charm.

The most popular type of paste brooch in the colonies, however, was the twisted-heart breast or bosom pin. One of Gilbert Stuart's earliest portraits showed a young man wearing such a brooch mid-way down his white stock.[16] The brooch was open in the centre. The bar of the pin came through to the front of the heart. The stock was passed through to the front, wrapped around the bar, passed to the back, and pulled down, thereby securing it without the necessity of a hook or piercing the fabric. Both men and women enjoyed wearing these hearts, as can be seen by the portrait of Mrs. Eunice Devotion (Colour Plate 28) who wears a similar brooch on her lace neck ruffle.

Made of clear pastes with a single topaz-coloured paste at the top was a brooch (Plate 24, left) owned by the Robbins family of Massachusetts. Though the heart setting is made of silver, the pin stem was made in gold as was often the case in the better eighteenth century jewelry. Another example (Plate 24, right), owned by the Knowles family of Deerfield, New Hampshire, was made of clear round pastes with a single larger square-set red stone at the top. The shape of the pin was more straight sided in style and was without the twist of the earlier rococo design, indicating the introduction of more elliptical shapes with the advent of neo-classical taste. The pin stem can clearly be seen coming to the front on this brooch. Many of these heart brooches had their fasteners changed when the original method of attachment was no longer understood. The pin stems were forced or resoldered to the back and a hook placed on the opposite side so that they could be clasped like pins that were pushed in and out of the fabric.

French paste jewelry, often made of smaller stones and fussier in its details than the

14. Cooke & Co., *The Md. Journal & Balto. Advtr.*, 20 Aug. 1773.
15. *Pa. Journal & Wkly. Advtr.*, 15 Dec. 1763.
16. Portrait at Museum of Fine Arts, Boston.

Plate 24. Heart-shaped paste brooches, owned by the Robbins family of Lexington, Massachusetts (left) and Knowles family of New Hampshire (right). The brooch with the red stone at the top was placed on a now tattered red silk ribbon to show how fabric was wrapped around the stem pin and brought down through to the back. Height 1¼in. and 1⅛in. Photograph by David Bohl, Boston. Society for the Preservation of New England Antiquities.

Plate 25. Bright blue pastes set in scrolled rococo silver mounts were worn by Mrs. Metcalf Bowler in her portrait by John Singleton Copley about 1763. Her necklet had an impressive pendant (probably detachable) with a large tear-drop stone surmounted by three round stones. Height 50in., width 40¼in. Gift of Louise Alida Livingston. ©1995 National Gallery of Art.

English, found its way to the colonies via England. Philip Hulbeart advertised French paste necklaces and earrings in 1761 in the same advertisement with English paste buckles imported by him from London.[17] There is evidence to suggest that in colonial eighteenth century parlance the term 'French' with regard to jewelry often meant that it was made of paste.

Martha Washington acquired a pair of French earrings from the London jeweler, Grymes, in 1760 for only five shillings, confirming that they must have been paste. Over the next few years, she acquired a number of 'French' necklaces and earrings. The most significant paste jewelry was purchased in 1770 for Martha's daughter Patsy Custis. It was a complete set consisting of a necklace, earrings, a sprig pin and hair combs, with pins and buttons for the stomacher, all for £25, which for paste was a tidy sum.[18]

Paste jewelry could also be purchased in a variety of colours. In 1759, at the time of her marriage, Martha Washington received an 'emerine' necklace from the London shop of Susanna Passavant. A decade later a green hoop ring was purchased from Gurdon and Son for daughter Patsy. Both items were undoubtedly made of paste.[19] Earrings and necklaces were available in aquamarine, green, red, black, and blue paste.[20]

By 1774, John Hector was able to make paste jewelry in his own shop in Charleston, South Carolina. Not only could he set all kinds of jewelry by the same methods employed in London, including paste buckles, but he could sell them for no more than they cost imported from London and Birmingham. Furthermore, he guaranteed that they would last twice as long.[21] Jeremiah Andrews of Philadelphia also made his own paste buckles for ladies' and gentlemen's shoes, knees, and stocks, on the shortest notice.[22] There was enough demand that jewelers such as Abel Buell in Connecticut kept a number of brilliant paste buckles and earring drops on hand in their shop.[23]

Nevertheless, in spite of these imports and domestic productions, Thomas Gwatkin, a professor at the College of William and Mary in Virginia, complained:

> Fashion reigns here with despotic sway. New modes are imported full as soon as they are conveyed into Counties at a distance from London. The ladies generally wear a great number of rings upon their fingers which are seldom of any value. And indeed I have seen but few jewels or even paste of superior quality since my residence in this Country.[24]

17. Hulbeart advertisement *Pa. Gaz.*, 5 Nov. 1761.
18. Two 'french Necklaces' and '1 three round Oval ditto' were purchased from the London firm of Heath in 1763. In 1764, George Washington ordered a 'french Necklace & Earings' for Martha. In 1766 'a handsome french Necklace & Earings – not to exceed 21' shillings was ordered. GW *Invoices & Letters 1755-66*, pp. 49, 81, 96, 142; Fitzpatrick, *Writings of Washington* 3:23.
19. Washington invoices, pp. 11, 59.
20. John Mecom adv. *The N-Y Mercury*, 23 May 1763.
21. *S.C. & Am. Gen. Gaz.*, 16 Dec. 1774.
22. *Md. Journal*, 13 April 1779.
23. Wroth, *Abel Buell of Connecticut*, p. 35.
24. *Wm & Mary Quarterly*, Third Series, *IX*, 1 Jan. 1952. Trivia, p. 84.

Plate 26. This portrait of Mrs. Jacob Ogden includes a clasp similar to that made by John Gardner (see Colour Plate 30). Her clasp fastens two strands of gold beads. Portrait attributed to Joseph Steward (1753-1822), Connecticut, c.1794. Height 37⅛in., width 33½in. (overall). The Connecticut Historical Society, Hartford.

Quartz

Colourless natural gemstone quartz, popularly called crystal, had been used in jewelry to simulate diamonds before the better types of glass were developed and it had respect and value of its own. In comparison with paste, crystal feels cold to the touch, has a higher transparency but less brilliance, and is slightly harder and more durable, allowing it to take a sharper polish than paste. Crystal taken from deposits in the Clifton limestone near Bristol, England, was used in seventeenth and eighteenth

Colour Plate 29. Above left. Cypher and crystal jewelry. Ring, with gold band, set with crystal over wire twist cypher, flanked by small stones. Earrings, with cypher and crystal over red foil. Owned by Mrs. Stephen Robbins of Lexington, Massachusetts in the mid-18th century. Diameter ¾in (ring). Photograph by Mark Sexton. Peabody Essex Museum

Colour Plate 30. Above right. Gold clasp for a four-strand necklace, c.1760, bearing the engraved monogram EH on the back for its original owner. It is marked IG in a rectangle on the back by its maker John Gardner (1734-1776) of New London, Connecticut. The clasp is set with crystal over twisted wire borders and cypher over red foil. A similar clasp can be seen in the portrait of Mrs. Jacob Ogden (Plate 26). Length 1⁵⁄₁₆in. The Connecticut Historical Society, Hartford.

Colour Plate 31. The gold clasp for this bracelet is set with a flat plait of dark brown hair on which the script initials EW are laid and covered with a piece of polished quartz with a faceted edge. It is thought to have been owned by Elizabeth Wormeley of Virginia. American, c.1760-80. Colonial Williamsburg Foundation.

century English jewelry and became known as Bristol stones or 'Bristows'. A contemporary English verse made reference to their use as substitute diamonds:

> Haires curl'd ears pearl'd with Bristows brave and bright
> Bought for true diamonds in his false sight.[1]

Bristol stones were occasionally specified by name in the newspaper advertisements of colonial American jewelers, but not often enough to give evidence that there was much of a market for them there. Perhaps many of them were passed off as diamonds and not always acknowledged for what they really were. In Philadelphia in 1753, Charles Dutens imported fine Bristol stones that he could make into lockets, solitaires, stay hooks, earrings, buttons and mourning rings.[2]

In Philadelphia in 1759 crystal jewelry was imported from London. John Leacock offered a variety of forms ranging from 'white and brown chrystal stone buttons set in gold, with or without scollops' to 'crystal coffin stones and cyphers for mourning rings'. He had crystal tops and drops for earrings, and his waistcoat crystal buttons could be set in silver, with nine stones in each, or set with a single stone. His stone solitaires could be set in silver or a less expensive metal. He also had gold cyphers for crystal buttons that could be foiled ruby or white.[3]

1. Quoted from Lenton's *Young Gallant's Whirligig*, 1629, by Lewis, pp. 32, 75.
2. *Pa. Journal or the Wkly. Advtr.*, 14 Oct. 1753. A ring with two Bristol stones on each side of a central heart-shaped garnet was stolen from the New York shop of Otto de Parisien in 1765. *The N-Y Mercury*, 20 May 1765.
3. *Pa. Gaz.*, 25 Jan. 1759.

New England jewelers found these items popular as well and kept on hand a stock of crystal cypher earrings and buttons or links of buttons, set in silver or gold. Earrings could be made of a single button. Top and drop earrings could be made of a small button with a pendant button of a slightly larger size attached below. Rings could also be set with these same buttons. Daniel Parker was one of several Boston jewelers around 1760 who offered 'Cypher and Brilliant Button and Earing Stones of all Sorts', 'Brilliant earing top and drop Christials', 'Locket Stones', as well as watch crystals.[4]

Numerous examples of crystal and cypher jewelry survive (Colour Plate 29). Held in a fitted collet with posts, the crystals were backed with red foil and contained little black squares on which were laid gold-twist cyphers. These buttons shared a close relationship to the crystal and cypher clasp (Plate 26 and Colour Plate 30) owned by Mrs. Ogden in Connecticut. One of the most beautiful crystal and cypher jewels (Plate 11) was owned in Boston. It featured a deep and brilliant-cut stone with a distinct cypher and neatly looped border.

Plain crystal, as opposed to crystal and cypher, jewelry was also readily available at the same time. In Massachusetts, a fascinating list of the jewelry kept in George Roger's desk in 1748 included a girdle buckle with twenty-six brilliant-cut crystals, a pair of crystal earrings with three drops, a ring set with seven crystals, a crystal heart hook, as well as a pair of cypher buttons set in gold.[5]

Crystal was also used for seals. Pyramidal crystal seals with gold loops and triangular crystal block seals set in silver were but a few of the designs available.[6] William Bateman, who specialized in stone seal engraving in New York in 1774, offered to engrave coats of arms, crests, cyphers, figures, heads and fancies. He even had a book of heraldry from which gentlemen who did not know what their arms might be could search without charge and pick one out.[7]

Lewis Ducray, a London lapidary who was working in Philadelphia in 1771, cut indigenous crystal as well as paste and other stones for local jewelers. He boasted, 'Such gentlemen and ladies as would choose this country Chrystal, may have it cut superior to any imported'.[8]

Although the designation 'stone' was often applied in colonial times to transparent crystal as well as paste, it was also used to describe other kinds of non-transparent quartz such as chalcedony or agate. Mocha stone was a variety of agate that could be the same as moss agate, but generally referred to a stone with black or brown dendritic markings. The name came from the port of Mocha in Yemen on the Red Sea, the source of fine coffee as well. Mocha jewelry appeared with some frequency in mid-eighteenth century America, especially in rings and sleeve buttons. Mocha stones suitable for earrings as well as rings were offered by Dutens and Harper in Philadelphia in 1755.[9] Sometimes the mocha stone was surrounded with garnets. John Mecom advertised mocha rings with garnet clusters in New York in 1763 and in Charleston 'a neat Mocco Stone Ring, set round with Garnetts' was lost in 1782.[10]

Cornelian, sard and onyx, all varieties of chalcedony in different colours, were often used for seals because their hardness lent itself to sharply defined cutting. Charles Dutens had fine cornelians engraved with doves, poses, and other devices that he recommended for both gold seals and men's rings in 1753. Cornelian seals set in gold and silver were imported from London and advertised by John Leacock in 1759. Scotch pebble referred to a variety of quartz, often agate, used in traditional Highland jewelry and imported to colonial America largely in the form of buttons.[11]

4. *Boston N-L*, Joseph Edwards, Jr., 21 Mar. 1765; John Towzel, 5 Nov. 1767; *Boston Gaz.*, Parker, 6 Nov. 1758; 12 Feb. 1761; 10 Sept. 1764.
5. Cited by Jobe & Kaye, *New England Furniture*, pp. 227-28; Suffolk Co., Mass., Probate Records, old series, *41*, 404.
6. *Pa. Journal*, 17 May 1763.
7. *The N-Y Gaz. and the Wkly. Mercury*, 7 Nov. 1774.
8. In addition, he also cut the glasses for miniature picture frames and sold a variety of artificial flowers. *Pa. Journal*, 4 Apr. 1771.
9. *Pa. Gaz.*, 18 Feb. 1755.
10. *The N-Y Mercury*, 23 May 1763; *The Royal Gaz.*, 1 June 1782.
11. *Pa. Journal or Wkly. Advtr.*, 4 Oct. 1753; *Pa. Gaz.*, 25 Jan. 1759; *The Md. Journal & Balto. Advtr.*, 20 Aug. 1773.

Gold and Silver

For thousands of years gold has been the metal of preference for jewelry. Not only valuable because it is rare, gold has a unique bright yellow colour and is capable of receiving and retaining a lustre. In its pure state it is chemically inactive and will not tarnish in air as silver does. Both silver and gold are very malleable and can be easily shaped and decorated. Tensile strength and ductility allow them to be drawn into amazingly long fine wires without breaking. Both can be alloyed to improve on certain qualities.

Gold and silver were the chief inducements to many of the first Europeans who came to America. Captain John Smith complained that it was the gold-seekers 'with their golden promises' that made everyone who came to Virginia a slave to the search. 'There was not talke, no hope, nor worke, but dig gold, wash gold, refine gold, load gold'.[1] It would be two centuries before any substantial amount of gold would be found in the United States. However, coins and old jewelry made of gold and silver could be melted down and remade into new jewelry.

The work of the Richardson family of Philadelphia illustrates the types of jewelry colonial goldsmiths made of solid precious metals. In addition to rings discussed earlier (pages 23-31), buttons and buckles were among the objects most frequently made of gold and silver. A pair of nicely shaped silver buckles a little over an inch long were cast and marked by Francis Richardson of Philadelphia about 1721 (Plate 27). They were engraved with an inscription indicating that they were worn by Elizabeth Paschall on 11 May 1721, her wedding day.[2] Buckles for shoes, knees, and stocks got progressively more ornate as the eighteenth century advanced. Their design became more rococo as the fashion for flowers and scrolls became more popular. Francis' son Joseph made smoothly curved plain gold buckles, for his more Quakerly customers as well as swirly foliated and encrusted buckles for those who had 'gone English' (Plate 28).[3] He also imported buckles from London for his mid-eighteenth century patrons, on at least one occasion sending a pattern to show his supplier exactly what he wanted.

1. *Proceedings of the Va. Colony in The Travels, Adventures and Observations of Captain John Smith*, from the London edition of 1629, *I*, 169.
2. Fales, *Richardson*, pp. 13-15.
3. *Ibid*, pp. 147-19.

Plate 27. Pair of silver shoe buckles worn by Elizabeth Paschall on her wedding day, 11 May 1721, according to the engraved inscriptions on the back of the buckles. They were made and marked (FR in a heart) by Francis Richardson (1681-1729), Quaker goldsmith of Philadelphia. Length 1¼in. The Historical Society of Pennsylvania.

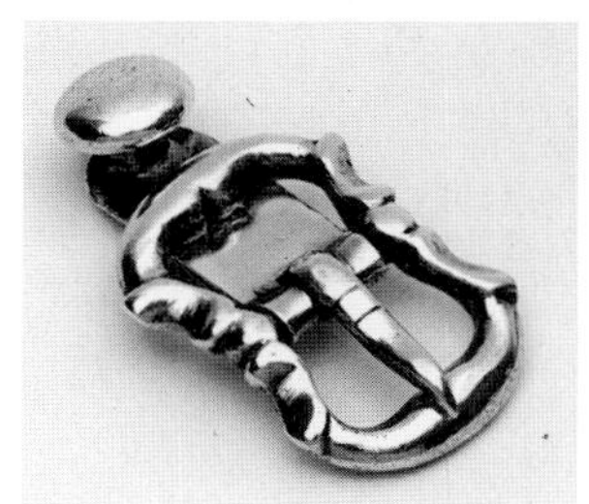

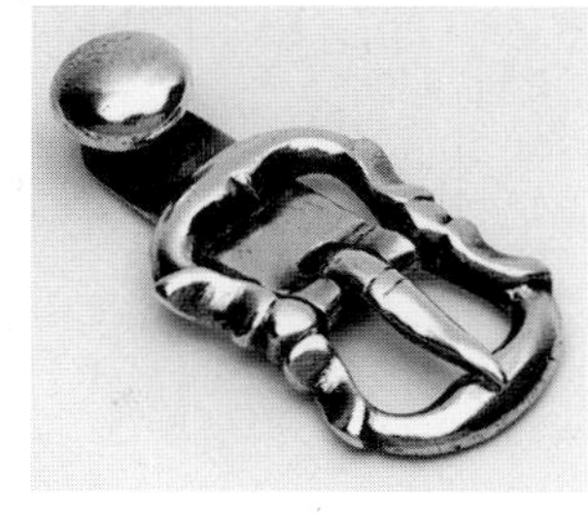

Plate 28. Gold shoe buckle made by Joseph Richardson (1711-1784), Philadelphia goldsmith, c.1750-1760, and cast with a pattern of scrolls and leafage, gadrooning and shells characterized by Richardson as 'wrought' or 'carved'. The Quaker goldsmith imported buckles from How & Masterman of London for resale in his shop. These provided him with up-to-date fashions he could then use to cast his own buckles. Marked IR in oval. Length 1¼in. Gift of Walter M. Jeffords. Yale University Art Gallery.

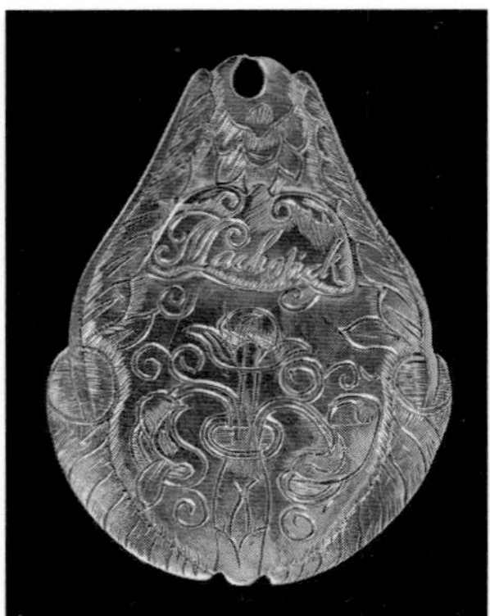

Plate 29. Silver badge, engraved on front Ye King of *and on the back* Machotick, *ordered by the Virginia General Assembly in an act of March 1661/62, to be given to Indian chiefs as a form of identification for their safe passage in areas settled by the English. This badge was found in 1964 when an Indian site was excavated at Camden in Caroline County. The engraving depicts flowers and foliage typical of mid-17th century decorative arts. Vines grow out of the cornucopias on each side of the base of the badge. Height 2½in., width 2in. The Collection of the Virginia Historical Society.*

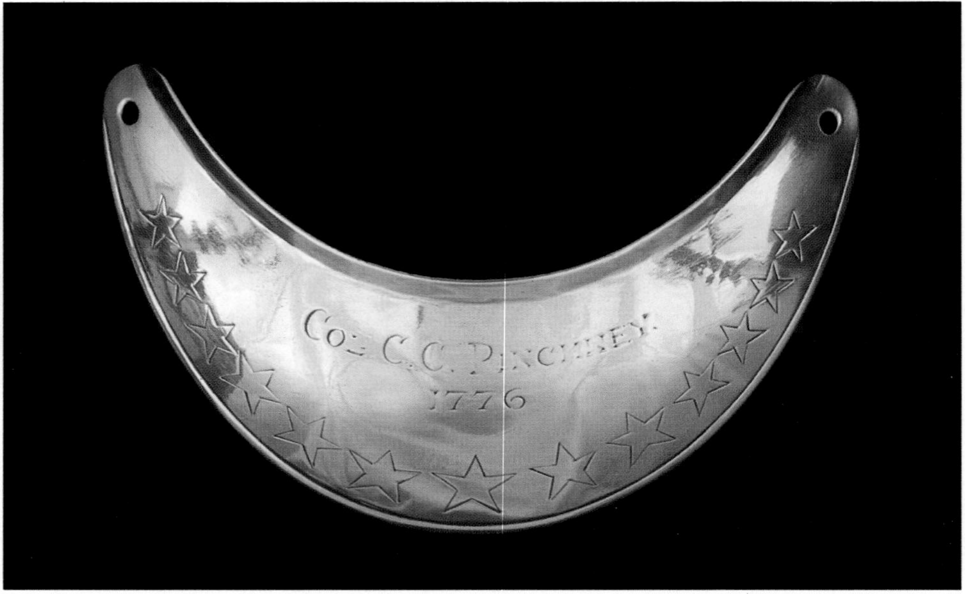

Colour Plate 32. Silver gorget made and marked (I[.]VANALL in rectangle) by John Vanall who was working in Charleston, S.C. c.1749-52. It was owned by Charles Cotesworth Pinckney whose name, rank and date of 1776 were later added with thirteen stars for a border. Length 5½in. Photograph by Terry Richardson. The Charleston Museum.

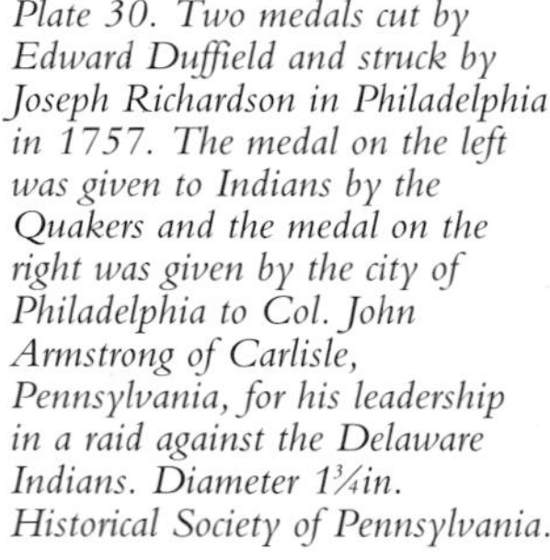

Plate 30. Two medals cut by Edward Duffield and struck by Joseph Richardson in Philadelphia in 1757. The medal on the left was given to Indians by the Quakers and the medal on the right was given by the city of Philadelphia to Col. John Armstrong of Carlisle, Pennsylvania, for his leadership in a raid against the Delaware Indians. Diameter 1¾in. Historical Society of Pennsylvania.

Buttons were made in circular shapes, cut from flattened pieces of silver or gold, with a simple attachment loop soldered to the back. During the middle decades of the eighteenth century, they were often octagonal in shape with the edges turned under to form a rim. These were embellished with engraved rosettes or scrolls.[4] Two buttons could be linked together to form what we call today cuff-links. The Richardsons and their customers called them links of buttons. Joseph Richardson sold hollow and solid buttons, silver as well as gold. In 1760 he ordered a socket die and punches 'for Stamping silver or gold buttons the Siz & form of the Patterns herein Incloased'.[5]

Joseph Richardson provided customers with silver seals for four or five shillings and for watch chains he charged an additional ten shillings. More often, however, colonial seals seem to have been imported. Andrew Belcher, of Milton, Massachusetts, had amassed a small collection of seals by the end of the colonial era. He had a seal for his gold watch, three for his silver watch, and a triangular seal set in gold, not to mention the four family seals with handles that were used at the desk and not worn.[6]

Silver medals were presented on special occasions to Indian chiefs by the French, Spanish, and English governments, in an effort to win their loyalty and help in gaining territory in the new world. In 1661/2 the Virginia General Assembly issued

Colour Plate 33. Portrait of Ann Claypoole (1760-1832), daughter of Joseph Claypoole, attributed to James Claypoole, Jr., Philadelphia, c.1767. Her two-strand, coral bead necklace was worn with its gold clasp in front. Coral, considered to be helpful in preventing sore throats and other maladies, was often given as a present to babies and young children. Height 20¼in., width 16$\frac{1}{16}$in. Private Collection.

small silver badges to the Indian chiefs under their protection for purposes of identification (Plate 29). In 1710 Queen Anne sent medals bearing her image as a pledge of her protection and a reminder to them of their loyalty to her.[7] Cherokee chief Cunne Shote was portrayed about 1763 with an assortment of English medals, gorget, arm and wristbands, added to his native ornaments of bead necklaces, feather head-dress, and scalping knife.[8]

Very few medals were struck in gold and silver by colonial goldsmiths, but both Joseph Richardson in Philadelphia and Daniel Christian Fueter in New York struck silver medals for presentation to the Indians (Plate 30). The Fueter medal was designed with a view labelled Montreal on one side, commemorating the successful attack on that city during the French and Indian Wars in which several hundred Indians had taken part. Two sets of the medals were presented by Sir William Johnson to the ranking Indian Chiefs.

The dies for the medals struck by Richardson were cut by a clockmaker, Edward Duffield. One medal was presented by the city of Philadelphia to Colonel John Armstrong who led a surprise attack against the Delaware Indians in 1756. The other was presented by a Quaker organization, The Friendly Association of Regaining and

4. *Ibid*, p. 136.
5. *Ibid*, p. 234. He also imported crystal and cypher buttons from London for resale.
6. A.L.Cummings, *Rural Household Inventories*, p. 242.
7. *Marks of Achievement*, p. 28.
8. See *Boston Prints and Printmakers 1670-1755*, #136, Bradford F. Swan, 'Prints of the American Indians', p. 268.

Plate 31. *Gold beads and clasp, c.1720-50, marked on the back of the box clasp P•V•D in oval for Peter Van Dyck (1684-1751). The top of the clasp is engraved with a bird. The hollow beads appear to be earlier in date and have little rings of filigree forming a floral pattern at each end of the beads where they meet two small plain spacer beads. Length 24½in. (beads), ¾in. (clasp). Yale University Art Gallery, The Mabel Brady Garvan Collection.*

Preserving Peace with the Indians by Pacific Measures, in 1757.

As a Quaker and a member of The Friendly Association, Joseph Richardson was responsible for producing literally thousands of pieces of jewelry for presentation to the Indians. The leading article was the brooch, but he made arm and wristbands, earbobs, hair plates and bobs, crosses, moons, rings, and gorgets. One gorget made by Richardson was engraved with a scene of a Quaker offering a peace pipe to an Indian.[9]

Some of this jewelry was buried with the Indians when they died or was passed on to successors. The silver gorget found in an Indian grave in Macon County, North Carolina, was made in 1755 by Barent Ten Eyck of Albany whose father Koenraet Ten Eyck was making gorgets early in the 1730s.[10] Gorgets were worn by white warriors as well. Colonel Charles C. Pinckney's silver gorget was made and marked by Charleston goldsmith John Vanall about 1750 (Colour Plate 32).

For the ladies, simple gold and silver earrings were a popular item and jewelers often kept them on hand. A pair of gold wire earrings and two pair of silver earrings 'with Bob' were ordered in 1763 from Jonathan Payne of London by George Washington.[11] Two years earlier, Martha Washington and her five-year-old daughter Patsy had had their ears pierced.[12] The earrings were made with a hinge so that the wire at the top could be pushed through the ear and the ring snapped close to close (see Colour Plate 82).

The Richardsons and other colonial goldsmiths made gold clasps (or lockets as they called them) to fasten their necklaces. Oval in shape and boxed to allow the entrance of a spring catch, the clasps had extensions on each side with holes drilled through for fastening the chains or beads. The early extensions were shaped to conform to the holes and had rings soldered on the top side over each opening to finish them off. The top of the clasps were engraved with rosettes and borders in the first decades of the eighteenth century. In the middle decades they were decorated with rococo scrolls, floral sprays, and baskets of fruit (see Plate 92).

Necklaces made of gold beads were very popular throughout the century and were made by many goldsmiths and jewelers. Each bead was made of two hollow hemispheres of gold soldered together. One necklace (Plate 31) had a clasp marked by goldsmith Peter Van Dyck of New York. The necklace had twenty-five large gold beads with filigree around the openings of each pierced hole, interspaced with two smaller beads graduated slightly in size. A less common type of clasp was marked by Jacob Boelen II, of New York. It was made of flat, oviform pieces with filigree scrolls applied on top and serrated beaded edges. Several necklaces, marked on their clasps by Newport, Rhode Island, goldsmiths, have single strands of gold beads in two different sizes.[13]

Plate 32. *Children's rattles were often worn around their necks, suspended from ribbons or chains, to keep them from being damaged. Made of silver or gold, the rattles were fitted with a whistle at one end, a smooth piece of coral suitable for teething, and any number of bells to ring. This example was given by Mrs. Mary Livingston of New York to her granddaughter Mary Duane c.1765-70. It was made of gold by a Swiss goldsmith and jeweler working in New York between 1754 and 1779. Fueter's mark, DCF in an oval and N:YORK in conforming outlines, is stamped on the underside of the whistle. The repoussé work is especially elaborate and may have been executed by a specialist chaser named John Anthony Beau who worked for Fueter about 1769. Length 5 5⁄16in. Gift of Mrs. Francis P. Garvan, James R. Graham, Walter M. Jeffords and Mrs. Paul Morse. Yale University Art Gallery, The Mabel Brady Garvan Collection.*

Plate 33. *Above. Pendant, heart-shaped, Portsmouth, New Hampshire, c.1776. Captain Samuel R.C. Moffatt died in 1816 at New Orleans at the age of forty. The pendant is said to have been made to contain his caul. The Moffatt coat of arms is engraved on one side. Height 2⅛in. Gift of Robert T. Moffatt. Museum of Fine Arts, Boston.*

Plate 34. *Left. Silver pendant chains made about 1756 by Samuel Parmalee (1737-1807) of Guilford, Connecticut. His mark (S•P in a cartouche) appears on the back of the heart-shaped plaque. Owned originally by Ann Cushing, whose name is engraved on the plaque with the date 1756. The chain may have held a watch or a pendant. Length 1¼in. (heart), 10⅞in. (each chain). Gift of Miss Emily Chauncy. Yale University Art Gallery.*

Plate 35. *Silver love token, made by Richard Brunton (? - 1832), Connecticut engraver, commemorating the marriage of Lydia Griswold Phelps and Col. Jonathan Humphreys on 31 October 1782, on the obverse the figure of Justice. Biblical verses from the last chapter of Proverbs are engraved around the borders. The Connecticut Historical Society, Hartford.*

Most of the strings of gold beads that have survived from the colonial period have beads of uniform size. A string of gold beads of small size with a heart-shaped stone locket was advertised as lost in Boston in 1732.[14] Edward Lang of Salem, who made numerous strings of gold beads, charged Richard Derby in 1769 a little over three pounds for his gold necklace.[15]

Gold beaded necklaces are often seen in eighteenth century portraits of American women. Two early New York portraits of young ladies around 1730 show them wearing single strand necklaces with the gold clasp worn in the centre front.[16] Of special interest is the necklace visible in the portrait of Mrs. Jerusha Ogden (Plate 26) of Hartford, Connecticut, painted about 1794 by Joseph Steward. Mrs. Ogden wore two strands of gold beads with the clasp placed centre front, where its design could be appreciated.

Gold clasps often held strands of coral beads. These were very popular during the seventeenth and eighteenth centuries when it was believed that coral had therapeutic properties. Coral was worn to prevent illness and ward off evil spirits. Many early American children are portrayed with strands of coral around their necks (Colour Plate 33). The smooth, oblong cylinders of coral beads were imported from England, and England in turn was supplied by Italy. The Mediterranean Sea was the most important source of the finest coral. Joseph Richardson preferred a medium-sized bead for the necklaces he made. When strung there were nine beads to the inch.[17]

Children were also given rattles (Plate 32) made of silver or gold with bells attached in the middle, a whistle in one end and a polished stalk of coral in the other end for teething. These were often the present of doting grandmothers to well-born babies

9. Harrold E. Gillingham, *Indian Ornaments Made by Philadelphia Silversmiths*, p. 25.
10. Fales, *Early American Silver*, pp. 182-83.
11. GW *Invoices & Letters 1755-1766*, p. 49.
12. The Mount Vernon Ladies' Association of the Union, *Annual Report*, p. 21.
13. Kathryn C. Buhler and Graham Hood, *American Silver Garvan and other Collections in the Yale University Art Gallery, II*, 53; Bohan, #40, #44. Fales, *American Silver in the Henry Francis du Pont Winterthur Museum*, #46. Rhode Island School of Design.
14. Dow, *Arts & Crafts*, p. 47.
15. 28 November 1769, Salem and Essex County Misc. Mss., Library, PEM.
16. Susanna Truax by unknown artist, 1730, Plate 8; *Young Lady with a Rose* attributed to Pieter Vanderlyn 1732, Plate #9 *(Am. Naive Ptg. of the 18th & 19th C,*
17. Fales, *Richardson*, p. 144.

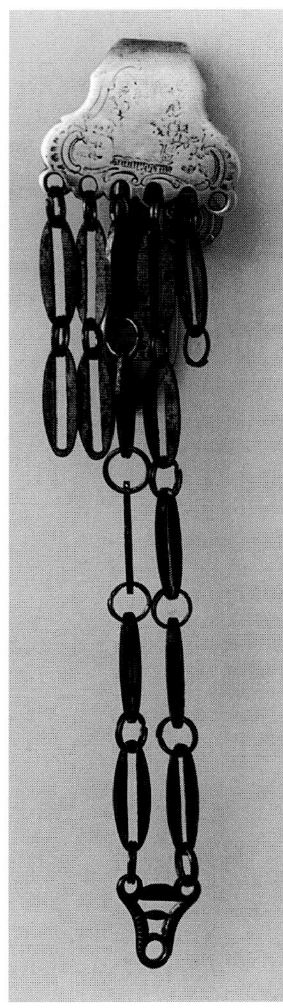

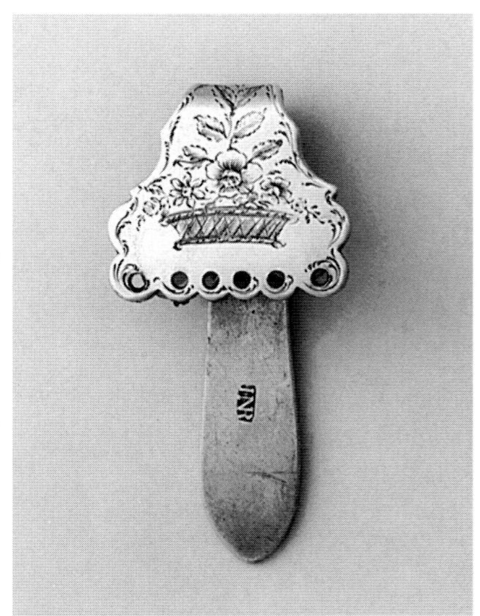

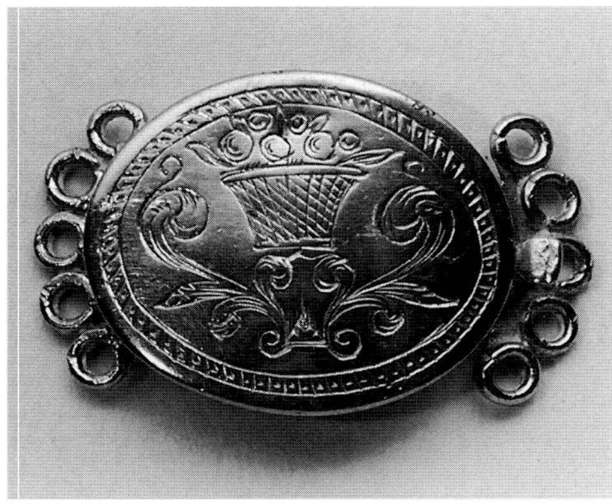

Plate 36. Gold locket, made by Joseph Richardson, Philadelphia, c.1750. Marked on back IR in a rectangle. Engraved with initials EC for Elizabeth Coultas. Winterthur Museum.

Plate 37. Chatelaine hooks made and marked by (right) Joseph Richardson about 1765 and (left) his son Joseph Richardson Jr. about 1780, Philadelphia, for their wives. Each hook could hold up to six chains. Length (right) 2$\frac{5}{16}$in., (left) 5$\frac{3}{8}$in. Courtesy, Philadelphia Museum of Art.

who could wear them suspended around their necks on a ribbon or a silver or gold chain. Such a rattle was described in *The Rape of the Lock* by Alexander Pope in 1714:

> Her infant grand-dame's whistle next it grew,
> The bells she jingled, and the whistle blew.[18]

Called a coral and bells, this delightful object was offered for sale by many American goldsmiths. Some were of their own workmanship and some were imported. The elaborately embossed fashions of the mid-century could be produced more efficiently and economically in the large workshops of London. Nevertheless, a number of American-made examples have survived, some of commendable craftsmanship. The family portrait of the Isaac Winslows of Boston, painted by Joseph Blackburn (w. 1752-74) shows Mrs. Winslow holding both their baby and the infant's coral and bells.[19] A second-hand 'very handsome Gold Whistle, with Bells and Coral' was sold at public auction in Boston during the summer of 1762.[20]

More unusual was a heart-shaped pendant made about 1776 of two convex silver plaques joined together by a thin silver strip (see Plate 33). According to family tradition, it contained the caul of Captain Samuel R.C. Moffatt of Portsmouth, New Hampshire, who died at the age of forty in New Orleans. It was engraved with his name and birthplace on one side and on the other with his coat of arms and surname.[21] The caul was considered by some as lucky, and was supposed to be a preservative against drowning.

While elaborate chatelaines were most often imported to the colonies, simple gold or silver hook plates and chains were made and marked by American goldsmiths. These were called 'hearts' in the early eighteenth century because the hook plate was often heart-shaped at that time. Joseph Richardson made a chatelaine hook for his wife Mary about 1765. It was engraved with a delicate plaited basket of flowers and was equipped to hold six chains and accoutrements. His son Joseph, Jr., followed tradition and made one for his bride Ruth Hoskins in 1780 (Plate 37).

18. Canto V, lines 87-96.
19. MFA, Boston.
20. *Boston Gaz.*, 23 Aug. 1762, Dow, A & C, p. 65.
21. Buhler, *Am.S.MFA, II*, 492, #441.

Colour Plate 34. The fashionable Mrs. Samuel Quincy of Boston wore two brooches on her wide lace collar. They appear to be made of marcasites set in silver, a newly introduced material enjoying popularity in the third quarter of the 18th century. Her portrait was painted by John Singleton Copley about 1761. Height 35½in., width 28¼in. Bequest of Miss Grace W. Treadwell. Courtesy, Museum of Fine Arts, Boston.

Alternative Materials

Just as there were substitutes for diamonds, there were substitutes for precious gold and silver. From medieval times, alchemists attempted to turn base metals into gold. Christopher Pinchbeck (1670-1732) succeeded as well as anyone in this impossible task. About 1720, the London watchmaker invented an alloy that was roughly five parts copper to one part zinc. It had a golden colour and was quite suitable to the manufacturing of parts for the clock and watch business. Because of its desirable colour and because it maintained a bright and unoxidized appearance relatively well, the alloy became used for watch cases, chains, chatelaines, buckles, clasps, and for setting pastes and other kinds of inexpensive jewelry. It could also be covered over with a gold wash that was hardly discernible as it wore off. The alloy came to be called pinchbeck and worked so well that by 1733, after the death of its inventor, Pinchbeck's son had to warn customers about the cheap imitations that abounded.[1]

Pinchbeck gilt buckles were being sold in Philadelphia by Dutens and Harper as

1. Becker, *Antique and 20th C. J.*, pp. 65-67.

early as 1755. Edmund Milne offered pinchbeck-set seals and watches. Philip Hulbeart imported and sold pinchbeck chains in 1761 and two years later his executors sold 'Pinchback *[sic]* and bath metal Buckels' for his estate. Bennett & Dixon in New York got their buckles from London and Birmingham, claiming they were the best, while Charles Oliver Bruff employed a London jeweler who could make all kinds of pinchbeck buckles in Bruff's shop, so that he could sell them cheaply by the dozen. Thomas Hilldrup also offered pinchbeck jewelry in Hartford in 1774 and Abel Buell had in stock, in his New Haven shop in 1775, pinchbeck brooches, rings, hair lockets, and buckles.[2]

Towards the end of the colonial period, marcasite jewelry was introduced. Made of iron pyrite which, when cut, is highly reflective, marcasite became quite popular in the mid-eighteenth century. When it was set in closed-back silver mounts, it gave the effect of diamond jewelry. Imported marcasite necklaces and earrings were for sale in Timothy Berrett's shop in Philadelphia in 1772, and the following year Baltimore's Cooke & Co. offered tortoiseshell and horn combs neatly set with marcasites, as well as necklaces and earrings.[3] Marcasites could also be used to surround *coque-de-perle* and mother-of-pearl jewelry (see pages 43 and 44).

It is quite possible that the two distinctive brooches that adorn the lace collar on the dress of Mrs. Samuel Quincy in her portrait by Copley about 1761 (Colour Plate 34) were made of marcasite. Copley's ability to capture the essence of materials with paint supports the impression that these were intended to be something that looked like silver and diamonds but was not.

Chatelaines, étuis, seals, and watches could all be made of a variety of metals from gold and silver to pinchbeck and copper gilt. The chatelaine that belonged to a colonial dame of the de Peyster family in New York was made of copper gilt.[4] The chatelaine consisted of a triangular hook plate that fitted over a belt and from which were suspended the various small and useful objects a woman might need for daily household chores: a case for sewing instruments, a thimble, a needle case, keys, and seals. Watches, pin cushions and étui cases could be worn in this way as well. Mrs. de Peyster's chatelaine included a thimble holder and an étui. It was decorated in repoussé on the hook plate with allegorical figures in rococo cartouches. A gold étui was given as a wedding present by William Plumsted of Philadelphia to his bride Mary McCall when they were married in 1753.[5]

Enamelled jewelry, which had been very popular in the seventeenth century, continued to be made in the mid-eighteenth century, but less frequently. In the 1750s Charles Dutens sold enamelled earrings with mother-of-pearl drops. Black and blue enamelled necklaces and earrings were available in New York in 1763. It is likely that these enamelled pieces resembled some of the necklaces, rings, and pendants made a century earlier and discovered in the famous Cheapside Horde that was found under a house near St. Paul's Cathedral in London in 1912. Brooches, watch seals and trinkets made of enamel and pinchbeck were being sold in Philadelphia at John Carnan's shop in 1771.[6]

American jewelers were able to perform routine enamelling tasks such as were required for inscriptions in black or white enamel on mourning rings. However, it is doubtful that many were qualified to do very intricate enamelling in the colonial period. It was for this reason that Charles Oliver Bruff touted the London jeweler working in his shop who knew the secrets of enamel work.[7]

2. *Pa. Gaz.*, 18 Feb. 1755; *Pa. Journal*, 15 Dec. 1763; 17 March 1763; *N-Y Gaz. etc*, 26 Aug. 1771; *N-Y Mercury*, 16 Dec. 1765; *Conn. Courant*, 5 Dec. 1774; Wroth, p. 35.
3. *Pa. Packet*, 30 Nov. 1772; *The Md. Journal and Balto. Advtr.*, 20 Aug. 1773.
4. Museum of the City of New York, probably English with side pendants added c. 1830.
5. Anne Hollingsworth Wharton, *Heirlooms in Miniature*, p. 13.
6. *Pa.Journal* –1771; *N-Y Mercury*, 23 May 1763, John Mecom adv.; Tait, *7000 Years*, pp. 178-81.
7. *N-Y Mercury*, 16 Dec. 1765.

Jewelers

By the end of the Colonial period, the jeweler's business had been firmly established. From the meagre beginning, when one jeweler came to Virginia in 1608 and went home again for lack of customers and materials, a century later there were jewelers in every major city and in many of the less populous areas as well. For much of this period, the goldsmiths doubled as jewelers (Plate 38) but by the mid-eighteenth century more and more men who specialized in making and repairing jewelry were hanging out their own shop signs.

Boston

For example, in Boston in the seventeenth century, it was the goldsmith who was most often the purveyor of jewelry. Jeremiah Dummer and John Coney provided mourning rings (see Plates 5 and 6), but on occasion supplied gold and stone earrings, coral and pearl necklaces, and other sorts of rings. This tradition persisted into the eighteenth century when there were dozens of goldsmiths like the Hurds, Edwards, and Reveres, who were capable of making gold and silver jewelry and setting stones. The patriot Paul Revere is not only best known among these goldsmiths, but his account books survive to tell us how he combined the two trades and what he charged for his jewelry.[1]

Beginning in the early 1760s, Revere's first accounts were for such things as a Freemason medal, silver buckles, and turtleshell jacket buttons, more often than for silver plate like canns, teapots and casters. Small items like hooks and eyes, stone buttons, and funeral rings made as good a profit for the young goldsmith as the larger items like whistles and bells.

Mr. Williams was one of Revere's best jewelry customers in 1762. He bought a gold necklace for £2.10.8, with a locket costing seventeen shillings; one odd gold button worth five shillings and four pence; a pair of spectacle frames and glasses for three shillings; some silver spoons costing a little over two pounds; and a turtle shell ring lined with gold for nine shillings. It should be noted parenthetically that Revere was correct in using the word turtle instead of tortoise. The material that jewelry was made from came from a kind of marine turtle, often the hawksbill turtle of the West Indies, not from the land turtle called tortoise. Actually the material is not shell but the organic, horny top plates covering the upper shell of these creatures.

From 1763 to 1767, John Singleton Copley, America's first significant artist, provided a new dimension to Revere's jewelry production when he asked the goldsmith to make gold cases and bracelets for the miniature portraits he was painting of Boston's residents. Copley usually paid about £2 for the gold used in the bracelets and £1.8.0. for the cost of Revere's labour. Soon Revere was providing the glass to cover the miniatures and setting them as well. The cases could be made as pendants in the simplest of frames or enclosed in an oval locket with a clasp that was fitted with openings on each side to hold a bracelet's chains or strings of pearls. In spite of the fact that Revere sometimes noted on Copley's account whose portrait the bracelet was to contain, no surviving examples have been attributed to Revere as yet. A Copley miniature of Samuel Cary still remains in its original frame which is made as a clasp and

1. Paul Revere Ledgers (1761-1797), Massachusetts Historical Society.

Colour Plate 35. The American jeweler's shop was often in his house. Exterior view of the shop of James Craig (?-1794) at the sign of the Golden Ball in Williamsburg, Virginia. Craig advertised as a newly arrived jeweler from London in September 1746. His shop carried silver wares and watches as well as jewelry. Colonial Williamsburg Foundation.

retains its spring catch. The clasp is fitted for a nine-strand bracelet.[2] Revere also provided artist Richard Jennys with a gold bracelet as well as a gold picture frame, both set with glasses in 1764. In 1767 he made two gold bracelets for George Brinley, one for Jonathan Jackson in 1768, and another for Mr. Fitch in 1774.[3]

Occasionally Revere made a gold brooch like the one Thomas Brattle bought in 1766 for £1.12.0., or the one for Captain John Tilley in 1772 which cost four shillings more. He made what he called burying rings, death's head and enamelled rings, some of them set with stones (see Colour Plate 8). He also set a stone locket, but by the time of the Revolution he was spending much more time making silver and engraving prints than he was making jewelry.

We need to know much more about the mid-eighteenth century men working in Boston who called themselves jewelers instead of goldsmiths. William Cario (1712-1769) was one of them. Born in Boston, he worked there from 1735 to 1738 and advertised that he made all sorts of jeweler's work and sold fine sword blades as well. A small sword with a silver hilt wrapped with twisted silver wire is attributed to him. It has a French blade and was made about 1735.[4] Cario moved to Portsmouth, New Hampshire, where his son William Cario, Jr. (1734-1809) continued as a goldsmith and jeweler. None of the father's jewelry has been identified. His son was a maker of church silver and a lovely snuffbox given to his second wife shortly after their marriage in 1768 (Plate 39). The box is made of silver with turtleshell and mother-of-pearl.[5]

Only the names are known of jewelers Stephen Winter, Asabel Mason, Joshua Eames, and the partnership of Roberts and Lee, all of whom worked in colonial Boston.[6] Slightly more information can be culled from advertisements to shed light on the extent of John Dexter's business. He sold loose stones as well as the foil with which to back them and, in 1757, expected a large assortment of jewelry to arrive.[7]

Between 1754 and 1758, Joseph Hiller was advertising in the *Boston Gazette* all sorts of jeweler's work. The son of a goldsmith, he conducted and lectured about electrical experiments as well. In 1758, Jonathan Trott's jewelry shop was robbed of a large gold

2. *Antiques*, Sept.1958, pp. 237-41.
3. PR Ledgers.
4. Harold L. Peterson, *American Silver-Mounted Swords 1700-1815*, pp.8-9.
5. Henry N. Flynt and Martha Gandy Fales, *The Heritage Foundation Collection of Silver and New England Silversmiths*, pp. 176-77; Charles S. Parsons, *New Hampshire Silver*, pp. 20-21, 87; *Boston Gaz.*, 23 Oct. 1738.
6. Stephen Winter, self-styled jeweler, is known primarily from his advertisement in the *New England Wkly. Journal* on 27 January 1741. Asabel Mason, a jeweler from London, was insolvent when he died in 1752 (*Boston Gaz.*, 19 Dec. 1752.).
7. *Boston Gaz.*, 7 Nov. 1757.

WHEREAS the Shop of the Subſcriber was the laſt Night broke open, and the following Articles ſtolen, *viz*

34 pair of wrought Silver Shoe Buckels.— 20 pair of ditto, Knee ditto.— 6 pair plain Shoe ditto. — 2 Silver Snuff-Boxes. — 1 ditto Tortoiſe Shell Top.— 2 Silver Pepper Caſtors, ſtamp'd I. E. — 12 Tea Spoons, ſame ſtamp. — 2 large ditto, Name at length ; 9 ſtock Buckles ; 3 gold Necklaces ; 5 gold Rings ; 1 Cream pot, ſtamp'd I. E. ; 1 Punch-ladle, ſame ſtamp ; ſeveral pair Stone Buttons ; 3 pair briliant Stone Earings, ſet in Gold ; 5 pair Cypher ditto ; ſeveral ditto ſet in Silver ; ſeveral ſtone Rings ; a Box with gold Beads ; 3 pair Tea Tongs ; gold Earings ; 2 pair ſmall Buckles,R. ; 1 pair old Tea-Tongs I. M. 1 old Spoon ; 3 Child's Whiſtles ; 1 pair ſmall Scales and Weights ; 1 pair gold Buttons ; 1 ſilver Pipe.

Whoſoever will make Diſcovery of the Thief or Thieves, ſo that they may be brought to Juſtice, and that I may recover my Goods again, ſhall receive TWENTY DOLLARS Reward, and all neceſſary Charges paid by

Joſeph Edwards, *Jun'r.*

N. B. If any of the Articles ſhould be offered to Sale, it is deſired they may be ſtop'd, and Notice given to *J. E.* *Boſton, March* 19. 1765.

Plate 38. Left. Advertisement of Joseph Edwards, Jr. (1737-1783) concerning a robbery at his shop, in the Boston News-Letter, *21 March 1765. He was the third generation of Boston silversmiths named Edwards. Items of jewelry stolen included gold necklaces, rings, brilliant stone earrings, cypher earrings and plain gold earrings. He also lost a silver snuff box with a tortoiseshell top, probably similar to one made by William Cario illustrated in Plate 39.*

Plate 39. Above. Silver snuff box with inlaid lid of tortoiseshell and mother-of-pearl, backed with horn. Made by William Cario, Jr. of Portsmouth, New Hampshire, c.1765. It is inscribed 'The property of Lydia Cario 1769'. He married Lydia in 1768. Length 2⅞in. Smithsonian Institution.

necklace, a pair of stone earrings set in gold, and several sets of silver shoe buckles, giving us some idea of the goods he kept on hand. From 1758 to 1765 John Welsh made jewelry, had coral beads for necklaces and loose stones to set with red and white foil, and sold supplies to other jewelers and goldsmiths. Alexander Crouckeshanks came from London to Boston in 1768 and was able to make or mend jewelry. Joshua Eames is known as a jeweler only by his obituary in 1772. Roberts and Lee, in that year, were supplying country goldsmiths with imported jewelry and made or repaired it as well.[8]

More is known about the Boyers. James Boyer (1700-41) was a Huguenot jeweler who came from London in 1722. He boarded at the dancing-master's house on King Street and was able to carry on his trade there, setting all manner of stones in rings and other kinds of jewelry. He married the daughter of a wealthy merchant, Daniel Johonnot, in 1724, but when he died in 1741, he was insolvent. Their son Daniel (1725-79), on the other hand, was successful at the jeweler's trade by combining it with goldsmith's work. This dichotomy of occupation can be seen in the fact that he called himself a jeweler in the advertisements and a goldsmith in his will.

From 1754 to 1758, Daniel Boyer was clerk of the market and in 1762 he was fourth sergeant in the Artillery Company, while carrying on his trade. He married Eliza Bulfinch, had only daughters and no son to carry on the family trade. However, one of his daughters married Joseph Coolidge, Jr., who trained as a goldsmith, became a jeweler and ultimately a merchant.[9] Some of Daniel Boyer's silver is known – a few pieces of church silver and an occasional domestic piece like a porringer or spoon – but not much has survived considering his long working period, and this suggests that he spent more of his time at the business of jewelry. A gold mourning ring bearing his mark made in 1779 has a plain band with a rudimentary winged death head engraved on it.[10]

Daniel Parker (1726-1785) was one of Daniel Boyer's biggest competitors. Born in nearby Charlestown, Parker established his shop on Merchants' Row in Boston in 1752. A greater variety of silver survives bearing Parker's marks. He also had no son to carry on his trade but is believed to have trained his nephew Isaac. Isaac Parker (1749-1805) moved to Deerfield, Massachusetts, about 1774 where he and his apprentice John Russell served the town as jewelers and founded a silver and cutlery industry that continues in that area today under the name of the Russell-Harrington Cutlery Company.[11]

8. Ibid., 5 Mar. 1754; 9 Jan. 1758; 6 Nov. 1758; 16 Oct. 1758; 17 Dec. 1765; 10 Aug. 1772; *Boston N-L*, 19 Nov. 1772. A silver spoon and a silver punch ladle at the MFA, Boston, have been attributed to Trott and Crouckeshanks respectively. Buhler, II, 647; I, 379.

9. Flynt and Fales, p. 162; Buhler, *Am.S.MFA, I*, 330.

10. Buhler, *Am.S.MFA*, I, 331, #291. See also Buhler and Hood, I, 156-7.

11. Flynt & Fales, p. 293; Buhler, *Am.S.MFA*, I, 332-5; Buhler & Hood, I, 162.

Both Boyer and Parker were able to create a good business by importing quantities of ready-made jewelry from London. Inexpensive jewelry like paste, crystal and cypher earrings, buttons and rings, crystal and stone foiled buckles and brooches were sold in their shops along with jewelry made of diamonds, garnets, amethysts, and topaz. Coral beads and coral for whistles and bells and silver thimbles with steel tops proved popular imports too.

Like many jewelers, Boyer and Parker carried watches and were capable of doing repair work, importing watch crystals, main springs, hour hands, fusee chains and enamelled dial plates. Parker also sold scales and weights. At the same time, they imported the tools needed for making silver as well as jewelry: skillets, forging and raising anvils, hammers, vices, shears, pliers, files, spoon teasts, draw plates, dividers, burnishers, gravers, blow pipes, drill stocks, blades, hollowing stamps, freezing punches, polishing stones, crucibles, death head and heart-in-hand ring swages.[12]

Boyer's son-in-law Joseph Coolidge, Jr. (1747-1821) had established his own jewelry shop at the foot of Cornhill by 1771. That year he imported from London some lovely jewelry: rose- and star-shaped earrings made of garnets or paste; sprigs and pins made of garnets, paste, and marcasite; and turtleshell combs either plain or set with pastes. Spurs as well as buckles, cornelian and mocha buttons, pinchbeck items and 'teeth brushes', indicate that he had something for everybody.[13]

As we have seen, jewelers like William Cario and Isaac Parker fanned out from Boston to Portsmouth, New Hampshire, and western Massachusetts in the mid-eighteenth century where they would have less competition from other jewelers and goldsmiths. Ebenezer Austin worked as a goldsmith/jeweler in Charlestown, Massachusetts, until about 1761, when he moved to Hartford, Connecticut.

By the end of the colonial period, there were men serving as jewelers in many of the rural towns of New England, but their business was more like that of the seventeenth century goldsmith/jeweler than it was of the specialized mid-eighteenth century jeweler that the colonial capitals were fostering.

New York

Like Boston, New York had its families of goldsmiths and occasional jewelers. Three generations of Ten Eycks and Lansings had worked in Albany and in New York city, and there were several generations named Van Dyck, Le Roux, Boelen and Wynkoop who were able to supply their customers with baubles. Already, however, the city was showing evidence of its growing cosmopolitan nature. To the large portions of Dutch and English settlers were being added steady influxes of other nationalities, German, Swiss and French. As a result there were more specialist jewelers in New York than in New England.

Several of the New York goldsmiths hired jewelers from London to work in their shops. In 1746, Thauvet Besly had Peter Lorin working with him. Lorin was able to set all kinds of jewels, particularly the four most precious gems – diamonds, rubies, emeralds, and sapphires – in rings, earrings, solitaires, lockets, aigrettes and seals. By 1751, Peter Lorin was working on his own at a house in Crown Street, providing gentlemen and ladies with any kind of jeweler's work.[14]

Charles Oliver Bruff (1735-1817), the son of a silversmith, was born in Maryland and came to New York about 1763 by way of Elizabeth, New Jersey. He married Mary Le Telier and set himself up as a goldsmith and jeweler at the sign of the Teapot and Tankard in Maiden Lane. He, too, employed a jeweler from London who

12. *Boston Gaz.*, 28 Oct. 1765; *Boston N-L,* 22 Oct. 1767. The miscellaneous papers and account book of goldsmith Zachariah Brigden (1734-1787) at the Beinecke Library, Yale University, reveal that during the last decade of Boyer's career, from 1766 to 1777, Boyer purchased silver wares made by Brigden for resale to his own customers. In turn, Boyer supplied Brigden with tools, buckle chapes and numerous rings, some enamelled and some set with stones, a set of cypher stones, plated buckles, gold and coral beads, earrings, and lockets. Hilary Anderson brought this information to my attention.
13. *Boston N-L,* 9 May 1771.
14. *The N-Y Wkly. Post Boy,* 10 Nov. 1746; 13 May 1751.

understood how to make and mend any kind of diamond or enamelled work, both areas in which American goldsmith/jewelers were deficient. Bruff ordered precious stones from London especially for use by this new jeweler. In addition to the range of goods offered in Boston, Bruff's shop could now produce enamelled lockets and hair plaited in true lovers' knots. By the summer of 1763, he had not only an English but also a French jeweler working for him. In 1772, Bruff had added an earring to the tankard and teapot on his shop sign and featured diamond and enamelled work among the jewelry in his advertisements (Plate 40). He offered to mend ladies' fans and to put glasses in watches for a shilling a piece. He made dies to stamp gold, silver, pinchbeck or brass buttons with his own design.[15]

Next Bruff fitted up a lapidary mill and announced he was ready to cut any kind of stone. He offered to purchase old jewels, rough crystals, paste, and any sort of old stones. He also had for sale, in different sizes, the four most precious gems plus amethyst, garnets, onyx, stones and paste of all colours. He could make snuff boxes of onyx or mother-of-pearl. To expand his business further, Bruff urged country jewelers to buy their stock from him because he could supply them cheaper than anyone else in the city and he would make it a point to fill their orders quickly.[16]

That Bruff engaged in lapidary work is of special interest. Lapidarists were few and far between in the colonies.[17] Great Britain frowned upon the Americans' importation of raw materials and tried to force them to import goods manufactured in or shipped through England. Gems and minerals had a value in their natural state and so fell into a different category.

In 1768 a news item appeared in *The New-York Gazette* which pointed out that there was a rising interest on the part of the people there in inventing and promoting manufacturing in the colonies. To this end, millstones and grindstones equal, if not superior, to their British counterparts were being set up in such quantities that imports would be discouraged. Lapidaries would soon be supplied with beryls, topaz, garnets, amethysts, and crystals of New England origin. Samples of this native rough material had been cut here and set in rings sold to gentlemen of taste who found they were not inferior to those imported from England, so the article said.[18]

In spite of the inevitable journalistic hyperbole, there was in fact a basis to the newspaper account which was inspired in large part by the work of Abel Buell (1742-1822), a Killingworth, Connecticut, goldsmith, jeweler and inventor. Just two months before the item appeared in *The New-York Gazette,* Buell had announced in the *Boston Gazette* that 'he hath discover'd the true method of grinding and polishing chrystals and other stones of value, viz. Rubies, Garnets, Topaz, Amethysts, white and brown Chrystals, &c...and that he has [specimens] of the above kind of stone in the native State; as also ground, polish'd and set'.[19] Earlier, in a petition to the Connecticut Assembly, Buell had exhibited a ring set with precious stones which he had cut himself. The Reverend John Devotion of Saybrook, Connecticut, referred to Buell's achievement when he wrote to the Reverend Ezra Stiles of Yale that in the 'matter of cutting amethysts and other native stones our Killingworth lapidary's "Invention equals his curious neat workmanship"'.[20]

In addition to lapidaries, seal cutters were needed in the colonies. Charles Bruff employed a man to cut seals in stones and recommended them to his customers and to country jewelers. Various designs were offered from heraldic devices like arms and crests to figures and heads. English literary figures were popular, among them Shakespeare, Milton, Newton and Pope. So were the heroes of classical antiquity –

15. *The N-Y Mercury,* 3 Jan. 1763; *The N-Y Gaz. or the Wkly. Post-Boy,* 9 June 1763; *The N-Y Gaz. & the Wkly. Mercury,* 25 May 1772.
16. *The N-Y Gaz. & the Wkly. Mercury,* 24 Jan. 1774.
17. Lewis Ducray, the London lapidary working in Philadelphia in 1771, was an exception to the general situation, offering to cut rubies, topaz, emeralds, garnets, crystal, and paste. *Pa.Journal,* 4 April 1771.
18. *The N-Y Gaz. Extraordinary,* 4 Feb. 1768.
19. 7 Dec. 1767.
20. Wroth, pp. 32-35.

Charles Oliver Bruff,

Gold-Smith and Jeweler, at the fign of the Tea-pot, Tankard, and Ear-ring, the corner of King-ftreet, near the Fly-Market,

HAVING employed a Jeweler from London, who underftands making or mending any kind of diamond or enamel'd work in the Jewelery way; alfo makes and mends all manner of ftone buckles, ftone rings, ear-rings, broaches, feals, folitairs, hair jewels, lockets enameled; makes all manner of fleeve-buttons, mourning rings of all forts, trinkets for Ladies rings or lockets, plain or enameled gold necklaces, or ftone of all forts; he makes all forts of pinchbeck buckles, and fells them cheap by the dozen or pair. Whereas the faid BRUFF, has had his work undervalued by three different Silver-fmiths of this city, by one I loft three

Plate 40. *Charles Oliver Bruff advertised in the* New-York Mercury *on 20 April 1767 as a jeweler as well as a silversmith. He noted that he had employed a jeweler from London who could make or mend any sort of diamond or enamel work.*

DANIEL FUETER,

SILVER SMITH and JEWELLER, next Door to Mr. Peter Curtenius, facing the Ofwego Market.

Has lately imported:

A Beautiful Affortment of Jewellery, which for Elegance and Tafte is greatly fuperior to any Thing hitherto brought to this Place; Confifting of a great Variety of Rings, fet Knot Fafhion, Entourage, Clufter, &c. Viz. Brilliant Diamonds and Rofe Diamonds, of all Sizes; Rubies, Topazes, Emeralds, Saphirs, and all Kinds of precious Stones, warranted. Ear-rings of all Sizes, Fafhions and Prices; Pafte Shoe and Knee Buckles, fine Twezer Cafes, and Snuff Boxes of curious Workmanfhip. Alfo a genteel Parcel of Silver Work, Tea Pots, Milk Pots, Sauce Boats, Shoe and Knee Buckles, and other Articles too numerous to mention, all extremely Cheap.

N. B. The faid DANIEL FUETER, importer of the above Goods, who was bred a Jeweller and Goldfmith, will give full Satisfaction to thofe Gentlemen and Ladies who will honour him with their Cuftom: and will undertake to execute on the fhorteft Notice, and as cheap as may be done in London, any Orders he receives in the feveral Branches of Jewellery, and Gold or Silver Smith's Work; being furnifhed with the beft of Workmen, and all Requifites for that Purpofe.

Alfo he will make exact Affays of all Sorts of Ores and Metals; and will perform Refining and Gilding in the neateft Manner. He gives ready Money for old Gold and Silver. 53--61.

Plate 41. *Daniel Christian Fueter, Swiss goldsmith and jeweler who came to New York from London, advertised in the* New-York Gazette, or, the Weekley Post-boy *on 10 March 1763, specifying the kinds of precious stones he could use in various settings (knot fashion, entourage or cluster).*

Homer, Socrates, Hannibal, Mark Antony, Caesar and Plato, as well as any number of gods and goddesses. Bruff's advertisement illustrated a swivel seal cut with his own initials in script. Cyphers were available too. Recently he had bought some Egyptian pebbles that he planned to make into seals and snuff boxes.[21]

With the outbreak of the Revolution, Bruff, ever the opportunist, turned to the making of swords to supply the militia companies that were being formed and tried to hire silversmiths, whitesmiths, cutlers, chape forgers and filers, instead of lapidarists. He decorated small swords with beautiful green grips made of dyed bone or ivory. Broad swords were embellished with the heads of William Pitt and John Wilkes, both Englishmen who had championed the colonists' cause. Some had mottos inscribed on them: 'Magna Charta and Freedom' came with Pitt's head and 'Wilkes and Liberty' for the other. Bruff immodestly claimed them to be all manufactured by him and the most elegant swords ever made in America. He offered to pay cash for old sword blades and ivory.[22] Nevertheless, before the war ended Bruff had gone over to the British; and when the end came he migrated with other American Tories to Nova Scotia. He was soon advertising at the sign of the Teapot, Tankard and Cross Swords, where he continued the work of a goldsmith and jeweler.[23]

Jewelers dependent upon importing large quantities of jewelry from England were greatly affected by the Stamp Act taxes levied by Parliament in 1765, repealed in 1766, and the Townshend Acts passed in 1767. The colonists resisted these import duties by agreeing to ban the purchase of the goods affected until these acts were repealed. The nonimportation agreement resulted in a ban of luxury goods and an on-again, off-again trade situation. When he came from London to work in New York in 1769, Thomas Richardson brought jewelry and materials necessary to his trade, and proceeded to start selling his wares. The Committee of Merchants responsible for enforcing the ban had offered to raise money to offset his losses if he would store his goods temporarily instead of selling them. When he refused, he was taken to a scaffold erected in front of the Liberty Pole where he was made to agree and to beg for pardon. The following month Richardson was open for business offering jewelry and silversmiths' work at lower prices than elsewhere and seeking to buy old gold, silver, diamonds or any curious stones. He went back to England the next year and returned with a fresh shipment of all kinds of English-made jewelry, including plated and pinchbeck buckles and Singleton's Cock spurs.[24]

21. *The N-Y Gaz. & the Wkly Mercury,* 18 July 1774.
22. Ibid. 19 June 1775; 8 July 1776.
23. Donald C. Mackay, *Silversmiths and Related Craftsmen of the Atlantic Provinces,* pp. 45-6. Relatively few silver objects have survived bearing Bruff's mark. Many of his customers were probably Tories who lost their valuables or took them with them when they left the country.
24. *The N-Y Chronicle,* 14 Sept. 1769; *The N-Y Gaz. & the Wkly. Mercury,* 30 Oct. 1769; 12 Nov. 1770.

Simon Coley, another goldsmith/jeweler from London, got into greater trouble. His 'daring Infractions' and his 'insolent and futile Defense of those inglorious Measures', inflamed patriotic New Yorkers in 1769 and he was forced to acknowledge his crime, beg for pardon, and store the equivalent of the goods he had sold and all he still had of what he had imported contrary to the nonimportation agreement. Shortly thereafter he gave public notice that he would be leaving the city with his family. Ironically, two years earlier, when the repeal of the Stamp Act had taken place, Coley had made several 'very neat Fancy-Rings' especially to be worn at the celebration of that happy occasion.[25]

Jeremiah Andrews, yet another London jeweler working in the city at the time, capitalized on these earlier incidents. He announced that shopkeepers and traders who were at a disadvantage because of the nonimportation agreement could be helped by him. He would cheerfully do his part by making every article of jewelry himself, as cheap and of as good materials as could be imported from London. By 1779, Andrews had migrated to Philadelphia where he appealed to local customers, as well as to nearby Maryland patrons, to buy jewelry of his own manufacture. Included in his repertoire were ladies' paste shoe buckles, men's knee and stock buckles, garnet hoop rings and other kinds of rings, lockets and brooches made plain or with stones, very neat hair work and mourning rings.[26]

There can be little doubt that the nonimportation agreement was responsible for the influx of trained jewelers into New York as well as the increased local production. Whitehouse and Reeves imported fashionable London patterns for ladies' paste shoe-buckles instead of the buckles themselves and promised to keep anything they sold in repair for two years without charge. Another employee in their shop, also from London, specialized in the art of working hair in the design of 'sprigs, birds, figures, cyphers, crests of arms', all guaranteed to be equal to any made in London. Whitehouse and Reeves claimed to have 'had the honour to serve a number of the first families of distinction in London'.[27]

Jeweler James Bennett had arrived from London in 1768 and opened a shop in the house of cabinetmaker Thomas Griggs, where he offered jewelry, watches, trinkets, gloves, brocade and satin shoes, and pistols. By 1771 he had formed a partnership with another Londoner named Dixon and expanded his services to include lapidary work, saying that they 'had engaged some of the best workmen in these branches, that could be had in any part of England, and are determined to work as cheap and good as in the City of London'. They imported such finery as necklaces, earrings, egrets, sprigs, pins for ladies' hair, rings, lockets and brooches, stone, paste, garnet and marcasite buckles, and London and Birmingham pinchbeck buckles. The partnership lasted only a year, but Bennett continued alone, pointing out to his customers that he was 'the only real maker in this city of Ladies shoe buckles, ear-rings, egrets, sprigs and hair pins, seals, necklaces, combs, crosses, and lockets, sleeve buttons and bracelets, &c.' He also called attention to the fact that he made mourning rings set with any sort of stone with hair worked in landscapes.[28]

Best known for his work as a goldsmith, Daniel Christian Fueter (1720-85) had arrived from London in 1754 but he was actually a political refugee from Switzerland and had only worked in England for six years. He had been trained as a jeweler as well and imported for his New York customers 'A Beautiful Assortment of Jewellery, which for Elegance and Taste is greatly superior to any Thing hitherto brought to this Place' (Plate 41). There were entourage, cluster and knot rings made of brilliant and rose-cut diamonds of all sizes, rubies, topazes, emeralds, and sapphires. His shop was

25. *The N-Y Gaz. & the Wkly. Mercury,* 24 July, 4 Sept. 1769; 16-23 March 1767.
26. *Rivington's N-Y Gaz.*, 25 May 1775; *Maryland Journal,* 18 April 1779.
27. *Rivington's N-Y Gaz.*, 29 Sept. 1774; *The N-Y Gaz. & the Wkly. Mercury,* 2 Jan. 1775.
28. *The N-Y Gaz. & the Wkly. Mercury,* 3 Oct. 1768, 8 May 1769; 5 July 1773; 26 Aug. 1771; 6 Aug. 1772.

staffed with only the best workmen and equipment. Fueter continued to say he was from London in his advertisements for many years, no doubt because London jewelers were more highly regarded. In 1769 he hired a fellow Swiss, John Anthony Beau, from Geneva, who specialized in chasing, to help him make snuff boxes and watch cases. Fueter's son Lewis also joined him in the business that year, carrying on alone after his father was permitted to return to Berne.[29]

Goldsmith/jeweler Myer Myers (1723-1795) was born in New York of Jewish parents. In addition to making gold and enamelled mourning rings, several of which survive, he sold gold rings with stones and silver and gilt seals as well as earrings made of gold and pinchbeck. In 1763, in partnership with Benjamin Halsted he imported diamond rings, garnet hoop rings and brooches, along with ready-made plate. He also employed an English servant named Lewis Meares who was a jeweler and could engrave, but who ran away.[30]

Some of the most exciting jewelry to be found in New York was in the shop of a German, Otto de Parisen, who came from Berlin to New York about 1763. One afternoon in the middle of May in 1765 a daring robber had taken from his shop a small square shagreen box in which were a large number of beautiful rings. There was a diamond ring with a heart-shaped central stone surrounded by sparks. There was a ring in the shape of a flower pot set with diamonds, rubies, emerald and topaz. Another ring had a heart-shaped sapphire with an emerald and two sparks above it in the form of a crown. Parisen's losses included an octagonal garnet and a square-cut emerald both set in rings with sparks on each side, and another long heart-shaped garnet set with two Bristols on each side. Even the brown stone ring sounded especially nice, since it was cut with a roman head and encircled with sparks.[31]

Philadelphia

On the eve of the Revolution Philadelphia was the largest city in the American colonies. However, its growth as a jewelry centre had been retarded somewhat by the fact that it was not founded until the end of the seventeenth century and that it had a majority of Quakers who were taught that the plain life was the good life. In the first few decades of settlement, Francis Richardson, Quaker founder of a dynasty of goldsmiths, made only the most useful sorts of jewelry like rings and lockets that had sentimental overtones, or practical items such as pincushion hoops and thimbles, buttons and buckles, chains and spectacles. In 1719 he went to London to purchase goods for resale to augment his business: silverware, gloves and looking glasses. He bought coral for necklaces and rattles, probably from goldsmith James Thompson on Lombard Street. From Matthew Judkins, a goldsmith who tipped bottles, he got little glass bottles that could hold water and flowers, to be placed in a lady's stomacher. Francis' sons Frank and Joseph and his grandsons Joseph, Jr., and Nathaniel continued doing business in this way throughout the century.[32]

Posy rings, seal rings and mourning rings were stock in trade for Joseph Richardson and occasionally he set a ring with hair, a stone or crystal. He sold chains by the inch, but he also imported watch chains, occasionally impressing in sealing wax the pattern he wished to be sent. He kept on hand in his glass display case a few simple gold bobs for the ladies' ears. However, his big business was in buckles (Plate 28). In the 1730s and '40s they came wrought, cross-barred and threaded. By the 1750s and '60s most of them were pierced and carved and came from How & Masterman in London.

29. *The N-Y Gaz. & the Wkly. Post-Boy*, 10 March 1763; *The N-Y Gaz.& the Wkly. Mercury*, 13 July 1769; 30 Jan. 1769; 21 May 1770; *Rivington's N-Y Gaz.*, 12 May 1774.

30. *The N-Y Mercury & the Wkly. Post-Boy*, 10 Nov. 1763; 9 April 1753.

31. Bad luck struck de Parisien again in 1774 when his furnace caught fire and his house burned down. *The N-Y Gaz.*, 14 March 1763; 20 May 1765; *The N-Y Journal or the Gen. Advtr.*, 9 Feb. 1769; *The N-Y Gaz. & the Wkly. Mercury*, 25 April 1774; *Rivington's N-Y Gaz*, 12 May 1774.

32. Fales, *Richardson*.

Juſt imported, and to be ſold by

JOHN DAVID, GOLDSMITH,

The fourth Door from the Drawbridge,

A Neat Aſſortment of JEWELLERY, conſiſting of paſte ſhoe, knee, and ſtock buckles, hair pins, ſet combs, very neat paſte and garnet broaches, paſte and garnet ear-rings, ſtone ſleeve buttons, of different ſorts, ſtone ſeals, chaſed and plain bells and whiſtles, coral necklaces, ſilver ſoup and punch ladles, ſilver and ſteel top thimbles, with a quantity of large and ſmall ſilver work, which he will diſpoſe of on the moſt reaſonable terms.

N. B. He gives the full value for old gold and ſilver. ¶

Plate 42. John David was a silversmith working in Philadelphia in the mid-18th century who occasionally imported an assortment of jewelry from London to sell in his shop, as specified in the Pennsylvania Gazette, *21 October 1772.*

Charles Dutens advertised as a jeweler from London in Philadelphia in 1753, and formed a partnership with one of Richardson's apprentices, David Harper, who concentrated on the silver goods. Dutens had previously set up shop in New York about 1751 where he had made all sorts of rings – mourning, enamelled, motto, fancy, etc. – as well as earrings, solitaires (meaning breast brooches, not rings, in those days), stay hooks, seals and lockets. More importantly, he set diamonds, rubies, emeralds and sapphires, garnets, amethysts, and topaz, or any other kind of stone, which he imported from London. He stretched his income by teaching children French.

In Philadelphia, Dutens and Harper offered some jewelry that was not often mentioned by other advertisers at the time, such as enamelled earrings, with three drops of mother-of-pearl, and single drops. They also had 'fili-green' rings and chains for scissors. 'Ivory eggs instead of smelling-boxes' and pinchbeck gilt buckles and necklaces were also stocked by Dutens and Harper. The fine cornelians they had for gold seals and men's rings were engraved with doves and poses. They added opals and jacinths (hessonite garnets) to the precious stones Dutens could set with sparks and carried fine Bristol stones for setting in lockets. The partnership ended when Charles Dutens went to the West Indies in 1757.[33]

Edmund Milne (1724-1813) had worked for Charles Dutens, and perhaps had been an apprentice in his shop. When Dutens left, Milne set himself up in the business. His shop sign at first was a crown and a pearl. After a successful buying trip to England, he added two more pearls to the sign. The Crown and Three Pearls indicated a greater emphasis on jewelry. No one offered a longer list of imported jewelry in the colonies. In addition to diamond ornaments, some of the more intriguing baubles he had in his shop were brooches set with Brazilian topazes and double-heart brooches set with green or green and white stones. He had mocha bracelets surrounded with garnets and three- and single-drop earrings made of garnet and crystal. Some of his cornelian seals were in Roman settings and his enamelled gold heart-shaped lockets were set with garnets. There were enamelled snuff boxes in the shape of birds, fruit, flowers, and some in the shape of a shoe. There were China smelling bottles and ivory patch boxes, Masonic medals, corals and bells, grape rings, turquoise bead necklaces, and paste necklaces with drop earrings to match. What a terrible temptation it must have been to pass by or to enter Mr. Milne's shop on Second Street.[34]

A very good picture of what a colonial Philadelphia jeweler's shop actually had in it can also be gleaned from a small account book found among the papers of Joseph Richardson. In it Richardson kept a record of goods that he and his colleague Philip Syng sold for the benefit of jeweler/goldsmith Philip Hulbeart's estate in 1763. Of equal interest is who bought what, since other Philadelphia goldsmiths and jewelers took the opportunity to pick up items that would be of use in their own business. George Drewry purchased a lot of chapes and tongues for use in buckles of his own make or for repairs. A jeweler from Barbados, Samuel Alford, got old gold. Michael Brothers bought a parcel of punches. William Young, one of Richardson's apprentices, was able to get twenty-four gold rings with three months in which to pay

33. *The N-Y Gaz. Revived in the Wkly. Post-Boy*, 4 March, 3 June 1751; *Pa. Journal or Wkly. Advtr.*, 4 Oct 1753; *Pa. Gaz.*, 18 Feb. 1755, 29 Dec. 1757.
34. *Pa. Journal & the Wkly. Advtr.*, 15 Dec. 1763

for them. Six months later he had to return sixteen of them that had not sold. Stephen Reeves purchased twenty-seven gold rings and four pairs of gold buttons, as well as a great many tools he needed to furnish his own shop – crucibles, scorpers, files, binding wire, a touchstone, and a blowpipe for soldering.

At the time of his death, Philip Hulbeart had in his shop numerous pieces of wrought silver, a pair of French plate candlesticks and a pair of enamelled candlesticks. Among the jewelry there were turtleshell rings, jet beads, a gilt brooch, a pair of 'Dropt Clustered Gold Ear Rings', a pair of stone earrings without any drops, a garnet and diamond ring, and French paste necklaces and earrings.[35]

Theodore Carbin (Karbin), who bought scorpers from Hulbeart's shop, was a jeweler who had been born in Germany and worked in Philadelphia from about 1758 until 1775, when he returned to Stuttgart. His house and shop were on the south side of Chestnut Street across from the Turk's Head. He was successful enough to advertise occasionally for an apprentice and he knew how to gild all kinds of jewelry. Carbin also understood a little about how to promote his imported jewelry. His brilliant and rose-cut diamonds were advertised as 'very neat', his emeralds were 'exceedingly fine', his topaz curious and his amethysts charming.[36]

Another interesting Philadelphia jeweler whose advertisements promised unusual items was George Christopher Dorwig. He made gold rings 'out of which Water springs'. The sort of person who bought such a trick ring would have been the sort to build a garden with sprinklers in it that would be activated by an unwary visitor when he walked through a meandering path in a mid-eighteenth century English country-house garden. Dorwig's wedding rings were most curious, he said, and of an entirely new invention. One hesitates to speculate.[37]

Maryland

Like a number of Philadelphia jeweler/goldsmiths, George Dorwig moved south to Maryland, establishing ties in Baltimore about 1773. Here he followed Southern precedents by selling tickets at his shop for a lottery to 'Those who wish to hazard a Harvest of Gold, Silver and Jewels'. It must have proved profitable to Dorwig since, when he thought he would retire from business in 1788, he announced that he would dispose of his stock by lottery. He divided his goods into first, second and third class prizes. First class tickets sold for a half dollar each and prizes included spoons, buckles, pincushion hoops with chains, plain gold rings, garnet rings valued at ten shillings apiece, and strings of the best coral necklaces. Second class consisted of better items like a silver teapot and three-stone garnet rings. Third class was best of all with pairs of silver cans and salts, whistles with bells, sets of gold sleeve buttons and double strings of coral beads. The following year he sold the remainder of his stock, again by lottery, and his set of tools.[38]

William Whetcroft, an Irish goldsmith from Cork, came to Annapolis, Maryland, about 1766 and advertised himself as a jeweler and lapidary. Perhaps he did not find as much business there as he would have liked for the following year we find he kept a shop in Baltimore as well. While minding stores in both towns, he encouraged customers by keeping the work he sold in good repair at no extra charge to them and by paying the highest prices for gold and silver and 'Baltimore-Stone'. He gave up the Baltimore shop in 1769 and concentrated on his Annapolis business, importing large quantities of silver plate as well as jewelry. He had 'beautiful paste necklaces with ear-

35. Fales, *Richardson*, pp. 202-06; ms. #, DMMC, Winterthur.
36. *Pa. Journal or Wkly. Advtr.*, 1 June 1758; 1 May 1766.
37. Dorwig also said he could make old stones appear like new. *Pa Gazette,* 1 Aug. 1765.
38. *Md. Journal and Balto. Advtr.*, 13 July 1784; 17 Oct. 1788; 1 Sept. 1789.

rings to match them in cases' and 'settings for miniature pictures and bracelets set round with garnets [see Colour Plate 16], diamonds, topaz, garnet, amethyst, cornelian, and hoope rings'. His little box lockets or clasps, if made of gold, were set with garnets and, if of silver, set with marcasites. The greatest part of his wares, he said, he made in his own shop and if perchance a stone should happen to fall out of any of his jewelry, he would reset it gratis. When the war came along, Whetcroft turned his talents to manufacturing iron.[39]

It is interesting to note that in 1778 William Faris (1728-1804), goldsmith and watchmaker in Annapolis, offered a negro for sale who was 'A likely young fellow, by trade a Silversmith, Jewellery, and Lapidary' with the recommendation that there were few, if any, better workmen in America.[40]

Christopher Hughes and Company was probably the most important jewelry firm in Baltimore at the end of the colonial period. At the sign of the Cup and Crown on the corner of Market and Gay in 1773, Hughes sold silver ware and jewelry such as Macaroni shoe buckles; ladies' rose or knot buckles; fashionable rings set with diamonds, topaz, emerald, sapphires, amethysts and garnets for both men and women; garnet and paste fancy-work earrings; and brooches set in gold and silver; paste and marcasite necklaces and earrings; and red and white foil lockets set in gold. Briefly, in 1774, he was allied with John Carnan, a Philadelphia jeweler/goldsmith, but this partnership was soon dissolved.[41] A detailed description of some of the better pieces of jewelry stolen from Hughes' shop during the night of 7 August 1775 indicates the quality of his merchandise: emerald and topaz rings set with four diamonds on the sides; garnet cluster rings; clusters with landscapes; a heart-shaped garnet ring with a twist shank; top and drop as well as star earrings set with garnets in gold.[42]

On the eve of the Revolution, four jewelers and a lapidary were shipped to Maryland from London, along with eight silversmiths, a goldsmith and numerous watch and clockmakers, to serve as indentured servants. However, there is no record of any of them establishing their own shop afterwards.[43]

Virginia

One of the earliest jewelers in Williamsburg was a crafty Scotsman named Alexander Kerr who had a novel approach to his business long before Dorwig got the idea in Maryland. Lotteries had been exceedingly popular in Virginia from the time of the first settlement in Jamestown. On 19 August 1737, in the *Virginia Gazette,* Kerr proposed a lottery of jewelry. The advertisement (Plate 43) explained how the sale of tickets would be handled and what the prizes would be. The prizes, listed in order of value ranging from sixty-two pistoles to two, could be viewed at his house or store prior to the drawing. The most valuable prize included three items: a large brilliant-cut diamond ring with two sides diamonds; a solitaire or breast jewel with a large amethyst in the centre, and with a large amethyst drop, three garnets, four emeralds and nine rose-cut diamonds (surely a splendid piece); and a chased gold box with an Egyptian pebble top and bottom. Next came another similar diamond ring, a mother-of-pearl and gold-chased snuff box, and a fine stone seal in a gold mount. Other distinguished jewels to make mouths water were a large rose-cut diamond ring with an emerald, diamond and ruby on each side of it; a scrolled ring with a large diamond and eight smaller ones; a ring with three emeralds and two rubies; and a hoop ring set with ten emeralds and ten diamonds.

39. *Md. Gaz.*, 3 Dec. 1767; 13 May 1773; Pleasants and Sill, *Maryland Silver 1715-1830,* pp. 74-76.
40. *Md. Journal,* 3 Nov. 1778.
41. A pair of silver knee buckles bearing Carnan's mark is at The Maryland Historical Society. Jennifer Faulds Goldsborough, *Silver in Maryland*, p. 131, #134.
42. *The Md. Journal & theBalto Advtr.*, Aug. 1776.
43. Pleasants & Sill, pp. 278-81.

PROPOSALS

For the Sale of s[…]dry valuable Jewels, and Plate, amounting to Four Hundred Pistoles. By Way of LOTTERY. For which

THERE are to […] Four Hundred Tickets, at a Pistole each, Eighty […] which will be Prizes; which will be Four Blanks to One Prize:

The greatest Prize is of Sixty Two Pistoles Value; the Second, of Forty Pistoles; the Third, of Thirty; the Fourth of Twenty Pistoles Value; and the rest of the Prizes gradually decrease in their Value, to the Number of Eighty Prizes, in all, 'til they come down to Two Pistoles, which are the lowest Prizes; so that every Adventurer has, for One Pistole, a Chance for a Prize of Sixty Two Pistoles; and if he draws but one of the lowest Prizes, he gets double the Value of his Money.

The Goods are rated at the common saleable Prices; and may be seen at any Time between this and the Day of Drawing the said Lottery, at my House or Store, in Williamsburg.

Alexander Kerr.

N. B. *The said Lottery is propos'd to be drawn some time in the next* October *General Court: And Tickets will be deliver'd out for the same, the next Week.*

A List of the PRIZES, in the said LOTTERY.

N°.		Value, in Pistoles.
1	ONE large Brilliant Diamond Ring, with a small Brilliant on each Side; One Solitair, or Breast Jewel, set with One large Amethist in the Middle, One large Amethist Drop, Three Garnets, Four Emeralds, and Nine Rose Diamonds; One Gold chas'd Box, with an Egyptian Pebble at the Top and Bottom; Value of them,	62
2	One Brilliant Diamond Ring, with a small Brilliant on each Side; One Mother of Pearl Snuff-Box, set in Gold, chas'd Plates on the Top, and studded on the Bottom; One fine Stone Seal, set in Gold,	40
3	One large Brilliant Diamond Ring, with a small Brilliant on each Side; a Gold Toothpick Case, with chas'd Plates,	30
4	One Mother of Pearl Box, set in Gold, with chas'd Plates on the Top, and studded on the Bottom; One Gold Toothpick Case,	20
5	One Ring, with a large Rose Diamond in the Middle, One Emerald, One Diamond, One Rubie on each Side,	15
6	One Hoop Ring, with Ten Diamonds and Ten Emarlds set round the Hoop,	13
7	One Scroll Ring, with One large Diamond and Eight smaller,	13
8	One Ring with One Emerald and Six Rose Diamonds, and One Gold Toothpick Case,	10
9	One Ring with Four Diamonds, Three Emeralds, and One Silver Toothpick Case,	7
10	One Ring with Three Emeralds, and Two Rubies, and One Silver Toothpick Case,	7
11	One Gold Toothpick Case, One Ring with a Garnet and Two Diamonds,	6½
12	One Ditto, and Six Tea Spoons, and Tongs,	6
13	One Ditto, and One pair of Gold Buttons,	6
14	One Ring with an Emerald, Four Diamonds, and a Silver chas'd Box,	5½
15	One Ditto with a Garnet, Two Diamonds, and a Silver chas'd Box,	5
16	One Ditto,	5
17	One Gold Toothpick Case,	4
18	A neat Silver Toothpick Case, chas'd in the Corinthian Order, with a Seal,	4
19	One Ring with an Amethist, ingrav'd,	4
20	One Head set in Gold,	4
21	One Ditto,	4
22	One Ditto,	4
23	One Silver Box, chas'd, and gilt on the Inside,	2½
24	One Ditto,	2½
25	One Ditto,	2½
26	One Ditto,	2½
27	One Ditto,	2½
28	One Ditto,	2½
29	One Ditto,	2½
30	One Ditto,	2½
31	One Silver Toothpick Case, and One false Stone Ring,	2½
32	One Ditto,	2½
33	One Ditto,	2½
34	One Ditto,	2½
35	One Ring with a Garnet and Two Diamonds, One Ivory Box,	2½
36	One Ring with a Garnet, and Two Diamonds, One Ivory Box,	2½
37	One pair of Stone Buttons, set in Gold,	2½
38	One pair of Ditto,	2½
39	One pair of Ditto,	2½
40	One pair of Ditto,	2½
41	One fine Brilliant Christal Buckle,	2
42	One Ditto,	2
43	One Ditto,	2
44	One Ditto,	2
45	One Mother of Pearl Box, and One small Girdle Buckle,	2
46	One Ditto, with a Silver Girdle Buckle neatly work'd,	2
47	One Cook Shell set in Silver, and One work'd Buckle,	2
48	One Stone Ring, and a Patch Box, with a Looking-Glass in the Top,	2
49	One Ditto,	2
50	One Ditto,	2
51	One Ditto,	2
52	One Ditto,	2
53	One Stone Ring, and One Ebony Mull, with Silver Rims and Hinges,	2
54	One Toothpick Case, and One pair of Gold Studs,	2
55	One Ditto,	2
56	One Ditto,	2
57	One Ditto,	2
58	One Ditto,	2
59	One Ditto,	2
60	One pair of Stone Ear-Rings,	2
61	One Ditto,	2
62	One Ditto,	2
63	One Ditto,	2
64	One Chas'd Mettle Box, gilt, with a *Bachus* on the Top,	2
65	One Toothpick Case, One Neck Buckle, One Ivory Box,	2
66	One Ditto,	2
67	One Ditto,	2
68	One Toothpick Case, One Mother of Pearl Box,	2
69	One Ditto,	2
70	One Toothpick Case, One Neck Buckle, One Ivory Box,	2
71	One Ditto,	[illegible]
72	One pair of Gold Buttons ingrav'd, One Ivory Box,	2
73	One pair of Ditto,	2
74	One pair of Ditto,	[illegible]
75	One pair of Ditto,	2
76	Six Tea Spoons, and Tongs,	2
77	Ditto,	2
78	Ditto,	2
79	Ditto,	2
80	One Silver Box, with a Paste Egyptian at the Top,	2

Williamsburg: Printed by W. PARKS. By whom Subscriptions are taken in for this Paper, at 15 s. *per Ann.* And BOOK-BINDING is done reasonably, in the best Manner.

Plate 43. Jeweler Alexander Kerr listed a whole page of bijoux which could be won in the lottery he put together in Williamsburg, Virginia, according to his advertisement in the Virginia Gazette, *19 August 1737. Photograph courtesy of The Virginia Historical Society.*

Plate 44. Illustration from Denis Diderot's Encyclopedie *published in Paris in 1776, showing the interior of a shop in which small work and jewelry was produced. Leather drop cloths were attached to the work bench and grids were placed on the floor to catch the filings and other tiny pieces of precious metals so they could be reused. The forge was fanned by a large bellows operated by the man in the background melting the metal. Hammering, soldering with a blowpipe and the setting of gems were other tasks shown here. American jewelry shops were less elaborate but made use of similar production techniques. Colonial Williamsburg Foundation.*

As the lottery list progressed to the two pistole prizes, the gems became less valuable, the number of snuff boxes and toothpick cases increased and they were made of silver rather than gold. Crystal and false stones entered the picture. Still there were intriguing things like a tiny patch box with a looking glass in it and a silver box 'with a Paste Egyptian at the top'. After four months of ogling and speculation, the lottery was drawn at last and Mrs. Dawson was the elated winner of the gorgeous breast jewel. Unfortunately, Alexander Kerr died the following year. He was extolled for his proficiency in business and the respect he commanded from his friends. A sale from his estate included rings made of diamonds and other stones, snuff boxes of a variety of materials, and gold toothpick cases. He is remembered for his goldsmithing as well. He was the maker of the silver chalice and dish presented to St. Paul's Church in Edenton, North Carolina.[44]

By 1746 James Craig had established himself in Williamsburg at the sign of the Golden Ball (Colour Plate 35). Craig was a jeweler from London who was able to supply his customers with diamond jewelry, as well as more mundane items like silver buckles, silver plate, toys, and cutlery. It was from him that George Washington bought garnet earrings in 1766 and mourning rings in 1769.[45] Like many of the jewelers in northern colonies, he became an agitator for American manufactures at the time of the nonimportation agreement; but, in his agrarian society, his stand is noteworthy.

Craig and his fellow jeweler/goldsmiths in Williamsburg – Patrick Beech and James Geddy – combined a little silversmithing and jewelry making with more importing and repairing. James Geddy (1731-1807), whose shop has been restored to operation in Colonial Williamsburg, billed Colonel William Preston in 1771 for a variety of things probably typical of the jeweler's business there at the time. The Colonel had bought several pairs of ear bobs, a pair of large strong buckles, a stone ring, an odd earring, a pair of silver studs, a large strong spoon (for his mother) and a pair of knee buckles.[46]

The colonial south was closely tied economically to England, exchanging crops for manufactured goods. The density of craftsmen per capita was considerably less than in the northern cities. In general, there were only one or two jewelers working in southern towns at any given time, as was the case in rural settlements of the northern colonies. These men continued to be jacks of all trades, filling the position of goldsmith, silversmith, jeweler, watch and clockmaker (Plate 44).

Charleston

Charleston, South Carolina had a surprisingly large number of jewelers and goldsmiths working there during the colonial period. Visitors to the city frequently remarked on

44. George B. Cutten, *The Silversmiths of Virginia,* pp. 199-202.
45. GW Ledger A, Lib. of Cong.
46. Cutten, *SSS. of Va.,* pp. 194-98. See *Va. Mag. of Hist. & Biog. 49,* 106.

Juſt imported in the Little-Carpenter *Capt.* William Muir, *from* LONDON, *and to be ſold by*
JONATHAN SARRAZIN,
At the Tea-Kettle and Lamp, the corner of Broad and Church-ſtreet;

A freſh and large aſſortment of jeweller's work, and ſterling made plate, *viz.*

SILVER caſters in ſilver frames, double flint ditto in ſilver frames, ditto in wooden frames with ſilver tops; chaſed, gadrooned and plain coffee-pots, ſauce-boats, tea-pots, ſugar-diſhes, milk pots, punch ladles, ſalt cellars, tweezer caſes, lancet caſes, tooth-pick caſes, pocket-book locks, ſnuff boxes, nutmeg grators, waiters, tankards, pint mugs, punch ſtrainers, ſoup and table ſpoons, tea ditto in ſhagreen caſes, pencil caſes, pincuſhion rims and chains, ſilver handle knives and forks in ſhagreen caſes, gold and ſilver ſhirt buckles ſet with cryſtal and garnets, ſilver ſhoe, knee, and ſtock buckles, ditto ſet with ſtones, ſilver hilted ſwords and cutteaus, joint and knob wires, ſword belts and buckles, pinchbeck buckles in ſets, diamond ear and finger rings, ſtone ſtay hooks, cryſtal, French paſte, coloured ſtone and pearl necklaces and ear-rings, mock garnet ditto, Marmaduke Storr's beſt mens and womens gold and ſilver watches, hair lockets and other trinkets for ladies watches, gold, ſilver and ſteel mens and womens watch chains, gold and ſilver ſeals with figures of maſonry, leather mounted fans, ſalt-cellar glaſſes, chaſed gold buckles, glazier's ruling diamonds, hat buckles, coral beads, anodyne necklaces for teething children, and many other articles too tedious to enumerate, which he will ſell at *ten for one*, any articles above 20 s. ſterling coſt, and allow 5 *per cent.* diſcount for prompt payment.

He continues to make and mend all kinds of jewellery, and motto rings as uſual. D

JOHN PAUL GRIMKE Jeweller, is removed from Mr. *Patchebel's* to the Houſe wherein Mr. *William Buttler* lived in *Tradd ſtreet*, next Door to Meſſrs. *Stead, Evance* & Comp. where he intends to work in Jeweller's Work as before: He has likewiſe juſt imported in Capt. *Wedderburn* from *London*, a freſh aſſortment of Brilliant and Roſe Diamonds, Rubies, Emeralds, Saphirs, Jacints, Topaz's, Amethiſts, Turky Stones, Garnets, and ſome ready made Rings He has alſo ſome Rooms to let.

NB Loſt in or near *Tradd ſtreet* by the ſaid *J. P. Grimke*, a pair of Diamond Scales: Whoever brings it to him ſhall have 40 *ſh.* reward.

Plate 45. Jonathan Sarrazin imported jewelry as well as silver from London for resale in his shop in Charleston. Among the treasures were diamond ear and finger rings, French paste, coloured stone, and mock garnet. Also available were pearl necklaces and earrings, Marmaduke Storr's watches, chased gold buckles, coral beads and anodyne necklaces for teething children. South-Carolina Gazette, *7 January 1764.*

Plate 46. Advertisement of John Paul Grimke, Charleston jeweler, which appeared in the South-Carolina Gazette, *12 September 1741, in which he specified the various gems he had imported for use in his jewelry. Courtesy of Museum of Early Southern Decorative Arts.*

the elegance of Charleston society. Peter Purry commented in 1731 that 'the People of Carolina...are all rich, either in Slaves, Furniture, Cloaths, Plate, Jewels, or other Merchandise'. Josiah Quincy, Jr., of Boston, observed in 1773 that the grandeur and splendour of Charleston surpassed all that he had seen or expected to see in America, and that its fashion, elegance, gaiety, and wealth were without parallel.[47]

The remarkable number of jewelers in the city may also have been influenced by the fact that, from the days of DeSoto and the beginning of settlement in Charleston in 1670, there had been persistent rumours of rich silver mines in South Carolina. In 1700, Solomon Legare (1674-1760), one of the colony's first resident goldsmiths, was among those who petitioned the Lords Commissioners for Trade and Plantation that they might be permitted to exploit the mines. Solomon Legare's father Francis was a Huguenot jeweler who migrated via England to Braintree, Massachusetts, in 1691, where he died in 1710 disappointed that his son had left his home and married without his approval. Little is known of Solomon's work, but he died in 1760 aged eighty-seven with a substantial estate appraised at more than £18,000.[48]

While there were a few Huguenot jewelers in colonial Boston and New York, there were more in Charleston. The Huguenot Sarrazins were a two-generation family of jewelers. Moreau Sarrazin (1710-1761), the father, was established on Broad Street by 1734. Louis Janvier (?-1748), a goldsmith who came from France via London, lived with Sarrazin part of the next year until he was able to set up his own shop. In addition to Sarrazin's jewelry, gold and silver work, he was also an engraver, producing a plan of St. Augustine in 1742 for the provincial government. In 1746 Sarrazin formed a short-lived partnership with William Wright, a goldsmith who worked there from about 1740 to 1751.

By 1754 Sarrazin's son Jonathan joined him in the business. They began importing large quantities of jewelry and silver (Plate 45). Gold and silver shirt buttons set with

47. Francis W. Bilodeau, *Art In South Carolina 1670-1970*), p. 216.
48. Burton, pp. 105-10.

crystal and garnets, diamond ear and finger rings, French paste, coloured stone and pearl necklaces, and earrings made of mock garnet were among the treasures Jonathan Sarrazin (?-1811) offered after his father's retirement and subsequent death in 1761. Marmaduke Storr's best London watches, made of gold and silver for men and women, were imported especially for his customers. In addition to coral necklaces, Sarrazin carried anodyne necklaces for teething children.[49] These were used as charms to ward off pain or sickness. Alexander Petrie was a competitor of Sarrazin and was also importing jewelry. When Petrie retired in 1765, Sarrazin bought out all of his stock and, after Petrie died, bought his negro silversmith named Abraham. Sarrazin's imprisonment by the British during the Revolution put an end to his once-flourishing family business.

John Paul Grimke whose business has been discussed (pages 34 and 47) had come from London to Charleston in 1740 and set up his shop on Elliott Street at the sign of the Hand and Ring (Plate 46). That very year a great fire raged through the colonial capital and his shop was lost. It was enough to make him decide to go back to England, but he reconsidered and stayed and the next year resumed his importations of jewelry and silver. He married in 1744 and three years later his wife died. Once again he determined to sell his possessions at public auction and leave the province, but he stayed on and married again. During the 1750s and '60s, he flourished. He took on more workmen, including a fine chaser. When the Stamp Act was passed, Grimke's health failed and he threatened to leave, but with its repeal, his health was restored and he stayed on, retiring at last in 1772, a successful Charleston jeweler in spite of himself.[50] The selection of precious gems offered by Grimke outshone that of all other colonial jewelers and ranged from brilliant-cut and rose-cut diamonds, sapphires, rubies, and emeralds, to amethysts, garnets, topaz, and turquoise.[51] The floral brooch set with most of these stones and the garnet-studded miniature frame illustrated in Colour Plates 13 and 15 may well have been made by Grimke.

Nicholas Smith, another London jeweler who came to Charleston about 1762, managed to carry on his jewelry and silver trade even during the war years. In the middle of the British occupation in 1781, he was able to receive a shipment of a large quantity of elegant jewelry.[52] Smith had worked in partnership about 1775 with George Smithson who made swords as well as jewelry. It was Smithson who provided quick delivery of mourning and wedding rings during wartime conditions for people who found themselves in a hurry. Smithson's sympathies lay with the British, however, and he soon left South Carolina for the West Indies.

Philip Tidyman arrived from London early in 1764 bringing with him a large supply of jewelry and plate. Because he employed able workmen, he could deal on very low terms, which meant that his jewelry could be purchased at wholesale prices for cash. Based on many advertisements and long lists of goods imported to his shop, Tidyman had a very successful business. He offered the large sum of a hundred pounds as a reward for information leading to the return of three diamond hoop rings stolen from him in 1766. When he died in 1780, he was a man of substantial means.[53]

Yet another English jeweler to find prosperity in colonial Carolina was James Alexander Courtonne (1720-93) who announced in the *South Carolina Gazette* on 3 March 1751 that he continued 'to sell, make and mend all sorts of jeweller's work, diamond and motto rings', that he would give the highest price for gold and silver, and would value jewels in a just manner. Courtonne, though born in London, is believed to be the son of French Huguenot refugees who fled to London after the

49. *S.C. Gaz.*, 7 Jan. 1764. Burton, pp. 163-9.
50. Burton, pp. 73-8.
51. *S.C. Gaz.*, 12 Sept. 1741.
52. Burton, pp. 173-5.
53. Ibid., pp. 182-4.

Revocation of the Edict of Nantes. His wife Ann Sabb died in 1773. A mourning ring inscribed 'Ann Courtonne, Jan. 7, 1773, aet. 50' and owned by a descendant is thought to have been made by him in her memory. Although Courtonne imported jewelry from London from 1755 on, he advertised that he had 'made several rich pieces of jeweller's work not inferior to any, and continues to make and mend in that Branch'. When war broke out, he and his son enlisted in the Charleston militia and took the Oath of Fidelity and Allegiance, but after the siege of the city, when it seemed that the rebel cause was lost, he petitioned to be reinstated as a British subject.[54] John Miot (1740-91), who made 'all [the] kinds of Jewellery used in this Province', followed the same course of vacillating loyalties, but when peace came he was banished and his property was confiscated.[55]

Patriot John Hector, a jeweler on Church Street, wrote at length of the necessity of encouraging American manufactures. He said that he would offer only work that was begun and finished in this place, and that his articles would not only be as cheap as those imported from London and Birmingham, but he would also guarantee them to last twice as long.[56]

Clearly, at the end of the colonial period, American jewelers were determined to break their English ties, political and professional. While jewelers carried on as best they could or switched to other productions, such as swords or ironware, it would not be until after the end of hostilities that they could get back to business as usual. When they did get underway again, the lessons learned from the Stamp Act and the nonimportation agreement remained imprinted in their consciences. It would take time, but Americans were determined to control their own destiny.

John Norton, a London merchant, received a letter from one of his Virginia clients in 1770 in which the American pointed out that English trade restrictions had taught the colonists that they could make many things for themselves and do without many of the other things that were not essential. The Virginian boasted, 'I now wear a good suit of Cloth of my Son's wool, manufactured, as well as my shirts in Albemarl & Augusta Counties, my Shoes, Hose Buckles, Wigg, & Hat etca of our own Country, and in these We improve every year, in Quantity as well as Quality'.[57]

Luxury items were the first things that had to be curtailed when the war came. John Adams wrote from Philadelphia to his wife Abigail in Braintree, Massachusetts, on 20 September 1774, 'Frugality, Œconomy, Parcimony must be our Refuge. I hope the Ladies are every day diminishing their ornaments, and the Gentlemen too'. A few weeks later Abigail replied, 'I have spent one Sabbeth in Town since you left me. I saw no difference in respect to ornaments'. If John Adams could have had his way, he would have banished forever from his beloved country all luxuries such as gold, and precious stones, because he had seen in France how riches had corrupted.[58]

The war cost dearly. Families were divided into Loyalists and Patriots. Many were killed and many were driven from their homes. Much of the colonial American jewelry was taken to England and other countries by fleeing Tories. Some was melted down or sold to pay for the war. 'During the War', we are told, 'after divine service on a Sunday, or on a Thanksgiving Day – contributions were often taken in church for the benefit of the Continental Army. Cash, finger-rings, ear-rings, and other jewelry –...were frequently thus collected – in New England particularly, in large quantities'.[59]

If, with the war, Americans lost their Crown and their jewels, they more than compensated by losing their dependence as well.

54. *S.C. Gaz.*, 3 Mar. 1751; Burton, pp. 40-42.
55. Burton, pp. 125-6.
56. Ibid., p. 87.
57. Mason, *John Norton*, p. 122, letter from W. Nelson, 24 Jan. 1770.
58. L.H. Butterfield et al, *The Book of Abigail and John*, pp. 77, 80, 217.
59. I.W. Stuart, *Life of Jonathan Trumbull, Senior*, cited by Wharton, p. 102.

PART II

FEDERAL JEWELRY 1775-1825

Introduction 1775-1825

With independence came innovation. No longer was American trade channelled solely through England. New ports throughout the world were open to direct contact and commerce. Products and resources from European countries and the Far East were available to Americans without the taxes formerly superimposed on foreign goods by England. Yankee sea captains were eager to set sail and war-starved Americans were more than willing customers for the luxuries the ships carried home.

In the first years of independence, England was still the major source of United States imports. More than three and a half million pounds' worth of British exports were taken to that country, one fifth the value of goods imported to Britain from the United States. However, trade with France and Holland grew, and ventures to China met with immediate success.

Ideas were imported as well, especially from England and Europe. The new government was based on the ideals of the Roman republic and the Enlightenment as interpreted by the founding fathers. Neo-classicism, which had begun to make an appearance in America immediately prior to the outbreak of war, caused a revolution of its own in cultural and artistic matters. Fuelled by printed designs and new-fashioned articles for everything from architectural details and house furnishings to wearing apparel, the taste for the classical swept over the foundling nation.[1]

Inspiration from ancient Rome was organized into a totally new art form by the gifted Robert Adam in England. Thomas Jefferson embraced the new style wholeheartedly, declaring the out-dated, pre-war approach to design a 'burden of barbarous ornament'. In its place came order, simplicity and symmetry. Contrasting geometric designs and delicate ornamentation permeated new buildings, wall paintings, furniture and tablewares. Festoons and swags, bowknots and bell-flowers, rosettes and paterae found their way into the arts of the young republic. Light delicate fabrics in light delicate colours covered people as well as things.

Jewelry reflected the new dictates of fashion. Necklaces and bracelets were designed in festoons and delicate fretwork patterns. Rows of pearls and occasionally diamonds formed the beaded borders of brooches and rings. Gold and white was an especially popular combination of colours, hence there was an overwhelming preference for gold jewelry embellished with white pearls. In general, diamonds were of less interest

1. 'A lady in Philadelphia' was among the first subscribers to Heideloff's *Gallery of Fashion* which began publication in London in 1794. Soon afterwards, a subscriber from Charleston, South Carolina, and one other American signed up for the fashion guide. Bury, I, 38-39.

Colour Plate 36. Opposite. During the Federal period, the use and variety of jewelry increased considerably. The daughter of John Stoughton of Boston, Louisa Carolina Matilda Stoughton, was married to the Spanish chargé d'affaires Don Josef de Jaudenes y Nebot in Philadelphia in 1794, the year that Gilbert Stuart (1755-1828) painted her portrait. An elaborate festoon necklace of tiny pearls and red gems, complementary top and drop earrings, a pair of matching bracelets, a wrought gold chain which holds a large gold locket, a chatelaine with bibelots attached, a gold watch and large golden snowflake medallions on her frizzed hair – all proclaim an era of increasing wealth and luxury. Length 50⅝in., width 39½in. Metropolitan Museum of Art, Rogers Fund, 1907.

than topaz and amethyst which harmonized with the colours of high-waisted, filmy dresses that appeared in American cities. To these were added contrasting colours such as burnt umber and black, suggested by Etruscan wall painting. As a result amber, coral, jets, and cornelian became increasingly fashionable. Clear royal blue and brilliant emerald green were stunning accents enamelled on gold lockets, watches and rings or on silver and pinchbeck chains. Clasps became oval or rectangular in shape and bore engraved or enamelled motifs taken from classical mythology and literature. Wedgwood plaques were moulded with classical sculptural figures and set into jewelry.

No decorative motif was more in demand than the American bald eagle, chosen as the symbol of the Great Seal of the United States in 1782. The stars and the stripes of the American flag became elements of design as well. These motifs were cheerfully placed on jewelry along with ancient devices such as the dove of peace, baskets of fruit, cornucopias, and figures of Hope and Justice. It was in the selection of designs from the abundance of examples served up abroad that the distinctive taste of Americans began to assert itself. Their choice of designs revealed what had meaning for Federal Americans and what they chose as emblems of aspiration.

Although importation of foreign-made jewelry was extensive in the first few decades of the Federal period, more and more jewelry was being produced in this country. New kinds of personal items such as miniatures and hair work were being made on a large scale. Although diamonds had gone out of style temporarily due to wars here and abroad, some diamond work was still carried on in American cities. By the nineteenth century, American jewelers were actively competing with British manufacturers in producing pearl, jet, and filigree jewelry. However, suites of jewelry made of topaz and amethyst, as well as watches and chatelaines, were often imported from England and France.

Whether it was imported or made in the United States, Americans wanted their jewelry to serve a purpose beyond that of being decorative. The idea of owning jewelry that portrayed loved ones or that contained a tangible connection to those dearest was most appealing to them. The symbols and inscriptions they chose to adorn their jewelry were usually selected with close attention to their meaning and expressed privately held ideals. Some jewelry had religious significance. In this way they were able to justify owning such luxuries. Early presidents and their wives, along with the politically important and the wealthy, set the pace. For the most part they elected to be fashionable but restrained.

As might be expected in a country dedicated to the individual, there was a desire to make all things available to everyone. Various kinds of jewelry were made to suit any pocketbook. Substitute materials such as cut-steel, shell, agate, anodyne and amulets found their way into fashion. Gold-plated jewelry was introduced. Rolled gold and silver was available, making the jeweler's task much easier. By the end of the Federal period, the roots of mass-production and the jewelry industry were spreading in eastern seaboard cities. The conversion of the individual shop to factory operation had begun. The emergence of an American style in jewelry was under way.

Miniatures

'I have a request to you which I hope you will not disappoint me of, a miniature of Him I best Love. Indulge me the pleasing melancholy of contemplating a likeness'.

So Abigail Adams wrote to her husband in 1780. John Adams was in Paris during one of their long separations necessitated by his active role in the Revolution. They had tried to get a satisfactory miniature of him in their own country, but it was such a disappointment that Abigail could not stand the sight of it. It looked, she said, more like 'a cloisterd Monk, than the Smileing Image of my Friend'. Abigail hoped that he would have the new one set in France too, because she thought it would be better done there than at home.[1]

The Revolution fostered a keen desire for miniature portraits among many Americans due to the repeated separations and deaths that war inflicts. No other form of jewelry was more treasured or more highly developed in Federal America than was jewelry set with miniature paintings. Many of their best artists turned their hands to little likenesses.

The miniature portrait, as a private memento intended for a loved one, had taken form during the Renaissance. It was not until the eighteenth century that this combination companion and charm became a widespread part of the artist/jeweler's art. Miniature portraits were related in essence to portrait medals and to the classical portrait gems set in rings. Painted on vellum or cardboard during the reign of Henry VIII, they were subsequently set in jewelled pendants and rings. Early in the eighteenth century the use of ivory was introduced, thereby contributing a greater permanence and preciousness to these cherished objects. At that time, too, it became the custom to place a lock of hair inside the gold or silver case enclosing the miniature.[2]

In the second quarter of the eighteenth century miniature portraits began to gather momentum in the American colonies. Many of them were put into English-made cases. About 1724, for instance, the Reverend Henry Addison of Maryland sent a miniature to his son in London along with instructions for having the picture copied by a fine artist and set in a gold frame so that it could be suspended from a ribbon worn around the neck.[3]

An early Charleston miniature, painted on ivory and originally set as a clasp on a bracelet, portrayed Mrs. Jacob Motte. It is believed to have been painted by Jeremiah Theus who was working in Charleston from 1740 until his death in 1773. Theus called himself a 'limner', the term that had been used to mean one who painted in miniature.[4] 'Face painter' Mary Roberts of Charleston made a miniature portrait of a member of the Gibbes or Shoolbred family some time prior to the artist's death in 1761 (see Colour Plate 15).

Some artists in America advertised that they made miniatures specifically to be set as jewelry. Brooks & Warrock in Norfolk, Virginia, announced 'The most striking Likenesses, taken in Miniature, For Lockets or Bracelets, at from 10 to 20 dollars each'. They even offered to go to customers in the country to take the likeness if the customer would provide the transportation.[5] William Birchall Tatley announced in

1. Butterfield, p. 265.
2. Harry B.Wehle, *American Miniatures*, pp. 3-6.
3. Wharton, pp. 35-6. The frame was to be engraved with a memorial inscription to a young woman who had died in 1724 at the age of twenty-five. Addison also ordered four 'lockets for ladies to be worn about the neck with a crystal in each, covering an urn made of the hair I send you herewith'.
4. Wehle, pp. 7, 13-14. Lewis Turtaz, working in Charleston in 1767, called himself a limner and miniature painter. He charged £20 for a head and bust, £10 down and £10 on delivery. *SC Gaz.*, 30 March 1767.
5. *Norfolk Herald*, 26 May 1796.

Colour Plate 37. Miniatures of Martha Washington's children by her first marriage, set in gold bracelet clasps designed to hold up to nine strands, probably made in Philadelphia, c.1780. The portraits of John Parke Custis (1754-1781) and Martha Parke Custis (1755-1773) were painted by Charles Willson Peale (1741-1827) in 1772. Height 1⅝in. Mount Vernon Ladies' Association, Mount Vernon, Virginia.

1774 that he painted portraits in miniature for bracelets or small enough to be set in a ring.[6]

American artists could import frames, bracelets, and rings from abroad or purchase them from a local jeweler. For his miniatures, John Singleton Copley bought both frames and bracelets in gold from Paul Revere (see page 63). Joseph Dunkerley, another Boston miniaturist, who rented a house from Revere, painted a little portrait of his landlord's wife Rachel (Plate 47), and the gold locket enclosing it is believed to have been supplied by Revere.

Most miniaturists undoubtedly knew how to set their pictures in cases. A few artists learned enough of the goldsmith's work to make their own cases, just as a few goldsmiths learned to paint miniatures. Charles Willson Peale of Maryland was one of the former. In 1765, Peale made a trip to Boston where he visited Copley and presumably saw some of his work in miniature. It was about this time that Peale painted his first miniature, a self-portrait. When he went to London to study with Benjamin West in 1767, he painted miniature portraits in order to support himself. He struck a deal with a jeweler on Ludgate Hill for whom he painted miniatures of country clients for two guineas a head. The jeweler then got the business of mounting the ivories in cases. Peale eventually learned how to set miniatures himself and occasionally during the Revolution he not only made the gold cases, but moulded and ground the glasses for them as well.[7]

In 1772 Peale painted miniatures of Mrs. Washington and each of her two children Martha (Patsy) and John (Jack) Parke Custis. During the war, Peale visited Washington's camp and made a miniature of the General. In 1780 Mrs. Washington wrote to Peale:

Plate 47. The gold pendant set with a miniature painting of Rachel Revere of Boston is believed to have been made by her patriotic husband Paul Revere. It has an oval shape decorated with gold beading, with a little bead of gold at the base and a delicate scalloped border engraved on the back. The portrait is attributed to Joseph Dunkerley, a miniaturist working in Boston about 1785, when he rented a house from Revere. Length 1¾in., width 1⅛in. Bequest of Mrs. Pauline Revere Thayer. Courtesy, Museum of Fine Arts, Boston.

Colour Plate 38. The portrait of Mrs. Robert Morris of Philadelphia, painted by Charles Willson Peale about 1782, includes miniature portraits set in chain bracelets, one of her husband and one of her father. Her extremely fashionable hat is studded with stars and a crescent pin probably was set with pastes. Courtesy, Independence National Historical Park.

> I send my miniature pictures to you and request the favor of you to get them set for me. I would have them as bracelets to wear round the wrists...I would have the three pictures set exactly alike, and all the same size. If you have no crystals yourself, if they can be had in the city, I beg you to get them for me.

Peale replied,

> The Jeweler promises me to have the bracelets done in a few days. I have begged him to take the utmost pains to set them neatly. As no foreign glasses were to be had, I have moulded some of the best glass I could find and got a Lapidary to polish them, which I hope will not be inferior to those made abroad. I have cut the Pictures to one size, and mean to go a little further than you are pleased to direct, – that is, to have spare loop-holes for occasional use as a Locket, – and the additional expense is inconsiderable.[8]

The miniatures (Colour Plate 37) were accordingly set as clasps fitted to hold nine-strand bracelets, perhaps of delicate gold chain, or to be sewn to wrist ribbons. It is

6. *The N-Y Gaz. and the Wkly. Mercury*, 8 Aug. 1774.
7. Charles Coleman Sellers, *Portraits and Miniatures by Charles Willson Peale*, pp. 59-65.
8. Quoted by Wharton, pp. 79-80, from Rembrandt Peale's memoir.

believed that Martha Washington wore the miniature of her son Jack on her right wrist and the image of Patsy on her left wrist.[9] The cases are engraved with Adamesque swag borders with faceted outer borders. The backs have guilloche borders executed in chasing and wigglework. At Mount Vernon, along with the miniature clasps of the children, there is also a miniature of George Washington set as a pin/pendant in a gold box frame with an opening in one side to admit a spring catch for a clasp. There are no opposite side fittings, indicating that the frame has been reworked. At the top is a hinged loop and, soldered to the back, is a simple pin with a hook. This may have been the third miniature that Peale had originally set in a bracelet clasp when he did those of the two children.

A similar pair of bracelets with miniatures set in clasps can be seen in the portrait Peale painted in 1782 of Mrs. Robert Morris of Philadelphia (Colour Plate 38.). On her right wrist is the portrait of her husband whose great wealth had helped to finance the Revolution. On her left wrist is the miniature of a man believed to be her father. The bracelets were formed by multiple strands of chains. These were called portrait bracelets by Claudius Chat, a Parisian jeweler working in Philadelphia in 1791, who also provided 'Padlocks for d[itt]o'.[10]

Abigail Adams wanted to have portrait bracelets made with miniatures of her two sons, John Quincy and Thomas Boylston Adams, to be set with their 'Hair in cypher' on the back. John Quincy Adams had been appointed Minister to the Netherlands in 1794 and Tom went with his brother to the Hague. There they found a British miniaturist named Parker who provided them with the portraits, but putting the hair into the back of the clasps was 'beyond the skill of the Dutch Jeweler'. Nevertheless their mother was delighted with the bracelets and thought the likenesses were very good, John Quincy's (Colour Plate 39, left) more flattering than Tom's. 'I can say with as much truth as the Lady of old', she wrote to them, 'Here are my Jewells'.[11]

In addition to miniature portraits, miniature scenes and emblems were painted for use in jewelry. While Judge John Lowell of Newbury, Massachusetts, was serving at the Continental Congress in Philadelphia in 1782, he sat to Charles Willson Peale. Lowell's miniature portrait, now at the Museum of Fine Arts, Boston, is backed by an emblematic miniature painting. Two angels display Hymen's torch and a marriage chaplet over a large tree (representing John Lowell) and a smaller tree (representing his third wife Rebecca Russell Tyng). On the right is the Temple of Love and on the left is an allée of six trees of diminishing size, representing the Judge's three sons and three daughters. Chopped hair of gold and brown is worked on to the trees.

Joseph Barrell of Boston ordered a pair of bracelets set with miniature paintings from England for his wife Sarah in 1786. Barrell was a successful entrepreneur as well as a sensitive, discerning man when it came to matters of taste. Not only did he specify the kind of jewelry he wanted, he specified what the design of the miniature painting would be. Rings, bracelets, brooches and earrings were personalized for him by the firm of Stephen Twycross in London, illustrating details of his familial joys and disappointments. Moreover the mottos on the jewelry also expressed Barrell's own feelings.

The pair of bracelets (Colour Plate 40), with delicately painted miniatures in the clasps, reveal the degree of Barrell's involvement in their design. One clasp was deliberately painted in sepia to depict the sad loss between 1782 and 1786 of the first three children of Barrell's marriage to Sarah Webb. The Grim Reaper stood by their

9. Sellers, pp. 60-1.
10. *Pa. Packet,* 31 May 1791.
11. The lady of old was Cornelia whose story was told by Seneca. AA to JQA, 8 Oct. 1795; 23 Jan. 1796; Adams Papers. John Quincy confided in his diary years later that his miniature by Parker he considered one of the few likenesses of himself worthy of preservation. Andrew Oliver, *Portraits of John Quincy Adams and His Wife,* pp. 2, 28, 32. Family tradition states that Mrs. Adams wore the miniatures on bracelets of black velvet ribbon.

memorial urn and the three children appeared in the clouds above with a banner proclaiming, 'Here all is calm and but a moment parts us'. In the other clasp, the companion miniature was painted in the pretty colours of Watteau, with the sun shining down on Joseph and Sarah Barrell. Their three deceased children, not forgotten, were half-hidden in the landscape. In the foreground were Barrell's daughter Hannah (by his previous marriage) and son Charles, born in 1784, with a little lamb representing innocent baby Henry, born in 1786. The banner above expressed Barrell's sentiment, 'Long may these sweets remain'.[12]

In 1796, Joseph Barrell ordered from Twycross a set of jewelry with miniatures, surrounded by diamond sparks, for his daughter Hannah who was married to Benjamin Joy in 1797 (Colour Plate 41). The earrings had charming scenes showing Hannah's three eldest step-brothers at play on one and her three youngest siblings in innocence on the other earring. The bracelets, with their triple strands of small natural pearls, had scenes expressing Barrell's deepest thoughts. Under the title of *Enjoyment,* Barrell was shown with his daughter Hannah and his wife. On the other clasp, Barrell, in his sixties and in failing health, lifted high a ring, the symbol of eternity, and announced, 'I seek the end'. His life had been fulfilled and he was ready to move on.[13]

Not many purchasers of jewelry took such an active part in its design as Barrell did. Most were satisfied to make a choice locally of ready-made pieces without waiting for months for the order to be filled. They still could choose designs that expressed their sentiments and suited their situations. The appropriate initials and dates could be added to the design or a personal inscription could be engraved on the back of the case (Colour Plate 42). Large numbers of miniatures, set in brooches and pendants with painted symbols of love or mourning, bore initials and inscriptions that once held great meaning to the families who owned them.

Among the most handsome jewelry settings of miniature paintings available in the United States were the cases sold by John Cook & Co. of New York about 1800. One such case (Colour Plate 42, right) had a label inside stating that 'Miniature settings, Mourning rings, Lockets &c [were sold] by John Cook & Co. working Goldsmiths & Jewelers, No. 133 William-street, New York, on the shortest notice'. Cook & Co. was located on William Street from 1796 to 1801. The gold frame of the case had an elegant border with interlacing bands of pink and gold, dotted with seed pearls, against a bright blue background. On the reverse, a wide bright blue enamelled border *en guilloche* surrounded a glass-covered oculus containing a plait of medium brown hair on which were laid the flat gold cut-out script initials *IMD.* The enclosed miniature painting of John Maynard Davis is attributed to Jean François de Vallée, a French artist and silhouettist working in America between 1794 and 1815.

Several cases with similar broad bright blue enamelled borders contained miniatures of residents of Savannah, Georgia. While the frames had plain gold bands, the backs contained oculi with plaits of hair and flat cut-out script initials. One charming example (Colour Plate 43) had *Souvenir* in gold script above the initials SM. Its miniature depicted a maiden watching a ship sail away with the object of her affection.

During the last quarter of the eighteenth century more and more American artists began to specialize in painting miniatures. John Ramage, an Irishman who had studied at the Dublin School of Artists, arrived in America on the eve of the

12. Fales, 'Stephen Twycross', *Antiques,* March 1987, pp. 642-49. Stephen Twycross (c.1745-c.1822) had a New England connection. His brother Robert, a sea captain, regularly sailed there, married a girl in Dresden in the District of Maine, and had a son who was apprenticed to Stephen Twycross, eventually joining his firm. 'Stephen Twycross, London Jeweller, and his American Patrons' in *Jewellery Studies 6,* The Society of Jewellery Historians (London, 1993), pp. 37-43.

13. The brooch in the set appears to have been remade from a ring and resembles the pieces purchased earlier by Barrell, with its figure of Death and eye of Providence.

Colour Plate 39. Miniatures of John Quincy Adams (shown here, left) and Thomas Boylston Adams were painted in 1795 by Parker, an Englishman who was working in the Netherlands while John Quincy was serving as Minister to the Hague. Abigail Adams, their mother, had requested that the miniatures be set in bracelet clasps. As soon as Abigail Adams received news that her son John Quincy was engaged to Louisa Catherine Johnson who was then living in London, Abigail requested of them a miniature and a lock of her future daughter-in-law's hair (right). The likeness was probably painted by Samuel Shelly (1750-1808) in 1796, in London. Length of both 2in. Courtesy of the Diplomatic Reception Rooms, The Department of State, Washington, D.C.

Plate 48. Gold pendant containing a miniature scene, probably New York, c.1790-1800, set with seed pearls and mother-of-pearl, watercolour on ivory, owned by Catherine Clinton. Length $2\frac{1}{16}$in. Historic Hudson Valley, Tarrytown, N.Y.

Revolution and gained fame in New York as a miniaturist. Today he is noted as one who made his own chased gold frames (Plate 48). Although it is tempting to think that every Ramage miniature has a Ramage pendant frame, that is not true. He also imported cases as well as crystals and the ivory on which the miniatures were painted. In 1784, he received from London what he called 'The greatest variety for settings for pictures that ever appeared in America'. These included settings with gold beads, elegant chasing, engraving, enamelling, and cases rimmed with pearls, pastes, or garnets, costing from one to twenty guineas each.[14]

Charles Willson Peale taught his younger brother James to paint and gave up painting miniatures himself so that James could have this specialty as his own (Plate 103). A miniature self-portrait painted by James was placed in a pendant case back to back with a miniature on the other side of his wife and their infant daughter Maria.[15] For his brother, James painted a miniature portrait of Charles' wife the year she died. On the reverse he painted a memorial scene which was surrounded by a plait of Mrs. Peale's hair. It was signed and dated 1790 and is in its original gold frame.[16] James Peale's miniature of James Mackubbin of Annapolis dated 1798 is in a lovely pearl-rimmed frame. Within a standard-sized portrait that James Peale painted of Mrs. Edmond Rouvert in 1800, the artist showed her holding a miniature of her husband in her hand. It was suspended from a very long and delicate chain worn around her neck.[17]

14. *Royal Gaz.*, 15 Nov. 1780; *Independent Journal: or the Gen. Advtr.*, 24 Jan. 1784. Perhaps this explains why Wehle, pp. 29-30, felt that Ramage's miniatures were 'as a rule, in frames...more beautiful than those used by any other miniaturist in America'.
15. Wehle, p. 21, Plates V and VI.
16. *Antiques,* Nov. 1957, p.386.
17. Ibid., Feb. 1956, p. 100.

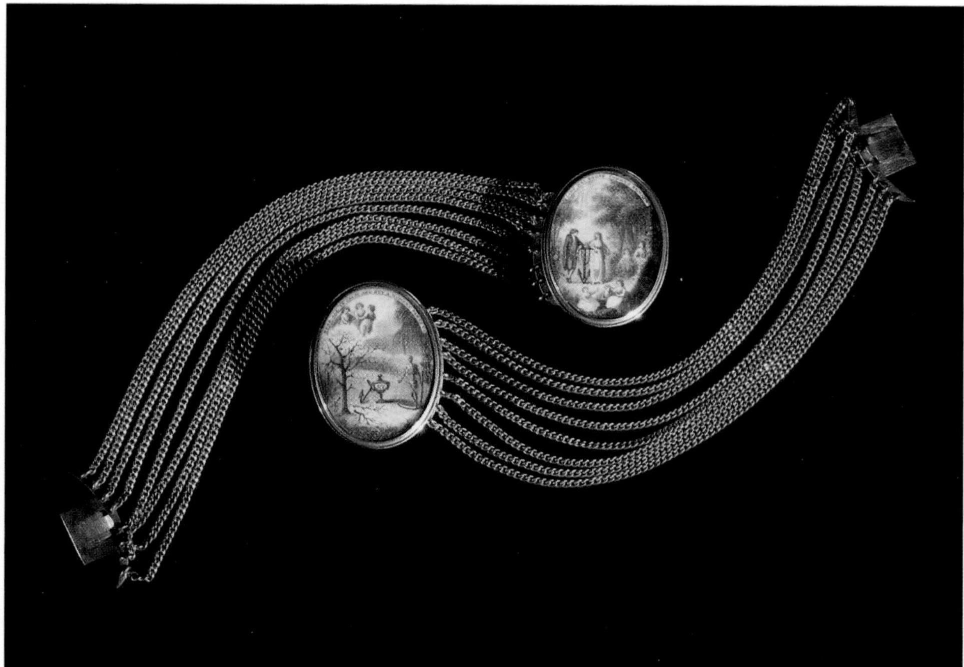

Colour Plate 40. Pair of gold bracelets, purchased by Joseph Barrell (1739-1804) of Boston from Stephen Twycross of London, c.1786, for his third wife, Sarah Webb (1752-1832). The clasps are set with miniature paintings depicting (left) the loss of their first three children and (right) Joseph and Sarah delighting in their three living children. Length 7¹⁵⁄₁₆in. Photograph by Paul Rocheleau by courtesy of The Magazine Antiques. *Webb-Deane-Stevens Museum.*

The method of wearing miniature pendants varied slightly according to where and by whom they were worn. In rural areas, ladies frequently wore their miniatures suspended from long, narrow ribbons sometimes looped around the neck and tied with a bow at the neck or at the top of the miniature (Colour Plate 44). In 1786, Mrs. John Sherman of New Haven tied a narrow ribbon or cord around her neck with a bow in front and then looped the long ends over to her left side so that her tiny miniature could be tied by another tiny bow and pinned over her heart.

Others wore their miniatures pinned over their heart, sometimes face down to preserve the intimacy of this love token. Mrs. Elijah Boardman, in her portrait by Ralph Earl, wore her gold-cased miniature without any suspension ribbon or chain. It was simply pinned over her heart, face down, for reasons of her own.[18]

The portrait Ralph Earl painted of Mrs. Homer Boardman of New Milford, Connecticut, in 1789, showed her with black faggoted ribbons as bracelets and narrower ribbon tied in a bow in the front of her neck, from which a gold locket was suspended. It too appears to be a miniature turned face in.[19] Several portraits by Charles Peale Polk about 1790 depict Virginia ladies wearing looped, very thin ribbons or cords with or without miniatures attached.[20] A portrait of Mrs. Marquis Calmes of Kentucky about 1806 shows her wearing a miniature of a woman over her heart.[21]

On a more pretentious level of the social scale, in Philadelphia, miniatures were worn dangling from strings of pearls or gold chains (Plate 49). Mrs. Thomas Lea wore her son's rather large miniature pinned face up over her heart, and hung from a long and loosely looped, doubled

18. c.1798. *Antiques*, Aug. 1986, p. 271. Henry E.Huntington Library and Art Gallery, San Marino, Calif.
19. Nina Fletcher Little, *Little by Little* (New York, 1984), Fig. 179, p. 136.
20. Gibbs, pp 53-103.
21. Poesch, *The Art of the Old South*, p. 160, painting by Jacob Frymire.

Plate 49. Miniature portrait of Fannie Hipkins Bernard of Port Royal, Virginia, who married William Bernard in 1789. Unknown artist, c.1789. Mrs. Bernard is lavishly adorned with pearls, feather aigrette, and wears two portrait miniatures. 2³⁄₁₆in. x 1⅝in. Courtesy of Museum of Early Southern Decorative Arts.

Plate 50. Mrs. Thomas Lea of Philadelphia wore her young son's miniature portrait suspended from a double gold chain and pinned over her heart. Her son's likeness was taken in 1794 by Adolph-Ulric Wertmuller (1715-1811), a Swedish artist working in Philadelphia from 1794 to1796. Her own portrait was painted in 1798 by Gilbert Stuart (1755-1828). Height 29in., width 24in. Anonymous gift, in the Collection of the Corcoran Gallery of Art.

gold chain (Plate 50). Although her portrait was painted by Gilbert Stuart about 1798, the miniature itself was painted a few years earlier in oils on wood by the Swedish artist, Adolph-Ulric Wertmuller, who came to Philadelphia in 1794. Originally cased in a gold frame as seen in the portrait, it is now in a carved frame.[22]

Men also wore miniatures. Captain Peter Le Breton, Jr., who was often at sea, wore a large miniature around his neck suspended under the bow of his stock.[23]

By the end of the eighteenth century, many accomplished artists were painting miniatures for jewelry. Both Thomas Sully and William Birch came from England. Sully was brought to Charleston by his parents in 1792 and was instructed in the art of miniature painting before he went back to England to study with Benjamin West. He returned to Philadelphia and became famous for his portraiture. In 1801, while in Norfolk, Virginia, he painted a miniature portrait of a jeweler named George Ott who had just come to town. On the back Sully signed it 'T. Sully Miniature and Fancy Painter'.

William Birch had been apprenticed to a London goldsmith before embarking on his career, painting miniatures in enamels. Birch came to Philadelphia in 1794. His best known enamel is the miniature he did of George Washington after Stuart's 'Lansdowne' portrait. An enamelled brooch (Plate 53) by him bore a scene of the Triumph of Independence.[24] Birch also enamelled a square miniature of Lafayette in 1824 when the much admired Frenchman came to the United States on a triumphal tour.[25]

One of the most talented miniaturists working in America, Edward Greene Malbone was born in Rhode Island. Like many in his trade, he travelled from city to

22. Philadelphia Museum of Art: *Three Centuries of American Art,* #136, 147.
23. Delin portrait, Historical Society of Old Newbury.
24. PMA, *Philadelphia,* p.236, #195
25. Wehle, Plate XIX.

Plate 51. Above left. Portrait of a man of the Hunter family, attributed to Edward Greene Malbone, 1803. Set in gold and pearl pendant, Length 2¾in., width 2⅛in. The Col. Alexander F. and Jeannie C. Stevenson Memorial Collection, gift of Mary Louise Stevenson, 1963.74. Photograph ©1993, The Art Institute of Chicago.

Plate 52. Above right. Memorial pendant with miniature painting of grieving woman leaning upon the gravestone of Sarah Sully and believed to have been painted by her son Thomas Sully (1783-1872) who became a well-known artist in the United States. Both of his parents were actors who brought him from England to Charleston in 1792. Sully travelled continuously to the major cities on the eastern seaboard painting miniatures as well as pictures. Diameter 1½in. Yale University Art Gallery.

Plate 53. Left. William Birch (1755-1834) enamelled this scene of the Triumph of Independence on copper and had it set into a gold clasp. Signed lower left, W.B. Length 1⅞in. Philadelphia Museum of Art, Purchased: Temple Fund.

Plate 54. Right. Portrait and eye miniatures, painted by Edward Greene Malbone (1777-1807), of Maria Miles Heyward, Charleston, S.C., 1802. Length $3\frac{15}{32}$in. (portrait), $\frac{11}{16}$in. (eye). Photograph courtesy of National Gallery of Art.

city in search of commissions. Between 1794 and 1801 he worked in Boston, New York, Philadelphia, and Charleston. In the latter city in 1802 he painted one of the most rare and interesting varieties of miniatures – the eye miniature (Plate 54). The Malbone example represented the eye of Maria Miles Heyward and was set in a small round breast pin with a twisted rope border.[26] The fashion for a tiny painting of an eye of a loved one is said to have been set in England shortly after 1800 when Richard Cosway, a leading English miniaturist, painted eye miniatures for the Prince Regent and Mrs. Fitzherbert to exchange. The identity of the beloved could only be recognized by one who cared deeply.

The miniature of the eye of Aimée de Breuys of New Orleans, painted by an anonymous American artist, was set with seed pearls in a round pendant case. A lock of hair and her initials were placed in the back of the case about 1810.[27]

While eye miniatures were set in rings as well as brooches, portrait heads were the

26. Poesch, p. 162.
27. This miniature is at the New Orleans Museum of Art, New Orleans, Louisiana. Cynthia Duval, *Infinite Riches: Jewelry Through the Centuries*, p. 87, illus. p. 34. An eye miniature painted by Joseph Wood (c.1778-1830) is at the Rhode Island School of Design. Wood worked in New York and travelled to other cities seeking patrons.

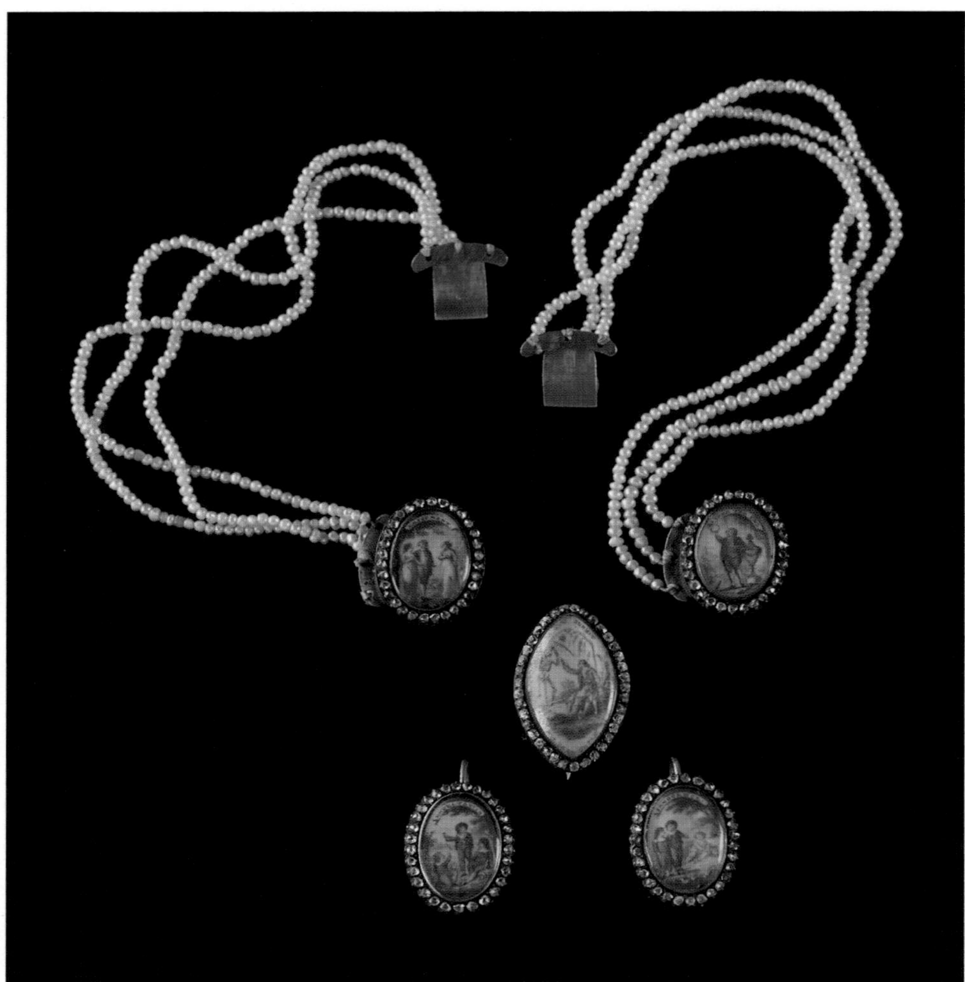

Colour Plate 41. Jewelry set with miniatures of family scenes, ordered by Joseph Barrell from Stephen Twycross of London in 1796, probably for his eldest daughter Hannah on the occasion of her marriage to Benjamin Joy, Jr. in 1797. Diamonds surround the miniatures. Height $\frac{11}{16}$in. (bracelet clasps), $\frac{15}{16}$in. (brooch). Photograph by David Bohl, Boston. Courtesy of the Society for the Preservation of New England Antiquities.

more typical choice for ring-set portraits (see Colour Plate 59, right). As early as 1779 an American reference was made to 'a miniature Picture of a Lady in a Ring set in Gold'.[28] A marquise-shaped miniature was painted by Robert Fulton to be set in a ring. The subject was Mrs. David Hayfield Conyngham (Mary West). It is said to have been painted with her own hair ground fine.[29]

When George Washington died on 14 December 1799, several jewelers offered rings set with miniature portrait heads of the first President (Plate 55, top). Engravings by Charles B.J. Févret de Saint-Memin, reduced from the crayon drawing he had made of Washington the year before, were sometimes coloured to look like painted miniatures and set in gold rings.[30] Simon Chaudron, a Philadelphia jeweler, offered rings with an elegant portrait of Washington as early as 4 January 1800.[31] Another Philadelphia jeweler, John B. Dumoutet, advertised on 27 January 1800, in the *Federal Gazette* that he had 'a quantity of those Rings so much in demand, with striking likenesses of the late General Washington, in uniform dress'. On 18 February Dumoutet was calling attention to the fact that rings had come on the market bearing false likenesses of Washington, but that he was 'the only person in Philadelphia that is in possession of the [engraved] plate with a true likeness of General Washington in uniform dress'. John Cook & Company in

28. *Royal Gaz.*, 18 Aug. 1779. A three-guinea reward was offered for the return of this lost ring.
29. Wharton, pp. xvi, 141, illus. opp. 140.
30. The original copperplate for these prints is at the National Portrait Gallery, Washington, D.C.
31. *Federal Gaz.*, 4 January 1800.

Colour Plate 42. Group of Charleston memorial and miniature pendants, obverse and reverse. Left to right: James Robertson, 1803; Dorothy Vanderhorst, 1786; miniature portrait of John Maynard Davis (c.1756-1827) painted by Jean François de Vallée (w. Charleston 1803-1806), in gold case with printed label inside of John Cook & Co., 133 William Street, New York, 1796-1801. Length 2$^{11}/_{16}$in. (pendant on right). Photograph by Leland Cook by courtesy of The Magazine Antiques. *The Charleston Museum, Charleston, South Carolina.*

New York also claimed that they had 'an approved Miniature Profile of the late General' in lockets as well as rings.[32] The ring shown here (Plate 55, top) has an oval bezel with a striking enamelled dentate border in black and white.

The ring bearing Lafayette's portrait on ivory, in its original shagreen case, has been exhibited in America at special celebrations honouring the French who served the Revolutionary cause. His watercolour portrait was set in a rectangular bezel with canted corners. As George F. Kunz pointed out in his history of rings, portrait rings were especially in vogue at the time of the French Revolution. Robespierre, as well as Washington, were popular as a subject, but those bearing the phiz of Franklin found special favour in France.[33] Portrait rings set with miniature heads of John Quincy Adams

32. The *N-Y Gaz. and Gen. Advtr.*, 22 Jan. 1800. Davida T.Deutsch, 'Washington memorial prints', *Antiques CXI* (1977) 331. Six 'Washington likenesses in rings' were stolen from William Elvins' jewelry shop in Baltimore on 6 March 1800. *Am. and Daily Advtr.*, 7 March 1800.
33. *Antiques,* August 1957, p. 109; Kunz, *Rings* , pp. 76-77.

Plate 55. Group of gold portrait rings and mourning rings. Centre top: George Washington (1732-1799), set with engraving by Charles Févret de Saint-Memin, Philadelphia, 1799. Upper right: Martin Van Buren (1782-1862). Upper left: John Quincy Adams (1767-1848). Lower left: memorial featuring the figure of Hope. Lower right: set with a locket to contain hair. Diameter ¾in. The Metropolitan Museum of Art.

Plate 56. Silhouette portrait of Governor James Bowdoin (1726-1790) painted by John Miers (1757-1821) of London, c.1805, set in gold ring. Believed to have been made for the Governor's widow when his son James was in England, possibly after a miniature painted by John Singleton Copley. A larger silhouette of the Governor was also painted by Miers on plaster. Miers was highly regarded by well-to-do Bostonians and he made silhouettes of a number of that city's notables. Length about 1⅞in. (bezel). Photograph by David Bohl, Boston. Gift of Clara Bowdoin Winthrop. Massachusetts Historical Society.

in an oval bezel and Martin Van Buren in a canted rectangle are also known (Plate 55).

The same machines used to make profile portraits enabled silhouettes to be mechanically drawn with greater accuracy. Shades, as these silhouettes were called, became a fad and were done in all sizes and degrees of complexity. A painted silhouette mounted in a gold ring was signed by John Miers (1757-1821), an English artist of the turn of the century (Plate 56). According to family tradition, the profile of Governor James Bowdoin was made for Mrs. Bowdoin after the Governor's death in 1790. Miers most likely painted the profile when their son James Bowdoin III was in London for a few months in 1805. The Governor's profile was unmistakable and Miers may have used a miniature brought by Bowdoin to serve as a guide.[34]

'The celebrated Miers of London' was extolled in a Boston advertisement of 1811. Silhouettist William M.S. Dole knew Miers' work and painted large profiles on chalk or composition in the style of the London artist.[35] Occasionally silhouettes were placed in pendants and worn as pins or suspended from chains (Plate 57). Pendant silhouettes of Eunice and David Crittenden were cut about 1825 by Ezra Wood (1798-1841), a profile cutter in Buckland, Massachusetts.[36]

As the Federal period progressed, miniatures set with diamonds appeared more frequently in America. In 1804 John Lovett & Son, jewelers in New York, called special attention to an elegant diamond miniature setting they had.[37] In 1795 Philip Parisen described a gold bracelet 'with a ladies miniature set round with diamonds'.[38]

The miniature given to General Henry Dearborn of Maine in 1822 by Don Juan VI was encircled with twenty-four sizable diamonds. (Colour Plate 45). The pendant loop was embellished with four more brilliant diamonds. The King of Portugal chose this method of thanking the first American ambassador to his country for saving his life during an uprising. General Dearborn must have cut quite a swath when he appeared in full-dress uniform wearing the King's miniature as well as his own Cincinnati Eagle decoration.

By 1825, miniatures were growing both larger and rounder, more closely

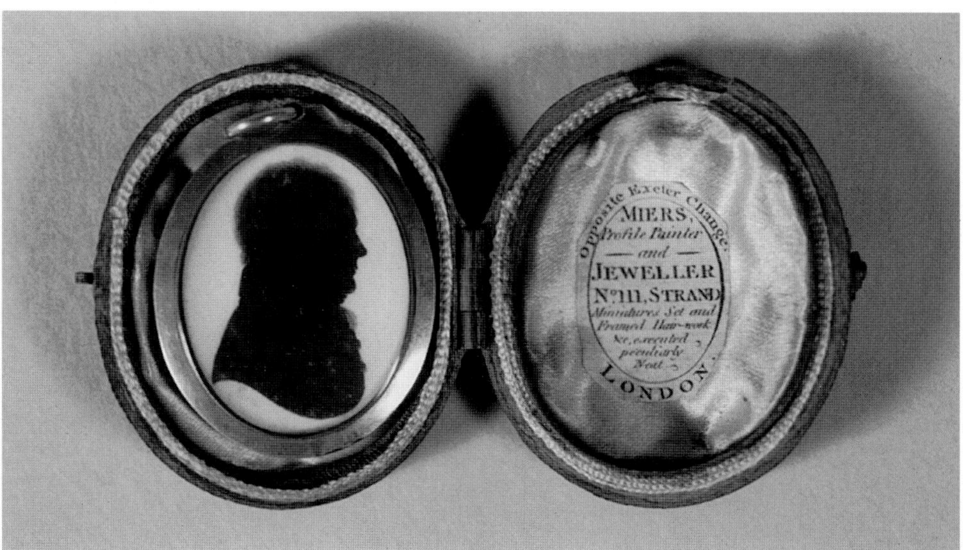

Plate 57. Silhouette of Mr. Day of Hartford, Connecticut, painted by John Miers of London, c.1800, and set in a gold pendant. The original box bears the printed label of Miers, profile painter and jeweler at No. 111, Strand, London. Length 1⁵⁄₁₆in. The Stowe-Day Foundation, Hartford.

Plate 58. While miniature frames of the late 18th century tended to be plain gold or classical in detail, in the 19th century they became more elaborate, often with heavily worked rococo revival designs and made of gilt metal, as can be seen in this portrait of Royal Ralph Hinman, painted by Anson Dickinson (1779-1852), in Litchfield, Connecticut in 1807. Length 2¹⁵⁄₁₆in. The Connecticut Historical Society, Hartford.

resembling watch cases of the same period (see Colour Plate 69). Engraved and enamelled ovoid cases were replaced by circular cases that had chiselled borders and milled bezels. While the earlier cases were usually made of gold, many of the later examples were made of gilded copper. Tapering pendant loops were replaced by wider, straight-sided loops or by rings attached to knobs, in the same manner that rings were attached to the stems of contemporary watches.

The transition in cases can be seen in the miniature of Royal Ralph Hinman of Litchfield, Connecticut, which is dated 1807 (Plate 58). The case had rounded ends but the miniature still maintained an oval format in its painting. The frame was chiselled by hammers and punches into an overall pattern of roses and leaves. The pendant loop still tapered, but it too had chiselled decoration. The miniature of Mrs. Rawlins Lowndes of New York, attributed to Henry Inman, in the mid-1820s,

34. The MHS also owns a large silhouette of the Governor painted on plaster and signed by John Miers. Miers' trade label boasted that he 'Takes the most perfect likenesses either to hang in frames, or upon ivory, for rings, pins, lockets, bracelets, etc.' Charlotte Gere, et al., *Rings Through the Ages*, p. 119. Shirley Bury, *Jewellery Gallery* , pp. 107, 216. A ring and a pair of gold brooches enclosing silhouettes by Miers are in the V & A Museum. One of the brooches is fitted on the back with a locket containing hair.

35. Alice van Leer Carrick, *Shades of Our Ancestors*, pp. 16, 34.

36. *Antiques*, Aug. 1942, p. 70.

37. *N-Y Evening Post*, 7 March 1804.

38. *Charleston City Gaz.*, 21 Oct. 1795. Philip Parisen was the son of colonial New York jeweler Otto de Parisien who, William Dunlap said, 'made monstrous miniature pictures'. Dunlap thought the son did better. Philip Parisen asserted that he used an entirely new method to take the most correct likeness in miniature which could be 'reduced upon whitened Ivory to set in rings, lockets, etc.' He offered gold bracelets and lockets for miniatures on the lowest terms. Dunlap, *History I*, 160; *The N-Y Daily Advtr.*, 15 June 1791.

Colour Plate 45. A handsome gold frame set with diamonds surrounds the miniature portrait of Don Juan VI of Portugal, who gave the brooch to General Henry Dearborn (1751-1829) for saving his life during an uprising there in 1822. Diameter 3in. Maine Historical Society.

showed the increasing integration of the new florid style of heavily encrusted cases.[39] The decoration was more dense and the pendant loop was of uniform width.

Previously, miniatures painted on ivory were limited in size to the shape of the animal's tusk or else had to be pieced together. In the nineteenth century, a method was found to cut the tusk on the bias, giving it a wider shape. A different solution was found by Archibald Robertson, a Scottish artist who had come to New York in 1791. He discovered a method of painting with watercolours on a particular kind of hard and well-polished marble, which could take any size or shape desired. In 1804 he obtained a patent from the newly established United States Patent Office to secure his discovery.[40]

The developments that allowed miniatures to become larger and larger led to their demise as pieces of jewelry. As they were turned into cabinet pictures, they were often set into larger rectangular frames made of lacquered wood, with an inner border of gilt and stamped metal. A suspension ring with an ornament was placed at the top of the frame so that it could be hung on the wall if desired. Others were set in folding cases to keep the paint colours from fading. With the increase in size and style of framing, the miniature became less suitable for jewelry. The fashion ebbed only to be revived periodically whenever there was a special commemorative occasion such as the Centennial celebration (see pages 302-306). Then these much treasured family pieces were brought out of hiding, sometimes reset in more fashionable styles or with hair bracelets, and worn as proudly as if they were multicarat diamonds.

Colour Plate 43. Brooch with miniature painting of a young woman watching as her loved one sails away and on the reverse side an oculus holds a plait of hair with Souvenir *and the initials* SM *cut out of flat gold and laid on top. Owned in Savannah, Georgia, c.1800. Telfair Academy of Arts and Sciences, Inc.*

39. Martha R. Severens, *The Miniature Portrait Collection of the Carolina Art Association,* Gibbs Art Gallery (Charleston, 1984, p. 145.

40. Archibald Robertson (1765-1835) had studied with Sir Joshua Reynolds. With his brother Alexander (1772-1841), he established the Columbia Academy of Painting in New York. Archibald was a director of the American Academy and wrote a treatise on the graphic arts published in New York in 1803. A third brother Andrew acquired fame as a miniaturist in London. Gottesman, *1800-1804,* pp. 9-15; *1777-99,* pp. 16-17; George C. Groce and David H. Wallace, *The New-York Historical Society's Dictionary of Artists in America 1564-1860,* p. 540. J.J. Foster, *Miniature Painters, I,* 85-86.

Colour Plate 44. This portrait of Mrs. John Sherman and child indicates that pendants and lockets with miniature paintings were often worn on long narrow ribbons, instead of chains, and were tied with tiny bows at the neck. Portrait painted by Abraham Delanoy, New Haven, Connecticut, 1786. Height 41in., width 33½in. Courtesy of Marguerite Riordan.

Plate 59. Samuel Folwell (1764-1813) was employed as a hair worker by jeweler Joseph Cooke in Philadelphia about 1787, but soon opened his own shop. This gold locket contains one of Folwell's trade labels. The memorial scene was dedicated to Walter Brook who died in 1798. Daughters of the American Revolution Museum, Washington, D.C.

HAIRWORK

Along with the alliance of the jeweler and the miniaturist, there developed a third related specialist, the hairworker. By the last half of the eighteenth century, the hair of a loved one was being neatly plaited and woven, or was worked into pretty designs, and placed in the back of framed miniatures under an oculus. The backing for these hair designs was usually a thin sheet of ivory or glass.[1] Gradually hairwork became an art of its own and moved from the back of pieces of jewelry to the front where it was set like a jewel in lockets, brooches, bracelets and other kinds of jewelry.

Lugubrious as it might sound today, hair was cherished because it was the one attractive part of the human body that did not decompose after death. It provided a tangible remembrance of a loved one. The hair was sometimes chopped up and mashed into the paint used to decorate the ivory plaques of miniatures. 'Hairwork for Lockets, Rings and Bracelets, in natural or dissolved hair', was offered along with miniature paintings by Francis Rabineau in 1796 in Newark, New Jersey.[2] Artist Thomas Sully mixed chopped hair with watercolour paint to make the memorial pendant brooch honouring his mother (see Plate 52). Its design bore the figure of a grieving woman leaning upon a funeral urn, a motif that had become traditional for both miniatures and hairwork pieces.

Charles Oliver Bruff, in 1763, had been one of the first jewelers to employ in his shop a hair-worker from London who could plait hair into true-lovers' knots to be put in plain or enamelled buttons, rings and lockets. Other New York jewelers soon offered this work. John Dawson, not only plaited hair to any size or shape, but he also formed it 'after the new taste' to look like mocha (Colour Plate 46). 'Hair work'd in landskips' and set in rings was the speciality of Bennett and Dixon. George Smithson not only did landscapes with hair, but also formed flowers, all kinds of figures, mottos, posies and emblematic devices, 'without assistance [of] Coulers'. Miniaturist John Ramage found that the devices he very carefully worked in hair were so admired that he provided his customers with 'every article that its wore in' from rings, lockets, and pins for handkerchiefs and shirts, to bracelets, shirt buckles, and 'Buffonts'.[3]

While ready-made hair jewelry was imported or kept on hand by American jewelers, many customers preferred to supply the hair of treasured heads themselves. If they were not purchasing their memorials locally, they simply sent the locks of hair to

1. William Dawson advertised 'devises, done in hair on ivory or on Venetian glass'. *Pa. Packet,* 26 April 1793, Alfred Coxe Prime, *The Arts & Crafts in Philadelphia, Maryland and South Carolina,* II, 111.
2. *Wood's Newark Gaz. and N-J Advtr.,* 6 Apr. 1796, Prime II, 32. See also Ruel P. Tolman, 'A Document on Hair Painting', *Antiques,* March 1930, p. 231, and 'Human Hair as a Pigment', *Antiques,* December 1925, p. 353.
3. *The N-Y Mercury,* 3 Jan. 1763; 4 May 1767; *The N-Y Journal or Gen. Advtr.,* 6 Aug. 1772; *The SC Gaz.,* 3 Apr. 1775; *Independent Journal: or the Gen. Advtr.,* 24 Jan. 1784.

the maker, whether in America or abroad.[4] In 1796, Joseph Barrell ordered mourning jewelry from Stephen Twycross of London. Hetty Webb, his wife's sister who had lived with them off and on taking care of young Charles, had died. Barrell wanted two gold brooches made in her memory, one slightly smaller and suitable for Charles. Barrell sent the hair to be enclosed in the brooches and requested that Twycross take particular care in following his detailed directions so that the two brooches would 'form a counterpart to the family peice, which you executed some years since'.[5]

When the new jewelry arrived a year later, Barrell gave the small miniature (Colour Plate 47) to Charles and explained to him the significance the remembrance should have for him. 'The Broach I now present you is a memento of the Loss of your excellent Aunt Hetty, who is represented in it as takeing her last leave of you. I trust your feeling mind will never forget the many obligations you are under to her for her extreme care and kindness; she has left this World, and returned you to a Father who dearly loves you'.[6]

Occasionally there were complaints among the hairworkers that some in their trade did not bother to use the specially supplied hair in the designated jewelry. James Askew therefore felt called upon to point out that the memorial jewelry he made was 'worked with the real hair given' when he advertised his 'much improved art of railed Hair work'.[7] By the end of the Federal period, jewelers openly advertised that they would pay cash for human hair twenty to thirty inches in length and that dark brown and black hair was preferred.[8]

John and Hamilton Stevenson of South Carolina advertised hair designs executed in a manner that they claimed had never been attempted before, combining hair and colours. They also sewed hair on to silk to make bracelets, 'a method which preserves the Hair and Work to the latest ages'.[9] Even more remarkable were William Donovan's skills, whereby he took the combination of miniature and hairwork to its ultimate conclusion by offering to make likenesses wrought in hair.[10]

The process by which the standard motifs of hairwork were created was clearly explained in a little book published in 1871 when this art was revived.[11] First the hair had to be thoroughly cleaned. Curls were made with a curling iron that had been heated over the flame of a chamberstick candle. After cooling, the curl was glued to a palette and set under a weight. A little trimming and the curls were ready for decorating with a bit of filigree work and pearls. Twisted cording was made of gold thread coiled around a needle and then flattened. Directions were given for making feather designs, plaits, flowers, leaves, tomb and willow, basket of flowers, and wheat sheaves – all popular designs of the Federal period.

Samuel Folwell of Philadelphia was one of the American hairworkers who taught amateurs this art. In 1793 and 1794, he conducted a drawing school for young ladies, providing instruction in the art of working devices in hair, as well as painting and drawing. Folwell's wife Ann Elizabeth taught young pupils the skills of needlework and Samuel assisted them by adding background painting and inscriptions to their needlework pictures. Making occasional forays south, to Baltimore and Charleston, Folwell offered gold rings, lockets, bracelets, and snuffboxes set with hairwork or miniatures for three to four guineas each (Plate 59).[12]

Amateur memorials were also executed by young ladies in New England. Betsy Danielson's documented mourning pieces were painted with macerated hair.[13] In Salem, Massachusetts, a painted ivory memorial in a gold brooch, with hair set in the

4. Tolman, 'A Document', p. 231.
5. Joseph Barrell, Letter Book, p. 292. At the same time Barrell sent back the piece he wanted matched so that it would refresh the jeweler's memory and so that Twycross could repair the 'parts cleaving from the Ivory'.
6. *Correspondence and Journals of Samuel Blatchley Webb*, ed. W.C. Ford, vol. 3, pp. 204-5. Barrell's brother-in-law, Samuel Blatchley Webb, sought Barrell's help when he wanted to purchase rings in memory of his wife Eliza who had died while Webb was serving in the Revolution. Webb was 'confident that no person has a prettier fancy for designs of this kind than yourself', and asked Barrell to make up different designs for each of the five rings and forward them to the English jeweler. Webb also wanted to send some old gold to be used in making the rings since he had some old lockets, necklaces and other things that had been given to his wife that were 'very ancient' and so were no longer of any use. *Ibid*, pp. 25-26.
7. *Charleston Evening Gaz.*, 5 Oct. 1785.
8. Seymour & Williston, Cincinnati, *Western Spy*, 28 June 1816.
9. *SC and Am. Gen. Gaz.*, 18 Nov. 1774.
10. *Pa. Packet*, 15 July 1785.
11. A. Speight, *The Lock of Hair* (London, 1871). American edition Jesse Haney, *Hair Ornaments for Souvenirs and Jewelry* (NY, c.1872).
12. *Md. Journal Advertiser*, 26 Aug. 1788; *Charleston City Gaz. and Advtr.*, 2 Mar. and 17 May 1791; *Antiques*, Sept. 1985, pp. 526-27. Davida T. Deutsch, 'The polite lady…', *Antiques*, March 1989, pp. 742-753; 'Collectors' Notes', p. 616+. Michael Berry, 'Drawn Upon Sattin and Ivory: Mourning Designs of Samuel Folwell 1793-1813', in *Twenty-eighth Annual Washington Antiques Show* (1983), pp. 74-75.
13. Tolman, *Antiques*, Mar. 1930, p. 231.

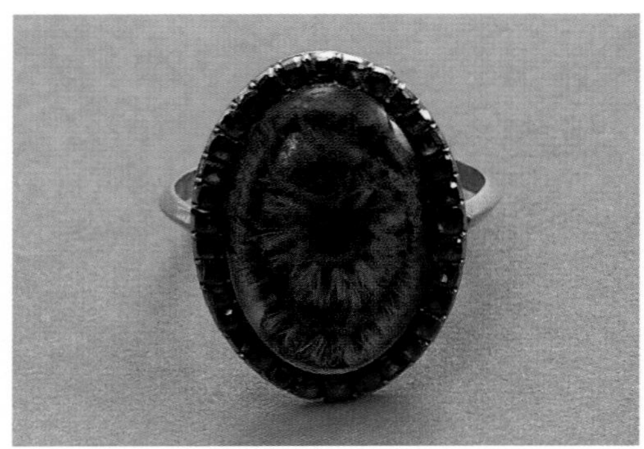

Colour Plate 46. Above. Ruby-bordered ring set with hair clipped and configured to look like mocha (agate), English, c.1765. Owned by the Lowell family of North Bucksport, Maine. Hinged locket on back of bezel. Length ¾in. (bezel). Photograph by Peter J. Theriault. Private Collection.

Colour Plate 47. Right. Brooch ordered from Stephen Twycross of London on 27 August 1796 by Joseph Barrell of Boston, in memory of his sister-in-law Hetty Webb who had cared for his son Charles. Barrell sent instructions as to the design for the painted miniature scene and enclosed a lock of hair, and presented it to his son who was then twelve years old. Length 1⅛in. Photograph by Paul Rocheleau by courtesy of The Magazine Antiques *and the Webb-Dean-Stephens Museum. Private Collection.*

Plate 60. (Above.) The bands of these bracelets made in Boston, c.1787, are formed by thin circles of tightly plaited hair joined together with hollow gold beads. The clasps are set with flat, cut-out initials placed on plaits of hair and covered with oval crystals. The script initials LH and IH memorialize the deaths of Lydia and John, the children of John and Dorothy Hancock of Boston. Lydia died in 1777 and John George Washington Hancock died in 1787. (Below.) Hair bracelet, c.1820, with gold fasteners and a gold locket over the clasp containing a plait of hair, engraved on the back A.E. / E.D.S. / L.C.E. Owned by a member of the Sedgwick family. The snap of the clasp is stamped F&G in a rectangle and an eagle, the mark of Fletcher & Gardiner who were working together in Philadelphia, c.1811-1827. Photograph by David Bohl, Boston. Massachusetts Historical Society.

back, is believed to have been worked by Dorcas Hiller in memory of young Sally Saunders who died in 1795 at the age of sixteen (see Colour Plate 61). A pair of bracelets with gold fasteners, holding two delicate braids of hair in such a way that they formed fat oval links, was made about 1787 in Boston (Plate 60, above). The clasps had oval settings containing flat gold script letters under their glazed clasps. On

Colour Plate 49. Memorial ring with enamelled border with the name of Noble Wimberly Jones and engraved Obt. 9 June / 1805 / Aet. 73 Ys. At the age of nine months, Jones came with his family from England to Georgia with James Edward Oglethorpe in 1733. The ring may have been made by Michael Germain, silversmith of Savannah c.1783-1806, who advertised hair work. Private Collection.

Colour Plate 48. Group of mourning rings made for funerals in Salem, Massachusetts. The ring (upper left) made in memory of four year old Eliza Gray in 1791 contained a plait of hair in an enamelled border with closely set garnets in an oval bezel. John Fisk's memorial ring, 1797 (upper right), is circular in shape and has a border of half pearls surrounding a plait of hair. Two kinds of rings were made for Priscilla Ropes' funeral in 1808 (centre row). Both have rectangular bezels with clipped corners. One has a thin flat tapering shank and the other has twisted wire shanks which would have been worth less than the solid gold shank. The solid band is engraved with another memorial and was reused in 1844. Jonathan Mason's ring (lower left) has a band of plaited hair set into a band of gold with a flat medallion in the centre engraved with his initials. The rococo revival ring (lower right) is set with faceted jet and, in the centre a small plait of hair is set in a heavily chased floral border. It was made in 1833 for the unidentified 'M.J.' Length $\frac{11}{16}$in., width $\frac{13}{16}$in. (Eliza Gray bezel). Photograph by Mark Sexton. Peabody Essex Museum.

the back of each was an inscription, one for each child of John and Dorothy Hancock. Baby Lydia died in 1777 and nine-year-old John George Washington Hancock died in 1787.[14]

Hair jewelry was given as a token of love as well as for mourning. In 1802, Eliza Southgate Bowne's friend Martha Coffin Derby of Salem, Massachusetts gave her 'a beautiful bracelet for the arm made of her hair; she is too good – to love me as she says, more than ever'.[15]

The earliest hair bracelet bearing the mark of an American maker that has come to light so far was stamped by the firm of Fletcher and Gardiner who were working in Boston from 1808 to 1811 (Plate 60, below). It had a narrow braided hairband and a circular centrepiece with gold fasteners engraved on the back with three sets of initials.

Of all the hairwork made in America, the most famous is that incorporating a lock from the head of George Washington. Long before he died, his hair was being harvested,

14. MHS #131. The bracelets were inherited by Mrs. Kingsmill Marr from a great uncle who bought them at one of the several sales of Hancock family effects.
15. *A Girl's Life Eighty Years Ago,* Clarence Cook, ed., p. 143.

Plate 61. Small brooch (left) with flat gold script initials IRT. Engraved on back in later script G.A. Thatcher / Bangor [Maine]. Length ⅞in. Rope bordered brooch, EMIP in flat gold script initials, in the style of the Merrimack Valley. Photograph by Peter. J. Theriault. Private Collection.

first for his wife and family, later for close friends and associates. Hair of every possible shade has been ascribed to his pate, more than ever grew there, in order to enhance the value of a piece of hair jewelry. It is useful to know that Washington had reddish brown hair. As he grew older and greyer, his hair appeared to be rusty grey.[16]

A locket added to the back of the setting of Martha Washington's diamond wedding ring (see Colour Plate 11) holds a swatch of her husband's mid-life hair. A large miniature pendant of George Washington, now at Mount Vernon, has a generous plait of reddish brown hair crossed with white hair in a simple gold frame. Another gold pendant brooch containing a loop of reddish brown and white hair is engraved on the back, 'Hair of George Washington cut by Martha Washington 1797 for Mrs. Oliver Wolcott great-grandmother of George Gibbs V'.[17]

When Washington died in 1799, he bequeathed three mourning rings, a hundred dollars each in value, to his friends Eleanor Stuart, Hannah Washington of Fairfield, and Elizabeth Washington of Hayfield. 'These bequests' were, he said, 'not made for the intrinsic value of them, but as mementoes of my esteem and regard'.[18] Requests for hair were made to Mrs. Washington after her husband's death and she obliged those she could. Among the successful supplicants was the Grand Lodge of Massachusetts. The Free Masons had written to her as soon as they had heard the news of his demise. The coveted lock was placed in a small gold urn made by Paul Revere that has been carried in the processions of installation ever since.[19]

Historian and gemmologist, George F. Kunz, in his book *Rings for the Finger,* tells of a gold ring made during George Washington's lifetime that contained a lock of his hair under a conical glass. Kunz described it as having a setting encircled with blue and white enamel with a square of red at each corner, around which was a border of thirteen pearls representing the number of original states of the Union. The ring was given by Washington to Lieutenant Robert Somers who later distinguished himself at Tripoli.[20]

Washington's death, like the Revolutionary War, contributed considerably to the increased demand for mourning jewelry, especially that embellished with hairwork. Mourning rings developed from simple gold bands embossed with symbols of death in the colonial period, into prettier, less morbid designs of infinite variety in the federal period (Colour Plate 48). The hair was usually plaited and set under a crystal or glass just as a gem would be. The shanks were flattened and widened as the eighteenth century drew to a close, the shoulders tapering to suit the diameter or shape of the bezel. Oval and shuttle-shaped bezels were fashionable as were rectangular bezels with canted corners. Pearls often encircled the hair and represented the tears of the bereaved. In some cases, an inner border was enamelled in black or white with the memorial inscription (Colour Plate 49). In other rings, tightly woven bands of hair were set in the outside of the shank.

At the end of the eighteenth century, the fashion for setting flattened-gold, script

16. A description of Washington's physical appearance given by a man who had seen him over the years noted that in the prime of life his hair was chestnut brown. The year before he died his hair was very grey. Daniel Ackerson's 1811 recollection published in *The Sun*, NY, 20 April 1889.
17. These pendants and the wedding ring are now at Mount Vernon.
18. *Antiques* May 1971, p.692.
19. Fales, 'An American Golden Urn', *Antiques,* May 1961, pp. 466-69.
20. Kunz, *Rings*, pp. 191-2. Kunz stated in 1917, 'Only two other rings containing Washington's hair are known of, one in Washington's Headquarters at Newburgh on the Hudson, the other in the Boston Museum.' A ring of this description without red enamel is at the Historical Society of Pennsylvania in Philadelphia.

Plate 62. The portrait of Mrs. Mary LeNord Plummer Smith of Newburyport, Massachusetts, includes her gold lace pin with gold script initials laid on a small plait of hair, characteristic of mourning pieces in the Merrimack Valley. In addition she wears large hoop earrings and a ring on the fore finger of her right hand. Portrait painted by William Jennys (w. 1793-1807), c.1805. Length 29in., width 24in. ©1985 Sotheby's Inc.

initials on top of the plaits of hair became prevalent both in America and elsewhere. In the Merrimack Valley area of Massachusetts, there appears to have been a jeweler who did a particularly strong business in this type of mourning jewelry, selling brooches and rings (Plate 61). They were distinguished by the lightly chased work on the cut-out letters, the fineness of the beading around the bezels, and the fatness of their oval shapes.[21] It is interesting to see that this specific type of mourning jewelry was minutely delineated in some of the portraits painted by William Jennys when he was working in the vicinity of Newbury (Plate 62).

Sentimental and fancy pieces of jewelry were also made to honour the living instead of the dead. These contained hair designs, but lacked obituary inscriptions. Samuel Brook, a Philadelphia jeweler, made the distinction when he advertised in 1793: 'Bracelets, Lockets, Rings, &c. &c. made in the newest fashions and hair laid in love,

21. A small clutch of these pieces is in the collections of the Historical Society of Old Newbury and the people in whose memory the jewelry was made have been identified as residents of the Haverhill-Newbury area.

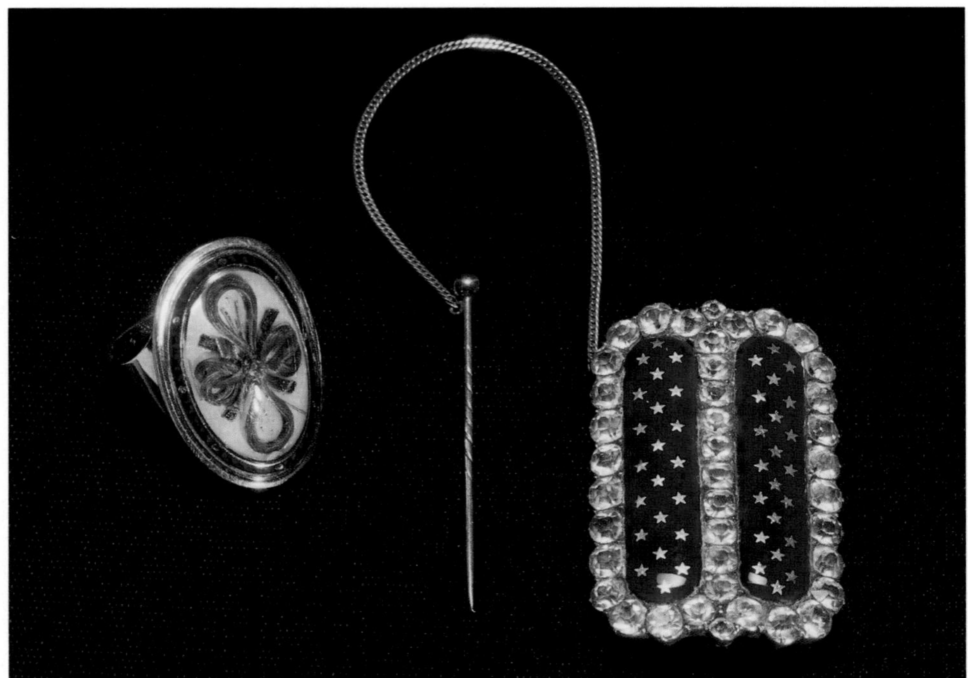

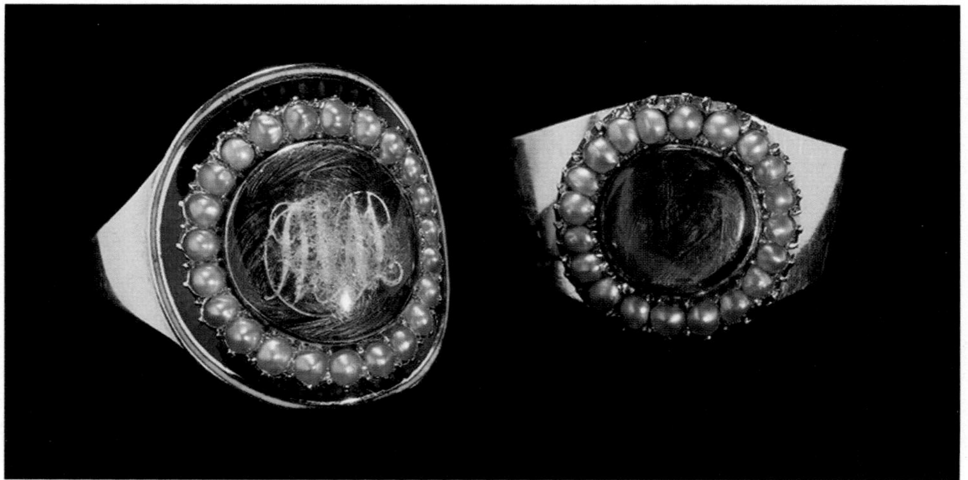

Colour Plate 50. Three hair-set gold rings and an enamelled turban brooch, attributed to the shop of Stephen Twycross of London, c.1800, and owned by New Englanders. (Upper left) Oval bezel with blue border and bowknot made of hair laid on an opalized ground, owned by Hannah Dawes Goldthwaite Newcombe (1769-1851). Original box labelled by Twycross. Length 1¼in. (bezel). (Upper right) Brooch with gold stars on a bright blue field surrounded by pastes, owned by Hannah Dawes Lucus (1743-1803). Length 1¼in. (Lower left and right) Two rings made in memory of 'William Dawes / ob. Feb. 25, 1799'. One with hair and pearls, the other with additional gold script initials WAD (probably for Dawes' son William M. Dawes and his wife Abby) and blue border. Length 13/16in. (bezels). Photographs by Paul Rocheleau by courtesy of The Magazine Antiques. *Massachusetts Historical Society.*

mourning, and fancy pieces'.[22] A ring that could be described as a love piece was presented to Hannah Dawes Goldthwaite by her uncle when she was married in 1800 (Colour Plate 50). The large oval bezel contains a very stylish true-lovers' knot, garnished with a little ruffle of gold, and laid on an opaline background. The border is enamelled in rich blue and studded with gold. The ring is still housed in its original

22. *Federal Gazette*, Phila., June 10, 1793.

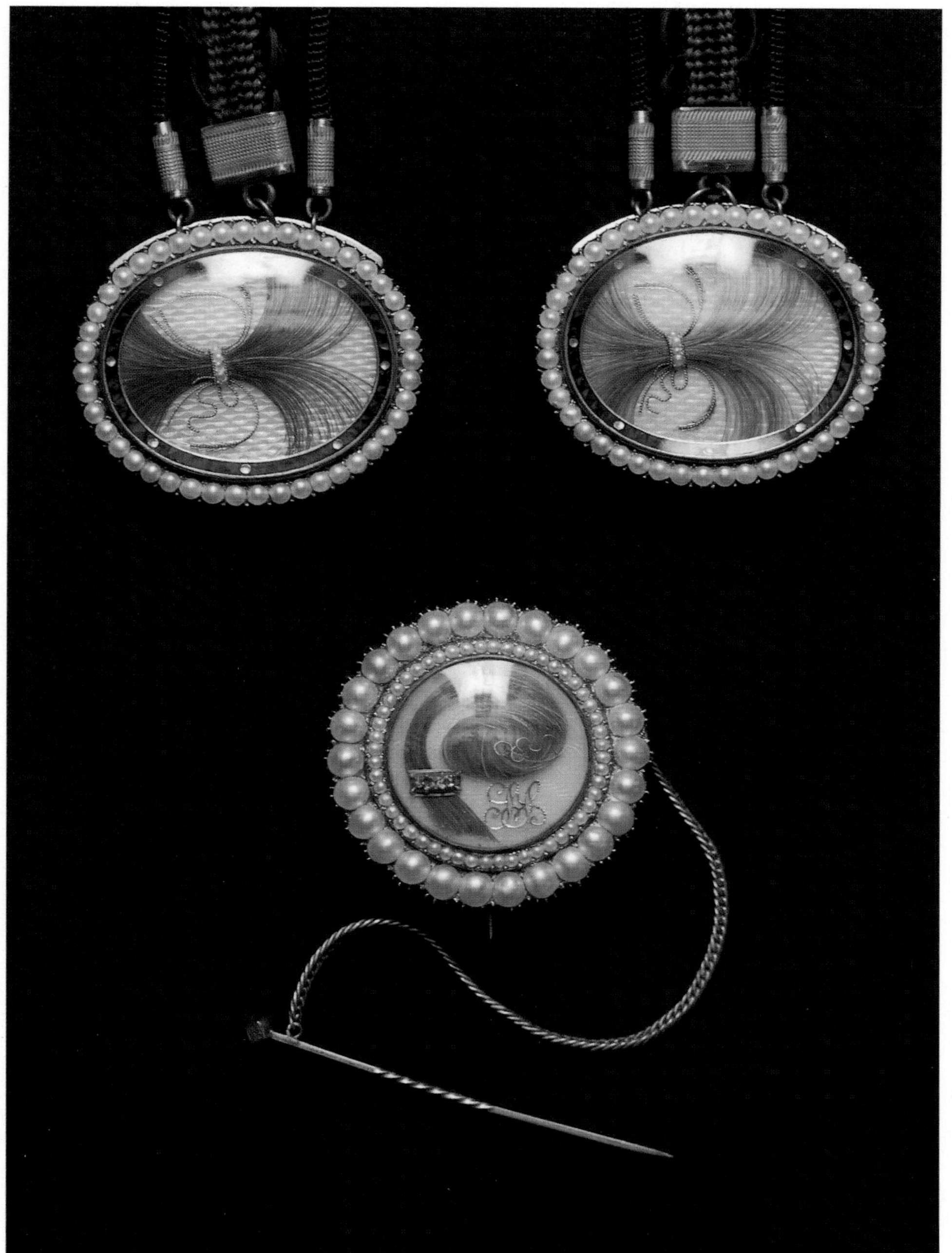

Colour Plate 51. Pair of clasps and brooch owned by Elizabeth Tuckerman Salisbury (1768-1851), Worcester, Massachusetts, made by Stephen Twycross, London, c.1800-1802. Set in gold with pearl borders enclosing fancy designs in hair laid on opalescent guilloche background. The clasps have blue borders while the brooch has gold script letters SS for her husband Stephen Salisbury. The bill for the brooch from Twycross dated 5 January 1802 survives, as does the original box for the clasps with the Twycross label. Diameter 1⅗in. (brooch). Bequests of Stephen Salisbury III Estate. Worcester Art Museum, Worcester, Massachusetts.

red leather box labelled by London jeweler Stephen Twycross, purveyor also of Joseph Barrell's miniature jewelry (see Colour Plates 40 and 41).

Stephen Twycross provided the love and fancy pieces owned by Elizabeth Salisbury of Worcester, Massachusetts. In 1802, Mrs. Salisbury purchased a pearl brooch (Colour Plate 51) for £6.10s. that included a sophisticated feathery scroll of hair held

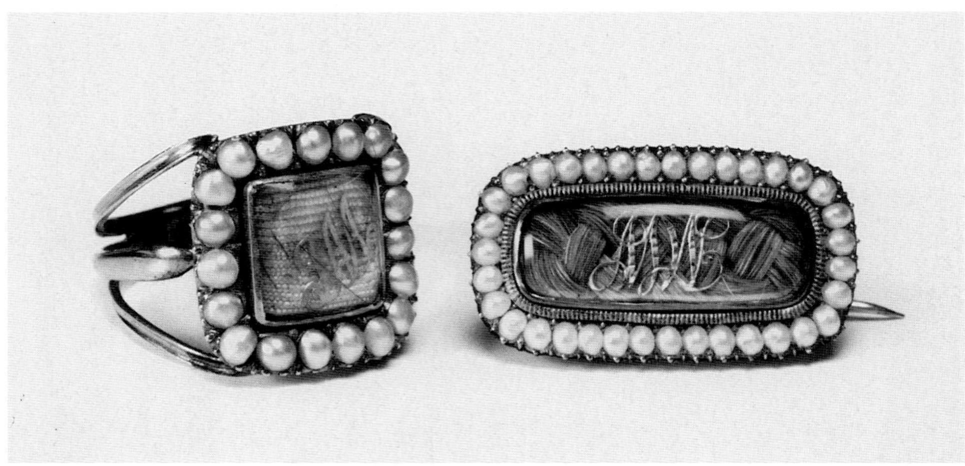

Plate 63. In 1812 Mercy Warren, John and Abigail Adams exchanged locks of hair to restore their long-time friendship which had been disturbed by political differences. Abigail, using gold sent to her by her son, had a ring set with the hair of both Adamses and their initials for Mercy, and a handkerchief pin for herself that had a plait of Mercy's hair and her initials. Photograph by David Bohl, Boston. Massachusetts Historical Society.

by a barrette set with pastes.[23] The initials of her husband Stephen, who was still very much alive, were cut out of flattened gold and placed in the crook of the scrolled hair with a little twist of gold wire laid on top. The composition was set on an elegant diaper-patterned ground that was covered with a layer of opaline glass to give it a rich, jewel-like effect. In England, glassworkers had recently learned the secret of making opaline by carefully cooling the batch of glass to allow tiny particles to separate out, giving it a milky, opalescent effect. It is doubtful that this sort of glass was part of the American jeweler's repertoire at the time. 'Elegant devices of hair on opal' imported from Liverpool were advertised by the jewelry firm of Dyer & Eddy in Boston in 1804.[24]

Mrs. Salisbury also purchased a pair of bracelets with clasps that were related in design to her brooch (Colour Plate 51). The hair was arranged as a wheat sheaf held by a barrette studded with pearls, and laid on translucent opaline over an engine-turned metal plate. Instead of the double ring of pearls on the brooch, the bracelet clasps had an inner border of gold-studded royal-blue enamel. Originally the clasps held eight-strand bracelets, but these were replaced in the mid-nineteenth century with intricate braids of finely woven hair.[25]

Hair for jewelry was exchanged between friends as well as close relatives. John and Abigail Adams and Mercy Warren, widow of James Warren, had been good friends for over forty years. Mrs. Warren had championed the patriots' cause during the Revolution by writing plays. In later years she and the Adamses had a difference of opinion over political matters which they patched up by exchanging locks of hair. Mercy Warren sent a lock of hair to the Adamses. Abigail, using gold sent to her by her son, had a handkerchief pin made with Mercy's lock. She also had a ring set with the combined locks of both Adamses (Plate 63). The pieces were embellished with pearls. On 30 December 1812, Abigail sent the ring to Mercy 'as a token of love and friendship'. Mrs. Warren was especially touched that the hair of both John and Abigail was included in her ring which, she said, she would wear with pleasure as a valuable expression of their regard, a daily reminder of 'friends who have been entwined to my heart by years of endearment, which, if in any degree interrupted by incalculable circumstances...we have more to think of than the partial interruption of sublunary friendships'.[26]

Very few eighteenth century examples of hair necklaces have survived due to their fragile design. A necklace made of rectangular links of hair chain with gold fasteners

23. Salisbury Family Papers, American Antiquarian Society, Worcester, Mass.
24. *Columbian Centinel,* Boston, 3 Oct. 1804.
25. Fales, 'Federal Bostonians', pp. 644-649.
26. She was gratified that Abigail would wear her 'faded lock...on her bosom as an eternal mark of her regard, it cannot but be pleasing to a mind who considers true friendship as one of the best cordials of human life'. Mercy Warren to Abigail Adams, 26 Jan. 1813. MHS *Collections* Series 5, IV, 502-03; Proc. 72, 436.

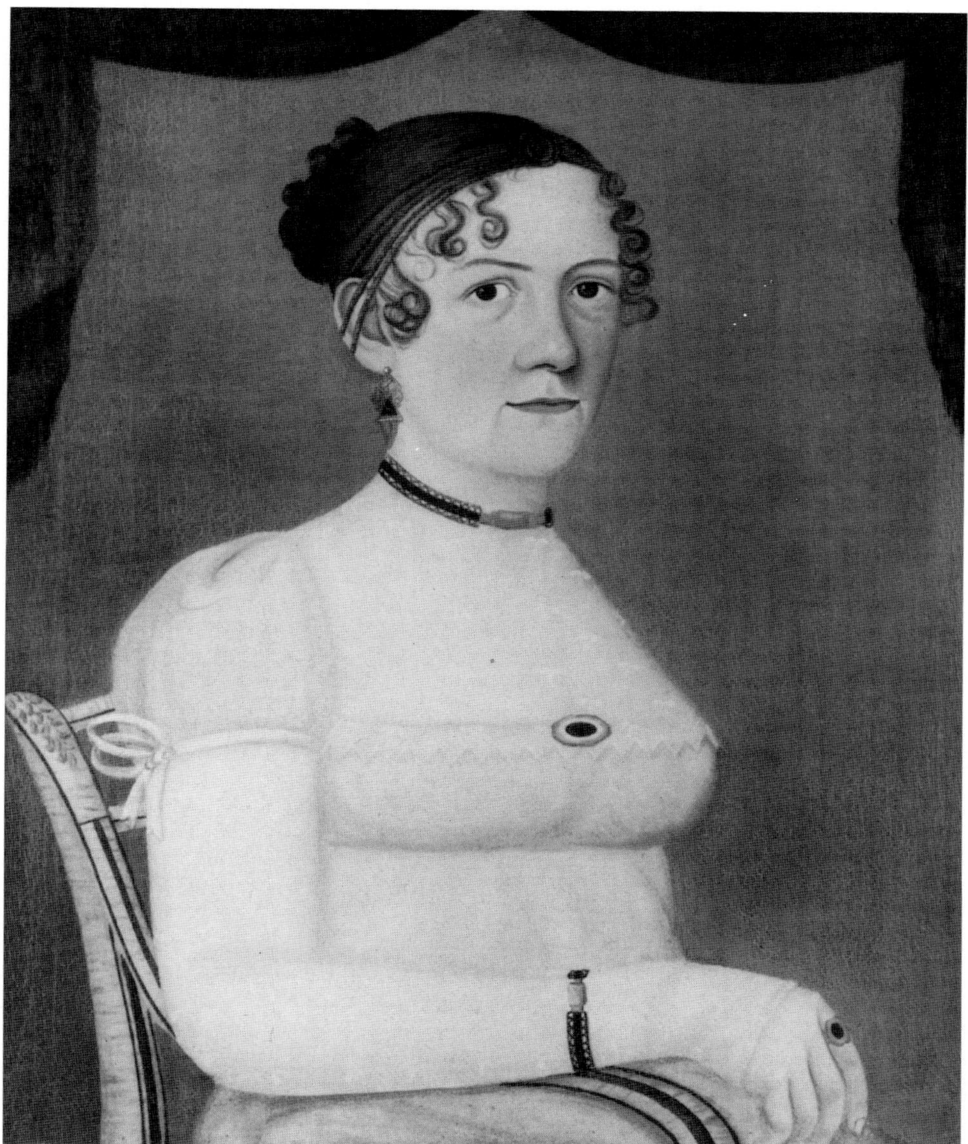

Plate 64. A Massachusetts lady whose portrait was painted about 1815 wore a wide range of hair jewelry, from the finely braided bands worn around her head and fastened in front with a clasp to the looped bands of her necklace and bracelet (also clasped in front) and including a ring on her right fore finger. Her gold drop earrings may also have been set with a triangular plait of hair. Length 24in., width 19⅝in. ©1987 Sotheby's Inc.

between each link can be seen in the portrait of an unknown lady painted by Asa Park of Lexington, Kentucky.[27] This sort of hair jewelry, woven in wide flat plaits, or later in hollow tubes, was called 'elastic' because it was flexible and yet held its form. The term was used in an advertisement in 1808 by Fletcher & Gardiner of Boston. An elastic bracelet with their marks stamped on the clasp was made for the Sedgwick family (Plate 60, below). Fletcher & Gardiner sold elastic ear hoops, watch chains, neck chains, and even festoon necklaces, with fine gold mounts and set with cornelian and pearl centres.[28] These were suggested as New Year's presents, not funeral gifts.

A summary statement of the variety in hair designs available in early nineteenth century American jewelry shops is to be found in a wooden chest (Plate 104) fitted with drawers containing samples of hairwork and mourning miniatures to suit the taste of everyone (Plate 64).

27. Nina Fletcher Little, *Little by Little* (New York, 1984), Fig. 161, p. 125.
28. *Col. Cent.*, 28 Dec. 1808.

Colour Plate 53. Miniature portrait of Mrs. James H. Heyward (1786-1867) of Charleston, South Carolina, painted by Edward Greene Malbone (1777-1807), c.1806. On her head is an aigrette made of seed pearls said to have been sent to her by her godmother in England as a wedding present. Length 3¼in., width 2⅜ in. ©Mr. and Mrs. Donald J. Quinn, Kansas City, Missouri.

Pearls

Colour Plate 52. Seed pearl jewelry owned by Martha Washington. The bird pin may have been purchased in Philadelphia c.1790. Seed pearl crosses and top and drop earrings were very popular at the turn of the 19th century. Length 1¾in. (cross). Mount Vernon Ladies' Association, Mount Vernon, Virginia

Beading, or 'pearling' as it was sometimes called, was an important decorative motif in neo-classical design. It appeared as edgings on everything from architectural details to furniture and silver. We have seen how small pearls were used as strands for bracelets and half-pearls were used as borders on lockets and clasps (see Colour Plate 50). Tiny pearls less than a quarter of a grain in size, exported from India and China, could also be drilled and strung on horsehair. Hair from a living horse, preferably a white one, was used for stringing. These delicate ropes of pearls were then attached in openwork patterns to templates cut out of thin sheets of mother-of-pearl. The designs were primarily of flowers and leaves, fretwork and flourishes. Bracelets, brooches, head ornaments, earrings, and necklaces were made during the Federal period (Colour Plate 52). They could be purchased separately or *en suite.*

One of the first forms of jewelry to be made in this way was the earring. Cluster earrings made of seed pearls had become fashionable by the end of the colonial period.[1] A second rosette, slightly larger, was often suspended from the cluster to create both a top-and-drop earring and more motion. During the nineteenth century, the difference in size of the two rosettes was more pronounced, with the drop becoming noticeably larger. Another popular style of seed-pearl earring in the Federal period was the simple hoop earring made with a single line of pearls. Young Abigail Adams wore such a pair of pearl hoops when she sat to Mather Brown for her portrait in 1785.[2] 'Rich Pearl Set and strung Ear-Hoops' as well as tops and drops were advertised in Boston in 1810.[3]

Pearls traditionally were associated with purity and love. When John Stoughton's daughter Matilda was married in 1794, Gilbert Stuart carefully depicted her wide, festooned necklace, made of seed pearls and red gems, along with the many other jewels she wore for her portrait (see Colour Plate 36). Another bride, Decima Cecilia Shubrick, was married to James H. Heyward in Charleston, South Carolina, in 1806. She wore a seed-pearl tiara sent to her from England by her godmother as a wedding gift.

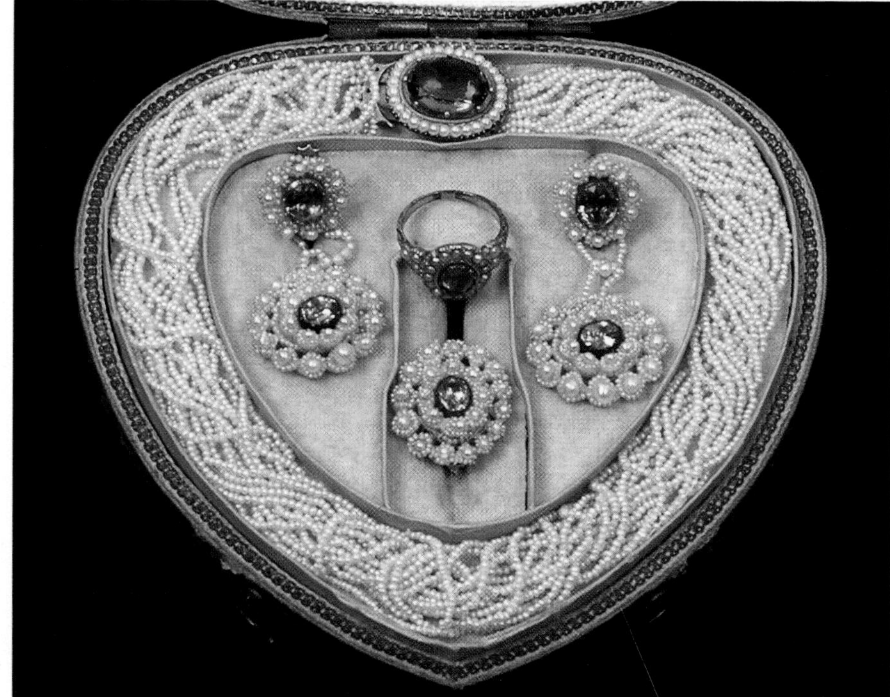

Colour Plate 54. Far left. Seed pearl parure first worn by Eleanor Coffin when she married John Derby, the son of Elias Hasket Derby of Salem, Massachusetts, in 1801, thereby establishing a tradition that Derby brides continued into the 20th century. A tiny bit of hair is set in a locket on the clasp of the bracelet. The flower aigrette is similar to one worn on a bandeau by Mrs. James H. Heyward (Colour Plate 53). Photograph by Mark Sexton. Peabody Essex Museum.

Colour Plate 55. Above right. Necklace and earrings set with seed pearls and garnets. English, c.1775, worn by Elizabeth Pelham at a ball in Newport, Rhode Island, in 1775 in honour of Lord Percy, the representative of the Prince of Wales. Miss Pelham was chosen to open the ball with Lord Percy. Later in the 19th century the fragile earrings and pendent cross were reinforced with decorative gold work to strengthen the set so that it could be worn again. Photograph by Arthur Vitols, The Helga Studio. Gift of Mrs. Theron R. Strong, descendant of Miss Pelham. Museum of the City of New York.

Colour Plate 56. Left. Seed pearl and amethyst earrings and small brooch, American or English, c.1822, to which were added over time an amethyst paste ring and a large amethyst-set clasp, the latter engraved 'Thomas Pearsall to Lavinia Coles, June 17, 1822', to commemorate their wedding. The twisted strands of seed pearls were added with the necklace clasp and the screw back fasteners for the earrings. Belonged to ancestors of the donor. Gift of Mrs. Stanley B. Ineson, 54.404.1 a-e, .2. Photograph by Arthur Vitols, The Helga Studio. Museum of the City of New York.

Edward Greene Malbone, who was in Charleston in 1806, painted an exquisite miniature of the bride with her veil attached to a bandeau decorated with a seed-pearl spray of flowers (Colour Plate 53). The bandeau was outlined with larger pearls. With this headdress, the bride wore pear-shaped pearl earrings.[4] It was reported in 1806 in New York that one bride's pearls had cost fifteen hundred dollars.[5]

Sets of seed-pearl jewelry, imported from England or made in America, became fashionable as wedding gifts to brides. As early as 1795, a set of pearl jewelry was advertised by jeweler James Jacks of Charleston, S.C. Consisting of a pair of earrings, an elegant necklace, and three pins, the set cost thirty guineas.[6] The earliest surviving suite of bridal seed-pearl jewelry with an American history is the parure of Eleanor Coffin who married John Derby of Salem, Massachusetts, in 1801 (Colour Plate 54). The

---

1. Copley portrait, c.1765, Prown #159.
2. Oliver, p.47; owned by George C. Homans.
3. Davis & Brown, *Col. Cent.*, 9 July 1810.
4. Wharton, p. 150. 'Rich Pearl and Gold Bandeaus for the hair' were advertised in New York by John Cook & Co. on 3 Oct. 1800 *(Commercial Advtr.)*.
5. Eliza Southgate Bowne, *A Girl's Life*, p. 215, letter to Octovia Southgate, 8 Nov. 1806.
6. *City Gaz. & Daily Advtr.*, 5 Oct. 1795.

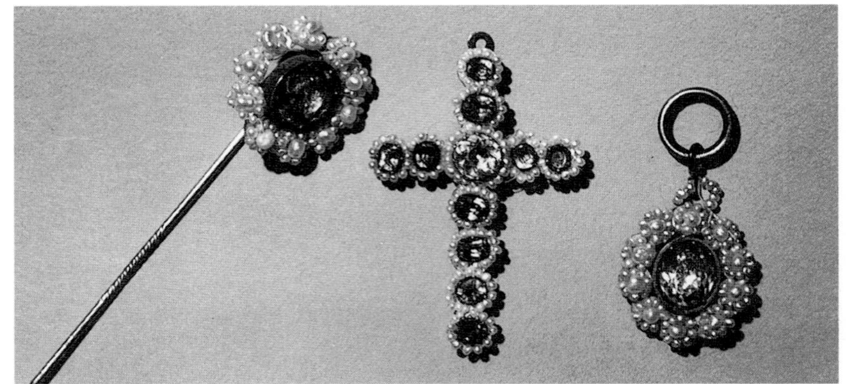

Plate 65. Seed pearl and topaz jewelry owned by the Buchey family and believed to have been made about 1815 by Jean Baptiste Buchey of Philadelphia. The stick pin was probably made from an earring or small pin in the last part of the 19th century. The earring's pendent ring shown here is also a later addition. Photograph courtesy of F.J. Dallett. Heirs of the late L.L. Robinett.

bracelets and necklace were formed of wide delicate, diapered bands of tiny pearls. Rosettes were constructed with pearls of slightly larger sizes to add dimension. The same symmetrical rosettes formed a pair of top and drop earrings, a brooch, and the centrepiece of a large asymmetrical floral spray. To add to the enchantment of the aigrette, the rosette was attached to the spray by means of a trembler to allow it to quiver. The parure was worn by subsequent Derby family brides, one of whom was Elizabeth Parsons Derby. She attached a note to the case of the parure stating that she wore these pearls that had belonged to her husband's mother on the evening of her marriage in 1864. Oddly, this still popular wedding gift was considered by some to be unlucky if worn on the actual wedding day. Empress Eugénie wore pearls at her wedding in spite of the superstition and everyone knew how tragic her life turned out to be.[7]

Although English jewelry historians note that the vogue for seed-pearl jewelry ended early in the Victorian era,[8] the fashion continued in the United States into the Colonial Revival period and the last decade of the nineteenth century. It is still not unusual for an American bride to wear her ancestral seed-pearl set.

By 1810, Fletcher & Gardiner were making their own pearl jewelry in Boston. 'Rich strung pearl Head Ornaments and Earrings; Pearl and Cornelian Neck-Clasps and Bracelets; Pearl set Broaches, Pins, Bracelets and finger Rings' were among their own productions. The firm imported 'a complete assortment of PEARLS of every size...and can now accommodate their customers with pearl work of every description, at prices much lower than English work of the same patterns and quality'.[9] At the same time, Fletcher & Gardiner imported a limited amount of pearl jewelry, in part to serve as patterns for their own manufacture. Included among the imports were finger rings, brooches, lockets, and bracelets richly set with pearls and one 'elegant pearl Sprig and Wreath'. When the firm moved to Philadelphia in 1811, Thomas Fletcher continued to manufacture pearl work and felt that it was one of the few types of jewelry that could be made and sold in America for less than the price of imports.[10]

Jean Baptiste Buchey (1782-1849) specialized in making seed-pearl jewelry. He had come from Paris to New York with his father in 1793. About 1805 he moved to Philadelphia and continued with his specialty until about 1818 (Plate 65). William Frost of Providence, R.I., was another producer of seed-pearl jewelry, advertising about 1810 that his firm of Frost & Mumford manufactured pearl jewelry.[11]

Coloured gems were often added to seed-pearl jewelry. Garnets added drama to the designs. A beautiful necklace and pair of earrings were worn to a ball in Newport, Rhode Island in 1775 by Elizabeth Pelham (Colour Plate 55). Miss Pelham had been chosen to open the ball with Lord Percy, the honoured guest. Beneath the added nineteenth-century incrustation of gold granulation can still be seen the original design of the jewelry. The necklace was made of interlacing serpentine bands set with tiny pearls and garnets, forming narrow ovals laid end to end. A similarly formed pendant cross was attached to the centre of the necklace. The earrings were set with a circle of large garnets surrounded by seed pearls, with graceful pendant drops.

Gradually, as the eighteenth century ended, topazes were used with pearls more often

7. Dirham, Misiorowski, and Thomas, 'Pearl Fashion Through the Ages', *Gems and Gemology*, Vol. 21, No. 2 (Summer 1985), pp. 72-73.
8. Becker, *Antique and 20th C. J.*, p. 72; Charlotte Gere, *Victorian Jewellery Design*, p. 202; Margaret Flower, *Victorian Jewellery*, p. 19.
9. *Col. Cent.*, 3 Jan., 11 Apr. 1810. On 18 Aug. 1810, Fletcher & Gardiner announced that they had 10,000 real pearls on hand 'which they will manufacture into ornaments'. *Col. Cent.*.
10. *Aurora Gen. Advtr.*, 19 Dec. 1811. Deborah Dependahl Waters, 'The Workmanship of an American Artist: Philadelphia's Precious Metals Trades and Craftsmen, 1788-1832', Ph.D., pp. 81-84.
11. Flynt & Fales, p. 222.

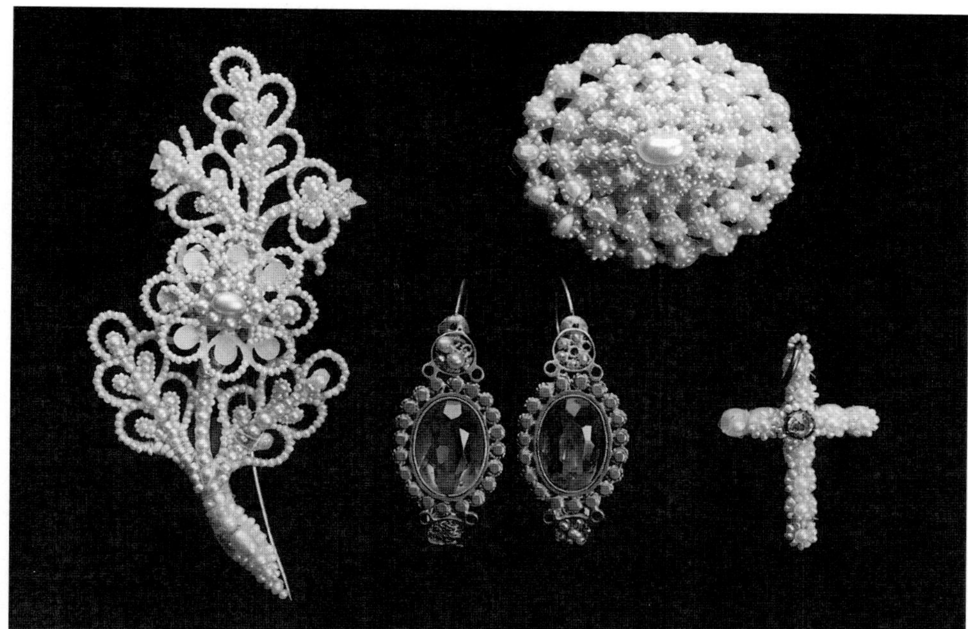

Plate 66. Group of topaz and pearl jewelry, early 19th century, American. (Left) The floral spray has lost some pearls in the central rosette, revealing the mother-of-pearl template to which the strung pearls were sewn. (Right) Cross pendant with central topaz. Length 1¼in. (Centre) Cluster brooch with large central pearl. Photograph by David Bohl, Boston. Society for the Preservation of New England Antiquities.

than garnets (Plate 66). It was a natural combination of colours in an era when gold and white were so frequently juxtaposed in architectural and interior design. Other choices of stones were cornelian or paste. In 1810, Fletcher & Gardiner of Boston had a set of cornelian and pearls – necklace, bracelets, four brooches, tiara, clasps, and three pairs of earrings – that could be worn in three different combinations.[12]

Amethysts also appeared in seed-pearl sets (Colour Plate 56). Thomas Pearsall gave an amethyst and pearl parure to Lavinia Coles on 17 June 1822. Symbolically housed in its original heart-shaped red leather case, the parure included a festoon necklace, a pair of earrings with detachable pendants, and a small brooch. At a later date a better amethyst was added to the necklace clasp and a paste ring was added to the set.

Some jewelers offered mock or imitation pearls instead of real pearls. In 1804 in Boston, combs made of 'Real and imitation of pearl and gilt crescent tops, with antique characters' were offered by Dyer & Eddy. These could be bought singly or in sets and were mounted on combs made of mock or real tortoiseshell, plain shell or horn. R. &. H. Farnam advertised 'mock Pearl and ornamented Combs; Slides and Crescents" on 5 Jan. 1805. A. Dumesnil sold 'English mock pearl beads' as well as common mock pearls.[13] 'Real and fine imitation Pearl, festoon Neck Laces, with Topaz in centre' were offered by Dyer & Eddy in 1805.[14] Davis & Brown suggested pearl jewelry set with cornelians or topaz for New-Year's presents.[15]

Pearl jewelry came in a variety of shapes and sizes. One of the more unusual types of hair ornaments was in the form of an arrow. These were slides that were made in two parts with the point of the arrow on one part and the fletching and a pin on the other half. A safety chain connected the two parts which were joined together by passing the pin through the hair and into the shaft of the arrow. Crescent-shaped pins were made in the same way. Boston jewelers sold pearl-set arrows and crescents slides.[16]

Pairs of small pearl pins were often worn on each shoulder where the sleeve joined the bodice of high-waisted dresses (see Colour Plate 67). Dyer & Eddy advertised 'Pearl set and Gold Twin Breast Pins'.[17] Abigail Adams chose pearl jewelry for her court appearances. She purchased three pearl pins and a pair of pearl earrings while her husband John was serving as U.S. envoy in London. 'The cost of them', she wrote to her niece in 1786, 'no matter what; less than diamonds, however'.[18] On another occasion, Mrs. Adams mentioned that while she was in England she had bought her jewelry from a Quaker jeweler named Savory in Cheapside, London.[19] Joseph Savory's trade card of 1783 is in the Heal Collection, The British Museum.[20]

12. *Col. Cent.*, 6 Oct. 1810. Davis & Brown, Boston, advertised 'Rich London pearl, topaz, cornelian and brilliant set' jewelry either 'sets or separate'. *Col. Cent.*, 1 Dec. 1810.
13. *Col. Cent.*, 3, 20 Oct. 1804; 5 Jan. 1805.
14. *Col. Cent.*, 27 Feb. 1805.
15. *Col. Cent.*, 6, 17 Jan. 1810.
16. *Col. Cent.*, Dyer & Eddy, 20 Oct. 1804; R. & H. Farnam, 5 Jan. 1805. See Tait, I, 23; II, 20-21.
17. *Col.Cent.*, 20 Oct. 1804.
18. McClellan, p. 259.
19. AA to TBA, 11 Feb. 1795, Adams Papers, MHS.
20. Sir Ambrose Heal, *The London Goldsmiths*, pp. 35, 238; Arthur G. Grimwade, *London Goldsmiths 1697-1837*, 652.

Colour Plate 57. Two sets of amethyst and gold jewelry owned in Massachusetts, probably imported from England or France, early 19th century. (Left) Tiara, earrings, bracelets and necklace owned by the Ropes family. Length about 7¼in. (bracelet). (Right) Festoon style necklace and bracelets, owned by Elizabeth Derby, ancestor of the donor. Both families lived in Salem and Boston, Massachusetts. Gift of Mrs. Joseph A. Ropes and Gift of Miss Martha C. Codman respectively. Courtesy, Museum of Fine Arts, Boston.

Colour Plate 58. Set of aquamarine and gold jewelry owned by Elizabeth Crowninshield of Salem, Massachusetts, probably English, c.1820. Length 1¾ in. (pendant). Photograph by Mark Sexton. Peabody Essex Museum.

Topaz, Amethyst and Aquamarine

Topaz and amethyst, stones popular in ancient times, were favourite coloured gemstones for Americans of the Federal period. Although topaz comes in many colours it was yellow topaz, the colour of the gold it was set in, that was especially agreeable to lovers of the antique style. Edward Preble, Commodore of the American fleet in the Mediterranean, purchased two pairs of earrings and two topaz breast pins while in London in 1804, no doubt as presents for members of his family in Maine.[1]

'Real topaz' was often specified in the advertisements of American jewelers in the first decade of the nineteenth century. However, citrine, a transparent yellow quartz, was frequently sold as topaz. American jewelers offered imitation topaz in the form of gold-foiled pastes. While most topaz jewelry was undoubtedly imported in finished form from England, Fletcher & Gardiner of Boston imported quantities of 'fine topaz' which they made into jewelry to suit their customers' taste.[2]

Mrs. James Monroe of Virginia purchased topaz jewelry while she and her husband were in France where he was serving as the United States minister to France from 1794 to 1796 (Plate 67). Tradition states that the jewelry was made by Napoleon's court

1. E. Preble, *Memo Book*, 1803-05, MEHS, courtesy of Laura Sprague.
2. *Col. Cent.*, 3 October 1804, Dyer & Eddy; 5 Jan. 1805, R. & H. Farnam; 1 Dec. 1810, Davis & Brown; 18 Aug. 1810, Fletcher & Gardiner. *Federal Gaz.* (Phila.), 7 Nov. 1800, John B. Dumoutet.

Colour Plate 59. Gold filigree earrings set with pink stones, owned originally by Mrs. Thomas Bulfinch, mother of Boston's leading architect, Charles Bulfinch, early 19th century. Length 1¾in. overall. Gold ring mounted with a miniature painting attributed to Nathaniel Hancock who was working in Salem in 1792 and in 1809, of Susannah (Hiller) Foster who married Nathaniel Foster in 1775. Photograph by Mark Sexton. Peabody Essex Museum.

Plate 67. Tiara, earrings and necklace set in gold with citrines, often mistaken for topaz at the time, purchased by Mrs. James Monroe in France where her husband was serving as Minister from 1794 to 1796. Photograph courtesy of Museum of Early Southern Decorative Arts. The James Monroe Museum, Fredericksburg, Virginia.

jeweler. Whether true or not, the set is neatly made and consisted of a tiara, earrings, and necklace. Round and pear-shaped stones were used in the earrings and tiara, the latter with a base row of oval stones set end to end to match the necklace. Round stones form the clasp of the necklace which has a pendant cross with pyramidal terminations. Tiny gold beads were added sparingly to punctuate the design of the individual pieces. A second and similar necklace owned by Elizabeth Monroe had a pendant cross formed of oval stones with pear-shaped stones hung on either side.

Mrs. Monroe, whose husband became President of the United States from 1816 to 1824, also owned a set of amethyst jewelry. In Boston, Dyer & Eddy advertised 'Amethyst set Broaches, Finger Ring and Ear Jewels'.[3] Amethyst is a variety of quartz and was found in large quantities in Siberia and Brazil. Another President's wife, Dolley Madison, had a pair of earrings with amethysts 'hung in chains in the shape of a letter M' and an amethyst pin to go with them.[4]

An amethyst parure owned by a member of the Ropes family in Massachusetts included a necklace, a pair of bracelets, a pair of drop earrings, a comb, and a brooch that could also be worn as a pendant on the necklace (Colour Plate 57, left). A pair of chain bracelets and a necklace set with large medallions of amethysts framed with *cannetille* work were owned by Elizabeth Derby of Salem (Colour Plate 57, right). Like the jewelry owned by the Presidents' wives, the amethyst jewelry owned by these Massachusetts ladies was said to have been imported from France.[5]

3. *Col. Cent.*, 20 Oct. 1804.
4. Maud Wilder Goodwin, *Dolley Madison*, pp. 167, 262.
5. Topaz and amethyst jewelry at Middleton Place in Charleston, S.C. includes a tiara said to have been worn by a member of the family at the Russian Court in 1820.

Plate 68. Two brooches set with pastes in the shape of a crescent and a butterfly, English, c.1790, owned by the Lee family of Virginia. Length 1⅞in. (crescent), 1½in. (butterfly). Robert E. Lee Memorial Association. Stratford Hall, Virginia.

Diamonds and Paste

The revolutions in America and France caused a temporary lull in the purchase and use of diamond jewelry. There were, of course, those whose wealth survived the ravages of war. Some still had their diamonds or could afford to buy new diamond jewelry if they chose to do so. Joseph Barrell of Boston was one of those whose fortunes were improved through privateering and who bought jewelry set with diamonds for his family soon after the war ended (see Colour Plate 41). Matilda Stoughton apparently married her jewels (see Colour Plate 36). The wife of the Spanish chargé d'affaires in Philadelphia, she was described by one of her contemporaries at a party as being 'brilliant with diamonds'."[1] Some post-war jewelers, particularly in Virginia and South Carolina, advertised diamonds for sale or purchase. Diamond hoop rings and cluster rings continued to be fashionable. Also popular were diamond-set miniature cases.

It was not until the last years of the eighteenth century that diamonds began to regain their former position of desirability. Importers of substantial quantities of jewelry, such as John Jacks in Philadelphia, offered an occasional 'brilliant Diamond Necklace and Earrings, price 2000 Dollars' or a watch in a diamond-studded case, with a chain for $1,000.[2] In 1801, it was noted in a New York newspaper that 'diamonds are again much in fashion in Europe'.[3] This observation was prompted by the desire to sell what was called a superb diamond watch chain suitable either to someone of great wealth or to a speculator.

Instead of buying diamond jewelry from a local jeweler, some Americans preferred to send directly to England themselves. In 1803, States Dyckman of Boscobel in New York sent a diamond and emerald ring to be converted into a brooch, with some extra diamonds added to it in the process. The work was done by the London firm of William Watson, goldsmith, jeweler and watchmaker in the Strand.[4]

The influence of French fashion was felt again as the country recovered from the Revolution. In 1813, it was observed by a Londoner that even though President James Madison was a man of small fortune, both his house and his wife were decorated in the French taste. 'His wife has a profusion of finery, Diamonds &c. which it is believed are the effects of French liberality', another English critic observed in his diary.[5]

Gradually, in the first decades of the nineteenth century, American jewelers began to make diamond jewelry in some quantity. Thomas Fletcher, first in Boston, then in

1. Marshall B. Davidson, *The American Heritage History of American Antiques*, p. 67.
2. *Fed. Gaz.* (Phila.), 15 April 1797. Prime II, 122.
3. *N-Y Gaz. & Gen. Advtr.*, 7 Oct. 1801.
4. Watson was located at No. 149 near Somerset House. Ian Pickford, ed., *Jackson's Silver and Gold Marks*, p. 257, gives Watson's dates as 1801-1809 and spells the surname with two tees. The bill from Watson is at Boscobel Restoration, Inc., Garrison-on-Hudson, N. Y.
5. Farington Diary, cited by F.J.B.Watson, 'French 18th Century Art in Boston', *Apollo*, Dec. 1969, p. 479.

Colour Plate 60. Group of paste jewellery owned in Charleston, South Carolina, probably English. The pair of shoe buckles (below), c.1770, were worn by Adam Gilchrist (c.1761-1816). Length 2¹⁵⁄₁₆in. The shoe buckle (upper right), c.1780, was worn by General Francis Marion (c.1732-1795). Length 2¹⁵⁄₁₆in. The scrolled hat pin (upper left), c.1790, was owned by General Christopher Gadsden (1724-1805). Length 2⅞in. Photograph by Leland Cook by courtesy of The Magazine Antiques. *The Charleston Museum, Charleston, South Carolina.*

Philadelphia, offered to make diamond jewelry in handsome designs to suit his customer's taste.[6] The Thibaults of Philadelphia also advertised diamond jewelry, in addition to the pearl work in which their shop specialized. William Frost of Providence featured diamond jewelry in his advertisement in 1810.[7]

Because diamonds had become less fashionable for a few decades, paste was not as much in demand during the Federal period as it had been during the mid-eighteenth century. Among long lists of imported goods, Fletcher & Gardiner had only 'a small invoice of Pastework'.[8] Some American women chose to wear paste jewelry instead of diamonds, not only because of the cost, but because they felt it was wrong to indulge in such luxuries. As mentioned on page 111, Abigail Adams, whose husband was opposed to all forms of extravagance, purchased pearls – three pins and a pair of earrings – to wear for court occasions while her husband was representing the United States in England. 'The cost of them — no matter what', she wrote to her niece in 1786, 'less than diamonds, however'.[9]

Paste buckles were extremely popular, especially for shoes. It was the last hurrah as it turned out, since the shoe lace was about to render shoe buckles obsolete.

6. *Col. Cent.*, 6 Oct. 1810.
7. Flynt & Fales, p. 222.
8. *Col. Cent.*, 28 Nov. 1810.
9. Cited by McClellan, p. 259.

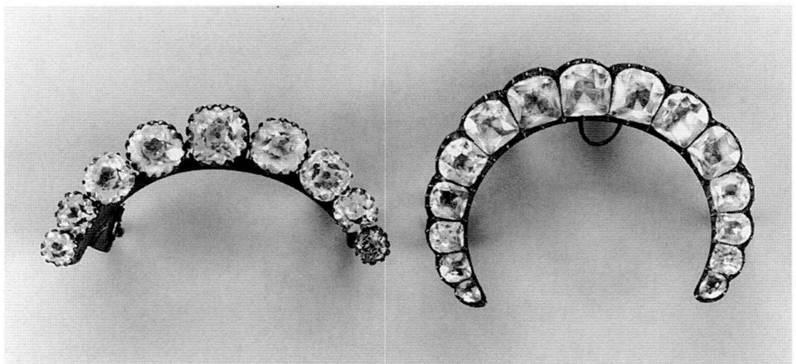

Plate 69. Left. Group of paste jewelry owned in the Boston area, English, c.1780-1800. Turban pin, star shaped. Bequest of M.A. Elton in 1888. Spray pin and cross with closed-back silver settings. Round star-like brooch with silver settings and gold back. Gift of Miss Georgiana G. Eaton. Courtesy, Museum of Fine Arts, Boston.

Plate 70. Above. Crescent brooch (left) with collet and post settings and neatly fitted pastes, English, c.1790. 1½in. x 1¾in. Brooch (right) with space between stones, early 19th century. Photograph by David Bohl, Boston. Courtesy of Society for the Preservation of New England Antiquities, Boston, Massachusetts.

Colour Plate 61. Group of early 19th century jewelry owned in Salem, Massachusetts. Pin in the form of a flower sprig set in silver with small rose diamonds, probably English, c.1810. Length ¾in. Ring set in silver with six pastes and a small citrine, topaz or gold foiled paste in centre, American. Diameter ¾in. Two pairs of sleeve buckles set with pastes, probably English, c.1800. Gold Brooch set with a miniature painting said to have been made by Dorcas Hiller of Salem, c.1795. Painting done with hair pigment in colours on ivory with a weeping mourner at the tomb of SS (Sally Saunders) who died on 16 July 1795 at the age of sixteen. Hair set under a crystal on back. Length 1⅞in. Photograph by Mark Sexton. Peabody Essex Museum.

However, they went out in the proverbial blaze of glory. Because buckles represented a quaint former fashion, a great many pairs of shoe buckles have survived, frequently in their original boxes. They could be quite elegant (Colour Plate 60). Their shapes were taken from neo-classical designs – geometric round, oval, and rectangular forms – or had lightly undulating or swagged borders. While set in silver, they frequently had gilt inner borders and bright-cutting. Bright blue enamel borders were fashionable too. Although most of these buckles were still imported from England, Van Voorhis & Coley were among a number of American jewelers who were proudly proclaiming their own manufactured paste buckles, well made, available in any pattern, and equal to any made elsewhere (Colour Plate 61).[10]

Hat or turban pins and buckles, as well as other bits of decoration for the head dress, were also frequently made of paste (Plate 69) One jewelry firm pointed out that their imported 'Combs, ornamented with Paste, set in silver and plated', formed 'most fashionable figures'.[11] Crescents and stars, arrows and slides were all desirable paste ornaments for the coiffure available to Federal Americans (Plate 70). Before the end of the Revolution, the style-setting Mrs. Robert Morris of Philadelphia wore a crescent in her overwhelming hat (Colour Plate 38). Whether it was made of paste or diamonds is indistinguishable from her portrait. A turban pin, later converted to a stick pin, once ornamented the head of a Massachusetts lady (Plate 69). Its floral shape shows how well paste could be cut to fit the form exactly, a feat that would have been expensive and wasteful if cut in diamonds.

A spray pin set more as it would have been if diamonds had been used can be seen in Plate 69. Here the pin had the form of an aigrette in miniature and relied more on the silver mounts than on the stones for its floral design. It had no fasteners on the back of it, indicating that it was meant to be sewn on to the headdress or garment.

A brooch set in silver and backed with gold looked very much like its diamond cousins (Plate 69). Its pastes were elaborately faceted and graduated to give form to its design. Twisted heart brooches were still being made at the end of the eighteenth century.

Earrings, finger rings (Plate 71) and bracelets were also set with pastes. Frequently rings were set with gold-foiled stones in an attempt to mimic the topaz jewelry currently popular.

Judging from the documentary evidence as well as the dearth of surviving diamond jewelry, it is apparent that many Americans of the Federal period preferred pastes, topazes, pearls, and amethysts to diamonds.

10. *N-Y Daily Advtr.*, 1 Sep. 1785. Gottesman I, 77.
11. *Col. Cent.*, 3 Oct. 1804.

Plate 71. Gold ring set with a cluster of pastes, English or American, c.1800. Partially effaced engraving inside band, 'This ring belonged to / Dolley Madison wife of the fourth / President of the United States'. Diameter 10/16 in. Photograph by Peter J. Theriault. Private Collection.

Plate 72. Mrs. Alexander Garden (1767-1817) of Charleston, South Carolina, wore a little cut-steel waist buckle set with a blue and white Wedgwood medallion in her miniature portrait painted by Adam Buck (1759-1833) in 1803. She also wore a cornelian bead necklace. Length 28in. Gibbes Art Gallery.

New Materials

The demand for jewelry embellished with scenes or motifs taken from classical antiquity led Josiah Wedgwood (1730-1795) to produce small stoneware plaques that could be set in buckles, buttons, brooches, chatelaines and other ornaments. In 1764 the enterprising Staffordshire manufacturer, noted primarily for his tablewares, had introduced a fine-grained ceramic which could be stained with metallic oxides in such colours as sage green, lilac, and the most popular light blue. This material he called jasper after a variety of quartz which is found in various colours. Relief decoration on these plaques was most often executed in white and showed portraits and classical scenes or motifs, following the designs carved in cameos and intaglios (Colour Plate 62). Capitalizing on the cameo craze, Wedgwood in effect was producing costume jewelry for the mass market utilizing mechanical means, turning out relief designs like moulded frosting decoration for cakes.

The delicacy of the modelling of the relief designs Wedgwood produced can be seen in a buckle of elongated oval shape owned in New England (Colour Plate 62). Two female figures stood within a white floral border studded with cut-steel beads and mounted in an elaborately bordered cut-steel frame.[1] Simpler in concept is the cut-steel comb with a Wedgwood rosette affixed to the middle of the cut-out decorative portion of the hair ornament (Colour Plate 63).

While Wedgwood plaques could be joined to mounts made of gold and silver, more often they were applied to marcasite or cut steel which kept the cost down.

1. A similar pair of belt clasps was purchased a century later by Baltimoreans William and Henry Walters in Vienna in 1878. *Walters Art Gallery Jewelry Ancient and Modern,* #648, p. 229.

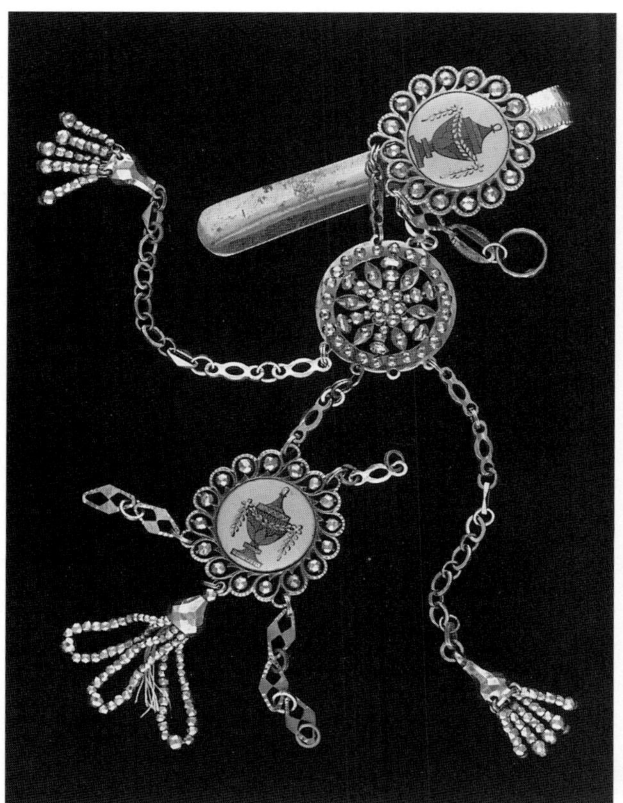

Plate 73. Chatelaine, pinchbeck chain with Wedgwood plaques, English, c.1790. Length 7⅞in. Owned by Mrs. Stephen Salisbury. Photograph by Stephen Briggs. Bequest of Stephen Salisbury III Estate. Worcester Art Museum.

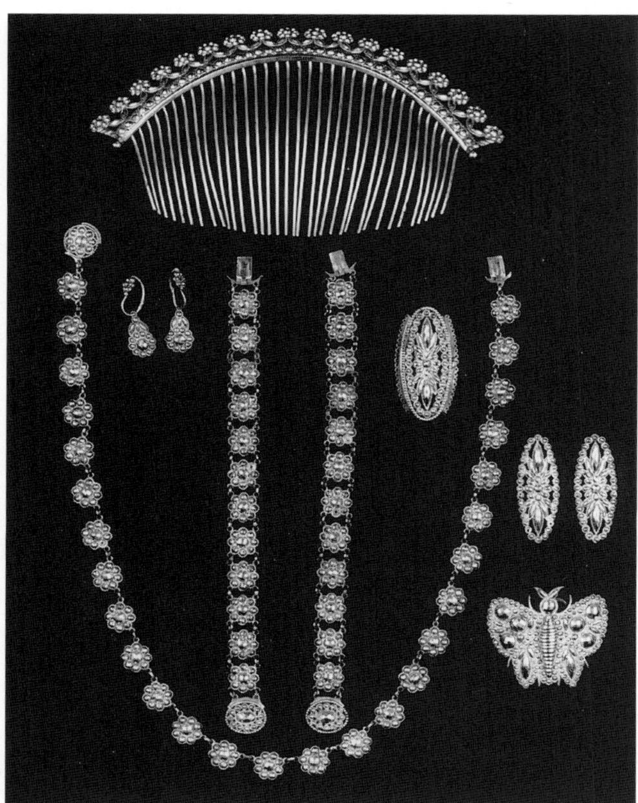

Plate 74. Cut-steel parure worn to the Lafayette Ball in New York city in 1824, English, c.1820. Tiara, pair of earrings, pair of bracelets, pair of brooches, clasp and necklace. Rosette designs mixed with paterae. Butterfly pin probably added to the set at a later date. Length 2⅛in. (brooch). New-York Historical Society.

Wedgwood was a frequent collaborator with another English entrepreneur, Matthew Boulton (1728-1809), of Birmingham, who made jewelry of cut-steel as well as of Sheffield plate. Individual studs of steel were intricately faceted, polished, and riveted, individually and close together, to the desired form of jewelry (Plate 73). While cut-steel jewelry was introduced in the 1760s, it became more fashionable during the neo-classical period, especially in France where it was substituted for the fine jewelry that the wealthy French families had been asked to turn in to the nation's Treasury.

Abigail Adams used cut-steel beads sewn on black velvet ribbon for a necklace which she wore to a ball in London in 1786, while her husband was United States envoy there. She reported to her niece that the steel ornaments were 'much in fashion and brought to such perfection as to resemble diamonds'.[2] When Lafayette made his grand tour of the United States in 1824, he was honoured at a ball given at Castle Garden in New York on 14 September. So far had cut-steel jewelry advanced in favour that one of the ladies present was adorned with a large set consisting of a tiara in the form of a floral band, a pair of pendant rosette earrings, a necklace, a pair of bracelets, a large oval clasp and a buckle in the shape of a butterfly (Plate 74).

A smaller set, made of steel, iron and brass, had an elegant tiara, a necklace, and a pair of drop earrings trimmed with graduated medallions featuring Roman heads (Colour Plate 64). The pieces were japanned at the time they were made to preserve a uniform colour. Iron jewelry was beginning to enjoy a limited amount of respectability. Made as early as 1804 in Germany at the Royal Berlin Factory, it was given in exchange for gold jewelry to help finance the cost of defence against

2. McClellan, p. 259.

Colour Plate 62. Cut steel waist buckle made by Matthew Boulton (1728-1825) of Birmingham, England, in collaboration with Josiah Wedgwood (1730-1795) who provided the blue and white jasperware medallion. English, c.1790. Length 3½ in. Photograph by James Garvin. New Hampshire Historical Society.

Plate 75. Brooch with a medallion portrait of a somewhat Continental looking George Washington, appealing to the American market. Cast iron with gold filigree setting. Probably German, c.1820. Length about ⅞in. Courtesy of The British Museum, Hull Grundy Gift.

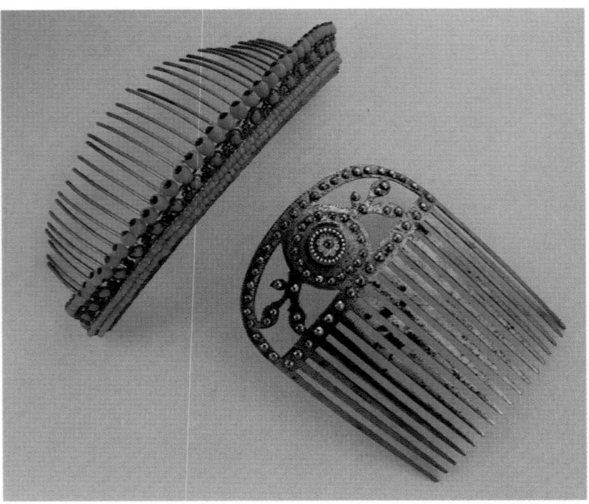

Colour Plate 63. Hair comb made of cut steel by Matthew Boulton c.1790, and set with a jasperware medallion made by Josiah Wedgwood. Length 4 1/16 in. Tiara, European, c.1815-1825, made of gilt brass and set with faceted and round coral beads. Owned by the Denaux family of Charleston. Length 5 11/16 in. Photograph by Leland Cook by courtesy of The Magazine Antiques. *The Charleston Museum, Charleston, S.C.*

Colour Plate 64. Parure, French or German, c.1820, made of cut steel and iron, japanned and gilt decoration. Owned by the family of the Reverend James Dewar Simons (d.1814) of Charleston. Photograph by Terry Richardson. The Charleston Museum, Charleston, S.C.

Napoleon in 1813. Iron jewelry was also made in France and became suitable for mourning and a symbol of constancy.[3] A portrait medallion of Washington was cast in iron about 1820 and set in a burst of gold filigree to be worn as a brooch (Plate 75).

3. Clifford, *Cut-Steel and Berlin Iron Jewellery*; Tait, *I*, 28. Iron jewelry is believed to have been produced in the eighteenth century in Silesia as well as France.

Colour Plate 65. Mrs. John Quincy Adams' tiara was made to accommodate either a coral top or a jet top. Probably bought in England, c.1815. Smithsonian Museum.

AMBER, CORAL AND CORNELIAN

Amber

One of the few organic materials historically used as gemstones, amber is a fossilized resin that was exuded from an ancient variety of pine tree millions of years ago. Amber is harvested from the sea or mined from the earth. It is found primarily in the area of the southern shores of the Baltic Sea. Warm to the touch and worn by the sea or cut and polished, the surface of amber is smooth and soothing to the touch. It can be clear and transparent or cloudy and included. Most highly prized by some collectors are pieces of clear amber that have ancient bits of flora and fauna, especially insects, entombed in a gemmy time capsule.

As the Greek word for amber *(elektron)* suggests, friction against a piece of this material can cause static electricity. This property undoubtedly encouraged the belief that amber had protective and healing capabilities, which in turn prompted its use in jewelry. Necklaces were believed to cure throat ailments and earrings to prevent headaches.

Amber had been important to the ancient Greeks and Romans and so it is not surprising that during the neo-

Colour Plate 66. Portrait of Mrs. John Quincy Adams (1775-1852) by C. Robert Leslie (1794-1859) in which she wears the coral-set comb in her hair, a twisted red bead necklace with gold clasp in front, and beaded tassel earrings. The portrait was painted in 1816 while her husband was serving as Minister to the Court of St. James in London. Length 42½in., width 32¾in. Courtesy of the Diplomatic Reception Rooms, the Department of State, Washington, D.C.

classical period amber enjoyed a revival in popularity. In its most common colours of yellow, orange, and brown, and even in its oxidized state of reddish hues, amber reflected the palette of classical art. From the Middle Ages and the era of amber guilds in what is now Poland, amorphous lumps of amber were turned and faceted into beads for necklaces. It was in this form that it was first worn in America by early colonial women (see page 21).

While by no means plentiful, some amber jewelry was imported to the newly formed United States. 'Real amber Ear Jewels and Necklaces, to match' were advertised in Boston in 1804. A pair of pendent earrings and a brooch in burnt orange amber were worn by Mrs. Stephen Gore of Waltham, Mass., with a necklace of large elliptical links of both yellow and orange amber. Amber jewelry made a nice present to take home for friends and relatives. Commodore Edward Preble of Portland, Maine, purchased numerous strings of amber and amber ear drops while he was in Naples from 1803 to 1805.

Coral

Organic like amber and reddish in colour like cornelian, coral also enjoyed a resurgence of interest toward the end of the neo-classical period. Coral bead necklaces had never gone out of fashion due to their amuletic associations. In the colonial period, coral beads were smooth, somewhat cylindrical in shape and imported through England from Italy to America.

In 1783, Joseph Richardson, Jr. (1752-1831), of Philadelphia, in partnership with his brother Nathaniel (1754-1827), ordered coral beads for resale from John Masterman & Son of London, requesting '20 Oz. small size Corral beads interspersed with longer pieces.' In their next order early in 1785 they asked that the beads be smaller and 'mixed with long pieces as they are much better liked here than all round ones.' In a later order that year they pointed out that 'the Pipe Coral is so very different from what we desired & so very unsaleable here, that we have taken the liberty of sending them back to you.' They also enclosed with the letter several beads to show their English suppliers exactly what they wanted. This proved successful. After Nathaniel left the partnership, Joseph continued to order the small coral beads from Masterman in 1791 and 1792. He strung the beads in his own shop and furnished them with engraved gold clasps.[1]

By the Federal period, 'Dog Teeth and Coral Arms' were offered for necklaces and were imported directly from Europe.[2] Branch coral was strung for necklaces and bracelets, while the slightly curving, pointed 'dog's teeth' were often mounted with a ferrule and pendant loop for use as fobs.

During this period, coral beads were frequently faceted. An 'assortment of cut coral' and combs was advertised in Philadelphia in 1824 by Louisa Morelle Gravelle as having recently been shipped to her for sale at her jewelry and fancy store on Chestnut Street.[3] The gilt tiara worn by Mrs. John Quincy Adams had several rows of faceted coral beads mounted on top of, between, and below a metal band of paired C-scrolls (Colour Plate 65). The Adamses lived in London while Mr. Adams served as United States Envoy Extraordinary. When they were there, Charles Robert Leslie painted portraits of the couple in 1816. He included the tiara in Louisa Adams' picture (Colour Plate 66).[4] This

1. Fales, *Richardson*, pp. 302-3.Joseph Richardson, Jr., Letter Books, Winterthur Museum Library.
2. Ephraim Hart, NYC, *The Daily Advtr.*, 8 July 1803.
3. Waters, p. 144.
4. JQA had wanted Leslie to include his new seal that he had just purchased from seal engraver R.W. Silvester, but for some reason Leslie declined to do so. Oliver, pp. 57-64.

tiara was seen by a great many Americans when the portraits were exhibited in Philadelphia the following year. The tiara was further publicized by an engraving of Louisa's portrait that appeared in Longacre & Herring's *National Portrait Gallery of Distinguished Americans 1834-1839.*[5] A similar gilt tiara made of faceted and round coral beads was worn by a member of the Denaux family in Charleston, South Carolina (Colour Plate 63).

Western tribes of Indians at this time were using coral in their jewelry. Spanish conquistadors had persuaded them that it was superior to the pieces of red spiny oyster from the Gulf of Mexico that the Indians had traditionally used. The Spaniards imported and sold the coral to Zuni and Hopi people who combined it with silver, shell and turquoise beads. The Navajo used this imported coral alone in necklaces. However, coral was not included in the list of eighteen objects that were considered sacred to them.[6]

Cornelian

Like amber and coral, cornelian, or carnelian as it is often spelled today, suited the neo-classical taste. Its reddish colour was in keeping with the current fashions, and had also been a favourite of ancient Greeks and Romans. While it was often used as a secondary element with pearls or carved into a seal and set in gold, cornelian was also shaped into primary forms of jewelry such as beads and pendants.

Mrs. Harrison Gray Otis of Boston wore her cornelian cross suspended from a necklace of medium-sized pearls when her miniature portrait was painted in 1804 (Colour Plate 67).[7] The cross was decorated in the centre with a precious topaz surrounded by seed pearls, a dentate ferrule at the top and seed pearls on the pendant loop. The cornelian beads that were inherited with the cross by Mrs. Otis' descendants may have been substituted for the pearl necklace later in the nineteenth century when the barrel clasp was attached. However, it may have been original and purchased at the same time. Cornelian necklaces were advertised in Boston in the early nineteenth century.

Cornelian bead necklaces were specified as having been imported from Liverpool in 1810 for the customers of Jones & Pierce in Boston. The same year Fletcher and Gardiner offered 'Cornelian Necklaces and Drops to match; Crosses' and interchangeable sets. They also had top and drop earrings of cornelian set in unburnished gold of their own manufacture. During the summer Fletcher and Gardiner had received a shipment from England that included a supply of five hundred cornelians to make into jewelry to suit their customers' wishes. They also had on hand a few necklaces of the less common white cornelian. A. & G. Welles offered cornelian head ornaments.[8]

In 1804, States Dyckman, who had built a splendid home called Boscobel at Garrison-on-Hudson, New York, purchased a variegated cornelian necklace and a pair of plain cornelian earrings. These were ordered from London jeweler and goldsmith, Thomas Wirgman, from whom Dyckman also bought rich silverware.[9]

Stone seal cutter Thomas Brown of New York offered the 'highest price given' for cornelians he could cut, engrave and set in gold seals in 1803. In his advertisement in *Mercantile Advertiser* on 17 December he offered to cut the stones with 'Heads Fancy Figures, Emblematical Subjects, Cameos & engraved in the best manner. He charged

5. H.R. D'Allemagne illustrates a similar tiara in a fashionable portrait of 1817 in *Les Accessoires du Costume et du Mobilier* (Paris 1828) 3 vols., *I,* Plate LIII.
6. GIA Colored Stones Course, Assignment 33, p. 8. Exactly how soon after 1540 coral was introduced to the Pueblo Indians in N.M. and Arizona has not been determined. The earliest documented reference to this trade is dated 1822. Modern Indian jewelers have returned to the use of the traditional red spiny oyster or abalone, and coral today is only occasionally used by the Zuni in New Mexico.
7. A similar necklace with cross was illustrated in the London *Lady's Magazine* in 1805, indicating that Mrs. Otis kept up with the latest styles. See Bury I, 34, Plate 9.
8. *Col. Cent.*, 3 Jan., 11 April, 30 June, 18 Aug., 6, 31 Oct. 1810.
9. Ms. 1149, Invoice of Thomas Wirgman, goods shipped from London to New York for Dyckman, 14 Feb. 1804. Boscobel.

Colour Plate 67. Miniature portrait of Mrs. Harrison Gray Otis, painted in 1804 in Boston by Edward Greene Malbone (1777-1807) in which she wears a pearl necklace with a cornelian cross. The centre of the cross is set with a topaz ringed with little pearls. An alternate necklace made of cornelian beads and the pendent cross survive. Fletcher and Gardiner, Boston jewelers, advertised in 1810 interchangeable sets of cornelians and pearls; cornelian necklaces and drops to match and crosses; and fine imported topazes. Length 1½in. (cross). Photograph by David Bohl, Boston. Society for the Preservation of New England Antiquities.

six dollars for engraving coats of arms, five dollars for crests and cyphers, and two dollars for cyphers alone. He had in his possession books on heraldry containing about 50,000 names from which his customers could select a coat of arms without the benefit of the Heralds' College in England.

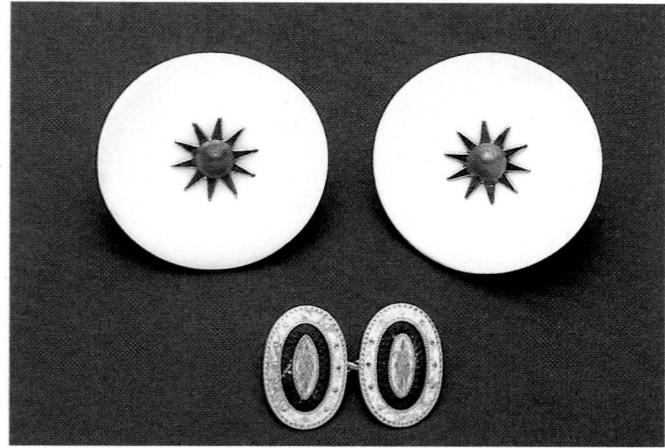

Colour Plate 68. Conch shell buttons owned by George Washington, set with a gold star and a silver bead, American, c.1790. Diameter 1¼in. Blue-enamelled gold cuff links, owned by Washington, English, c.1790. Mount Vernon Ladies' Association, Mount Vernon, Virginia.

Jet and Shell

Jet

Jet was used in the Stone Age for jewelry. Periodically over the centuries it has been returned to favour, notably by the Greeks and Romans who considered it a talisman. Pliny said that jet could do everything from staving off snakes and hysteria to detecting epilepsy and virginity.[1] Although it is so brown that it looks black and it polishes up to a glassy sheen, jet is a form of coal fossilized from a specific ancient variety of the araucarian tree. A particularly good deposit of jet was to be found in Whitby in Yorkshire, England. The invading Romans discovered this source and acquired a taste for jet jewelry and carved ornaments.

Jet was included in the list of rates for products exported to the Colonies as fixed by Parliament in 1660. Portraits of early colonial women occasionally include necklaces and bracelets of black beads possibly made of jet (Colour Plate 6). In the eighteenth century France produced much of the jet used for jewelry, the centre of this industry being the department of the Aude, in the southwest part of Languedoc.[2] At one time there were 1,200 workers employed in the jet trade.[3]

About 1800, when the lathe was introduced to its production, jet jewelry began to be marketed on a large scale. Because of its colour, jet became popular for use in mourning jewelry, along with onyx and black glass. An early example of an American ring had a faceted jet on each side of an oval mount containing a plaited lock of hair.[4] In 1807 Mrs. Richard Derby of Salem, Massachusetts, bought a jet finger ring from Philadelphia jeweler James Black. A motto was engraved inside its band. Mrs. Derby paid rather dearly for the jet ring at $7.50 plus fifty cents for the box.[5]

Thomas Fletcher believed that jet jewelry was one of the types of jewelry Federal American manufacturers could match against their English competitors. By 1810 he was making brooches, finger rings and earrings of jet and black enamel, 'of patterns entirely new'.[6] The faceted jet stones were set in gold mounts in designs very similar to those set with pearls, forming borders around a central setting of jet or hair under glass (Plate 109, lower right). The leaf-shaped setting was a characteristic one of the early nineteenth century. Bezels were often chased to give the effect of beading or filigree. Top and drop earrings were composed of a small rosette with an optional larger rosette drop (Plate 109, centre). The closed back was fairly shallow and slightly convex to accommodate the central stone.

A very desirable form in jewelry of this period was a jet-set tiara. Mrs. John Quincy

1. *Natural History*, quoted by Helen Muller, *Jet Jewellery and Ornaments*, p. 3.
2. Jedidiah Morse, *The American Universal Geography*, II, 252.
3. Louis Dieulafait, *Diamonds and Precious Stones*, p. 207.
4. In the collection of the MMA, New York.
5. Misc. Mss., Salem and Essex Co., 12 March 1807, Library, PEM. James Black advertised that his shop was on South Street in Philadelphia and that he made 'every article in the gold and hair fancy line'. *Fed.Gaz.*, 14 Feb. 1798.
6. *Col. Cent.*, 6 Oct. 1810.

Plate 76. Portrait of Sarah Ann Reeve Waterhouse of Brooklyn, New York, c.1835. Mrs. Waterhouse wears top and drop earrings, a small crescent lace pin and a ring, all set with small black jets. She has another ring on the third finger of her left hand, and a heavy gold rope chain loosely draped across her bodice, holding the gold watch she has tucked into her wide belt. When she died in 1877, she bequeathed her gold watch and chain to her son Albert. Length 37½in., width 31in. ©1986 Sotheby's Inc.

Adams had a tiara made so that it could be fitted either with coral as shown in Colour Plate 65 or with a coronet of jet. This was no doubt very useful to her in an age when mourning restrictions could strike at any time, rendering colourful jewelry inappropriate.

The early jet jewelry was generally made of small stones in delicate designs. Plate 76 shows top and drop earrings, crescent pin and cluster ring. As it became more popular, the pieces of jet became larger, the designs heavier, and it was more often carved than faceted. It would be several generations until jet jewelry reached its apogee in the second half of the nineteenth century.

Shell

In 1793 jewelers in Philadelphia and New York advertised jewelry made from sea shells. Conch shell, clam shell, cylinder shell and mother-of-pearl were all used to make fancy buttons in settings of gold, silver, and plated or gilt metal. Lemuel Wells of New York used cylinder shell for bracelets, hat pins, cestus buckles, clasps, rosettes, and buttons for the sleeve, coat and vest. James Byrne offered all kinds of conch-shell jewelry that he could supply in quantities for exportation.[7] George Washington was predisposed to buy American-made products whenever possible and could well have bought his coat buttons in either New York or Philadelphia (Colour Plate 68). His concave buttons were mounted with a central star cut out of gold with a silver bead in the middle. There was a twisted gold wire border around the outer edges.

The pearl lining found inside mussel shells was used by Gardiner Baker in New York for making hundreds of sleeve buttons. He appealed to customers by pointing out that they represented an original American manufactory utilizing the shell of the American pearl mussel 'in its native unpolished state...a most excellent proof that the fresh water brooks of our country afford a valuable article of convenience and ornament'.[8]

7. Peter Geley, *Pa. Packet*, 25 Jan. 1793; James Byrne, *New-York Daily Advtr.*, 3 Jan. 1793; Lemuel Wells, *N-Y Daily Advtr.*, 19 June 1793.
8. *The Herald* (NY, 27 Nov. 1794.

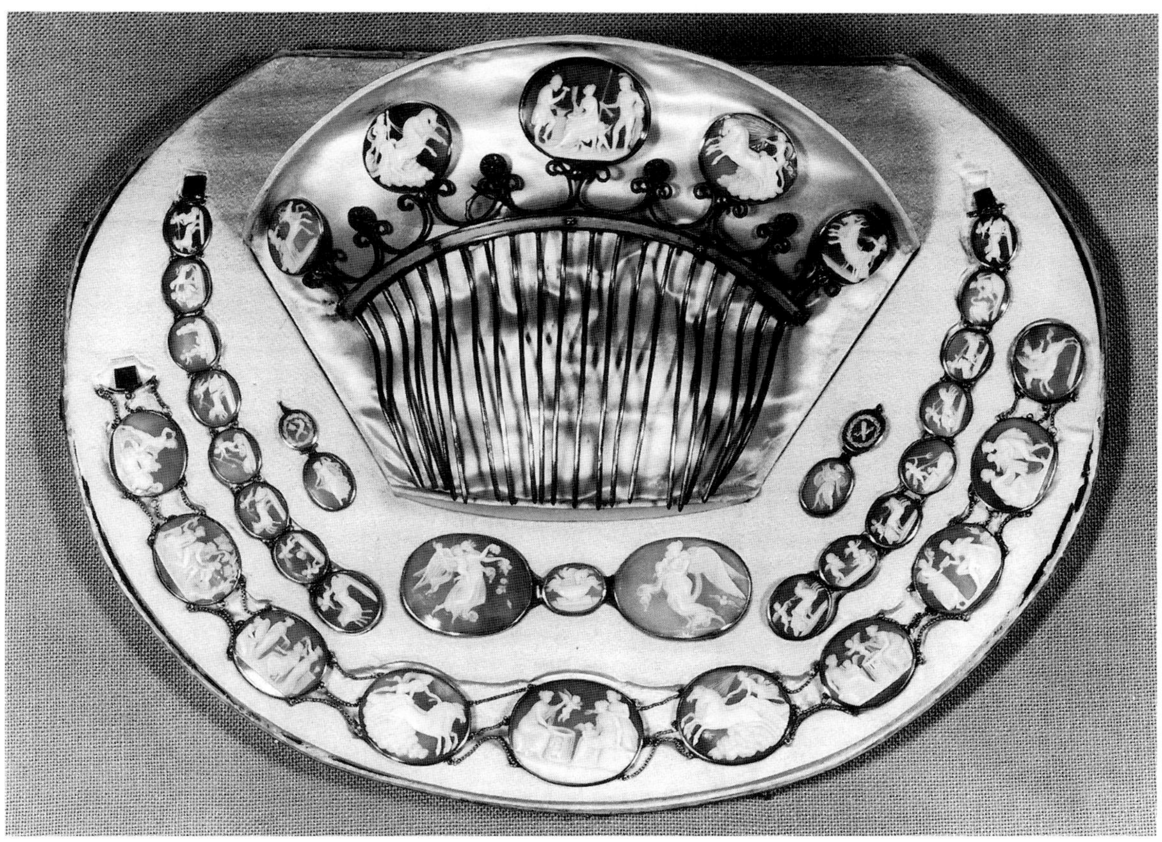

Plate 77. Cameo parure,Italian, c.1820, a wedding gift to Jane Peele when she married Stephen Phillips of Salem, Massachusetts. Mounted with shell cameos cut with classical figures and scenes, including figures of 'Night' and 'Day' which are derived from sculpture by Thorvaldsen who was working in Rome in the early 19th century. Photograph by Mark Sexton. Peabody Essex Museum.

In the early years of the nineteenth century, shell-carved cameos set as jewelry made their appearance. The love of cameos had its origin in the Greek and Roman tradition which had already been revived several times before, notably during the medieval and Renaissance periods. Its reappearance at the end of the eighteenth century was prompted by archaeological discoveries at Roman sites in combination with Robert Adam's interpretation of a neo-classical style and the relief designs of the Wedgwood-Boulton collaboration (pages 118-120). Napoleon Bonaparte became enamoured of the Roman cameos that had come to light at the time of his campaign in Italy in 1796. His empress Josephine began to wear cameos as jewelry in brooches and in her hair.

At the same time, in Italy, the carving of shell cameos was revived. A splendid example of finely carved cameo jewelry can be see in Plate 77. Consisting of a necklace, a pair of bracelets, a pair of top and drop earrings, a belt buckle and a tiara, the parure was made up of oval cameos carved with a variety of classical scenes. The festoon necklace had ten cameos connected by three rows of gold chain. The buckle cameo was carved after the sculpture of Night and Day by Thorvaldsen, the Danish sculptor who worked in Rome and influenced a number of aspiring American artists. The top of the earring was carved with a laurel wreath enclosing a quiver of arrows crossed with Cupid's bow. This classical design, symbolic of marriage, was especially popular in Salem, Massachusetts, where it was carved or painted on furniture during the Federal period. It is appropriate that this parure was purchased by Stephen Phillips of Salem about 1822, as a wedding present for his bride Jane A. Peele.[9]

9. They were married on 7 November 1822. A similar necklace is shown in Becker, *Antique and 20th C. J.*, Fig. 12.12.

Colour Plate 69. Two chatelaines owned by Charlestonians in the last decade of the 19th century. (Left) Purchased by Mrs. Gabriel Manigault from Green & Ward of London in 1792. Length 9⁷⁄₁₆in. (Right) French macaroni *style chatelaine acquired for Mrs. Charles Cotesworth Pinckney while her husband was in Paris on government business in 1797. Her watch was made by Lepine of Paris. Length 9¹⁄₁₆in. Photograph by Leland Cook by courtesy of* The Magazine Antiques. *The Charleston Museum, Charleston, South Carolina.*

Watches, Fobs, Seals and Trinkets

Prior to the Revolution, only wealthy Americans enjoyed the luxury of a watch, and even then there was a question if it would keep good time. Colonials were totally reliant upon England for their watches. Local self-styled watchmakers might be able to repair timepieces, or even put them together, but the basic parts had to be imported. Peter Faneuil not only purchased his watches from London, but he sent them back to be repaired and returned to him with spare crystals.[1]

It was not until the Federal period that artisans, many of whom had just recently gone to the United States from Great Britain and Europe, began to advertise more frequently watches of their own manufacture. It was in this period that accuracy in time-keeping instruments was increasing dramatically and that the precision watch was being developed. Previous mechanisms had been bulky in their roundness, but now the works were flattened so that they could be worn in narrow pockets. An early eighteenth century discovery of a method of piercing jewels for use in the pivot holes in watches permitted the jewelling of the train which became more widespread after 1775. Watches, now being offered for ladies as well as gentlemen, became more decorative, and therefore more like jewelry than simply utilitarian mechanisms.

Over the years, George and Martha Washington both owned several watches, all of which came from abroad. While Washington's watch was repaired in London on one occasion, watchmakers in Virginia were usually employed for this task.[2]

In 1785, George Washington ordered 'a handsome and fashionable gold watch' for his wife. He requested that the hour and minute hands on it be set with diamonds. Washington was a moderate man and shunned ostentation; the diamonds were not for

1. His gold watch 'of Graham's make', chain and seal were valued at £125 when he died in 1743. Weeden, *II*, 621, 629, 909. Graham was an innovative watchmaker of London and nephew of the famous Thomas Tompion.
2. Washington purchased a watch for himself in 1766 from Benjamin Sebastian of London and had a gold case made for it by John Waldron, London watchmaker. In 1767, Sebastian repaired and altered his watch. In 1771, Washington got a watch from Thomas Lawson, watchmaker, London. In 1772, Mrs. Washington's watch was repaired by Charles Turner, Alexandria; in 1780 by John Short, Norfolk; in 1783 by Edward Sanford, Alexandria. Edward Sanford also engraved a silver seal with Mrs. Washington's arms, perhaps to be worn on a chain with her watch. *GW Ledgers A and B; Britten's Old Clocks and Watches and their Makers*, pp.421, 492; Cutten, *SSS. of Va.*, pp. 20, 24.
3. GW, Mount Vernon, to Wakelin Welch, in *Writings of GW 28,* (Wash. D.C. 1938), 326, 496.
4. This case is marked and attributed to London goldsmith Samuel Jerman (free 1764), Grimwade, pp. 268-69, 562.
5. *Writings of GW 30,* 141-42.
6. Ledger B, 18 Aug. 1787; Benson J. Lossing, *The Home of Washington*, pp. 31, 221.
7. Lossing, p. 408.
8. Ibid., pp. 220-21.
9. Joseph Barrell, *Letter Book*, p. 84. Joseph Barrell, the father, placed the order for Hannah's gold watch and key with the firm of Chater in London (Britten, p. 351).It was to be new-fashioned but very plain with 'a neat face with common figures instead of Roman for the hours'. The chain was to be made of steel or any other more fashionable metal, but not of gold (Barrell, *Letter Book*, pp. 81-84). Barrell had purchased a new horizontal watch for himself from Chater earlier in the year (pp. 40, 55-56, 83). It was a large, double-cased watch with no second hand. The figures were to be as large and plain as possible to accommodate Barrell's failing eyesight.

show, but to make the hands easier to see. With the watch, he ordered 'a fashionable chain or string, such as are worn at present by Ladies in genteel life'.[3] The watch's outer case was embellished with enamelling in blue, white and gold with an amusing multicoloured miniature scene of Actaeon surprising Diana at her bath.[4] In 1793 a second outer case was made of solid gold for this watch and the arms of Washington impaling Dandridge (Martha's maiden name) were engraved on it. Shortly thereafter, Mrs. Washington decided to give her watch and chain to her granddaughter, Eleanor Parke Custis. It was replaced by a new horizontal watch accompanied by a chain and key in 1794.

'I wish to have a gold watch procured for my own use', wrote George Washington in 1788,

> not a small, trifling (nor finically ornamented one) but a watch well executed in point of workmanship; and of about the size and kind of that which was procured by Mr. Jefferson for Mr. Madison (which was large and flat) I imagine Mr. Jefferson can give you the best advice on the subject, as I am told this species of watches, which I have described, can be found cheaper and better fabricated in Paris than at London.

Plate 78. Lepine watch, seal fob and key owned by George Washington, made in France c.1789. The cornelian seal is cut with the Washington coat of arms. Photograph courtesy of Mount Vernon Ladies' Association, Mount Vernon, Virginia.

Washington made his request to Gouveneur Morris who was then in France, as was Thomas Jefferson, the American nation's new minister to France. With the watch, Washington wanted only a handsome key.[5] The watch procured for him was manufactured by Jean Antoine Lepine, a Parisian watchmaker favoured by Louis XV and Voltaire, as well as by Jefferson (Plate 78). Washington had purchased a new gold watch chain from Joseph Cook & Co. of Philadelphia in August 1787.

Portraits of the President show him wearing a key and a fob seal. The seal for his new watch bore his coat of arms engraved in white cornelian and the key had a polygonal piece of red cornelian in its handle.[6] Washington had two older seals engraved with his initials, one of which was lost on the battlefield at Braddock's defeat in 1755. In the inventory of Washington's estate in 1799, the Lepine watch is listed as '1 Gold watch, chain 2 seals & key' valued at $175.[7] Bushrod Washington inherited these items from his uncle and subsequently bequeathed the watch to his friend Robert Adams.[8]

Watch keys were originally shaped like coffee-grinder handles, but by the seventeenth century had assumed their more familiar straight shape, with a little finial or with an optional central medallion, and an open handle that served as a suspension ring or could be attached to one. Late eighteenth century keys often had flat geometrical medallions engraved with devices, the form later taken for the Phi Beta Kappa key in 1806 when the Society's medals became watch winders (see pages 135-136). Such keys could also be set with a cabochon gem or a slice of agate.

In 1793, Hannah Barrell of Massachusetts asked that her gold watch key be made in the form of a very handsome urn with crystals on both sides to contain a plaited lock of her father's hair, specifying that none of the grey hairs be taken out of the lock.[9] The frames for stone-set keys became more elaborate and featured heavily embossed or cast classical motifs. With the advent of stem winders and setters in the late nineteenth century, watch keys became obsolete.

The trinkets that were added to watch chains were delightful in design and revealing in selection. A New York lady of the 1780s had a gold watch with a steel chain to which was attached a miniature portrait of a bewigged man dressed in crimson velvet; three gold seals; a gold heart-

Plate 79. Gold fob seal, made about 1790, attributed to Paul Revere (1735-1818), Boston, Massachusetts, unmarked. The seal pivots and is engraved on one side with the monogram NG with floral pendants, and on the other side with the Greene arms, crest and motto, probably for Nathaniel Green, a known customer of Revere and Register of Deeds in Boston in 1789. Length 1$\frac{13}{16}$in. Yale University Art Gallery, University Purchase.

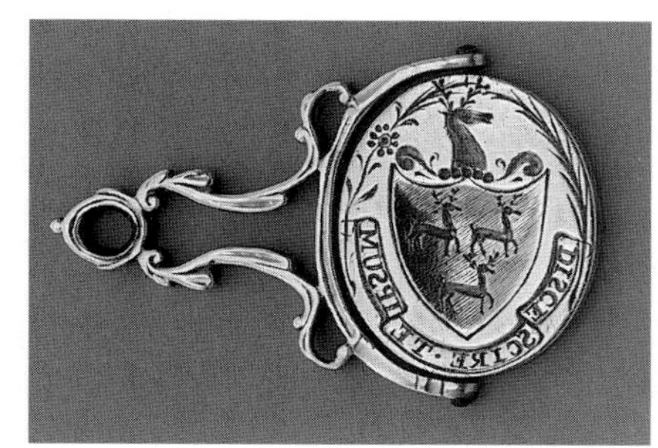

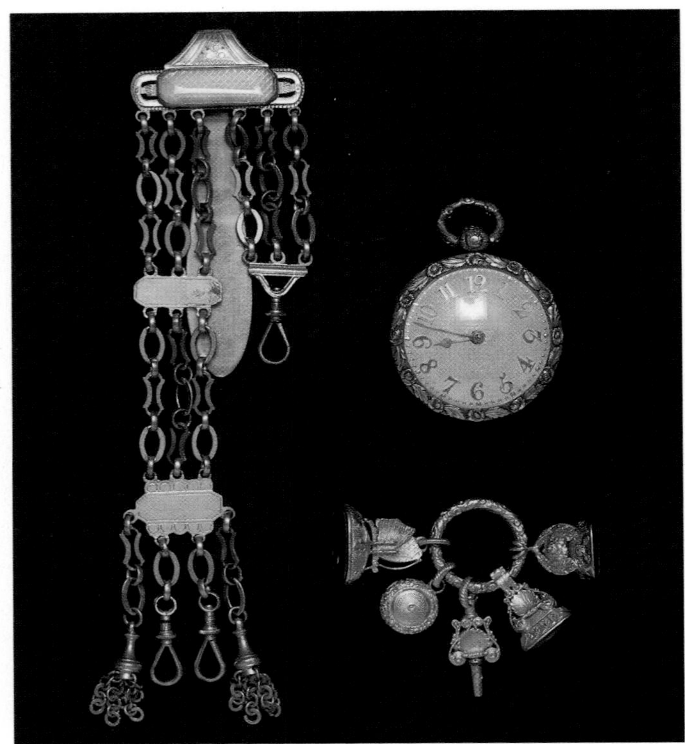

Colour Plate 70. Clinton family chatelaine made of gold-coloured metal, probably pinchbeck, with blue and white enamel. Valance-like design at top of hook carrying two white hardstone seals and a watch made by D. Jennings, London, c.1790. Belonged to Catherine Clinton, daughter of Governor George Clinton, who married Major-General Pierre Van Cortlandt in 1801. English, c.1800. Length 8½in. Bequest of Joseph B. Brenauer, 46.229.9. Photograph by Arthur Vitols, The Helga Studio. Museum of the City of New York.

Colour Plate 71. Gold chatelaine, watch and fobs owned by Elizabeth Tuckerman Salisbury of Worcester, ordered by her husband from Stephen Twycross of London for her fiftieth birthday in 1818. The watch is signed inside by Twycross. Diameter 1⅝in. The fobs are heavily ornamented and three of them are jeweled. Bequest of Stephen Salisbury III Estate. Worcester Art Museum.

shaped locket containing a plait of dark hair; and a plain gold key. Two of the seals were red cornelian, one engraved with a rose and the other with a globe and the motto 'La Veus'. The third seal was white cornelian with the motto 'L'Envie'.[10]

Agate and cornelian seals decorated the watch chains of two South Carolinians. One was purchased for Mrs. Gabriel Manigault from Green & Ward, watchmakers at 1 Ludgate Street, London, in 1792 (Colour Plate 69, left).[11] Their bill for a gold verge watch in a pearl-rimmed, transparent-green, enamelled case included an enamelled chain ornamented with pearls. There was also a locket for hair in the middle of the chain; a watch key and a seal engraved with a device; and a gilt skeleton case. The total cost of the watch and its concomitant paraphernalia was a little over £50. The watch and chain were suspended from a hook that was worn over a waist band or belt.

Another arrangement for wearing watches was made without a hook and was slung over the belt with a watch on one end and fobs suspended from separate chains on the other end. This type is known as a *macaroni*. A Lepine watch and chains of this variety (Colour Plate 69, right) were purchased in France, probably by Charles Cotesworth Pinckney when he was in Paris with the American commission at the time of the XYZ affair in 1796-97. It too had translucent emerald-green enamelling and pearl borders, but was made with flexible multiple strands of gold chain which would fit comfortably when looped over the waist band. While both of these sets of watch equipment are called chatelaines today, this is a nineteenth century term unused by Federal-period jewelers and watchmakers who were simply selling watches, chains, seals, keys and trinkets (Colour Plate 36).

A blue-enamelled chatelaine was owned by Catherine Clinton, daughter of New York's Governor Clinton (Colour Plate 70). The rectangular bar at the top of the hook was decorated with swags and resembled the design of Adamesque window

10. *Royal Gaz.*, NY, Nov. 17, 1781.
11. Britten, p. 391; Culme, pp. 194-5, says Green & Ward were in partnership 1787-1804.

Colour Plate 72. Paul Ambrose Oliver's gold watch, with its gold chain and cornelian seal fob, was an object of fascination for his young daughter Mary Ann. Portrait painted by James Peale, c.1810, Philadelphia, Pennsylvania. Vose Galleries of Boston.

valances. Its elegant chains are fire gilt and enamelled in black and white. The pearl-rimmed watch was made by D. Jennings of London, about 1790.[12]

Elizabeth Salisbury's chatelaine hook (Colour Plate 71) was embellished with a plaque of opaline paste to match her brooch and bracelet clasps, all of which came from the shop of Stephen Twycross of London (see Colour Plate 51). For her fiftieth birthday in 1818, Mrs. Salisbury received from her husband a gold watch, five fobs and a heavily wrought suspension ring. Elaborately worked gold was becoming more popular than enamelled and engraved surfaces. Even the face of her watch was decorated with finely worked gold instead of enamel. There were repoussé roses in place of pearls.

The three fob-seals accompanying Mrs. Salisbury's watch were set with gems. One had an amethyst cut with a dove (the Salisbury family crest), and the motto 'Affection has wings'. On top of the seal a delicately-formed butterfly perched, ready to flutter to a loved one. The second seal was engraved with a hand holding a pen, 'The tongue of the absent'. The third bore a squirrel with an acorn, 'The kernel lies within'. The order for this watch equipment was placed on 18 May 1818, by Stephen Salisbury 'to be neither large nor very small – a gold face – Chas'd Back – with a Gold [Chain?] Seals Keys and trinketts complete – the Seals to be of various precious stones Engraved in the best manner similar to those sent to Mr J Salisbury (one of which had a fly) (another an owl etc. – the watch and every article belonging to it to be of the newest fashion, and very best workmanship and materials – it is also particularly requested that it be a good time piece'.[13] A tiny gold locket with engine-turned decoration contained a circlet of white hair laid on a tightly-woven plait of dark hair to further personalize Mrs. Salisbury's set of trinkets. The fancy watch key had a lyre-shaped handle with a convex shell at its centre.

Diamonds, which had been out of fashion during the revolutions in America and Europe, returned to favour at the turn of the century and found their way on to cases and chains for watches. In Charleston, a lady's repeating watch and chain set with ninety large diamonds was offered for sale at 350 guineas. In Philadelphia, a watch and chain with brilliant diamonds cost $1,000, and in New York a superb diamond watch chain was offered to anyone of great wealth or a speculator.[14]

Most precious of all perhaps was a finger-ring watch set with fifty diamonds. Watchmaker David R. Launy offered it for sale in New York in 1802. He described it as being smaller than a six-penny piece, and 'notwithstanding its size', he said, it 'is a composition of taste, and on the whole, is the finest jewel a Lady can wear'. Launy was selling the ring watch second-hand for $300, 'only a little more than half its first cost'.[15]

False watches, or *faux montres* as they were called by American jewelers, came into fashion at the end of the eighteenth century. These were cases that looked like watches but contained no works. Instead they held a miniature painting or a lock of hair. These were sometimes worn in tandem with a real watch. William Dawson, a Philadelphia jeweler, advertised *faux montres* and said he could mount miniature paintings in them 'without doing the slightest injury to the picture'.[16] Hunn & Co. advertised *faux montres* among jewelry 'Chiefly of their own Manufacturing' in 1796, when they moved from New York to Charleston.[17] In England, these were called *Fausse Montres*.[18]

12. Joan Evans, *English Jewellery from the 5th Century A.D. to 1800 (London, 1921)*, Plate B, #5, a similar chatelaine enamelled with green, white and pale blue.
13. SFP, Box 18, folder 3, SSI to ETS.
14. *City Gaz. & Dly. Advtr.* (Charleston), 5 Jan. 1796; *Fed. Gaz.* (Phila.), 15 Apr. 1797; *NY Gaz. & Gen. Advtr.*, 17 Oct. 1801.
15. *N-Y Evening Post*, July 1802.
16. *Pa. Packet*, 26 Apr. 1793.
17. *Charleston City Gaz. and Advtr.*, 10 Dec. 1796.
18. Tait, I, p. 86.

Societal Jewelry

Cincinnati

America's most important piece of historic jewelry is the Diamond Eagle of the Society of the Cincinnati (Colour Plate 73). This illustrious Society was formed on 10 May 1783, at Newburgh-on-the-Hudson, as the Revolutionary army was preparing to disband. The officers who had served under George Washington agreed to form a society to perpetuate their friendship and to assist each other after they separated and returned to civilian life. They took their name from Lucius Quintus Cincinnatus, the Roman general. When his country called, Cincinnatus had left his farm, led his army to victory and then returned to his agricultural pursuits, refusing the honours the Senate wanted to shower on him. The parallel with George Washington was unmistakable. Washington was unanimously elected President General of the new-born Society.

The Society selected their emblematic devices at the first meeting. Cincinnatus was pictured receiving a sword from three senators. A plough was nearby and in the background his wife stood at the door of their house. The reverse side of the emblem showed a rising sun, open gates to a city, vessels entering the port, and the figure of Fame crowning Cincinnatus with a wreath. Major Pierre Charles L'Enfant was chosen to create the design. It was his idea to take the shape of the medal from the bald eagle of the newly chosen Great Seal of the United States, with the Society's heraldic devices borne on its body. He recommended that the body of the eagle be gold. The head and tail should either be made of silver, enamelled or set with diamonds, since the bald eagle is distinguished from all others by its white head and tail. His design accepted, L'Enfant made watercolour sketches (Colour Plate 74) of the eagle for each of the State Societies. Washington charged L'Enfant with seeing to the execution of the design in France when he arrived there in December 1783.[1]

Lafayette and the other officers of the French army and navy, who had served in the American Revolution, had been invited to join the Order and to form a branch of the Society in France. The French naval officers presented George Washington with the Diamond Eagle (Colour Plate 73). In their letter of presentation dated 26 February 1784, the officers, represented by the Count d'Estaing, asked the President to accept this American eagle, the symbol of Liberty.[2]

Richly set with diamonds, some of which were one and a half carats in weight, with emeralds and rubies studding the laurel wreath, Washington's Diamond Eagle is believed to have been made by Nicholas-Jean Francastel, master goldsmith in Paris. The medallions bearing the Society's emblems were beautifully enamelled in bright colours. The eagle was suspended from a military trophy of crossed flags and cannons which in turn hung from a loop set with large diamonds. When Washington died in 1799, the inventory of his estate included 'one diamond Eagle' estimated at $387 and 'three gold Cincinnati Eagles' worth $30. At Mrs. Washington's request, the Diamond Eagle in its original red morocco case was given to Washington's successor as President General of the Society, Alexander Hamilton, and subsequently became permanently attached to the office of the Society's President General.

The gold eagles made for the original members of the Society were cast by Duval and finished by Francastel (Plate 80). On 5 May 1784, Duval, gold medallist and engraver in Paris, charged the Society four Louis each for the forty-one Eagles.[3]

1. Edgar Erskine Hume, 'General George Washington's Eagle of the Society of the Cincinnati', *The Numismatist XLVI*, No. 12, Dec. 1933, pp. 749-59.
2. Hume.
3. Documents preserved by the Society of the Cincinnati, Washington, DC.

Benjamin Franklin was in France at the time and saw the medals. He thought that they were 'tolerably done'. Not everyone agreed. Some found fault with the inelegant and incorrect Latin inscriptions. They thought that if the universities could not produce better students, the mottos should have been in English. Others objected to the name of the Society, since only a few officers like Washington had served without pay. As to the bald eagle, there were those who thought the Eagles looked more like turkeys. Franklin said he would rather have seen the turkey as the national symbol than the eagle. After all, he said, the turkey was found in no other country, and even if turkeys were a little vain and silly, they still had a better character than the eagle.

Jefferson and Adams expressed concern that an attempt was being made to form a hereditary aristocracy since membership in the Society was based on primogeniture. To them it smacked too much of nobility for a newly established democratic republic. Others complained that those who were not 'embellish'd with a broach' would be unfairly marked. Washington took these criticisms seriously. He refrained from wearing his Eagle publicly and did not have it included in his many portraits.[4]

The gold Eagles purchased by the founding members of the Society of the Cincinnati have been passed from generation to generation, usually from father to son, along with their membership in the Society. Some still have their original blue watered-silk ribbons, two inches wide, edged in white, from which they were suspended. The Eagle's head and tail were enamelled in white, as was the inscription, and the medallions were enamelled in colours.

To the officers of the Revolution, the Eagles were the equivalent of the Golden Fleece emblems of European nobility. Many of them had portraits painted in which they proudly displayed their Eagles. The miniature portrait of Lieutenant Alexander Murray by James Peale, at the Metropolitan Museum of Art in New York, had a well-delineated Eagle suspended from his coat lapel. James Peale himself was portrayed by his brother Charles Willson Peale wearing his badge in the privacy of his studio. Charles Cotesworth Pinckney's portrait bust by William J. Coffee depicted him in military dress with the Eagle of the Cincinnati suspended from its ribbon rosette. John Trumbull's portrait bust by Robert Ball Hughes in 1834 included a carefully sculpted Eagle attached to his toga!

In normal dress, the ribbon was passed through the buttonhole in the lapel and held in place by a bar pushed through the gold ring affixed at the top end of the ribbon. The original ribbons included a rosette at the top made of the same French silk. Washington's Eagle retained its generous, pleated rosette made of three diminishing circles of striped-edge ribbon, centred with a covered button.[5] The pattern of the watered silk and its original rich blue colour can be clearly seen in Ralph Earl's portrait of Captain John Pratt.[6] Gilbert Stuart portrayed Major General Henry Dearborn in 1812 with his Eagle suspended from double bows formed of the ribbon.

The French Eagles were completed early in 1784. By December, Philadelphia jeweler Jeremiah Andrews took pleasure in informing the members of the Cincinnati that he had made a number of medals and that many of the Society's members felt his were superior to the imported Eagles. He took orders for medals at both his shop and the shop of jeweler Isaac Wagster in Baltimore. Two months later, Andrews called on George Washington and showed him one of the Eagles he had made, in the hope that the members of the Society would be encouraged to buy the medals from him. Several years later Andrews travelled to Georgia where he stopped in Savannah and in Augusta, selling Eagles and other jewelry. By the autumn of 1789 he advertised

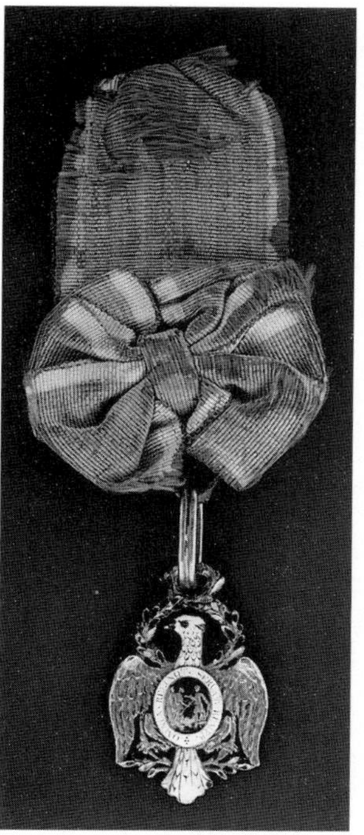

Plate 80. George Washington's Gold Eagle, the membership badge of The Society of the Cincinnati, cast by the French medallist and engraver Duval in Paris in the spring of 1784 and embellished by Nicholas-Jean Francastel, master goldsmith. Made for each of the forty-one original members of the Society. By December Jeremiah Andrews, a Philadelphia jeweler, advertised that he had made some of these medals and could supply members with them. Length 1¹⁄₁₆in., width 1in. Photograph by Adams Studio Inc. Museum of the Society of the Cincinnati, Anderson House, Washington, D.C.

4. Hume; John Bigelow, *The Complete Works of Benjamin Franklin, VII*, 444-5. Garry Wills, *Cincinnatus*, pp. 140-142. The Cincinnati member's eagle appears inWashington's portrait by Edward Savage, 1790 (at the Fogg Art Museum, Harvard University, Cambridge, Mass.). However, considering the large number of Washington portraits, the gold eagle is conspicuous by its absence.
5. Hume, pp. 53-54.
6. Tillou adv. *Antiques*, Jan. 1980, p. 117.

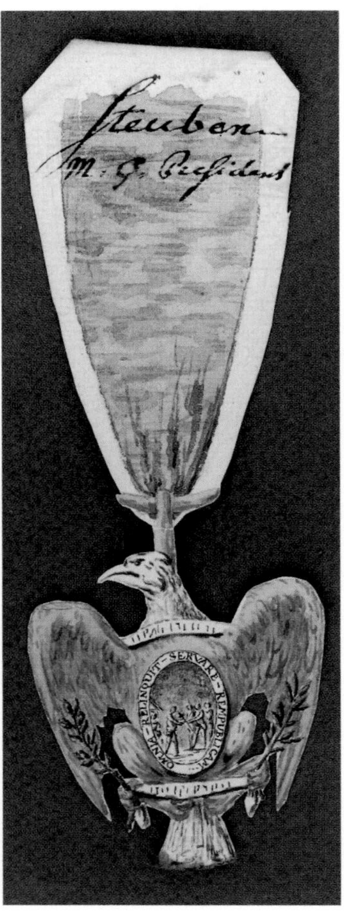

Colour Plate 73. Right. Diamond Eagle of the Society of the Cincinnati, presented to George Washington, President General, by the French naval officers of the Society on 26 February 1784. A trophy of crossed cannon and flags set with diamonds attaches the Eagle to the pendant loop. The medal is set with emeralds and rubies, four diamonds about 1½ carat each, five about 1 carat, in addition to numerous smaller diamonds. It is believed to have been made by Nicholas-Jean Francastel, Parisian master goldsmith. Length 3in. Photograph by Adams Studio Inc. Museum of the Society of the Cincinnati, Anderson House, Washington, D.C.

Colour Plate 74. Far right. Watercolour sketch of the member's medal of the Society of Cincinnati, painted in 1783-84. The emblem on the obverse side shows Cincinnatus receiving a sword from three Senators, with his wife standing by the door of their house. The design was created by Major Pierre Charles L'Enfant, French engineer and member of the Society. Length 5in., width 1$\frac{9}{16}$in. Photograph by Adams Studio Inc. Museum of the Society of the Cincinnati, Anderson House, Washington, DC.

'Three only of the Eagles of Cincinnati, with the proper ribbon, remain unsold, of American make', and by January he was down to one.[7]

The next generation of members was supplied by jeweler John Cook of New York who not only manufactured the Gold Eagle of the Society but also imported a bolt of the Society ribbon which he sold either with the medals or by the yard to those whose ribbons were frayed. Cook asked that all orders be placed by 1 May 1802 in order to be finished in time for 4th of July festivities.[8]

Military Decorations

Gentlemen of the Federal period had few ways of wearing jewelry. The dictates of fashion restricted them to cuff-links, studs, buttons, buckles, stickpins, rings, watches and fobs. The only recourse for non-royalty who longed for extravagant dress lay in choosing a military career and winning medals. In the half-century after independence was declared, the form of military dress became increasingly elaborate Colour Plate 75). In each major city there were jewelers who specialized in providing military accoutrements.

In Boston, Ebenezer Moulton sold fancy sword hilts of silver and gilt, silver-mounted or plated hangers, plated scabbards, sword blades, silver and gold lace, cord, epaulettes, tassels and sword knots.[9] Thomas Fletcher's military stock included plumes and counter straps in addition to epaulettes, sword knots, tassels, vellum lace and Prussian binding.[10]

Prior to the Revolution, most swords were imported, although eighteenth century American silversmiths occasionally made silver hilts for these weapons. Swords made after the adoption of the Great Seal of the United States often had silver eagles' heads

7. *Md. Journal, or Balto. Advtr.*, 17 Dec. 1784; George Washington, *Diary*, cited by Buhler, *Mount Vernon Silver*, pp. 46-7; George B. Cutten, *The Silversmiths of Georgia, together with Watchmakers & Jewelers*, p. 69.
8. *N-Y Evening Post*, 11 March 1802.
9. Inventory of Moulton's estate, 1824, Docket #19011, Essex Co. Probate Court, Salem, Mass.
10. *Col.Cent.*, 9 Nov. 1808.

on the pommels. While Ephraim Brasher is believed to have set at least one sword handle with amethyst eyes in a dog's head pommel, it was not until the Civil War that lavishly bejewelled American swords became the officer's mark of great distinction.[11]

Eagles adorned hats as well as swords and other military accoutrements. John Cook & Co. of New York advertised that he had a newly designed die for striking silver eagles for American cockades.[12] These were to be worn as badges in place of the more common rosettes and knots on cocked hats with wide upturned brims.

Epaulettes provided richness to military dress. In 1796, yellow and white epaulettes were made by Marcus Merriman of New Haven, Connecticut, and could be bought for two to five dollars.[13] James Jack's gold and silver epaulettes were imported from London to Philadelphia and were correspondingly more costly, but there was a wide range in price from four to eighteen dollars. He carried officers' sashes and sword knots to go with silver-mounted, gilt or plated swords.[14]

Colour Plate 75. A fifth-generation Louisianian, Antoine Jacques Philippe de Marigny de Mandeville (1811-1890) served as an officer in the French army. His portrait by Jean Joseph Vaudechamp in 1833 illustrates the variety of military regalia provided by jewelers, from epaulettes, braid and buckles to swords. Length 46in., width 35in. Louisiana State Museum, Purchase gift of the Friends of the Cabildo.

After the War of 1812, the officers' uniforms became more extravagant. Red and white wings, belt plates and mountings, and cockades added flourishes to dark uniforms.[15] A star made of silver and gold thread or plated metal decorated the front of the coat collar and the top of the epaulette. The lines of buttons an officer had to have sewn on his coat became ever longer and more superfluous. Buttons, like belt buckles, were stamped with insignia identifying United States army and navy men.

Phi Beta Kappa

The Phi Beta Kappa Society was organized at the College of William and Mary in Williamsburg, Virginia, on 5 December 1776. Its purpose was to honour academic achievement. A small square silver medal was designed to be worn by its members. The medal was engraved with the initials SP, for Societas Philosophiae, below which was added the date of the establishment of the Society. On the other side were engraved the Greek initials standing for Phi Beta Kappa, with a hand in the lower right corner pointing to three stars in the upper left corner. The stars represented friendship, morality and literature (i.e. learning).

One of the original medals of the Society was owned by Peyton Short and was subsequently given by his great-grandson to the College of William and Mary. Elisha Parmalee, a graduate of Yale, was made an honorary member of Phi Beta Kappa while he was living in Virginia in 1780. When he returned to New England he brought with him two medals and two charters so that branches of the Society could be instituted at Yale, 1780, and Harvard, 1781 (Plate 81) While most of the medals were made of silver, or occasionally gold, the medal owned by the Reverend E.D. Griffin, Yale 1790, was made of brass. Instead of having an integral round suspension loop, Griffin's medal had an oval ring attached to the top and was embellished with a swag of husks.

The Yale chapter was responsible for changing the Phi Beta Kappa medal into a

11. Harold L. Peterson, *The American Sword 1775-1945*, pp. 30-31.
12. *The N-Y Gaz.*, 30 June 1798.
13. Peterson, *Am. Sword*, p. 5.
14. *Fed. Gaz.* (Phila.), 27 Nov. 1797; Prime II, p. 123.
15. MS. account of Military Stock bought from John J. Low of Boston by jeweler William Fenno of Worcester, 1824-27, AAS.

Plate 81. Phi Beta Kappa medals, obverse and reverse, owned by members Zechariah Howard (above) and Benjamin Pickman (below), Harvard Class of 1784. Width 1in. Courtesy of Alpha Chapter, Harvard University.

watch key. Ebenezer Leonard's 1798 silver medal had a stem added at the top with a swivel and ring attached. In 1806 Nathaniel Chauncey's gold insignia had developed into a key with the addition of a stem for winding a watch attached to the base. In some cases the owner's name, college and class were engraved on the key. Harriet Beecher Stowe's brother Edward was elected to Phi Beta Kappa in 1819 and desired a watch chain for his key which his family could ill afford. His father Dr. Lyman Beecher cautioned him against foppery.[16]

The Harvard chapter continued the original design of the medal, but used the date of the chapter's founding instead of that of the Society. After 1820 the Harvard medals had heavier moulded edges on thicker cast medals and attached rings. Raised roman letters were substituted for the previously engraved script, and panels were incorporated on which the names of the owners could be engraved. It was not until the end of the nineteenth century that the Harvard chapter substituted gold keys for silver medals. With minor variations, such as the number of stars representing the number of active Alpha chapters, medals and then keys were accepted by each of the chapters of Phi Beta Kappa as they were instituted.

The jewelers who made these various medals and keys are as yet unidentified in most cases. However, in 1831 the chapter at Brown University paid Franklin Richmond, a jeweler and watchmaker in Providence $2.95 each for making fourteen medals or keys for the Alpha of Rhode Island founded in July of that year. Subsequent keys were engraved by George W. Babcock and showed much greater initiative on the part of the members of the Rhode Island chapter by introducing local details such as the state seal, the federal eagle and a seashell.[17]

Medals

The Phi Beta Kappa Society medal set a precedent for other nascent societies at colleges and schools where similar forms of member's medals were designed. For example, in Maine, Bowdoin College's Peucinian Society, organized in 1805 to promote literature and friendship, had a little bib-shaped medal with its symbol of pine trees engraved on one side.[18] In turn, a similarly shaped medal was made to honour students who excelled in their studies at the Portland Academy (Plate 82, top). Distinctive sunburst medals were presented to students in the private school kept by the Misses Dupee (Plate 82, middle two). All of these medals were probably produced by a jeweler in Portland, where other silver wares were characteristically decorated with the same wigglework borders.

Awards of merit became very popular during the Federal period. A silver medal was presented in 1791 to Joseph Johnson for being the best Latinist in his class at the College of Charleston, South Carolina. This medal bears its maker's mark which is unusual. Most are the work of unknown jewelers.[19] Exceptionally well documented is the gold medal presented to young Victorine du Pont, daughter of Eleuthere Irenée du Pont of Wilmington, Delaware, when she was attending Mrs. Rivardi's Seminary in Philadelphia in 1807 (see Plate 92). Her father had proudly written to a relative, 'she is Madame Rivardy's best pupil; every month her name is at the head of her class in every subject, though there are pupils who are much older and have been in school longer than she, and I have no doubt that next month that she has earned the school's first prize'.[20] The medal was engraved with a victory wreath and the motto 'Desert Rewarded' on one side and on the reverse with her name in a banner and a hand holding the scales of Justice. The engraver of her medal, Francis Shallus, also decorated Masonic jewels .

16. Forrest Wilson, *Crusader in Crinoline*, (Phila., London, NY, 1941) pp. 54, 59.
17. William T. Hastings, *The Insignia of Phi Beta Kappa* (Washington, D.C., 1964, 1968).
18. Laura F. Sprague, *Agreeable Situations*, Fig. 123.
19. The mark is ascribed to John Kershaw, working in Charleston, c.1789-91. Burton, p. 101.
20. Fales, *ASWM*, #63.

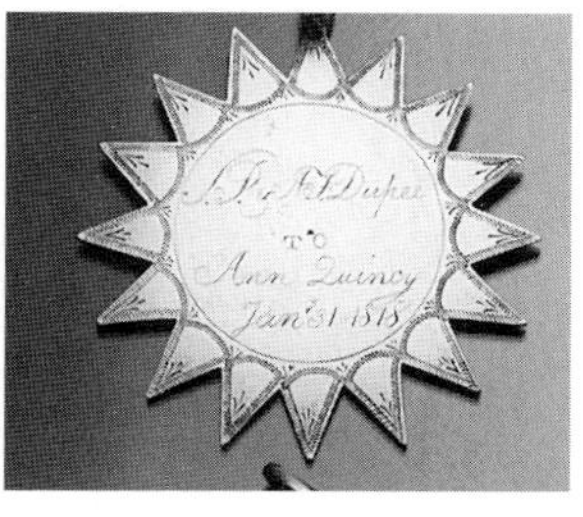

Plate 82. *Silver school medals, three of which were awarded to members of the Quincy family, Portland, Maine, 1818, by the Misses Dupee (middle two) and by the Portland Academy (top). The octagonal medal (bottom) was awarded in 1822 by the Boston Latin School to E. Deblois for a translation. Photograph by Peter J. Theriault. Private Collection.*

Boston Latin School, an intermediary public school established by 1635 for qualified students between the ages of nine and seventeen, used silver medals to encourage excellence on the part of its students (Plate 82, bottom). Benjamin Franklin established a fund when he died in 1790 to provide silver medals for distribution to students at the equally venerable Boston Grammar School. The rewards were presented for skill in reading and writing. It became customary for the recipients to be invited to have dinner at Faneuil Hall with the Mayor, Aldermen and School committee. In 1822 the female students were given equal rights to medals at the School.[21]

Organizations apart from academia began to distribute medals honouring excellence. In 1820 the Massachusetts Charitable Mechanic Association awarded three silver medals for the best work exhibited by apprentices. The Maine Charitable Mechanic Association began awarding medals in 1826 on a regular basis (Colour Plate 76). Made by Charles Farley and engraved by D.G. Johnson of Portland, their marks of achievement were also presented to the most skilful of apprentices.

Humane societies honoured acts of kindness and heroism in a similar fashion. In 1812, the Merrimack Humane Society of Newburyport, Massachusetts, presented a gold medal which graphically illustrates the comical heroism of old William Coombs who cast vanity aside, threw off his wig and plunged into the Merrimack River to save a drowning boy.[22]

Masonic

After the Revolution, fraternal societies such as Freemasonry, which had been introduced into the colonies about 1730, began to flourish. Due to the ritualistic nature of Freemasonry, a whole body of symbols was selected and was basic to the organization and the teachings of the order. These symbols appeared on their membership certificates, their regalia, the walls of their meeting places and on their medals or jewels. At the same time, these emblems helped popularize concepts of the Enlightenment and played a part in the dissemination of the ideals that led to the Revolution and the establishment of a new form of government based on natural rights and equality.

Because Freemasonry developed out of craft guilds, many of its symbols represented the tools of the stonemasons, such as the trowel used for spreading the cement to unite a building; the square representing virtue; the level, equality; and the plumb, uprightness. The chisel, which represented the benefits of discipline and education, could be explained with a gemmological simile: 'The mind, like the diamond in its original state, is rude and unpolished; but as the effect of the chisel on the external coat soon presents to view the latent beauties of the diamond; so education discovers the latent virtues of the mind and draws them forth'.[23]

Architectural principles were used to explain truth, beauty, nature and reason through lasting examples of stonemasonry, such as the images of pyramids, temples and cathedrals, and reflected the current interest in classical architecture. The ionic, doric and corinthian orders symbolized for the Masons the attributes of wisdom, strength, and beauty. The entrance to King Solomon's temple was suggested by a pair of pillars supporting globes, and the floor of the temple was represented by black and white tiles symbolizing good and evil. Mathematical and scientific principles contributed to Masonic devices such as the letter G for geometry. To all of these were added religious, heraldic, and philosophical symbols, providing a rich panoply for the jewels that were part of the Freemason's regalia.[24]

In 1762 silver brooches set with stones especially for Freemasons had been imported

21. Abel Bowen, *Bowen's Picture of Boston*, 3rd ed. (1838) pp. 29-33.
22. John J. Currier, *History of Newburyport, Mass.*, II, 130-131 (Newburyport, Mass., 1909).
23. Scottish Rite Masonic Museum of our National Heritage, *Masonic Symbols in American Decorative Arts*, pp. 9-13, 17-39; Alan Gowans, 'Freemasonry and the neoclassic style in America', *Antiques* (Feb. 1960), pp. 172-175.
24. Gowans. The emblems of the Lodge of Free Masons of New York were stolen in 1737 and included among them were a small silver square, a level, a plumb, rule and pen, insignia of the Master, Wardens and Secretary. *N-Y Wkly Journal*, 14 Nov. 1737.

Colour Plate 76. Right. Silver medal awarded by the Maine Charitable Mechanics Association in Portland to John W. Smith for the second best boot in their exhibition of 1826. Made with an integral pendant loop. Marked at top FARLEY in rectangle with an eagle in oval on each side, for Charles Farley (1791-1877) of Portland. Diameter 3in. Maine Historical Society.

Colour Plate 77. Far right. Masonic emblem originally owned by Captain Bartol of Portland, Maine, probably acquired abroad, c.1800. Diameter 3in. Maine Historical Society.

Plate 83. Below. Set of silver medals for Masonic officers, made by Paul Revere (1735-1818), of Boston, for the Washington Lodge in Roxbury, Massachusetts, in 1796. Photograph by David Bohl, Boston. Washington Lodge, A.F. & A.M., Lexington, Massachusetts.

from London and offered for sale in Annapolis, Maryland. However, the jewels were more often made locally. The sale of a Freemason's medal was the subject of the first entry in Paul Revere's extant account books.[25] At first, only the Masters and Wardens of each Masonic Lodge were adorned with jewels suspended from white ribbons, but gradually each officer acquired a different jewel.

By the end of the eighteenth century, Paul Revere, himself a Mason, was making complete sets of jewels such as those made for the Washington Lodge in Roxbury, Massachusetts, chartered in 1796 (Plate 83). The Master's jewel was in the form of a square. A level was the emblem worn by the Senior Warden and a plumb by the Junior Warden. The Treasurer was represented by crossed keys, the Secretary by crossed pens, the Chaplain by a Bible, the Stewards by cornucopias, and the Tyler by crossed swords. After the Revolution, the American Lodges began to develop their own vocabulary and devices. Revere added to the Masters' and Wardens' emblems a sunburst of sixteen rays pointing to the sixteen oval links in the surrounding chain, symbolizing the new nation of sixteen states, Tennessee having been admitted as the sixteenth state in the same year that the Washington Lodge was chartered.

Former Masters of Masonic Lodges were given the Past Master's jewel designed with a quadrant conjoined with an open compass. These were often embellished with elaborate settings made of pastes or precious gems. An example set with a green paste at the top of the silver compass had an additional medal suspended between compass legs. The medal part, probably imported from France, was cast ormolu with a bowknot at the top and set with green, blue, white, and yellow pastes. The American-made quadrant supporting the medal was veneered on top with gold and marked on the back with the maker's name, Jenkins.[26]

During the Federal period Masons occasionally had personal jewels made, often to commemorate their initiation, and designed to suit their owner's preference. In the mid-eighteenth century, a faction developed within the Freemasons with degrees of the Mark Lodge and Royal Arch Masonry. This gave rise to Mark jewels consisting of an individualistic design. The Mark jewels were usually round or shield shaped and were engraved with the initials HTWSSTKS, referring to the Hiramic legend which was part of the ritual. Samuel Cabot, a Boston merchant, became a Master Mason while he was in Paris. His gold Mark jewel (Plate 84, left), presumably made in Paris, was engraved on one side with his name and the designation of his French Lodge. On the reverse was his personal rebus, the arms of Cabot: three chabots (sculpins) with a scallop shell crest. Lockwood N. DeForest, a member of Jerusalem Chapter No. 13 in Bridgeport, Connecticut, had a silver Mark jewel engraved with his emblem, a three-masted schooner under sail flying a pennant and an American flag (Plate 84, top).

Colour Plate 78. Silver crowns, similar to those presented by the French in Canada, were occasionally distributed to Indian leaders in the district of Maine. Crosses dangle from the top of the crown and primitive wriggle-work patterns and piercing cover the surface. Photograph courtesy of Maine Humanities Council Resources. Collections of the Bangor Historical Society.

Plate 84. Masonic and school medals. (Top) Silver medal, 1826, owned by Lockwood N. De Forest, Jerusalem Chapter No. 13, 8 June 1826. Unusual central design of sailing vessel with engraver's name C. Foote below. (Below) Gold medal with elaborately engraved vignettes containing Masonic devices. Inscribed for Noah S. Bagley, Rittenhouse Chapter, No. 11. (Left) Gold Mark Mason medal obtained by Samuel Cabot while he was in Paris and attending Loge No. 2. Bears the Cabot arms on one side (three chabots, a rebus for Cabot). (Right) Gold school girl medal, c.1825, engraved with a piano and awarded for 'Progress on Music'. Photograph by Peter J. Theriault. Private Collection.

More unusual were the Masonic jewels that were composed of complicated designs crafted out of wax, gold wire, tiny pearls and other materials and set into a pendant shaped like a watch (Colour Plate 77, right). Captain Bartol of Portland, Maine, owned such a jewel about 1800.[27] Another Masonic sea captain, Samuel Doten of Plymouth, Massachusetts, wore a Masonic stickpin when he posed for his portrait.[28]

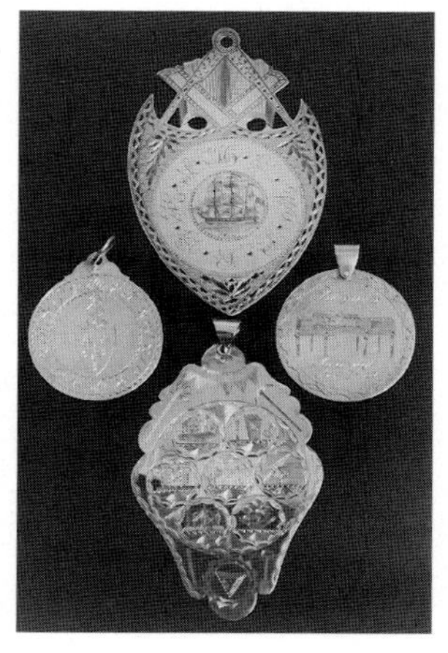

Jewelry for Indians

The Indians constituted one of the most troubling problems facing President Washington upon his inauguration in 1789. The government was eager to establish control over the situation. As a gesture symbolic of transferred loyalties, the government offered to exchange new United States medals for medals that the Indians had received previously from other governments.[29]

Great importance was attached to these medals by the Indians, not just as indications of their allegiance, but because they were sometimes regarded as amulets that would protect them from danger and illness. Because the medals were presented on special occasions, often marking important conferences or the signing of treaties, and because they were presented only to chiefs and other important men, a value was assigned to them that continued after the death of the recipient. If they were not buried with the original owner, they were passed on and treasured by worthy successors.

The first presidential medal was issued in 1789 (Plate 85). It was engraved on one side with the Great Seal of the United States, with thirteen stripes on the shield, thirteen arrows in the left talon of the eagle and thirteen stars above. On the other side, an Indian, with feathered headdress and draped blanket, discarded his tomahawk to accept the peace pipe passed to him by Minerva, representing America.[30] Subsequent designs for these medals took into consideration Indian concepts of government. The figure of Washington was substituted for Minerva in deference to Indian chiefs who had never heard of Minerva and who would have found the idea of a woman placed in a high position offensive.

25. *Md. Gaz.*, 11 Nov. 1762. PR Ledgers, 3 Jan. 1761, MHS.
26. In a private collection.
27. A similar Masonic jewel was advertised in *Antiques*, Jan. 1984, p. 63. It was engraved on the back 'RWM 1802 Swan Tavern – 5'.
28. *Antiques*, June 1975, p. 1048. The artist Charles Delin who was working in the Netherlands in the early 19th century painted many portraits of American ship captains while they were in that area on business.
29. Bauman L. Belden, *Indian Peace Medals Issued in the United States 1789-1889*, pp. 5-29. The English government had done the same thing after taking Canada from the French when it substituted English Indian medals for the French.
30. See Francis Paul Prucha, *Indian Peace Medals in American History* (Madison, Wis., 1971).

Plate 85. George Washington peace medal, silver, presented in 1789. Attributed to Joseph Richardson, Jr., of Philadelphia, and perhaps engraved by James Smither, Jr. Length 5¼in., width 4⅛in. Winterthur Museum.

Plate 86. Above. Osage warrior, portrayed by Charles Févret de Saint Memin, c.1795. The Indian wears a silver arm band and elaborate ear decorations. Winterthur Museum.

Plate 87. Right. String of six silver gorgets worn as a breast ornament by a Choctaw Mississippi native. One of the gorgets is marked by Charles A. Burnett who was working in Alexandria and Georgetown, near Washington, D.C. from 1785 to 1845. Length 6in. between joints (bottom). Museum of the American Indian.

Plate 88. Silver arm band made c.1815 for the Penobscot Indian trade by Zebulon Smith (1786-1865) whose mark Z. SMITH in serrated rectangle appears on the inside edge. Smith migrated from Ipswich, Massachusetts, to Bangor and Ellsworth, Maine. The zig-zag designs and pierced work are typical of jewelry made for Indians in northern Maine and the south-eastern part of Canada, around Montreal and Quebec. Height 5⁵⁄₁₆in., length 9⅝in. Yale University Art Gallery, The Mabel Brady Garvan Collection.

The 1792 medals depicted Washington offering the pipe to an Indian already wearing an oval medal, arm and wrist bands, and pendant earrings. However, the artist also endowed the Indian with ostrich plumes instead of the stiff feathers of native birds that were traditionally worn. Ostrich feathers were only occasionally imported for presentation to the Indians who valued them greatly. This design, with two intertwined trees and a ploughman tilling the field, became the model for the presidential medals of 1793 and 1795. Some of these medals were marked by Joseph Richardson, Jr., of Philadelphia, whose father had made Indian jewelry forty years earlier (see Plate 30).

The presidential medals were simply made, cut out of sheets of rolled silver, to which was soldered a thin rim and a suspension ring. The engraving was executed in a hasty and repetitious way. Because of the large quantities of Indian jewelry ordered by the federal government, these medals and other ornaments became the first jewelry in the United States to be mass-produced on a large scale. Joseph Richardson, Jr., sublet some of his production of Indian jewelry to other silversmiths working in the area, such as John B. Dumoutet and William Gethen. Dumoutet had 1,000 oz. of sterling Indian ornaments for sale on 7 November 1800.[31]

Richardson's accounts suggest that specialists were employed also to do the engraving, thereby dividing the labour for greater efficiency and economy. In 1795, Richardson paid engraver James Smither, Jr., more than £600 for work done by him, some of which may have been for monograms and decoration of Richardson's domestic productions as well as Indian jewelry. In 1796, Richardson billed the government for thirty pairs of arm bands, sixty pairs of wrist bands, thirty-six gorgets, 360 brooches, 114 ear bobs – a total of 690 items, of which 216 were engraved with eagles. The eagles on the arm bands and gorgets cost two shillings each to engrave, while the wrist-band eagles only cost one shilling threepence each.[32] In other cases Richardson made hair pipes and finger rings as well.

While the Washington presidential medals were hand made for the most part, subsequent presidential medals were made of two silver shells struck from dies and then soldered together with a collar. A suspension loop was added at the top.[33] On one side was a profile, half-length bust of Thomas Jefferson with his inaugural date 1801. The reverse displayed a pair of clasped hands, a universal gesture of friendship and trust. On the Indian's wrist was a beaded band emblazoned with the United States eagle and on the other wrist, the cuff of a military officer. Many of these medals were taken by Lewis and Clark on their expedition from 1804 to 1806 and distributed as they crossed the country from St. Louis to the Pacific. This general design was repeated for presidential medals by subsequent administrations until 1889.

Plate 89. A silver crown serves as a hat band for Sarah Molasses, daughter of John Neptune, Lieutenant Governor of a Penobscot Indian tribe living near Bangor, Maine. In addition to the silver ring, round brooches, a cross, ear bobs and other trade jewelry, Sarah Molasses wore bead necklaces and two distinctive strung bead collars. Her portrait was painted in 1825 by Jeremiah Pearson Hardy (1800-1887) of Bangor. Length 31in., width 31in. Photograph courtesy of Maine Humanities Council, Portland. Courtesy of The Tarratine Club, Bangor.

Jewelry was also presented by individuals who dealt with the Indians, sometimes as a reward for their help and sometimes to promote trade. Daniel Carrell, a Charleston jeweler offered 'a great variety of Indian work cheap and expeditious' in 1794.[34] Jeweler Michael Letourneaux, who had spent several years in Canada, in 1797 offered to supply traders and merchants in New York with ornaments that were 'adapted to the modern taste of the Indian native of the various tribes; not only in the style to gratify their vanity, but to advance a more important object to those concerned in the fur skin trade'.[35]

In 1810, the Superintendent of Indian Affairs, John Mason, ordered five thousand pieces of silver jewelry from a St. Louis silversmith named Antoine Danjen which were to be sent to the Fort Madison trading house. Included in the order were ear wheels, crosses of various sizes, finger rings, and breast brooches four inches in diameter. For the Fort Osage trading house, Mason ordered earbobs for fifteen cents a pair and very cheap hair plates. In 1827 the Columbia Fur Company obtained silver hat bands, sets of moons, wheels in two sizes, wampum moons, and gorget sets.[36] Gorgets of this sort (Plate 87) were made by Charles A. Burnett of Georgetown, D.C. in 1820 for the Superintendent of Indian Affairs on behalf of the frontier trading stations, along with arm bands, brooches and earrings.

Ornaments made for the north-eastern Indians differed considerably from the official jewelry made for the federal government. These north-eastern examples followed the style of the Canadian-made Indian jewelry and actually were better suited to the tastes of the Indians since they bore abstract patterns executed in wigglework. Jewelry presented to the Abenaki Indians who engaged in the fur trade often had pierced geometric designs like those on an arm band made by Zebulon Smith of Bangor, Maine (Plate 88).

Circular ornaments for the north-eastern Indians were made with a single pin fastened to one side of the central opening for attachment purposes. One example clearly shows on its reverse side that it was made from a United States coin dating between 1807 and 1815.[37] Silver crowns appear to be a north-eastern Indian preference (Colour Plate 78). Such a silver crown was worn on a top hat by Sarah Molasses, a Penobscot Indian and daughter of John Neptune, the Lieutenant Governor of his tribe, living in the area of Bangor, Maine (Plate 89). Sarah wore hers around a high hat with a plume on top. Her assortment of silver circular ornaments, earbobs, and her cross intermingle with necklaces and beads in a visually revealing mixture of cultures.

31. *Phila. Gaz. & Daily Advtr.*
32. JR, Jr. Receipt Book; Ledger, 29 Oct. 1796, DMMC Winterthur.
33. Belden #15.
34. *S.C. Gaz.*, 18 Dec. 1794.
35. New York, 22 May 1797, *Time Piece; and Literary Companion;* Gottesman II, 70, #200.
36. *Antiques*, July 1958, pp. 60-61.
37. Sprague, Fig. 122.1.

Colour Plate 79. Portrait of a woman attributed to Ruth W. and Samuel A. Shute, itinerant artists who travelled to New Hampshire, Vermont and upstate New York in the 1830s taking likenesses. To accentuate the jewelry worn by the sitter, the artists cut out and applied gold foil to her earrings and the ring worn on her left index finger. Her hair combs were made of tortoiseshell. The ribbon worn around her neck to serve as a watch chain may well be made of tiny glass beads worked in a stylised floral pattern, often made by young women for loved ones. Length 25⅞in., width 19⅞in. Old York Historical Society, York, Maine.

Colour Plate 80. Portrait in miniature of 'Mumbet' (c.1742-1829), painted by Susan Sedgwick in 1811. Susan's father-in-law Judge Theodore Sedgwick of Stockbridge, Massachusetts, was instrumental in procuring Mumbet's freedom under the bill of Rights of the 1780 Massachusetts state constitution. She was the first slave to be freed in this way in the state. Thereafter she was known as Elizabeth Freeman and became a paid domestic servant of the Sedgwicks. She is shown wearing a string of gold beads subsequently remade into a bracelet (see Plate 92). Length 3in., width 2⅛in. Massachusetts Historical Society.

GOLD AND SILVER

STOLEN. '400 gold finger Rings; 8 gold miniature Setting[s]; 200 pair gold Ear-Rings; 8 gold, plain and enamelled Watches; 1 Silver Watch; 4 gold Watch Chains; 6 gold Seals; 6 gold Breast-Pins…buttons…sleeve buttons… 6 fine gold Necklaces; 6 Beaded Necklaces, set in gold,…60 feet gold chain; a number of gold Watch Chains, Lockets, and Necklaces, and 1 silver mounted Pocket-Book'.[1]

The itemized list of jewelry stolen in 1803 from Philadelphia jeweler John Bouvier presents a realistic picture of the kinds of solid gold jewelry in fashion during the Federal period and kept on hand by many jewelers in American cities. Rings were by far the most popular item, followed closely by earrings. Only a relatively small number of watches, seals, breast pins, lockets, and necklaces were kept in stock, but gold chains were available and simply cut from reels.

A nineteenth century historian remarked that in the early years of the Republic, 'The most persistent ornament was a string of gold beads, the size of peas, worn about the neck. Thirty-nine was said to be the customary number. This gave rise to

1. *Commercial Advertiser,* 1 Jan. 1803.

Colour Plate 81. Above. Gold chains were turned into earrings as well as necklaces and served to suspend lockets or watches and fobs, as this portrait of Elizabeth C. Courtney (1752-1813) bears witness. The portrait was painted by James Earl about 1795 in Charleston, South Carolina. Length 37in., width 29½in. Gift of the Lida R. and Charles H. Tompkins Foundation. Daughters of the American Revolution Museum, Washington, D.C.

Colour Plate 83. Left. Portrait of Captain Simon Forrester, Jr. (1785-1807) of Salem, Massachusetts, includes two emblems of his days at sea. A small gold anchor is worn on his shirt and a gold ring is worn in his ear. He died at sea returning from the East Indies. The portrait is attributed to port painter Charles Delin (1756-1818) of Maastricht and Amsterdam, Netherlands, c.1800-1807. Delin's other sitters wore similar emblems, including Masonic devices. Length 21in., width 17in. ©1993 Sotheby's Inc.

Colour Plate 82. Group of gold jewelry owned by the Washington family. Two rings set with pearls, with blue enamelling around central pearl (left) and central diamond (right), c.1790. Memorial ring (centre) set with hair, American, c.1860. (Below) Pair of hoop earrings, American, late 18th century. Mount Vernon Ladies' Association, Mount Vernon, Virginia.

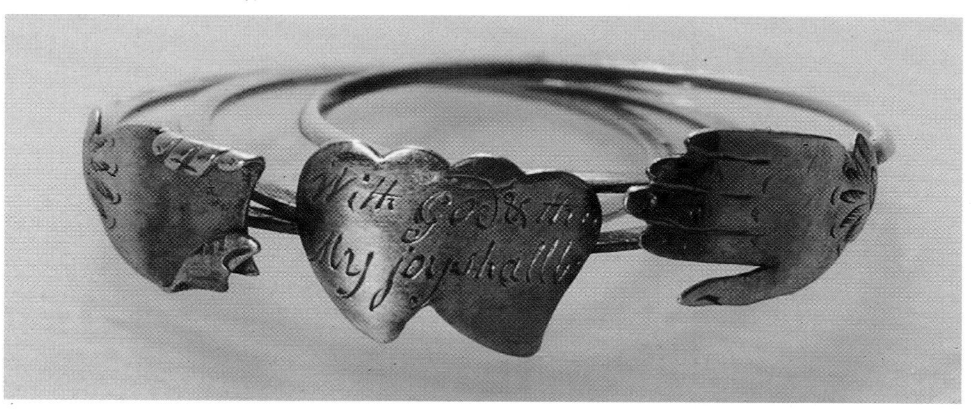

Colour Plate 84. Wedding ring made by jeweler John Vogler (w. 1803-1827) for his wife, Winston-Salem, North Carolina. Courtesy, Old Salem.

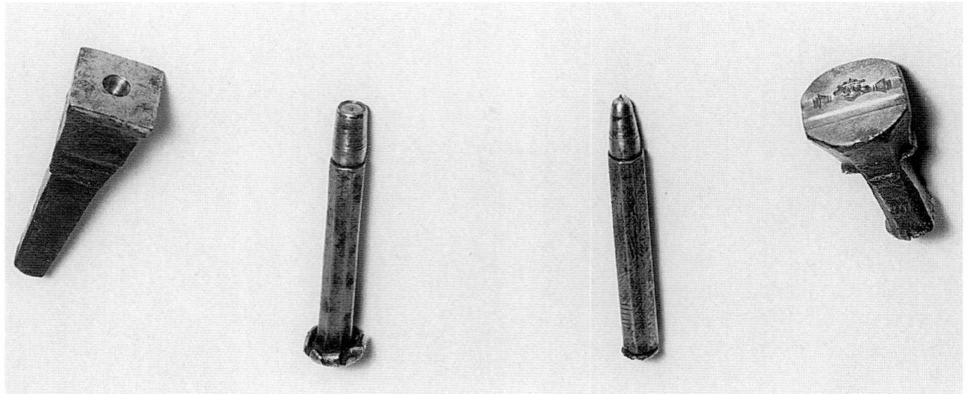

Plate 90. Tools used by Daniel Burnap of Connecticut, late 18th century, to make beads and (far right) to decorate the band of a ring. The Connecticut Historical Society.

the saying that an old woman was "so poor she hadn't a bead to her neck"'.[2] For some, gold beads represented an investment and were a means of accumulating wealth, as they still are in some areas of the world. As the standard of living rose in the United States, not only did the number of gold bead necklaces increase, but also the size of the beads grew larger as the nineteenth century progressed. The prevalence of gold beads in the portraits of American women reinforces the idea of their widespread popularity. In rural areas where the sitter wanted the viewer to know that her beads were made of real gold, the artist occasionally cut gold leaf and pasted it to the portrait so there could be no mistake (Colour Plate 79). Little girls too were given gold bead necklaces. Beads could be added as they grew older.

Any jeweler or silversmith was capable of making these hollow gold beads. Americans had been producing such necklaces in the late seventeenth century. However, by the post-Revolutionary period, the busy city jewelers had less time for this finicky work and often arranged for country colleagues with more time than customers to make the beads for them. Daniel Rogers (1735-1816), a goldsmith in Ipswich, Massachusetts, made large quantities of gold beads for a number of shops in Boston and Newburyport between 1796 and 1800.[3]

Daniel Burnap (1759-1838) of Connecticut, although a clockmaker by preference, made gold bead necklaces as well. The tools he used to make the beads (Plate 90) have survived, as has his written description of the steps taken to flatten a strip of gold, cut out rounds of metal, punch a central hole in each of them, and then hammer them up half-way, anneal them, and finally hammer them the rest of the way into half-globes that could be joined together like two hollow halves of a grapefruit.[4] By the end of the Federal period, these gold beads were being turned out by manufactories. Among the products of Newburyport, Massachusetts, gold beads represented a significant part of the forty to fifty-thousand dollars' worth of precious metal articles produced in 1825.[5]

Gold beads were also imported from England during this period. In 1800 John Cook & Co., jewelers in New York, had 'cut' gold beads imported from England and available in their shop. These they sold by the dozen or the gross.[6] The new fashion for cut beads referred to faceted beads shaped like cut stones. This method of finishing gold beads, chains and other flat surfaced jewelry was achieved by means of a

Plate 91. Gold beads from the necklace of Elizabeth 'Mumbet' Freeman who gave the beads before she died to Catharine Maria Sedgwick (1789-1876), daughter of Thomas Sedgwick. Miss Sedgwick had them remade about 1840 as a two-strand bracelet with gold spacers and a new gold clasp engraved with rococo revival scrolls and the name 'Mumbet'. Length 5¾in. Massachusetts Historical Society.

Plate 92. Gold cuff links attributed to James Butler, c.1760. Diameter ½in. Gold school medal by Francis Shallus, Philadelphia, c.1807. Gold beads and clasp by Samuel Casey, South Kingstown, Rhode Island, c.1765. Gold clasp by Joseph Richardson, Philadelphia, c.1765. Silver gilt Masonic medal, by William Hollingshead, Philadelphia, c.1780. Gold teaspoon by Daniel Van Voorhis, New York and New Jersey, c.1800. Winterthur Museum.

rotating lap which cut the gold away.[7] The overwhelming preference, however, was for the traditional smooth, round beads made in America. Nathaniel Vernon & Co. made a large assortment of gold beads, both cut and plain, that he warranted were made of good gold and yet much cheaper than any others sold in the city of Charleston, South Carolina.[8]

The clasps for gold necklaces changed in shape from the rounder forms of the mid-eighteenth century lockets to pointed oval or rectangular clasps of the turn of the century (Plate 92). The extensions on each side of the clasp no longer conformed to the shape of the holes drilled to receive the strands of the necklace and no longer had fillets soldered around the openings. The tops of plain gold lockets were engraved with sentimental and neo-classical motifs or with patriotic devices like the American eagle. The plaited basket of flowers and fruit was another popular design. Borders often were bright-cut, as were the edges of contemporary silver ware.

2. Weeden II, 859-60.
3. Rogers supplied Ebenezer, Joseph, and William Moulton, William Homes, Robert Evans, David Tyler, Isaac Townsend, Joseph Loring, Samuel Minott, and Samuel Davis with gold beads. Account book, Library, PEM. See also Fales, EIHC, Jan. 1965, pp. 75-84.
4. Penrose R. Hoopes, *Shop Records of Daniel Burnap, Clockmaker,* p. 117.
5. Peter Benes, *Old-Town and the Waterside,* p. 55, #31. John Cheever speaks of gold-bead factories in *Wapshot Chronicle.*
6. *Commercial Advtr.,* 3 Oct. 1800.
7. Wrigley, *The Art of the Goldsmith and Jeweller,* pp. 138-139.
8. *City Gaz. & Daily Advtr.,* 16 Oct. 1801.

Chains were widely worn as necklaces in the Federal period. Many were made to hold pendants, miniatures, or watches and fobs. Others were festooned across the throat. Both can be seen in the portrait of Mrs. Courtney of Boston (Colour Plate 81). She wore her miniature memorial scene on a long, delicate gold chain outside her collar. Her necklace was composed of swags of large links of varying sizes. Her gold earrings appear to be made of gold links of chain as well. Joseph Philips, a jeweler who had recently come to Baltimore from Paris, advertised 'Gold, gilt, and Fancy Chain Earrings' in 1791.[9]

During the Federal period, earrings were often gold hoops with a hinge to the top so that they could be fastened through pierced ears (Colour Plate 82). Plain gold hoops were worn by men as well as women. For men who went to sea there was a particular penchant for pierced ears and the wearing of earrings (Colour Plate 83). Nautical folk-lore fostered the belief that earrings would ward off evil spirits. They were permitted in the U.S. Navy until early in the twentieth century.[10] In 1903, social historian Alice Morse Earle wrote, 'It was a safe inference, until recent times, that an American man who wore ear-rings had seen the world and been round the Horn; and I am told it was as common for sea-farers (whether ship captains or supercargoes, or men before the mast) to have their ears pierced as to be tatooed'. She told of a woman who inherited her grandfather's portrait painted by Gilbert Stuart and who was so embarrassed by the earrings he was wearing that she had them painted out.[11] From the portraits of Franco-Americans painted by Saint Memin between 1798 and 1805, it would appear that the custom of wearing earrings was especially favoured by the French.

While stone knob earrings were considered old-fashioned by the end of the eighteenth century, gold knobs and drops were still available. However, the drops often were a little longer and more elaborate than the earlier examples.[12] Cut knobs were available to match the cut bead necklaces. Filigree was becoming popular for gold earrings (Plate 93). Little coils of twisted gold wire were soldered together to form a mesh set within a long narrow frame of gold. In addition to the hinge to open the earrings, a spring wire was sometimes added to create pressure and tighten the fit. In 1797, James Jacks imported filigree earrings from London, along with filigree necklaces, locket chains and rings.[13]

Gold rings were jewelers' best sellers. Many were plain gold bands, the standard wedding ring such as Mrs. Courtney wore. In Charleston, S.C., wedding rings were available either plain or cut.[14] Others were 'twist rings', that is, two bands joined together. Victorine du Pont's wedding ring was made of two thin flat bands intertwined so that by twisting they fell into place and formed a single ring (Plate 94). One band was engraved with her name and 'Novembre 1813', the date of their marriage on 9 November. The other band was engraved with her husband's name, Ferdinand Bauduy. It is thought that the individual bands were worn separately by a man and his intended and then were joined together to be worn by the bride after the marriage. These so-called 'alliance' rings were especially favoured in French-flavoured New Orleans. Characterized by the thinness of the two conjoined bands, alliance rings can be readily identified in portraits of Louisiana women throughout the *ante bellum* period (see Colour Plate 95).

By the end of the eighteenth century, 'Twist Rings with double and single Heart Stones' and gold rings with single or double hearts were offered by American jewelers from New England to Georgia see (Plate 7).[15]

9. *Md. Journal,* 4 Nov. 1791
10. In 1992, the Navy, Army and Air Force changed the policy so that earrings may be worn when these service men are in off-duty attire.
11. Earle, II, 456.
12. Isaac Davis, *Col. Cent.*, 1 April 1818.
13. *Fed. Gaz.*, 15 April 1797.
14. Michael De Bruhl, *Charleston City Gaz. & Advtr.*, 7 Aug. 1798.
15. Thomas Harland in *Connecticut Gaz.* (New London), 7 April 1796; Edward Griffith in *Columbia Museum & Savannah Advertiser,* Georgia, 12 December 1797, courtesy of MESDA.

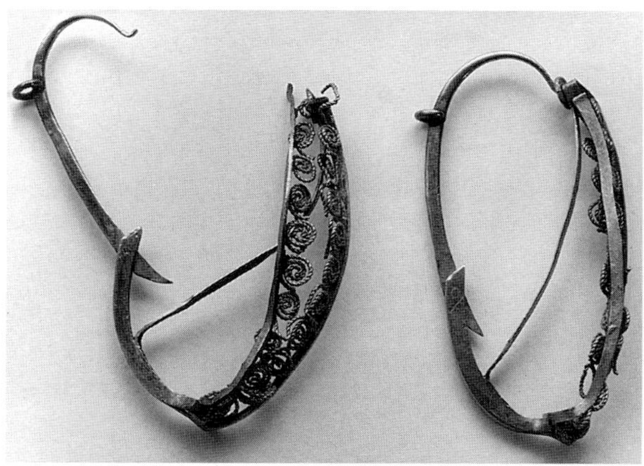

Plate 93. Gold filigree earrings worn by Victorine du Pont (1792-1861) of Wilmington, Delaware, c.1830. Probably French. Length 1¼in., width ¹¹⁄₁₆in. Winterthur Museum.

Plate 94. Gold twist wedding ring, French or American, c.1813. Engraved on one ring with name of Victorine du Pont and date November 1813 and the other with the name of her husband Ferdinand Bauduy. Diameter ²⁵⁄₃₂in. Winterthur Museum.

Heart-and-hand rings, popular in colonial America in the mid-eighteenth century, apparently went out of fashion in most of Europe during the eighteenth century. In America they became traditional forms, as they did in Ireland and elsewhere, and goldsmiths have continued to make them to the present day. John Vogler, the Moravian goldsmith working in Winston-Salem, North Carolina, about 1803 to 1827, made a charming example of a gimmel ring for his own wife in 1819 (Colour Plate 84). Inscribed underneath the hands on paired hearts was the verse, 'With God & thee/ My Joy shall be'.[16] The account book of William Fenno, a Worcester jeweler, shows that between 1824 and 1827 he sold a number of heart and hand rings, some of which he described as 'fine' and others 'coarse'.[17]

A swage used in making heart-and-hand rings is among the extant group of tools owned by Daniel Burnap (Plate 90, left). The straight gold band of the ring was placed on top of the swage which was held in a vice. It was then hammered from the top side until the die registered its engraved design on the surface. The impression could be improved by engraving or chasing. Then the ring was shaped over a ring mandrel, cut to size and soldered together.

Burnap's swage appears to have had a great deal of use but his account book records the sale of only three 'Hart in hand' rings for which he charged about 12 shillings apiece. This would suggest that he may have augmented his business by making these rings for other jewelers to sell, in the same way that he and other goldsmiths, living outside the city, wholesaled the gold beads they made to city goldsmiths.[18]

A silver spoon has survived bearing on the back of its shaft the maker's mark of George Arnold and on the back of its handle the relief impression of a heart held by two hands.[19] Arnold, an Uxbridge, Massachusetts, silversmith, who was working about 1809, obviously owned the swage and evidently produced heart-and-hand rings as well as spoons. The swage design may have been added to indicate that the spoon was a wedding present.

Gold bracelets and brooches, both imported and locally made, were frequently advertised by American jewelers. Michael Roberts of Philadelphia imported gold pins in addition to ladies' bracelets and buckles.[20] John Deverell, formerly a partner of James Dunkerley in Boston, established a manufactory there in 1788 in which he made gold bracelets and brooches as well as gold lockets, pins and rings.[21]

Buckles could be cast in moulds and therefore were easily produced in any shop. An imported buckle could be taken apart and used as the pattern to be impressed in the casting sand. Plain buckles and those set with pastes continued to be made by Federal jewelers some of whom designed their own moulds. Thomas Fletcher made cestus

16. Old Salem, North Carolina.
17. William Fenno, Account Book, AAS.
18. Hoopes.
19. Illustrated in Louise C. Belden, *Marks of American Silversmiths in the Ineson-Bissell Collection*, p.34.
20. *Indep. Journ: or the Gen. Advtr.*, 7 October 1785.
21. *Mass. Spy*, 21 Aug. 1788.

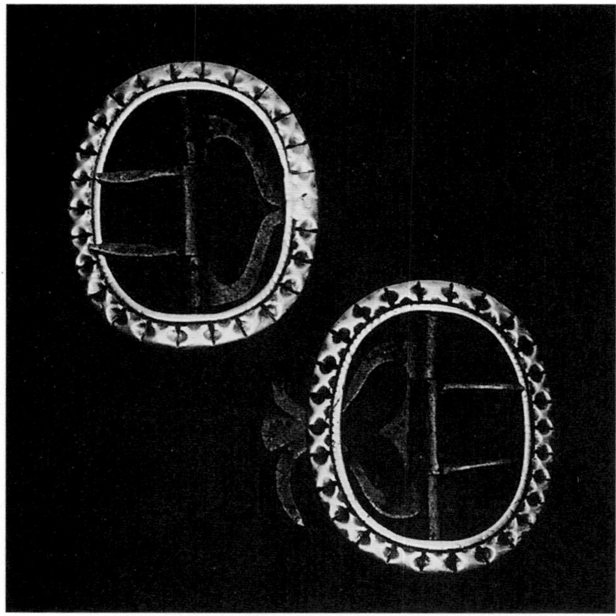

Plate 95. Pair of silver buckles made c.1785 by Timothy Gerrish (1749-1815), in Portsmouth, New Hampshire. Marked on back T•G, and engraved IP. Private Collection.

buckles of his own pattern. Some New Hampshire silversmiths specialized in making silver stock, knee and shoe buckles in the post-Revolutionary period. Of oval or rectangular shape, the buckles were often carved to look as if they were set with faceted stones (Plate 95). John Ward Gilman of Exeter left more marked examples of this kind than all the other buckles produced by his competitors, among whom were Mark Nelson, William Parker and Samuel Drowne.[22] The latter decorated his buckles with chased swags and rosettes.

While amulet and anodyne jewelry was available during the eighteenth century, it seems to have enjoyed renewed interest about 1818. Amulet earrings 'with real Fine Gold Wires and Tips' were advertised in the United States. So were sets of 'real London Amulets' made by J. & G. Richards. 'None other are genuine', a Boston jeweler cautioned. What the sets were made of is unknown, but there were necklaces, bracelets, earrings and ornaments. Also offered were amulet miniatures of Washington and Franklin.[23] The fashion travelled inland as well. Amulet earrings were advertised in Clarksville, Tennessee, the following summer.[24]

A change in the finish of gold jewelry occurred during the Federal period. The usual method of finishing had been to polish and burnish the metal to give it a soft bright lustre. With renewed interest in the antique style, a 'dead gold' finish was offered. It was a duller finish that gave the jewelry an appearance of age. In Boston, both 'burnished and dead gold Ear Hoops' were offered by Dyer & Eddy along with 'unburnished gold elastic Bracelet Bands and Neck Chains'. Davis & Brown spoke of their fine gold filigree ear hoops as being unburnished. 'Dead Gold Ear Drops and Bosom Pins' were specified by R. & H. Farnam.[25]

Gold-plated jewelry was beginning to be made early in the nineteenth century. John Hayden of Boston discovered a method of gilding metal 'with pure gold, in a superior manner'. On 28 July 1810, he announced that he made and kept on hand 'Patent BEADS for necklaces, covered with pure Gold equal in appearance and conveniency to real Gold Beads, which being made by a new process will wear a long time, and answer equally the purpose of real Gold Beads'. These Hayden claimed were the first such beads to be made in this country or elsewhere. Among those who read his advertisement was one person who was so impressed that within a week twelve strings of these patent beads were stolen from Hayden who then warned that the beads were so well executed that they would deceive any would-be purchaser. The only way to tell the difference was to test them with aquafortis.[26]

22. Parsons, *NHS*, pp. 27-30.
23. *Col. Cent.*, 28 Feb. 1818, Stoddard & Frobisher; 19 Dec. 1818, Robt. J. Brown & Co.
24. *Wkly Chron.*, 28 June 1819.
25. *Col. Cent.*, 20 Oct. 1804; 5 Jan. and 27 Feb. 1805; 1 Dec. 1810.
26. Ibid., 28 July and 4 Aug. 1810.

Plate 96. Mourning brooch made by goldsmiths Rowland Parry and James Musgrave (w. 1792-95) and hairworker Jeremiah Boone, Philadelphia, 1792. In memory of the two McConnell children whose mother Ruth is shown in mourning. Length 2¼in. Photograph courtesy of Museum of Art, Rhode Island School of Design. Collection of Daphne Farago.

JEWELERS

When John Lord Sheffield made his 1784 report, *Observations on the Commerce of the American States,* he predicted that jewelry, plate, buckles, watch chains, and the like would continue to be imported to the United States from Sheffield and Birmingham. 'In France', he said, 'they are either too costly, or too badly designed and finished, to suit the American taste; whilst the British manufacturers of these articles have so far succeeded, in uniting the solid and useful with the showy and elegant, as to have the preference, even in France'.[1] While this assessment was correct for the years immediately following the Revolutionary War, American jewelers were beginning to manufacture their own goods, frequently assuring customers that their products were equal to those of Birmingham.

Major changes were beginning to affect the American jewelry business. The influx of foreign jewelers that had begun prior to the Revolution not only continued, but increased. While some goldsmiths/jewelers had imported jewelry from England for resale before the war, many post-Revolutionary jewelers imported vast quantities from England as well as from other European sources. The diversification of wares sold by jewelers was unlimited. The jewelry store as we know it today began to appear. Furthermore, signs of the impending industrial revolution were becoming ever more apparent.

In England during the last quarter of the eighteenth century, Matthew Boulton had begun to convert the jewelry and metal trades in Sheffield and Birmingham from individual shop production to organized factory output. He developed the machinery and power for factory production. He also realized the benefit of dividing tasks among labourers and encouraged specialization in production. European artisans were brought to work in Birmingham. Boulton and others in England sought to protect their trade secrets by encouraging the passage of an act in 1785 that prohibited both the exportation of tools and the emigration of artisans.[2] Judging from the jewelers' advertisements in American newspapers of the period, this act did little to stem the tide of emigrant workers, but was undoubtedly of some help in slowing the transmitting of innovative designs in machinery. American jewelers had been hiring

1. *Observations on the Commerce of the American States* (London, 1784), p. 31.
2. Eric H. Robinson, 'Problems in the Mechanization and Organization of the Birmingham Jewelry and Silver Trades' in *Winterthur Portfolio* (1973) pp. 65-101.

English and European specialists for at least a decade before the war and, after gaining independence, continued to do so at a much greater pace.

Among the first men to attempt the establishment of a factory for making jewelry and silverware in the United States were Joseph Cooke and William Donovan of Philadelphia. Cooke, who had recently arrived from London, advertised his new wholesale and retail manufacture and commission store in August 1784. William Donovan announced the opening of his manufactory in January 1785. Donovan said he had been at great expense in bringing experienced artists from different manufacturing towns in Europe to work in his factory. He pointed out that, if this manufactory was well patronized, it would result in 'lessening the prodigious and impoverishing importations of articles in that line'.[3]

Both Cooke and Donovan emphasized the production of miniatures and hairwork. These were among the specialized jewelry items that lent themselves to the sort of factory that was based on division of labour requiring different skills. While Donovan's enterprise apparently did not last long, Cooke's was more successful. In 1786 he publicly thanked his customers for their encouragement and patronage. In addition to his 'Federal Manufactory and European Repository', in 1788 he opened a warehouse on Second Street to accommodate the large quantities of goods he was importing from Europe and England. He boasted of the number of workmen he employed. In this emporium, hairwork in any device, mourning rings and lockets, portrait and miniature painting, jewelry set with miniature painting, and engraving, could all be produced and sold. The extent of his operation can be measured by the fact that he wanted to employ an additional twenty to thirty journeymen goldsmiths, jewelers, engravers, buckle and chape makers, small workers, lapidaries, and other mechanics. He also wanted to hire a watchmaker accustomed to jobbing for repairing and cleaning watches and a foreman whose duties would include instructing apprentices. He even employed an accountant and a man who spoke different languages to help foreigners transact their business with him.

A public controversy with one of the Cooke's employees, Samuel Folwell, led to the publication in the *Pennsylvania Packet* of interesting details regarding how the factory was operated. Samuel Folwell (1764-1813), an artist from New Hampshire, was employed as a hairworker by the company about 1787.[4] Cooke said he would pay Folwell 7 shillings 6 pence per day. In comparison, the cost of the ivory on which the miniature was painted was sixpence. Folwell claimed that jewelers and silversmiths who were unable to perform hairwork themselves had to employ others who were specialists to do the work for them and then charged more than the people who did the work. Cooke claimed that he had taught Folwell everything he knew about the art, but was not impressed by the latter's abilities and so declined to continue employing him. Folwell retorted that as for Mr. Cooke being a master, Cooke knew as much about the business of a hairworker as the fabled ass knew of the lyre.[5] In an effort to circumvent the middle man and the factory system of production, Folwell opened his own shop and proclaimed himself to be the only real hairworker in Philadelphia. This assertion was quickly disputed by Cooke and two of his colleagues, Joseph Anthony and hairworker Jeremiah Boone (Plate 96).

Joseph Cooke combined with his manufactory output a line of merchandise shipped to him from Birmingham, Sheffield, London, and Europe, 'which, for beauty, elegance, fashion and taste do credit to the manufacturers, and far excel

3. *Pa. Journal*, 11 Aug. 1784; Carey's *Pa. Evening Herald*, 25 Jan. 1785.
4. Davida T. Deutsch, *Antiques*. Samuel Folwell.
5. *Pa. Packet*, 10 June 1786; 26, 29 Mar. 1788.

Plate 97. This elegant building at the corner of Third and Market Street was erected in Philadelphia in 1794 by Joseph Cooke to accommodate his expanding jewelry business and his raging ambition. Two service levels were below the ground level store and two floors above were public rooms. The upper floor and garrets were to be used by lodgers. The project soon failed when Cooke became bankrupt. This view was engraved by William Birch of Philadelphia, c.1798. Length 13in., width 11in. The Historical Society of Pennsylvania.

anything of the kind ever imported into this city'.[6] Because of his long residence in England, Cooke had connections that made it possible for the patterns of the latest fashions to be forwarded to him as soon as they appeared in Paris or London.

Cooke counted George Washington among his customers, supplying him with eight of the newly patented Argand lamps in 1793. Earlier he had sold Washington a gold watch chain, silver spoons, and silver bottle holders on wheels made in Cooke's manufactory. So delighted was Cooke with the presidential patronage that he had to be restrained from displaying Washington's arms over his shop in the manner of English firms patronized by the royal family. A forthright letter from Tobias Lear saying that the President would find such an action very disagreeable put an end to the idea.[7]

Had Cooke been endowed with fewer delusions of grandeur and greater mechanic genius, he might have become an American Matthew Boulton. However, he began building and developing real estate, to lease or sell, in the hope that it would prove profitable so that he could continue 'to beautify the city'.[8] The extravagant, seven-storey building that Cooke erected in 1794 at the corner of Third and Market Streets was a precursor of today's multi-purpose complex. There were two underground service floors, ground-level stores, two floors of public rooms, with the top floor and garrets intended for lodgers. Built under the direction of master carpenter John Butler, the structure was featured in one of the select views of Philadelphia engraved by William Birch as the city appeared about 1800 (Plate 97).

Unfortunately, Philadelphia was not quite ready for Joseph Cooke. When he could not get enough investors in his grand scheme, Cooke tried to convert the building into three houses. When this failed to attract buyers or renters, he tried a lottery with the building and jewelry as prizes. Even this did not elicit the necessary number of chance takers. In the end Cooke became bankrupt, his projected large-scale jewelry enterprise was doomed, and he disappeared into oblivion.[9]

Sporadic attempts at large scale production occurred elsewhere. Their rise and decline is typified by Daniel Van Voorhis and his associates in New York. In 1784, the same year that Cooke first opened his business in Philadelphia, the firm of Van Voorhis, Bayley and Coley advertised in New York City as 'Real Manufacturers' of

6. *Pa. Journal,* 11 Aug. 1784.
7. GW Ledger B, 18 Aug. 1787; Buhler, *M.V.S.* (Mt. V., 1957), pp. 60-62.
8. Prime II, 99-111.
9. The building was demolished in 1838. Cooke's story is documented by Prime II, 99-111 and Waters, pp. 117-118.

Plate 98 Trade card of Joseph Anthony, Jr. (1762-1814), goldsmith and jeweler in Philadelphia, c.1789. Anthony advertised miniature pictures set in lockets, devices in hair as well as mourning rings, and jewelry in the latest fashion and most elegant taste. He also bought old gold, silver and diamonds for reuse in his own production.

gold, silver and jewelry. They, too, claimed to have procured the best workmen from Europe. The following year Bayley left the firm and continued manufacturing the same products. He was also able to execute a process he called water-gilding. Van Voorhis and Coley maintained their production at Hanover Square. The partnership of Van Voorhis & Coley ended in 1787. Between 1787 and 1790, Daniel Van Voorhis exchanged work with William Verstille, a peripatetic portrait painter and miniaturist. Verstille provided Van Voorhis with devices, portraits, hairwork and cyphers. Among the devices were two used in rings purchased by Martha Washington in 1790.[10] In return, Van Voorhis supplied Verstille with settings, bracelets, lockets and glasses for lockets, breast pins and rings.

Daniel Van Voorhis continued his business as a jeweler, goldsmith and watchcase maker until 1802, with a short-lived partnership in 1791-92 with Garret Schenck.[11] Van Voorhis and Coley offered hairwork of any device, paste buckles of any pattern, and had a good lapidary especially employed to repair paste buckles. They offered to supply other jewelers, whether in the city or in the country, on very reasonable terms.[12]

Advertisements of immense quantities of imported jewelry, silver, plated wares and fancy goods peppered newspapers in major cities. England was sending a flood of goods to the United States in response to the demand caused by the euphoria of citizens starved for the luxuries denied them during the Revolution. Unlimited credit was extended to American merchants.[13]

Joseph Anthony, Jr. (1762-1814), of Philadelphia, stocked his Market Street shop with silver, plated ware, jewelry and cutlery that came directly from the English manufactories. The jewelry consisted of fancy lockets, rings, bracelets, necklaces and fancy earrings, in addition to two hundred different patterns of plated shoe and knee buckles. At the same time he produced some jewelry and silver in his own shop (Plate 98).[14]

James Jacks (w.c.1784-1822) imported English goods to his shop in Charleston, South Carolina, on an even larger scale than Joseph Anthony, if the number of inches of newspaper advertising is a valid measure. The jewelry was quite elegant: gold enamelled necklaces and earrings; and diamond bracelets, lockets, watch chains, and hoop and cluster rings. From 1797-1800 Jacks was in Philadelphia, at first and briefly in Cooke's building and then at 192 Market Street which, he was quick to point out, was next door to the President's house. Thousands of dollars of jewelry imported

10. Connecticut Historical Society *Bulletin 25,* Jan. 1960, pp. 24-31.
11. *Indep. Journal: or the Gen. Advtr.,* 18 Dec. 1784; Gottesman II, 75.
12. Ibid, 9 July, 1 Sept. 1785; Gottesman II, 76-77. Paul von Khrum, *Silversmiths of New York City 1684-1850,*, p. 132.
13. Weeden II, 818.
14. *Pa. Packet,* 7 Dec. 1790.

MANUFACTORY.

JOHN E. & LEWIS C. MICHEL, respectfully inform their friends and the public in general, that they have established, at No. 301 *King-street*, sign of the double *Gold Heart*, a Manufactory of JEWELLERY and SILVERSMITH'S WARE, in all its various branches, upon a scale much more extensive than any in this State; where they will engage to give satisfaction to those Ladies and Gentlemen who may favor them with their notice. As Ladies may have a reluctance to enter into the shop, they will be attended to next door. No. 303. All orders from the country will be punctually attended to, and executed with great dispatch.

October 16 20

Plate 99. Advertisement of John E. & Lewis C. Michel, manufacturers of jewelry and silver, which appeared in The Charleston Courier, *South Carolina, 16 October 1822. Courtesy of Museum of Early Southern Decorative Arts.*

from London filled his shop. Dozens of watches; gold earrings, festoon necklaces, medallions, and lockets; diamond and pearl sets; all in addition to ordinary jewelry such as strings of red and white beads, and men's buckles and cuff-links.

The list of non-jewelry goods that Jacks imported was twice as long. There were tortoise and ivory snuffboxes, whist sets, military dress items, swords, guns, pocketbooks, watercolours, backgammon tables, compasses, spy glasses, travelling desks, clocks, japanned tea urns and trays, picture frames, sterling silver, plated silver of all sorts, Matthew Boulton's patent candlesticks, glass candelabra, and even 'Imperial Paintings'. In short, Jacks was carrying the same kinds of things that one might find in a leading jewelry firm today. It is not surprising, considering the huge inventory, that by 1800 Jacks was bankrupt and selling off his goods and property to return to Charleston.[15]

During the Federal period there were more jewelers and silversmiths working in Charleston than at any other time in the city's history. The number peaked with about seventy precious metal workers in 1800. Although many like Jacks enjoyed limited financial success, others were able to establish longer lasting firms. John and Lewis Michel established a jewelry and silver manufactory at the sign of the Double Gold Heart (Plate 99). In 1822 they advertised that since ladies might be reluctant to enter their manufacturing shop, they would serve them in a building next door.[16]

Such extensive importation as Cooke, Anthony, Jacks and others engaged in engendered a sense of competition among ambitious Americans. As a result, a growing force of entrepreneurs began to organize and mechanize the jewelry business. Increasing specialization led to the rise of jewelers who did not produce silverware, watchmakers who did not make jewelry, men who were opticians not silversmiths who sold spectacles, and men who were skilled at lapidary work or enamelling and were not involved in the other aspects of the jewelry trade. John Grayson's shop in New York at the Sign of the Spectacles was devoted to lapidary work and spectacles, and extended to scientific glasses for instruments, and glasses for miniatures, lockets and rings.[17] Thomas Pons (1757-1827) of Boston, who had learned the 'European' method of making jewelry from James Dunkerley in 1786, gave up his jewelry and silver work in favour of the spectacle business in 1810.[18] There were shops that manufactured a single kind of item, as in the case of Thomas Reynold's seal manufactory in Philadelphia. There were men, such as Joseph Richardson, Jr., who produced hundreds of articles of jewelry for presentation to the Indians and paid other men to engrave this jewelry.[19]

Along with specialization came a change in marketing. No longer did the city jeweler make jewelry for his local clientele alone. Production was increased to supply other jewelers and merchants, not only in the manufacturer's own area, but for shipment to distant customers as well.

Epaphras Hinsdale (1769-1810) is credited with being one of the pioneers in the United States jewelry industry. Hinsdale came from Hartford, Connecticut, to Newark, New Jersey, in the 1790s. By 1801, he had established himself as an enterprising jeweler on Broad Street. In the next few years, he hired enough workers to manufacture sufficient jewelry to supply jewelers not only in Newark, but in Norwich and Hartford, Connecticut; New York city and state; Philadelphia;

15. *Fed.Gaz.*, 15 April 1797; 28 Mar. 1798; *Pa. Packet*, 13 Nov. 1799; Burton, pp. 91-96.
16. *Courier*, 16 Oct. 1822; Burton, p. 120-1.
17. *NY Gaz. & Gen Advtr.*, 5 April 5, 1801, Gottesman, 1800-04, p. 103.
18. *Boston Patriot*, 4 April 1810. Flynt and Fales, p. 302.
19. Fales, *Richardson*, pp. 159-61.

Alexandria, Virginia; and Augusta, Georgia. Newark was an ideal location for Hinsdale's enterprise. Expenses were minimized outside the big cities, but access to the market place was easy. Not only was Newark near both New York and Philadelphia, but it was also accessible by land and water to other centres along the east coast.

E. Hinsdale & Co. produced good gold jewelry at a price that made it possible for others to buy and still be able to sell at a profit. Among the jewelry the company produced were brooches, bracelets, earrings, necklaces, and chains. When Epaphras Hinsdale died in 1810, the company's assets in gold and tools were worth over $6,000, there were accounts due of almost $16,000, and he was a wealthy man. Among the customers were Marquand & Harriman and J. & A. Simmons of New York; Chaudron & Co. and John J. Parry in Philadelphia; and Charles A. Burnet in Alexandria. Epaphras Hinsdale's partner and former employee, John Taylor, established an outlet shop in New York under the name of Taylor and Hinsdale in 1804.[20] Hinsdale's approach to the jewelry business was the opposite of John Cooke's. Instead of beginning on a large scale, Hinsdale began in a small way with a modest number of employees and eventually a partner. From this manageable beginning, his enterprise took root and developed into a major industry several generations later.

Marchais La Grave, a French jeweler, is believed to have been responsible for establishing New York's first successful manufactory of jewelry. He brought with him when he came to New York a group of skilled French workmen and started producing gold jewelry in 1812.[21] Gold filigree jewelry had come into fashion and was something that American jewelers were not accustomed to making. Instead, they had been forced to import it. By concentrating on this desirable kind of jewelry, La Grave prospered.

The pioneer of the jewelry industry in Providence, Rhode Island, was Nehemiah Dodge. His location was well suited to success, being central to Boston, Connecticut and New York. In 1794 Dodge established a shop in Providence, advertising himself as a goldsmith, jeweler, clock and watch maker. He manufactured and sold 'gold necklaces, knobs, twists, gold rings, miniature cases, and fancy jewelry'. Before long he had learned to make a less expensive grade of jewelry by using plated gold. Nehemiah's uncle, Seril Dodge, is suspected of being the innovator of the process of soldering thin sheets of gold on a sheet of copper using silver solder.[22]

William R. Bagnall, an early historian of the American jewelry industry, noted that 'filled' jewelry was made at a very early date in Providence. According to Bagnall, 18 karat gold was used for the face of the piece of jewelry which was stamped out of a very thin ribbon of gold in the desired pattern. This shell was filled with a solder made of pewter. The back was made of an inferior grade of gold. When finished the face of the jewelry had a fine lustre and a well-defined design. It could also be reasonably priced. Filled jewelry quickly became very popular. Later Providence jewelers also learned how to plate gold or silver on to an alloy of copper and brass which could then be rolled to the required thinness.[23]

The Providence jewelry business grew very rapidly. By 1810, when the first national census was taken, there were a hundred employees in the jewelry business there. The annual production had reached $100,000. By 1815, employment had jumped to 175 workmen and the yearly production to $300,000.

Success breeds imitation. Nehemiah Dodge claimed that his secrets of manufacture

20. Carl M. Williams, *Silversmiths of New Jersey (1700-1825),* pp. 92-98; William R. Bagnall, *The Manufacture of Gold Jewelry* , pp. 14-15. Bagnall notes that their jewelry was made of solid gold of a fineness no less than 16 karats. The inventory of Hinsdale & Co., 1810, included a supply of hair and cornelians that presumably were used for settings in some of the jewelry.
21. Bagnall, p. 16.
22. Charles H. Carpenter, Jr., *Gorham Silver 1831-1981,* pp. 20, 273. Gilbert S. Suzawa, 'Seril Dodge: Real Jewelry Industry Pioneer?', *URI Alumni Quarterly,* Summer 1979, pp. 26-28. Suzawa also suggests that the Dodges may have been using the 'close-plating' technique to cover jewelry with silver plating.
23. Bagnall, pp. 18-20.

Plate 100. John B. Dumoutet (1761-1813), goldsmith and jeweler, had his advertisement printed on silk. Dumoutet worked in Philadelphia in the 1790s and in Charleston, South Carolina from 1801-1813.

were stolen from him by the men who introduced these methods in Attleboro, Massachusetts. The jewelry industry was started there in 1821 by the firm of Draper, Tifft & Co. Soon there were others who took up the business, among them Richard & Price. Attleboro became, along with Providence, Newark and New York, one of the four centres of the United States jewelry industry in the nineteenth century.[24]

While all this industrialization was getting under way, there were still local jewelers working on a smaller scale. Some had been born to the trade and trained by their fathers. Others were apprenticed in established shops in the cities. There was, however, a sizeable number of immigrants already skilled as jewelers who were coming from England or more often from France. The French Revolution contributed heavily to migration to the United States. A feeling of kinship for their allies in arms caused Americans to welcome the French and to patronize them. France had been the recognized leader in the art of the jeweler for centuries, as well as the chief arbiter of taste.

French surnames abound among jewelers in post-Revolutionary America. More of these emigrés came to Philadelphia, no doubt because it was the capital city. There we find Chat & Poincignon, Descuret, Dumoutet, Bouvier, Ravel, Brasier and Gaudichaud (Plate 100). Other French jewelers came by way of France's Caribbean colonies. From Santa Domingo, where there was continuous political upheaval, came the Thibaults, the Bucheys and Simon Chaudron.[25]

New York, the seat of government during 1789 and 1790, drew its share of French jewelers: Letourneaux (via Canada), Bellodière, Bis, Barrière and Cauchois. Charleston, South Carolina, had always attracted French jewelers due to its Huguenot population. Here one found emigré jewelers named Boudo, Cabos, Duplat, Fillete, Flottard, Michel and Peysson. Also added to the seaboard cities were a few jewelers from Germany, Switzerland or elsewhere in Europe. The result was a decidedly more cosmopolitan aspect to the jewelry, whether it was imported or made in America.

With a rising number of jewelers in the major cities, more jewelry was available than was needed to satisfy the local demand. Some of the enterprising artisans solicited merchants and shippers as did John Cauchois of New York. They pointed out that their jewelry was well suited for the French and Spanish islands in the West

24. Bagnall, pp. 16-21.
25. See Waters.

Indies, thus extending their market well beyond their city confines.[26] One of the most widely publicized articles of jewelry destined for the islands was a crown made by a Philadelphia jeweler for presentation to Dessalines when he had himself crowned as emperor of Haiti in 1804. Made at the behest of Philadelphia merchants, the crown was shipped to Haiti on the American vessel *Connecticut*. Such was Dessalines' reputation for cruelty in massacring the French soon after his coronation that Simon Chaudron, a French jeweler who had lived in Santo Domingo before coming to Philadelphia, felt called upon to deny publicly the rumour that the crown had been made in his shop. Chaudron was among those who advertised jewelry suitable for the Spanish and West Indian markets.[27]

To take advantage of developing markets and to avoid the competitiveness of the older cities, some jewelers moved to new areas of settlement that were being opened up in northern New England, in the west, and in the south. Members of the Moulton dynasty of silversmiths of Newbury, Massachusetts, for instance, moved to Ohio, New Hampshire and Maine. There they supplied jewelry, along with silverware, watches and related items, repeating the role of jewelers in the early colonies. Philadelphia jewelers moved to Maryland, Kentucky, South Carolina, Georgia and Louisiana. John B. Dumoutet established a shop in Charleston and ultimately moved there from Philadelphia in 1802. From this location he travelled to North Carolina to extend his business. In 1819, Anthony Rasch moved from Philadelphia to New Orleans where he made diamond jewelry as well as silver ware. In this way, through the constant movement of jewelers and their products, the prevailing fashions of England and the Continent were made available beyond the major cities of Federal America.

American jewelers produced an abundance of mourning jewelry, hairwork, miniatures and gold beads during the first decades of independence. With the help of emigré jewelers, they were able to produce some of the same kinds of fancy jewelry that were being produced in England or western Europe. We know that diamond as well as paste jewelry was made, as was pearl, jet and filigree jewelry.[28]

Thomas Fletcher, in partnership with Baldwin Gardiner, began to manufacture jewelry in Boston in 1808. At the end of the first year their sales amounted to $14,000 and their stock was worth about $9,000.[29] The firm made pearl and stone-set jewelry as well as solid gold jewelry, plain or filigree. They imported assortments of pearls, diamonds and other precious stones, and offered to pay cash for diamonds, pearls and other gems.[30] On 30 June 1810, Fletcher & Gardiner advertised in the *Columbian Centinel* that they had lately received a supply of pearls and cornelians as well as 'rare and beautiful gems, which they will manufacture into Ornaments of any kind...Specimens may be selected at the Manufactory, No. 43 Marlboro' Street'.

Other items manufactured by Fletcher & Gardiner were waist clasps. In 1810 they introduced 'Cestis clasps' of their own design, presumably with amatory emblems embossed on them. These were described as richly chased, made of fine gold or silver, and optionally set with cornelians. They made miniature settings, gold watch chains, seals and keys, tortoiseshell combs and elastic hairwork necklaces, bracelets, and ear hoops.[31] At least one piece of jewelry, an elastic hairwork bracelet, has survived bearing the mark of this firm (Plate 60). Considering the number of splendid examples of fine silver made by Fletcher & Gardiner that have been identified and that corroborate their advertising claims, it is only a matter of time until examples of good jewelry will be identified as their work.

26. *Commercial Advtr.*, 2 Jan. 1800.
27. C.L.R. James, *The Black Jacobins* (NY, 1963), p. 370; *Aurora,* 3 May 1805. *Fed. Gaz.*, 4 Jan. and 17 Feb. 1816. See also Waters, pp. 25-27.
28. William Frost (1792-1872) and his partner Henry Mumford advertised in Providence as manufacturers of diamond, pearl, paste and jet jewelry, about 1810. Flynt & Fales, p. 222.
29. Letter of Thomas Fletcher to his father 12 Nov. 1809, cited by Waters, p. 78.
30. *Col. Cent.*, 3 Jan., 11 April and 6 Oct. 1810.
31. Ibid., 3, 13 Jan. and 3 Mar. 1810.

Plate 101. Above left. Trade card of Thomas Fletcher (1787-1866), Chestnut Street, Philadelphia, manufacturer of silver plate and jewelry and importer of clocks, watches and fancy goods. The trade card was originally engraved by Young & Delleker, c.1822, for Fletcher & Gardiner. In a later state c.1838-39 the name was changed to Thomas Fletcher. Length 6¼in. Courtesy, The Winterthur Library: Joseph Downs Collection of Manuscripts and Printed Ephemera, No. 63 x 13.

Plate 102. Above right. Illustration of a jeweler's shop, from The Book of Trades, or Library of the Useful Arts, *published by Jacob Johnson, Philadelphia and Richmond, 1807.*

Fletcher & Gardiner also augmented their own products with rich imported jewelry, plated silver, fine cutlery, fancy goods and watches. They made a special arrangement with Boston watchmaker, John Tolman, to repair the watches the firm sold. Some of the timepieces were imported from Roskell in England. The English jewelry that they imported included some of the same kinds of jewelry that they made themselves – gold filigree, pearl and cornelian necklaces, bracelets, tiaras, earrings and brooches. In addition they imported mourning jewelry with black enamel and jet; and jewelry made of topaz, brilliants and paste.[32] Fletcher and Gardiner formed a short-lived partnership with John McFarlane, once Fletcher's employer, in 1810. McFarlane provided capital and made the selection of goods at the English manufactories to be shipped to Boston.[33]

In 1811 Fletcher & Gardiner moved to Philadelphia in search of wider patronage. Statistics show that in 1810, Pennsylvania produced five times as much gold and silver work and jewelry as Massachusetts did, indicating a more encouraging climate for jewelry manufacturers in Philadelphia.[34] Fletcher decided that he could best compete with English jewelry manufacturers of pearl work, filigree and jet. At the same time, he decided that his best profits and competition rested in the manufacture of fine silver wares.[35] As his trade card indicated, he struck the balance of his business between the manufacture of silver plate and jewelry on the one hand and the importation of clocks, watches and fancy goods on the other (Plate 101).

The road to success for the jeweler of the Federal period, whether he had a large business or a small one, was full of potholes. The credit extended so liberally by

32. Ibid., 3 Jan., 28 Nov. 1810.
33. Waters, pp. 78-93; *Col.Cent.*, 6 Oct., 28 Nov. 1810.
34. *Niles Weekly Register* (Baltimore), 9 July 1814, p. 327, cited by Elizabeth Ingerman Wood, 'Thomas Fletcher, A Philadelphia Entrepreneur of Presentation Silver', *Winterthur Portfolio III* (Winterthur, 1967), p. 137.
35. Waters, pp. 81-84. These conclusions were drawn by Fletcher when he went to England in 1815 to buy for his firm.

English producers of jewelry, plated wares and fancy goods, led to bankruptcy for some of the American jewelers whose ambitions were greater than their resources. Towards the end of the Federal period, the War of 1812, with its embargoes, trade blockades, and curtailments of commerce, limited the number of people who could afford to buy jewelry. The British destruction of the new capital in Washington and attacks on other cities mitigated against a normal routine as well as against a luxury market. The lack of an organized currency during the war was yet another serious economic deterrent. The Second United States Bank was finally instituted in 1817 but had to be reorganized in 1819. That year a major panic occurred due to rampant speculation, overextended investments, withdrawal of credit and the collapse of foreign markets. Those engaged in the jewelry business suffered severe if not fatal setbacks.[36] Only the best organized jewelry firms survived.

Other government policies affected the jewelry trade as well. Tariffs were placed on imported jewelry. This served as an encouragement to American manufacturers to produce their own wares, but for those who relied on importation for their profits, the tariff represented a real hardship. John Lowe of Charleston tried to circumvent the problem. He was found guilty of evading the payment of duties required by the United States Revenue Laws and of selling his smuggled jewelry over a three-year period. As a result, his shop goods were seized, condemned and sold at public auction, returning some $4,000 to the government.[37]

Daniel H. Dodge, a Philadelphia jeweler dealing with gem-set jewelry and watches, failed in 1819. He found work again as the foreman of Fletcher & Gardiner's manufactory until 1823. Then he resorted to thievery, stealing not only from his employers but from the firm of Ward & Miller as well. He was indicted but jumped bail and vanished.[38]

Fletcher & Gardiner managed to continue despite Dodge's perfidy and other economic setbacks. Younger brothers of both original partners joined the firm and Fletcher and Gardiner were able to extend their business from Boston to North Carolina.[39]

In 1820 Fletcher and Gardiner employed a work-force of eighteen and were still growing. While in England on a buying trip in 1825, Thomas Fletcher had visited Roskell's watch company in Liverpool, a fused plate manufactory, and Sheffield plants where he had a chance to study the potential of the steam-powered rolling mill and the down fall press. In Birmingham he visited Matthew Boulton's Soho Works and admired the quality and fine patterns of their wares. It was reassuring to him to see that his Philadelphia workmen were accomplishing their tasks in a manner comparable to Boulton's men. It was not long before Fletcher would have steam power in his own workshop. By 1820 his Philadelphia manufactory employed seven men, two women burnishers and nine boys and produced $100,000 worth of gold and silver wares and jewelry a year. Another Philadelphia manufactory, Thibault & Bros., made only jewelry and had the same number of men and boys working for them, producing $40,000 worth of goods during the same year.[40]

The Newark jewelry business, while being one of the first to market goods to distant places, was slow to develop in terms of specialization and industrialization. For several decades, Newark jewelry continued to be made in the age-old handcraft tradition with each workman completing each of the steps in the making of an individual piece.[41] By 1826 there were only twenty-two workers recorded as being employed in the jewelry trade in Newark.

36. Waters has delineated in detail the effect of the Panic of 1819 on the precious metal trades and craftsmen in Philadelphia.
37 *The Daily Advtr.*, 27 July 1803; Gottesman 1800-04, p. 101. Burton, pp. 113-14.
38. Waters, pp. 88-89.
39. Baldwin Gardiner's brother Sidney, joined the firm. Thomas Fletcher's brother, Charles, who had started his own jewelry store in Philadelphia in 1817, joined with another brother, George, in 1818 to start their own jewelry manufactory. They supplied their jewelry wholesale at attractive prices. George dropped out of the firm about 1824, but Charles Fletcher continued on for a few years until he joined Fletcher & Gardiner as their travelling representative, selling their jewelry and their good name from Boston to North Carolina. Waters, pp. 81-86.
40. Census of 1820, cited by Waters, pp. 129-30.
41. Susan E. Hirsch, *Roots of the American Working Class: The Industrialization of Crafts in Newark, 1800-1860*, pp. 4, 11, 25, 31-32.

Plate 103. Miniaturist James Peale (1749-1831) had a portable work table to assist him in this delicate work. He also had special spectacles with 'near and distance focus in each eye' provided by Philadelphia optician John McAllister who told Thomas Jefferson in 1806 that 'for painting miniatures [the lenses] answer extremely well'. [John Wilmerding, 'America's Young Masters', The Walpole Society Notebook *(South Portland, Maine, 1987, p. 40).] Portrait of James Peale painted by his older brother, Charles Willson Peale, about 1789. Mead Art Museum, Amherst College. Bequest of Herbert L. Pratt, class of 1895.*

John Taylor, Epaphras Hinsdale's partner and successor, greatly expanded the business. While continuing the firm of Taylor and Hinsdale in New York with Epaphras' son Horace Seymour Hinsdale, Taylor formed another partnership about 1817 with Isaac Baldwin in Newark.[42] During an epidemic in New York in the summer of 1822, Taylor & Hinsdale moved back to Newark temporarily. They rented a store on Broad Street where they sold pearl, jet, and gold jewelry; silver teasets and flatware; and plated goods.[43] Several other Newark jewelry firms had shops in New York as well, moving back and forth, and in and out of partnerships with abandon.

George R. Downing began manufacturing gold watch seals in Newark about 1812. Gradually he introduced other kinds of jewelry. In 1821 he opened a shop on Reade Street in New York where he continued to prosper under the firms first of Downing & Phelps (1812-1824) and subsequently of George R. & Benjamin Downing (1829-1833) and Downing & Baldwin (1832-1850). George Downing also continued to advertise in the Newark *Sentinel.* He offered for sale gold jewelry, solid or filigree, and set with pearls, paste or jet, all of his own manufacture.[44]

Providence jewelers felt the impact of the economic problems of the second decade of the nineteenth century more than their colleagues to the south. Having expanded their trade to a greater extent, they had more to lose. Nehemiah Dodge, Ezekiel Burr, John C. Jenckes and Pitman & Dorrance had increased their production from buckles, gold beads and finger rings to include 'breast pins, ear rings, watch-keys and

42. Bagnall, p. 15; Dorothy T. Rainwater, *American Jewelry Manufacturers,* pp. 8, 234.
43. *The Sentinel* (Newark), 24 Sept. 1822.
44. Bagnall, p. 16; von Khrum, p. 40; Rainwater, *AJM,* pp. 8, 78, 234; Newark *Sentinel,* 24 July 1827.

Plate 104. Hairworker's box with drawers containing samples of the art, American, first half of the 19th century. Height 6¼in., width 13⅞in. Winterthur Museum.

other articles', according to a brief history that appeared in the Providence city directory in 1856. By 1815 they had been joined by other firms. From an industry of 175 employees and production of $300,000 in 1815, the trade dropped drastically in the next two years and was nearly abandoned. However, in 1818 the business was resuscitated, increasing so rapidly by 1820 that there were 300 workmen producing jewelry worth $600,000 in Providence.

By 1825 Providence had outstripped all other attempts to establish a jewelry industry in the United States. In addition to jewelers, goldsmiths and silversmiths, there were refiners, watchmakers and lapidaries all working together to produce diamond, paste, pearl, jet, and garnet jewelry, solid gold jewelry and watch cases. Davis & Babbitt advertised as 'Jewellers and Lapidaries' who manufactured 'in a Superior style of workmanship, Gentlemen's Watch Seals, Chains and Keys, &c.' At the same time, they specialized in setting all kinds of precious stones in gold mounts and kept most kinds of jewelry on hand that they sold wholesale. They also purchased gems locally as well as precious stones in the rough which they could cut into any shape and polish. Frost and Mumford advertised as 'Manufacturers of Diamond, Pearl, Paste, fine and Jet Jewelry at Wholesale'. Sturgis & Davis too specialized in the jewelry and lapidary business, purchasing all kinds of precious stones in their original state.[45]

As the Federal period drew to a close, the American jewelry industry was well established. There were large-scale entrepreneurs now in addition to the old-fashioned, general, local jewelers. 'Manufacturing' and 'working' jewelers, as they were now called, had begun to organize the trade along the lines established by Matthew Boulton in England at the beginning of the period. American ingenuity, combined with a liberal patent policy, was bringing great changes to the production of jewelry. Mass production, which had begun with the making of beads, buckles, mourning jewelry, Indian trinkets, miniatures and hairwork, gradually spread to other areas of the industry. Steam engines, rolling mills, die-stamping, and the plating of metals were beginning to change the fabrication of jewelry and every other line of metal work.

45. *Prov. City Dir.*, 1824; *Prov. Gaz.*, 25 Apr. 1820.

PART III

MID-19TH CENTURY 1825-1875

Colour Plate 85. Gold and enamelled bracelet in the Gothic style, American, c.1840-60. Set with a miniature portrait of Samuel Blatchley Webb of Wethersfield, Conn. In February 1779, Webb's likeness was taken by Charles Willson Peale of Philadelphia for Webb's second wife Elizabeth Bancker whom he married on 20 October 1779. A replica was made of the portrait during the 19th century for Webb's descendants. Photograph by John Giammatteo. The Webb-Deane-Stevens Museum.

INTRODUCTION 1825-1875

The mid-nineteenth century was a time of boom or bust in America. Celebration, expansion and the discovery of gold and silver marked the period from 1825 to 1875. Exuberance was matched by wild fluctuations of fortunes and economic extremes. To this volatile cauldron was added the bitter devastation of the Civil War.

The era began with the 50th anniversary of United States independence and concluded with the Centennial celebration in 1876. On 4 July 1825 Thomas Jefferson and John Adams had died within hours of each other, closing the door on the most historic chapter in American history. The Marquis de Lafayette came from France to join in the commemoration. He made a grand tour and at each stop noted the progress of the nation. The same year the National Academy of the Arts of Design was established to encourage the arts in America. Through education and standard setting, the members hoped to elevate public taste and to dignify artists by honouring them with awards. Another wave of neo-classicism washed over the country. This time the emphasis was on Greek as well as Roman models. American homes resembled Grecian temples and were filled with Grecian urns.

It was an age of invention and scientific discovery as well as of sentiment and romanticism. Roads were improved and the means for transportation and communication were accelerated. Ideas travelled like wildfire along the newly opened pathways, creating a more homogenous national style. Villages and towns in the hinterlands were well stocked with many of the luxuries found in the cities. As the nation prospered, more people were able to enjoy the increasing productivity of their burgeoning industries, including that of the developing jewelry industry.

More Americans were able to travel abroad than ever before where they could sample firsthand the products of other nations and make comparisons with the progress of their own country. Frequently they returned with souvenirs, house furnishings, art work, jewelry and clothes, creating a market for these goods which enterprising merchants soon began importing.

Changes in fashion abroad were reflected in the United States. New modes in dress

caused changes in jewelry. Gowns changed from the neo-classical style of filmy, high-waisted, columnar fashions made of a minimum of fabric, requiring light and delicate jewelry. New wide-shouldered, long wasp-waisted, crinoline lined, full-skirted, puff-sleeved gowns, made of yards and yards of fabric, demanded more substantial, larger ornaments. Soft colours gave way to deep, strong colours. Coiffures changed from wispy, loose hair cut short or done up in the back, to long hair parted and formed into rolls, ringlets, loops and buns that called for a multiplicity of decorative combs to hold the hair in place. Long earrings, elaborate necklaces and chains, wide decorative belt buckles to suit broad belts, and brooches to fasten lace fichus or shawls were balanced by bracelets that fitted comfortably below long full sleeves, and by numerous decorative rings, not simply a single wedding or mourning ring.

In England, the return to dress and styles more sympathetic to the fashions of the mid-eighteenth century has been attributed to Queen Victoria's ascent to the throne in 1837, and with it the return of romanticism and the revival of the more feminine rococo style. In the United States this movement was reinforced by the 50th anniversary of independence. Americans looked back to the age of their grandparents. They began to bring out relics of the pre-Revolutionary period and took pride in the possessions of their past. Silversmiths embellished teasets with eighteenth century roses and scrolls and jewelers worked the same motifs in gold and enamel for a new generation of jewelry lovers. Old jewelry was reset, miniatures were given new settings in modern bracelets, and clasps were renewed. The 1783 miniature of General Samuel B. Webb, for example, was reset in a very stylish enamelled and articulated bracelet exhibiting gothic arches (Colour Plate 85). The gothic element of rococo style played a decorative role in the mid-nineteenth century.

Colour Plate 86. Gold half-set made by Edward Burr, manufacturing jeweler in New York, c.1836-1850s. Set with pearls and diamonds against a bright blue enamel ground with a floral pattern reminiscent of French rococo designs of the late 18th century. Original box imprinted inside lid, E.W. BURR / 573 B.WAY / NEW-YORK. Length 2¼in. (brooch). Photograph by Peter J. Theriault. Private Collection.

Another popular revival was the use of blue enamelled medallions set with diamond studded sprigs and monograms. This design had been fashionable in France and England in the late eighteenth century. A brooch and matching earrings in this style were made by Edward Burr of New York after 1848 when he moved from Ann Street to Broadway (Colour Plate 86).

Flowers, singly or in bouquets were appropriate for every sort of jewelry whether set with diamonds or carved out of coral. Americans who preferred their jewelry to carry some sentiment cheerfully embraced the clichés of mid-nineteenth century romanticism. They loved anything miniature. Tiny little books that explained the symbolism of flowers were published everywhere. When Miss S.C. Edgarton published *The Flower Vase; containing the Language of Flowers and Their Poetic Sentiments* in Lowell, Massachusetts in 1844, she admittedly used *Flora's Interpreter* as her model, but claimed 'though imitating we have not copied'. Americans also indulged themselves in exchanging tokens of friendship. Their jewelry bore secret messages of affection in cryptic initials as well as in the language of flowers.

By the mid-century archaeological jewelry came into fashion. In 1858, Boston jeweler Samuel Crosby advertised Etruscan gold jewelry for sale.[1] Ten years later he offered Roman and Byzantine in addition to Etruscan ornaments.[2] During this period

1. *Transcript*, 22 Dec. 1858.
2. Crosby and Morse, *Transcript*, 17 Dec. 1868.

Plate 105. Half-set in the Roman style, with bulla motifs superimposed on classic architectural designs and vase-shaped drops. In original box imprinted by Crosby & Morse of Boston, c.1860-1868. Width 1½in. (brooch). Photograph by David Bohl, Boston. Society for the Preservation of New England Antiquities.

the firm of Castellani in Italy continued to make reproductions of antique Etruscan and Greek jewelry discovered during archaeological excavations. Twisted wire decoration and granulation embellished these antique shapes and forms. The Civil War slowed the pace of the newly introduced designs, but their popularity resumed after peace was restored in 1865 (Plate 105).

Gold continued to be the most desirable material for use in good jewelry. Silver was still used to mount white and colourless stones, but this tradition was waning and gold was increasingly used for setting all stones or at least for the back structure. Mass-produced jewelry was often made of plated or gilded metal. New methods of rolling a sandwich of two sheets of gold with a base material in the middle were developed and this prefabricated filled gold could be supplied as jewelers' stock.

Gold of two or three different colours could be used in a single design to make a more naturalistic effect. Pink or red gold was made by adding copper to the alloy while green gold was alloyed with silver. Together with the usual yellow gold, these different colours could be mixed to provide shading and contrast. The colour of gold could also be enhanced by use of chemical processes known as wet and dry colouring (see page 267).

In addition, the surface of the gold could be given different finishes. The metal could be polished, lapped (cut), or burnished as had been done traditionally. New finishes were developed that stippled or frosted the entire surface to give a subtle pitting overall, referred to as a 'rich bloom'. Engraving, engine-turning, chasing and embossing continued to be used in decorating jewelry, but machines were developed to perform these tasks by rolling the metal through presses or stamping the metal by means of a drop press.

Enamelling, an ancient technique of ornamenting with coloured glass, became more prevalent in mid-nineteenth century jewelry. One of the simplest methods of enamelling was to engrave the surface of the metal with the desired design and then to fill the recessed areas with coloured fusible glass. Most jewelers could perform this task and did so frequently when making mourning rings with inscriptions. This process was employed widely for making bracelets with strapwork designs in the 1860s and 1870s.

An enamelled set consisting of brooch and earrings made in Providence about 1850 was described by a man in the trade forty years later as having been sold 'in larger quantities than any other patterns in the same class of jewelry' (Plate 106, figs. 7 and 8). 'They were made', he said, 'by G. & S. Owen in 18-karat stock with engine-

was filigree gold, in which were set stones of different color, coral, garnet, imitation pearls or white stones. At the present day, the pattern will strike one as somewhat barbaric, but its popularity forty years ago is easily understood when we remember that in

FIGS. 7 AND 8. BROOCH AND EARRING SET.

addition to the symmetry and real beauty of the article itself the public had not been educated to dilettantism, and a false appreciation of proportion that the present-day public has.

The exceedingly pretty sleeve buttons, Fig. 6, attained a remarkable popularity that

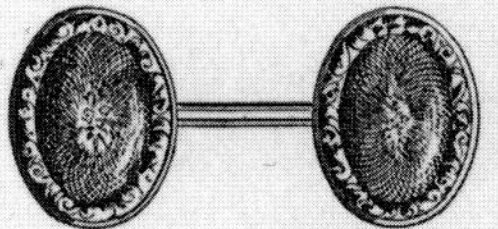

FIG. 9. SLEEVE-BUTTON.

the sales of them numbered among the thousands. The same conceit is at the present time, to some extent, employed in earrings. An exaggerated form of the Greek honeysuckle similates the conventional shell. As sleeve links, nothing perhaps could be neater and prettier; still the pattern in this class of jewelry has had its day, or, as the writer believes, its preliminary existence; for that it will be resuscitated he feels certain.

The set, breast-pin and earrings, Figs. 7 and 8, was sold forty years ago in larger quantities than any other patterns in the same class of jewelry. They were made by G. & S. Owen, in 18-karat stock, with engine-turned centers. The setting, indicated by the black scroll work in the illustration, was of black enamel. The effect of this black enamel work on the gold background was much admired in the old days, though to the present generation it would be perhaps too sombre and staid. The dimensions of the breastpin were exactly twice those of the earrings. The patterns in both cases were counterparts of each other.

FIG. 11. CHILD'S ARMLET.

The sleeve-button represented in Fig. 9 will be remembered by any person who was in the trade forty years ago as a style that was in everybody's stock. Nearly all the manufacturers of a general line of jewelry made it. It was a filled button having a gold front with a chased edge, and with engine turned and plain centers. Such a pretty design as this must have been, one would think, should prove salable during any decade of time.

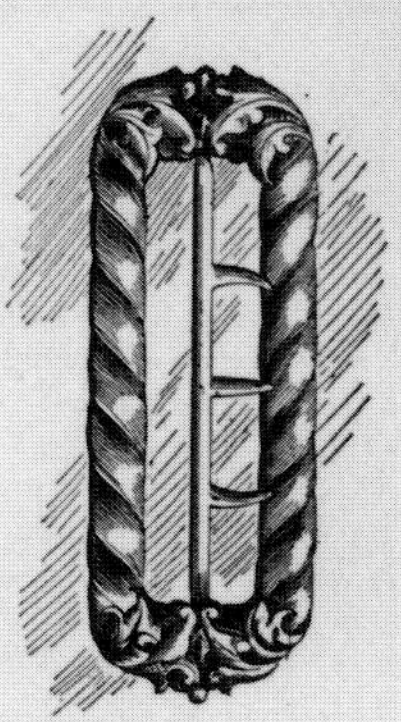

FIG. 10. BELT BUCKLE.

At the time of which we are speaking belt buckles and slides of various widths were very much used, and in many instances belt clasps were quite extensively made and sold. The illustration, Fig. 10, represents a characteristic buckle of that period. It had an 18-karat front on a silver back. The design is plainly depicted. The clasps referred to were made of the width of the ribbons worn, and the two portions were hooked together after the manner of the ordinary hook and eye.

An article of jewelry which is apparently dead, buried and forgotten is the baby's armlet, illustrated in Fig. 11. This article was used for looping at the shoulder the short sleeves then worn by the new-born generation. The one depicted here was about the widest made, and undoubtedly the most popular style produced. The width of the chains varied from that of the one in the illustration.

FIGS. 12 AND 13. WATCH-KEYS.

about one-half inch, to less than one-quarter inch. Armlets were made of other kinds of chain than the one shown. Some were made of bands of gold with pins and pointed backs. While one may readily understand that a design, however popular, may decline in favor, it is not so clear to his mind why a class of jewelry, once a staple, should die out. Perhaps a brave manufacturer who should start to manufacture babies' armlets would not wake to learn that his enterprise had brought failure.

As is well-known, stem-winding watches were unknown forty years ago. Though horologists may have sighed and experimented to produce a mechanism more convenient in its construction than the keywind watch, that historical article held full sway. Thus it will be readily appreciated that many kinds of watchkeys were in vogue. The drawings Figs. 12 and 13 represent the most popular styles that then existed. These keys were made by John Bowden, New York, forty years ago. Similar styles and sizes were made by all concerns that manufactured a general line of jewelry. The keys, as may be inferred by an inspection of the engravings, were quite massive in character, the treatment of the design being very bold. The keys in numerous instances took the place of the charms now worn. The flat portion forming the top was usually a slab of onyx or other stone. These keys were of gold, with the exception of the shank, which was of steel. Apropos of watchkeys, it may be stated that imported ratchet keys, to prevent the winding of the watch in the wrong direction, were quite popular, especially among women. They were not as large as the other keys, and were made of enameled or plain gold.

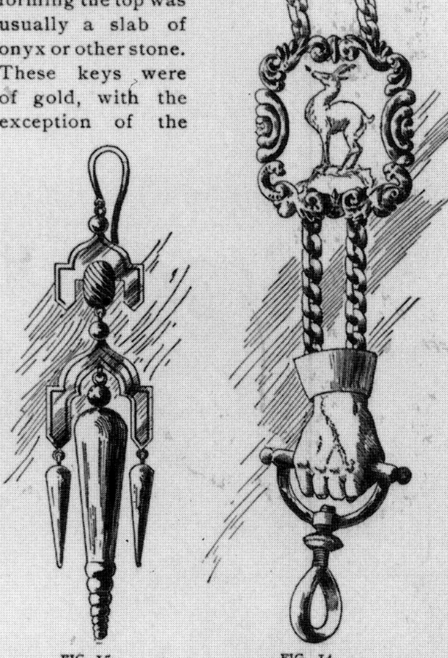

FIG. 15. FILLED EARRING. FIG. 14. LADY'S GUARD CHAIN.

At the time of which we are speaking long chains, such as illustrated in Fig. 14, were much assumed by ladies; they were known in the trade as guard chains. The majority of these chains had a hand and swivel connected together as depicted in the cut. They also had a slide, which enabled the chain in being worn about the neck to be safely secured if desired by the wearer. The hand, swivel and slide were stuck in dies and filled with copper solder. Curb chains were for the most part used, but many fancy patterns were in vogue, and old-time jewelers will vividly recollect the then familiar names and styles—"Greek," "Adelaide," etc.

The earring illustrated in Fig. 15 is a characteristic pattern of this class of jewelry that was forty years ago very popular. Such

Plate 106. Illustrations from an article entitled '40 Years Ago', published in Jewelers' Circular XXIV, *No. 1, 3 February 1892. Photograph courtesy of Janet Zapata.*

Plate 107. Group of New England made mourning jewelry, c.1810-1846. (Top) Brooch enamelled with rococo revival shells, scrolls and flowers. Engraved in memory of I. Amory who died 4 September 1832 and C. Amory who died 20 July 1831. Width 2in. Bequest of Maxim Karolik. (Centre, each end) Pair of earrings set in gold with faceted jets, c.1825. Length about 1¾in. Gift of Miss Catherine Waters Faucon. (Centre) Brooch in the shape of a bowknot made of a belt with buckle, set inside loops with two different locks of hair. Chased gold borders, surrounding black enamel, and compartments outlined with pearls. Engraved on back for William S. Wetmore, Jr., who died at the age of 2½years, and John D. Rogers who died 27 August 1846, age 25 years. Length 1⅛in. Bequest of Maxim Karolik. (Lower left) Gold shield-shaped ring with black and white enamelled bezel, set with a rectangular locket holding a plait of hair. Inscribed for I. Amory 1832. Diameter ¹¹⁄₁₆in. Bequest of Maxim Karolik. (Lower right) Pin set with faceted jets and leaf-shaped locket containing braided hair. Engraved on back D.D.H. Weld and E.W. Weld Obt. Aug. 29th 1809. Length about 1⅛in. Gift of Miss Catherine Waters Faucon. Courtesy, Museum of Fine Arts, Boston.

Colour Plate 87. Tiffany pin, c.1875, enamelled in grisaille with cherubs gathering grapes from the arbour and placing them at the foot of a statue of Bacchus. Marked on back TIFFANY & CO. May have been mounted in a more elaborate gem-set border. Length 1½in. Photograph by Peter J. Theriault. Private Collection.

turned centers. The setting, indicated by the black scroll work on the gold background was much admired in the old days, though to the present generation it would be perhaps too sombre and staid. The dimensions of the breast pin were exactly twice those of the earrings. The patterns in both cases were counterparts of each other'.[3]

Special training was required for executing champlevé enamels. The design had to be cut away to form sunken areas with thin ridges separating the areas that would be filled with enamels of different colours. The enamels were applied in powdered form and then fused on to the metal. William Cummings in California produced belt buckles with champlevé enamelling in 1868 (see Colour Plate 160).

Another technique used for jewelry was called 'Painters' enamel'. This was a surface type of enamelling, usually on a slightly concave, thin sheet of copper to prevent warping when fired. A thin layer of enamel was fused over the surface and then painted with enamels in a similar fashion to painted porcelains. Since the process was originated in Limoges, it was often known by that name. Shadows were created by painting a layer of white enamel over the dark background which then fused and became grey. The process of painting and fusing continued until the design was completed. Watch cases were among the best examples of this type of enamelling. The French and the Swiss excelled in this work, and manufacturers of jewelry in the United States imported enamel work and set it in their own mounts (Colour Plate

3. 'Fashions in Jewelry Forty Years Ago,' *The Jeweler's Circular and Horological Review*, 3 Feb. 1892, XXIV, No. 1; Rainwater, *AJM*, p. 222.

Colour Plate 88. (Top) Pair of black enamelled earrings, gold, French, c.1840. Back stippled light blue. Length about 3⅞in. Gift of Miss Mary Haven and Mrs. Waldo Ross. (Centre) Small pendant in the form of St. George and the Dragon. Hungarian, bought in Budapest in 1897. Length about 3in. Bequest of Mrs. John H. Thorndike. (Lower right) Delicate filigree earring, top and drop, open work design. French or American, c.1825. This earring appeared in the miniature portrait of the original owner Mrs. Franklin Haven, painted at the time of her marriage in 1826. Length about 1¼in. Gift of Miss Mary Haven and Mrs. Waldo Ross. (Left) Small brooch in the form of a diving bird, bearing in its beak a pendent heart-shaped locket containing hair. American or English, c.1840. Across the wings is a sentimental message spelling out in gems 'Regard', i.e. ruby, emerald, garnet, amethyst, ruby, diamond. Here however the second stone (an emerald) has been replaced by a garnet by someone who was not privy to the secret code. Length about 1⅝in. Gift of Mrs. Henrietta Page. Courtesy, Museum of Fine Arts, Boston.

87). 'Ornaments in the Louis XVI style are all the rage…ornaments of pink enamel, with Cupids painted in grisaille, or two shades of gray – such are the favorite ornaments this season', reported the Boston *Transcript* on 27 January 1868.

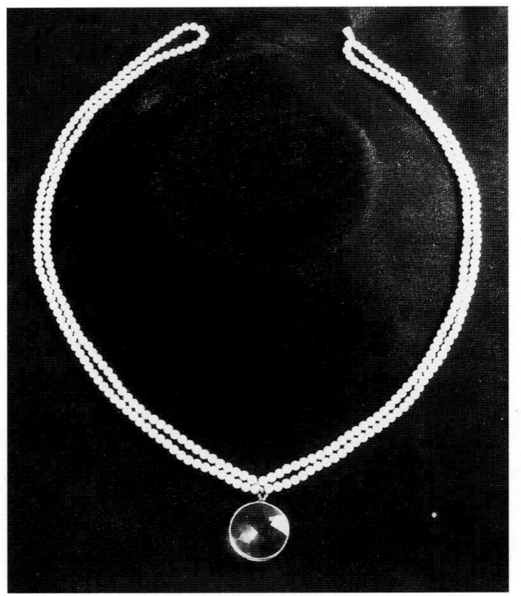

Plate 108. Ferronnière owned by Angelica Van Buren, but not the one shown in her portrait. It is set with a glass amethyst and artificial pearls (Colour Plate 89). Smithsonian Museum.

New Fashions

Ferronnières

One of the most captivating and short-lived fashions in jewelry in the second quarter of the nineteenth century was the ferronnière. This was an ornament for the forehead. A pearl or some other jewel was suspended from a headband formed of strings of pearls, a ribbon, gold bandeaux or chains. The name came from the portrait *La Ferronnière* attributed to Leonardo da Vinci, in which 'the blacksmith's wife' wore a similar ornament on her forehead.

Once blessed by Queen Victoria's use, the ferronnière made its way to other aspiring heads. Shortly after Angelica Van Buren, daughter-in-law of President Martin Van Buren, attended Victoria's coronation in 1838, she was portrayed with a pearl ferronnière (Colour Plate 89). A ferronnière with a glass amethyst and a band of artificial pearls was also owned by Angelica (Plate 108). President Tyler's wife was wearing a ferronnière when she sat for a portrait.[1] Among the ferronnières offered for sale by Tiffany's in its first catalogue in 1845 some were made of jet.

In 1898 Alice Morse Earle recalled the fashion for these jewels. 'It gives to every countenance', she observed, 'a curiously submissive look, as if the jewel were hung on a slave. It was originally an Oriental fashion, but had been most popular in France in the seventeenth century. The ferronnière was generally a fine gold Venetian chain, but might be made of velvet ribbon, of silken cord, of strings of beads, or tiny vines of artificial flowers'.[2]

A decade later, Mary S. Parker wrote a verse about the jewelry worn by Salem, Massachusetts, women of past generations. One set of topaz jewelry included a necklace

With ear rings too, which matched, and pendant,
All sparkling with a fire transcendant –
And lastly, a ferronnière
To droop upon her forehead fair.[3]

The fashion was dependant upon a compliant coiffure and as soon as the hair style changed, the ferronnière was gone as quickly as it had come, the jewels discarded or converted into a bracelet or a necklace.

1. John Wilmerding, 'White House Collection of American Paintings', *Antiques*, July 1979, p. 137.
2. Earle, II, 793.
3. *Small Things Antique* (Salem, Mass., 1909), p. 12.

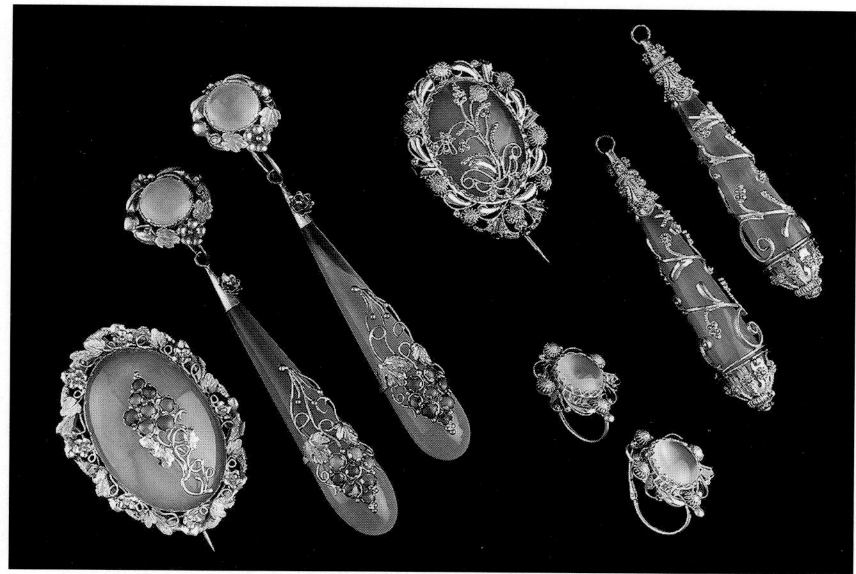

Plate 109. Chalcedony earrings with detachable pendants and brooches, English, c.1830-40, owned by Elizabeth Salisbury, Worcester, Mass. Set on left with turquoise flowers. Length about 3¾in. (earrings). Photograph by Stephen Briggs. Bequest of Samuel Salisbury III Estate, Worcester Art Museum, Worcester, Mass.

Other hair ornaments that were fashionable at mid-century were wreaths of water lilies, geraniums and gold ears of wheat. Diamond stars accented wreaths of white grapes and coral studded white lilacs. 'Feathers are also worn for evening coiffures; but flowers or resillés [hairnets] of gold, coral or pearls, are more in favor', the Boston *Transcript* reported on 24 March 1858.

Buckles

The delicate little oval or round buckles of the Federal period were inadequate for wide fabric belts of the mid-nineteenth century. The new buckles were rectilinear and were placed vertically to receive the wide sash. Many were made of gilt metal or more humdrum materials. Stylish waists, however, sported buckles that were made to match the jewelry with which they would be worn.

Mrs. Elizabeth Salisbury (1768-1851) of Worcester, Massachusetts, owned several decorative buckles (Colour Plate 90). Prettiest of all was her gold buckle enamelled with turquoise-coloured grape clusters to match her chalcedony earrings which were also ornamented with grape motifs (Plate 109). This buckle was purchased from Jones, Lows & Ball of Boston on 17 October 1835 for $22 along with a gilt and enamel buckle costing only $3.[4] Several years later she acquired a gold filigree buckle from the same firm (the firm's name changed to Lows, Ball & Co. from 1840-46).

In the mid-1850s, the California Jewelry Co. in San Francisco made buckles of local gold that were enamelled in blue and black, and engraved in the gothic style. The design of the buckle was patented by William Cummings. (see Colour Plate 160).[5]

Earrings

In addition to the eighteenth century styles that were revived for earrings, the most startling new design in the second quarter of the nineteenth century was the elongated drop known today as a torpedo pendant because of its shape. These pendants tapered smoothly from the top, widening slightly as they got longer, and finished with rounded endings. They could be detached from their round tops if a less noticeable earring was warranted. Some of the pendants were bracketed or enclosed by light, stamped metal frames. The earrings were fastened to the ear by passing a wire shaped like a shepherd's crook through the pierced earlobe. Materials popular for these earrings ranged from chalcedony (Plate 109) and mosaics to the more unusual sea urchin spines set in gold filigree (Colour Plate 92).

4. SFP, Box 56, Folder 3.
5. Christie's #7640, lot 141, 22-23 Jan. 1993, similar buckle marked by Wm. U. Bohm and not enamelled.

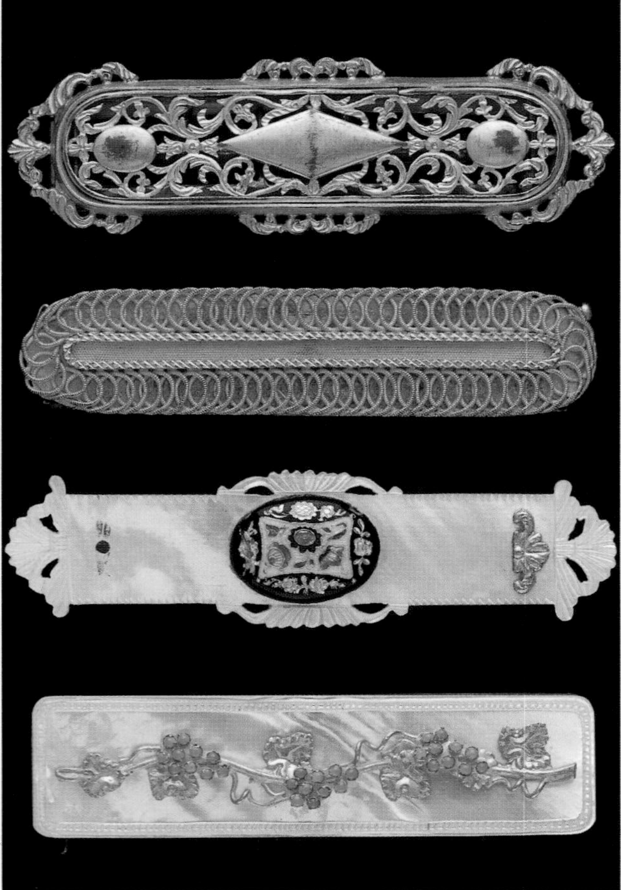

Colour Plate 89. Above left. New fashions in jewelry appear in the portrait of Angelica Singleton Van Buren, daughter-in-law and official White House hostess for President Martin Van Buren, painted in 1842 by Henry Inman (1801-1846). Most noticeable is the jeweled ferronnière dangling over her forehead. Her three-strand pearl necklace is centred with a lozenge-shaped medallion and set with an amethyst and a pendant pearl. Length 42¼in., width 33⅝in. White House Historical Association.

Colour Plate 90. Left. Group of four waist buckles for wide belts owned by Mrs. Elizabeth Salisbury of Worcester, Mass., c.1835-1845. Mrs. Salisbury bought a gold and enamel buckle on 17 October 1835 from Jones Lows & Ball, Boston, for $22, possibly the buckle shown here decorated with applied turquoise-enamelled grape clusters. Several years later she purchased a gold filigree buckle from Lows, Ball & Co., the name of the firm from 1840 to 1846. Length about 3¾in. (coiled wire buckle). Photograph by Stephen Briggs. Bequest of Stephen Salisbury III Estate. Worcester Art Museum, Worcester, Mass.

Colour Plate 91. Above right. A Massachusetts lady wore the most fashionable of inexpensive jewelry when her portrait was painted about 1835, probably by Erastus Salisbury Field (1805-1900). Her watch was held in place by a long woven bead tape to which were attached gilt fasteners and her watch key. Her wide gilt belt buckle was placed vertically in the latest mode. Elongated top and drop earrings and a lace pin were set with what appears to be black and white agates mounted in light gilt frames. Her husband's matching portrait (not shown here) included a similar agate pin which he wore on his shirt. Length 30in., width 26in. Abby Aldrich Rockefeller Folk Art Centre, Williamsburg, Virginia.

Colour Plate 93. Right. *A pair of earrings in the form of grape-like clusters and leaves, suspended from a cluster top, were worn by an unidentified woman in this portrait painted by Franz Fleishbein (c.1802-1868) in 1842. The Bavarian artist worked in New Orleans from 1834 to 1868. The earrings, and her necklace, appear to be made of glass beads and are similar in concept to the so-called mulberry earrings made by Joseph F. Chattellier of New York. Length 36¼in., width 29in. Purchase gift of the Friends of Cabildo, Louisiana State Museum.*

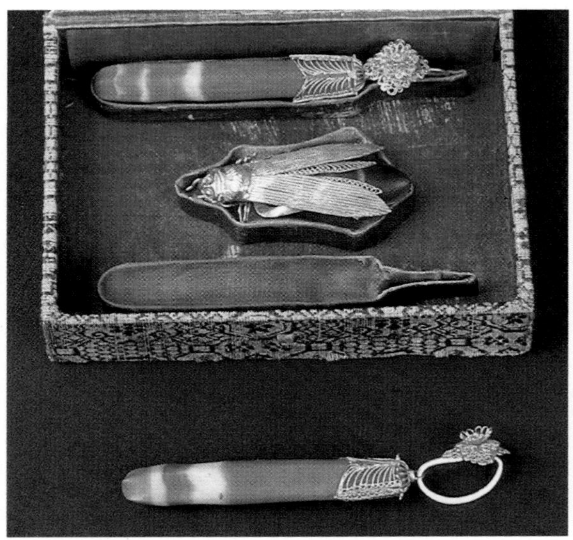

Colour Plate 92. Above. Set of pendant earrings and brooch in the shape of a large insect, Italian, c.1840-60. The body of the insect and the elongated drops of the earrings are made from the polished spines of a sea urchin. Details of the design are added in gold filigree. Owned by the Manigault family of Charleston, S.C. Private Collection.

Colour Plate 94. Right. Beaded necklaces with crosses suspended from oblong pendants were worn by two of the children of New Orleans commission merchant Louis A. de Barjac and his wife Celine. The eldest daughter proudly wears her spectacles as well. The portrait was painted by Franz Fleishbein in 1839. Length 35¾in., width 29in. Louisiana State Museum.

Colour Plate 95. Above right. Marie Josephine Lennen (1816-1842) wore a necklace with a pendent dove carrying a heart in its beak, a derivation of Saint Esprit motifs. She also wears a buckle-style ring made with a wide band of woven hair, as well as a plain gold wedding ring on her third finger, left hand. Her portrait was painted by L. Scotia in 1841. Her husband Lézin Becnel was a fourth generation farm owner in the German coast section of the Mississippi River above New Orleans. Length 29in., width 23⅝in. Louisiana State Museum.

Feb. 3, 1892. AND HOROLOGICAL REVIEW. 75

FASHIONS IN JEWELRY FORTY YEARS AGO.

A REVIEW OF SOME OF THE STYLES IN JEWELRY THAT WERE ALMOST FADS, FOUR DECADES AGO.

THAT which we term modern fashion is pre-eminently a work of reconstruction, or, if we may be allowed the term, of resurrection. Gold work, as well as the other industrial arts, as ceramics, furniture, painting, and binding, exists largely upon the past. The tendency of modern fashion is to

FIG. 1. FILIGREE BOW PIN.

return to the past of comparatively recent date, having sprung up with the romanticism of about a half century ago. Fashions in jewelry are not the result of independent fancy. It is not solely because the designer possesses a fertile imagination that a manufacturing firm attains success in its productions. An untrammeled imagination in the matter of designing may be compared to a spirited racer rampant; both may cover much ground in a short space of time, but the course they take may be the reverse of

FIG. 2. REVOLVING BOX PIN.

a desirable one. The industrial arts are dependent one upon the other, the laws of harmony governing them all. The designer in each branch must study the prevailing fashions in the others.

Whoever was the wise man who said there is nothing new under the sun was responsible for an aphorism that is more than a half-truth. Originality in the matter of art is too often nothing more than a reconstruction, the "cock-eyed Madonnas" of one period being the serious-countenanced shepherdesses of a later period. And originality in gold and silver work is scarcely more than a transformation. However, while the foregoing may be asserted as facts, hundreds, yea, thousands, of fashions and styles in jewelry lie apparently dead, though really only dormant, waiting to be roused from their slumber. Perhaps a satisfactory compensation awaits the man who produces a volume whose pages shall comprehend descriptions and illustrations of a fraction of the departed styles in jewelry, with an analysis of the causes of their rise and decline. A bulky volume could be written on the subject. A thorough understanding of the science of fashion—fashion is a science as much as many of the ologies—must prove of inestimable benefit to the designer and manufacturer of jewelry.

In such an article as this it is impossible to even specify the fashions and styles of jewelry that have had their day of popularity since the commencement of jewelry manufacture in America until the present time. Therefore a period—forty years ago—which was perhaps more fruitful of popular fashions than even the preceding decade, which witnessed the revival of romanticism in all branches of industrial art, has been chosen, and some of the salient styles which were then very fashionable will be described or enumerated.

FIG. 5. MULBERRY EARRINGS.

For several months past bow-knot jewelry has been a fad. We see its prototype in Fig. 1, and who shall say that the bow pin depicted did not have its prototype. This illustration is taken from the design book of fifty years ago, of JosephF. De Guerre, who was the first filigree worker in the United States. His workshop was located in Reade St., New York. As may be seen, the bow pin was made of filigree gold, with a rosette or other setting in the center. As evidenced by the book referred to, bow pins were made a half century ago in numerous styles, no less than ten different patterns being here delineated.

Forty-seven years ago Mr. Cunliff entered the factory of G. & S. Owen, Providence, R. I., and began to make what are known as box

FIGS. 3 AND 4. BOX PINS.

pins. Mr. Cunliff is still making the same articles. During all these years this fashion in jewelry has existed, sometimes more potently than at others. The illustration herewith depicts a revolving box pin, Fig. 2, that was very popular four decades ago. The box revolved upon a pivot, and had a glass front and a glass back, which adapted the article to contain hair in one side and a miniature in the other. The background of both interiors was composed of silk arranged in checker pattern, as indicated.

These articles were made in 18-karat gold, and large quantities of them were sold. In this connection box pins Figs. 3 and 4 may be specified. The former was the regulation box pin with glass front, to contain mementoes in the shape of hair, picture, or the like. The latter was older than the other and won great popularity by means of its design. The edge, as may be seen, is a continuous vine of bunches of grapes and leaves, unusually rich and striking. It seems that such a pattern would be very acceptable at the present day. These two styles were also in 18-karat gold.

Regarding the mulberry earring, Fig. 5, Joseph F. Chattellier, New York, its manufacturer, had orders on his books for 1,800 pairs at one time, so great was its popularity. The illustration is slightly larger than the original. The ground work of the article

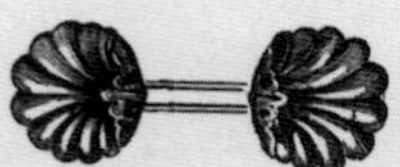

FIG. 6. SLEEVE BUTTONS.

Plate 110. Illustration from an article published by Jewelers' Circular *in 1892, discussing mulberry earrings fashionable about 1850 (fig. 5). Figs. 2-4 show a very popular type of revolving box pin of the same date, which allowed a locket to be set with a photograph and a lock of hair or another photograph. Photograph courtesy of Janet Zapata.*

Feb. 3, 1892. AND HOROLOGICAL REVIEW. 79

earrings were made in various shapes, and answered the popular demand if they were long and showy. This style of earring would be entirely obsolete in America but for the wearing of them among the lower class of Italian immigrants.

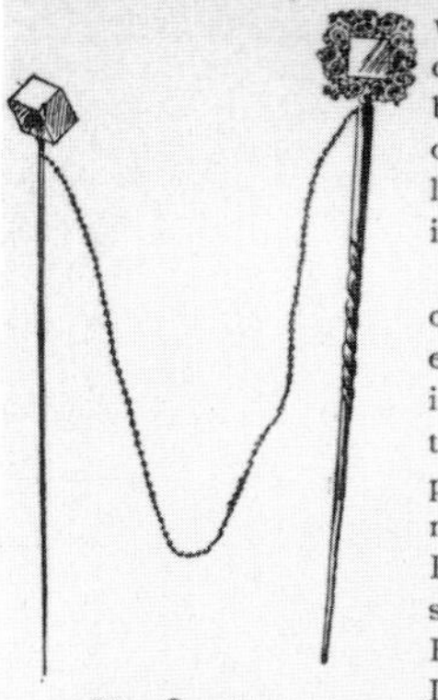

FIG. 18. CUFF PIN.

Swing seals, an old fashion in jewelry, were produced in enormous quantities, a number of pioneer jewelry manufacturers, as Palmer, Richardson & Co., Alling Bros. and Carter & Doremus, being identified with their manufacture. Fig. 16 represents a characteristic type once very much in demand. Mention of these swing seals brings to mind the once familiar fob chains which divided the demand for gentlemen's chains about equally with vest chains. Both these class of chains had heavy trimmings filled with copper or silver solder.

Hoop earrings, such as seen in Fig. 17, were extensively worn; they ranged from the cheap, plain, filled die hoop to the stylish large "Duncan," or plain red gold and filigree hoops, with or without precious stones. The one shown was made by Joseph De Guerre, as far back as fifty years ago. In his pattern book before referred to, from which this illustration is taken, the writer saw drawings of various styles and shapes in this jewelry. This book also contains many patterns of cuff pins, such as illustrated in Fig. 18. Ladies in those days wore large flowing sleeves pinned together at the cuffs. These pins were used for this purpose. Styles similar to this are found in jewelry stocks at the present time.

Besides the fashions illustrated several others may be specified. Fob buckles were a feature of the trade forty years ago; they are now almost obsolete. In those days the very few necklaces worn were generally of filigree work, ornamented with imitation

FIG. 16. SWINGING SEAL.

opals topazes, etc. Bracelets, for the most part, were stiff, half-round bands, some plain and some engraved. However, there were a good many flat glove bands, which were made of thin, flat pieces of gold, wide in front and tapering to the back; they were

FIG. 17. HOOP EARRING.

held together by a slide and eyelet hole. They were worn, as may be inferred, to cover the arm below the glove. Link bracelets to some extent were made in die work.

In the days we are writing of comparatively few watches were sold to women, the fashion instead being to wear a locket at the end of a long chain. Large quantities of these articles were sold. Their purpose was to contain hair or a miniature. These lockets were about the size of watches, and large, oval, open-faced ones were much used to hold miniatures, which were pointed, as the daguerrotype had not yet been invented. A small box of glass at the back was intended to contain hair.

Plate 111. Illustration from Jewelers' Circular *article, discussing hoop earrings and filigree made about 1850 by Joseph De Guerre of New York. Photograph courtesy of Janet Zapata.*

Mulberry pendant earrings were popularized by Joseph F. Chattellier of New York (Plate 110). At one time he had orders for 1,800 pairs. Made of gold filigree, they were set with stones of various colours such as garnet or coral and imitation pearls or diamonds.[6] A related design was set with red stones and golden grape leaves (Colour Plate 93). Hoop earrings 'ranged from the cheap, plain, filled die hoop to the stylish large "Duncan," or plain red gold and filigree hoops, with or without precious stones' which were worn extensively. Joseph De Guerre of New York was one of the producers of these designs about 1850 (Plate 111).[7]

During the third quarter of the century, vase-shaped pendants were attached to oval or arched tops and suspended from them were fringes or chain tassels. A typical earring of the mid-century (see Plate 106, fig. 15) was made of filled gold 'and answered the popular demand if they were long and showy. This style of earring would be entirely obsolete in America [in 1892] but for the wearing of them among the lower class of Italian immigrants'. So said a man in the jeweler's trade recalling in 1892 the fashions that had prevailed about 1850.[8] Ball drops were popular in gold, coral or jet. Hoops made of plain gold or studded with beads sometimes had balls of coral or other decorative materials suspended inside the hoop.

Necklaces

Festoon necklaces continued to be popular up to the mid-century, filling the space opened up by the ever widening necklines. Necklaces were formed of narrow bands that widened toward the centre to feature a medallion flanked by foliage and scrolls

6. *JC*, 40 yrs., p. 77.
7. De Guerre was listed in New York directories from 1808 to 1850, according to von Khrum, p. 37.
8. *JC*, 40 yrs., p. 78.

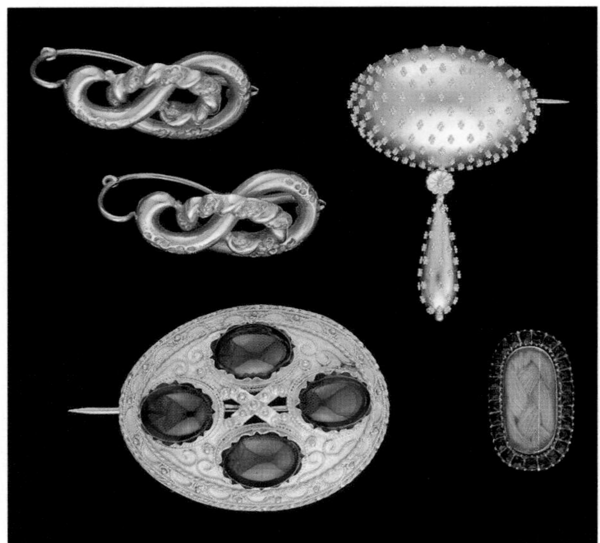

Colour Plate 96. Brooches and earrings owned by the Salisbury family. (Upper left) Earrings in serpentine form, gold filled, c.1850. Length about 1¼in. (Lower left) Brooch with gold fill mounts, twisted wire and granular decoration, set with cabochon garnets. Length about 1⅞in. (Upper right) Gold brooch with clusters of granules giving the impression of embroidery, with tear drop pendant. Probably English, c.1860. Length about 1⅛in. (Lower right) Small brooch set with jets, containing a plait of blond hair, American, c.1830. Length about ⅞in. Photograph by Stephen Briggs. Bequest of Stephen Salisbury III Estate. Worcester Art Museum.

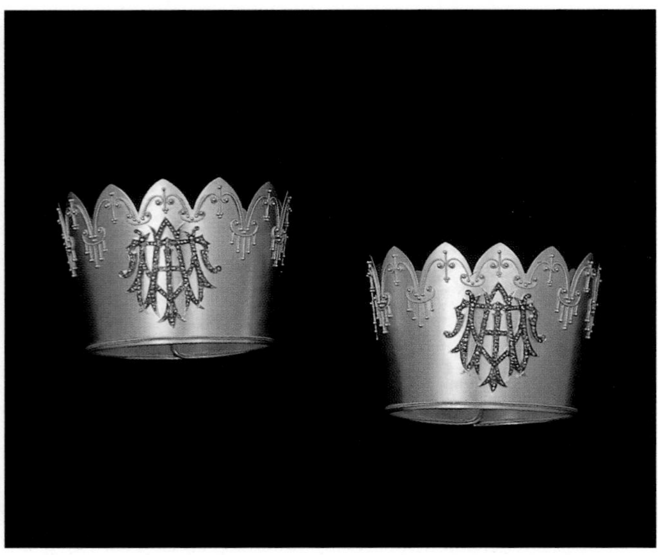

Colour Plate 97. Pair of manchette bracelets made by Thomas Kirkpatrick, New York, c.1871. Wide gold gothic bands resembling lace cuffs, initialled with diamonds 'MAT' for Mary Amelia Tweed, eldest daughter of William Marcy Tweed, and his gift when she was married in May 1871. Original box labelled by Thomas Kirkpatrick, N.Y. who was listed as a jeweler at 305 Broadway in the 1870-1871 city directory. Photograph by Arthur Vitols, The Helga Studio. Gift of Mrs. John W. Mackay and Reginald P. Rose, 70.94.3 a b. Museum of the City of New York.

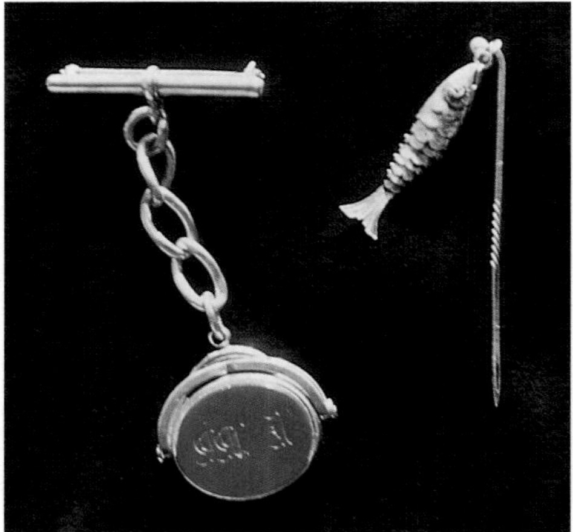

Colour Plate 98. Seal fob and stickpin owned by Washington Irving (1783-1859). Gold fob, American or English, c.1840, with bloodstone seal. Silver stickpin, European, c.1825-50. Historic Hudson Valley, Tarrytown, N.Y.

Colour Plate 99. Right. A cabochon-set brooch with a fringe of elongated pendant drops in the archaeological style and matching earrings, worn by Mrs. Frank Wagener (1843-1919) in her portrait by François Bernard in New Orleans in 1867. Her husband, a native of Germany, ran a frame shop and art gallery on Canal Street in New Orleans. Length 24in., width 20in. Louisiana State Museum.

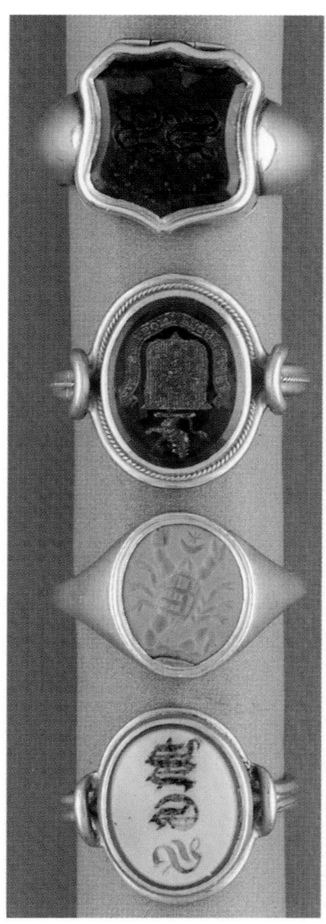

Colour Plate 103. Gold chain necklace and pendant cross, from Tiffany & Co., Union Square, New York, given by Brutus J. Clay to Pattie Amelia Field, 20 February 1872. Private Collection.

Colour Plate 100. Above left. Group of Salisbury family gold signet rings. Shield-shaped ring set with bloodstone engraved in gothic script SS for Stephen Salisbury II. Engraved inside band ES / ob[t] Oct. 19th 1851 / AE. 83 yrs. Apparently bought by him in memory of his mother Elizabeth Salisbury. Diameter about 1in. Ring with entwined band, set with amethyst cut with lion crest. Diameter about 1in. Ring cut with an insect for a seal, in box labelled by Shreve, Brown & Co., working together in Boston from 1857-1860. Ring set with cornelian cut with initials MGS in gothic script for Mary Grosvenor Salisbury (1800-1864) who married Stephen Salisbury in 1855. Diameter about ⅞in. Photograph by Stephen Briggs. Bequest of Stephen Salisbury III Estate, Worcester Art Museum.

Colour Plate 102. Above right. Multicolour beaded watch and fob tape, made by Laura for her brother William H. Long as 'A memento of affection', 14 March 1833. Shown here with a silver-cased watch made in London by Charles Cabrier in the third quarter of the 18th century. This watch was owned in Maine in the 1830s and is backed with watch papers inserted in the case by watchmakers William H. and Samuel Blood of Thomaston, Maine. Total length of watch tape 52in., diameter 2in. (watch). Photograph by Peter J. Theriault. Private Collection.

Colour Plate 101. United States Military Academy ring, 1864, made by Ball, Black & Co., New York. Shield-shaped bloodstone signet engraved with a laurel wreath crossed with a sword and the legend UNO ALIAM, the class motto. Shoulders embossed with military trophies. Engraved on back 'U.S. M.A. / John K. Elliott/ Graduating Class / 1864'. Elliott was a Pennsylvanian who served during the Civil War and died in 1871 as a result of battle injuries. Diameter ¹¹⁄₁₆in. Photograph by Peter J. Theriault. Private Collection.

and sometimes garnished with pendants (Plate 135). Single pendants suspended from narrow bead or chain necklaces were popular for less formal occasions.

The de Barjac children (Colour Plate 94) in New Orleans wore matching bead necklaces with jewelled crosses suspended from them. In Louisiana, Catholic women often adorned themselves with emblems of their faith. In 1841, Mme. Becnel was portrayed wearing a gold and gem set St. Esprit pendant. The bird, representing the

Plate 112. A native of Ireland and emigrée to New Orleans, Mrs. John Delamore (c.1805-1869) was portrayed in 1860 by L.A.A. Meuser, a German artist. She wore a pair of hoop earrings distinguished by a more elaborate twist than usual, and a crucifix suspended from the slide chain attached to her watch and tucked into her waist band. A knot brooch held her lace collar in place. Like many in the South, she wore a variety of rings on several fingers. Length 36in., width 29in. Louisiana State Museum.

Holy Ghost, held a heart suspended from its beak (Colour Plate 95). Often the heart held a locket enclosing hair. In 1860, Mrs. John Delamore of New Orleans had a crucifix which she wore on a watch chain (Plate 112). Pearl-set onyx crosses were popular in the 1870s and were worn by Catholic and Protestant alike (see Plate 175).

Lockets

Lockets enjoyed great popularity as pendants and were often embellished in the 1860s with monograms in gold or set with diamonds.[9] Locket rims were mass-produced using the same machinery employed for making watch case rims. Lockets and brooches were made with identical frames and had fasteners so that they could be pinned or suspended. Many lockets were equipped with cases to hold hair or a likeness of a loved one. During the Civil War, lockets frequently held photographs of a uniformed husband or son.

Among novelties in lockets was the type imported by Ball, Black & Co. of New York. It was set with a crystal engraved on the back in intaglio with the head of a Skye terrier and then coloured. The crystal was set in a spiked collar and had a belt around it (Plate 113).[10]

9. 'A Gold Locket with the letter S in diamonds on a black face' was lost in Boston in 1868. Boston *Transcript*, 19 Dec. 1868.
10. Illus. from Mme. Demorest's *Monthly Magazine*, May 1867; Gere, *A.&E.J.*, p.153.
11. Marsh & Bigney, 1883 catalog, pp. 256-264.
12. *JC*, 40 yrs., p. 77.
13. #31,931, H.Kipling, NY 1861.

Plate 113. Lady's locket set with a reverse crystal intaglio of a Skye terrier head in a belted dog-collar frame. The intaglio technique is believed to have originated in England with Thomas Cook, a seal engraver in Clerkenwell, and by the early 1860s was an established novelty. Advertised in Mme Demorest's Monthly Magazine *in May 1867 by Ball, Black & Co. of New York. Courtesy of The New York Public Library.*

Brooches

Brooches were set in rococo revival frames made of scrolls and flowers, cusps, or smoothly curved corners in the 1840s. They often were set with floral designs such as mosaic or enamelled bouquets. Knotted patterns appeared in brooches, earrings and rings and were often formed by the body of a snake (see Plate 132). Mid-century brooches were shaped into circles, squares, lozenges or domed ovals worn horizontally. These were plain gold or set with stones such as carbuncles, and often had one or more long thin pendants.

Cameo settings for brooches enjoyed an unprecedented vogue in American jewelry of the mid-century. They could be set in the narrowest of gold frames conforming to the outline of the carved shell cameo, or mounted in an elaborate frame set with pearls and fine gems to enhance the onyx of which they were carved.

Many brooches were fitted with a suspension ring at the top so that they could be worn as pendants on a necklace. They also could have rings placed on the lower edges to support one or three pendants. The customer could thereby choose the degree of elaboration of the piece.

A form of brooch known as a bar pin made its appearance, heavily ornamented in the Roman style, in the third quarter of the nineteenth century. Horizontal bars of gold were engraved with Japanese or floral designs, while others were given granulated and twisted wire ornamentation. Raised borders were sometimes added. Other bar pins had scalloped outlines with fans or balls at each end. They might be set with medallions, cameos or gems.[11]

The revolving box pin became popular in the 1840s and continued to be made to the 1890s (Plate 110, figs. 2-4). The box had glass on both the front and the back of it to hold a plait of hair on one side and a miniature or picture on the other side. The box was attached to the frame on pivots so that it could be reversed if desired. Made of 18-karat gold and lined with a chequered silk interior, these pins were made in quantities by G. & S. Owen of Providence. The favourite design was one encircled by a border of bunches of grapes and leaves.[12]

Bracelets

It was no longer necessary for bracelets to be worn in matching pairs, one on each wrist. If two were worn, they often did not match. The bands were wider and often bulged in the centre to accommodate sizeable medallions or gems (Plate 114). The medallion might be enamelled and studded with diamonds forming a monogram. Matched bracelets made a reappearance in the 1870s in the band bracelets engraved with strapwork patterns accentuated by black enamel in the background.

To make the bracelets more comfortable to wear, the bands were divided into sections joined by hinges or made more flexible in a variety of ways. The sections could be overlapped or extensible by means of a lazy-tong arrangement or threaded with elastic. They could have cylinders alternating with plaques. The bracelet could also be made of braided hair or, alternatively, coiled spring wire that could be covered with a suitable outer material.[13] Bands resembling straps or belts were adjustable to the size of the wrist.

Plate 114. Gold and blue enamelled bracelet, made in Philadelphia in 1849, set with a large opal surrounded by clusters of diamonds. Philadelphia Museum of Art.

In the 1860s machine-produced chain was being used for the

Plate 115. Pair of cuff buttons and studs, tortoiseshell, with (below) conjoined SS appliqué, one of silver and one of gold, and piqué tendrils, and (above) with a single applied gold gothic S with floral scrolls in piqué. Owned by Stephen Salisbury II (1798-1884) of Worcester. American, c.1860-80. About 1⅛in. x ⅞in. and 1¼in. x ⅞in. Photograph by Stephen Briggs. Bequest of Stephen Salisbury III Estate. Worcester Art Museum, Worcester, Mass.

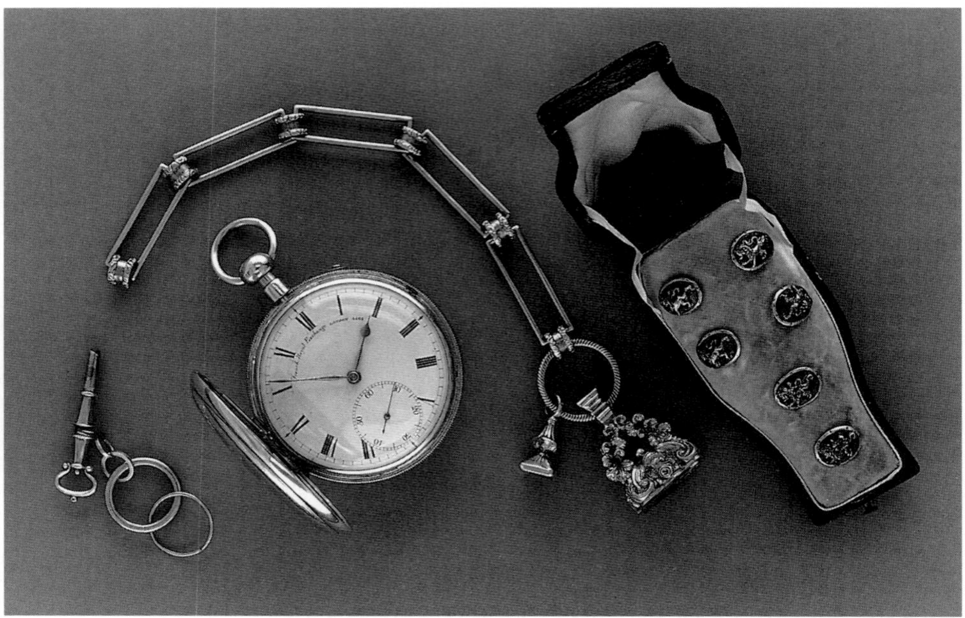

Plate 116. Watch and seal fob owned by Stephen Salisbury II (1798-1884) of Worcester, and probably the seal purchased by him from Rundell, Bridge & Rundell of London on 10 December 1830, described in the bill as 'A chased gold seal with Topaz, Engraving Crest & Cypher on d[itto] in medal[l]ion' at a cost of £5.15.6. Diameter 2in. (watch). Set of gold studs with lion passant design, in original box imprinted by Jones, Ball & Co. 226 Washington / 1 Summer St., Boston, who were in business together under this name from 1852 to 1854. Diameter about ½in. Photograph by Stephen Briggs. Bequest of Stephen Salisbury III Estate. Worcester Art Museum, Worcester, Mass.

construction of bracelets. Joseph Christi received a patent in 1864 for manufacturing two narrow chains connected by crossbars.[14] The patent of P.M.C. Beziel of Paris utilized a sandwich of metal consisting of a sheet of iron or other metal between sheets of gold for forming chains that could be used in making bracelets. After the forming process, the base metal was removed by dissolution in acid.[15] In 1872 William Edge of Newark patented an improved form of bracelet in which woven-metal chain was used as an ornamental covering for a simple band bracelet. The edges of the chain work were turned over the edges of the band.[16] Providence jewelers improved upon bracelet design by manufacturing chain that was spirally twisted.[17]

A short-lived fashion for bracelets simulating the dentate fabric cuffs on clothing emanating from France about 1860 found limited success in the United States.[18] Called *manchettes,* they were shaped with the deeply-pointed upper edge of a crown. A pair made of gold with beaded decoration and the initials MAT worked in diamonds was given to Mary Amelia Tweed, the eldest daughter of Tammany Boss William Marcy Tweed of New York, possibly at the time of her wedding in May 1871 (Colour Plate 97). The cuff bracelets were bought from Thomas Kirkpatrick, one of New York's up and coming jewelers.

Men's Jewelry

In 1856, the Boston *Transcript* reported on 'the fashionable extravagance indulged in by masculine "Young America"', noting the 'extravagant quantity of jewelry' that Newport gentlemen were wearing. Mosaic and gold vest buttons the size of a quarter and studs the size of dimes were worn in addition to a watch, with a heavy chain dangling charms, keys and seals. Coral coat clasps were fastened through the buttonhole. Rings were worn on both hands, and large signet rings were *de rigueur.* A gold-headed cane completed the picture of elegance.[19]

Plate 117. Portrait by an anonymous American artist, c.1835, of Sea Captain Maxwell B. Chase who wears a very popular type of shirt pin with a pearl-set square head on a short stem. Length 29in., width 24⅛in. Gift of Edgar William and Bernice Chrysler Garbisch. Courtesy, Museum of Fine Arts, Boston.

Cuff links, studs and shirt pins were among the most popular indulgences (Colour Plate 98). Plain gold cuff links and studs were commonly stocked by jewelers and could be personalized with engraved initials (Plate 115). Stephen Salisbury II owned a set of rich gold cuff links and studs embellished with a lion passant that he bought from Jones, Ball & Co. in Boston about 1853 (Plate 116). The original box bears the address of this firm at 226 Washington Street from 1852-54. In 1874 Isaac Pforzheimer of New York designed sleeve buttons that could be set with any prefabricated letter of the alphabet. These proved to be a big success and continued to be made into the twentieth century. Studs or buttons were usually plain and round, with gold mounts, set with currently popular materials, whether gems or jet, mosaics, or coral.

Shirt pins in the 1830s and 1840s had short stems and heads that were stylized flowers or single stones set in a geometric bezel (Plate 117). Occasionally the design pertained to the man's profession or affiliation. Sea captains chose anchor shirt pins while Masons chose emblems of their society. As the century progressed and the pins were used to hold foulards and scarves, the stems became longer and were scored or twisted part way up the stick to keep them from slipping out of the fabric.

Seal fobs were among the few essential pieces of jewelry for watch-owning gentlemen. Stephen Salisbury II purchased his watch and seal fob while travelling abroad shortly after his father's death in 1829 (Plate 116). Although his watch was purchased from J.M. French in London, his seal fob was from Rundell, Bridge & Rundell, the firm he considered to be the best in the city. The seal was mounted in a cusped bezel and a richly chased mount. It was engraved with a demi-lion rampant, his family crest, and the initials SS in gothic script. The bill specified that the gem used for the seal was topaz, but it was actually citrine.[20]

Swinging seals that pivoted within the frame of the fob were produced in great quantity by American jewelers such as Palmer, Richardson & Co., Carter & Doremus, and Alling Bros., all Newark firms (Plate 111, fig. 16).[21]

14. #41,175.
15. #62,178.
16. #133,145.
17. #149,823-4-5-6 and #155,941.
18. Henri Vever, *La Bijouterie Française au XIXe Siècle,* III, 396.
19. 20 Aug. 1856.
20. SFP, Box 24, Folder 4, 13 Dec. 1830; Box 56, Folder 1, 10 Dec. 1830. The fob cost £5.15.6.
21. *JC,* 40 yrs., p.79.

Rings

The first American book devoted to the history of rings was published in New York in 1855. Written by a lawyer named Charles Edwards, the work was entitled *The History and Poetry of Finger-Rings.* Edwards included an explanation of the manner of wearing rings in America. If a gentleman wore a ring on his left hand and first finger, it meant he was looking for a wife; if worn on the second finger, he was engaged; if worn on the third finger, he was married; and if worn on the fourth finger, he did not want to be married. If a lady wore a diamond or a hoop on her first finger, it meant she was not engaged; on the second finger, she was engaged; on the third finger, she was married; and if worn on the fourth finger, she was determined to die unmarried. To this Edwards added, 'The last is seen about once in an age'.[22] This canard was published with illustrations and other passages from Edwards' book in *Godey's Lady's Book* and in numerous newspapers in the United States.

American portraits of the mid-nineteenth century indicate a variety of ways of wearing rings, but offer no proof that such a method of message sending was known or widely held in that country. However, it was during this period that customs pertaining to engagement and wedding procedures began to solidify. The plain gold posy rings had given up their engraved inscriptions of endearment and the gimmel, twist and hand-and-heart rings had gone out of fashion, except in New Orleans where the twists remained in fashion during the *ante bellum* period. By 1848 a New York etiquette book recommended that a wedding ring, if used, should be plain and gold, and the gift of the bridegroom.[23] Large and ornate rings were considered in bad taste.

Many engagement and wedding rings were set with gems chosen for the beauty of their colour or their fashionableness. Garnets, amethysts, emeralds and diamonds were popular settings for these rings, used either as solitaires or combined with pearls (see Colour Plate 110). A new style of ring made its appearance, called a name ring by Edwards. A sentimental code was based on the first letter of each gem, the gems being set in order to spell out a message. The most common was 'Regard' – ruby, emerald, garnet, amethyst, ruby, diamond. 'Dearest' was another favourite. The name of the loved one could also be spelled out in stones, provided it was not too long or full of odd letters.[24]

While only the wealthiest American women could hope for a gold wedding ring in previous centuries, mid-nineteenth century middle class brides could expect them, and other kinds of rings as well. The plentitude of gold rings can be illustrated by the fact that at the 1841 Mechanic's Exhibition in Boston an enormous cake weighing 3,300 pounds was baked with fifty gold rings in it, an unthinkable extravagance in earlier days. Slices of the cake were sold to those who hoped to eat their cake and have a ring too.[25]

The smooth shanks of the Federal period rings gave way to thicker ornamental surfaces in the mid-century. One jeweler described them as 'heavy chased gold rings'.[26] The bezels featured knotted designs and the shoulders were often worked in rococo-revival scrolls and leafage. The half-hoop ring of the eighteenth century was revived, frequently set with a larger stone in the centre. In the second quarter of the nineteenth century, bezels were sometimes lozenge-shaped and turned on the side so that the long points of the lozenge tapered into the shoulders (see Colour Plate 110).

The signet ring received continued attention in the mid-century. Several signet rings are among the Salisbury family jewels, one set with an 'amethyst' cut with a lion crest and another with an insect (Colour Plate 100). Another signet ring was

22. p.54. Edwards attributed 'Love's Telegraph, as understood in America' to an English publication called *Family Friend,* II, 132.
23. C.P. Huestis, *The Art of Good Behavior,* p. 49, quoted by Rachel Jean Monfredo, *American Finger Rings / Representing Bonds of Relationships,* pp. 6-14.
24. Edwards, pp. 55-56.
25. *Transcript,* 24 Sept. 1841.
26. These were offered by J.G.L. Libby for $1 to $5 each. Boston Evening *Transcript,* 26 Dec. 1840.

purchased in 1851 in memory of Stephen Salisbury's mother Elizabeth, and was engraved with her initials and date of death. It had a shield-shaped bezel and was set with a bloodstone cut with his initials in gothic script. One ring was cut with the initials of Mary Grosvenor Salisbury who married Stephen Salisbury II in 1855. It had an entwined double band, as did the amethyst ring. She also owned a signet ring with her initials cut in cornelian.

The signet ring was appropriated by societies and schools for emblematic rings in the mid-nineteenth century. The tradition apparently began at West Point about 1835, and was followed by the United States Naval Academy several decades later (Colour Plate 101). At first the rings were purchased privately and were an elective part of the official graduating ceremony. The Military Academy rings were seal rings with class mottos. The class of 1835 motto was 'Amicitias Periculque Foldus'. The designs of the rings were selected on an informal basis as were the manufacturers until 1869 when the first competition took place among the cadets and a vote was taken on the design. Class rings continued to be made individually until the end of the century.[27] Many of the earliest rings were made by Ball & Black and its successors.

The first Naval Academy class rings were used at the 1869 graduation, but it was not until 1881 that these rings were distributed at the time of the graduation ceremonies.[28] The design of the Naval Academy rings followed the general pattern of the military rings, but nautical symbols were substituted. In both Military and Naval Academy rings, the stone used for the setting was often bloodstone, an obvious choice due to its symbolic meaning. For centuries this gem had been worn in battle as an amulet to help prevent the loss of blood. Tiffany produced many of the later Naval and Military Academy rings (Colour Plate 244).

Fraternal organizations followed the precedent of the academy class rings. Among the first was the order of the Freemasons which had a long tradition of symbolic jewels.[29]

During the Civil War, soldiers wore rings that could identify them, and prisoners often spent their hours carving rings from the bones of their food. Sailors on whalers whiled time away by carving rings from ivory and others formed rings out of silver or copper coins with the help of a marlin spike.[30]

Innovations in ring designs led to all sorts of oddities. A ring that could also serve as a watch key was invented and patented by Elihu Bliss, a Newark jeweler, in 1857.[31] Other rings were used for more devious purposes. A gambler, for instance, might have a ring with moveable parts so that it could display any one of the four card suits he might want his partner to lead. Thieves owned rings that had dog's head bezels. The ear of the dog was extended and well sharpened so that it could severely cut a victim if he were struck with it. We are told that the New York Chief of Police in the 1850s, if he caught someone with such a ring, clipped off the sharp ears from the ring before releasing the owner. Some thieves had rings equipped with cutting hooks or spring-lancets, so that the thief could cut the pocket of his intended victim.[32]

Innovations were made in the technology of ring making. Machines were invented to diestamp rings. Virgil Draper received his patent for such a mechanism in 1865.[33] Machines for engraving decoration on rings were invented. Straight-sided band rings were most easily produced by machines. To add some appeal to these plain bands, Frederick W. Martin of Massachusetts patented a design for a ring that had a musical clef and a few bars of music engraved on it (Plate 118). The design could be enamelled on either the intaglio or the relief surface.[34] A machine for producing rolling stock for finger-ring manufacturers was patented in 1872 by John S. Palmer of Providence.[35]

FIG. 1

FIG. 2

Plate 118. A bar of music decorates a wide band ring, a design patented by F.W. Martin of Springfield, Mass., 2 July 1872. U.S. Patent Office, 5970.

27. In 1897 the design changed from an engraved seal to an optional ornamental stone setting. A standard motto, 'Duty, Honor, Country' was adopted. Henceforth the Military Academy crest appeared on one shoulder of the ring and the class crest on the other. Letter from Mrs. Marie T. Capps, Map and Ms. Librarian, Dept. of the Army, USMA, West Point, NY., to author, 10 Nov. 1987.

28. Later it became customary to acquire the rings during the junior year. John Loring, *Tiffany's 150 Years*, pp. 130-31; Monfredo, pp. 50-56.

29. Monfredo has pointed out the close relationship between the Masonic fraternity and the US Military Academy and suggests that rings may have been used by Masons earlier than the Academies. pp. 36-52.

30. Edwards, p. 31.

31. US Pat. Off. #18,033, 25 Aug. 1857.

32. Edwards, p. 145.

33. US Pat. Design #2,063, 5 Sept. 1865.

34. Design Pat. #5,970, 2 July 1872.

35. Pat. #124,971, 26 Mar. 1872.

Plate 119. Mrs. John Quincy Adams' fetter chain with clasp in the shape of a hand. Smithsonian Institution.

By 1875 companies had grown up that manufactured nothing but rings. Clark & Coombs, first in Providence and then in New York, advertised as 'Makers of Rings'. They produced gold, plated and gold-filled rings of all sorts.[36]

Watches and Chains

The American watch industry had its origins in the 1830s when Henry and James Pitkin began manufacturing watches in Hartford, Connecticut, and later in New York. Their machinery was crude and their production limited. Patents were granted to a number of American watchmakers in the mid-nineteenth century for designs with unusual features of their own invention. In 1850 Edward Howard and Aaron Dennison of Boston started what soon became the Waltham Watch Co., inventing the machinery for making watch parts that, with a few alterations, is still used today.

Silver watches were shipped from England and Switzerland with their cases, but gold watches usually received their cases in America. William Warner of Philadelphia is credited with being the first American watchcase maker, beginning this business some time before 1812. Philadelphia continued to be one of the leading producers of gold watchcases. Among other watchcase makers in the city were Warner's successor T. Esmonde Harper; E. Tracy & Co. which supplied the American Watch Co.; and Jacot & Brother which supplied importers and jobbers.[37]

In 1856 there were eleven firms manufacturing watchcases in Philadelphia. Together they employed more than 300 workers and produced about 500 cases a week valued at $20,000 or a million dollars a year.[38] The gold used to produce a week's worth of cases cost at least $14,000. Newark jewelers also produced a great many watch cases as well as ornamental chains. In 1851 it was reported that about fifty workers in Newark were engaged in manufacturing watchcases.[39]

Among the patents issued to Providence jewelers were machines for forming watch and locket rims. Other mechanisms performed the tasks of burnishing and engraving.[40] Both Providence and Newark jewelers patented machinery for making ornamental chains.[41] By the 1870s the designs for chains were being patented as well as methods for their manufacture.

Increased production of American watches greatly increased the demand for the jewels used in watch movements. Each watch made use of seven to twenty-one jewels. Garnets, rubies and sapphires were used for this purpose. These gems were imported and usually were cut to shape abroad. However, the Waltham Watch Co. cut its own material. In addition, the industry required large quantities of diamonds to slit and drill the watch jewels.[42]

Swiss productions had challenged the market for French and English watches and were now competitive in both price and accuracy. Brackett, Crosby & Brown advertised in the Boston *Transcript* on 26 December 1849 that they had been appointed agents of the house of Malignon in Geneva and 'have just received a large

36. Rainwater, *AJM*, p. 62.
37. Edwin T. Freedley, *Philadelphia & its Manufactures*, pp. 345-347.
38. Boston *Transcript,* Mar. 8, 1856.
39. *The Sentinel,* 25 Feb. 1851.
40. Pat.#17,515; #17,416 (1857).
41. #25,837 (1859); #19,497 (1858); #20,183 (1858); #32,159 (1861); #34,564 (1862).
42. Geo.F. Kunz, *Gems & Precious Stones*, p. 319. By the early 1890s Kunz reported that the annual jeweled watch production in the United States had reached about 1,200,000 requiring approximately twelve million jewels (7,000,000 garnets, 5,000 each of rubies and sapphires, valued altogether at $300,000). These stones had to be flawless, of decided colour, and harder than quartz. Kunz hoped that American gem material would soon be utilized in American-made watches.

Plate 120 *John Henry and his wife emigrated from Ireland to New Orleans. His portrait by L.A.W.Neuser, painted in 1859, includes fancy shirt buttons and a slide chain attached to his watch which he pocketed in his waistcoat. Both he and his wife wore three rings on different fingers in their portraits. Length 36in., width 28¾in. Louisiana State Museum.*

assortment of Watches, plain and richly enamelled with paintings by the first artists for Ladies and Gentlemen; Watch jewels, Pompadours, Chatelaines, Bracelets, &c...The house of Malignon is known by all travellers to Geneva to be the best, and their goods to be of the finest quality and most exquisite finish'. 'Fine London and Geneva Watches' were touted in Boston by John B. Jones' jewelry store in 1856 and were promoted for holiday presents.[43] Jones claimed that their watches were made 'by all the celebrated makers'.[44] Watches made by the 'celebrated' Adams of London were specified by another Boston firm which also carried French watches.[45]

Samuel T. Crosby recommended a wide assortment of watches from 'the low-priced Swiss to the most elaborately balanced English masterpiece of mechanism'. He sold watches made by Charles Frodsham, F.B. Adams & Sons and E.F. Brandt.[46] Frodsham was well known for watches of the highest quality. By 1860 there was a special watch department in Crosby's store with an experienced man in charge of repairs to maintain the English, Swiss and American watches he sold.[47]

Palmer & Bachelders offered watches made by Frodsham, Adams, David Taylor, Russell and Sons, and Jules Jurgensen, and they were the New England agency for Patek, Philippe & Co. of Geneva. American watches were also stocked and could be purchased with gold or silver cases. Movements could be purchased without cases. They had low priced watches for the trade or for export. The firm hired S.W. Bailey, who had worked at Bailey, Chapman & Co., to supervise the watch repairing department.[48] C.L. Thierry specialized in manufacturing watch cases. In the Boston *Almanac* for 1867, he advertised engine-turning, polishing, springing and all kinds of repairing as well as gold and silver plating.

Salisbury Brothers & Co. of Providence supplied watches and other kinds of jewelry to dealers, jewelers, gift shops, dollar stores and Indian trading expeditions.[49] On the other side of the continent, California jewelers were selling Jurgensen and Perregaux watches.[50]

Early in the 1830s, there was a fad for making beaded ribbons that could be worn around the neck to keep watches from getting out of hand. Young ladies were encouraged to string these ornamental bands for their family members. Many had pretty floral patterns and inscriptions worked into the design commemorating for whom and when they were made (Colour Plate 102). They had gold fasteners and were worn by both men and women (see Colour Plate 79).

Long chains used for watches were made so that they served as necklaces as well as watch holders. The chain could be looped around the neck and then draped over the chest and attached to the watch so that it could not possibly slip away unnoticed. Often the watch was placed into a man's vest pocket or a lady's wide waistband for added protection (Plate 119).[51]

To make the chain stay in the proper position, a bar was added that could slide up and down, shortening or lengthening the chain as desired (Plate 120). These slides, as they are called today, could be set with gems or otherwise ornamented. They first appear in American portraits in the 1830s. Chains with slides were mass produced by

43. Boston D.E. *Transcript,* 20 Dec. 1856, Jones Shreve Brown & Co.
44. Ibid., 28 Dec. 1856.
45. Broadhead & Co., Ibid., 25 March 1856.
46. Ibid., 22 Dec. 1858.
47. Ibid., 8 May 1860. Lincoln's watch chain, Calif. gold, c.1861, illustrated in Sotheby 100 yrs., p. 157.
48. Ibid., 24 Dec. 1860.
49. Frank Leslie's *Illustrated Newspaper,* 12 April 1862.
50. Levison Bros. California Jewelry Co., 1 Jan. 1875. Edgar W. Morse, ed., *Silver in the Golden State,* p. 6.
51. See Blunt portrait of Lady on Red Sofa, c.1833, Sotheby's #5375, lot #79.

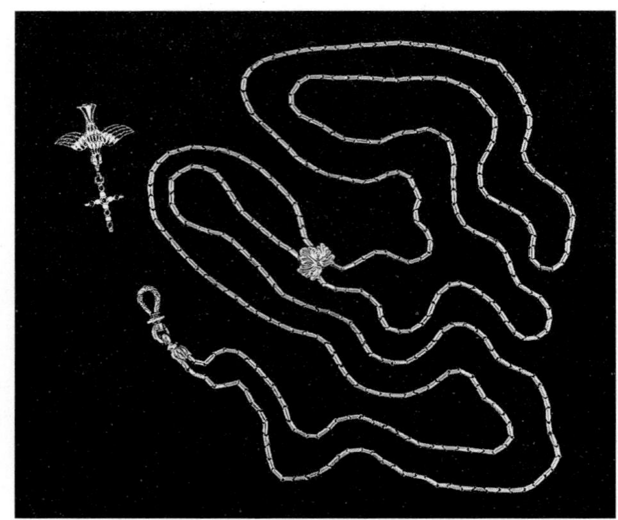

Plate 121. Slide chain, gold fill, with maple leaf slide, American, c.1860-70. Length 25¼in. (double). Box imprinted W.D. Fenno & Son, jewelers in Worcester between 1860 and 1869. Owned by the Salisbury family. Dove and cross pendant, gold with black and white enamel on gilt metal. Box imprinted Jones, Lows & Ball, in business in Boston, c.1835-39. Length 1⅜in. Photograph by Stephen Briggs. Bequest of Stephen Salisbury III Estate. Worcester Art Museum, Worcester, Mass.

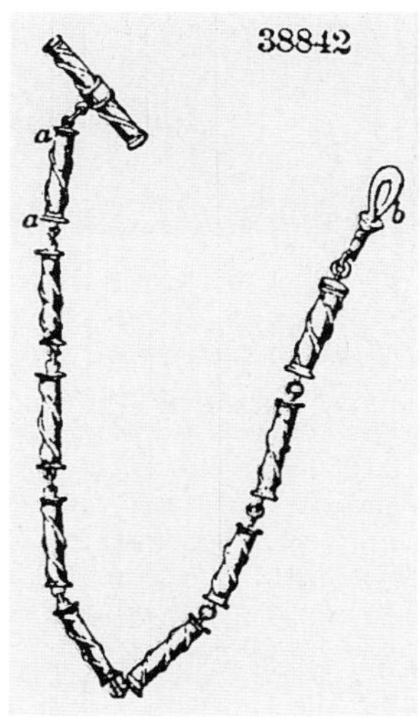

Plate 122. Design for an ornamented watch chain patented by Egbert S. Richards, Attleboro, Mass., No. 38,842, 9 June 1863.United States Patent Office.

American manufacturers and sold by jewelers throughout the country (Plate 121).

During the mid-nineteenth century, the specialist chainmaker and his product overwhelmed the market place. Jewelers sold ever-increasing miles of gold link chain in a variety of patterns. Chain was usually sold by the length. J.G.L. Libby advertised 'fine gold chain from $1.50 to $4. per foot', all made under his immediate supervision.[52]

The traditional method of making chain consisted of drawing wire to the desired thickness, winding the wire around a mandril of the desired dimension and then cutting the coils into separate links that could be joined together (loop in loop) and then soldered at the joints. Curb chains, which were popular in the late eighteenth century, were formed by giving each link a twist so that the chain could be flattened with a mallet and each link would be held in its proper position.[52]

Individual chainmakers became known sometimes for a particular type of chain. About 1830 Jabez Gorham in Providence designed a pattern that was called Gorham chain. His son knew it as Gadroon chain.[54] About the same time and in the same city, Adnah Sackett invented machinery to produce Adelaide chain.[55]

In the mid-nineteenth century, machines were developed to mass produce chains, both solid and hollow links, in various shapes and configurations. Providence gained an early lead in making chains by machine. In 1857, a machine for making ornamental chain was invented by E.H. Perry of Rhode Island and was patented by George Haseltine of Washington, D.C. The machine was sold by Haseltine, who had subsequently moved to London, to John T. Goode, leading chainmaker in Birmingham, England. Two years later, Haseltine patented a machine for making snake chain which he also sold to Goode.[56] The snake chain was made from stamped sheet metal blanks with arms that interlocked with each other and required no solder.

Not to be outdone, Charles W. Dickinson of Newark patented a machine for making loop chains in 1858.[57] Providence returned the challenge. James Lancelott of Cranston and South Providence patented several improvements in ornamental chainmaking in 1859.[58] In 1860 he took out a patent in England where his address was given as Essex.[59] Lancelott is said to have worked in Birmingham as well. Isaac Lindsley of Providence offered other improvements in the machine manufacture of gold chains which allowed the arms of 'convexo-concave' links to be formed as the links were stamped out of the strip of sheet metal.[60]

More complex and more decorative chains were made by machinery patented by Egbert S. Richards of Attleboro, Massachusetts, in 1863 (Plate 122). A skeletal frame of metal was produced that could contain ornamental stone or glass.[61] Virgil Draper of North Attleboro patented a device for swaging chain links in 1865[62] and William F. Davis patented a machine that would automatically connect links of ornamental chain.[63]

52. Boston *Transcript,* 26 Dec. 1840.
53. Thomas B. Wigley, *The Art of the Goldsmith and Jeweller,* Fig. p. 117.
54. Carpenter, *Gorham,* p. 25.
55. Rainwater, *AJM,* p. 106.
56. Bury I, 365.
57. #19,497.
58. #23,303 and 25, 837.
59. Bury I, 366, 438.
60. #29,503.
61. #38,842. Design patents issued to Richards in 1863 included #1757, 1758 and 1761. See also L. Towne's chain for ornament 1864, #44,899.
62. #50,200.
63. #151,362.

Diamonds

The taste for diamonds increased dramatically in the mid-nineteenth century. It was fed by rising fortunes, new sources of stones and protective tariffs that encouraged the production of diamond jewelry in the United States. Additional factors included more skilled jewelers, improved methods of faceting and more flattering ways of setting stones.

In 1828, the tariff levied on imported manufactured goods encouraged American jewelers to import unmounted stones and to design and make the settings themselves. Palmer & Clapp of New York was only one of a number of firms that began to specialize in diamond jewelry of their own manufacture. Between 1829 and 1833, they employed a dozen or more jewelers and supplied other jewelers with a variety of diamond work.[1] The diamonds they used were brilliant and rose cut, single or double cut, and occasionally table cut. Their average cost was about $35 a carat, larger diamonds ranging from $50 to $80 and smaller diamonds bringing between $25 to $30 to the New York trade. Occasionally yellow diamonds were used and they usually cost $50 a carat. Rose-cut diamonds were still being set in closed-back settings, but there was an increasing demand for brilliant-cut diamonds set in 'transparent' or open backs. Infrequently a basket setting was requested for a pin or a ring.

A typical pendant earring had a pear-shaped drop and a top that could be worn separately. It was gemmed with a number of small graduated diamonds, often with tiny gold scrolls between each of the diamonds (Plates 123-130). Another popular style was the earring with a cluster top, a pear-shaped drop and a horizontal asymmetrical scroll in between. In the middle of the pendant was a pear-shaped diamond. More unusual was a pair of earrings set with four dozen brilliant diamonds with three diamonds suspended from the pendant. Diamonds mounted in a lozenge at the top of the earring dangled a sunburst of diamonds suspended from attached scrolls. The size and number of diamonds in this design varied from thirty-five to forty-five stones and the cost for the pair might be $300 to $400. Another elaborate design featured elongated diamond shaped pendants and tops. Earrings with a grape motif were also popular in the 1830s.

Pendant crosses set with diamonds were very desirable and came in a variety of shapes. A straight-armed Latin cross had a cluster of diamonds at the transept, while a crosslet was made with clusters of three diamonds at the end of each diamond studded arm.

Studs, rings and small pins were made by the dozen. A popular style of mounting rings placed a half-carat diamond in a double bordered circular bezel with an enamelled bifurcated shank. Cluster rings, hoop and half-hoop rings continued to appeal to the New York trade. Both rings and pins were set with stones arranged in a diamond formation. A standard style for pins had a central rose or single cut diamond in a plain double border, with a straight stem and tiny furls at the base. Flower pins with rose diamond centres and enamelling were especially appealing and were ordered a hundred at a time by one customer of Palmer & Clapp. More unusual was the diamond crescent pin or a small diamond cross pin.[2]

By 1840 it was not unusual for a city jeweler such as J.G.L. Libby of Boston to

1. Design/account book 1829-1833, owned by a descendant of Henry W. Clapp of Greenfield, Mass., who was in partnership with James Palmer at 145 Reed Street from 1823-1835. von Khrum, p. 97; Francis Thompson, *The History of Greenfield, Mass.*
2. The account book of New York jeweler James S. Mott for the years 1833 to 1844 reveal that he was buying gem-set jewelry for resale from a number of manufacturing jewelers in New York. Chamberlin & Ellis supplied pins (some set with brilliant diamonds and some with imitation diamonds), brilliant and rose cut diamond rings (hoop and half hoop designs) and 'dangle top and drop earrings'. N-YHS Library, 20 June and 27 Aug. 1835.

1 pr Diamond E Rings Scroll pattern (Brilliants

Cary Mtg

Dimonds 5 & 3/4 cts @ $35 = $201.25
Mounting & Gold 33
$234.25

Cary Mtg

1 Finger Ring Scroll pattern (Brilliants
9 Dimonds 2 cts & 1/8 $35 $74.37
Mtg & Gold 7
$81.37

Cary Mtg

1 Pin Scroll pattern (Brilliants
9 Diamonds 1 & 1/4 cts @ 35 $43.75
Mtg & Gold 6
$49.75

Cary Mtg

1 Ring Detached pattern Roses
11 Stone 3/4 cts @ 30 $22.50
Mtg $3 Gold & charge $3 6
$28.50

Cary Mtg

1 Pin Detached pattern Roses
17 Stone 1/2 1/8 cts @ $30 $18.75
Mtg $3.50 Gold $1 4.50
$23.25

Plates 123 to 130. Designs for diamond jewelry, drawn in the record book of the jewelry firm established by James Palmer & Henry Wells Clapp at 145 Read Street in New York City from 1829 to 1833. Courtesy of William Lanford, thrice great grandson of Henry Wells Clapp.

1 cross Transpt close set (Brilliants

Sawin Mtg 3½ cts @ 35 $122.50
Mtg & Gold 15.00
$ 137.50

12 Scroll pattern collar Buttons (Brilliants
Carey Mtg 12 Dimonds Single cut 1 ct $30.00
Mtg $15 Gold $11.25 26.25
$ 56.25

6 Transpt Dimond pins (Single cut Brilliants

Edward Mtg 36 Dimonds 4¼ cts @ $30 — $127.50
Mtg & Gold @ $4 — 24
$ 151.50

Carey Mtg 1 Pin detatch pattern (Brilliants
17 Dimonds 1¾ cts $35 $61.25
Mtg $3.50 Gold $1 4 50
65 75

6 pins Chased Borders & Shank (Rose
Sawin Mtg 24 Dimonds 2 cts @ $25 $50
Mtg & Gold &c

Esnaill mty

36 Single cut Dimonds for pins 6#
Weigh 1ct 1/8 1/16 @ $32 $38.00
Mtg & Gold @ 4 24
$62.00

Lawn Mtg

24 Single cut Dimonds for plain pins
Dimonds Weigh 2ct 1/2 @ 32 $80
Mtg & Gold @ $175 42
$122

Lawn Mtg

24 Rose Dimonds plain pins
Dimonds Weigh 1ct 1/2 @ 30 $45.00
Mtg & Gold @ $175 42
87

Carey Mtg
pr $20 +

Rose Dimonds for F Magill

Esnaill Mtg

24 Brilliants 2 pins Trand/r
3ct 1/2 1/8ct @ $38 $137.75
Mtg & Gold 10.00
$147.75

Pavin Mty

44 Briliants for 4 Ear Rings
2 Dimonds Weigh 2 1/2 1/8 1/32 $60 $162.12
42 do do 3 1/2 1/8 1/16 1/32 35 $130.14
Mty 20 Gold $5 25.00
$317.26

Eding altrd by taking out Large Stone in the Drops

Esmalt Mty

78 Rose dimonds
Weighing 4 cts $30 $120.00
Mty & Gold

Not made

Esmalt Mty

54 Dimonds for 6 Rings Transpt
Dimonds 2 1/4 1/8 35 $83.12
Mty & Gold By Esmalt 3 18
$101.12

Pavin Mty

1 Center Briliant 2 cts $60 — $120
34 Briliants 2 & 3/4 35 96
Mty 5th Gold $5 10
$226.00

Sawin Mty

12 Rubys & Emeralds $16
6 Rose dimonds 35
6 Single cut do 35
Mty 10 $ Gold $17 42
Done
$128

Barry mtg $12 -

Made of Rose diamonds for H Margaret

Carey mtg

26 Brilliants for Ring & Single Stone

Diamonds 3 1/2 cts — 30 $105.00

Carey mtg — 3/1 — 36.00

Gold dw 36 — 27.00

$ 168.00

1 Large Diamond 2 1/2 cts 60 $ 150.00

Carey mtg

diamond

9 Small do 1/16 20 1.87

Gold $1.50 mtg $3.00 4.50

$ 156.37

Carey mtg

24 Single cut Diamonds for Buttons

Diamonds 2/4 & 1/8 cts @ 30 $ 71

Gold $24 $ mtg 1 $ 24 48

$ 119

Carey Mtg

3 Rings Brilliants 27 Dimonds
Weigh 2 1/4 1/16 @ $35 = $80.93
Mtg @ 3 10 $10.50 Gold — 3 50 14
$ 94.93

Carey Mtg

3 Half Hoop Briliants 15 Dimonds
Weigh 3 cts 35 $105.00
Mtg @ 2 $6 Gold — 3 9
114
Gold 3 3 50 $150
Lirre

1 pair Ethings 66 Briliants
5 carrats Diamonds @ 35 $175
Mounting 20
Gold 5
$ 200.00

1 pair Single Stone Basket Setting
Weigh 1 1/2 1/8 1/16 @ 65 — $ 109.68
Mtg $2 50 gold $1 3 50
113 18

Rilen

1 Ring Single Stone Basket Setting
Weigh 1 1/4 1/8 1/32 @ 65 = 91.81
Mtg $2 Gold $1 3

H & B
Nov 1830
$130

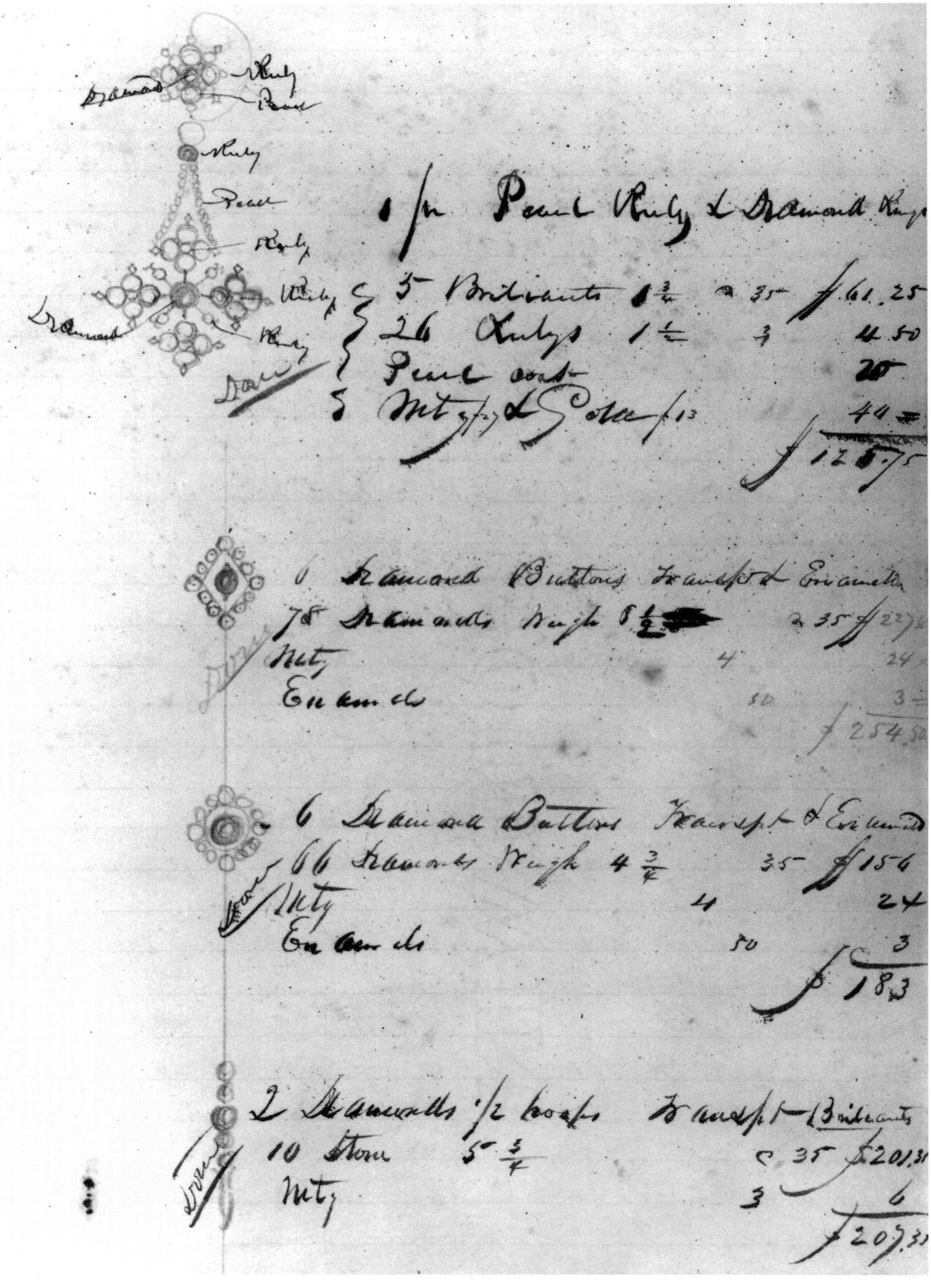

Diamond — Ruby — Pearl

Ruby

Pearl

Ruby

Ruby

Diamond — Ruby

Done

1 pr Pearl Ruby & Diamond Rings

5 Brilliants	1 3/4	@ 35	f 61.25
26 Rubys	1 1/2	3	4.50
Pearl cost			20
Mtg & Gold f 13			44
			f 12[illegible].75

Done

6 Diamond Buttons Transpt & Enamelled

78 Diamonds Weigh 6 1/2	@ 35	f 22[illegible]
Mtg	4	24
Enamels	50	3
		f 254.50

Done

6 Diamond Buttons Transpt & Enamelled

66 Diamonds Weigh 4 3/4	35	f 156
Mtg	4	24
Enamels	50	3
		f 183

Done

2 Diamonds 1/2 hoops Transpt Brilliants

10 Stone 5 3/4	@ 35	f 201.31
Mtg	3	6
		f 207.31

8 Rose Diamond Rings
54 Stones Weigh 1 1/2 @ 30 $45
Done Mtg 4 24
Enamels 0.25 1 50
$76.50

1 Pair Diamond Earrings Brilliants
66 Diamonds in Drops 4 1/2 1/8 @ 35 $161.87
21 Do in Spins 1 3/4 35 61.00
Mounting 25
Enamels 50 2 50
$251.37

24 Pins fild mill chased Shanks
24 Brilliants Weigh 3 3/4 1/8 @ 30 $116
Done Mtg @ 18 54
$170

12 Brilliants for Buttons fild mill Enamelled
Done 12 Stones Weigh 4 1/8 @ 35 $143.75
Mtg @ 150 18
Enamels 25 3
$164.75

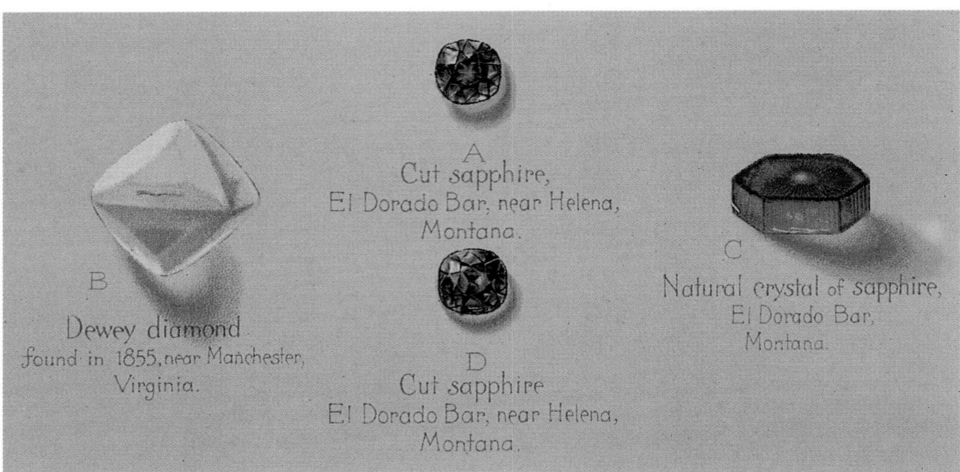

Colour Plate 104. Illustration of gemstones found in the United States, published in George F. Kunz, Gems and Precious Stones of North America *(New York 1890), Plate I. The Dewey diamond (left) was found near Manchester, Virginia in 1855. The three sapphires were discovered in Montana. Length 8¾in; 5½in.*

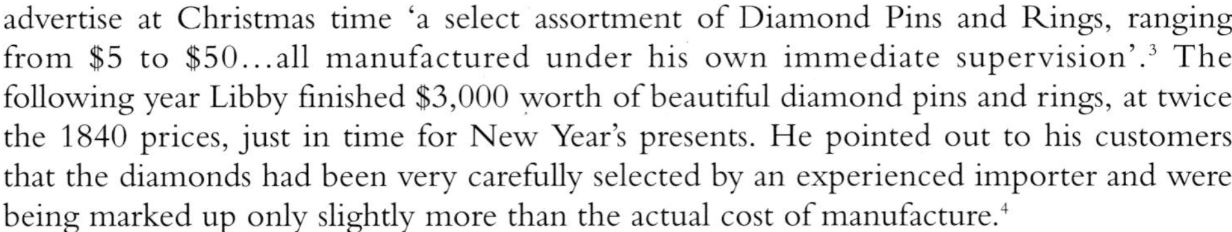

advertise at Christmas time 'a select assortment of Diamond Pins and Rings, ranging from $5 to $50...all manufactured under his own immediate supervision'.[3] The following year Libby finished $3,000 worth of beautiful diamond pins and rings, at twice the 1840 prices, just in time for New Year's presents. He pointed out to his customers that the diamonds had been very carefully selected by an experienced importer and were being marked up only slightly more than the actual cost of manufacture.[4]

In July 1841 a fancy ball was held in Boston at Faneuil Hall to honour the Prince de Joinville. While most of the ladies were ornamented with flowers, one unmarried woman had diamonds looping the sleeves of her black velvet dress, and an unnamed matron was blazoned with a parure of diamonds.[5] Such reports as this appearing in local newspapers, along with accounts of jewelry worn at the Court of Queen Victoria, did much to fan the growing interest in significant jewelry in this country.

It was also in 1841 that the Revenue Bill passed by the Senate raised the duty on imported jewelry and precious stones that were already mounted in jewelry. This further stimulated American jewelers not only to import stones but to cut and set them themselves.[6] The first American firm credited with dealing exclusively in diamonds was Randel & Baremore, founded in New York in 1840. They were also seriously engaged in diamond cutting.[7]

The role played by Charles L. Tiffany in the promotion of fine diamond jewelry for multitudes of Americans can not be exaggerated. In the 1840s, the firm had developed its reputation for carrying only better jewelry (Plate 131). A special goldsmithing shop was established so that the firm could produce its own jewelry in house. During the collapse of Louis Philippe's regime in 1848, John Young, the partner charged with purchasing for Tiffany's in France, was able to take advantage of the glut of diamonds that were being sold by fleeing nobility. It was a dangerous business, but among the many jewels acquired by them at this time were some of the crown jewels of France and the jewels of the King's wife Maria Amelia.[8] Marie Antoinette's diamond girdle is believed to have been one of the treasures that was acquired at this time and broken up into smaller pieces of jewelry for Tiffany's customers. It was this coup that won for Tiffany the title of the King of Diamonds.

3. Boston *Transcript*, 26 Dec. 1840.
4. Ibid., 22 Dec. 1841.
5. Ibid., 26 Nov. 1841.
6. Ibid., 13 Aug. 1841.
7. During the early years of their partnership, they were at several different locations, but in 1854 they established themselves at the corner of Maiden Lane and Nassau Street where the firm remained very active in the diamond business for more than half a century. Von Khrum, p. 106.
8. Joseph Purtell, *The Tiffany Touch,*, pp. 21-22.

Plate 131. Tiffany & Co. hair bracelet, New York, 1851. Tightly plaited strands of hair are braided into a thick coil bracelet band with gold collets at each end, attached to a medallion clasp with the monogram M outlined in diamonds. Engraved on fastener MEM / 10th July 1851. Diameter 2½in. Courtesy New-York Historical Society.

Colour Plate 105. Design for a brooch to be made by Tiffany & Co., late 1860s, with diamonds in scrolled leafage and what appears to be a pendent black pearl. John Loring's Tiffany's 150 Years *(New York: Doubleday, 1987).*

Colour Plate 106. Tiffany & Co. design for a spray of lily of the valley, set with diamonds, tied with a bow, and pendent tear-drop pearl. John Loring's Tiffany's 150 Years *(New York: Doubleday, 1987).*

The establishment of a branch of the firm in Paris, under the direction of their new partner Gideon F.T. Reed, allowed Tiffany to purchase diamonds and other jewelry for his customers on a less revolutionary basis. The firm's expansion dovetailed neatly with the rising fortunes of American entrepreneurs. In 1852 Tiffany advertised that 'the advantages of having their own house in Paris, and their own manufactories of

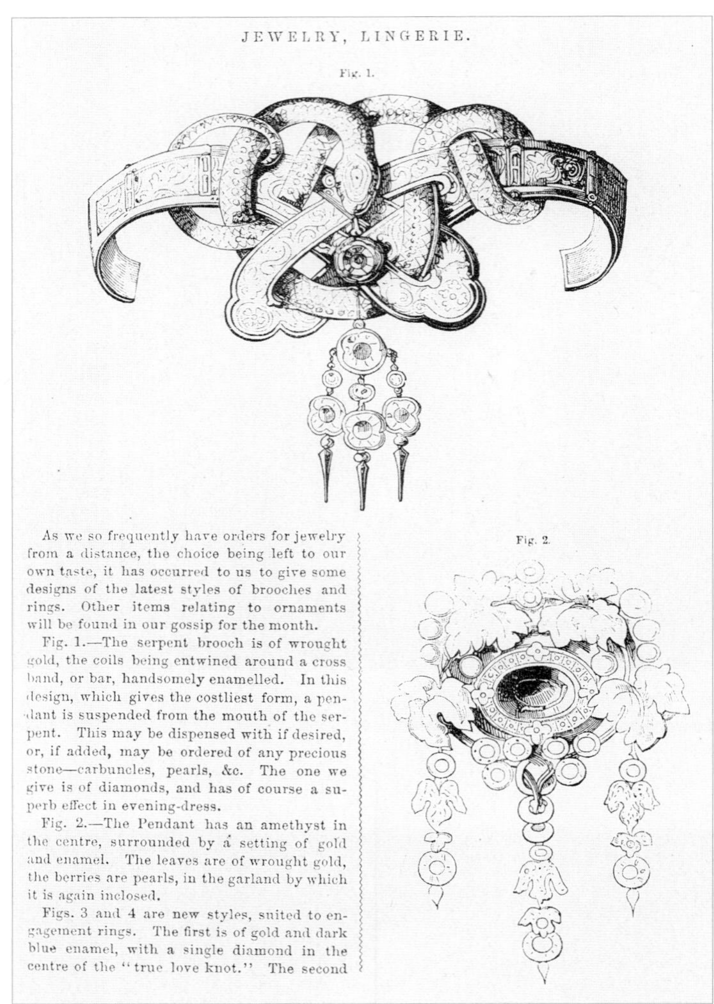

JEWELRY, LINGERIE.

Fig. 1.

As we so frequently have orders for jewelry from a distance, the choice being left to our own taste, it has occurred to us to give some designs of the latest styles of brooches and rings. Other items relating to ornaments will be found in our gossip for the month.

Fig. 1.—The serpent brooch is of wrought gold, the coils being entwined around a cross band, or bar, handsomely enamelled. In this design, which gives the costliest form, a pendant is suspended from the mouth of the serpent. This may be dispensed with if desired, or, if added, may be ordered of any precious stone—carbuncles, pearls, &c. The one we give is of diamonds, and has of course a superb effect in evening-dress.

Fig. 2.—The Pendant has an amethyst in the centre, surrounded by a setting of gold and enamel. The leaves are of wrought gold, the berries are pearls, in the garland by which it is again inclosed.

Figs. 3 and 4 are new styles, suited to engagement rings. The first is of gold and dark blue enamel, with a single diamond in the centre of the "true love knot." The second

Fig. 2.

Plate 132. Illustration of a brooch with detachable pendant, published in Godey's Lady's Book, *February 1857, p. 163, Fig. 1. Serpent entwined around a cross band that is 'handsomely enamelled'. It is set with diamonds but could be made with carbuncles or pearls instead. Courtesy, The Winterthur Library: Printed Book and Periodical Collection.*

Jewelry, Silver Ware, &c., here [in New York] enable them to offer inducements in prices and qualities,...such as cannot be offered by any other house in the trade'.[9]

The availability of diamond jewelry in New York in 1854 is apparent in the list of goods being auctioned in New York that year by William Irving. Included were elegant diamond rings (solitaire and cluster), crosses each set with eleven large brilliant cut diamonds, and diamond brooches and pendants.[10] Occasionally diamonds were advertised in more unusual ways. 'A lady appeared at a recent ball at Congress Hall, Saratoga, with a $10,000 set of diamonds, besides other jewelry, upon her person. They were not her own, however, but belonged to a dealer who hoped to find a market for them among the fashionables, and took this method of advertising them'.[11]

By mid-century, jewelers in smaller cities throughout the United States were also able to offer their customers diamond jewelry. F.H. Clark & Co. of Memphis, Tennessee, advertised jewelry of 'all kinds repaired, and new made to order, including superior Diamond work'.[12] *Godey's Lady's Book,* published in Philadelphia, received so many requests for jewelry from out-of-town subscribers who left the choice of design to the editor, that they decided to include illustrations and descriptions of the latest fashions for rings, brooches and bracelets (Plate 132). They further suggested that purchases be made through J. E. Caldwell, jewelers in Philadelphia.

1859 was the year that the Diamond Wedding occurred in New York, inspired no doubt by accounts that had appeared in American newspapers of the jewelry lavished upon Queen Victoria's daughter the year before when she married Prince Frederick

9. *NY Times,* 1 Jan. 1852.
10. Ibid., 10 Jan. 1854.
11. Boston *Transcript,* 22 Aug. 1856.
12. *Raney's Comm. & Bus. Dir.,* 1860.

Plate 133. The 'Diamond Wedding' procession. The bride wears her Tiffany diamond and pearl parure, the gift of the bridegroom who wears an enormous diamond solitaire as a shirt pin. Frank Leslie's Illustrated Newspaper, *22 October 1859.*

Plate 134. Diamond and pearl parure made by Tiffany & Co. for the wedding of Don Estaban Santa Cruz de Oviedo and Frances Amelia Bartlett which took place in New York, 13 October 1859. Frank Leslie's Illustrated Newspaper, *22 October 1859.*

William of Prussia.[13] 'The pomp of wealth, the majesty of loveliness and the splendor of gems', described the marriage of Frances Amelia Bartlett of New York to the wealthy Cuban Don Estaban Santa Cruz de Oviedo on 13 October 1859.[14] The wedding and the jewelry created an enormous stir (Plate 133).

Foremost among the jewels bestowed by Oviedo was a parure created by Tiffany & Co. for her bridal jewelry (Plate 134). The necklace and bracelet were composed of four strands of sizeable and fine pearls. In the centre of the necklace was a large lover's

13. Boston *Transcript*, 11, 16 Feb. 1858.
14. Frank Leslie's *Illus. News.*, 22 Oct. 1859, p. 319.

Ministère
de la
MAISON
de
L'EMPEREUR

Chancellerie

No 852.

St Pétersbourg le 20 Février / 4 Mars 1859.

Monsieur

Sa Majesté l'Empereur de toutes les Russies, mon Auguste Souverain, Se plaît à Vous gratifier d'une tabatière ornée de Son chiffre et enrichie de diamants, en retour des différentes armes dont Vous avez fait hommage à Sa Majesté ainsi qu'à Leurs Altesses Impériales les Grands Ducs de Russie.

Vous voudrez bien m'accuser la réception du cadeau Impérial mentionné, que je m'empresse de Vous transmettre, ci-près.

Recevez, Monsieur, l'expression de mes civilités.

Le Ministre de la Maison de l'Empereur [illegible]

Mr Colt.

... Etats Unis. Amérique

Colour Plate 107. Jewelry presented to Col. Samuel Colt in the 1850s by foreign rulers in appreciation for Colt's manufacture of the revolver. Gold repoussé snuff box, with multicoloured enamel to set off the diamond monogram of Alexander II. Engraved in Cyrillic 'From Alexander II, Emperor of All Russians to Col. Samuel Colt'. Cluster diamond ring has central reserve with dark blue enamel and initial A in diamonds, the gift of Alexander I in 1854 when he was Russian Grand Duke. The lozenge-shaped ring was the gift of Alexander's father, the Emperor Nicholas and bears his monogram, N with a crown above. Gift of Mrs. Samuel Colt (Elizabeth Hart Jarvis), 1905. Wadsworth Atheneum, Hartford, Conn.

Colour Plate 108. Diamond solitaire, ½in. in diameter, weighing 7⅛ karats, the gift of Charles Albert, King of Sardinia, to Col. Samuel Colt. This diamond was reset (both mounts survive) as an engagement ring for Colt's wife. Gift of Mrs. Samuel Colt (Elizabeth Hart Jarvis), 1905. Wadsworth Atheneum, Hartford, Conn.

knot sparkling with diamonds, from which was suspended a pear-shaped pearl to match the pendant pearl earrings. The bracelet was centred with a diamond-shaped medallion of pearls and diamonds. The interplay of lozenge shapes with round shapes was used to great effect in the brooch where faceted diamonds contrasted with smooth round pearls and a large kite-shaped pendant diamond contrasted with the pendant pearls in the other pieces of the set. 'Never in this country has there been seen a bride dressed in more royal robes than those of the bride of Thursday' gushed *Leslie's Illustrated Newspaper.* Miss Bartlett was even compared favourably to the Empress Eugénie of France, having 'the same style of face, the same drooping of the eyelids, the *spirituelle* aspect of countenance, the same color and manner of wearing the hair'.[15]

Featured among the trousseau jewelry were several sets from Ball, Black & Co. that were considered to be 'of surpassing magnificence and originality of style' (Plate 135). The *Illustrated Newspaper* was granted sketching privileges prior to the wedding and was able to furnish the public with exclusive detailed drawings of the most important pieces of jewelry purchased by the groom to meet his bride's every need. The elaborate diamond jewelry included a parure made up of rosettes, volutes and diamonds set 'in a rain' (falling in streams of raindrops). The necklace, brooch and hair ornaments were light and airy, with trails of tapering raindrops. The bracelet and earrings, while sympathetic in design, were more substantial looking and more tailored. The tops of the

15. 22 Oct. 1859, p. 320.

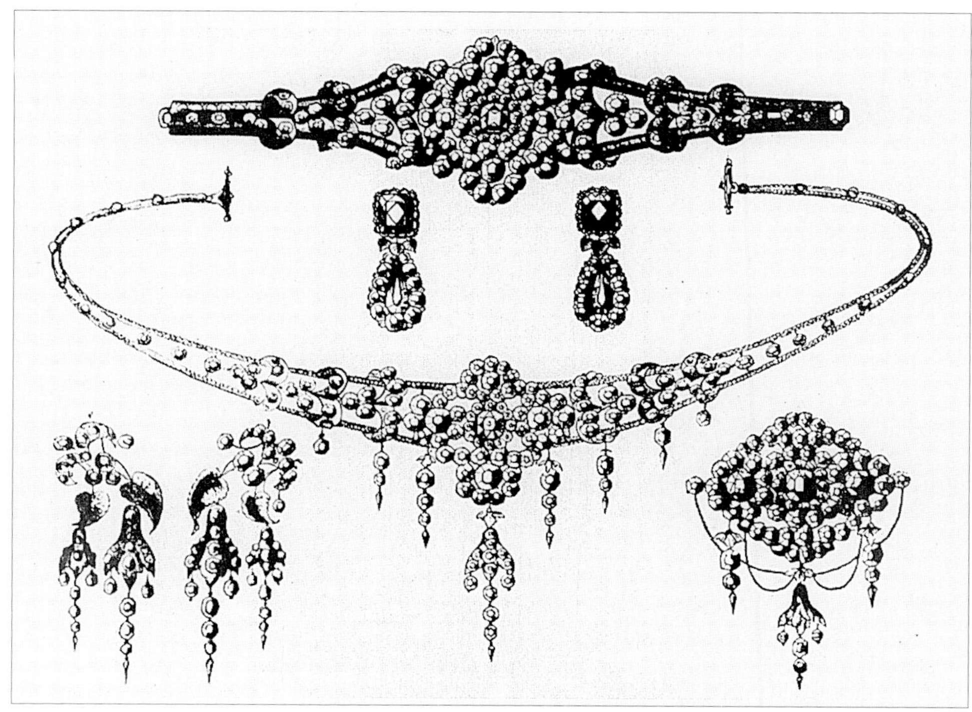

Plate 135. Set of diamond jewelry, made for the Oviedo and Bartlett wedding of 1859 by Ball, Black and Co. of New York, said to have been of 'surpassing magnificence and originality of style'. Frank Leslie's Illustrated Newspaper, *22 October 1859.*

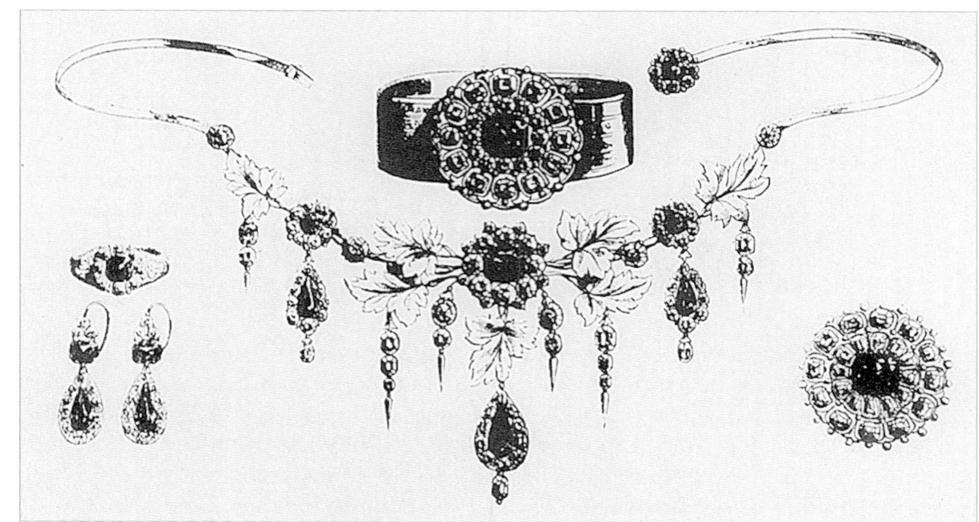

Plate 136. Diamond and ruby set made by Ball, Black and Co. as part of the wedding trousseau of Frances Amelia Bartlett in New York 1859. Frank Leslie's Illustrated Newspaper, *29 October 1859.*

earrings were set with large rectangular diamonds from which were suspended perfectly matched pear-shaped diamonds outlined with smaller diamonds.

Ball, Black & Co. supplied several other diamond parures studded with coloured gems. One featured emeralds with black pearl pendants. A suite in the Moorish style was mounted with emeralds and diamonds. Another was made of rubies and diamonds (Plate 136). There was a set of cameos and diamonds, a set of acorn clusters made of diamonds and purple pearls, and a coral parure (Plate 137). A pair of everyday diamond earrings and several diamond and sapphire rings also came from Ball, Black.

Tiffany provided some of the lesser jewelry in the groom's gift. The diamond covered Swiss watch and its matching chatelaine and charms were enamelled in the blue colour for which Geneva was known. A particularly fine onyx cameo was skilfully cut with the profile of Medusa and mounted in a frame of large diamonds. Tiffany's also made a blue-enamelled demi-parure in the antique Pompeian style. The brooch was described as having 'very rare diamonds set in three horizontal medallions, with smaller medallions pendant by brilliant chains'. The earrings were similar but had single medallions. 'The work upon this is such as can be done by only one artificer in the United States, though the design is but a single specimen from the antique *repertoire* of Tiffany & Co.' observed the *Illustrated.*[16] The groom's only piece of jewelry was the breastpin he wore at his wedding. The solitaire diamond in the pin reportedly cost $6,000 and it also came from Tiffany's.

Between the two New York firms, the Oviedo jewelry was estimated to be worth about $90,000. In 1882 the occasion was still remembered as the 'Diamond Wedding' when the widow Oviedo was remarried in New York with little pomp. There was no mention of the jewelry she wore at her second marriage, but the public still recalled the richness of the ornaments at her first marriage.[17] Indeed it had been as much a tribute to the wealth of the Cuban groom as it was to the American jewelers who had produced it and the lovely blonde bride who inspired the gift.

It was in Boston that the first and most important contributions to the diamond business were made. The man responsible was Henry D. Morse (1826-1888). Starting out as an engraver and silversmith in his father's shop, he soon began to specialize in jewelry. He became interested in diamonds. He wanted to learn how to bring the age-old art of diamond cutting as practised in Amsterdam to his country and to perfect the art. As his reputation spread, diamonds were sent from all over the United States to be cut at the Morse Diamond Cutting Company which he had established in Boston.

With the discovery and export of large quantities of diamonds from South America about 1870, there was an unprecedented supply of diamonds available. Through

16. Ibid., p. 320.
17. *The Sun*, 6 Sept. 1882.

Plate 137. Rich jewelry made for the 'Diamond Wedding' on 13 October 1859 by Ball, Black & Co. Diamonds were used with emeralds, black pearls, cameos or coral jewelry suitable for every social occasion. Frank Leslie's Illustrated Newspaper, *5 November 1859.*

experimentation and the application of the laws of science, Morse was able to bring diamond-cutting to a previously unknown state of perfection. His shop foreman, Charles M. Field, developed the steam-driven machinery that allowed the stones to be cut and polished precisely at the correct angle. Morse developed what would be known as the American cut. Diamonds had never before sparkled with such brilliance.

The development of American diamond cutting had an immediate effect on the amount of diamonds imported to the United States and the production of diamond jewelry. In 1867 Americans imported over $1,300,000 worth of loose diamonds and other gems and only $291 worth of stones set in gold or other metal. The amount of loose unset gems increased by $1,000,000 in 1871, while there was only $256 worth of imported mounted stones. The amount of rough uncut diamonds was so small that it was not reported until 1873 when $176,426 worth of rough was imported along with almost three million dollars' worth of cut but unset stones.[18]

Simultaneously, the number of jewelers setting and selling diamond jewelry increased throughout the United States. Methods of setting this most precious stone changed so that the beauty of the diamond was further enhanced. The open-back setting that had come into fashion in the early part of the nineteenth century became more universal. This allowed light to enter the diamond through the facets, thereby increasing the brilliance. At first, the open-setting was achieved by cutting out the back of the collet. This was followed by the prong setting, either cut into the collet or soldered on to the side of the collet.

Solutions were found for mass-producing settings. As early as 1832, a method of setting diamonds had been patented by Philadelphia jeweler John Dickinson.[19] In 1857, Isaac Lindsley, a Providence jeweler, patented a means of stamping out settings for mounting diamonds that could at the same time raise 'points or studs' which served as prongs to hold the stones. This, he claimed, produced a superior setting, gave greater brilliance to the diamonds, and the cost of the labour involved was no greater than it would be for the setting then being used in making cheap jewelry.[20] New York City jeweler Francis Stefani formed settings with a bezel that had two fixed claws and two removable claws, the latter being attached by screws.[21] For the most part, good diamond jewelry continued to be set in individually crafted mounts. By the third quarter of the nineteenth century, relatively little mounted diamond jewelry was being imported. Most of it was being set in American shops.

18. Ten years later, imported rough had climbed to 2½ times that value, and the value of cut unset stones had increased in the same proportion. Kunz, *Gems,* pp. 113-14.
19. Henry Ellsworth, *A Digest of Patents,* p. 411.
20. #18,288, 29 Sept. 1857.
21. #58,501, Oct. 1866.

Colour Plate 109. Emerald and diamond ring, diamond and ruby coronet brooch, with detachable scrolled brooch, owned by Mrs. Jefferson Davis, whose husband was President of the Confederacy during the Civil War. Smithsonian Institution.

Coloured Gems

Colour Plate 111. Rings belonging to the Salisbury family of Worcester, Mass., probably purchased in Boston, c.1850-1860. Ruby ring with twisted gold band. Ring with cruciform bezel set with emeralds, wheel-shaped band. Ring with large diamond flanked by smaller diamonds, engraved inside band SS to NHL April 29th 1850, and given by Stephen Salisbury II to his second wife Nancy Hoard Lincoln when they were married in 1850. Ring set with ruby, engraved band. All about ¾in. diameter. Photograph by Stephen Briggs. Bequest of Stephen Salisbury III Estate. Worcester Art Museum, Worcester, Mass.

With the rococo revival and the return to naturalism, a great variety of gems of all colours reappeared in American jewelry. Garnets, amethysts, aquamarines and topazes continued in favour. Emeralds, rubies, opals and turquoises received renewed attention. All of these gems were offered by J.G.L. Libby of Boston in 1840 for use in rings manufactured under his immediate supervision.[1] Rings and small pins were the objects most often purchased and so it was in these items that people often had their first opportunity to enjoy the use of brightly coloured precious stones.

Solitaire rings, shirt pins and buttons could be purchased in plain, enamelled or chased settings with the customer's choice of gemstone, whether ruby, emerald, pearl or diamond. Some had scroll settings and others were designed to look like a little flower set with diamond petals (see Plates 123-30). A variety of coloured stones could also be used in the same piece of jewelry; rubies, emeralds and pearls being a favourite combination in rings.[2]

In the 1830s the idea of using the first letter of each gem's name to spell out a

Colour Plate 110. Group of gem-set rings, Boston, c.1850-1870. Bow-tie ring, ruby and pearl, black enamel outlining, machine decorated straight flat band. Emerald cabochon ring with open-work shoulders. Lozenge-shaped bezel, black enamel background, set with rubies and pearls. Diameter ¾in. Rose cut garnet and gold hoop ring, inscribed inside the band 'Remember the Giver'. Photograph by David Bohl, Boston. Society for the Preservation of New England Antiquities.

Colour Plate 112. (Left) Turquoise and pearl studded gold locket, monogrammed on reverse MEL for Mamie E. Lamont, later Mrs. James R. Jesup, c.1871. Gift of Harry Harkness Flagler, 51.20.4. (Centre) Gold brooch with cameo carved with charioteer and horse drawn chariot, surrounded by diamonds, four oriental pearls and four emeralds, with detachable pendant set with a cameo head. French, c.1860, owned by Mrs. August Belmont, Sr. (née Caroline Slidell Perry). French eagle head mark on pin. Length 2in. Bequest of Eleanor Robson Belmont, 80.36 a b. (Right) Brooch set with old mine cut diamonds and oval opals, accented with green enamel, owned by Mrs. Charles A. Lamont, c.1870, mother of the donor's wife. Gift of Harry Harkness Flagler, 51.20.1. Photograph by Arthur Vitols, The Helga Studio. Museum of the City of New York.

Colour Plate 113. Ruby and opal ring in mount with chased decoration, engraved inside the band 'M.L. / July 29th 1856'. Diameter ¾in. Pair of gold earrings, set with turquoises and seed pearl in centre, in the form of a flower. Length ¾in overall. Photograph by Mark Sexton. Peabody Essex Museum.

Colour Plate 114. Gold scrolled hollow bracelet with hinged band, set with opals and emeralds, American, c.1863-4. Given by Charles Otto Witte to Charlotte Sophia Reeves of Charleston, as an engagement present. Diameter 1¾in. Photograph courtesy of the Charleston Museum, Charleston, S.C. Private Collection.

Colour Plate 115. Gold brooch (left) in open scroll-work, stamped setting with pendant drop, set with cabochon garnets. Brought from London before 1847, according to family tradition, by Joseph Silvester of Danvers, Mass., for his daughter Luella Stacey, on the last of his visits to England. Length 1⅞in. (brooch). Bohemian garnet brooch set in gilt metal frame, mass produced and sent in great quantity to the United States for resale. Diameter 1 9/16in. Photograph by Mark Sexton. Peabody Essex Museum.

sentiment came into fashion. Ruby, emerald, garnet, amethyst, another ruby, and a diamond, set in the proper order, spelled 'regard'. Rings set accordingly became known as regard rings. The New York firm of Palmer & Clapp first made regard rings in 1833.[3] Regard rings were offered among jewelry in the newest style in Boston in 1848.[4] The same message was intended to be sent by the gold filigree brooch made in the form of a dove carrying a heart, and the sentiment in stones across its outspread wings (see Colour Plate 88, right).

By mid-century, rubies and emeralds were considered appropriate stones for use in engagement rings. An emerald and diamond engagement ring was presented to Varina Howell by the Confederacy's future president Jefferson Davis when they were

1. Boston *Eve. Transcript*, 29 Dec. 1840.
2. Henry W. Clapp and James Palmer, Design/Account Book, *passim*.
3. Ibid., 107, 121. In some of these rings the diamonds were rose cut and in others were single cut. The cost of making them was a little over $6. each.
4. Advertisement of Eben Cutler, Boston *Transcript*, 20 Dec. 1848.

married in 1845 in Mississippi. Mrs. Davis also owned a ruby and diamond brooch that survived the Civil War (Colour Plate 109).[5] Palmer & Clapp made several emerald-cut emerald rings with rectangular bezels set with a border of diamonds.[6]

Among the Salisbury family jewelry in Worcester, Massachusetts, is an emerald-cut ruby ring in a gold setting marked with the Paris eagle stamp used from 1847 throughout the century. Another ring featured a tiny cross set with emeralds (Colour Plate 111). On 14 July 1843, Lows Ball & Co. billed Mrs. Stephen Salisbury for a diamond and emerald ring valued at $23.[7]

Samuel T. Crosby of Boston advertised that he had rubies, emeralds and pearls available for jewelry to be made by his firm in Boston in 1856 and Tiffany's called attention to their receipt of 'a lot of fine Old Spanish Emeralds' in 1868.[8]

The long drop earrings popular at this time had tops consisting 'of one large precious stone – as an emerald, a ruby, or a sapphire – set round with five pearls or brilliants', according to *Godey's Lady's Book* in 1856.[9]

Opals

Opals were rarely seen in American jewelry until the second quarter of the nineteenth century, and even then were not for superstitious people. Sir Walter Scott's romance *Anne of Geierstein,* published in 1829, publicized the long-held fear that opals caused misfortune. They were thought to be unlucky for all who could not claim opals as their birthstone. However, opals received the blessing of Queen Victoria and others who, unintimidated, indulged themselves in the unusual beauty of opals.

Opal is an amorphous silica and therefore enjoys endless variety and colour. To John Ruskin the opal in its uncut state presented 'the most lovely colours seen in the world, except those of clouds.'[10] Historically opals came from mines in northern Hungary. Samuel T. Crosby said his opals came from there and from Central America.[11] It was not until 1849 that opals were discovered in New South Wales in Australia and that the most beautiful opals in the world subsequently came to light. The increase in supply lowered the cost of opals and they became more available to Americans.[12]

Small brooches were made in the 1830s with diamond centres, four opals set at the cardinal points, and studded with eight little rubies. Other pins were set in clusters with an elongated opal in the centre surrounded by ten diamonds.[13] Men also enjoyed opals set in gold shirt pins. Theodore S. Harris of Boston described his as being in a gold setting without a shank, confirming that they were made both ways at that time.[14]

The beauty of the flashing colours of opals was often enhanced by accenting the stones with other coloured gems such as rubies and emeralds. (Colour Plate 113). Opal and emerald brooches and earrings could be purchased by lottery in New York in 1862.[15] A medallion of opals and emeralds decorated the clasp of a hollow, hinged gold bracelet given as an engagement present about 1863 by Charles Otto Witte of Charleston, S.C., to his bride Sophia Reeves (Colour Plate 114).

Opals surrounded by diamonds proved to be another happy combination. A bracelet with a gold and blue enamelled band was tapered to receive a large oval opal surrounded by clusters of diamonds (see Plate 114). One of the richest pieces of diamond and opal jewelry was made for Mrs. Charles A. Lamont of New York

5. The brooch was accompanied by a box imprinted with the name of the Broadnax firm.
6. P&C.
7. SFP, Box 57, Folder 2.
8. Boston *Transcript,* 31 Dec. 1856; *Evening Mail,* 7 Dec. 1868.
9. Vol. 53, p. 288.
10. Lecture on 'Colour', cited by Marcell N. Smith, *Diamonds, Pearls, & Precious Stones*, p. 72.
11. *Transcript,* 31 Dec. 1856.
12. 'Among precious stones there is not one more pure or chaste than the opal. Yet it is no longer the supreme gem of fashion, solely for the reason that it is less costly than formerly'. Unidentified clipping, Tiffany Archives, 1855-75.
13. P&C, pp. 94, 102.
14. *Transcript,* 6 Feb. 1868.
15. J.H. Winslow & Co., Frank Leslie's *Illus. News.*, 12 April 1862.

(Colour Plate 112, right). Two large and beautiful opals were centred on a diamond bow with extra loops at the top. Instead of emeralds there were beads of green enamel. In addition, icicles were added on each side above the pendant drop.

Lacking a Queen to emulate, Americans at the President's New Year's Day reception in 1876 took special note of the opals and diamonds enhancing Mrs. Ulysses S. Grant's gown.[16]

Garnets

Garnets were used more as garnishes than featured gems in the post-Federal period. They were often used with other stones, and especially with pearls, in finger rings (Colour Plate 110). Mrs. Elizabeth Salisbury of Worcester bought a pearl and garnet bracelet from Jones, Ball & Poor in 1847.[17] By mid-century the flat-cut garnet was superseded in popularity by the cabochon cut and the size of the stones grew larger and larger. These garnet cabochons were often called carbuncles, although the term could be applied to other large red stones as well.

About 1847 Captain Silvester of Danvers brought home from England for his daughter a pendant brooch made of hollow gold scrolls lightly engraved and set with carbuncles (Colour Plate 115). Carbuncles were very effective when mounted in Etruscan style frames in the 1860s and 1870s (see Colour Plate 96). Garnet jewelry was advertised by Levi Gay for holiday presents in Boston in 1868.[18] That same year a competitor had imported 'Paris garnet sets, extra fine'.[19]

With the revival of old styles in jewelry, there was a rebirth of the Bohemian garnet trade. These dark red stones were faceted and mounted in clusters to form flower heads and were joined together somewhat in the manner of Martha Washington's garnet jewelry a century earlier (see Colour Plate 18). Earrings, brooches and necklaces were very popular, and star and crescent pins were added to the repertoire in the 1870s. Because of the wide availability of the Bohemian garnets and the cheapness of the settings – gilt metal or a low grade of gold – it quickly became a favourite form of mass-produced jewelry.

Amethysts

Amethysts, like garnets, grew ever larger during the nineteenth century. In 1857, *Godey's Lady's Book* illustrated a pendant brooch featuring a large oval amethyst mounted horizontally, surrounded by chased gold leaves with pearl berries and accented with enamelling (see Plate 132).[20] In the 1870s it became fashionable to encrust amethysts, setting them with little diamonds. Stars, anchors and flowers were the most popular designs for encrustation (Colour Plates 116 and 117).

Turquoises

Because it looked like a piece of the clear blue sky that had fallen to earth, turquoise was called 'sky stone' by the first inhabitants of the American south-west. These native Americans had developed their skills as miners and craftsmen hundreds of years before the arrival of the Conquistadors. Archaeological ruins of A.D. 1,000 indicate that the Indians in the Cerrillos Hills south-west of Santa Fé, using the most primitive tools, were capable of producing remarkably well-carved, drilled and polished beads

16. Boston *Transcript,* 3 Jan. 1876.
17. It cost $25. SFP, Box 57, Folder 3, 30 Aug. 1847.
18. Levi B. Gay, Boston *Transcript,* 17 Dec. 1868.
19. Palmer, Bachelders & Co., Boston *Transcript,* 30 Mar. 1868.
20. Vol. 54, p. 163.

Colour Plate 116. Amethyst, gold and pearl brooch with matching earrings, American, c.1865-85. Amethysts encrusted with pearls in eight-pointed stars and set in fleur-de-lis shaped prongs with beaded base. Scrolled knife-edge bracket attached to the base with foxtail fringe. Black enamelling and bright-cut borders. Replacement screw fasteners on earrings. Owned in Boston. Length 3in. (brooch). Photograph by Dennis Griggs. Private Collection.

and pendants of turquoise for use in necklaces, bracelets and anklets. Through trade these objects were passed along to the Aztecs and Maya to the south.

In the seventeenth and eighteenth century, turquoises were often called 'turkey stones' after the country where they were revered as talismans. It was from Turkey that these stones were shipped to the rest of the world. Historically, the greatest source of turquoise used for jewelry was the Nishapur area of Persia (Iran). Usually shaped into cabochons, turquoises were used to form beaded borders or to provide a touch of blue in a multicoloured design.

In the nineteenth century, turquoise enjoyed several periods of popularity in jewelry. At first it was used as an accent, studding floral repoussé designs or outlining the form of birds (see Plate 109). Increasingly they became pavé-set to provide whole shapes and splashes of bright colour. A set of jewelry sold by Bailey & Kitchen of

Colour Plate 117. Amethyst ring, American, c.1880, encrusted with a diamond-set anchor. The shoulders of the gold band are engraved with a chevron pattern. Diameter $\frac{11}{16}$in. Photograph by Peter J. Theriault. Private Collection.

Colour Plate 118. Tiara and earrings with turquoise beads, pavé set in leafy scrolls, sold by Bailey & Kitchen, jewelers working in Philadelphia, c.1833-1846. Originally owned by Mary ap Owen (Shields) Stedman of Philadelphia. Pearls decorated the matching earrings as well as the wheel-shaped earrings set with wedge-shaped sugar loaf turquoises, popular about 1870. American. Length 3³⁄₁₆in. (drop earrings). The Connecticut Historical Society, Hartford.

Colour Plate 119. Above. Locket, Massachusetts, c.1878, made of filled gold and set with five sugar-loaf turquoise beads. Etruscan style wire work. Engraved on back with superimposed initials EMJ and engraved inside lid of locket 'E M Johnson / from / Father / Dec. 25, 1878'. Family tradition states that her father, a jeweler in Springfield, made the pendant for his daughter. Length 2in. Photograph by Peter J. Theriault. Private Collection.

Colour Plate 120. Above right. Turquoise brooch and earrings in the Egyptian style, owned by Mrs. Bruce Price (Josephine Lee Price), a gift from her mother while they were on a grand tour of Europe in 1872. Probably French. Gift of Mrs. Price Post, 54.115.3 b-d. Photograph by Arthur Vitols, The Helga Studio. Museum of the City of New York.

Philadelphia about 1840 was pavéd with turquoise furls and leafage (Colour Plate 118). The tiara, which was a *peigne avec pendeloques,* had the added exotic feature of gold drops suspended on chains from each side.[21] The earrings were similarly fashioned from stamped, hollow gold worked into scrolls in the rococo revival style. These could be worn as small floral earrings with turquoise centres or with long swelling pendent drops attached. The pendants were embellished with alternate leaves of pearls. Although the design gave the appearance of being massive and weighty, the hollow gold rendered them quite light.

Turquoises could be simulated in enamel. In 1835, Mrs. Elizabeth Salisbury purchased a handsome gold belt buckle (see Colour Plate 90) with enamelled 'turquoise' grape clusters from the Boston firm of Jones Lows & Ball.[22] Both 'Enamelled and [real] Turquoise Brooches, Ear-Rings, Bracelets and Finger Rings' were advertised in 1848 by Brackett & Crosby of Boston.[23] Eben Cutler also sold 'Turquoise painted' brooches, bracelets and earrings.[24] Turquoise was rarely used as the only stone in a ring, appearing instead with pearls and coloured gems. The combination of turquoise and ruby signified a pledge of love.

The pairing of turquoise and pearls continued to be popular during the mid-nineteenth century. Wedge-shaped cabochons of turquoise were set into wheel designs, in vogue about 1870, with a pearl suspended in the centre and three pearls set in the roof-like design above (Colour Plate 118). A Springfield, Massachusetts, jeweler made a pendant locket in the Etruscan style for his daughter in 1878 with the same kind of roof-top (Colour Plate 119). It was set with small sugar-loaf turquoises and embroidered with filigree work.

By the third quarter of the nineteenth century, turquoise jewelry was set in silver or in steel, rather than in the traditional gold settings. The New York *Sun* recommended it as a novelty for holiday presents at Christmas time in 1876.[25] With the interest in archaeological jewelry, particularly in Egyptian designs, turquoise began to appear inlaid in designs of the Pharoahs (Colour Plate 120). The bracelet made in the form of a flexible serpent to encircle the arm, which had first become popular in the 1840s, had its body sheathed in closely set turquoise cabochons. Alternatively, only the head or the eyes of the snake were set with turquoise.[26] American fashion reporters recommended turquoise jewelry especially for blondes 'to whom they are particularly becoming'.[27]

A demiparure of turquoises and pearls was worn by Mary Eliza Backus at her wedding to Dr. John Howard Lever at Newtown, New York in 1874. The set is believed to have been purchased at Tiffany's and is now at the Museum of the City of New York.

---

21. Vever, *I,* 253.
22. It cost $22. SFP, Box 56, Folder 3.
23. Boston *Transcript,* 2 Dec. 1848.
24. Ibid., 20 Dec. 1848.
25. 1 Oct., 17 Dec. 1876.
26. SPNEA, snake bracelet, #1930.1029.
27. TA, unidentified clipping, c. 1855-75.

Colour Plate 121. This American freshwater pearl necklace is set in gold galleries with thirty-two round, undrilled pearls. The circular gallery wire of the largest pearl is engraved 'November 30, 1858'. The previous year Unio pearls had been found in Paterson, New Jersey. The pearls are graduated in size from about ¼in. to ½in. in diameter. Photograph by D. Hargett. Courtesy of Gemological Institute of America.

Pearls

The delicate seed pearl jewelry that had made its appearance in the United States during the Federal period became firmly entrenched in American fashion during the mid-nineteenth century. While women in England and France are said to have abandoned the seed pearl parure, Americans were making them a matrimonial institution.[1]

The discovery of American sources for pearls in the 1850s probably contributed to the continuing production of this popular form of jewelry.[2] The lustrous Unio pearls found at Notch Brook, near Paterson, New Jersey, in 1857 were large and valuable. They caused a pearl fever and a nation-wide search for fresh water pearls. 'Within one year pearls were sent to the New York market from nearly every State', reported George F. Kunz of Tiffany's. From a peak of $15,000 worth of pearls in 1857, this trade dwindled to about $1,500 worth in 1863. There was a lull in the production until 1868. Then interest was revived when the abundant Little Miami River pearls were found.[3] A necklace made of twenty-seven graduated American fresh water pearls ranging in diameter from 5.25mm to 11.50mm. set in enamelled gold galleries was inscribed 'November 30, 1858', the year after the Paterson discovery (Colour Plate 121).[4]

The demand for seed pearl jewelry was such that Henry Dubosq, Jr., a Philadelphia jeweler, felt it worth while to devise and patent an improved method for its manufacture.[5] Because of the delicate construction of this jewelry, with its openwork templates cut from thin slices of mother-of-pearl, damage was not infrequent. Dubosq's solution was to give the plaques of seed pearls a supporting structure by riveting metallic

1. Jewelry historians state that the vogue for seed pearl jewelry began to wane in the 1840s. Flower, p. 19, says 'These early years of Queen Victoria were the last in which extensive use was made of seed pearls'. Becker, *Antique and 20th C.J.*, p. 72, and Charlotte Gere, *V.J.D.*, p. 205, agree. Conversely, Gilbert Levine argues that during this period the gentry and the rising middle class were not so interested in new styles and that in England 'Suites of seed pearl jewelry were still being sold for young unmarried women'. *The Jeweler's Eye* (N.Y. 1986), p. 18.

2. A.H.Grundy, notes that Scottish parures made of fresh water pearls from the Tay and Spey Rivers were very much in vogue from 1800 to 1850 and were sold by Scottish jewelers such as MacKay and Chisholm in Edinburgh. *Apollo,* Oct. 1959, Fig. IX, p. 83. These Scottish pearls were depleted by mid-century.

3. Kunz, *Gems,* p. 231.

4. *Gems & Gemology,* Spring 1989, p. 37.

5. Henry Dubosq was one of a number of family members working as jewelers in Philadelphia. From 1818 until at least the 1850s, Henry Dubosq, Jr., was listed in the Philadelphia City *Directories*. Maurice Brix, *List of Philadelphia Silversmiths and Allied Artificers from 1682 to 1850,* p. 32. See also Rainwater, *AJM,* p. 79. In 1892, an article in *JC* XXIV, No. 1, p. 80, recalled Dubosq's pre-eminence in strung pearl jewelry.

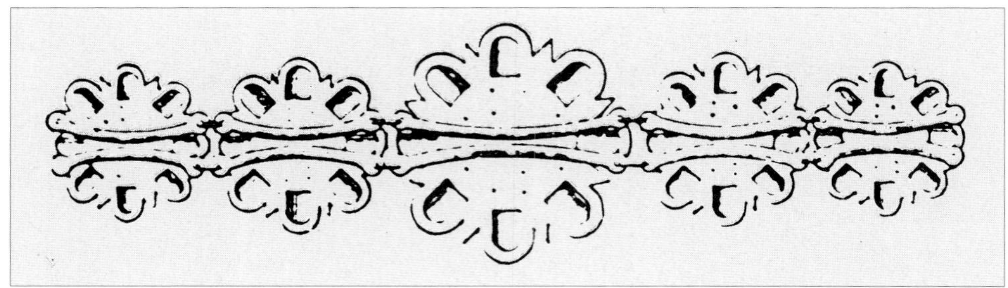

Plate 138. Design for constructing strung pearl jewelry, issued to Henry Dubosq of Philadelphia, Pa., 26 April 1859. United States Patent Office No. 23,760.

bars to the backplates and linking the ends of the bars to each other (Plate 138).

The designs of seed pearl parures changed from the regimented symmetrical patterns of the neo-classical period to the more loosely festooned and romantic motifs of the mid-nineteenth century. Cornucopias and circular flower heads gave way to swirled rosettes and a naturalistic variety of flowers. To the closely spaced pearls on the stems were added openwork leaves. Necklaces were swagged in single or double rows, and pendent rosettes were added in the centre. The bracelets, instead of having wide interlaced bands, now had triple strands with a woven fret or flower pattern flanked by straight strings of pearls. As the supply of fresh water pearls increased, the parures became larger in concept as well as in size, and there was greater variety to the pieces in the set. The layers of pearls became thicker and more three-dimensional, and larger pearls were added to the design (Colour Plate 122).

The early nineteenth century use of garnets, amethysts or topazes to add accents to the seed pearl jewelry gradually disappeared. *Gleason's Pictorial Drawing Room Companion* at Christmas time in 1853 explained, 'We do not affect colors; they give a cheap effect at all times, and deteriorate the finest complexion, while pure white is unequalled in appropriateness and delicate beauty under all and every circumstance'.[6] *Gleason's* remarks were prompted by the Tiffany display on view at the Crystal Palace exhibition in New York which the writer thought so beautiful he had the jewelry drawn for illustration (Plate 139). 'This style of ornament for the ball-room is exceedingly chaste and effective, and is probably the most becoming jewelry that a lady can wear', *Gleason's* added, pointing out that this sort of jewelry was now being rapidly revived. Tiffany's seed pearl jewelry was lavish in the number of pearls used per square inch. The tops of the earrings had not one but two drops. The brooch was

6. The article continues, 'In England, and on the continent, we understand that pearls are being generally adopted'. 24 Dec. 1853, p. 412.

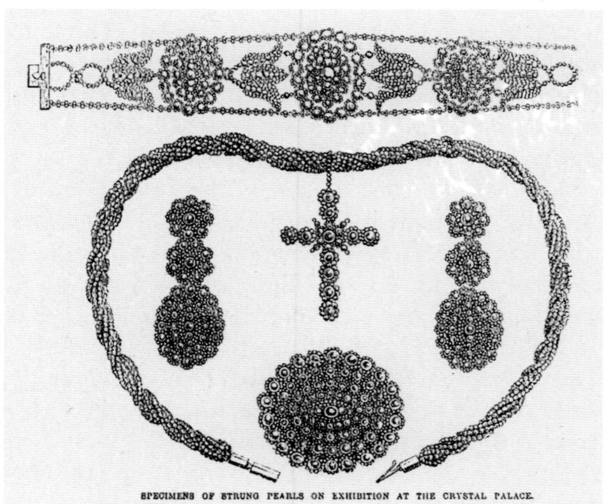

Plate 139. Seed pearl suite of jewelry made by Tiffany & Co. for the New York Crystal Palace exhibition in 1853. This illustration appeared in Gleason's Pictorial Drawing-Room Companion *on 24 December 1853.*

Plate 140. In her photograph taken in 1861 by Matthew Brady, Mary Todd Lincoln wears double lobed earrings, necklace with pendant, breast pin, and pair of bracelets, all part of the set purchased from Tiffany & Co. by her husband (see Colour Plate 123). New-York Historical Society.

a fulsome oval medallion solidly encrusted with pearls of various sizes. Similar medallions punctuated the openwork design of the bracelet and were interspersed with large trumpet tulips. Tiffany departed from the usual matching necklace and instead used twisted multiple strands of pearls. The horsehair and mother-of-pearl templates could be uncomfortable around the neck. Indeed some sets survive with fabric backing sewn in place to correct this fault. The twisted ropes of pearls were supple and smooth. To the rope could be attached a delicate pendent seeded Latin cross *pommée,* crossed again in the centre and made up of little stylized blossoms.

The attitude of Americans toward their seed pearl jewelry was described in a literary contribution to *Godey's Lady's Book* in 1857. In the fiction, a young lady was preparing to attend her first party since the death of her father. As she dressed, her mother 'opened a jewel-case...and taking from the velvet cushion a necklace and bracelets of pearl, she clasped them around the throat and wrists of her daughter. 'Oh, mother! your bridal jewels?' 'They are not misplaced here, I think, Ellen, for your dress is very simple; and these will be a happy relief'. Ellen refrained from wearing her mother's seed pearl spray for fear of being conspicuous.[7]

In 1861 President Lincoln purchased a seed pearl set for his wife from Tiffany's for $530 (Colour Plate 123). In place of the usual strands of pearls connecting the rosettes or medallions, the bracelet bands were made of articulated plaques of gold with a continuous engraved stripe of rococo ornament running through the middle. A large medallion with slightly smaller medallions on each side was decorated with concentric rows of matched pearls. The spacers between the smaller medallions of the necklace were little hexafoil gold flowers. Mrs. Lincoln wore the parure including the matching earrings to the Inauguration in 1861 (Plate 140). This led to copies of the set by another American, the prominent Washington jeweler M.W. Galt & Bro.[8]

7. *Godey's Lady's Book 54,* 1857.
8. His imprint was stamped inside the original fitted box containing a similar parure. Information courtesy of Patricia C. Sheehan, Harry H. Solomon Co., Inc., Boston, Mass. See also Arthur Guy Kaplan, *Official Identification and Price Guide to Antique Jewelry,* 6th ed., p. 592.

Colour Plate 122. Peabody family pearls, 1845, include a necklace, earrings and four brooches in the florid rococo style. The original earring fasteners were replaced by screw backs. Length 3in. (earrings). Photograph by Mark Sexton. Peabody Essex Museum.

A splendid seed pearl spray (Plate 141) set with a trembler in the eighteenth century manner had its original box marked 'Tenney/ Rich Jewelry/ 251 Broadway, Cor[ner] of Murray St.' William I. Tenney was a jeweler working at this address in New York from 1828 to 1852, where he was joined in the latter year by David I. Tenney.[9] A red velvet case contained the seed pearl necklace, brooch and earrings given to Fanny Arnot by her future father-in-law when she married R.S. Palmer of New York in 1864. Kate Beekman's parure came from Starr & Marcus who were jewelers at 22 John Street in New York. Her necklace was backed with velvet to keep it from scratching.[10]

Ella Brooks Carter married Charles Warren Cram in 1869. Her blue velvet box of wedding jewelry was stamped on top with her maiden name and the date 29 April 1869, and was imprinted inside with Tiffany's name and Broadway address (Colour Plate 124). The floral brooch had a wonderfully convoluted shape with nicely bevelled edges on the backplates. It had a detachable pendant and earrings to match.

The histories of these examples confirm the report that appeared in the New York *Evening Mail* on 17 December 1870: 'The Pearl Sets are exquisitely beautiful and constitute an appropriate and elegant present to a young bride'.[11] When General

9. Darling Foundation, *New York State Silversmiths*, p.175; and von Khrum, p. 127.
10. These two parures are at the N-YHS.
11. TA. The prices ranged from $100 to $1500, the report added.

Plate 141. Seed pearl spray with flower heads and leaves in open work mounting. Original box labelled TENNEY /RICH JEWELRY / 251 Broadway Cor[ner] of Murray St. / New York. William I. Tenney was working as a jeweler in New York c.1828-1852. Smithsonian Institution.

Colour Plate 123. Abraham Lincoln purchased this set of seed pearl jewelry from Tiffany & Co. in 1861 for his wife who wore it to his Inauguration as President of the United States (see Plate 140). The set cost $530. Small gold blossoms separate the graduated oval pearly bosses. The gold bands of the bracelet are articulated and have engraved scrollwork running freely across the segments. Photograph from Tiffany's 150 Years *book by Doubleday. Courtesy, Special Collections, Library of Congress.*

Colour Plate 124. Seed pearls half-set with brooch and pendant, and pendent earrings in original box imprinted by 'Tiffany & Co., 550-552 Broadway', a wedding gift to Ella Brooks Carter 29 April 1869, when she married Charles Warren Cram. Gift of their daughter Mrs. Edward C. Moen, 62.234.1 a-c. Photograph by Arthur Vitols, The Helga Studio. Museum of the City of New York.

Sherman's daughter was married on 1 October 1874, the description of her wedding included the fact that her elegant set of pearls was the bridal gift of her mother. With it she wore a comb in her hair and carried a fan, both items that her mother had used on her wedding day.[12] By the 1890s seed pearl sets 'mounted in *tumuli*' were said to be 'the spoil of every bride'.[13] Americans had appropriated this old-world jewelry and made it an integral part of their own manufacture and traditions.

12. Boston *Transcript*, 2 Oct. 1874.
13. Journalist Lucy Benedict, cited by Penny Proddow and Debra Healy, *American Jewelry, Glamour and Tradition*, p. 17.

Plate 142. Two mourning brooches made for Mrs. Elizabeth Salisbury of Worcester, Mass. in memory of her husband Stephen who died in 1829. One (left) was purchased in Boston from John B. Jones in September 1829. The other (right) was purchased for her in 1830 by her son while he was in London from Rundell, Bridge & Rundell. Photograph by Stephen Briggs. Bequest of Stephen Salisbury III Estate. Worcester Art Museum, Worcester, Mass.

Hair and Mourning Jewelry

When Elizabeth Salisbury's husband died in Worcester, Massachusetts, in May 1829, she gave serious thought to the kind of memorial jewelry she should buy. Stephen Salisbury's estate was charged for a finger ring and sixteen brooches, all of which were set with jet and were provided by jeweler John B. Jones of Boston. In September Jones sold Mrs. Salisbury a round brooch with graduated jets set around a lock of hair (Plate 142, left). Still she thought she could do better abroad. Her son was in Paris and she wrote to him that she was unable to find a mourning pin that she 'consider'd rich enough for myself – nor do I think we shall find one here, and I have thought lately, that I would ask you to have one prepared for me, either in France or England, that is in Paris or in London'. She enclosed a lock of her husband's hair for her son to have placed in the mourning pin, requesting 'something rather large, if it is proper', something like the brooch worn by one of their relatives only 'richer and handsomer'. Anticipating her son's reaction, she added, 'what very few ornaments I wear, ought to be handsome you know'. With the pin, she wanted a pair of earrings. Months later her son wrote that he had purchased a brooch for her from Rundell, Bridge & Rundell, 'the first Jewellers in London' (Plate142, right). When it arrived, Mrs. Salisbury thought the brooch might not be 'sufficiently mourning', but people told her that pearls were appropriate mourning apparel. 'If so', she said, 'there is nothing to be wish'd. The Broach is eminently beautiful'.[1]

Jewelry made or set with hair continued to be very popular with Americans, whether as expressions of friendship and love or of mourning and remembrance. A greater variety of forms were made of hair in a greater variety of designs and were increasingly non-funereal in content. The customary rings, brooches, necklaces and bracelets continued, but in the mid-nineteenth century there were also earrings, watch chains, charms and other trinkets made of hair. Compared with increasing machine and mass-production, hair ornaments remained a very personal form of jewelry.

While most of the earlier hair jewelry was delicate in design and sparing in its use of materials, mid-nineteenth century jewelry was much more substantial in size and more lavish in its use of hair, gold fittings and large clasps sometimes mounted with oversized stones such as citrines or pastes. Instead of two-dimensional flat plaits of hair,

1. SFP, Box 23, Folder 7; Box 24, Folders 5 and 7; Box 55, Folder 3.

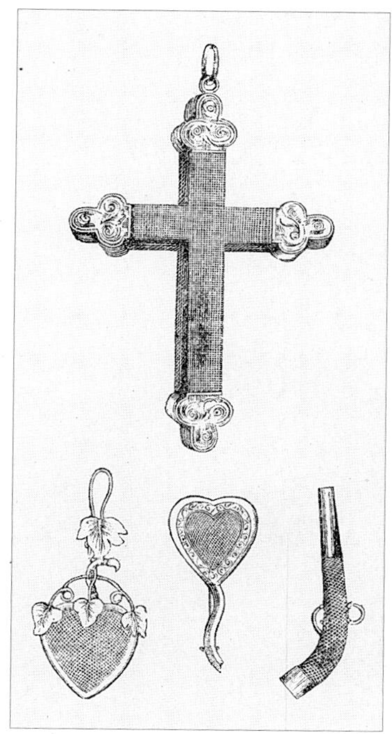

Plate 143. Godey's Lady's Book, *Philadelphia, January 1861, p. 86, illustrated ornaments made from hair that could be purchased from the publisher. Courtesy, The Winterthur Library: Printed Book and Periodical Collection.*

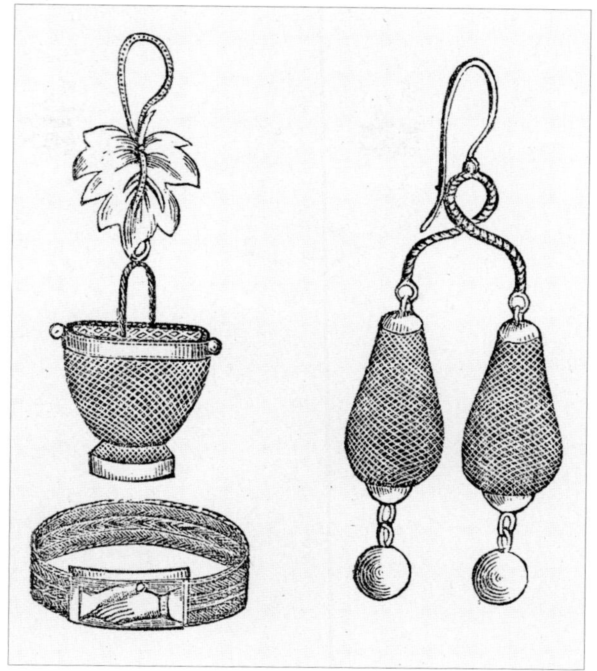

Plate 144. Earrings made with woven hair and a ring with a hair band and a cental design of clasped hands were among the types of jewelry that could be ordered from Godey's Lady's Book, *as advertised May 1861, p. 476. Courtesy, The Winterthur Library: Printed Book and Periodical Collection.*

the hair was now puffed up into woven tubes that could be shaped into a multitude of three-dimensional forms.

Godey's Lady's Book actively promoted the use of hair jewelry, citing English writer Leigh Hunt's much quoted sentiment. 'Hair is at once the most delicate and lasting of our materials, and survives us, like love. It is so light, so gentle, so escaping from the idea of death, that with a lock of hair belonging to a child or friend, we may almost look up to heaven and compare notes with the angelic nature – may almost say: "I have a piece of thee here, not unworthy of thy being now."'[2] *Godey's* offered to supply their subscribers with hair jewelry in many shapes and forms. Breast pins, earrings, bracelets and fob chains were available along with rings costing as little as $1.50 and necklaces as much at $15. In each issue *Godey's* listed the date that items had been sent to customers who were identified by their initials: 'T.A.C. – Sent hair fob-chain, hair necklace and cross, and hair bracelet with Daguerreotype clasp 14th'.[3]

In 1861, *Godey's* illustrated the various designs available (Plate 143). Charms, studs and sleeve buttons could be ordered. Crosses in two styles were offered. One was a cross *fourchée* with engraved gold trefoil mounts at the end of each arm and a rectangular-sectioned cross of woven hair. The other cross was made of tubular bulbous sections with gold fasteners and a circular centre. There was a watch fob key in the shape of a miniature powder horn. In addition to charms representing faith, hope and charity (cross, anchor and heart), there was a tiny drum, complete with lacings, and a Masonic compass and square. Rings were available in an adjustable belt-and-buckle form or in wide woven bands of hair with variously shaped central mounts. One ring featured the clasped-hand motif familiar from earlier fede rings (Plate 144). Earrings could be in the shape of a bell with pendant balls suspended

2. Vols. *50,* 1855; *52,* 379, 1856; 380, 1861.
3. *Godey's Lady's Book and Ladies' American Magazine, 54,* 380, 1857.

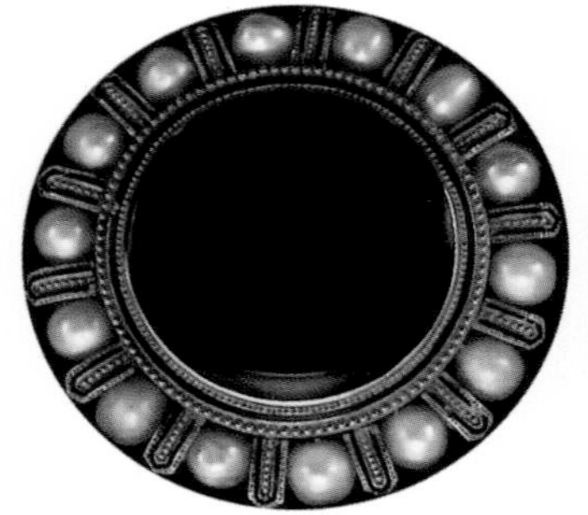

Colour Plate 125. Gold brooch, set with a plait of auburn hair in memory of Cornelia Ray Hamilton who died in 1867. Made by Tiffany & Co. Gold setting mounted with whole pearls separated by black enamelled epaulette motif. Obituary inscription engraved on back. Original box imprinted inside 'TIFFANY & C° / 550 Broadway 552 / NEW YORK'. Paper label on back of box inscribed 'Gold & pearl breast pin / with C. Hamilton's hair – / given to me by Mother / January 1868'. Photograph by Peter J. Theriault. Private Collection.

Colour Plate 126. Group of mid-19th century jewelry owned in Louisiana. (Left) Woven bead necklace with pendant cross. (Right) Bracelet made of coiled hair with enamelled clasp set with design of pansies inside a wreath. (Centre, below) Woven hair brooch with botoné *cross set with pearls and three pendent drops with gold borders and beads, with original box imprinted 'Paris / L. Charleux B*[te] *[Bijoutière].' (Centre, above) Rectangular brooch with carved shell cameo of a hand clutching a bouquet of flowers which, like the ivory pendant (below, left) is related to the* immortales (see Plate 146). *Louisiana State Museum.*

from an oval boss or more simply a little basket or three pear-shaped pendants dropped from a gold leaf. Shirt pins were heart-shaped with a curved stem or oval with a straight stem.[4]

For those who were creative or perhaps did not want to purchase a mass-produced hair jewel, Godey's provided information for do-it-yourself subscribers. The magazine gave no specific instruction in how to make each item, but did list the pattern number of the plait required and specified the amount and kind of materials needed for each item of jewelry. For a bracelet made of nine tubes divided into thirds and plaited like a pigtail, the subscriber needed '16 strands; 10 hairs; 1 oz. bobbins; 4 oz. balance; No. 9 mould; [and] plait No. 15'. The clasps and other fasteners had to be bought as well. The snake bracelet was more difficult, requiring significantly more material, a special mould seven inches long, 'No. 1 at one end, decreasing to No. 5 at the other'. In addition to the great variety of bracelets, there were recipes for Albert chains, rings, bows for brooches and three-pieced brooches.[5]

A number of jewelers continued to specialize in the manufacture of hair jewelry. *The Boston Almanac and Directory* in the 1860s listed V. Brandly, Gray & Libby, Jordan & Wilder, Louis Christen and Guild & Delano. Most were listed separately as hair jewelers, but Guild & Delano were identified under the general heading of jewelers as well. Gray & Libby still took pains to say that they manufactured hair jewelry to order in 1860. 'By furnishing the hair, rare Keep sakes will be made up of superior workmanship'. They particularly recommended it for Christmas and New Year's presents as 'there is nothing more suitable for a gift (from one friend to another'). One of their competitors in this line was a Mrs. Stuart who suggested that anyone who was planning to give a gentleman a vest chain braided from their own hair should stop in to see her before making their purchase.[6] Abby Pennell, a Maine girl who spent many years at sea with her husband

4. 1861, pp. 86, 183, 283, 380, 476.
5. Ibid. and p. 544 (1860). See also Bragg & Wilder, *Savannah's Antique Hair and Mourning Jewelry*, pp. 9-11.
6. Boston *Transcript*, 3 March, 20, 31 Dec. 1860.

Colour Plate 127. Two woven hair bracelets, c.1850, American. The snake has a filled gold head and fasteners and its head is set with turquoise beads and garnet eyes. Length 7½in. The wide band bracelet has a large oval gold clasp fitted with a miniature portrait of William Allen of Charleston, Painted on ivory by Pierre Henri who was working in Charleston, c.1790-1793. Length 7⁵⁄₁₆in. Photograph by Leland Cook by courtesy of The Magazine Antiques. *Courtesy of The Charleston Museum, Charleston, S.C.*

Captain John, took the opportunity when their ship came into New York in 1860 to get him a watch chain made of her hair.[7]

The American Civil War drastically increased the variety and demand for hair jewelry. It is inconceivable that anyone could have offered more patterns of hair jewelry than James E. Brinsmaid of Burlington, Vermont. His customers could select from more than three hundred designs, but he warned them to do so while there was still time if they wanted them for the holidays.[8] In 1874 Blockinger in Boston boasted that both the braidings and the gold mounts for his hair jewelry were all of his own manufacture.[9]

A small manual illustrating over eighty designs for *Hair Ornaments for Jewelry and Souvenirs* was published in New York about 1871. This provided trade secrets for jewelers as well as amateurs. It appears to have been an unacknowledged American edition of Miss Alexanna Speight's 1871 publication *The Lock of Hair,* to which was added a preface suitable for Americans and certain spelling changes.[10]

Mid-nineteenth century jewelry set with hair made great use of enamelling and jewels. For example, a bracelet made in 1851 by Tiffany's had diamonds set in the

7. Coffin, Robert P.T., *Captain Abby and Captain John* (NY 1939), p. 173.
8. Cited by Lilian Baker Carlisle, *Vermont Clock and Watchmakers Silversmiths and Jewelers 1778-1878,* p. 76, from *Burl. Times,* 26 Dec. 1863.
9. Boston *Transcript,* 30 Sept. 1874.
10. See Bury II, 682-68. A copy of the English edition is in the British Museum Library. A copy of the American edition is in the Kent State Library in Ohio.

Plate 145. Two gold hair brooches owned in Maine, c.1850. (Left) Twisted rope border around band of jet, owned by 'M.A. Deering' whose name is engraved on the back with her street address, has a sheaf of hair under an oculus. Length 1¼in. (Right) Outer border of faceted jet around border of pearls, plaited hair under crystal. Engraved on back 'Chas. T. Evans / Ob^{t} at sea, / Sept. 20th 1852. / AE. 39 Yrs.' Safety chain and stick pin added. Length 1⅝in. Photograph by Peter J. Theriault. Private Collection.

initial on top of the locket on its clasp (see Plate 131). The shapes were often rectangular or round. Oval shapes were elongated or widened. Wide bands of enamelled inscriptions in black or white had large letters often in gothic script, IN MEMORY OF. Chased gold borders were popular and featured leaves, flowers and scrolls. The jewelry could be set with faceted jet (Plate 145) or garnets so dark that they looked black. Pearls continued to form suitable borders and sometimes appeared in double rows. The bezels of rings were often shield shaped while brooches and clasps were cusped in the gothic style (see Plate 107). Among the prettiest of the small enamelled memorial brooches was one that had a white floral spray and a modelled outer border featuring shells and leafy scrolls. Another had the loops of a belt in the form of a figure eight with two lockets in the loops containing hair of two different colours and outlined with graduated pearls.

When Tiffany's produced hair jewelry, the result could be quite elegant (Colour Plate 125). A brooch the firm made in 1868 had a border of pearls pinned and freestanding between little epaulettes of gold and enamel. The plait of lustrous auburn hair was covered with crystal so highly polished that the hair took on a jewel-like appearance. Engraved on the back was the legend 'Cornelia Ray Hamilton born Dec. 26th 1829. Died Dec. 1st 1867'. The maroon leather box that came with the brooch was imprinted by Tiffany & Co. and had a paper label pasted on it saying '...breast pin with C. Hamilton's hair – given to me by Mother January 1868'.

In spite of Queen Victoria's deep mourning for Prince Albert, the mid-century saw a gradual easing of the restrictions of mourning customs in America. Perhaps this was accelerated by the enormous losses of life caused by the American civil war and the need to get on with life. There continued to be two periods of mourning, referred to as first or deep mourning, in which black and some white apparel was worn exclusively for a year, and second mourning or half-mourning which was adopted by distant relatives or for the second stage of mourning. Grey and pale lavender became acceptable tints for bereavement clothing. *Godey's* had noted in 1857, 'we think the present taste is to lighten a garb, grave, at best, by color rather than ornament'.

However, 'the present taste' varied in different areas of the United States. Godey's felt that Philadelphians tended 'to carry mourning to extremes... much more than any of their Atlantic neighbors. In New York, it is too gay; in Boston, fashion is by

Plate 146. Memorial floral arrangement or immortale *made of wax and cloth, featured a cross and a hand holding a clutch of flowers, reminiscent of the New Orleans memorial brooches set with floral wreaths and pansies worked in chopped hair. Pendant ivory crosses were favoured here. This* immortale *was made by Blanche Dumestre in memory of her husband Capt. Alexis Dumestre of New Orleans, c.1884. Length 17½in. The Historic New Orleans Collection 1977.317.2.*

no means so arbitrary as elsewhere. People are inclined to have minds of their own, and follow feeling and convenience rather than form'.[11] *Godey's* recommended that any ornaments worn in mourning be 'few and plain'.

In New Orleans, with its strong Catholic population, mourning jewelry resembled *immortales* (Plate 146). These were funereal arrangements made of wax and various materials, filled with symbols of affection and everlasting life. The cross or crucifix was a central element (Colour Plate 126, left). A hand holding a bouquet of flowers was carved into a shell cameo (Colour Plate 126, centre, above). Memorial wreaths with pansies ('think of me', in the language of flowers) were made with chopped hair and set into jewelry. In addition to locally made mourning jewelry, hair ornaments made in Paris had appeal for the French immigrants in New Orleans (Colour Plate 126).

In Chicago, the fancy was for wide lacy bracelets, with elastic tubings, appliquéd on top. Photographs of the family of Mr. and Mrs. Cyrus Hall McCormick, including two sons and a daughter, were set in a band of brown braided hair.

Brooches with borders of pearls or jet were appropriate everywhere, as were plain enamelled gold brooches. Jet and imitations of jet were thought to be most appropriate. This view was repeated two decades later when the fashion reporter for a Boston newspaper recommended that 'Jet, relieved with gold and pearls, is fashionable for second mourning'.[12] Irish bogwood jewelry was an acceptable substitute for jet, as were onyx and black and white banded agates.

11. 54, 192 (1857).
12. *Sat. Eve. Gaz.*, Boston, 26 March 1876.

Colour Plate 128. Pair of bracelets set with mid-18th century miniature portraits of Sir George and Lady Anne Houston of Savannah, Georgia. Articulated gold bands made about 1860-70. Owned by relatives in Savannah. Courtesy, Museum of Early Southern Decorative Art, Winston-Salem, N.C.

PORTRAIT JEWELRY

With the rococo revival came a sporadic fashion for jewelry set with miniature paintings. Portraits appeared as medallions in bracelets, now more often worn singly than in pairs. The bracelet band was formed of flexible materials such as articulated discs or woven hair, rather than chains or strings of pearls. Old miniatures were sometimes reset in new bands. A miniature painted in 1779 by Charles Willson Peale of the Revolutionary General Samuel Blatchley Webb of Connecticut was put into a bracelet of gothic design with overlapping enamelled ogivals (see Colour Plate 85). In Georgia, a pair of miniatures of Sir George Houston and Lady Anne Moody Houston were fitted with bands made of cylindrical sections that had an overall stippled pattern of the type made about the time of the country's centennial celebration (Colour Plate 128).

One of the most ambitious and interesting examples of miniatures in jewelry was a festoon necklace made of portraits of the nine children of Thomas Seir Cummings (1804-94), miniaturist and artist, presumably for his wife Jane Cook (Colour Plate 129). The necklace appears to have been composed about 1841, judging from the ages of the children depicted who were born between 1823 and 1840. The two oldest children form a centrepiece protecting the memory of little Charles F. Cummings who had died in 1831 at the age of six or seven. The box clasp was covered with rococo-revival repoussé decoration. Cummings, a pupil of Henry Inman, has been called 'the last of America's fine practitioners' of the art of miniature painting.[1] William Dunlap, historian of early American arts, said 'I know that a miniature painted by an artist like Mr. Cummings, and treated as miniatures ought to be – that is, kept as we keep jewels, only for occasional gratification – will lose neither force nor freshness for centuries'.[2]

As miniature paintings became larger and were more often used as cabinet pictures, their place in jewelry was taken by the photograph, a new art medium that made its début in the form of the daguerreotype in 1839. Monsieur L.J.M. Daguerre, a French artist, invented the method of taking a likeness by means of silvered copper-plates developed over heated mercury. The technique was immediately brought to the United States by Samuel F.B. Morse, himself an artist and inventor, who had been working along the same lines. So successful was this innovation that it soon put miniature portraitists out of business.

1. Newark Museum, *Classical America*, p. 194.
2. *History of Arts II*, 2, 399-402.

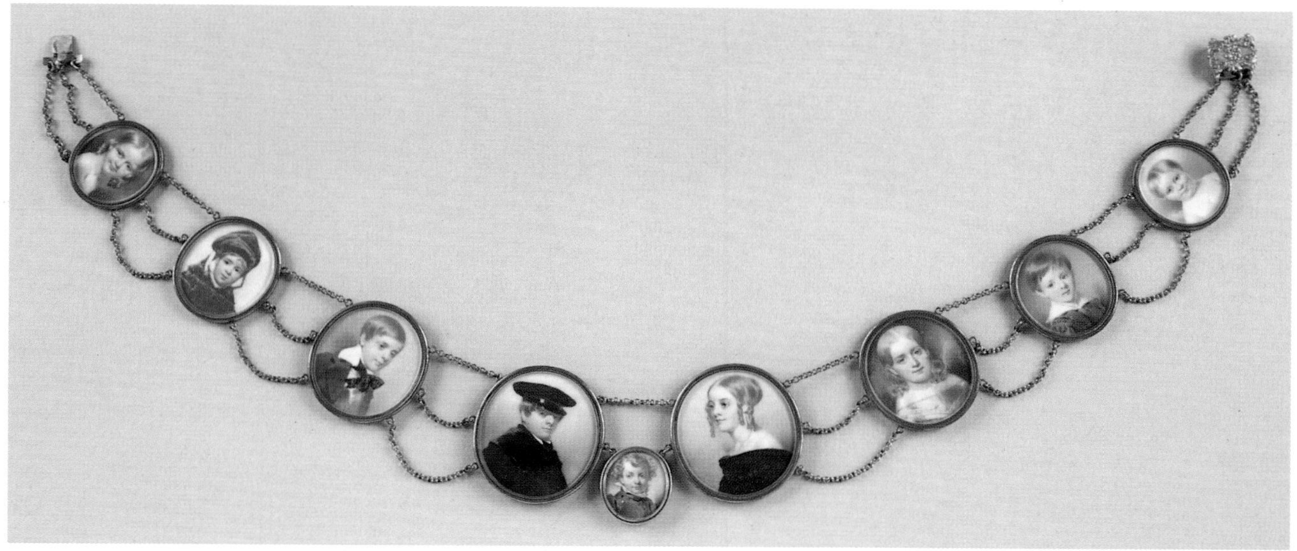

Colour Plate 129. Necklace set with miniature portraits of the nine children of artist Thomas Seir Cummings (1804-1894), c.1841, for his wife. The ornate gold clasp is worked with rococo revival ornament. Length 17½in. Photograph by Paul Warchol. Gift of Mrs. Richard B. Hartshorne and Miss Fanny S. Cummings, 1928, Courtesy, Metropolitan Museum of Art. All rights reserved, ©1985.

Among the first to establish a daguerreotype studio were Albert Sands Southworth and Josiah Johnson Hawes. They proved also to be among the most accomplished Americans to work with this medium. Their 'Artist's Daguerreotype Rooms' were patronized by illustrious Bostonians as well as foreign notables and their daguerreotypes were often set in jewelry.[3]

John Quincy Adams was 'facsimiled' as he called it by a number of daguerreotypists, including Southworth in Boston and Philip Haas in Washington. An early photographic profile portrait of Adams was set in a bracelet, along with photographs of other notables (Plate 147).[4] The portrait of his father John Adams, which was also included in the bracelet, was not taken from life; the elder Adams had died in 1828 before the technique was invented. It was copied from an earlier likeness and shows

3. Pamela Hoyle, *The Boston Ambience*, pp. 1-3; *Britannica Ency. of Am. Art*, pp. 430-31, 531-32.
4. Oliver, pp. 281-87, Fig. 127.

Plate 147. Bracelet with compartments holding early photographic images of A.D. Bache, Benjamin Pierce, John Quincy Adams, Sauss, John Adams and Louis Agassiz, notables of the Boston area, c.1845-61. On the reverse side are locks of hair belonging to the subjects, except that the thread of hair in the back of the balding John Quincy Adams came from the head of Daniel Webster instead. Length 7½in. Gift of Mrs. Albert Thorndike. Photograph by David Bohl, Boston. Society for the Preservation of New England Antiquities.

Plate 148. Daguerreotype brooch with image of George P. Greer. Length 1⅛in. Gift of George C. Winslow. Photograph by David Bohl, Boston. Society for the Preservation of New England Antiquities.

him as he appeared about 1800. Louis Agassiz, first on the left in the bracelet, was appointed professor of zoology at Harvard in 1848. In the back of each frame a swatch of hair was placed on a plaited background. Presumably these are locks from each of the heads portrayed, except in the case of the very bald J.Q. Adams. The back of his case contained the hair of Daniel Webster. The bracelet appears to have been made up of stock lockets that were hinged together, and attached to a few links to bring it to proper size.

As miniaturists had done, daguerreotypists advertised that their pictures were suitable for jewelry. In 1848, J.J.P. Davis kept on hand at his gallery in Boston a large assortment of both gold and plated lockets. A few years later, Briggs & Knapp recommended their ambrotypes for settings in lockets and pins.[5] Mr. Ormsbee of Boston took daguerreotype portraits, using ivory or ivory paper, which he then had coloured by a miniaturist without disturbing the likeness.[6]

For the convenience of their customers, some jewelers set up Daguerrean Galleries in their stores to encourage the sale of jewelry to hold the photographs. W.H. Deshong was provided with a whole suite of rooms, specially built for his needs and handsomely furnished, at F.H. Clark & Co., a jewelry store in Memphis, Tennessee, in 1860.[7]

Subscribers to *Godey's Lady's Book* could order hair bracelets that had clasps made to contain daguerreotypes.[8] Daguerreotype and photographic jewelry was particularly treasured during the Civil War. Numerous lockets still contain the images of lost sons, husbands and sweethearts.

The most telling indication of how popular photographic jewelry had become was the large number of patents secured for these designs. One jeweler designed a miniature locket to look like a tiny photograph album, with spaces for pictures in the leaves. The outer sides of the locket were fastened to the body in such a way that it could be opened wide enough to display the whole picture.[9]

An Englishman, Walter Bentley Woodbury of London, developed a method of using photography in the making of jewelry which he patented through the United States Patent Office in 1866.[10] He produced a metallic mould from a transparent positive from which a cast was made in porcelain, plaster of Paris or similar white material. Into this white cast a dark and semi-transparent material was forced. The surface was then ground off to achieve a smooth surface.

At the time of the Centennial a 'dioramic locket' was invented by Albert W. Pherson of North Attleboro. It had a perforated locket case, equipped with a stop-spring and a pivot, combined with a rotary disc and lens glasses displaying pictures.[11] In 1878, William B. Closson designed a finger ring that had 'eye and light openings' leading out of its socketed head. Inside the head there was a lens and a picture secured by a perforated cup or guard.[12]

---

5. Boston *Transcript,* 1 Jan. 1848; *Boston Almanac,* 1856, p. 202.
6. Ibid., 28 July 1853.
7. Benjamin H. Caldwell, Jr., 'Tennessee Silversmiths', *Antiques* (Dec. 1971), p. 908.
8. 'Sent hair fob-chain, hair necklace and cross, and hair bracelet with Daguerreotype Clasp', Vol. *54* (1857), p. 380.
9. Patent # 46,788, 14 March 1865, E.N. Foote, New England Village, Mass.
10. #77,231. This was an improvement upon his earlier patent in the same year.
11. #175,494. 1876.
12. #203,323.

Designs from Abroad

The mid-nineteenth century was a period in which Americans enjoyed the luxury of indulging in the products of other countries. Foreign countries mass-produced local specialities in jewelry and sold them as souvenirs to tourists. The ornaments brought home by travellers created a market for these regional designs. Jewelers in the United States, seeking an expansion of their trade, imported the same baubles and offered them for sale in foreign-made settings or in mounts of their own manufacture. Often the designs inspired American jewelers to make similar jewelry. The material used in tourist jewelry was quite varied. It ranged from shells and onyx to gems and minerals, coral, jet, iron, bogwood and lava.

Tortoiseshell Jewelry

The rich brown colour of the turtle's shell, flashed with patches of sunshine, had a continuing appeal to Americans. Commonly known as tortoiseshell, the material actually came from the back of the hawk's-bill turtle. These marine turtles were abundant in warm coastal areas, and provided a natural substance well suited to the manufacture of combs for the hair. Shells were imported from the West Indies and China, the latter source providing the best quality.

Both shells and ready-made tortoiseshell combs came from China and India in the nineteenth century. Salem ships started bringing back these items in the early days of their post-colonial trade with those countries. Benjamin Shreve had special orders to purchase combs on behalf of Charles Thorndike who even provided Shreve with drawings of the sizes and designs of four different styles of combs. Those purchased on his behalf came from the shop of Yushing in Canton in 1819. At the same time Joseph Tilden ordered a large quantity of uncarved tortoise shells which he expected to sell on the European as well as American market.[1] In 1835 S.K. Gifford ran an illustrated advertisement in the Providence *Advertiser* showing examples of his new assortment of elegant American and Canton shell combs.[2]

American comb makers were able to compete with foreign manufacturers by adapting their designs to suit American taste. French combs did not strike their fancy as well. Furthermore, American comb makers changed their styles continuously, especially in the finely carved combs which they updated every six months.[3]

The era of the decorative tortoiseshell comb began in earnest when women abandoned their caps and bobs, and wore their long hair done up in elaborate coils and plaits. About 1825 it became fashionable to bring the hair looping up from the back to the top of the head in a sort of pompadour. Large decorative combs were used to keep the hair secured at the crown, while side combs were used to keep the hair below in place. It was this new coiffure that put life into the comb industry.

The extent of the growth of the decorative hair comb industry is suggested by the advertisement of Isaac Davis at the Boston Comb Store in 1823. He had plain shell combs, cut top combs, and wrought top India combs. These could be purchased individually or in sets with side combs. In addition, Davis had on hand thirty dozen combs 'of the circular or high patterns', made of rich coloured shell, for retail or

1. Carl L. Crossman, *The China Trade*, pp. 6, 12. Thorndike requested carved tops; plain, square and rounded tops; large and small combs. Tilden ordered between 500 and 1,000 uncarved shells.
2. 25 Sept. 1835.
3. Freedley, p. 407.

Colour Plate 130 *Tortoiseshell bracelet with pendants and tiny gold key to unlock the heart pendant clasp. Made in Ceylon and bought at Point de Galle in 1854. Piqué tortoiseshell bracelet with inlaid gold stars and heart-shaped locket, American, c.1860. Length about 6in. Bogwood brooch carved with a castle, inscribed on back 'Druin'. Length 2⅝in. Pair of jet earrings, with locket for hair in centre drop, engraved on back of one earring 'L.C.F. / Obt. Apr. 27, 1837'. Length 2in. Earrings made of Whitby jet and bought in Paris about 1867. Length 2½in. Photograph by Mark Sexton. Peabody Essex Museum.*

Colour Plate 131. *Dark tortoiseshell chain and pendent locket; light tortoiseshell chain and pendent cross; American, c.1870. Locket deeply cut with superimposed initials. Length 2in. (locket), 19½in. (cross chain). Photograph by Peter J. Theriault. Private Collection.*

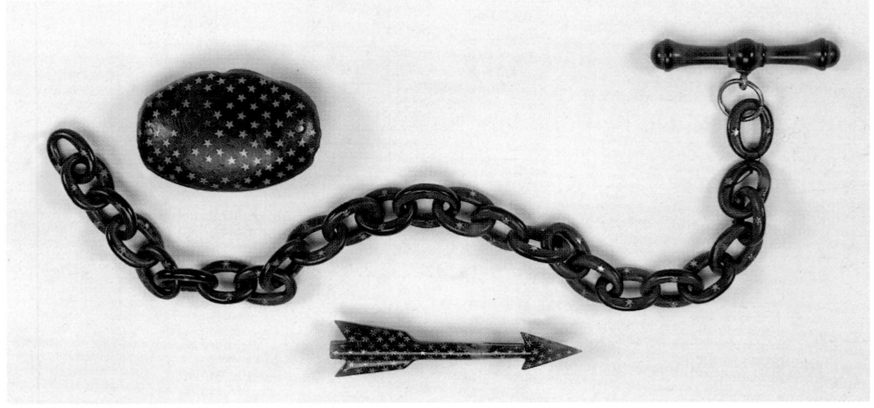

Colour Plate 132. *Above left. Group of tortoiseshell jewelry with piqué gold stars, north-eastern United States, c.1860-80. Buckle (upper left), arrow pin, one of a pair (below), width 2¾in.; watch chain (centre), c.1868. Length 9½in. Society for the Preservation of New England Antiquities.*

Colour Plate 133. *Above right. Hair comb made of vulcanite (a substance made of india-rubber combined with sulphur and heated), invented in 1836 by Charles Goodyear (1800-1860) of New York and patented on 15 June 1844. Marked on back, I.R. COMB C[o] Goodyear 1851. Financial problems forced Goodyear to sell licences and establish royalties for less than value. Vulcanite jewelry was one of the most popular substitutes for jet and tortoiseshell. Length 4¼in. (overall). Photograph by Fred Furkel. Private Collection.*

Colour Plate 134. *Left. Helmet conch shell cameo, cut about 1835 with portrait bust of Andrew Jackson by George W. Jamison (?-1868), working in New York City as a cameo cutter from 1835-1838. The enamelled border bears the campaign slogan Jackson used,* The Union it must and shall be preserved. *The meandering border is made of yellow, rose and green gold. The cameo is signed below the cavetto, GJ in relief. Jamison exhibited 'Conchylia' portraits including one of Jackson at the National Academy in 1835. Length 2½in. (overall). Photograph by Peter J. Theriault.*

Plate 149. *John B. Jones sent this comb to President Andrew Jackson in 1831. Carved with United States eagle at top, portrait bust of Lafayette on left and George Washington on right. Andrew Jackson's portrait is in centre. Smithsonian Institution.*

Plate 150. *Tortoiseshell comb manufactured in Boston by Alfred Willard. Its original wallpaper-covered box is marked 'purchased in 1832'. Photograph by Amanda Merullo. ©1993 Historic Deerfield, Inc.*

wholesale. He paid cash for tortoiseshell, ivory and horns that could be used in his manufacturing. For those who could not afford combs of these materials, he had made 1,200 imitation combs ranging in price from twenty-five cents to a dollar.[4] Any of these would make fine New Year's presents, he promised. Further proof of the growing industry can be found in the list of manufacturers and dealers in American goods published in 1831 which named comb manufacturers in Massachusetts, Connecticut, Rhode Island, New York, Pennsylvania, Maryland and Kentucky.[5]

As a means of showing how American manufacturers were progressing, John B. Jones, a Boston jeweler, sent a handsomely carved high back-comb to President Andrew Jackson in 1831 (Plate 149). Carved with a swooping eagle, the tortoiseshell comb bore a well cut miniature portrait of Jackson, flanked by smaller profiles of Washington and Lafayette. Jones noted that in a short period of time, American manufacturers were making tortoiseshell objects that could compete in quality and price with products made abroad. The President, following Jones's suggestion, gave the comb to his niece Emily Donelson to wear. This comb may have been produced by Alfred Willard who operated the Boston Comb Manufactory at 149 Washington Street from 1831 to 1836. He packaged his decorative ladies' combs in half-round cardboard boxes covered with ornamental paper, to which he added a large label describing his products (Plate 150).[6]

Changes in technology as well as fashion encouraged the development of new designs for tortoiseshell combs. As early as 1817, David E. Noyes of West Newbury, Mass., then living in Philadelphia, obtained a patent on a machine he had invented for 'twinning horn and tortoise-shell combs', so that two combs could be cut from one piece of shell. Noyes also improved upon the cutting of the teeth of the saw.[7] In 1835 the foot-powered lathe was replaced by horse-powered lathes and a decade later horses were replaced by steam. Anson Peck of Boston, manufacturer of shell combs for wholesale and retail, provided 'Wrought Shell Back and Twist Combs; Long Round do; Neck do; Wrought and Plain Side do; Plain Shell Back and Twist do' in 1850.[8]

A.S. Jordan, another Boston firm producing and selling combs from the 1840s to 1870, received public notice for the fine workmanship of the combs and shell work that he displayed at the Mechanics' Exhibition in 1841. In addition to the combs he made

4. *Columbian Centinel,* 1 Jan. 1823.
5. Bernard W. Doyle, *Comb-Making in America,* p. 20.
6. Robert Gedney had a trade card advertising his 'New York Patent Comb Manufactory' on Pearl Street from which he shipped shell combs to Connecticut merchants. *Antiques,* Sept. 1933, p. 85.
7. Bury, I, 260, notes that Mr. Lynn invented a twinning machine for use by Stewart's, a leading comb factory in Aberdeen, Scotland, but this was ten years after Noyes patented his machine.
8. *Boston Almanac,* p. 188.

'from the latest London and Paris fashions', Jordan also offered to alter ladies' old combs to the newest, most fashionable patterns, plain or fancy.[9] Twist and cap combs were popular too. By the 1870s Jordan was receiving awards for his Premium shell combs.

Providence reported production of $30,000 worth of tortoiseshell combs annually in 1856.[10] By 1858, American combs were being exported to California, Mexico, the West Indies and Europe. In Philadelphia, where W. Redheffer obtained several patents for comb making, there were nearly two hundred workers producing $150,000 worth of hair combs.[11]

Tortoiseshell jewelry in a variety of forms was as popular as the combs. A large-linked bracelet, with two heart pendants and a cross attached to it, was made in Ceylon and purchased by a Salem woman when she was in Point de Galle in 1854 (Colour Plate 130). There is even a tiny key to unlock the hearts.

A description of the American manufacture of tortoiseshell jewelry was included by the famous educator Horace Greeley in his *Great Industries of the United States* in 1872.[12] After soaking the shell in warm water for forty-eight hours, it was cut into pieces, then stacked and pressed together until the desired thickness was obtained. Next, it was carved by hand or inlaid with gold. Inlaid tortoiseshell is called piqué and is related to the studding of leather or tortoiseshell watch cases of the seventeenth century. Piqué refers to the process of tracing the design on to the shell with a pattern of dots. The metal was inlaid into the shell when it was hot and could be pressed into the desired design. The piece was then polished with list wheels covered with layers of carpet material.

In 1871 Tiffany's displayed tortoiseshell jewelry at their Union Square store. The New York *Daily Tribune* called it 'an artistic triumph of American workmanship' in an area previously dominated by French and Neapolitan shell carvers.[13] Not only had the Americans 'caught the style' of the Italian craftsmen, but they had also improved upon the durability and finishing of the shell work by perfecting the machinery used in its manufacture. Particularly important was the American use of steam pressure, rather than heavy weights, to achieve greater compactness and strength. This also resulted in a better surface for intricate carving. Providence manufacturers were among the first to employ steam pressure for tortoiseshell work.

The relief carving on the examples exhibited by Tiffany's was very skilfully executed. A brooch with the profile of a Bacchante evoked high praise from the *Daily Tribune* which said 'the profile is sharply defined, the wreaths of flowers and bunches of fruit are distinctively marked, and the soft gloss of the surface, combined with the mellow tones of color, justify the artistic pretentions of the designer'. Etruscan forms and flowers and fruit were praised. Elaborate creole earrings and raised monograms were singled out for special notice. Monograms could be formed from shell relief, or gold relief, or by gilt engraving. The best monograms were boldly undercut to accentuate the outlines of the combined letters (Colour Plate 131). The colour of the tortoiseshell was important too. A mahogany hue was desirable but the brown, crimson and saffron shades were sought for their rarity. A matched set of earrings and brooch could cost as much as $65.

While English and Continental piqué tended to be very finely patterned with tiny dotted borders, American piqué was often set with bolder designs (Colour Plate 132

9. Boston *D.E.Transcript*, 1 Oct. 1841; 15 June 1842. Jordan was located at 2 Milk Street at the sign of the 'Original Golden Comb'.
10. *Providence Directory*, 1856.
11. Freedley, p. 407.
12. Horace Greeley et al., *The Great Industries of the United States*, quoted by Peter Hinks, *19th Century Jewellery*, p. 56.
13. 24 Mar. 1871.

Plate 151. Tortoiseshell bracelet with silver piqué inlay. Diameter about 2⅝in. Tortoiseshell gold earrings with applied gold rosettes. Diameter about 1⅛in. American, c.1860-80. Photograph by Stephen Briggs. Bequest of Stephen Salisbury III Estate. Worcester Art Museum, Worcester, Mass.

and Plate 151). Especially popular here were inlaid gold stars graduated to fit the shapes when necessary. Also fashionable among Americans were creole earrings, feather-weight chains, and smooth fat oval lockets.

At the Centennial Exposition, Milo Hildreth & Co. of Massachusetts displayed several showcases full of tortoiseshell combs, brooches, earrings, bracelets, lockets, chains and buttons. The lockets and buttons attracted special attention because they were set with inlaid gold monograms that were, according to one reporter, 'beautifully designed and executed, and the material was of very fine shades, lights, and tints'.[14]

Numerous substitutes appeared. Dyed horn often masqueraded as tortoiseshell. Samuel Sylvester and his wife in West Newbury, Mass., made a speciality of painting tin to look like the shell.[15] Vulcanite was introduced in the 1850s (Colour Plate 133). William A. Joslin of Boston advertised India rubber combs in 1856.[16] Most successful of all the substitutes was celluloid, invented in 1870.

Just as they were born of the coiffure, tortoiseshell combs and their imitators died from the change in hair styles and fashion in the late nineteenth century. Elaborate hair ornaments remained for formal dress, but daytime hair styles were loose and unfettered.

Cameos

The impetus for the cameo craze came from England and Europe. Napoleon's interest in Roman cameos was stimulated by his campaign in Italy in 1796. His empress Josephine decorated herself from head to hand with cameos set as jewelry. At the same time, in Italy, the carving of shell cameos had been revived. Here the supply of shells suitable for relief carving was plentiful and the tradition of sculpture was strong (see Plate 77). From this centre carved cameo jewelry was sold in quantities to visitors making the grand tour or was shipped to foreign ports in Europe, England, and

14. J.S. Ingram, *The Centennial Exposition*, p. 305.
15. Doyle, p. 23; example at Historical Society of Old Newbury.
16. Maine Register 1856-7, p. 40, advertising section.

Plate 152. Cameo necklace with five matching brooches, Italy, c.1840. Carved with classical figures and heads, set in gold frames alternating with scrolled pendants, all decorated with gold beading. Marked on tongue of necklace clasp. Length about 17¾in. (necklace). Gift of the Misses Cornelia and Susan Dehon in memory of Mrs. Sidney Brooks. Courtesy, Museum of Fine Arts, Boston.

America (Plate 152). Skilled Italian artists found their way to the same countries where they established firms of cameo cutters, thereby extending the market farther.

Great skill was needed to carve these medallions. Heroic scenes had to be reduced to miniature scale. The shell consisted of layers of contrasting colour and the dimensional effect was created by cutting away the layers so that the background revealed different colours contrasting with the relief design. Using drills of various sizes, the cutter worked the design to achieve a sculptural effect and then the piece was polished to give a high lustre to the background, care being taken not to erase any of the relief work. The helmet shell and the queen conch shell were frequently used for this work, the helmet yielding a rusty layer for the background and the queen conch revealing a pink field. The early nineteenth century examples are more frequently made of helmet shell, while the later nineteenth century cameos are more often made of conch shell.

In America, the revival of the art of cameo carving coincided with the rise of the first professional sculptors in that country. Some of the best sculptors augmented their major works with miniatures carved out of shell or stone. Like the miniature painter and the silhouettist, cameo cutters used tracing machines such as the physiognotrace and the pantograph.

In 1825, Horatio Greenough of Boston sailed for Italy to become a professional sculptor. He was the first of many American artists who studied with sculptors like Thorvaldsen in Rome and Bartolini in Florence. Greenough's footsteps were followed by another American from Massachusetts, Henry Kirke Brown, who was in Italy from 1840 to 1844. One of Brown's first students was William Morris Hunt who would later gain fame as a painter and a cultural leader. A rare survival of Hunt's work in cameo is a startlingly modern-looking bracelet set with finely carved profile portraits, not of classical heads but of Hunt and his three brothers (Plate 153).

Not all cameo cutters had direct contact with the original source of neo-classicism.

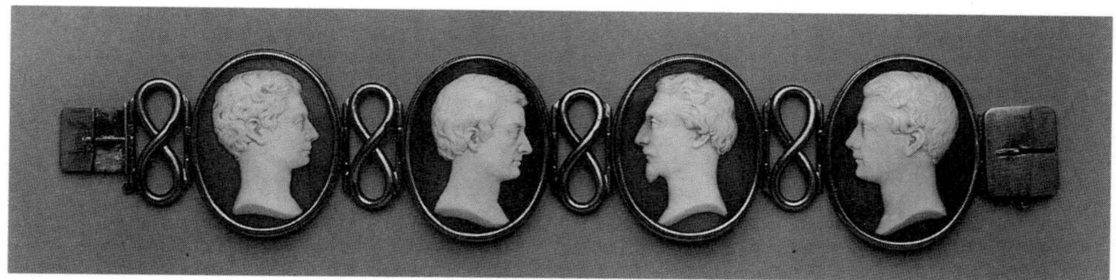

Plate 153. Gold bracelet, c.1855, set with cameos by American artist William Morris Hunt (1824-1879) who studied with the sculptor Henry Kirke Brown in Boston in the 1840s. Cameos depict (left to right) Hunt and his three brothers Richard Morris Hunt, the architect, John Hunt and Leavitt Hunt. About 7⅜in. x 1½in. Bequest of Miss Jane Hunt. Courtesy, Museum of Fine Arts, Boston.

Plate 154. Two portrait cameo brooches carved and set in Boston, by John C. King (1806-1882), a Scottish sculptor who worked in Boston most of his life. (Left) Benjamin Smith Rotch, 1844. Length 1⅞in. (including frame). (Right) Abbott B. Lawrence, 1843. Length 1⅝in. (including frame). Private Collection.

Instead they learned the craft second-hand from someone whose teacher may have had the contact. Others of the first generation of cameo cutters in America came from abroad. John C. King came to the United States from Scotland. By 1837 he was cutting cameos in New Orleans. In 1840 he went to Boston where he exhibited cameos and his sculpture at the Boston Athenaeum.

King was singled out of four sculptors working in Boston by the *Transcript* in 1842. He had recently completed a bust of a local dignitary that the reporter felt was an admirable work of art. Moreover, the newspaper observed, 'what delighted us most, on visiting Mr. K's studio a day or two since, were some small cameo likenesses – set in gold as breast pins – which were not only accurate copies of the originals, but in execution most exquisite'. If the progress in sculpture in the next decades progressed as rapidly as it had in the past decade, the *Transcript* said, our artists' work would bear the scrutiny of connoisseurs.[1] King's likenesses in cameo were cut in shell and carved with his name and the number of the cameo at the base of the bust. Some were engraved on the back with the date (Plate 154).[2]

Not many Americans could afford to buy full-scale statues, but a cameo was within reach. Purchasers of cameos helped the growing profession of American sculptors to make ends meet while working on more ambitious designs. At the same time cameos

1. Boston *D.E. Transcript*, 18 June 1842. The other three sculptors noted were Edward Augustus Brackett, Robert Ball Hughes and Henry Dexter.
2. Gertrude S. Cole, *Antiques*, Sept. 1946, p. 170.

See Colour Plate 134 on page 224

provided images of loved ones, as well as pieces of jewelry. In a period when miniature painting was declining and the photograph was still being invented, cameo likenesses filled a real need. Consequently, it was the portrait cameo, more than the carved classical motif, that was especially cherished and that today provides in miniature the range of skills and individual styles of nineteenth century American sculptors.

Andrew Jackson's profile bust was cut in cameo by George Jamison of New York (Colour Plate 134). In 1835, the National Academy exhibition included Jamison's 'Conchylia portraits' of which Jackson's likeness was but one. The wreathed setting carried an enamelled banner paraphrasing the President's famous rallying cry, 'The Union It Must and Shall Be Preserved'. Art critic William Dunlap pronounced Jamison 'a very ingenious artist in cameos'.[3] The maker of the mounting is not known. However, William Rose was listed as a cameo mounter in New York from 1839 to 1850.[4]

A shell cameo dated 1849, signed by J.A. Greenough, portrayed James Brown Thornton (1794-1873) of Maine. John A. Greenough, brother of Horatio Greenough, began as a granite cutter.[5] The irregular convex curve of the shell from which the profile of Thornton was carved was accommodated by its close-fitted plain gold frame, giving the brooch a less classical and imposing, more natural and human appearance. The same personal approach to portraiture in American cameos can be seen to an even greater degree in the likeness carved in 1853 by Benjamin Harris Kinney (1821-1888), a sculptor in Worcester, Massachusetts. His endearing portrayal of Mrs. Sarah H. Earle has some of the compelling realism and attraction that the better-known painted portrait of Whistler's mother would later command (Plate 155).

One of the most famous American sculptors to work in cameo was Augustus Saint-

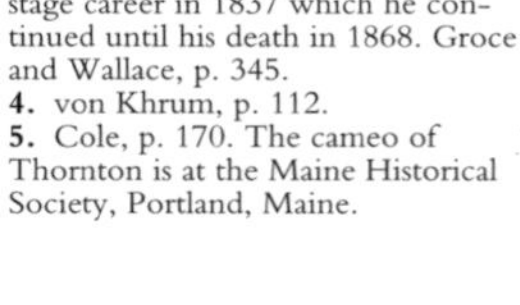

3. II, 472. Jamison began a successful stage career in 1837 which he continued until his death in 1868. Groce and Wallace, p. 345.
4. von Khrum, p. 112.
5. Cole, p. 170. The cameo of Thornton is at the Maine Historical Society, Portland, Maine.

Plate 155. Portrait cameo of Mrs. Sarah H. Earle, c.1853, by Benjamin Harris Kinney (1821-1888), of Massachusetts, a marble cutter and sculptor working in Worcester from 1843-1888. Signed and dated on back. Length $1\frac{3}{8}$in. Worcester Art Museum, Worcester, Mass.

Gaudens (1848-1907) who arrived in New York with his parents in the first year of his life. In 1861, he was apprenticed to a terrible tempered Frenchman named Avet. Avet supplied cameos to Tiffany and to Ball, Black & Co. After several years with Avet, Saint-Gaudens was apprenticed from 1864 to 1867 in the shop of Jules Le Brethon who had a stone lathe but no one skilled in using it (Plate 156). Le Brethon encouraged Saint-Gaudens to spend time modelling clay to develop his talents. Soon the young apprentice was taking drawing lessons at Cooper Union after work.

In 1867 Saint-Gaudens left for France, carrying his cameo-cutter's lathe with him, to study at the Ecole des Beaux-Arts. To support himself, he got a job cutting cameos at the shop of an Italian named Lupi.[6] While he was studying in Paris, he carved the cameo of William Root Bliss who was travelling in France in 1869 (now at the Boston Atheneum). Bliss's loose wavy hair combined with a wisp of a goatee give the portrait a memorable appearance. When Saint-Gaudens moved to Italy in 1870, he told a friend, 'They pay a lot more for cameos here than they do in Paris and they're a lot less demanding...I'm beginning to establish myself with some rich Americans and cameos for them are extra high priced'.[7]

Plate 156. Photograph of Augustus Saint-Gaudens working at his cameo lathe, c.1865. New York. Dartmouth College Library.

A cameo portrait of Mrs. William T. Walters of Baltimore (Plate 157) was cut in shell by the renowned Tommaso Saulini (1793-1864) in Italy. The profile was derived from a marble bust carved by the expatriot Maryland sculptor William H. Rinehart

6 Louise Hall Tharp, *Saint Gaudens & the Gilded Era*, pp. 15-32.
7. Ibid., p. 48.

Plate 157. Shell cameo brooch with bust length portrait of Mrs. William T. Walters (Ellen Harper, 1822-1862), attributed to Tommaso Saulini (1793-1864) of Rome, after a marble bust of Mrs. Walters carved in 1862 by William H. Rinehart (1825-1874), a Maryland sculptor and friend, living in Rome. The gold frame is marked with the double C. monogram of Castellani. Length 2⅝in. Walters Art Gallery, Baltimore.

Plate 158. Above left. Shell cameo brooch, carved with the figure of Spring after a marble relief sculpture by William H. Rinehart, a Baltimorean working in Rome. Italian, after 1874. Commissioned by William T. Walters and mounted in gold Italian frame. Length 2⁹⁄₁₆ in. Walters Art Gallery, Baltimore.

Plate 159. Above right. White and grey agate cameo of the Empress Josephine, carved by the Italian sculptress Teresa Talani, c.1797. Talani was born and trained in Rome and worked in Naples. Cameo acquired by William T. Walters (1820-1894) of Baltimore in 1892. Mounted in delicately chased gold frame with blue enamelled inner lining. Suspension ring added for use as a pendant. Signed at bottom [TE]RESA TALANI. Walters Art Gallery, Baltimore.

(1825-1874) in the year of Mrs. Walters' death in 1862. The strength of her features contrasts with the softness of her loose curls and lace scarf. The cameo is mounted in an oval gold brooch marked with the monogram of Augusto Castellani (1829-1914) whose family firm in Rome was famous for its jewelry. Mrs. Walters' husband purchased a number of other cameos. An oval cameo carved with a filmy figure of Spring scattering flowers was commissioned by William T. Walters in Rome (Plate 158). It too was based on a sculptural work by Rinehart, a marble relief executed in 1874. Walters collected several historic cameos as well. In 1892 he purchased an old cameo in a pendant (Plate 159). The cameo was cut in white and grey agate by Teresa Talani about 1797 and depicted the Empress Josephine. Talani worked in Naples.[8]

Fashion articles in American newspapers and magazines extolled the virtues of cameos as the ideal jewelry to be worn during the day as well as in the evening. Cameos became the Christmas present of choice. Two days before Christmas in 1869, the stalwart George Templeton Strong of New York went up town to do a little 'Christmassing' as he called it. Although he was determined to be parsimonious, not spending more than $20 for his wife's present, he unwisely found himself inside Tiffany's where, he confessed, 'I was inflamed by a pretty cameo brooch, and involved myself to the extent of $200. Never mind', he said, 'I won't do so again, and I think Ellie will be much pleased with this bit of wampum'.[9] Cameos from Tiffany's were still touted for Christmas presents by the New York *Times* in 1877. The newspaper pointed out that the cameos were carved in Italy by some of the finest artists there, 'but the beautiful mountings are the special design of Tiffany & Co.'[10]

At the Centennial Exhibition in Philadelphia in 1876, the Italian display of jewelry included several cases of rare and beautiful cameos. Francatti & Santamaria, a Roman firm established in London, was one of the exhibitors. Pio Siotto of Rome had a case showing cameos in the various stages of their production. 'First the shell medallion,

8. Walters Art Gallery, *Objects of Adornment,* #192, p. 173; #178, p. 166.
9. IV, 266.
10. 16 Dec. 1877. Illus. Fig. 8, Proddow, p.26.

Plate 160. Onyx cameo portrait of Mary Queen of Scots, carved by Augustus Saint-Gaudens, known as the Williams version, 1873. The gold frame is set with twenty diamonds spaced with ten pearls. The delicacy of the Queen's lace collar is a testimony to the sculptor's skills. Photograph by Jeffrey Nintzel, Plainfield, N.H. Collection of Saint-Gaudens National Historic Site, Cornish. N.H.

then the same with the design sketched upon it, then the design blocked out with the tool; after that, in the phases of development until the last, showing the head of Bacchus crowned with the vine, all in the very perfection of the art', observed a chronicler of the exhibit.[11] The German display featured an abundance of cameos in fine settings, primarily from Hanau and Pforzheim, the principal centres of cameo cutting. Nevertheless, 'the cameos exhibited by Starr & Marcus', according to one critic, 'were among the most exquisite in the world'.[12]

The Philadelphia Centennial no doubt caused those who still had no cameos to want one. By that time there were cameo cutters and jewelers in every major area of the country who could supply them. To celebrate the country's 100th anniversary, cameos were made with Martha Washington's face and the Victorian version of eighteenth-century costume. For the mass market, inexpensive cameos were made of imitation materials, the relief cast from a mould and glued to the contrasting background.

By 1876, American-made cameos were frequently carved out of black and white onyx and set in elaborate gold frames with pearls and diamonds. Black, Starr & Frost had a black and white onyx cameo so exquisite that the New York *Sun* described it to its readers. It was in the shape of an oval shell with a cupid inside, floating on a wave, the shell being black, cupid and the wave, white. It was set around with alternating diamonds and pearls. Below was suspended a larger diamond and pearl, one above the other. Another large diamond was set at the top in the pendant loop.[13] Saint-Gaudens' head of Mary Queen of Scots with her perky lace collar (Plate 160) reveals the artist's great skill in handling stone as well as the elegance and formality of the period.

11. McCabe, James D., *The Illustrated History of the Centennial Exhibition*, p. 419; Ingram, p. 522-23.
12. Ingram, p. 433; McCabe, p. 368.
13. 9 April 1876.

Plate 161. Earrings and brooch with carved onyx cameos in gold mounts and pearls, American, c.1880. Owned by Hattie Brazier Libby whose family lived in the Morse-Libby Victoria Mansion in Portland, Maine. Screw-back earring fasteners are substitutions. Length 1⅞in. (brooch). Photograph by Dennis Griggs. Private Collection.

Sets of cameos, including earrings and brooches, became commonplace and can be seen in many of the early photographs of the period. A pendant brooch set with the profile of an Elizabethan lady, accompanied by similarly set dangle earrings, was proudly displayed in the photograph taken of Mrs. Joseph Ralph Libby about 1880 (Plate 161).

When the end came to this fashion, it came quickly. In 1881 the fancy for cameos had been exceeded only by the passion for Limoges enamel jewelry. Two years later, it was reported in the New York *Times,* 'Cameos seem to have gone almost entirely out of date'.[14] A fashion commentator called attention to an intaglio ring engraved in sapphire that was worth only $125 because both cameos and intaglio rings had gone out of style. 'We have a peck or more of them', the jeweler was quoted as saying, 'antiques and modern, cut in many varieties of stone, and some of them quite valuable, but there is hardly any sale for them'.[15]

14. 27 Nov. 1881; 23 July 1883.
15. *The Sun,* 15 Jan. 1882.
16. Tait, *I,* p. 211.
17. *Antiques,* Sept. 1956, p. 252.

Cameos in Glass and Ceramics

The craving for cameos led to the substitution of man-made materials for shell and stone. As we have seen in Wedgwood medallions (see Colour Plates 62 and 63) manufactured cameos could be moulded or stamped out quickly, eliminating time-consuming carving by hand. Artistic skill was required only for making the initial master pattern.

As early as 1779, portraits of Benjamin Franklin had been made in clay in France. Most were set in snuff-box lids, but some were set in rings. About 1819 encrusted cameos, or sulphides as they were called, were made in England and encased in a clear flint-glass medallion.[16] This innovation was the idea of a London glass-maker, Apsley Pellatt, and was patented by him in 1831. Among the early busts produced by Pellatt were those of George Washington and Lafayette.[17] In France sulphides of Benjamin Franklin were still popular subjects (Plate 162).

Plate 162. Sulphide of Benjamin Franklin attributed to Apsley Pellatt who made clear glass cameos set with portraits made in a kind of white porcelain as early as 1819. Photograph by Taylor & Dull, courtesy of Historic Deerfield Curatorial Department. Private Collection.

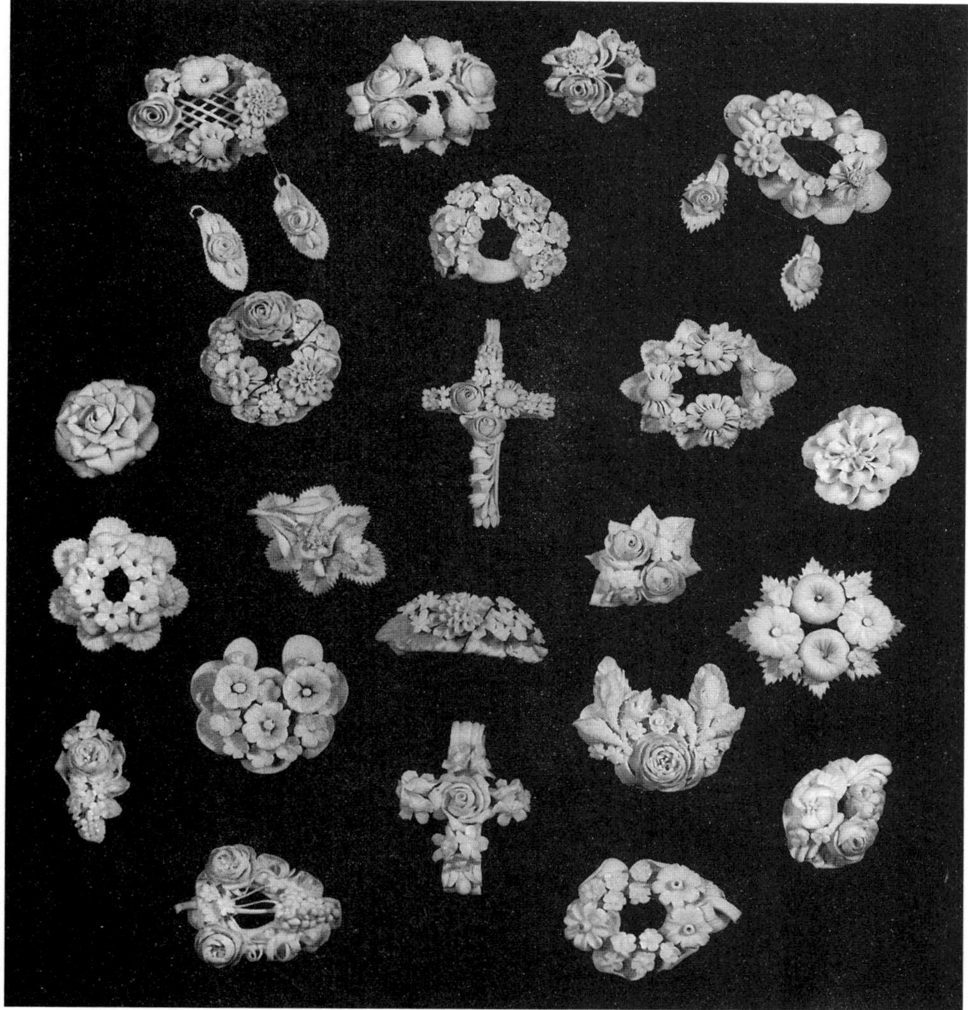

Plate 163. Group of parian jewelry with applied flowers, made by the Bennington Company in Vermont, c.1847-1858. In addition to brooches, earrings, stick pins and pendants, there were pieces made to be worn as bracelets with ribbon ties. Courtesy of The Bennington Museum, Bennington, Vermont.

While some of the encrusted cameos were three and four inches in diameter, smaller sulphides set as jewelry enjoyed a vogue during the second quarter of the nineteenth century. American glassmakers used sulphides in glass tablewares but apparently did not make jewelry of this sort.[18] Occasionally glass pendants were made with a small silver medal bearing the likeness of Washington encased in glass, instead of an encrusted cameo.

With the development of parian, cameos were sometimes formed of this new unglazed, soft, cream-coloured ceramic. At the famous Bennington factory in Vermont in the mid-nineteenth century, floral wreaths and other designs were made out of bisque porcelain and set as brooches (Plate 163).[19] One example was made for Jane Fenton Norton, the granddaughter of Jonathan Fenton, one of the Bennington potters, about 1850.[20]

18. Arlene M. Palmer, 'American Heroes in Glass: The Bakewell Sulphide Portraits', *American Art Journal, XI,* No. 1 (January 1979), pp. 4-26.
19. Richard Carter Barret, *Bennington Pottery & Porcelain.*
20. *Antiques,* Sept. 1925, p.152, Fig.6.

Lava

Vesuvius, the volcano east of the Bay of Naples, and the cities it had entombed attracted a great deal of attention in the nineteenth century. Between 1806 and 1814, at the instigation of the French government, excavations were made at Pompeii. The treasures that were revealed had a tremendous impact on the arts. No tour of Italy was complete without a stop at the ruins. Following fresh eruptions of the volcano in 1832, interest in Vesuvius heated up again. One enthusiastic American traveller climbed to the top of the volcano, an ascent that he said 'was about as steep as Park Street in Boston'. In a daring manœuvre, he collected a half cup of the molten lava, pressed a silver coin into it, and carried it home triumphantly to dazzle his friends.[1]

It is, unfortunately, human nature to want to pick up pieces of historic monuments. To capitalize on this foible, Italian artisans began to carve 'Vesuvian lava' into cameos for jewelry. The most common colour of the lava was a dull grey, sometimes tinted olive brown or beige. Often the cameos were carved from a lava look-alike, an easily cut stone from Monte Sant' Angelo in Salerno, Italy. Oval cameos were carved with classical heads and set in brooches, rings, and linked bracelets. Gargoyles, satyrs and cupids of uniform colour appealed to some, while others preferred the profiles of Italy's most famous literary figures, each in a different hue.

In a rare instance of lava jewelry custom-made for an American, Dr. John Bellinger had his own head carved into lava and set as a brooch (Colour Plate 135). It is possible that the lava portrait could have been cut from a shell cameo that had been previously carved with Bellinger's profile by R. Burrell in 1859, rather than from life.[2]

Lava jewelry could be obtained without ever setting foot in Italy. In 1861, a New York gift store advertised lava jewelry along with cameos, mosaics, coral, garnet and turquoise baubles.[3] Tiffany sold lava parures featuring bacchantes and amphorae-shaped pendants and drops (Colour Plate 136). The gold mounts for lava jewelry, whether made in Italy or in America, were usually quite modest. However, a lava brooch with the design of a winged Venus and Cupid, so deeply cut that it is almost free standing, has a very nicely granulated gold frame (Plate 164). It was sold in Boston about 1855 by Samuel T. Crosby.

1. Diary of Charles Brooks, Boston, 14Feb. 1834, as quoted in Boston *Daily Evening Transcript,* 2 Jan. 1852.
2. *Antiques,* May 1947, p. 344.
3. D.W. Evans & Co., 1677 Broadway, adv. in *Harper's Bazaar,* 1861. Flower, Fig. 15.

Plate 164. 'Lava' brooch sold by Samuel T. Crosby of Boston, c.1855-1857. Italian cameo of Flora and Cupid brandishing Hymen's torch, carved out of limestone, a substitute for lava. The depth of the carving is almost full round. Mounted in a gold filigree setting. Original box imprinted with address of Crosby's shop at 69 Washington Street where he was located between 1855 and 1857. Length 2¼in. Bequest of Mrs. Edward Jackson Holmes. Courtesy, Museum of Fine Arts, Boston.

Coral

Traditional forms of shell and stone cameos spawned cameos and carved ornaments made of other materials such as coral, lava, ivory, and ceramics. Coral jewelry was especially well liked because of its colour which ranged from red to pink to white. The yellowish-red colour that is called coral was less popular than the rosy-pink shades in the mid-nineteenth century, and the pale-pinkish white coral known as 'angel skin' became the favourite for young ladies. Coral was not complicated by multiple shallow layers of contrasting colour as were shell and stone. It could be carved into deeply dimensional or full-round ornaments. It came in a variety of shapes and textures: beads, cylinders, branches, and dog's tooth, to name a few (Colour Plate 137).

The coral trade was centred in the area around Naples. At Torre del Greco, situated on the slopes of Mt. Vesuvius near the ancient ruins of Pompeii, the art of carving coral had been taught from generation to generation for centuries. The supply of coral in the Mediterranean, whether harvested locally or available through trade, was plentiful.[1] Coral jewelry from Naples was considered the best and some American jewelers advertised specifically that they sold Naples coral.[2]

Because of its reputed therapeutic properties, coral had been used for beaded necklaces, especially for children. This practice continued well into the nineteenth century until Louis Pasteur's more scientific approach to germs and disease became accepted. Portraits of early nineteenth century American children frequently illustrated the use of both beaded and branched coral necklaces and bracelets (see Colour Plate 33). Women also continued to wear coral beads, either plain, faceted, or carved, but as the nineteenth century progressed, the size of the beads grew larger and larger. Coral négligés and beads were recommended for holiday presents by William Osborn of Providence in 1835.[3]

One of the first coral parures owned in the United States was brought back from Europe by Captain Nathan Endicott (Colour Plate 138). It was made of tiny beads the size of seed pearls and consisted of a necklace, two bracelets, a brooch and earrings. It was set with bright gold Etruscan work and cameos. In 1853 P. Raffaelli & Son of Leghorn, Italy, won a bronze medal for their display of coral jewelry at the Crystal Palace exhibition in New York, thereby helping to create an interest in the United States for these designs.

The rococo revival encouraged the use of floral coral jewelry. Rose heads were carved out of coral to great effect. Floral sprays could be made to look like a single flower with coral leaves attached to a single gold stem or could be fashioned into a bouquet with many stems. 'All ornaments of coral are much in fashion', the Paris correspondent reported to the Boston *Transcript* in 1856, and 'with a white toilette, a coral wreath for the hair, and a *bouquet de corsage,* are very becoming ornaments'.[4] Tiffany sold matching sets of brooches and top-and-drop earrings, with slight variations among the leaves and flowers of the separate pieces (Colour Plate 139). The effect of delicacy, asymmetry and the infinite variety of nature was enhanced by the fringed borders, carved on some but not all of the petals and leaves.

Godey's Lady's Book described the fashion for coral bracelets in 1855. They were formed of strands of coral wrapped around the arm several times, with long, full tassels of coral beads attached to them. Another style of bracelet called a sultan had gold cord woven with green silk and coral beads in a wide gothic band, with five little coral balls suspended on gold ribbons. This was recommended for summer wear.[5] A

1. Julius Wodiska, *A Book of Precious Stones*, pp. 104-09.
2. M.W.Galt & Co., *Washington* (DC) *Star*, 23 Dec. 1876.
3. Providence *Daily Journal*, 1 Jan. 1835.
4. 24 Nov. 1856.
5. *Godey's, 51,* 478 (1855).

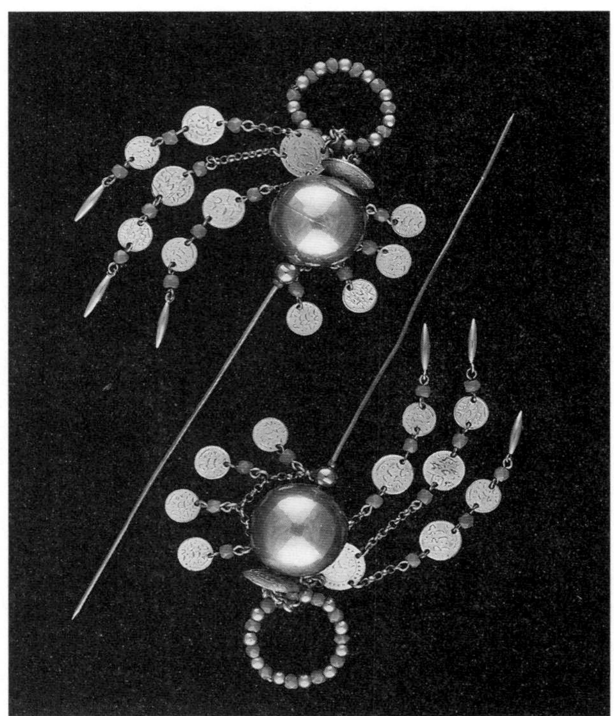

Plate 165. Gold and coral hat pins with cluster of 'Persian' coins, in box labelled by Jones, Shreve, Brown & Co., in business together in Boston from 1854 to 1856. Photograph by Stephen Briggs. Bequest of Stephen Salisbury III Estate. Worcester Art Museum.

more exotic form of coral jewelry was the set of hat pins set with clusters of 'Persian' coins, sold by the firm of Jones, Shreve, Brown & Co. about 1855 (Plate 165).

With the advent of the archaeological style, coral jewelry became more robust. Masques, rams' heads and elongated amphora, comparable to the designs found in Etruscan-style gold jewelry, became very desirable. By 1870, elegant sets of coral jewelry were especially recommended for Christmas gifts for 'sister and brothers' gifts'. The prices ranged from $50 to $375.[6]

While carved coral was produced in Italy (Colour Plate 140), it was not always made into jewelry there. Robert Phillips, the London jeweler, made so much coral jewelry that he was credited with extending its popularity and received a decoration from the King of Naples in 1870. Mid-century American jewelers were also putting Neapolitan coral into mounts of their own design (Colour Plate 141). Brooches, earrings and studs were made with bars of coral riveted to ornately chased, lobed, gold plaques and were held in place by applied clusters of leaves and berries. To these were suspended smooth pointed pendants, typical of archaeological motifs of the period.

Import records chart the popularity of coral jewelry in the United States. In 1868, the importation of manufactured coral was valued at a high of $62,270. The next big year was 1873 and, over the next four years surrounding the Philadelphia Centennial Celebration, imported manufactured coral remained strong. 'Coral jewelry is increasing in favor of late', the New York *Sun* announced in 1876, "...it looks very pretty with the cream lace so much worn'.[7] At the Exhibition, Oliveri of Venice contributed some fine coral jewelry to the Italian display and this may have helped to keep it in fashion.

At the same time, more and more unmanufactured coral was being imported and not only set in American-made mounts but carved into designs of American origin. In 1882, for the first time, more unworked coral was imported to the United States than manufactured coral. By 1888, almost $60,000 worth of unworked coral was imported while the value of manufactured coral was too insignificant to be specified.[8]

Coral cameos, cut in designs much like their counterparts in shell and stone, were very pleasing when well-modelled and polished. Set in elegant Renaissance-revival

6. *Evening Mail,* 17 Dec. 1870. TA.
7. 16 April 1876.
8. Kunz, *Gems,* p. 315.

Plate 166. Imitation coral cross pendant, moulded with winged cherub's head on transept. Shown in an early photograph of its original owner, Ardella Spaulding Chadbourne of Dover, Maine, who wore the cross suspended from a watch chain. Length 1⅞in. Photograph by Peter J. Theriault. Private Collection.

frames with borders of diamonds and pearls, the coral cameo heads such as that of Flora (Colour Plate 142) presented an appealing combination of classicism and naturalism. *Godey's* commended the beautiful coral cameos encircled with large pearls and suggested that diadems and necklaces made of small coral cameos were very effective for ball gowns of white, sea-green or amber.[9]

Imitation coral was made possible by the introduction of the first plastic material. Alexander Parkes in England produced cellulose nitrate in 1855 which he dubbed parkesine and promoted as a substitute for coral and other organic materials. His enterprise failed in 1868 and was taken over by Daniel Spill who invented xylonite and specialized in making simulated coral with it. John W. Hyatt and Isaac S. Hyatt, of Newark, New Jersey, patented their brand of cellulose nitrate in 1874. They called it celluloid. At first, it was used primarily for imitation ivory, especially for billiard balls, but it proved an excellent substitute for coral as well. The Hyatt brothers' celluloid made use of gum camphor and fine tissue paper.[10]

Two more patents were obtained in 1874 for coral simulants by other inventors. Daniel D. Smith of Syracuse had developed a compound exclusively for making artificial coral for jewelry that could be coloured and then moulded.[11] Smith's recipe called for gum copal and gum camphor. Julius Frauenberger's patent[12] could be used for making artificial coral as well as ivory and other similar articles. Celluloid coral jewelry rapidly gained popularity and sold for a sixth of the cost of real coral.[13] 'American corals' were mentioned in an English publication in 1877 and were said to be made from a secret formula devised by Kingman & Hodges of Mansfield, Massachusetts, from milk used in New York cheese processing plants.[14]

At the Philadelphia Exhibition in 1876 The Celluloid Manufacturing Company of Newark was given an award for its jewelry and other products. One observer said that the 'jewelry of imitation coral [is] so much like the real that it takes an expert to distinguish between them'.[15] Although it was possible to fabricate in celluloid all the various colours of coral, the manufacturers most frequently used bright or dark shades. They found that their copies of the expensive pink coral did not win popular approval.[16]

Moulded imitation coral was available in designs that appealed to the masses (Plate 166). The cherub head applied to the centre of a pendent cross looked very much like the china doll's heads mass-produced at the same time. The fashion for coral began to wane and when cameos went out of style about 1883, they took coral jewelry with them.[17]

9. *54*, 288 (1857).
10. #152,232 (23 June 1874); #156,353 (27 Oct. 1874).
11. #150,722.
12. #153,939.
13. NY *Sun*, 12 Mar. 1876.
14. Bury I, 380.
15. Ingram, p. 316.
16. *Journal of the Franklin Institute*, May 1879, p. 336.
17. *NY Times*, 22 July 1883.

Mosaic

The art of mosaic work took on a new life in the nineteenth century as a result of archaeological discoveries at Pompeii and other classical sites. The Vatican Factory and School, established in the sixteenth century to execute mosaic designs in St. Peter's Basilica, had been revived in the seventeenth century. In the nineteenth century, the Vatican School still produced the most skilful mosaic work. Spun filaments of coloured glass were cut into tiny tesserae which were affixed to a stucco ground held

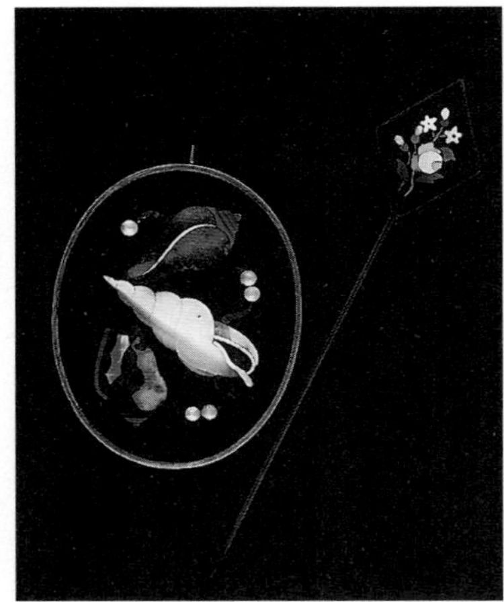

Plate 167. Above. Italian mosaic jewelry probably bought by Stephen Salisbury II when he travelled abroad in the 1850s. Stickpin with box imprinted BENEDETTO BERCHIELLI / mosaic maker / Firenze Lung. / Arno Acciajoli 12. Length 3¼in. Brooch in gold frame and mosaic in design of shells. Length about 2in. Photograph by Stephen Briggs. Bequest of Stephen Salisbury III Estate. Worcester Art Museum, Worcester, Mass.

Plate 168. Right. Cards of micromosaic buttons with views of classical buildings in original box imprinted L. GALLANDT / 7. PIAZZA di Spagna 7. / Rome. Set of buttons with bird designs. Diameter ⅝in. Photograph by Stephen Briggs. Bequest of Stephen Salisbury III Estate. Worcester Art Museum, Worcester, Mass.

by a metal or stone plate. The resulting plaques could then be mounted into jewelry.

The mosaic designs most popular with Americans consisted of floral motifs or were derived from classical architecture. 'Doves drinking at the fountain', a design in mosaic found at Hadrian's villa, was especially well liked and was referred to as 'The Doves of Pliny'. There were scenes inspired by Aesop and still-life compositions of flowers and fruit, some directly inspired by wall paintings at Pompeii (Colour Plate 143).

About 1840 mosaic-set jewelry began to appear in portraits of American women, most often in the form of brooches and earrings. It was considered appropriate for daytime dress.[1] Imitations were attempted with enamelling or with painting on wood. A reporter, who attended The Mechanics' Exhibition at Faneuil Hall in Boston in 1841, saw a breast pin on display that he thought at first was mosaic work. To his amazement, it was made of beads by Miss Mary E. Conant.[2]

On rare occasions, mosaics were custom-made for Americans. The small round brooch shown in Colour Plate 144 displayed the American eagle instead of the more usual dove. In the eagle's beak was a flag pole topped with a Liberty cap instead of the peace bough doves often carried in their beaks. The eagle was well executed and the American flag billowed in the breeze. The grey-blue background had a single row of lapis-coloured glass tiles outlining the design.

Increasingly pleasing to the grand tourists were mosaics depicting the most famous architectural sites in Rome. Jewelry set with the Coliseum or the Pantheon made a pretty souvenir in the pre-picture-postcard period. Stephen Salisbury II of Worcester, Massachusetts, toured Europe in the 1850s (Plate 167) and again in the 1880s. A set of mosaic buttons ornamented with classical buildings is in the Salisbury collection (Plate 168). The buttons were never removed from the card to which they were attached when they were bought. Their original box is imprinted with the name of the vendor, L. Gallandt, 7 Piazza di Spagna, Rome.

1. A mosaic earring was lost on a Saturday afternoon in Boston and a reward was offered for its return. *D.E. Transcript,* 16 Sept. 1841.
2. *Transcript,* 30 Sept. 1841.

Colour Plate 135. Lava jewelry set in gold frames, Italian, mid-19th century. The half set has the goddess of wine in the brooch and classical female heads in the earrings. The brooch (top, right) has a cameo carved with the head of Dr. John Bellinger of Charleston, S.C. Length 2½in. (brooch, upper left). Photograph by Leland Cook. Courtesy of The Charleston Museum, Charleston, S.C.

Colour Plate 136. Lava parure in the archaeological style, sold by Tiffany & Co., c.1860-80. Courtesy of Edith Weber & Assoc.

Plate 169. Brooches and earrings with micromosaic designs of flowers and landscape, in box imprinted by Jones, Shreve, Brown & Co., c.1854-1857. Length 1¾in. (oval brooch). Photograph by Stephen Briggs. Bequest of Stephen Salisbury III Estate. Worcester Art Museum, Worcester, Mass.

It was not necessary to travel to Rome to purchase these souvenirs. The more enterprising American jewelers imported mosaics. These could be set by an Italian jeweler or could be set by the jeweler importing them. A pair of mosaic earrings was bought by Mrs. Waldo Flint from the Boston jewelry firm of Shreve, Brown & Co., in 1859.[3] Mrs. Flint was related to the Salisburys. A pair of mosaic earrings, as well as a brooch, in a box labelled Jones, Shreve, Brown & Co. (Plate 169), are also in the Salisbury collection of jewelry at the Worcester Art Museum. This firm was in business from 1854 to 1857 when Jones left the firm. It is possible that Shreve, Brown & Co. continued using boxes with the firm's old name. In 1868 their successors Shreve, Stanwood & Co. advertised under the heading of Byzantine Mosaics '100 Sets Brooches and Earrings, received this day from Rome, at extremely low prices'.[4]

Tiffany also sold mosaics (Colour Plate 145). As might be expected, the design and workmanship of the jewelry they sold was of much greater distinction than the tourist items and most of the other jewelers' products. A brooch in an abstracted bowknot design was set with Egyptian motifs featuring a splendid pair of gold-inlaid beetles. The ogivals and volutes of the frame also were set with mosaics, as were the pendants. Graduated gold beads added the final Tiffany touch.

The Italian display at the Centennial Exhibition in Philadelphia in 1876 gave another boost to the market for mosaics. It included a portrait of Abraham Lincoln that was executed in glass tesserae. Cesare Roccheggiani won a medal for his exhibition of mosaics.[5] 'Since the Centennial, mosaic jewelry has risen in favor', reported *The Sun*.[6]

In 1880, Francis E. Meyer of New York city patented a somewhat crude imitation of mosaic for jewelry. His innovation consisted of a transparent face plate of glass

Plate 170. Brooch and matching earrings in the form of a Greek cross set with black and white mosaic tesserae. Purchased by a Bostonian from Castellani whose mark, an applied cartouche-shaped tag containing a monogram of two Cs, appears on the back of the brooch, c.1870. Length about 2in. (brooch; diameter about ¾in. (earrings). Gift of Miss Aimee Lamb and Miss Rosamond Lamb in memory of Mrs. Horatio Lamb. Courtesy Museum of Fine Arts, Boston.

having an opaque border and an outline of a central figure, combined with a central mosaic figure made of pieces of mother-of-pearl, or other suitable material, cemented to the face plate.[7]

Florentine Mosaic

Americans also liked the kind of mosaic work produced in Florence. Instead of the glass tesserae used in Roman micromosaics, Florentine mosaics were made of larger pieces of inlaid multicoloured stones. To distinguish between the two types, mid-nineteenth century American jewelers referred to the Roman micromosaics as simply mosaic. Stone inlay was called Florentine.[8]

Florentine mosaic jewelry was worked in pleasing designs, taking advantage of the natural colour and patterns of hardstones, and cut to fit like a simplified jig-saw puzzle. The mosaics could be used for decorating objects as large as table tops and as small as the head of a shirt pin. Varicoloured marbles, malachite, lapis lazuli, and cornelian were most often used for the patterns. Occasionally some other material such as mother-of-pearl or coral would be added to the jewelry design. Black marble was the most common background material.

3. Bill dated 26 July 1859, AAS.
4. Boston *Transcript,* 17 Dec. 1868.
5. Bury, I, 236-7.
6. New York, 17 Dec. 1876. Ingram, pp. 526-27.
7. #227,877.
8. D.W.Evans & Co. adv. *Harper's Bazaar,* 1861. Gere, *A. & E.J.* Fig. 15.

Plate 171. Jewelry owned by Harriet Beecher Stowe, c.1850-1860. (Upper left) Florentine mosaic brooch with spray of flowers in gold mount. (Below) Brooch and earrings with Roman micromosaics of popular classical ruins depicted in mosaic for tourists in Rome. (Above) Pair of love birds in mosaic in gold brooch with three elongated pendants. (Upper right) Carved ivory cross pendant, Italian or Swiss, with winged cherub's head. (Lower right) Pair of Scottish plaid pins, gold set with cairngorms, which Mrs. Stowe purchased for her twin daughters while she was touring in Scotland in 1853. Stowe-Day Foundation, Hartford, Connecticut.

Colour Plate 137. Carved coral hand holding a ring with coral fobs, Italian, c.1840-80. Owned by the Manigault family of Charleston. The bracelet on the carved hand is studded with turquoise beads as was the ring on one of the fingers. Photograph by Terry Richardson, courtesy of The Charleston Museum, Charleston, S.C. Private Collection.

Colour Plate 138. Coral parure, set in gold, and believed to have been brought from Europe to Salem, Massachusetts, by Captain Nathan Endicott in 1825. Probably made in Italy. Length 18in. (necklace); 1½in. (cameo). Photograph by Mark Sexton. Peabody Essex Museum.

Colour Plate 139. Carved floral sprays of coral for earrings and brooch with original box imprinted Tiffany & C°. / 550 Broadway 552 / NEW-YORK, where the firm was located from 1854-1870. The earrings retain their original shepherd's crook fasteners. Length 1⅞in. (brooch). Photograph by Dennis Griggs. Private Collection.

Colour Plate 140. Part of a set of coral and gold jewelry, Italian, c.1860. Worn by Sophie Sherman (Mrs. Robert Lenox Taylor) and by Margaret Lenox Taylor (Mrs. Alexander T. Van Nest), mother of the donor. Length 2¼in. (brooch). Gift of Mrs. Arthur N. Little, 35.226 b-d. Photograph by Arthur Vitols, The Helga Studio. Museum of the City of New York.

Colour Plate 142. Coral cameo head of Flora, set in brooch in gold mount with pearl border spaced by six diamonds. Cameo probably carved in Italy and mounted in United States, c.1860-70. Owned in Hingham, Mass. Length 1½in. Photograph by Peter J. Theriault. Private Collection.

Colour Plate 141. Set consisting of gold earrings, brooch and studs. Earring fasteners replaced. Small cylinders of coral are placed on ornamental gold plaques with applied clusters of leaves and berries. The original box is imprinted inside the lid, Ball, Black & Co. / 565 Broadway 567 / New York. Length 1 7/16in. (brooch). Photograph by Peter J. Theriault. Private Collection.

Plate 172. Group of Florentine mosaic jewelry, Italian, c.1860. Lilies-of-the-valley were popular with Americans when depicted in mosaic jewelry. The single blossom was set in a circular gold frame with a twisted flat strip of metal forming the border. The sections of the articulated bracelet band are stamped and engraved. Bracelet engraved 'MTB from WGD, June 15th 1856'. Length 5½ in. (bracelet). Smithsonian Institution.

The most striking designs in Florentine mosaics were floral sprays composed, for example, of single stalks of lilies-of-the-valley (Plate 172). In the language of flowers, lilies-of-the-valley meant the return of happiness.

Conchology was of special interest in the mid-nineteenth century and compositions of different sorts of shells were consequently popular designs for mosaics. Here (Plate 167) mother-of-pearl was inlaid to give the effect of the nacre inside sea shells or to give a realistic sheen to the pearls included in the design.

Florentine mosaics were considered appropriate for daytime wear and sometimes were lost during excursions into town. One proper Bostonian lost a 'Florentine Mosaic Stone' which fell out of her pin either on her way to church or while she was attending Sunday service. An unlucky Boston shopper lost her entire Florentine breast pin while visiting stores on Summer and Washington Streets.[9]

9. Boston *Transcript,* 12 Jan., 6 Feb. 1858.

Malachite and Lapis

Malachite, with its waves of dark and light emerald colour, and lapis lazuli, with its equally intense rich blue flecked with golden grains of pyrite, were sometimes used in Florentine work to add to its richness.[1] So appealing were these stones that solid pieces were cut into pleasing shapes, polished to a high smoothness and set into gold frames to be worn as jewelry. The beauty and gem-like quality of cut and polished malachite was called to the attention of Americans as early as 1826 by A.F.M. Willich when he published *The Domestic Encyclopedia.* Willich pointed out that it was eminently suitable for use in jewelry and had lately come into fashion.[2]

Set in simple gold frames with twisted rope borders, malachite and lapis were very effective in brooches and earrings. However, stone jewelry of all kinds was quite heavy and so was only appropriate for use on heavy fabrics and sturdy ears. Stunning in its simplicity was a brooch made of a lapis lazuli log with a long lapis drop suspended from it by means of a gold rope (Colour Plate 143). This was purchased in

1. 'A malachite Mosaic pin, set in gold' was advertised as lost in the Boston *Transcript,* 3 April 1868.
2. Philadelphia, 1826, *I,* 531.

Rome by Mrs. Francis H. Lee about 1870.

At the Philadelphia Centennial Exhibition, the Russian display included a handsome array of objects made of malachite, lapis and other valuable minerals such as jasper, labradorite and rhodonite. American 'ladies who have prided themselves upon possessing a single piece of ornament for the ear, or breast, or finger, containing a fragment of malachite or lapis lazuli', wrote one reporter, were stunned to see huge articles lavishly constructed of these exotic materials. There was a mantelpiece made of solid malachite ornamented with a mosaic design of fruit incorporating amethysts, agates and crystals. A circular table had a top made of lapis. This, no doubt, stimulated the fashion for jewelry made of these minerals.

Lapis lazuli was not found in the United States. Malachite of any quality was found only in Arizona where it occurred in combination with copper and was unfortunately used for its metal content rather than for ornamental objects.

A set of malachite owned by Mrs. Skolfield of Brunswick, Maine, included a brooch and a pair of cabochon malachite earrings mounted in a typical Renaissance-revival frame. A necklace formed of unmounted overlapping discs of malachite and matching ball cuff-links were added to the set, now at the Pejepscot Historical Society.

Quartz

Chalcedony, a kind of white quartz with a grey-blue cast, enjoyed a brief period of popularity in jewelry in the second quarter of the nineteenth century. In England, chalcedony was used in pendent Maltese crosses with vinaigrette compartments, some of which have inscriptions of the 1820s. While crosses such as these do not seem to have found favour in the United States, chalcedony earrings and brooches did. Mrs. Elizabeth Salisbury of Worcester, Massachusetts, had a special fondness for them and purchased several sets. One demi-parure was embellished with gold frames and filigree (see Plate 109). The brooch had a floral spray appliquéd on its chalcedony cabochon. The earrings had cabochon tops matching the brooch and long torpedo drops with gold granulated vines twining up their exaggerated length. Her second set was embellished with little cabochon turquoises forming forget-me-knots which, in the language of flowers, meant more than the obvious 'remember me'. Their formal meaning at the time was 'true love'.

Chalcedony formed the backdrop for bunches of grapes, carved from coral and capped with gold grape leaves, in a demi-parure owned by another Massachusetts lady (Colour Plate 147). The frame of the brooch had five different borders of twisted wire and rope. Tiny ball drops dangled from the earrings.

Onyx, banded agate and cornelian were the varieties of quartz most popular for jewelry in the mid-nineteenth century. Amuletic properties were assigned to agates. Cutters at Idar and Oberstein, Germany, turned out record quantities of these stones for use in jewelry. At the peak of production, some of the establishments there each exported $30,000 worth of goods in a year.[1] 'Elegant cut mineral goods from Oberstein, Germany... made of Onyx, Agate, Cornelian, and Mosaic' were advertised in Boston in 1868. Bracelets, necklaces and crosses were available, as were jewel boxes and cups.[2]

Black stones were considered appropriate for mourning jewelry. Mary Todd

1. Kunz, *Curious Lore,* p. 54.
2. Charles G. Brewster, *Boston D.E. Transcript,* 9 Dec. 1868.

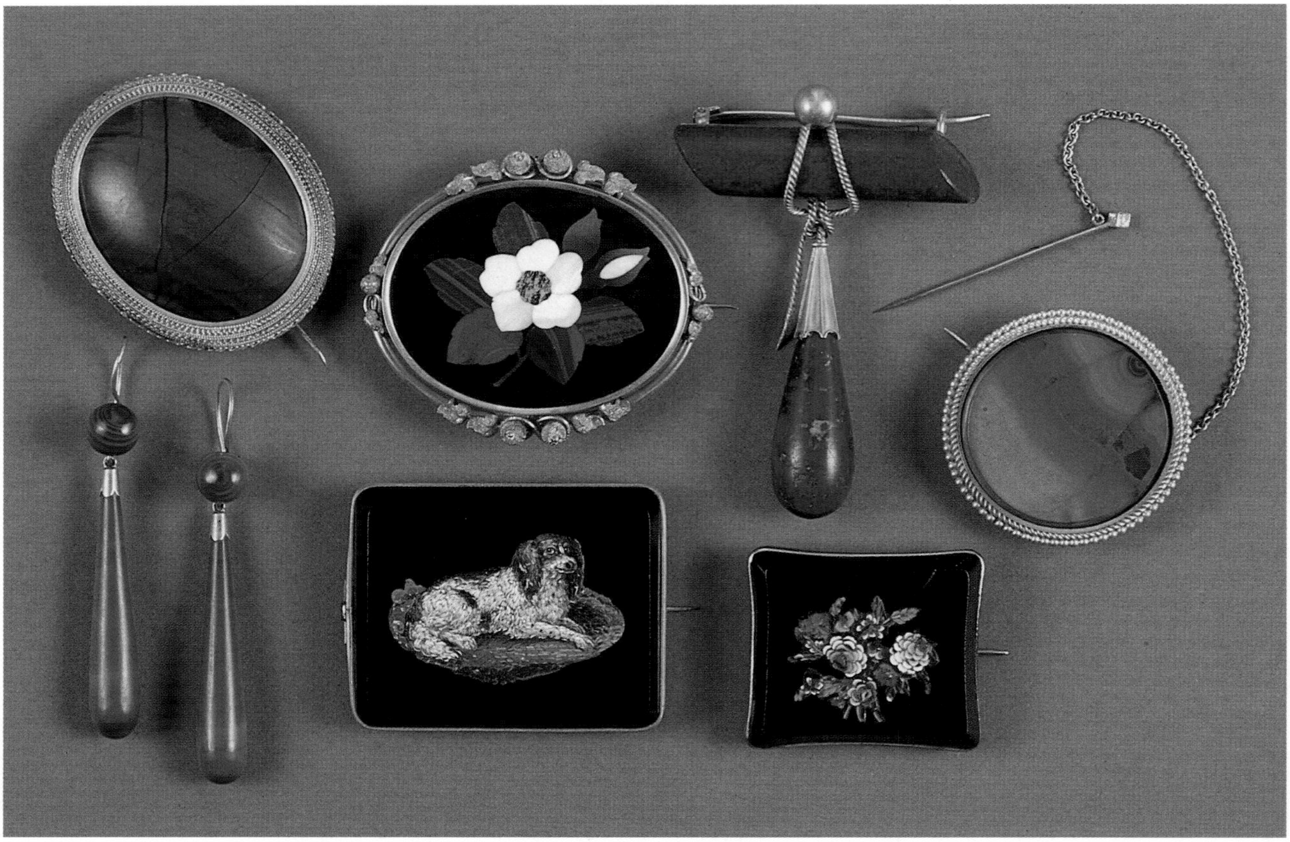

Colour Plate 143. Group of jewelry owned in the Salem area of Massachusetts, c.1845-1870. (Lower right) Roman micromosaic brooch with bouquet of flowers set in plaque of black onyx. Worn by Mrs. Mary Adams Cleveland, a wedding present in 1845 (Lower centre) Roman micromosaic brooch with spaniel on cushion, c.1850. Florentine mosaic, white flower with malachite leaves in oval gold frame with acorn design c.1860-80. Two malachite brooches, Russian c.1870, and elongated drop earrings. Swiss lapis lazuli brooch bought in Rome by Mrs. Francis H. Lee, c.1870. Length 2¾in. (lapis brooch overall). Photograph by Mark Sexton. Peabody Essex Museum.

Colour Plate 144. Small pin set with Roman micromosaic design of the American eagle bearing the flag of the United States, Italian, c.1870. Diameter 1in. Photograph by Peter J. Theriault. Private Collection.

Colour Plate 145. Pair of gold bracelets with Roman micromosaic plaques mounted in gold. Sold by Tiffany & Co., New York, c.1860-70. The back sections of the bracelets are articulated for greater comfort. Marked Tiffany & Co. ©1992 Sotheby's Inc.

Colour Plate 146. The Navigator's Wife, *as this unidentified American woman is known, wears a variety of jewelry current in America about 1830-40. Her top and drop earrings appear to be set with chalcedony. She wears matching bracelets that are set with large round clasps, and there are rings on the first and second fingers of her left hand. A small brooch secures her lace inset and a black beaded necklace is looped around her neck. Length 33⅛in., width 28in. Abby Aldrich Rockefeller Folk Art Center, Williamsburg, Virginia.*

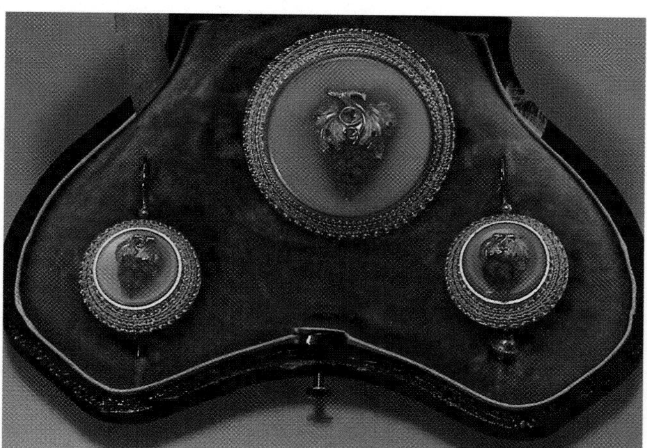

Colour Plate 147. Brooch with matching earrings, with chalcedony set with coral grapes in elaborate gold frames, Italian, c.1840-1860. Owned by a Massachusetts family. Diameter 1¾in. (brooch). Photograph by Peter J. Theriault. Private Collection.

Colour Plate 148. Right. Tiffany & Co. design, c.1880, for a necklace and pendant, earrings and bracelet, gold backed and linked, with onyx monogrammed in diamonds. The necklace and bracelet are articulated for greater comfort and lightness. Used with the permission of Tiffany & Co. All rights reserved.

Plate 173. Above. Mrs. Abraham Lincoln's onyx pendent watch was made for her use during the mourning period after her husband's assassination in 1865. The memorial stickpin, with Lincoln's head against a laurel wreath and cross, was also made for mourning. Smithsonian Institution.

Plate 174. Right. Pearl and onyx necklace with pendent locket and matching earrings, owned by Sarah Elizabeth Silsbee, also considered suitable for periods of mourning. Length 11in. (necklace); length 1¼in. (earrings). Society for the Preservation of New England Antiquities.

Lincoln wore an onyx mourning watch after her husband's assassination in 1865 (Plate 173). It was sculptured into bold geometric shapes. With this she wore an onyx and diamond ring. Plain rectangular bars or roundels of onyx were frequently embellished with seed pearls or diamonds (Plates 174 and 175).

Onyx and sardonyx, with their distinct layers of colour which could be enhanced by dye, were most often used for carving cameos (see Plate 161). A cameo pendant bearing a portrait of George Washington was carved out of onyx by Georges Bissinger, whose work was exhibited at Paris exhibitions in 1867 and 1878 (Plate 176). Bissinger took his likeness of Washington from the well-known bust produced about 1786 by Jean-Antoine Houdon, in which the first President of the United States appeared as a Roman hero.

Banded agates made handsome beads and sets of jewelry. Black or dark brown agates with a white ring in the centre could be worked to give the appearance of an eye and so were especially favoured by those seeking to ward off the evil eye. A set of banded agate, owned by Catherine Bergen Johnson (Mrs. Richard Van Wyck) of New York about 1870, had graduated beads with an oval pendant, ball earrings and a pair of square cuff buttons (Colour Plate 149)

Cornelians in shades of orange and reddish brown were frequently chosen for scarabs, seals and signet rings. A parure of gold jewelry in the antique style set with large scarabs carved out of cornelian was worn by Anna Eliza Henderson who had

Plate 175. Left. A large onyx cross set with pearls and suspended from a black velvet ribbon, fastened with what appears to be a diamond, was worn around the neck of Mrs. John Henry when her portrait was painted in 1875 by an unidentified artist. Length 84in., width 60¼in. Louisiana State Museum.

Plate 176. Above. Cameo of George Washington after Houdon, c.1878, carved in onyx by Georges Bissinger. Length 1¾in. The Milton Weil Collection, Gift of Mrs. Ethel Weil Worgelt, 1940 (40.20.17). The Metropolitan Museum of Art.

married Daniel Giraud Elliot in 1858 (Colour Plate 150). The necklace had a gold woven chain and a circular clasp decorated with grapes. The bracelet was formed of six hinged rectangular plaques, each set with a scarab. The earrings and matching necklace pendant had attenuated classical amphorae drops. One earring was lettered VIS and the other, MEA, together meaning 'my strength'. The pendant for the necklace was lettered ROMA, attesting to the set's Italian origin.[3]

3. The set was catalogued by the MCNY as bearing the mark of GM for Gaetano Melillo on the necklace but the mark has not been discerned. Giacinto Melillo (1849-1915) became manager of the Castellani workshop in Naples in 1870 and made similar jewelry in the archaeological style. Tait, I, 149-51; II, 251.

Scottish Pebble

Among the most popular forms of mineral jewelry were the brooches and bracelets made in Scotland in the mid-nineteenth century out of native stones. The Highlands had been endowed with romanticism by the stories of Sir Walter Scott and by Queen Victoria's love of her Balmoral retreat. The traditional tartan and kilt dress made use of interesting centuries-old annular brooches and witch's hearts. Plaid brooches and pins made in the shape of dirks and basket-hilted swords were used for fastening kilts and tartan stoles.

Contrasting stone inlays were cut, polished, and tightly fitted together in silver or gold mounts. This yielded endless variations of colour and pattern and created a sort of plaid of its own. Moss green, rust and grey agates were combined with pink or grey granite and often were set off with cairngorms, a kind of quartz found in the Cairngorm mountain range in Scotland.

Tourists travelling in the wake of Victoria inevitably acquired a souvenir of their visit. When Harriet Beecher Stowe was in Scotland in 1853, she visited Mr. Leslie's shop in Dundee where she saw the machinery for polishing granite in operation. Her brother noted that 'The Aberdeen granite and the Peterhead [are capable of] receiving a high polish. They even set it in brooches and breast pins'.[1] Mrs. Stowe bought two circular silver brooches, each set with three amber-coloured cairngorms, for her twin daughters who were then sixteen years old (Plate 171).

Baronial crests and Luckenbooth brooches, stag's leg pins and the cross of St. Andrews were favoured by British visitors. Americans apparently preferred simpler designs such as annular or ring brooches and sword or dirk pins. Bracelets formed of

1. Charles Beecher, *Harriet Beecher Stowe in Europe*, p. 49.

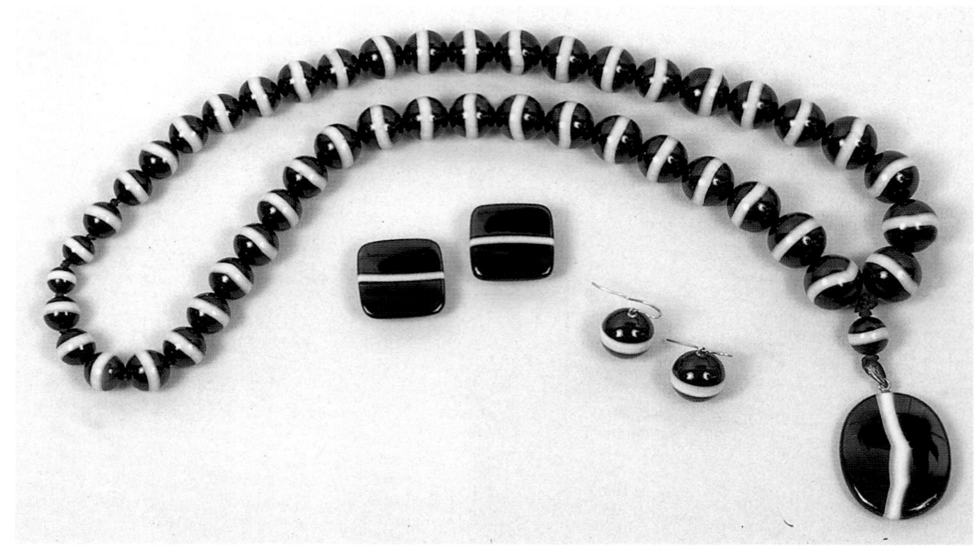

Colour Plate 149. Necklace, earrings and cuff buttons made of banded agates, probably cut in Idar Oberstein, c.1860-1880. Worn by Catherine Bergen Johnson (born 1829), mother of the donor. Length 16⅛in. Gift of Mrs. Henry de Bevoise Schenck, 36.276. Photograph by Arthur Vitols, The Helga Studio. Museum of the City of New York.

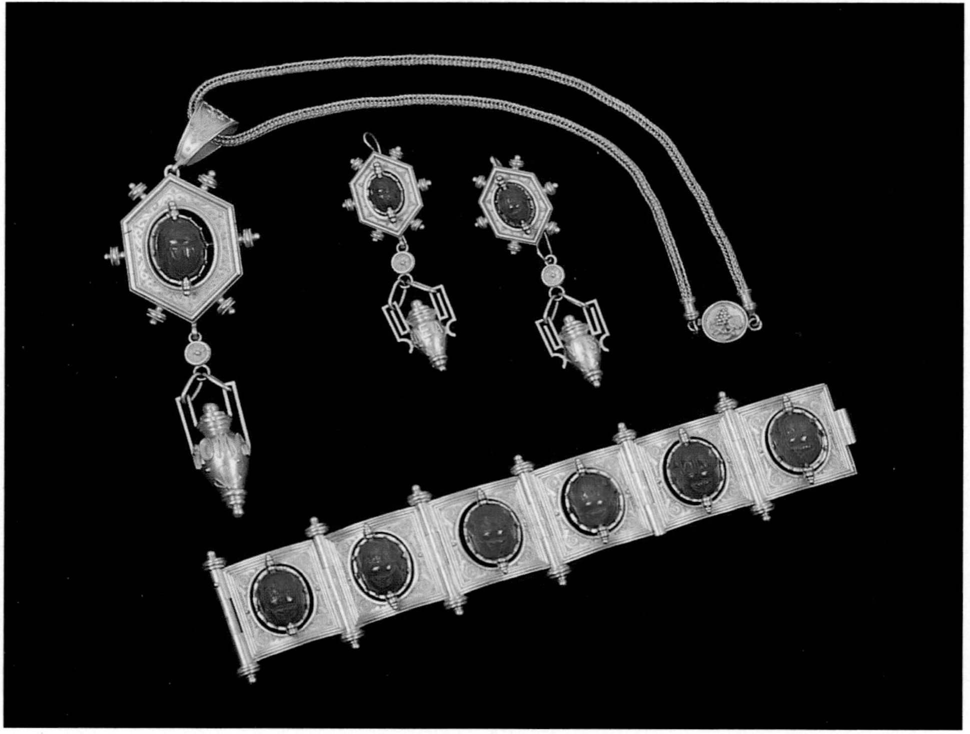

Colour Plate 150. Cornelian scarabs and gold parure, Italian, c.1865-75, in the archaeological style of Castellani and Giuliano. Applied lettering on pendant 'ROMA' and on earring 'VIS / MEA' (my strength). Worn by donor's mother Mrs. Daniel Giraud Elliot, married in 1858. Length 16¾in. (chain). Gift of Miss Margaret H. Elliot, 33.355.8 a-e. Photograph by Arthur Vitols, The Helga Studio. Museum of the City of New York.

double rows of cylindrical agates and fastened with heart-shaped padlocks sometimes had compartments to hold a lock of hair. These too were popular with Americans (Colour Plate 151). Chased leaf and scroll patterns decorated the scalloped ferrules and bezels of the metal mounts until the latter part of the nineteenth century when the designs became simpler and less traditional.

For those who liked pebble jewelry and could not afford to travel to the source, their local jeweler could be of service. Bigelow Brothers & Kennard advertised in Boston on 16 January 1856 that they had just received some handsome 'Edinboro' Shawl Pins, of new styles'.[2]

James Aitchison of Edinburgh, who specialized in Scottish pebble jewelry, brought a display of cairngorm and pebble jewelry to the Centennial Exhibition in Philadelphia

2. Boston *Transcript*, 16 Jan. 1856. A skater lost a Scottish pebble shawl pin on the way to or from the Pond in Jamaica Plain and offered a reward for its return in the Boston *Transcript* on 6 February 1858.

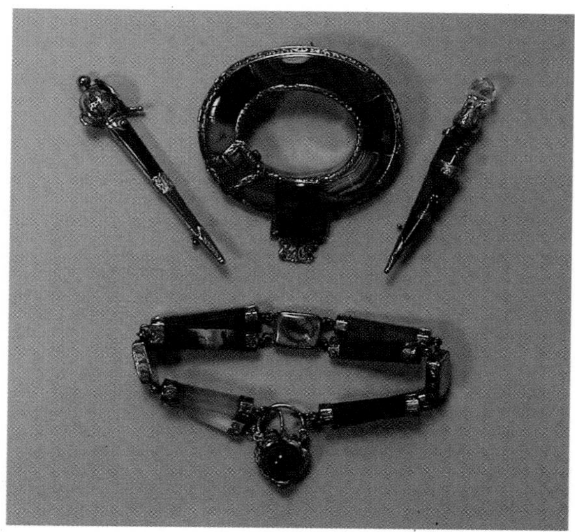

Colour Plate 151. Scottish agate brooch, sword pins and bracelet with heart-shaped locket clasp, owned in Maine, c.1860-1880. Dirk kilt pin is mounted with citrines. Diameter 2¼in. (ring brooch). Photograph by Peter J. Theriault. Private Collection.

in 1876. Included were designs of ram's heads with amethyst-tipped horns. The jewelry cost between two dollars and four hundred dollars a piece. Also on display was the biggest cairngorm crystal ever found. It was the colour of smoky topaz and the size of a small apple.[3] This exhibition, seen by people from all the United States, sparked further interest in pebble jewelry.

Inevitably the idea occurred to make pebble jewelry of stones native to America. In Colorado, local smoky quartz and citrine were sent abroad to be cut, then returned to be set in jewelry and sold to tourists at Denver, Colorado Springs, Hot Springs, Arkansas, and other Western resorts. George F. Kunz, Tiffany's gemmologist, thought the American designs were an improvement over the jewelry made in Scotland. Among the various shapes were horseshoes, shepherd's crooks, crescents and umbrellas.[4]

3. Ingram, p. 401.
4. Kunz, *Gems*, 109-133, 329-330.

Irish Bogwood

Just as the Italians made jewelry from local lava, so the Irish carved jewelry from their abundant bog oak. While this Irish jewelry was less eagerly sought by American tourists than the Italian baubles, it enjoyed a brief vogue particularly during the 1850s and early 1860s. Fossilized oak wood found in peat bogs is dark brown in appearance with a matt surface. A hint of the grain can be seen on its flat areas. Celtic designs were popular in bog jewelry, as were crosses and deeply carved floral designs. The English preferred the latter, while American tourists were partial to brooches and bracelets carved with Irish shamrocks, castles and harps.

At the Great Exhibition of the Industry of all Nations opened in 1851 by Victoria, Queen of Great Britain and Ireland, Irish bog oak jewelry set with pearls was displayed. In Boston in February 1852 Gray & Libby advertised bogwood bracelets in 'a variety of patterns, some quite new –– prices low'. Genuine Viner's bogwood bracelets, ordered directly from the manufacturer and highly perfumed, were offered by Jones, Ball & Poor.[1]

Edward Keevil, who manufactured bog oak jewelry in Dublin, advertised in Frank Leslie's *Illustrated Newspaper* in New York on 12 April 1862, that he exported brooches, bracelets and earrings, as well as necklets and charms 'set in Irish stones in endless variety', for as little as $2 per dozen. He could fill all orders by return mail due to his large inventory. Retailers needed only to supply a reference or send a draft payable to the Dublin Hibernian Bank.[2]

In the United States bog jewelry set with either pearls or Irish stones is seldom seen today.[3] More typical was the bracelet brought home from Ireland to Charleston, South Carolina, in 1856, now at the Charleston Museum. It was carved with castles

1. *D.E. Transcript*, 10 and 14 Feb. 1852. 'Viner's Perfumed Bogwood Bracelets' and other ornaments were sold wholesale and retail by James G. Hovey. *Transcript*, 17 Mar. 1852, St. Patrick's Day.
2. Keevil was located at 27 Merchants Quay in Dublin.
3. Becker, *Antique and 20th C. J.*, p. 74.

interspersed with shamrocks. A brooch brought back to Salem, Massachusetts, was inscribed on the back 'Druin', reminding us that the rites of the Druids were conducted in oak groves and that oak was regarded with peculiar veneration (see Colour Plate 130). The Skolfields of Brunswick, Maine, lived in England for a few years. When they returned, Mrs. Skolfield brought with her an Irish bogwood set of earrings and brooch, now at the Pejepscot Historical Society. The earrings were quite delicate considering the material involved. A little cross was suspended from the brooch.

In the 1860s dull black bog oak was a suitable material for mourning jewelry. Burlington, Vermont, jewelers were able to offer their customers bogwood bijoux in twenty different styles.[4] By 1876, it was reported in Boston that 'For persons in mourning the only jewelry that is admissible is the bogwood or Whitby jet, and some indulge in hair jewelry'.[5]

At the Philadelphia Centennial Exhibition, William Gibson of Belfast had what one American reporter called 'a fine display of Irish bog-oak jewelry'.[6] Jeremiah Goggin, purveyor of mediocre Irish bogwood by London standards, also exhibited at Philadelphia in 1876. His display included necklaces and tiaras, as well as brooches, bracelets and earrings, some set with local stones.[7]

While tourist jewelry of other countries continued to be made into the twentieth century, Irish bog jewelry came and went rather quickly and has not been reproduced in modern times.

4. Carlisle, p. 35.
5. *D.E. Transcript*, 3 Feb. 1876.
6. McCabe, p. 389.
7. Bury II, 536.

Jet

Good jet had been in short supply until the mid-nineteenth century. It was found by beach-combing or by tunnelling into the hills near the seaside resort of Whitby in Yorkshire, England.[1] Jewelry made of jet had been designed with little flat faceted pieces set into fancy gold and enamelled mounts, making the most of the least amount of the limited material. This fashion continued into the 1830s. A delicate pair of top-and-drop earrings made about 1837 was elaborated by openwork C-scroll frames (see Colour Plate 130). In addition, they were set with a tiny tear-drop shaped compartment containing a bit of hair under glass, in memory of eighteen-year-old 'L.C.F.' who died on 27 April 1837. Similar earrings were worn by Mrs. Paul Smith Palmer of Massachusetts, along with one of the popular crescent-shaped pins, in her portrait of the same date (Plate 177). Crescent jet rings were available too.[2]

In 1840, to meet the increasing demand, serious mining for jet began. Not only was more jet jewelry produced, but the individual pieces gradually increased in size. At the same time, the fashion in dress was for heavier and more voluminous fabrics, calling for more substantial designs in ornaments. Jet had the advantage of being light while looking bulky, so that it was more comfortable to wear.

In 1845, when Tiffany, Young & Ellis issued their first catalogue, they offered jet dress combs, bracelets, ferronnières, and tassels.[3] About 1850, jet jewelry was taken up by Queen Victoria. This, together with the display of jet jewelry at the Great Exhibition, assured the success of the Whitby industry. With the death of Prince Albert in 1861, only jet jewelry was allowed at court during the prolonged period of mourning.

Jet bracelets, necklaces and pins were imported by Jones, Ball & Co. of Boston in 1852.[4] In 1865, Tolman's in Boston announced that jet was 'now worn by all fashionable ladies in Paris, London and New York'. While there were deposits of jet in France, there were not enough to support the industry there. The French began producing imitations

1. Muller.
2. James Mott, jeweler in New York, bought crescent as well as regular jet rings from Chamberlain & Ellis on 25 June 1835. Account Book of James Mott, N-YHS.
3. *Catalogue of Useful and Fancy Articles*, New York, 1845.
4. *Transcript*, 31 Mar. 1852.

Plate 177 Crescent-shaped pins and top and drop earrings set with faceted jet were most popular in the 1830s and early 1840s. Mrs. Paul Smith Palmer used her crescent pin to hold her lace collar high upon her neck and placed it in a horizontal position, tips up, to correspond with the drops of her earrings. Portrait of Mrs. Palmer and her twins by Erastus Salisbury Field (1805-1900) who was working in the Connecticut Valley about 1835-1838. Length 38½in., width 34in. Gift of Edgar William and Bernice Chrysler Garbisch. ©1995 National Gallery of Art.

of jet in glass which could be mass-produced easily and sold very cheaply. Tolman's offered necklaces of real jet or imitation at prices from one dollar to $13.50 each.[5] At one point there was a store in Boston devoted entirely to this type of jewelry, the Jet Ornaments Jewelry Co. at 7 Green Street.[6]

Jet watch chains for ladies were also fashionable in the 1860s and 1870s, as were 'Fancy Jet Ball Hair pins'.[7] The jet was elaborately carved by hand or with lead wheels into ornate patterns or faceted into diamond-cut patterns. Some was left with a soft smooth matt finish and some received a high polish to give it a lustrous velvety finish. Tolman's advertised the new cut jet jewelry in a large variety of excellent styles in 1868.[8]

During the summer of 1870, a social columnist reporting from Newport, Rhode Island, praised the 'sensible' dress that prevailed there that season, approving the fact that 'Jet jewelry and black velvet trimming were never so much worn' heretofore.[9] Another reporter in New York noted, 'Jet jewelry is more fashionable than ever. Some of the styles are as finely cut as the cameo. The medallion sets are the favorites; these may be had with and without pendants. Necklaces with hanging ornaments are also popular.'[10] In Boston in 1874, the current fancy was for medieval jet crosses suspended from black velvet collars or ribbons with lace edging, tied in long loops with the ends trailing down from the nape of the neck.[11] John Vose & Co. of Boston specified that the jet he sold was from Whitby. He had for sale the stock of the W.T. Gale company, including sets, bracelets and chains at substantially reduced prices.[12]

The wearing of jet jewelry with black costumes was preferred. As one pundit explained, 'A mixture of color with jet and gold shocks good taste'.[13] Nevertheless, jet could be combined with other materials to great effect. Most frequently, pearls were used to outline the jet in rings and brooches. This combination was considered both appropriate and fashionable for second mourning, according to the *Saturday Evening Gazette*.[14] Cameos and mosaics were often set in carved jet frames. More rarely, a jet cameo was placed on a medallion carved from lava stone.

The London branch of an Italian firm received special notice at the 1876 Philadelphia exhibition for the jet jewelry that they set with cameos and mosaics. Francatti & Santamaria displayed these along with large jet wall ornaments deeply carved with medallion heads.[15]

5. Ibid., 14 Jan. 1865.
6. *The Boston Almanac & Directory* 1867, p. 177.
7. Tolman, *Transcript,* 14 Jan. 1865; H.A.Woodman, *Transcript,* 3 Mar. 1870.
8. *Transcript,* 16 Jan. 1868.
9. Ibid., 1870.
10. Clipping, TA Notebook, c. 1855-75.
11. *Transcript,* 24 Aug. 1874.
12. Ibid., 9 Oct. 1874.
13. Ibid., 17 Nov. 1874.
14. Boston, 26 Mar. 1876.
15. Ingram, p. 401.

Colour Plate 152. Pair of top and drop earrings with enamelled scenes of Switzerland in gilt channelled frames with scrolled brackets supporting the lower third of the elongated pendants. Made for the Swiss tourist business. Photograph by David Bohl, Boston. Society for the Preservation of New England Antiquities.

Colour Plate 153. Tiffany gold and enamelled card case and watch from Switzerland, gifts of Governor John Henry Kincaid to his wife in 1855. Watch works by Patek Philippe. The card case flips up to reveal a photograph of a man. Purse with similar engraving and diamond-studded ornament. Length 2⅞in. (card case). Smithsonian Institution.

Plate 178. One of a pair of cast iron bracelets given to Mrs. Henry Wadsworth Longfellow in the winter of 1851-52 by Countess Pulasky who came to Boston with her husband and Hungarian patriot Louis Kossuth. Its delicate rococo design is similar to bracelets made by Monsieur Simeon Pierre Devaranne (d.1859) in Berlin and may be the product of his foundry. Length about 7½in. Gift of Miss Alice M. Longfellow and Mrs. Joseph G. Thorp. Courtesy, Museum of Fine Arts, Boston.

Jet jewelry reached its height of fashion in the 1870s. The Whitby cottage industry had grown from two shops with twenty-five workers in 1852 to two hundred shops with 1,500 men, women and children in 1872.[16] Kunz studied the locations of jet deposits in the United States and noted that the jet from the Wet Mountain Valley of south-east Colorado could take as fine a polish as the best jet from Whitby.[17] It is believed that during the peak of Whitby's jewelry production, rough jet was imported from the United States to England, as well as Spain, to help meet the demand.[18]

In 1874, Louis Dieulafait pointed out, 'the imitations of this substance [jet] have largely taken its place; even the poor imitation of varnished glass is received with favour'.[19] George F. Kunz laid the demise of jet in jewelry to the use of black onyx and the low cost of its production at Idar Oberstein.[20] However, it was also due to the rise of mass-produced substitutes, such as vulcanite, crapestone and glass. Imitation jet jewelry was patented by Charles Downs of Providence in 1876.[21] Made of fusible enamel, the fake jet was die-struck with beaded or serrated edges.

When Queen Victoria finally gave up mourning in 1887, new fashions were lighter and more delicate in colour, and both jet and its imitations were relegated to the back of the jewelry box.

16. Muller, p. 14.
17. Kunz, *Gems*, p. 203.
18. Doris E. Kemp, 'Whitby Jet', *Lapidary Journal*, May 1986 (Vol. 40, No. 2) p. 38.
19. Dieulafait, p. 207.
20. Kunz, *Gems*, p. 203.
21. U.S. Pat. Off. #174,497.

Colour Plate 154. Group of China trade filigree jewelry in gold and silver. Silver posy holder in form of a cornucopia, with a straight pin and a finger ring to secure it. Original box labelled 'Cutshing, Gold & Silversmith; New Street.' in Canton. Length about 7⅛in. Pair of silver bracelets. Gold bracelet in form of two dragons, a speciality of Cantonese goldsmiths. Diameter about 2⅞in. Photograph by Mark Sexton. Peabody Essex Museum.

Berlin Iron Jewellery

Berlin iron jewelry is not often found in the United States today. Its rarity may be due to its fragility and the small value of the metal from which it was made. While Berlin iron was advertised for sale in America in the late 1840s, the goods were more often trays, cigar stands and match boxes than jewelry. John E. Abbott of Boston sold crucifixes and ring stands.[1]

Mid-nineteenth century iron jewelry was very light, with delicate tracery in naturalistic, rococo and gothic designs. A pair of bracelets (Plate 178) in this fashion was presented to Mrs. Henry Wadsworth Longfellow of Cambridge, Massachusetts, by the Countess Pulasky of Hungary when she accompanied her husband and Louis Kossuth to America during the winter of 1851. The *Boston Daily Evening Transcript* noted under 'Kossuthiana' that on 4 May 1852, the Count and Countess accompanied Kossuth to Cambridge, where they paid a special call on Professor Longfellow. Americans had sympathized with the Hungarian revolution of 1848 and, accordingly, they provided a grand reception for the visitors during their tour.

Meanwhile, at the Great Exhibition of 1851 in London, a number of German firms were displaying their iron jewelry. Monsieur Simeon Pierre Devaranne (1789-1859) of Berlin exhibited iron jewelry similar to Mrs. Longfellow's bracelets, with asymmetrical shells, scrolls and tiny flowers. Marked examples of Devaranne's work indicate that Mrs. Longfellow's gift came from his foundry.[2]

Berlin iron pins and bracelets were imported by D.P. Ives & Co. for his Boston customers in 1858, and advertised with fancy goods, jet and imitation bracelets.[3]

1. *Transcript,* 9 Dec. 1848.
2. Tait, *I,* 31; Kaplan, Price Guide, p. 29.
3. *Transcript,* 1 Mar. 1858.

Swiss Enamelled Jewelry

Like the Pallisers in a Trollope novel, Americans occasionally sought the healthy climate of the Swiss alps. Here, too, travellers were able to find souvenirs in the form of jewelry. The Swiss specialized in exquisite watches with increasingly refined works and beautifully enamelled cases. To match the watches Swiss jewelers created brooches, earrings, necklaces and bracelets that were enamelled on gold. Most popular abroad were the designs of Swiss girls in the traditional costumes of their cantons. Americans favoured landscape scenes, often painted on vertical plaques to allow the awesome Alps greater height in the enamelling (Colour Plate 152).

Harriet Beecher Stowe and her assorted relatives travelled through Switzerland in the summer of 1853. They were spiritually moved by the natural wonders of the landscape and skies, finding therein the glories of the heavenly Father. One of Mrs. Stowe's first stops in Geneva was at 'the celebrated Beautte's jewelry and bijou

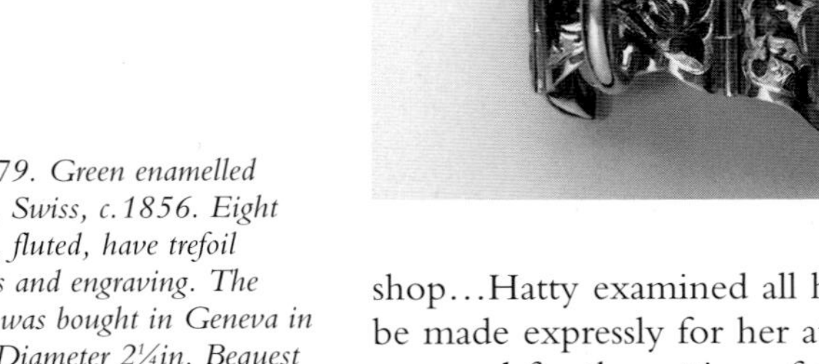

Plate 179. Green enamelled bracelet, Swiss, c.1856. Eight plaques, fluted, have trefoil piercings and engraving. The bracelet was bought in Geneva in 1856. Diameter 2¼in. Bequest of Miss C.L.W. French. Courtesy, Museum of Fine Arts, Boston.

shop...Hatty examined all his goods', her brother reported, and 'Engaged a watch to be made expressly for her at 60 francs cheaper than the same quality sell for here and arranged for the setting of the two cameos of herself and one of Mr. Stowe'.[1] Before the Stowe party left Geneva, M. Bautte had repaired a watch, set cameos, made several watches, and altered a chain as well as Harriet's bracelets.[2]

Alpine lake scenes ornamented the elongated earrings purchased by one of the Livingstons from Moulinie & Le Grandroy in Geneva, now at the New-York Historical Society. Knife-edge scrolls formed brackets on the pendants. A bracelet formed of rectangular plaques was bought in Geneva in 1856 and brought home to Boston by one traveller (Plate 179). Each plaque was fluted, pierced, engraved, and enamelled in green.

Swiss watches were introduced to Tiffany's stock in 1847.[3] In 1855, Governor John Henry Kincaid bought a Swiss watch and complementary card case from Tiffany's for his wife (Colour Plate 153). The works were by Patek Philippe. Framed in gold rococo scrolls, both objects were exquisitely enamelled with an emerald green ground and were set with diamonds. The watch and its suspension plaque were embellished with tiny pink roses.

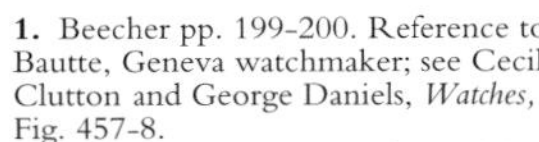

1. Beecher pp. 199-200. Reference to Bautte, Geneva watchmaker; see Cecil Clutton and George Daniels, *Watches*, Fig. 457-8.
2. Beecher, pp. 211-12 and 245-247.
3. Loring, p. 43.

Oriental

From the mysterious east came jewelry that was exotic both in design and materials. Trade and travel brought brooches and necklaces to Americans that were made of carved peach stones, ivory, bird's beaks, feathers and filigree. The trade, started in the post-Revolutionary period between the United States and China and India, received increased impetus in the 1840s with the opening of the Treaty Ports and the subsequent development of the American clipper ships. United States importation of jewelry and other China trade goods reached its height between 1840 and 1870 with more new ports being opened in 1860. Ships returned with much coveted goods for resale and with more personal objects selected by the captain and crew for the use of close family and friends.

Yankee traders quickly learned that silver and gold work could be bought from Chinese goldsmiths at great advantage. Not only was the cost of labour and material cheaper, but the gauge of the metal was often heavier. Furthermore, the gold was alloyed with silver instead of copper, usually 7 parts silver to 93 parts gold. The traders could make a profit simply by melting the metal and extracting the silver.[1] Since the Chinese government restricted the export of gold ingots, jewelry and especially gold chains became desirable commodities. The Chinese were good copyists and could produce silver and gold objects in the western fashion or in their own idiom.

The Chinese were especially noted for the fineness of their filigree work. Some observers thought it was because their hands were very small and lent themselves to this delicate work.[2] One westerner who spent many years in China commented that 'Their jewelry, too, admirably exhibits the delicate filigree work which agrees so well with their genius'.[3]

A pair of gold earrings, made with long drops formed of twisted coils and floral ornaments, was brought back to Boston by a member of the Atkinson family and is at the New England Historic and Genealogical Society. The original box for the

1. H.A. Crosby Forbes; John D. Kernan,; Ruth S. Wilkins, *Chinese Export Silver 1785 to 1885*, p. 27 +.
2. Ibid., p. 66, citing John Barrow, *Travels in China*, 2nd ed. (London, 1806), pp. 299, 307.
3. S. Wells Williams, *The Middle Kingdom*, 2 vols. (N.Y., 1883) *II*, 19, also cited by Forbes.

earrings was labelled by Wonshing of Canton about 1850. A gold filigree dragon bracelet was brought back from China by Edward Cunningham for his sister Mary Ann Cunningham who died in 1857. The intricacy of its design is testimony to the skill of the oriental craftsman.

Silver filigree exhibited a similar degree of technical achievement (Colour Plate 154). The lightness of the extruded metal made it suitable for posy-holders. These came into fashion in the mid-nineteenth century. A ring was attached to a small vase by a chain, so that the posy-holder could be hung from a chatelaine hook or worn on a lady's finger while she was dancing or otherwise occupied. An example from the shop of Cutshing of Canton also had a chain attachment for the long pin used to hold the bunch of flowers in place in the vase (Colour Plate 154).

The same patience and talent for working in small detail was required for jewelry carved from unusual materials. The beak of the helmeted hornbill *(Rhinoplax vigil),* a rare bird found in the East Indies, was highly prized by the Chinese. It had a subtle light honey colour and a pleasing smooth texture. Floral displays, scenes and figures could be deeply carved in this horn.[4] The carvings were mounted in gold plaques chained together to form brooches, earrings and bracelets (Colour Plate 155). A demiparure retains its original brocade box labelled by Hoaching of Canton about 1860 (Colour Plate 156) A bracelet with exquisitely carved high-relief, full bloom roses was set with gold filigree sections in the form of a coiled serpent slithering through flowers and tendrils.[5] It came from the shop of Leeching in Canton.

Plate 180. Tiger claw set, gold, monted in the 'English manner', consisting of necklace, earrings, brooch and bracelet. Acquired in Bombay by Miss Georgina Lowell Putnam of Boston about 1875. Width 3¼in. (brooch). Photograph by David Bohl, Boston. Society for the Preservation of New England Antiquities.

Leeching was also a dealer in ivory. A gold brooch set with an ivory carving of a bouquet of flowers bore his label (Colour Plate 156). Hoaching too was noted for his ivory carvings. Both these men were listed in tourist guidebooks and both, together with Yutching of Canton, exhibited their wares at the Philadelphia Centennial Exhibition of 1876. Their ivory carvings especially deserved attention, said one observer who was also impressed by the Chinese jade charms for watch chains and the carved tortoiseshell they displayed.[6] The Chinese also carved dried peach stones into beads of intricate design (Colour Plate 156). Among the Skolfield family jewelry in Brunswick, Maine, was a silver filigree bracelet set with carved peach stones.[7]

Tiger claw jewelry must have been one of the most eye-catching ornaments of the mid-Victorian period. From early ages primitive man used parts of wild animals to adorn themselves and to serve as talismans. By so doing they hoped to endow themselves with the superiority of that animal's strength. An Englishwoman living in India in the mid-nineteenth century reported, 'If you kill a tiger, the servants steal his claws as quickly as possible to send to their wives to make into charms, which both women and children wear around their necks. They arrest the evil eye and keep off maladies'.[8] American Indians of the period were portrayed with claws adorning their necks for similar reasons.

The British, with their developing interests in India, took up the custom of wearing jewelry crafted from trophies of the hunt such as tiger's claws. Americans followed suit. Miss Georgiana Lowell Putnam of Boston was given a whole set of this jewelry mounted in Bombay 'in the English manner', according to the inheritor of the parure (Plate 180). The claws were mounted with engraved and scalloped gold caps and

4. *Antiques,* July 1954, pp. 34-6.
5. Forbes, pp. 108, 129.
6. Ingram, pp. 573, 585.
7. Pejepscot Historical Society.
8. Fannie Parks, quoted by Susan Stronge, Nima Smith and J.C. Harle, *A Golden Treasury, Jewellery from the Indian Subcontinent,* p. 84.

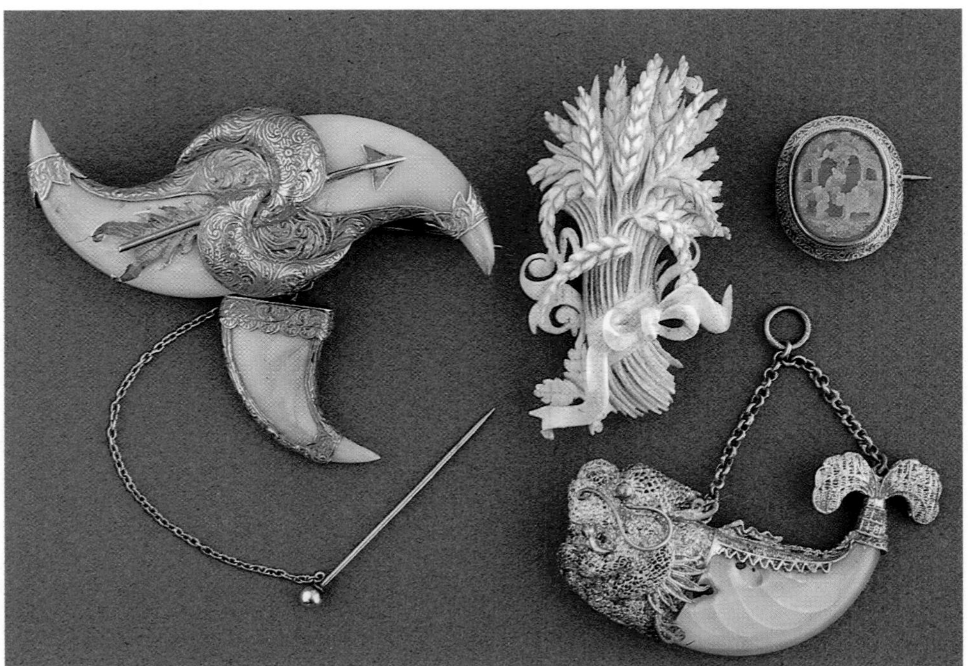

Colour Plate 155. Ivory was frequently exported from China to the western world where it was carved in familiar designs of the period. Brooch carved in the form of a sheaf of wheat, English, c.1850. Length 2¼in. Brooch made of tiger's claws in engraved gold mount with attached chain and stickpin. The tiger was killed at Singapore in the 1860s and the brooch was made for Elizabeth Gardner Putnam. Length 2⅞in. Pendant made of tiger's claw in gold filigree mount in the form of a dolphin, c.1870. Length 2¼in. (overall). Brooch carved from a helmeted hornbill's beak, mounted in gold filigree frame. Length ⅞in. Photograph by Mark Sexton. Peabody Essex Museum.

festooned together on two rows of chain to form the necklace and bracelets. The brooch was made of two conjoined claws pointing in opposite directions and draped with chain. Two diminutive claws were suspended from chains to form the earrings.

A similar brooch with an additional pendent claw was made for Mrs. William A. Putnam from a tiger killed in Singapore in the 1860s. More imaginative was the tiger's claw pendant with gold filigree mounts that was made to look like a wide-eyed fish (Colour Plate 155.). The grain of the claw was used to suggest the scales of the fish. Like John Brogden and other jewelers in England, Tiffany in New York sold tiger's claw jewelry in settings of their own devising (see Colour Plate 209). 'The tiger-claw pin and brooch [was] among Tiffany's most select wares, and set off with mountings of the finest design and workmanship' was highly recommended by the New York *Times* for Christmas presents.[9] In one Tiffany example, the gold mount that unified two claws was enamelled in Mogul colours of red, green and white, and spread like a canopy over the back of a caparisoned elephant. Touches of turquoise and black added to the richness. The claws were turned into a pleasing and unferocious ornament.

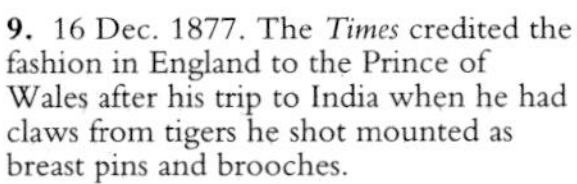

9. 16 Dec. 1877. The *Times* credited the fashion in England to the Prince of Wales after his trip to India when he had claws from tigers he shot mounted as breast pins and brooches.

Ivory

Ivory and ivory substitutes were moderately fashionable in mid-nineteenth century America. Some of the finest ivory jewelry owned there was imported from China, but it also came from England and Europe. An ivory brooch and matching earrings in the form of a wheat sheaf were owned in Salem, Massachusetts, about 1850 (Colour Plate 155, top centre).[1] English in origin, the set may have been a wedding gift. Wheat was a symbol of prosperity and a traditional marital blessing. The design had been a popular one in Salem since the late eighteenth century when it appeared frequently in the architectural and furniture details produced by carver and house builder Samuel McIntire. Crucifixes were another cherished form of ivory jewelry (see Plate 171). Harriet Beecher Stowe's cross was carved with a cherub's head and wings in the centre.

Bone was a frequent substitute for the expensive ivory which came from elephant tusks. Whereas elephant ivory is characterized by the infinitesimal crosshatching of its surface, bone is distinguished by its straight grain. Prisoners and sailors often filled

1. Similar example in Tait, *et al.*

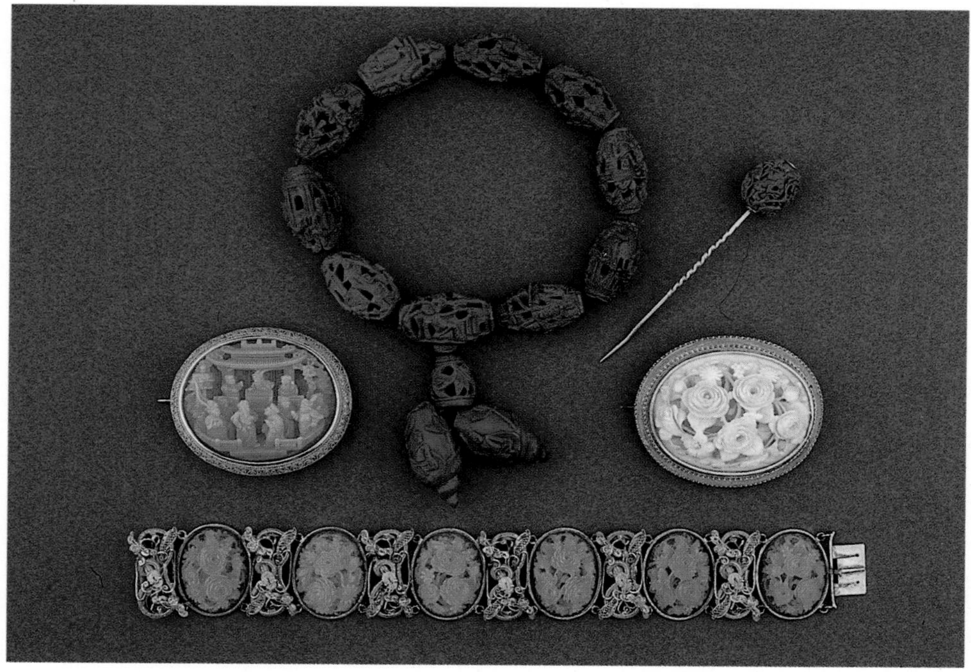

Colour Plate 156. China trade jewelry with American provenance, mid-19th century. Bead bracelet, c.1851, and stickpin carved out of peach stones. Original box for stickpin stamped inside 'LEE CHING / Hong Kong'. Length 3in. (stickpin). Brooch (right), gold, set with ivory plaque carved with distinctive flowers. Original box stamped LEECHING. Length 2⅟₁₆in. Brooch (left) carved in ivory with a courtly scene. Original box stamped inside HOACHING / CANTON. Length 1⅞in. Bracelet, gold filigree sections alternate with carved hornbill ivory sections of flowers. Length 7½in. Original box labelled by Leeching of Canton. Brought from China to San Francisco by donor's grandfather. Photograph by Mark Sexton. Peabody Essex Museum.

their tedious days by carving rings of bone, whale ivory or wood. Numerous bone and wooden rings survive from the Civil War period and are identified as to which prison camp held the carver captive.

Imitation ivory was made out of clay, porcelain and celluloid, all of which lack the graining and high lustre of ivory. Porcelain substitutes, popular in the 1850s, were made of a very fragile feldspathic porcelain which sometimes had a pearly glaze to give it a closer resemblance to ivory. In Ireland it was called Belleek. In England it was called Parian and was turned into jewelry primarily by Mrs. Mary Brougham. In America it was produced by the United States Pottery Company at Bennington, Vermont. Small floral brooches and earrings were made for a brief period, but they required very careful handling and had a low survival rate (see Plate 163).

Meerschaum, an ivory coloured, clay-like material, was carved into cameos in the middle decades of the nineteenth century. A desirable high relief could be obtained and Italian cameo cutters made good use of this advantage. A cameo of Italian manufacture was set on a gold filled, American made bracelet with rococo revival engraving on the wide band.[2]

In 1874 the Hyatt brothers of Newark, New Jersey, invented celluloid which made a very effective substitute for ivory out of gum camphor and gum cotton. They were so successful that the New York *Sun* reported on 26 November 1875, 'the material is now a regular article of merchandise'. In addition to lacking the grain of ivory and bone, celluloid was lighter in weight. 'White ivory ornaments are very pretty and much in demand in the place of jewelry', the New York *Sun* remarked on 1 October 1876.

W.M. Welling patented a method of making compressed ivory. This had the same weight and elasticity as ivory, but kept its shape and colour better. It was used successfully for jewelry, especially for sleeve buttons, as well as for billiard balls and checkers.[3] Welling was located at the sign of the Golden Elephant at 251 Centre Street in New York by 1855. His patent on compressed ivory was granted in 1879.

2. Now at the MMA.
3. New York *Times*, 1 Jan. 1886.

Gold and Silver

The first gold rush in the United States to produce any measurable results occurred in the 1820s in Georgia and North Carolina where surface mining recovered the first significant quantity of gold yet found. Deep mining was organized by the late 1830s. Several private mints were established in these two states and coins were minted there. Gold from these mines was soon being used for making watch cases and jewelry. At first the gold was sent from North Carolina to Philadelphia to be worked, but by the 1830s B.B. Lord & Co. in Athens, Georgia, advertised that he made these items from Georgia gold. Victor G. Blandin, who worked in Charlotte, N.C., said that he had begun using North Carolina gold for making jewelry in the French fashion. Even South Carolina jewelers used North Carolina and Georgia gold for making watch cases and jewelry.[1]

The discovery of gold in California in 1849 had an enormous effect on the history of jewelry in America. At Sutter's Fort in the lower Sacramento Valley in late January 1848, James W. Marshall erected a saw mill on a branch of the American River and in so doing discovered a nugget of gold. At the same historic moment, the acceptance of the treaty ending the Mexican War, effective in July 1848, ceded California, Texas, and the remainder of the American Southwest to the United States.

The immediate result was an unprecedented rush to El Dorado. People came by the thousands from all over the world to California, arriving by ship or coming overland from the South-west or Mexico. Most were young men in their twenties.[2] Many were simply adventurers, but many came because they were jewelers or in some way suited to work with precious metals (Colour Plate 157). Newark, New Jersey, for instance, where the jewelry industry was well established, supplied a number of jewelers who were listed in the 1850-51 Newark city directory with a California address. One man was listed simply as 'gone west'. John L. Moffat came to San Francisco from New York in 1849 and promptly made a spoon out of the native gold.[3] A goldsmith by trade, he established a smelting and assaying business in California.

Among the most interesting objects made in the first years of the Gold Rush was an immense commemorative ring (Colour Plate 158 and Plate 181) presented to President Franklin Pierce in 1852 by some of the San Francisco citizens. Weighing approximately half a pound, the solid gold ring was designed by George Blake and was valued at $2,000. The entire history of California was delineated in panels around the shank. The state's arms were emblazoned on the bezel against a field of the United States stars and stripes. The bezel had a lid beneath which was a box divided into nine sections, each containing a specimen from one of nine different successful mines in California, including the first significant gold strike made there in 1842 at a site about thirty-five miles north of Los Angeles.[4]

This extraordinary ring was made by the firm of Barrett & Sherwood who began their business in San Francisco on Montgomery Street in December 1849. Samuel Barrett and Robert Sherwood advertised as makers of jewelry and chronometers. Their firm was the innovator of gold quartz jewelry. On 27 August 1853, they announced that they had hired a celebrated lapidary from the east to make 'Quartz Rock' jewelry for them. They offered to buy gold quartz rock at prices 100-500% above its net gold value.[5]

1. James H. Craig, *The Arts and Crafts in North Carolina 1699-1840*, pp 58, 69. George B. Cutten, *Sss. of Ga.*, pp. 8-10. Burton, pp. 223-4.
2. David Lavender, *California*, pp. 31-4, 57, 59, 64.
3. Peter J. Bohan, *American Gold*, Yale University Art Gallery, 1963.
4. Ring illustrated and described in *Gleason's Pictorial*, 25 Dec. 1852, and by Kunz, *Rings*, pp. 84-5. A somewhat similar ring was described as made from specimens from Australian goldfields in April 1855. *Australian Jewelry*, p. 32.
5. San Francisco *Alto*. In an advertisement in the *San Francisco Directory* for 1861, Robert Sherwood proclaimed himself to be the 'inventor of the art of manufacturing quartz rock jewelry'. This information and the following concerning Barrett & Sherwood was supplied by Edgar W. Morse, Argentum, San Francisco.

In 1853 at the Crystal Palace Exhibition in New York, Barrett & Sherwood displayed some of their gold quartz jewelry.[6] George Templeton Strong admired their exhibit. He noted in his diary that 'there are many most covetable things scattered through the building – furniture, jewelry, bronze, and so forth, not to speak of various appetizing nuggets and bars and chunks from California'.[7]

So popular was the 'peculiar California industry', as one early historian of the trade called it, that immediately imitators cropped up, but Barrett & Sherwood maintained their name which the same historian boasted was 'known throughout the world for excellence and elegance'.[8] The firm had soon added diamond work and rich jewelry of their own manufacture and later stocked silver ware and plated goods, placing their retailer's mark on wares made by firms such as Gorham of Rhode Island and Vanderslice of San Francisco.

George C. Shreve & Company was another firm born of the Gold Rush that featured native quartz jewelry. Arriving in San Francisco from Salem, Massachusetts, in 1852, George and his half-brother Samuel soon offered 'Every description of California Jewelry manufactured to order'.[9] Among the items that they made of rich specimens of gold in its natural combination with quartz – white or black, opaque or transparent – were brooches, stickpins, earrings, lockets, bracelets, and sleeve buttons (see Colour Plate 223).

A jewel casket exhibited at the Paris Universal Exposition of 1878 revealed the heights that could be achieved by combining gold quartz with solid gold.[10] Made as a wedding anniversary present, the jewel box (7in. x 9in.) was formed of slices of polished gold quartz inlaid with gold and solid gold inlaid with gold quartz. Symbols taken from the California state coat of arms were combined with Western scenes such as a buffalo hunt.

Jewelry made from nuggets found by eager 'Forty-niners' provided another form of Gold Rush memorabilia. Robert W. Lord of Kennebunk, Maine, was one of hundreds who had a stickpin made from gold he found in California.[11] Gold panners from Vermont, like others elsewhere, sent small amounts of gold to the folks back home who then took them to their local jewelers to be made into wearable mementos. Brinsmaid's in Burlington advertised that they made rings of California gold and plain or engraved pins that could be set with diamonds or coloured stones.[12]

Gold was discovered in Plymouth, Vermont, in 1855. The strike produced only a little gold, but for a decade jewelers offered to make baubles of pure Vermont gold. In 1866 Clark Brothers, Rutland jewelers, seized the opportunity to set polished native marble in Vermont gold settings.[13] John Price, an optician in Newark, New Jersey, was in California in 1848 and 1849. When he returned to Newark he was able to offer his customers spectacles made of California gold 'of his own digging and manufacture'.[14]

Digger's brooches were a form of Gold Rush jewelry that originated in the California gold-fields and that was repeatedly reinterpreted at subsequent Gold Rush sites in the Black Hills of South Dakota, Australia, South Africa and Alaska before the end of the nineteenth century. The original California version (Colour Plate 159) consisted of a trophy of mining equipment: a crossed pick and shovel with a prospector's pan in the centre. Tiny nuggets of gold clung to the pan and the shovel, while grape leaves with curly vines decorated the sides.[15]

The Jewelers' Circular and Horological Review noted in its gossip column for May 1885

6. Edgar W. Morse, p. 4; Paul Evans, 'Gold Quartz: The Jewelry of San Francisco', *Spinning Wheel,* May 1977, pp. 8-10.
7. *Diary,* II, 132.
8. Hackett, Fred H., ed., *The Industries of San Francisco* (1884), p. 115.
9. Edgar W. Morse, p. 16.
10. Oakland Museum, California.
11. The Brick Store Museum, Kennebunk, Maine.
12. Carlisle, pp. 34, 69.
13. Ibid., pp. 34, 98.
14. J. Stewart Johnson, 'Silver in Newark', *The Museum,* New Series, *18,* Nos. 3 and 4, p. 28.
15. Australian miner's brooches (1851) featured complicated designs often including a sieve with a bucket swinging from it. South African brooches (1880s) had the name of the country embossed on the spade and occasionally had diamonds for decoration in addition to the nuggets. Alaskan brooches (1898), being the latest in design, were simpler with only a crossed spade and shovel, and ALASKA in plain sans-serif letters above. See Anne Schofield and Kevin Fahy, *Australian Jewelry;* Anne Schofield 'Australian Jewellery in the 19th and early 20th Century' and Linda Young, 'Westralian Digger Brooches', *The Australian Antique Collector,* Jan.-June 1983 and 1986 respectively.

Colour Plate 158. Commemorative ring presented to General Franklin Pierce, 14th President of the United States, by citizens of San Francisco in 1852. Designed by George Blake, this oversized ring weighing almost half a pound contained beneath the bezel lid nine compartments each of which held a pure specimen of gold ore found in California. On each segment of the ring band is an engraved design providing a pictorial history of California's natural resources. Diameter 2⅛in. overall. Photograph by James Garvin, courtesy of New Hampshire Historical Society. New Hampshire Public Library.

Colour Plate 157. Decorative hair comb made about 1850 of California gold with gold nugget borders occasionally set with gold quartz nuggets at the top and featuring a floriform clump of nugget in a central cartouche. Marked by W.A. Woodruff of San Francisco who advertised in August 1850 'Woodruff's Jewelry Shop'. Woodruff died later that year and his business was taken over by Jacks & Woodruff. The comb is engraved on the back 'E. Davis'. Length 4½in. (overall). ©Christie's, New York, 1993.

RING PRESENTED TO GEN. PIERCE.

It is already pretty widely known to the public generally that a number of the citizens of San Francisco have caused to be manufactured and forwarded to Gen. Pierce, a most valuable and unique present, in the form of a massive gold ring, as a token of esteem for the president elect. Of this ring our artist has herewith given us an admirable representation. It is a massive gold ring, weighing upwards of half a pound. This monster ring, for chasteness of design, elegance of execution, and high style of finish, has, perhaps, no equal in the world. The design is by Mr. George Blake, a mechanic of San Francisco. The circular portion of the ring is cut into squares, which stand at right angles with each other, and are embellished each with a beautifully executed design, the entire group presenting a pictorial history of California, from her primitive state down to her present flourishing condition, under the flag of our Union. Thus. there is given a grizzly bear in a menacing attitude, a deer bounding down a slope, an enraged boa, a soaring eagle and a salmon. the staffs crossed and groups of stars in the angles. The part of the ring reserved for a seal is covered by a solid and deeply carved plate of gold, bearing the arms of the State of California in the centre, surmounted by the banner and stars of the United States, and inscribed with "FRANK PIERCE," in old Roman characters. This lid opens upon a hinge, and presents to view underneath a square box, divided by bars of gold into nine separate compartments, each containing a pure specimen of the varieties of ore found in the country. Upon the inside is the following inscription: "*Presented to* FRANK PIERCE, *the Fourteenth President of the United States.*" The ring is valued at $2000. Our engraving gives a separate view of the lid, so as to represent the appearance of the top of the ring both when it is open and when it is closed. Altogether, it is a massive and superb affair, rich in emblematical design and illustration, and worthy its object.

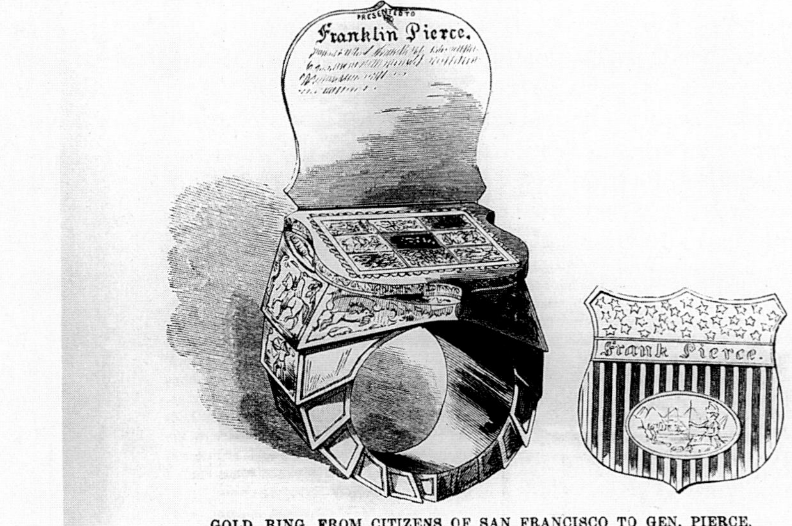

GOLD RING FROM CITIZENS OF SAN FRANCISCO TO GEN. PIERCE.

Plate 181. Illustration of the gold ring presented to President Franklin Pierce of New Hampshire which appeared in Gleason's Pictorial Newspaper, *25 December 1852. The author of the article referred to it as 'this monster ring' due to its size. Photograph courtesy of Boston Public Library.*

Colour Plate 159. Digger's brooch, made for the tourist trade, with appropriate symbols of the trade: a shovel crossed with a pick and a pan with gold nuggets in it, perhaps an indication of success for the wearer. Marked 14 K. Length 1⅞in. Photograph by Peter J. Theriault. Private Collection.

Colour Plate 160. Yellow gold belt buckle, made by the California Jewelry Co., c.1868, with blue and black champlevé enamelling. Marked on back of chape W. CUMMINGS. PAT^{D}. AUG. 1868 in intaglio. Length 2¼in. Photograph by Peter J. Theriault. Private Collection.

that 'Visitors to California are importuned at all points in that State to purchase specimens of the native productions of precious metals, decorative stones, etc.... Every California tourist feels in duty bound to bring away something to remind him of his trip to the Golden Gate'. This demand was met by California manufacturing jewelers who created such personal decorations as seal rings made of native stones, cuff buttons, scarf pins and watch charms. These same manufacturers were attempting to extend the range of their productions to include the same kinds of goods and styles available in the East. New York still held the balance of that trade but the California companies hoped to be able to supply the entire Pacific coast with jewelry made in San Francisco.[16]

One of the largest firms manufacturing jewelry in the San Francisco area was Levison Brothers' California Jewelry Co. on Sutter Street. Organized in 1857, it became the largest establishment of its kind on the west coast. 'The superiority of the products of the California Jewelry Co.,' claimed the author of *The Industries of San Francisco,* 'is conceded by the trade, and they are sent every where in the course of a large exporting business, or as souvenirs or samples of California taste or workmanship'.[17] Their special products included quartz jewelry. Having their own lapidaries and diamond setters, they could offer faceted native stones and diamond work as well as little trinkets.

In 1868 William Cummings patented a buckle design that was made by the California Jewelry Co. (Colour Plate 160 and Plate 182). The trick of the patent was that little rings were soldered on the back of the buckle where the three points or prongs came to rest, thus keeping the belt firmly secured from slipping when worn. The curvilinear shaping of the buckle was enhanced by scrolled reserves in the corners and finely worked side panels containing the seated figure of Minerva with the bear taken from the California coat of arms. Black champlevé enamel dramatized the design in the corners and a delicate addition of blue enamel highlighted the flowers engraved on a vertical line in the centre.[18]

From California the Gold Rush extended, on a lesser scale, to Idaho, Colorado, Montana and then into South Dakota. The Black Hills of South Dakota became the last site of a major gold strike in the United States. As early as 1877 jewelry with a distinctive grape leaf design was being produced in Deadwood and Lead by Edward La Beau, Squire T. Butler, the Thorpes and E.O. Lampinen who organized the Black Hills Manufacturing Co. (see Colour Plate 224).[19] Tradition maintains that the grape cluster

Plate 182. The patent for an improved belt buckle issued 11 August 1868 to William Cummings of Sacramento, California, concerned the rings added to keep the prongs from slipping out of place. United States Patent Office No. 80924.

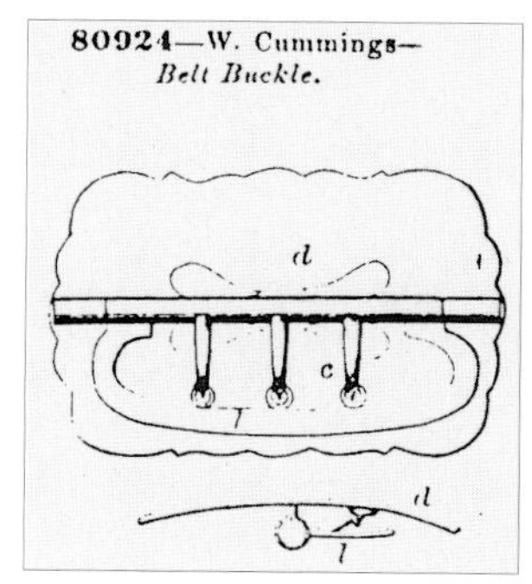

16. p. 105, courtesy Edgar W. Morse.
17. Fred H. Hackett, ed. *The Industries of San Francisco,* p. 141.
18. A similar though unenamelled buckle marked by William U. Bolm of San Francisco was sold at Christie's in New York on 23 January 1993.
19. Information supplied by Dayton W. Canaday, Director, South Dakota State Historical Society, 16 Aug. 1984. This grape-leaf design of jewelry continues to be made of tricoloured gold by Landstram's Original Black Hills Gold Creations.

Plate 183. Silver filigree brooch owned by the Salisbury family in Worcester, Massachusetts. Box imprinted Shreve, Stanwood & Co., working in Boston 1860-1869. Length about 1½in. Earrings made of steel woven wire, European, c.1835-1840. Box labelled Jones, Lows & Ball / Jewellers / 123 Washington Street [Boston], working together from 1835 to 1837. Length about 3⅜in. Photograph by Stephen Briggs. Bequest of Stephen Salisbury III Estate. Worcester Art Museum.

with leaves was chosen because there were wild grapes growing rampant in the Black Hills at the time of the first settlement of the area of Boulder Canyon, below Deadwood.

These golden geegaws were merely footnotes bearing witness to the great significance of the Gold Rush to the history of jewelry in America. From 1855 to 1860 alone almost sixty million dollars' worth of gold was transported by Wells Fargo from California mines.[20] Routinely, as ships arrived in New York from California, the *Times* announced the value of the gold to be delivered and to whom. $2,000,000 worth of gold arrived on the *Cherokee* early in January 1852 and another $1,000,000 came by the same ship at the end of the month. Occasionally the *Times* had to announce the amount of gold lost when a ship sank. After 1851, ships like the *Flying Cloud* were able to make the complete trip from San Francisco to New York in ninety days on a good run. More often the gold was shipped by one vessel to Panama, carried across the isthmus, and shipped on to New York by another vessel. When the railroad across Panama was completed in 1855, the process was accelerated. The final junction in Utah of the transcontinental railroad in 1869, commemorated by the driving of gold and silver spikes into the tie, allowed precious metal to be transported directly from the west coast to the east coast of the United States.

While the Gold Rush in California was basically over by 1857, silver had been discovered in the west as well. The most productive source, the Comstock Lode in western Nevada, was discovered in 1859 (see page 375). Over the next twenty years it is estimated to have yielded over $300,000,000 dollars in roughly equal amounts of gold and silver. The production of jewelry soared. The popularity of silver jewelry greatly increased in the late 1870s and early 1880s, and the market for both gold and silver jewelry was greatly expanded.

The Gold Rush in America coincided with the interest in antique gold jewelry produced by nineteenth century archaeological discoveries. As a result, an unprecedented amount of plain gold jewelry as well as Etruscan or Roman jewelry was made from the late 1850s onwards. For the most part these designs derived from the work of Fortunato Pio Castellani (1794-1865) and his sons Alessandro and Augusto of Rome who collected, studied and reproduced antique jewelry. As their interpretation of classical gold jewelry spread through Europe and England, it also came to the United States in a simplified version.

Gold jewelry of the mid-century was described by jewelers of this period by four different terms: Plain, Filigree, Etruscan, and Roman. These terms described the

20. Lavender, p. 75.

technique of manufacture and the finish given to the piece of jewelry. In the case of the terms Etruscan and Roman, the style and decoration of the piece were indicated as well.

We have seen that in the seventeenth and eighteenth centuries American goldsmiths had used a low-alloy, high quality of gold for making jewelry and they had finished it 'bright' by polishing and burnishing. At the end of the Federal period some American jewelers were offering a 'dead gold' finish in addition to the prevailing burnished finish (see page 148). The dead gold finish was an attempt to give the jewelry an antique, more classical appearance, the idea being that less bright was less new looking.

By the second quarter of the nineteenth century, new techniques of finishing gold were developed to give the metal different effects. As early as 1826, Fortunato Pio Castellani gave a lecture to the Accademia dei Lincei in which he discussed the chemical methods of colouring gold. Two methods predominated. One involved a chemical treatment that removed alloy from the surface of the metal leaving a thin layer of purer gold on top. The other method called gold colouring added a layer of pure gold to the surface of the object by the process of electrolysis or electroplating. According to Thomas B. Wigley's *The Art of the Goldsmith and Jeweller,* gold colouring was introduced by an unnamed Frenchman, and was first practised in England in the 1820s.[21]

Colouring gold became more prevalent as the fashion for Etruscan style jewelry and the electrolytic process became more widespread in the 1840s. Castellani's experiments to discover the methods used for the amazingly complex jewelry made by classical goldsmiths were furthered by the school of Italian archaeological jewelry Castellani established in the 1840s.

Not everyone in the United States liked the new finishes. In 1841 jeweler J.G.L. Libby took pains to explain to his customers in Boston that his jewelry 'was made with special reference to the quality of the gold, being warranted 18 karats plump. The complexion of them are *[sic]* not heightened by any chemical process whatsoever, and they are the natural color of the gold.'[22] In contrast, the following year John Gunn advertised that he could gild or silver by a 'magneto electric' process a number of objects such as 'Watch Cases, Spectacles, Chains, Thimbles, Fine Cutlery, & at low prices'.[23]

The chemical formulae for wet colouring differed from place to place. For American jewelry, the Etruscan finish called for dipping the completed pieces of jewelry in a solution of 8oz. saltpetre, 4oz. salt, 2oz. sal ammoniac, 4oz. muriatic acid and 2oz. water.[24] Dry colouring, in spite of its name, was executed in the same manner, but could only be done with jewelry made of 18 karat gold or finer. In addition a thin iron bar had to be used for stirring the solution which was a mixture of saltpetre, salt and alum. 'Finely finished French Etruscan Jewelry entirely new designs' was imported and advertised by Townsend & Toppan of Boston in 1868 under the heading of 'New Gilt Jewelry'.[25]

Another finish given to Roman jewelry in the 1860s and 1870s was called 'frosting'. This was achieved by subjecting the finished piece of jewelry to scratch brushing. The scratch brush was fixed in a lathe and turned at high speed. The object was held against the bristles which were lubricated with stale beer. The resulting surface was uniformly covered with infinitesimal pits, giving the jewelry a rich bloom, particularly attractive on plain gold brooches, bracelets and lockets.[26]

Granulation was one of the key ingredients in Etruscan jewelry. Minute beads of gold had been soldered individually to the surface of jewelry found in Etruria. The process by which this had been done was lost, but the Castellanis were dedicated to

21. Thomas B. Wigley, *The Art of the Goldsmith and Jeweller* (London 1898), p.147.
22. Boston *D.E .Transcript,* 22 Dec. 1841.
23. Ibid., 31 Dec. 1842.
24. The French formula omitted the sal ammoniac, and increased the amount of salt and acid. J.Parish Steele, *The American Watchmaker & Jeweler,* supplement, pp. 72-5. This handbook also gives the proportions for wet-coloured gold alloys of 15-20 karats.
25. Boston *Transcript,* 17 Feb. 1868.
26. For frosting, as well as dry and wet colouring processes, see Wigley, pp. 147-60. In 1879, a jeweler's frosting tool was patented by George B. Fittz, John Baxter and Mark E. Rowe of Attleborough, Patent #217,522.

Colour Plate 161. Silver filigree set, according to family tradition brought back to Salem, Massachusetts by Captain Benjamin Balch Jr. (1804-1863) from Russia where he called on the ship Glide. *Length 14in. (necklace). Photograph by David Bohl, Boston. Peabody Essex Museum.*

duplicating the method. Although they did not succeed altogether, they came closer than anyone else. In America, as well as elsewhere, there was a greater reliance upon the tightly twisted wires also found in Etruscan jewelry. Extruded wire was twisted and applied as borders or coiled into rings and cut into sections that could then be manipulated into decorative motifs and soldered on to the jewelry. The twisted wire decoration was better suited to mass-production than granulation.

Granulated grapes and applied grape leaves were among the most popular of the classical designs adapted to mid-nineteenth century jewelry. Occasionally the granulation formed an over-all pattern. Brooches were sometimes made with the beading uniformly spaced on the surface of the metal, giving it an embroidered effect (Colour Plate 96).

Filigree jewelry, skilfully executed by Etruscan jewelers, was given new fashion authority by the increasing interest in classical jewelry. At the same time, filigree was imported from the orient and elsewhere. While England made little filigree, the French and Italian jewelers supplied western markets. Under the title of 'Fillogram Articles', Tiffany, Young & Ellis listed as imported from France 'A select and elegant assortment of this new and favorite style, comprising all the novelties, as soon as they appear in Paris'. This entry in their 1845 catalogue also pointed out that both gold and silver filigree could be cleaned by washing in warm soap suds (Colour Plate 88, lower right).[27]

There were also American jewelers who made this drawn wire jewelry and some who specialized in this branch exclusively. William Nielson was manufacturing filigree jewelry in Boston in the 1840s.[28] His surname suggests that he was from Scandinavia, an area long noted for its tradition of filigree work (Plate 183, top).[29] Joseph F. De Guerre (w.1808-1850) made gold filigree jewelry at his shop on Reade Street in New York city. Among the jewelry sketched in his design book were ten patterns of bow-knot brooches (see Plate 111).[30]

Posy holders were popular items in filigree. In most cases this work was too delicate to be marked. However, boxes accompanying jewelry were sometimes imprinted with

27. Tiffany, Young & Ellis, *Catalogue of Useful and Fancy Articles.*
28. *Boston Almanac,* 1841-1850.
29. Vestlandske Kunstindustrimuseum, Thale Riis, and Alf Boe, *Om Filigran..*
30. von Khrum, p. 37; *JC,* 40 yrs., XXIV, 3 Feb. 1892, No. 1, p. 77. This article calls De Guerre the first filigree worker in the United States. However, Fletcher & Gardiner made filigree jewelry in Boston and Philadelphia about 1810 and Marchais La Grave in New York and George Downing in Newark, to name a few, made gold filigree early in the 1820s.

Colour Plate 162. Gold half-set by Bigelow Kennard & Co. of Boston, working c.1869-1881, with original box imprinted inside the lid with the name of the firm. Owned in Rockland, Maine. Length 1¼in. (bar pin). Photograph by Peter J. Theriault. Private Collection.

the shop's name and address, giving an indication of the provenance. A silver filigree posy-holder that came from the firm of Gelston & Treadwell in New York was given as a wedding present to Washington Irving's niece Charlotte when she was married in 1845 (Plate 184).[31] A gold filigree buckle was purchased from the shop of Lows Ball & Co. in Boston by Mrs. Elizabeth Salisbury of Worcester, Massachusetts about 1840-46 (Colour Plate 90). The most famous piece of filigree produced by an American firm was the silver horse and carriage made by Tiffany's as a wedding present for General Tom Thumb and his equally diminutive Lavinia Warren, both stars of P.T. Barnum's shows. Originally studded with real rubies and garnets, the horse and carriage was displayed in Tiffany's window for several weeks prior to their marriage on 10 February 1863.[32]

Ear drops and hoops, filigree and plain, were advertised as appropriate Christmas presents by Palmer & Bachelders in 1848 in Boston.[33] They were still being worn in that city twenty years later when 'A long gold EAR-DROP, with filagree ornaments' was advertised as lost.[34]

Plain gold earrings, brooches and bracelets were sold singly or in sets. The most usual combination was the half-set of earrings and brooch. Some of the jewelry without engraving or enamelling is remarkably modern in appearance (Colour Plate 162). A set made by Bigelow Kennard in Boston relied entirely upon the shapes of its bar pin and pendant loops, and the smooth reflective surfaces of the gold. Tiffany's made a similarly minimalist bracelet of squared

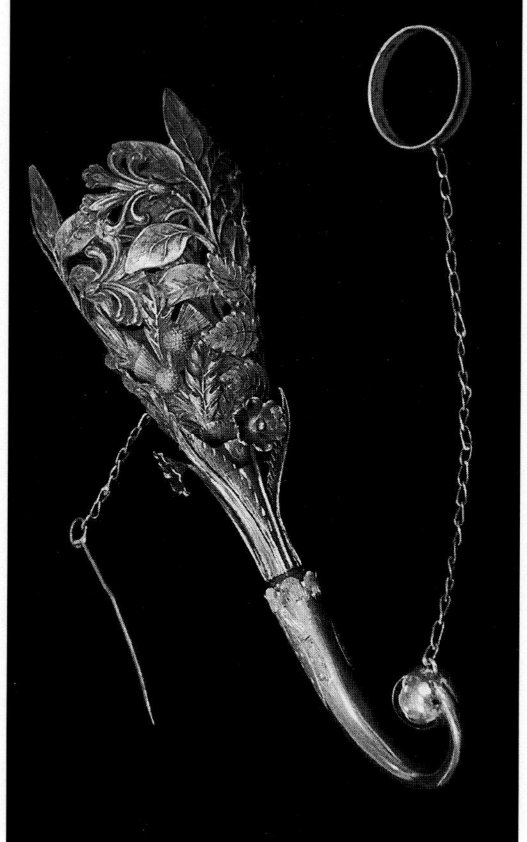

Plate 184. Silver bouquet holder in box labelled by Gelston and Treadwell of New York city, c.1845. The wedding gift of Washington Irving to his niece. Length 5⅛in. Historic Hudson Valley, Tarrytown, N.Y.

31. Jewelers Gelston & Treadwell were working at #1 Astor House, the address given on the box containing the posy holder, from 1844-48. von Khrum, p. 54. Jeri Schwartz, *Tussie Mussies: Victorian Posey Holders*.
32. Loring, pp. 47-49.
33. *Transcript*, 27 Dec. 1848.
34. Ibid., 6 Feb. 1868.

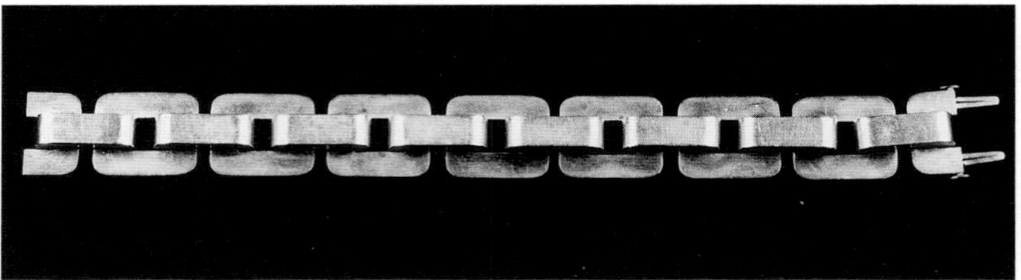

Plate 185. Left. Gold bracelet given to Harriet Beecher Stowe on 8 May 1853 by the Duchess of Sutherland on behalf of abolitionists in England in honour of Mrs. Stowe's contribution to the cause in her book Uncle Tom's Cabin. *Chain links in the bracelet were engraved with the dates of important legislation in England, to which Mrs. Stowe added appropriate dates for the American movement. Stowe-Day Foundation, Hartford, Connecticut.*

Plate 186. Above. Square link bracelet made by Tiffany & Co. coloured gold, about 1860-1870, anticipating mid-20th century designs. Courtesy, New-York Historical Society.

hollow gold links that would look as much in style today as it did more than a hundred years ago (Plate 186).

Jewelry made of gold coins was popular in the third quarter of the nineteenth century, also inspired by the archaeological jewelry of Castellani and others. At the grand ball at Newport, Rhode Island in August 1856, this new fashion was considered 'the oddest whim'. One of the belles wore a headdress consisting entirely of gold pieces the size of a half-eagle attached by delicate gold chains to her hair and hung down to her ears and neck. A reporter thought there might have been $100 worth of coins in all or about two hundred coins. It was 'decidedly a distingué conceit; the pretty young lady who wore them looked like an Indian Princess in her barbaric ornaments; and surely the fashion has economy to recommend it. Unlike most other feminine trinkets it will

Plate 187. Left. Gold medal made by Frederick Marquand & Brothers, New York, 1832, the anniversary of Washington's birth, for presentation to the Marquis de Lafayette. Length 6¼in. Courtesy, Winterthur Museum.

Plate 188. Above. Group of silver medals. (Left) The Franklin medal awarded to 'Henry A. Sawyer / 1857' cut by Francis N. Mitchell, Boston seal engraver, working 1841 to 1860. (Centre) Mechanical Fire Co. No. 1 presentation medal given to P.W. Loury 'by the members who visited Philadelphia Dec. 31, 1838'. Length 3⁵⁄₁₆in. (Right) Boston City medal, cut by Francis N. Mitchell, awarded to Ann I. Lyon in 1856. Diameter 1⁷⁄₁₆in. Photograph by Peter J. Theriault. Private Collection.

Plate 189. Silver medal marked by Samuel Kirk of Baltimore, Maryland, presented by the Reverend D.A. Payne to Miss Jane E. Jones of Montgomery County, Maryland, on 25 February 1850 for the second best piece of embroidery exhibited by people of colour. Marked SK & SON and 11 OZ. Diameter 2⅜in. The Bayou Bend Collection, The Museum of Fine Arts, Houston, Texas.

always be worth what it cost'.[35] An heirloom of the Gardner family of Salem was a cross made of Spanish American coins dating from 1744 to 1788.[36]

Gold and silver medals continued to be made throughout the mid-nineteenth century for presentations (Plate 187). Presidential 'Peace and Friendship' medals were designed for presentation to the Indians through the term of Zachary Taylor who died in office in 1850. His profile bust was cut by Henry Kirke Brown and the reverse side was cut by John Reich.

While many medals were designed as cabinet pieces, medals for youthful scholars and prize winners were still made to be worn (Plate 188). The Boston *Transcript* reported in 1858 that jeweler Abraham Hews, Jr., had recently made four beautifully designed gold medals to be presented to the graduating scholars at the Mystic Hall Seminary. 'They are elegant specimens of workmanship', the paper said, 'and will undoubtedly be highly prized by the recipients'.[37]

Rapidly proliferating organizations like the Mechanics Associations and the Agricultural Societies held annual fairs and awarded premiums to the outstanding exhibitors (Plate 191). Competition prizes were awarded by Fire Societies (Plate 188) and other volunteer organizations (Plate 189).

Keeping abreast of the times, Masons added rings to their regalia. Masonic designs progressed from classical and Greek revival motifs of the Federal and Empire periods to the eclectic Victorian styles of Gothic, Egyptian and Oriental, with ornate rococo revival motifs and heavy ornamentation.

In the nineteenth century it became more common for the quality of the gold to be specified and, in many cases, guaranteed by a mark struck on the piece of jewelry. Pure or fine gold is 24 karats. Alloyed gold is measured by the parts of gold compared to the parts of other metal. Good gold jewelry in the United States generally utilized gold from 10 karat fineness to 18 karat, 14 karat fineness being most usual. In England the word is spelled carat, so that gold marked with a K for karat usually indicates that the piece of jewelry is American made.

35. Boston *Transcript*, 26 Aug. 1856.
36. PEM, gold coin charm found at camp site, Morris Island, S.C. #107, 375.
37. 28 Jan. 1858.

Colour Plate 163. Above left. Masonic medal made by Guild and Delano of Boston, c.1879, specialists in jewelry for the Masons, set with a diamond, for Past Master Thomas Alden, of the Corner Stone Lodge, Duxbury. Photograph by Peter J. Theriault. Private Collection.

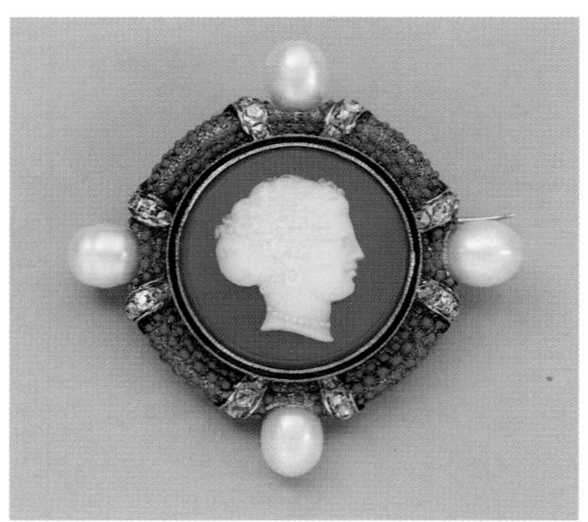

Colour Plate 164. Left. Carved pink chalcedony cameo with profile of a classical woman, mounted in a turquoise and diamond-studded tubular gold frame with four large pearls pinned at the cardinal points, c.1860-70. Original box bearing the Tiffany & Co. imprint with the address 550 Broadway where the firm was located from 1853-1870. Length 1¼in. Tiffany & Co. Permanent Collection.

Colour Plate 165. Above right. In 1856 the historic Charter oak tree blew over in a wind storm in Hartford, Connecticut. Charles L. Tiffany, who was born in Connecticut, bought some of its ancient limbs which he turned into gold mounted jewelry for his customers. This half-set retains its original box with the imprint inside the lid, TIFFANY & C^{O} / 550 Broadway 552 / NEW-YORK. Length 1⅞in. (brooch). It was originally owned by a woman who had lived near the tree when she was a child. Photograph by Dennis Griggs. Private Collection.

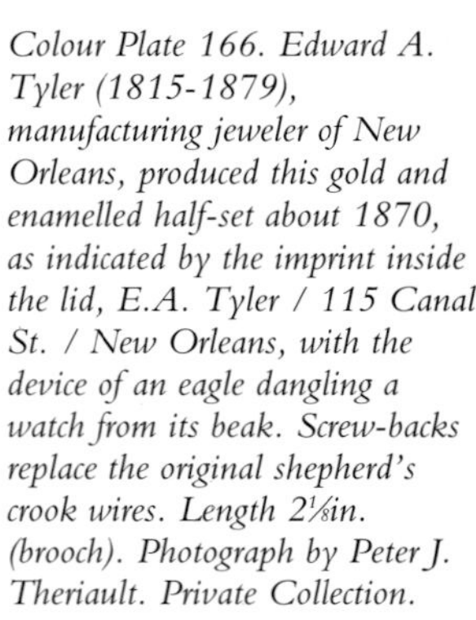

Colour Plate 166. Edward A. Tyler (1815-1879), manufacturing jeweler of New Orleans, produced this gold and enamelled half-set about 1870, as indicated by the imprint inside the lid, E.A. Tyler / 115 Canal St. / New Orleans, with the device of an eagle dangling a watch from its beak. Screw-backs replace the original shepherd's crook wires. Length 2⅛in. (brooch). Photograph by Peter J. Theriault. Private Collection.

Jewelers

The machine's conquest of American manufacturing dominated the mid-nineteenth century. Jeweler's work was affected significantly by changes in technology, but not to the extent that most industries were affected. Machines were used primarily to assist the jeweler in the performance of tasks, not to replace handwork altogether, and automatic machinery was looked upon with scorn by makers of fine jewelry.

Industrialization of jewelry manufacturing manifested itself in the use of steam engines (Plate 190) to power the equipment used in processing and preparing the metal, and for forming the stock used in making jewelry. At first, jewelers often shared the use of a steam engine, and moved their workshops into the building that housed the source of power. Drop presses were introduced to stamp out metal parts.

With the development of machinery came the increased ability to decrease the amount of precious metal needed by combining thin layers of gold with a greater proportion of base metal. Providence, Rhode Island, led the way in the production of cheaper jewelry made of filled or plated gold. Filled gold was made by stamping out the front of the piece of jewelry from a very thin piece of 18-karat gold. This hollow shell was then filled with pewter or similar base metal. Next the back, often made of less fine gold, was soldered on to the front. Because the front was made of fine gold and could be struck in carefully cut dies, it produced a very nice superficial appearance and so was appealing to the cost-conscious public.

Gold or silver plating could be achieved by uniting an ingot alloyed of copper and brass with a plate of gold or silver as much as one-fortieth the thickness of the ingot. The blocks of metal were bound together with iron wire and a flux of borax was introduced around the edges. When heated just enough to fuse the metals together, and not enough to melt the metals, the completed ingot could then be rolled out to the desired thinness for making jewelry. This procedure was referred to as the English method.[1]

Electroplating, in which gold or silver was deposited on the surface of an article by means of electric current, was introduced to the United States in 1842 as a result of successful experiments by Thomas Spencer of Liverpool, England, and Professor Jacobi of St. Petersburg, Russia.[2] Elkington Bros. in Birmingham, England, had been among the first to put the process to commercial use. They obtained several patents, notably one granted in 1840 based on the work of Alessandro Volta and Luigi Galvani.[3] At first electroplating was used in the United States for making silver spoons and forks, and subsequently for gold plated articles. By 1868 the process was so commonplace that *The American Watchmaker & Jeweler* provided directions and the formulae for both gold and silver electroplating with or without the use of a battery.[4]

Mass production inevitably led to specialization of tasks during the mid-century. We can chart the progress of each centre of jewelry manufacture by the number of specialists in allied skills who were working in each centre. Assayers and refiners

---

1. The French method involved putting gold or silver leaf on brass and joining the layers by means of heat and burnishing. Bagnall, pp. 18, 20.
2. Bagnall, p. 22.
3. Bury, I, 354.
4. Steele, pp. 51-5.

Plate 190. Engine Room, located in a separated area adjacent to the basement.

Plate 191. Grinder, located in the basement, in which waste gold was reduced to powder and then transferred to the amalgamator to separate pure gold from dregs.

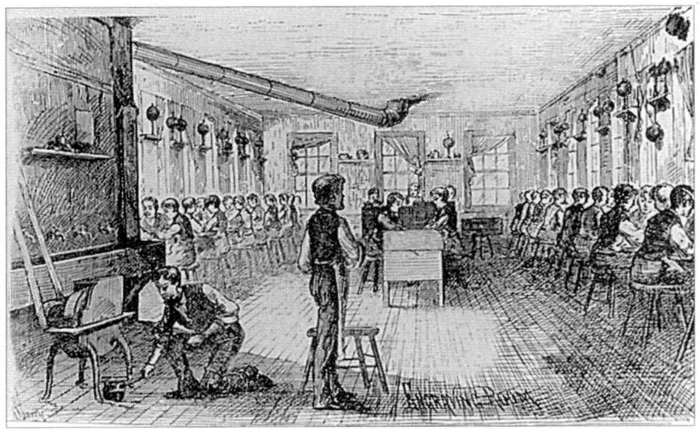

Plate 192. Engraving Room where articles to be enamelled were engraved with the design to be filled with enamel.

Plate 193. Enamelling where molten glass was coloured with various oxides of metal and then applied to the appropriate engraved areas, subjected to heat, cooled, and filed down.

Plates 190-193. Illustrations from William R. Bagnall's The Manufacture of Gold Jewelry *(New York 1882) showing processes of manufacture at Enos Richardson & Co. in Newark, New Jersey.*

appeared to grind up the shop sweepings, filings and other waste gold, transferring it to the amalgamator to separate the gold (Plate 191). The refined metal was then alloyed to the desired fineness between 10 and 18 karats, cast into ingots, and passed through powerful rolling machines to reduce it to the desired thickness.

Die makers and other toolmakers designed the equipment needed to shape the metal into the desired patterns for stamping machines or repoussé or relief. Parts were soldered together and decorative borders, twisted wire work and motifs were soldered on. Engravers prepared the articles for enamelling by designating the areas to be filled (Plate 192). Enamellers then prepared the paste of glass ground with metallic oxide of different colours, applied it, and heated the work to a temperature that would vitrify the enamel without melting the metal (Plate 193). Polishers and finishers then filed and ground down the surfaces, polished and finished the pieces, using polishing lathes (Plate 193, right). Finishing also included colouring the gold to what was called the Roman colour by means of an acid solution or using a scratch brush to pit the surface with thousands of tiny dots, giving the metal a frosted finish. Eventually the pieces were turned over to gem setters who were supplied by lapidaries with cut and polished cameos, gemstones and seals.

By mid-century, there were specialist watch makers, watch and locket case makers, chain makers, spectacle frame makers, ring makers, and bracelet makers, as well as makers of jeweler's stock, findings, settings, tools and machinery. Because of the fragmentation of the industry, there arose middle men to reunite and sell the various parts of the jeweler's trade. Jobbers and wholesalers entered the market to distribute various products to the non-manufacturing jewelers throughout the United States. The distinction between the manufacturing jeweler and the retail jeweler, which had developed at the end of the eighteenth century, now became a widely differentiated occupation.

Inevitably, the designer of jewelry became increasingly separated from the processes of manufacturing. The person who made the mass-produced jewelry was no longer the designer or the seller; nor did he have the sense of pride and achievement that the old-fashioned jeweler had since he was only contributing one step in the production. Trade unions began to be organized, as early as the 1850s in Newark, for mutual assistance and protection. Concerns began to surface for the conditions and fair pay of shop workers.

The retail store as an emporium of taste in a large and luxurious building that could accommodate all the customer's requirements became the rule rather than the exception. Often the stores in the major cities supplied jewelers in smaller towns, especially in the south and west.

Providence, Newark and Attleboro jewelry manufacturers specialized in less costly forms of jewelry. Newark, while turning out mass-produced jewelry in quantity, made more of their goods of solid gold and respectable fineness. Makers of fine jewelry continued to work in more traditional methods and materials. New York and, to a lesser extent, Philadelphia and Boston continued to be centres of jewelry production. California and Chicago developed their jewelry industries in the third quarter of the nineteenth century.

A survey of the major American jewelry-making centres in the mid-nineteenth century provides specific information about how this transformation of the industry came about.

Philadelphia Jewelers

Philadelphia jewelers had been well patronized during the Federal period, but with the transfer of the seat of government to the District of Columbia in 1800, the city lost some of its clout. Economic hard times, resulting from the War of 1812 and subsequent financial panics, caused a significant number of jewelers to move to other cities in the south and west. However, there continued to be a strong jewelry manufacturing business in Philadelphia.

In 1828 the precious metal workers in Philadelphia included thirty-one silversmiths, sixty-five watchmakers and sixty-one jewelers.[5] The city directories for the second quarter of the nineteenth century listed literally hundreds of people working at these trades, some for only a few years, others for decades.[6]

At the end of the Federal period, Fletcher and Gardiner were the leading silversmiths and jewelers in Philadelphia. Their success continued into the second quarter of the nineteenth century (see Plate 60). Although Sidney Gardiner died in 1827, the name of the firm remained Fletcher & Gardiner until 1836. They became known for their presentation pieces. Philip Hone of New York visited the shop of Fletcher & Co. in 1838 and declared 'Nobody in this "world" of ours hereabouts can compete with them in their kind of work'.[7]

5. Waters, p. 121.
6. Brix.
7. Diary, 1828-51, quoted by Wood, p. 166.

The emphasis on manufacturing silver wares began to overshadow Fletcher's jewelry production, some of which was subcontracted. Fletcher ordered chains from Taylor & Baldwin of Newark in 1833. The New Jersey firm was pleased with the business and gratified that there was 'anyone on the whole earth that wants better Jewellery than we have been compelled to make for the depraved market of late years'.[8] Unfortunately Fletcher & Co. encountered financial difficulties and by 1842 was out of business.[9]

The Thibaults, who had been making jewelry in Federal Philadelphia, continued into the mid-century as Thibault Brothers with Felix (Plate 194), Francis, Frederick and Francis, Jr. Eventually they merged with John Carrow, continuing through the 1860s as manufacturing jewelers. According to the 1860 census, Carrow, Thibault & Co. employed sixty-nine men and seven women in producing, with the assistance of steam power, $225,000 worth of bracelets, necklaces, rings and other jewelery.[10] John S. Carrow received a patent in 1875 for spring-prong clicks for bracelets.[11]

'The manufacture of Jewelry is largely and successfully carried on [in Philadelphia]', reported Edwin T. Freedley in his history of *Philadelphia and its Manufactures* in 1858, 'particularly the finer and the costly kinds, as Diamond and Pearl Jewelry'. Cameo, filigree and enamelled jewelry was also produced of such fine gold work and taste that people 'familiar only with the work of this description executed in New England' would have been astonished.[12]

Bailey & Co. was singled out among jewelry manufacturers for their highly commendable workmanship and their original designs. This firm was founded in 1832 by Joseph Trowbridge Bailey and Andrew B. Kitchen, manufacturing jewelers producing and selling jewelry and silver ware. Bailey & Co. gained a high reputation because they were first to use the higher British standard of 925 parts silver in 1,000 for their silver wares, rather than the American standard of 900 parts. An example of the kind of jewelry they sold can be seen in Colour Plate 118. This stamped gold set of earrings and matching hair comb was embellished with turquoise and designed in the Algerian style. About 1846, the firm became Bailey & Co., with a brother E.W. Bailey added to the partnership along with several other men.[13]

The firm of Caldwell & Bennett was established in the 1830s by James E. Caldwell (1813-81) and his partner James M. Bennett. In 1868, it was reorganized as J.E. Caldwell Co. and has continued on Chestnut Street to the present day. Caldwell's was the firm chosen by agents of *Godey's Lady's Book* to fill orders for jewelry placed through the magazine by subscribers.

By 1857, the total value of the gold jewelry made annually in Philadelphia amounted to $1,275,000. There were 17,000 workers employed in the making of gold and silver pens, spectacles, leaf and foil as well as fine jewelry. Fifteen lapidaries cut and prepared rubies, emeralds, sapphires and agates and large quantities of gems were imported from abroad for use in jewelry.

Gold chains were a significant part of the jewelry production. The four leading Philadelphia firms producing chains were Stacy B. Obdyke; E.C. Bonsall; Newlin, Bishop & Co.; and Dreer & Sears. The latter firm had been established in 1833 as Dreer & Hayes. Their manufactory, located in Goldsmiths' Hall on Library Street, was considered a model of completeness and arrangement. Well lighted and ventilated, it was powered by steam and equipped with the most up-to-date technology. They employed 125 workmen in 1857 whom they paid $70,000 a year. Their annual production of chains was worth $200,000. They also assayed and refined precious

8. Fletcher papers, 1833, HSP, quoted by Wood, p. 165.
9. Waters, p. 93; Wood, p. 168.
10. Waters, p. 174.
11. #169,775. Carrow was in partnership with Henry Dubosq from 1839-50. Brix, p. 33. John Carrow also was in partnership with Crothers from 1869-74 and Bishop from 1882-85. Rainwater, *AJM*, p. 58.
12. Freedley, p. 344.
13. Belden, *Marks*, p. 42. Bailey & Co. provided many southern jewelery stores with their silverware.

Plate 194. One of a pair of gold bracelets attributed by family history to Felix Thibault (1791-1841) of Philadelphia who made them for his second wife Anna Maria whom he married in July 1822. The Thibault family came from France via Saint Domingue and Haiti to Philadelphia about 1793 where three generations of the family worked as silversmiths and jewelers. The bracelets are made of stamped swirls, open work circlets with chased surfaces in floriform articulated sections. The Historical Society of Pennsylvania.

metals and sold bullion which added $300,000 worth of income to their business.[14]

George W. Simons & Brother dominated the pencil and pen case production of the precious metals business. Due to a disastrous fire that destroyed all of their tools and machines in 1856, they had to replace everything. As a result, their manufactory had the latest in machinery and appointments. They also made earrings, finger rings, bracelets, breast pins, charms, seals, thimbles and other small items. There were sixty workmen employed in 1857.[15]

After gold plate and jewelry, the making of watchcases and dials was the next largest part of the precious metals industry in Philadelphia. Silver watches were usually imported from England or Switzerland in their cases, but gold watches were usually put into American made cases. In addition, American made watches became competitive with European imports in the mid-century under the leadership of the American Watch Co. of Waltham, Massachusetts.[16]

William Warner started the first American production of watchcases in Philadelphia some time prior to 1812. By 1857, there were sixteen watchcase manufacturers there who made $942,000 worth of cases a year, and employed 294 workmen. 'In purity of Gold, in excellence of workmanship, and in elaborateness and beauty of ornamentation', Freedley said, 'the cases made in Philadelphia are not surpassed by any'.[17] Other watchcase makers included E. Tracy & Co. who supplied the American Watch Co. T. Esmonde Harper supplied Baltimore, Boston and New York as well as Philadelphia. He used an ingenious machine invented by a Swiss monk for engraving cases. Jacot & Brother produced about 6,000 cases a year and employed skilled Swiss workmen induced to go to America by Jacot who advanced the money for the cost of their expenses in getting there.[18]

Other specialities in Philadelphia included the making of gold spectacle frames and hair jewelry. McAllister & Brother was one of five well-known spectacle manufacturers and there were at least six hair jewelry manufacturers in 1857 including F. Fromhagen, Mrs. A. Green, F. Schalch, Charles Stubenrauch and Schmidt & Stubenrauch.[19] J.T. Midnight made bracelets, George P. Pilling made gold and silver combs. Diamond cutting was performed by F. Bohrer and diamond setting by Jacob Bennet. Engraving jewelry was the speciality of E.F. Baton and William F. Cavenaugh. Gold and silver chasing was executed by C.J. Smith and refining by Dreer & Sears. Jewelers' tools were made by H.H. Smith and jewelers' cases were made of morocco and velvet by G.F. Kolb and Peacock & Fickert.[20]

Manufacturing jewelers in Philadelphia obtained a number of patents from 1850 to 1875. A new type of bracelet clasp was designed by John Mansure in 1854.[21] John F. Mascher, a Philadelphia watchmaker, designed a spiral catch for breast pins in 1857.[22] Jewelry fasteners were patented by Charles Ferdinand Kolb and John T. Folwell.[23]

14. Freedley, pp. 344-45, 351.
15. Ibid., p. 345.
16. Ibid., pp. 345-46.
17. Ibid., p. 346.
18. Ibid., pp. 346-7.
19. Ibid., p. 348.
20. Ibid., pp. 455-90.
21. #10,973. Mansure is listed by Brix as a jeweler from 1844 to 1850, p. 50.
22. #17,800. Brix, 1845-50, p. 69.
23. #17,881. Kolb is not listed by Brix. #18,277. Folwell is listed by Brix from 1847 to 1850.

Henry Dubosq made a name for himself as a manufacturer of seed pearl jewelry. He patented an improved method for making this type of jewelry in 1859.[24] Henry Oliver patented the use of sun pictures on concave glass surfaces for use as settings in jewelry in 1859.[25] A spring joint for bracelets was patented by Henry Carlisle, Jr. in 1870.[26] A breastpin fastener was designed by John A. Lehman in 1871.[27]

In 1848 Philadelphia was noted for the elegance of its jewelry stores. George G. Foster wrote in *The New York Tribune* on 21 October that in this regard 'Chestnut-street fairly and decidedly outstrips Broadway'. He pointed out that 'The displays of costly and magnificent silver plate, jewelry, and bijouterie in the windows of Chestnut-street are positively dazzling. We have never seen anything to approach them in any other city of the United States'.[28] Ten years later Bailey & Co. completed 'a marble store', one of the finest on Chestnut Street.[29]

Boston Jewelers

In 1849 the prominent jewelry firm of Jones, Ball & Poor built a new store in Boston that surpassed anything in Philadelphia. Designed by architect S.P. Fuller, the store was the most state-of-the-art jewelry establishment in the country. Indeed one ecstatic reporter thought it would outshine the stores of Storr & Mortimer of London and Verdier of Paris. He even doubted if it had an equal in all the world.[30]

Almost 130ft. long and 30ft. wide, the building had a retail department that was entered from Washington Street and a wholesale department entered from Summer Street. This permitted ladies to make their selections without the disturbance of the essential commercial aspects of the business. There were separate offices for the partners and the bookkeepers. The workshop was located beneath the street level and was equipped for engraving, repairing and setting stones. There was a bathing room to assure the health, comfort and no doubt the appearance of their clerks. Not only was there a safe in the main part of the store, there was another downstairs for the use of customers who wished to store their chests of silverware and other valuables when they went out of town. In addition the entire building was heated centrally by a furnace.

Arthur Gilman, also an architect, supervised the interior decoration. The ceiling and the walls were frescoed. The interior was finished in the Elizabethan style, the cases and counters were white and gold. Plate glass was used profusely and when the show cases were filled, the report was that it rivalled the splendour of the *Arabian Nights* (Plate 195).

On the corner of the building at the second-floor level, a huge clock that could be illuminated at night was placed for the convenience of the public. Above it stood guard a large gold American eagle with its wings outstretched proclaiming the name of the firm at the Sign of the Golden Eagle. The store was pronounced 'a Model Watch and Jewelry establishment' and New Yorkers were advised to come and see it.[31]

When the new store opened in May of 1849, Jones, Ball & Poor announced 'New Store! New Goods!' both retail and wholesale, fine jewelry and rich silver goods which were 'manufactured under their immediate inspection'. The good gold jewelry they made themselves was set with pearls, jets, diamonds and stones. They also carried watches and clocks from London and Geneva, superior Sheffield plate, japanned and Britannia wares, papier mâché furniture, porcelain and Bohemian glass, bronzes and candelabra from Paris, and other fancy goods.[32]

24. #23,760. Brix p. 32-33. *JC*, 3 Feb. 1892, p. 80.
25. #23,042.
26. #108,683.
27. #119,860.
28. Waters, p. 173.
29. Freedley, p. 349.
30. *Selling Quality Jewels Since 1800: A History of Shreve, Crump & Low Co*, pp. 2-25.
31. *Transcript*, 25 Jan. 1849. The clock remains in the possession of the firm of their successor Shreve, Crump & Low at their present location at the corner of Boylston and Arlington Streets. It is now inside on the second floor.
32. *Boston Directory*, 1829-30, p. A4. Boston *Transcript*, 14 May 1849.

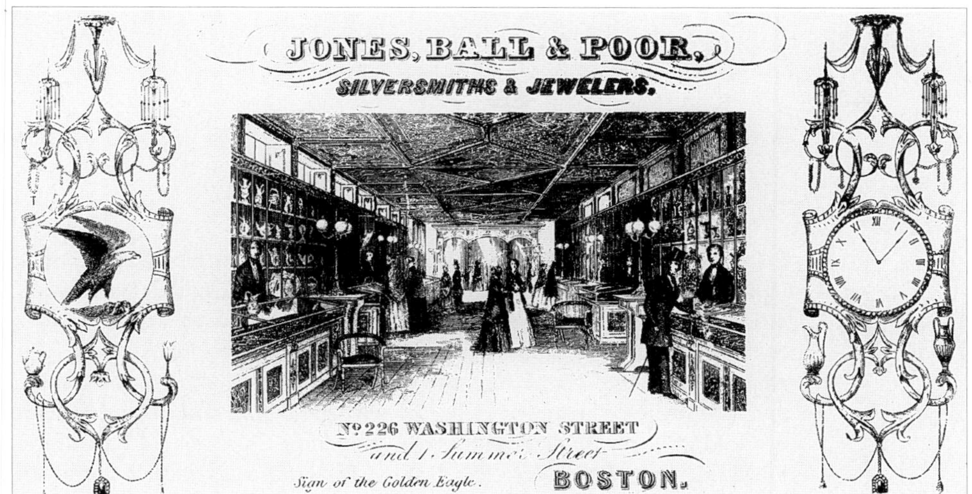

Plate 195. Interior view of the jewelry showroom at the firm of Jones, Ball & Poor. Boston Almanac, *1850.*

In 1852, Benjamin Shreve joined the firm and in 1869 Charles H. Crump was added to form the company of Shreve, Crump & Low. The jewelry made and sold by this firm was praised by the Boston *Transcript* which pointed out that it 'includes all the newest styles...and will be found unusually rich and brilliant'.[33] The quality of their jewelry increased as the years passed. Diamonds and other gems of all sorts were offered, as were rare stone cameos, and 'unique styles in Roman and other Jewelry'.[34] It was this firm that was in large measure responsible for the high reputation attached to Boston jewelers. 'The jewelers of Boston have always enjoyed the confidence of the people of all parts of the country to an unusual degree, and the reliance upon their integrity is now as extensive as at any former period', the Boston *Transcript* declared on 13 September 1856.

One reason for the quality of Boston jewelry was that it was made to suit specific standards. J.G.L. Libby had a large inventory of jewelry in his store, all of which he claimed was made under his immediate supervision. At Christmas time in 1840, he offered diamond brooches and rings, and rings set with emeralds, rubies, opals, amethysts, topazes, aquamarines, garnets, pearls and turquoises. Gold chain could be purchased by the foot. He had gold and stone head ornaments as well as silver and gilt combs. There were brooches made of cameos, mosaics or painted enamel, and gold beads, gold crosses and heavy chased gold rings.[35]

The distinction between jewelers and manufacturing jewelers was clearly delineated in city directories. In 1845 the *Boston Almanac* recorded twelve jewelers and another twenty manufacturing jewelers. The list did not include all of them. By 1856 there were fifty-two jewelers, twenty-eight manufacturing jewelers, sixteen hair workers and a lapidary. In 1860 the number listed included twenty-five jewelers and thirty manufacturers of jewelry. When the period closed in 1874, jewelers were listed under the inclusive category of Jewelry, Watches and Plate. There were 137 jewelers and fifty-six manufacturing jewelers. In addition there were three hair jewelry specialists, four watch manufacturers and numerous watch and watch case and glass makers, dealers and repairers. There were now people who specialized in making jeweler's findings; jeweler's trays; jewelry boxes and cases; ivory, horn and tortoiseshell dealers; assayers and refiners; a bracelet manufacturer (Greenwood & Young); diamond merchants, and gold and silver platers.

The biggest competition for John B. Jones' successors came from Samuel T. Crosby. In 1848 he was in partnership with Jeffrey R. Brackett. Seth E. Brown joined the firm the next year and in 1850 Brackett withdrew. The remaining partners took the opportunity to reduce prices on their stock of 'Rich Watches, Jewelry and Fancy Goods'.[36] By 1854, Crosby had established his own business at 69 Washington Street in the heart of the Boston jewelry trade. His advertisement in the Boston *Almanac*

33. 9 Dec. 1856.
34. Ibid., 19 Dec. 1868.
35. Boston *E. Transcript* 26 Dec. 1840.
36. *Transcript*, 9 April 1850. Belden, *Marks*, p. 125.

240 Washington St.,

Have in Store their Holiday Stock of DIAMONDS and GEMS of the finest quality. FINE WATCHES from the best makers. RICH JEWELRY and SILVER WARE, in great variety, and a new invoice of the celebrated Ekegren Watches. All at present values!

TWO GOLD MEDALS

—AND—

A SILVER MEDAL

Have been awarded them by the MASS. CHAR. MECHANIC ASSOCIATION, who are pleased to say in regard to DIAMOND CUTTING:

"The thanks of the community are due to them for their patience and perseverance in introducing this mechanical art into this city."

And in regard to SILVER WARE and JEWELRY, their report is:

CROSBY MORSE & FOSS, Boston, Mass.: Diamonds, Jewelry and Silver Ware. The Silver Ware consists of a great variety of useful and ornamental articles, the embellishments of which are very skillfully executed. The Jewelry is rich, chaste and of superior workmanship. WE DO NOT HESITATE TO PRONOUNCE THIS DISPLAY UNSURPASSED IN QUALITY AND STYLE. For the Silver Ware and Jewelry contributed, your Committee award a SILVER MEDAL.

Plate 196. Crosby, Morse & Foss of Boston advertised a holiday stock of diamonds and gems of finest quality and other rich jewelry. They boasted of their recently awarded gold and silver medals for their diamond cutting as well as their rich, chaste jewelry and the quality of their workmanship. Boston Evening Transcript, *9 December 1874.*

that year was boldly printed in gold against a brilliant blue background. It showed silver, clocks and glass ware, and a woman calling her friend's attention to a demi-parure in an open box. Crosby attempted to expand his trade as well as his reputation in neighbouring areas. He advertised in the *Maine Register* in 1857 jewelry made of diamonds, precious stones, in plain or elaborate settings of gold and silver. 'Articles of Gold of every conceivable form... Medium Quality, and Extra Fine Gold, Chains, Brooches, Ear Rings, Finger Rings &c...' could be bought from Samuel Crosby (see Plate 164).

Crosby got jewelry from various parts of the world to augment his own production. He had cameos from Rome, with pearl and fine gold settings; mosaics from Florence in ornamental or plain settings; and from Naples coral and lava in brooches, rings, bracelets, earrings and necklaces. From Germany, particularly Hanau and Frankfurt, he imported more coral, cameo and gold jewelry. Opals came from Bohemia and Central America, pearls, emeralds and rubies from the Orient. Diamonds were imported from India and Brazil.[37]

In 1858, Crosby introduced Etruscan gold jewelry. His watches were made by Charles Frodsham, F.B.Adams & Sons and E.F.Brandt.[38] He also carried 'all the approved kinds' of watches, from the low priced Swiss watch to the most elaborately balanced English masterpiece of mechanism.[39] In 1860 Crosby, by then allied with F. Hunnewell and Henry D. Morse (see pages 200-201) was awarded the highest prize for both design and workmanship at the autumn fair sponsored by the Massachusetts Charitable Mechanic Association. At Christmas time the firm staged its own first annual exhibition of holiday goods. Included were rich and elegant examples of jewelry in original mounts, set with stone cameos, pearls, diamonds and all kinds of other precious gems.[40]

The emphasis on precious stones was no doubt made possible by the presence of Henry D. Morse in the partnership. A man of many skills, he was devoting himself to the scientific study of gemmology and developing new revolutionary techniques for cutting gems. In a newspaper announcement on 8 May 1860, Crosby noted that a copartnership had been formed with Morse, the diamond jeweler who had been supplying the finest stones in Boston for the last twelve years. They were now able to offer a much larger stock of rare gems. Morse was also put in charge of directing their own workshop in new designs for settings. This, Crosby noted, gave their customers an advantage no other jewelry store in Boston could offer.[41]

Crosby & Morse had recently moved to 240 Washington Street, on the corner of Central Court. Their new granite building, although not as large as Jones', was tastefully designed specifically for their needs. Huge walnut cases held the massive silver pieces. By contrast, the cases on the counters were plain to offset the richness of the jewelry they contained. The ceiling was frescoed by Schutz who had gained fame in this trade in Boston. The manufacturing was carried out in rooms above the sales area. 'In the setting of diamonds, and in the production of the choicest descriptions of jewelry', the Boston *Transcript* opined, 'these partners have taken a high rank, and have received corresponding encouragement'.[42]

Crosby & Morse exhibited a case of jewelry at the Mechanics' Fair in 1865. There were cameo pins and pearls 'that would charm an eastern Queen' and the necklaces and bracelets were of exquisite workmanship.[43] In addition to displays of diamonds and watches, there was a Pompeian Show Room in which they displayed the Gorham silver they carried.[44] Many of the diamonds they sold they cut themselves, thanks to Morse's achievements in this area. 'Being the only Diamond Cutters in the country', they said they had 'superior facilities for obtaining Diamonds of the finest quality, and for reforming and making more brilliant those, that by being badly cut lack force and brilliancy'. Mr. Morse would, they pointed out, be 'constantly making new and original designs for jewelry, diamond settings, silverware and monograms'. The watch department was put under the direction of S.S Crosby, possibly Samuel's son, and Horatio Towne, who had previously been with Haddock, Lincoln & Foss.[45]

It was probably Morse who designed the advertisement that featured the bold vertical lettering, combining P with XMAS in the style of Castellani's Byzantine jewelry designs (Plates 196 and 197). For the Christmas holidays in 1868 their notice called special attention to the Byzantine and gold jewelry that they had for holiday presents, namely brooches, bracelets, earrings and buttons. In addition to Byzantine mosaics, they offered Roman gold and Etruscan gold jewelry.[46]

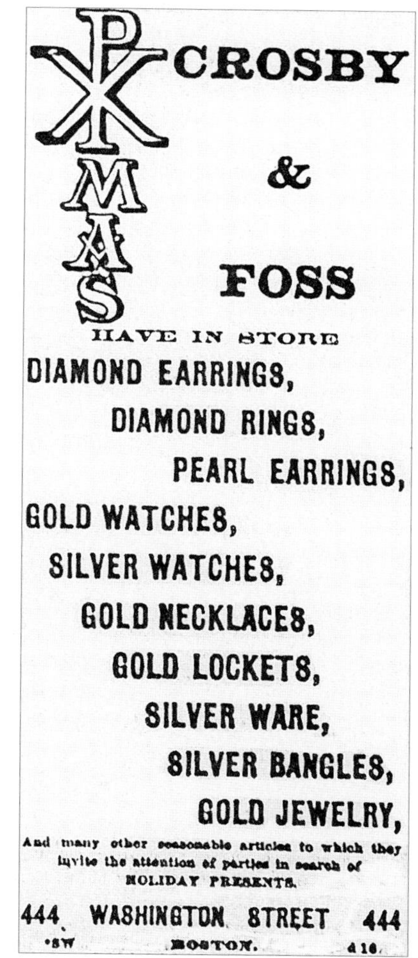

Plate 197. Henry Morse designed new and original jewelry, diamond settings and monograms for the firm of Crosby, Morse & Foss, in Boston, until the end of 1876. Boston Evening Transcript, *14 December 1876.*

As a service, Crosby, Morse & Foss provided insured safe deposit storage in the fire-proof vaults 'at their old stand'.[47] At the Massachusetts Charitable Mechanic Association Fair in 1874, the firm won two gold medals and a silver one. One was for their diamond cutting. It was said that 'The thanks of the community are due them for their patience and perseverance in introducing this mechanical art into this city'. In making the award for their jewelry, the committee said it was 'rich, chaste and of superior workmanship. We do not hesitate to pronounce this display unsurpassed in quality and style'.[48]

In 1876 a patent was obtained for the diamond-cutting machine developed by Henry D. Morse and Charles M. Field. Morse left Crosby & Foss and established his own diamond-cutting firm at 383 Washington Street, with Field as the foreman of the shop. He obtained rough diamonds directly from the mines to cut and polish in his own workshop. He kept on hand a large assortment of diamonds and other gems, cut and uncut, unset or in settings to suit the customer's taste.[49] Crosby & Foss moved to 444 Washington Street and continued to offer diamond jewelry, pearls, gold necklaces and lockets, gold and silver watches, silver bangles and silverware.[50]

Of slightly less renown but noteworthy were the firms of Palmer & Bachelders, Guild & Delano, and Bigelow Kennard, all firms that originated during the mid-nineteenth century. Palmer & Bachelders on Washington Street was formed in 1846 as a jewelry and watch business by Jacob P. and Julius A. Palmer with Augustus E. and Josiah G. Bachelders. They imported watches from London, Liverpool and Geneva, and in the 1870s featured Patek Philippe watches. They were agents for Boston-made watches as well.

The jewelry at Palmer & Bachelders included both 'domestic and foreign'. It ranged from diamond jewelry, pearls, and stone cameos to coral, ivory, cornelian

37. *Transcript*, 31 Dec. 1856.
38. Ibid., 22 Dec. 1858.
39. 29 Dec. 1856.
40. *Transcript*, 20, 31 Dec. 1860.
41. Ibid., 8 May 1860.
42. 7 May 1860.
43. Ibid., Supplement, 27 Sept. 1865. By this time, Hunnewell had left the firm and in 1868 Charles M. Foss, formerly of Haddock, Lincoln & Foss, joined Crosby & Morse.
44. Ibid., 1 July 1868.
45. Ibid., 1 July 1868.
46. Ibid., 17, 18 Dec. 1868.
47. Ibid., 12 Dec. 1872.
48. Ibid., 9 Dec. 1874.
49. Ibid., 14 Dec. 1876.
50. Ibid.

jewelry, and gold chains and bracelets. In addition they sold Parisian clocks and bronzes, silver and plated wares and opera glasses.[51] The silverware was produced by Gorham 'and other first-class manufacturers', but they made at least some of the jewelry themselves. They noted particularly their solitaire diamond and cluster diamond rings, ladies' brooches and earrings, as well as pins and studs for gentlemen. They mounted other kinds of gems too. Their gold jewelry included necklaces, lockets and gold-headed canes.[52]

Henry Guild was a manufacturing jeweler as early as 1846 and formed a partnership with T. Ingalls Delano. They sold cameo and mosaic sets and manufactured a variety of jewelry. They prided themselves on their work with diamonds and catered to the Masonic trade (Colour Plate 163). They also sold silverware.[53]

Bigelow, Kennard & Co. was started by John Bigelow in 1830. He was subsequently joined by his brothers Alanson and Abraham O. Bigelow, and M.P. and William H. Kennard. They imported watches, pearls and all kinds of gems. They manufactured fine jewelry as well as silverware. In 1864 they featured chatelaines with watches and leontine chains to match.[54] Jeweler Charles W. Kennard advertised 'Precious Stones, Pearls and Corals; Jewelry of original designs, and made to order'. He called attention to the fact that he had whole pearls and not simply the half-pearls so often used to form decorative borders and accents in jewelry.[55]

New York Jewelers

Two firms dominated the scene in mid-nineteenth century jewelry circles in New York. They were Ball, Black & Company and Tiffany & Company. In 1859, at the time of the Oviedo 'Diamond Wedding', these two firms vied to provide the bride with the most beautiful sets of jewels (see Plates 133 to 137). Ball, Black's history had begun in 1839 when Henry Ball joined with William Black and Erastus O. Tompkins in taking over the well-known firm of Marquand & Co. Black had been apprenticed to Marquand, and Tompkins had been a partner in the firm.[56] The new partners continued importing, making and selling jewelry and silverware at 181 Broadway. They also sold and repaired watches. They moved to 247 Broadway in 1848.

In 1860 Ball, Black & Company's store was chastely decorated on the first floor with faux ebony interior walls and white marble counters. A reporter noted that 'there are gems, pure and sparkling enough to delight the most critical of connoisseurs'. In addition they had for sale elegant silver wares, bronzes in the antique style, inlaid marble specimens, Parian statues, and paintings, one of which was worth $2,000.[57] Ball, Black was prestigious enough to attract a royal visit to its premises by the young Prince of Wales during his triumphal sojourn in the city in 1860. Further interest was created by *Mme. Demorest's Monthly Magazine* which frequently published illustrations of jewelry available at Ball, Black's (see Plate 113).[58]

In 1850, the jeweler Herman Marcus (1828-99) came to New York from Dresden, Germany. He had been trained by Ellemeyer, the court jeweler. Marcus did work for Ball, Black and for Tiffany. It is likely that he played a part in the designing and crafting of the elaborate jewels selected by Oviedo in 1859. In 1864, Marcus joined the firm of Theodore B. Starr (1837-1907).[59] Marcus & Starr were among the finalists chosen to submit designs for the vase to be presented to William Cullen Bryant in 1876. At the Philadelphia Centennial exhibition that year, they displayed a notable

51. Boston *Almanac,* 1859; *Transcript,* 27 Dec. 1860; 19 Dec. 1868.
52. *Transcript,* 16 Dec. 1870; 24 Dec. 1873; 9 Dec. 1874.
53. Boston *Almanac,* 1846-51; *Directory* 1840-80; *Transcript,* 23 Dec. 1865; 17 Dec. 1868. Rainwater, *AJM,* pp. 74, 111.
54. *Transcript,* 23 Dec. 1864; 14 Jan. 1865; 17 Dec. 1868.
55. Boston *Almanac* 1867; *Transcript,* 16 Dec. 1870.
56. von Khrum, pp. 9, 15, 86, 129.
57. Boston *Transcript,* 22 Sept. 1860.
58. Gere, *A.& E.J.,* p. 153, Fig. 45. Cortlandt W. Starr became a partner in the firm in 1874 when it was reorganized and the name was changed to Black, Starr & Frost. Two years later the store was moved to 251 Fifth Avenue.
59. Starr had worked for several New York jewelers before establishing his own shop in 1862 on John Street.

Plate 198. The first store occupied by Charles L. Tiffany, in partnership with John P. Young, occupied from 1837 to 1841 and located at 259 Broadway, then the centre of New York's shopping district. John Loring's Tiffany's 150 Years *(New York: Doubleday, 1987).*

assortment of jewelry. Their cameos were 'among the most exquisite in the world', according to one observer, 'and were selected with skill and taste'.[60] Marcus was a connoisseur of cameos without peer, according to his obituary.[61] Some of the cameos displayed had exquisite enamelled settings. An aigrette made of diamonds, a necklace of pink pearls with diamonds, and brooches of coral were among their treasures.

Although the firm of Ball, Black had a longer continuous history, it took Charles L. Tiffany very little time to catch up with them. Born in Killingly, Connecticut, in 1812, Charles forsook his father's textile business. In 1837, with a school friend John P. Young, he opened a stationery and fancy goods store in New York. Young had been working in a similar sort of store for several months, and Charles' father kindly provided a modest amount of financial backing for the two young men (Plate 198).

Located at 259 Broadway, their store was stocked with everything from stationery to knick-knacks. Tiffany's business sense led him to be one of the first to stock Chinese and Japanese goods as they came on the market. At first they imported inexpensive paste jewelry from Hanau, Germany. J.L. Ellis became a partner of the firm in 1841, bringing with his name enough capital to fund John Young as a European agent. The first result of this new arrangement was Young's discovery of a superior French paste jewelry known as Palais Royale. Tiffany quickly substituted it for the cheaper Hanau jewelry. Its success inspired him to go into the market for better jewelry. In 1845, the firm issued its first catalogue, taking the opportunity to emphasize its role as an importer of fancy manufactures from England, France, Germany and China. 'Elegant articles of taste and utility' were what they wanted to be known for carrying. Objects were chosen from the best producers and were often made to order, yet were newer and better priced, they claimed.

Jewelry still played a very small part in the store of 1845. Goods made of inlaid exotic woods, leather goods, ceramics, glass, bronzes, toiletries, chairs, cutlery and games all commanded greater attention. However, they listed 'A very beautiful collection of gilt, steel, jet and tortoise shell dress combs' and French filigree jewelry. Special attention was given to 'a limited number of every new style of Bracelets, Hair

60. McCabe, p. 368.
61. *JC*, 25 Oct. 1899.

Plate 199. From 1853 to 1870 Tiffany & Co. occupied a five-storey building at 550 Broadway. John Loring's Tiffany's 150 Years *(New York: Doubleday, 1987).*

Pins, Dress Combs, Head Ornaments, Chatelaines, Scarf Pins, Brooches, Shawl Pins, Chains, &c., &c., in gold and imitation'. A justification was included on the subject of imitation jewelry of the finest quality. If it had an excellent surface of gold that could be engraved and chased, as solid gold could be, then it was an acceptable substitute for the rapidly shifting fashions, and was 'very generally approved by people of rank, wealth and fashion, both in Europe and in this country'. Among the sundries listed were agate and cornelian rings, bouquet holders, bracelets, brooches, chatelaines, crucifixes, ferronnières, guard chains, jet jewelry, lockets, shirt studs and scarf pins.[62]

Tiffany began making good jewelry in house about 1848. At the same time, in Paris, John Young was able to take advantage of the fall of Louis Philippe by purchasing the jewelry of the king's wife Maria Amelia. Fleeing supporters of the king were also eager to sell Young their diamonds for cash. At some threat to his life Young was able to secure for the firm a portion of the French crown jewels including, it is thought, Marie Antoinette's diamond girdle. In addition he procured enough diamonds to stock the store for years to come, earning the title of the king of diamonds for his partner Charles Tiffany.

To insure continuation of such opportunities, Tiffany made Gideon F.T. Reed a partner and head of the office in Paris. Reed had been a partner in the Boston jewelry firm of Lincoln & Reed. In January 1852, Tiffany, Young & Ellis advertised their store at 271 Broadway in New York as well as Tiffany, Reed & Co., Rue Richelieu, No. 79, in Paris. They stressed that 'having their own house in Paris, and their own manufactories of Jewelry, Silver Ware, &c., here' offered advantages in better prices and quality than any other company in the business.[63] In 1851 they had been able to entice the gifted John C. Moore and his son Edward, who had been supplying silverware for rivals Gorham and Ball, Black, to work exclusively for Tiffany & Co. The Moores' shift made it possible for Tiffany's to boast of their services.[64] In 1853 Young & Ellis retired and the firm became Tiffany & Co.

In 1854 the store was moved into a large four-storey building at 550 Broadway (Plate 199). Like Jones, Ball & Poor in Boston a few years earlier, Tiffany also installed a conspicuous clock for the public's convenience. Supported by Atlas, rather than the gold eagle of the Boston clock, the Tiffany clock still reigns over the entrance to the store.

Tiffany had a special talent for anticipating the public's whims. In 1856, in Hartford, Connecticut, the giant oak tree that had served as a hiding place for the charter of the Connecticut colony in 1687 was finally brought to the ground by a terrible gust of wind. Such an attraction had this tree been, not only to that state but to patriots everywhere, that the tree was given a funeral service, complete with band, bells and eulogies. Tiffany immediately understood that pieces of this venerable oak

62. Purtell, pp. 14–27.
63. NY *Times,* 1 Jan. 1852.
64. Proddow, p. 30.

would be treasured relics. He acquired small plaques and pendants carved into oak branches, eagles and other symbolic motifs and had them set in simple gold mounts as brooches, earrings and bracelets (Colour Plate 165). This novel all-American costume jewelry proved very popular as soon as it was put on sale.[65] Countless other kinds of articles were made from the wood by other craftsmen including pianos, furniture, goblets, napkin rings and canes.[66]

When, after many mishaps, the transatlantic telegraph cable was successfully laid between America and Europe in 1858, Tiffany bought the remaining twenty miles of cable. He had it cut into pieces suitable for seals, watch fobs and other items (Plate 200). Four-inch long chunks of cable were mounted with brass ferrules and sold for fifty cents apiece, along with a certificate signed by Cyrus W. Field authenticating their origin. The day these novelties were put on sale there was such a crush of customers trying to get into the store, the police had to be called to maintain order.[67]

Plate 200 Cross section of the Atlantic cable which Tiffany & Co. had set in gold for use as a watch fob, c.1866. Length 1¼in. Winterthur Museum.

The Civil War only slightly altered Tiffany's course to supremacy. He immediately turned to providing military goods for the Union: swords and rifles, shoes and caps, epaulettes and badges. Tiffany's became the distributor of Derringer pistols in New York and the north-east. When the war was over, the demand for presentation swords for surviving heroes was intense. Tiffany's reputation was such that those making the presentation could hardly settle for less. Many of the swords were set with diamonds and were enamelled. The initials of the recipient, studded with diamonds, appeared on the guard in script or superimposed block letters.

In the absence of royal patronage, Tiffany received presidential patronage. Abraham Lincoln purchased a seed-pearl parure from the famed New York store at a cost of $530 (see Colour Plate 123). Mrs. Lincoln wore the necklace, earrings and bracelets to her husband's inauguration in 1861 (see Plate 140). Soon Tiffany was selling jewels to royalty. The rare pink pearl, the first to be found at Notch Brook, New Jersey, and acquired by Tiffany, he sold to the Empress Eugénie. It became known as the Queen Pearl.

Tiffany's next move was to challenge Europe's finest on their own turf, at the Exposition Universelle in Paris in 1867. To the dismay of the old-world exhibitors, Tiffany & Co. walked away with first place honours for their domestic silver. The London *Art Journal* was chagrined, but admitted that Tiffany's designs and workmanship were unsurpassed by any others submitted. They were neither too ornate nor too plain. 'The establishment of Messrs. Tiffany is the largest in the new world: it is of importance, therefore, that they should minister to pure taste in America...The exhibits hold their own beside the best of England and France'.[68] One art critic and designer singled out what was to be the common thread in American arts. 'While other exhibits rest principally upon rare and costly works, elaborated to the highest degree, this little display of the Americans rests upon humble work, proving that ordinary articles may be exalted and invested with a dignity that will entitle them to rank with the proudest achievements of industrial art'.[69]

Tiffany seized the moment and pointed out in his advertising that his firm was the recipient of the only award ever granted by a foreign country to an American manufacturer of silverware. Europeans now began ordering silver services from

65. Conn. Hist. Soc. *Bulletin, 49,* 125-127.
66. At the Centennial Exhibition in 1876, the Connecticut State display featured the history of the Charter Oak and thin slices of wood from the tree cut to one inch square were glued into the copies of *Connecticut's Souvenir of the Centennial Exhibition* on page 209.
67. Carpenter, *Tiffany,* p. 125.
68. Carpenter, *Tiffany,* p. 125.
69. Carpenter, *Tiffany,* p. 125.

See Colour Plate 164.

Tiffany's. The firm had become the purveyor of choice for wedding silver, presentations and jewelry.[70] Their business in diamonds at the New York and Paris stores was estimated to be a million dollars annually in 1869, and their retail sales at the New York store were valued at three million a year. George McClure was Tiffany's diamond expert and gemmologist whose knowledge was widely respected.

It was time to move up another notch on Broadway too. In 1870 Tiffany built a new palace at Union Square, at the corner of Broadway and 15th Street. Architect John Kellum designed the fireproof building for the newest technology. Built of iron, it was painted drab and had bronze and gilt pillars. George Templeton Strong, who had hoped that it would be an improvement over the unattractive church that was pulled down to provide the space for the store, thought the new building was hideous.[71] However, the impression of stability and safety became an asset for Tiffany's. The Boston *Transcript* reported that Tiffany's was the most complete jewelry store in the country, if not the world.[72]

The building cost about $750,000, occupied four lots, and was about 79 feet by 114. There were three floors below ground with five storeys above. The building was steam-heated by Harrison's finest engines which also powered the machinery in the workshops in the four storeys above the store. There was an elevator as well as a staircase connecting each floor.

The workshops provided the space and equipment for jewelers, engravers, stone engravers, polishers, box makers and watch and clock makers. The top floor was devoted to the setting of diamonds. For customers whose jewelry required repairing, all their needs could be met here. No longer was it necessary to take it to a jeweler who then had to turn it over to specialists in various locations, thereby increasing risk to the objects.

George Strong took a tour of the manufacturing areas of the new store which he found quite interesting. Mr. Magauran told him about the processes and equipment employed and he observed about five hundred men and women at work there.[73] Actually, there were approximately 750 workmen in addition to about fifty salesmen at that time. Tiffany's also provided an insured fireproof storage facility where customers could safely store their valuables when they went away.[74] The Strongs packed their things off to Tiffany's in the summer of 1872 when there was an outbreak of robberies. Ever with an eye on the ledger, Strong was happily surprised and a bit smug that their precious chattels were worth more than $8,000.[75]

Tiffany had enhanced his own image as well as that of New York. The new displays were breathtaking. The latest fashion in silverware was the finish introduced to this country by Tiffany called satin finish. Among the watches, those by Charles Frodsham were now sold exclusively in America by Tiffany's and cost from $500 to $1500. Fine French watches were in evidence too. The diamond jewelry was truly beautiful, but one reporter thought the unset diamonds were the outstanding feature. One tray in the safe room held diamonds valued at $350,000, of which two were the largest known in the United States and worth $10,000 each. Elsewhere there were magnificent pearls and a superb thirty-two carat sapphire.[76]

An observer of the scene 'saw a lady and a gentleman examining a precious stone set in a diamond circle. The woman's eyes were fixed upon the gem with a fascinated gaze...while husband, or what not, stood by, watching the tempted and the tempter. It was a picture of Adam and Eve in a jeweller's shop, with the devil in the shape of a

70. TA, N.Y. *Evening Post,* 7 Oct. 1869.
71. *Diary,* III, 43; IV, 211, 326.
72. *Transcript,* 14 Nov. 1870.
73. *Diary,* IV, 540.
74. *The World,* NY, 11 Nov. 1870, clipping, TA.
75. *Diary,* IV, 431.
76. *The World,* NY, 11 Nov. 1870, clipping, TA.

Plate 201. A glimpse of the stock in trade at Tiffany's in 1867 may be seen in this early photograph. Sets of jewelry, open jewel boxes, and festoons of pearls decorate the heavily carved furniture. John Loring's Tiffany's 150 Years *(New York: Doubleday, 1987).*

breast-pin'.[77] Strong would have appreciated the circumstances since he too stood in terror of Tiffany's. Yet he had to admit, after Tiffany let it be known that henceforth only real jewels would be sold there, 'Tiffany's customers will pay still larger sums, but they will secure a genuine article'.[78]

In 1874, Tiffany advertised in Boston newspapers. He offered a mail-order service to 'people out of New York' who could describe what they wanted in what price range. Tiffany's would then make selections from their stock and send them on approval.[79] Later in the year, Tiffany & Co. advertised as diamond merchants seeking Boston business. They noted that the discovery of diamonds in South Africa had caused a glut on the market of diamonds not always of the highest quality. Prices were lower than they had been since 1848. Tiffany's had used this circumstance to buy a large stock of the best white diamonds and could now offer the finest selection in the country.[80]

Charles Tiffany's mid-nineteenth century career had brought him from humble beginnings, selling cheap baubles, to a prize-winning, world-recognized purveyor of the finest goods a jewelry store could offer. He had done what no other American had done. Tiffany's was now engaged in the most innovative and important period in its already impressive history.

New York Manufacturing Jewelers

New York supported hundreds of jewelers in the mid-nineteenth century. Many had shops that carried jewelry made by other American manufacturers and jewelry that was imported, rather than their own products. Many were primarily watchmakers who sold some silverware and gold jewelry on the side. Others, however, were manufacturing jewelers who sold their goods wholesale to retail jewelers. In New York between 1825 and 1850 there were at least twenty-two men specified in city directories as manufacturing jewelers, and dozens identified only as jewelers, but who are known from other sources to have made jewelry.[81]

Men specializing in the precious metals industry in New York during this period included Platt & Brothers, gold and silver refiners; Brainerd & Arrowsmith, enamellers on gold; William E. Rose, cameo mounter; and six chasers of jewelry: Thomas H. Bridgwood, Louis Halbert, Benjamin C. Lotier, J.M. Marshall, Jonathan Smith & Son, and Frederick Moore, Jr. In addition, there were Wray & Sadd, diamond jewelers and Mark A. Swain, diamond setter. Wilson's *Business Directory* for 1849 listed 116 jewelers working on their own account in New York city south of 23rd Street.[82]

Although there have been no detailed studies of the jewelry industry in New York in the mid-nineteenth century, it appears that its manufactories and production were probably as great as those of Providence and greater than those of Newark. A comparison of patents on jewelry granted to men in these three cities indicates that

77. Boston *Sunday Courier,* 11 Dec. 1870.
78. *Diary,* IV, 211.
79. *Transcript,* 2 May 1874.
80. Ibid., 9 Dec. 1874.
81. Von Khrum found 2,546 names of silversmiths, watchmakers and jewelers or related craftsmen. He utilized published directories that he found were not all inclusive listings.
82. *Newark Sentinel,* 3 July 1849.

fifty-four were won for Providence, forty-five for New York and thirty-two for Newark.

New York patents in the 1850s concerned improvements in fasteners for earrings, safety clasps for bracelets, secure pins for brooches and lock joint fasteners for studs. Isaac Hermann, who registered his safety clasp for bracelets in 1857, was obviously interested in safeguarding the expensive jewelry he made. For a while he was the only jeweler in New York who both cut and set diamonds.[83] Hermann established his New York Diamond Cutting Co. in 1870.

Methods of setting stones in jewelry were the concern of several patents obtained in the 1860s. One was for setting stones in ready-made mounts, while another involved mass-produced mounts with two movable claws and two fixed claws.[84] Rings were another area of attention. A finger ring with a grooved inner face made of cast or rolled metal and edges widened to form a bearing surface upon the finger was the design of William H. Peckham who founded the Peckham Seamless Ring Co. in 1850.[85]

An interesting design for making coiled bracelets with spring wire was patented by H. Kipling in 1861.[86] Brooch fasteners were patented by Thomas W. F. Smitten, Frederick Catlin, Israel Farjean, William Sackermann and Robert James Pond.[87]

In 1871 George D. Stevens designed a guard chain for bracelets, provided with a middle stop and a sliding guard, and a neck chain with not only one but two slides.[88] The following year he patented a bracelet with a slot in the thumbpiece of its snap that would allow the addition of a tassel or some other kind of ornament, and a combination handkerchief and fan holder.[89] Another Stevens design was a new kind of spring guard for securing earrings in place.[90]

Shubael Cottle, a manufacturing jeweler specializing in fourteen karat gold jewelry and silver novelties, obtained a diverse range of patents. Some had to do with the processes of making the jewelry and jewelry bases.[91] Another was for a bracelet fastening that provided a cap to fit over the knob of the catch and a spring pin to lock the cap on the knob.[92] In 1874, he patented a design for making necklaces formed of alternate closed links and open spiral links. He assigned this patent to his firm Mulford, Hale & Cottle.[93] Shubael Cottle assigned a patent for making dies for manufacturing hollow rings to the firm in 1875.[94] Cottle also invented a machine for manufacturing collar buttons from rolled gold plate and for making watch cases. Cottle retired in 1878 and the firm continued as Hale & Mulford.[95]

New York jewelers were interested in combining forms, as Stevens' handkerchief-fan holder indicated. Auguste Weiller patented a breast pin that incorporated a small thermometer in 1871 and Friedrich Wachter combined a locket and smelling bottle in 1874.[96]

The advertisements of manufacturing jewelers in Wilson's *New York City Directory* of 1861 illustrate the range of their productivity. Beach & Powell simply described themselves as manufacturers of fine gold jewelry. H. Edinger & Son made gold chains. John D. Lennon specialized in 'Fine Gold Half-round and Flat Band Bracelets' which he always had on hand and could make to order. Emile Martin who came from Paris advertised as a 'manufacturer of Paris Fancy Jewelry'. He could set diamonds in any style and made coral and filigree jewelry as well. In 1863 Richard B. Cowley manufactured jewelry for wholesale and retail, specializing in regalia for fraternal orders such as the Free Masons, and Knights Templars. He also made fine jewelry to order.

At the other end of the spectrum, 'The Great Cash Jewelry House of New York' of

83. #18,245. Patent #183,474 on a diamond-cutting machine was assigned to Hermann in 1876 by Thomas F. Tully of New York.
84. #38,184 (1863) Samuel J. Smith; #58,501 (1866) Francis Stefani.
85. #82,546 (1868); Rainwater, *AJM*, p. 187.
86. #31,931 assigned to J. B. Behrman.
87. #81,835 (1868); #92,163 (1869) #108,578 (1870); #108,520 (1870); #122,192 (1871).
88. #111,489 and #118,294.
89. #123,740 and #129,871 (1872).
90. #148,996 (1874).
91. #133,762 (1872); #135,087 and #135,088 (1873).
92. #145,788 (1873).
93. #147,045. This firm also procured patents on finger ring designs, #89,455 (1869) Chester S. Ford to self and Lewis J. Mulford; Frederich Bohnenberger to Mulford, Hall & Cottle, #7,453 (1874).
94. #158,914.
95. Rainwater, *AJM*, p. 125.
96. #121,440; #152,197.

W.A. Hayward touted 'Great Bargains, especially in all kinds of Sets, Lockets, Bracelets, Rings, Pins, Studs and Buttons, Masonic Marks and all kinds of Emblems'. He recommended that potential customers send for his circular. C.P. Girton advertised his headquarters for cheap jewelry at 208 Broadway in Frank Leslie's *Illustrated Newspaper* on 12 April 1862. He made a complete line of jewelry, from all kinds of sets to lockets, bracelets, pins, rings and chains.

By 1875, there were 323 manufacturing jewelry firms listed in Wilson's Directory, some of which were New York outlets of firms in Providence and Newark and a few in Attleboro, Philadelphia and Boston. Only one of the manufacturing jewelers listed was a woman, Martha Seckendorf at 89 Prince Street. Miller Brothers of 11 Maiden Lane had a manufactory in Newark. Their goods included plain, engraved or enamelled Roman gold buttons, studs, and lockets set with amethysts, topazes, pearls, cameos, stones, onyx or coral. They specialized in initial jewelry.

There were three firms on Nassau Street in 1875 that specialized in enamelling jewelry. They were the firms of Conrad Brand, James C. Orr and John C. Scarry. Samuel Blatt specialized in making gold chain and Frederick Staudinger concentrated on bracelets. Jewelry made of vulcanite and celluloid were available from the Vulcanite Jewelry Co. at 191 Broadway and 53 Mercer Street and the Celluloid Novelty Co. at 196 Broadway. Those involved with the watch industry included ninety-two watch makers, twenty-six watch case makers, three case polishers including one woman, four crystal makers, one dial maker, four watch jewelers, fourteen makers of watchmakers' tools and five makers of watch and clock springs. In addition there were 316 dealers in watches and jewelry, at least nine of whom were women and some of whom are known to have been manufacturing jewelers as well. Importers of watches and jewelry were listed separately and were eighty-two in number. Philip Bissinger was listed as an importer of jewelry and agent for Bohemian garnets. Finally, Frasse & Co. supplied tools to the jewelry trade while others made jewelry trays and cases.

Newark Jewelers

Newark's jewelry industry had grown slowly but steadily in the 1830s. According to the 1830 census, there were only fifty jewelry workers there. The 1836 census recorded four jewelry establishments with one hundred wage earners and production valued at $225,060.[97] In addition to the thirty-four jewelers listed in the Newark Directory in 1838, there were allied craftsmen such as silverplaters and watchcase makers, as well as one lapidary. In advertisements in the Directory, Stephen B. Alling, Demas Colten, Jr., Taylor, Baldwin & Co., and Taylor & Nichols described themselves as wholesale manufacturers of all kinds of jewelry.

It was not until the 1840s that task differentiation gained ground in the manufacture of jewelry in Newark. Steam-powered machinery was introduced by 1849 for a few of the specialized operations such as the production of chains and watchcases. While men performed most tasks, women were employed to do the polishing. Wages were comparatively high for workers in the jewelry industry.[98]

The Gold Rush in 1849 had a marked effect on the jewelry business. Bars of gold were assayed and shipped directly from California to Newark. Moses Canfield was listed in the 1850-51 Directory with both his Newark address and the notation

97. Julia B. Smith, 'The Jewelry Industry in Newark', pp. 1, 4-5.
98. Hirsch, pp. 31-2.

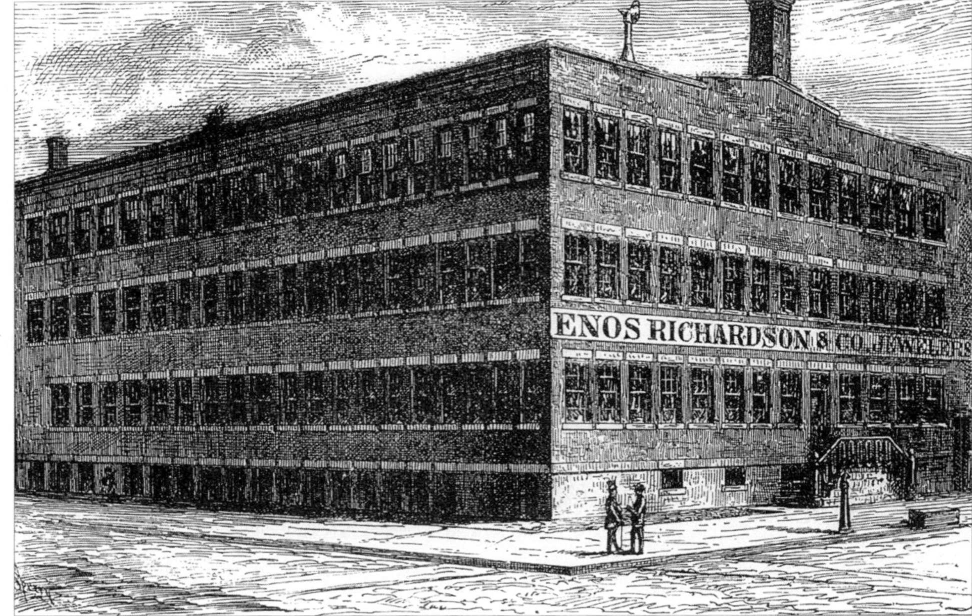

Plate 202 The Enos Richardson & Co. building, one of the leading jewelry manufactories in Newark, New Jersey, illustrated in William R. Bagnall's The Manufacture of Gold Jewelry *published in New York in 1882.*

'California'. The entry for Moses M. Osborn was 'gone west'. William Riker's partner George Tay became a forty-niner too.[99]

Supporting crafts began to proliferate. Lapidaries, engravers, and gold chasers were joined by bucklemakers, watch and watchcase makers and comb makers. There were other specialists such as moulders, pattern makers, tool makers, die sinkers, filers, platers and annealers.

In 1851 there were eighteen manufactories. The average wage of their six hundred workers, including boys, was approximately $12 a week. The average number of workers per firm was thirty-nine. The production for the year amounted to about $1,820,000. About fifty workers were employed in making watchcases alone. Chains and rings represented other important specialized products. That year there were five steam engines used for polishing and other tasks in the jewelry industry.[100]

During the 1850s small machines such as circular saws and lathes became more widely utilized. Diamond cutters and setters appeared in Newark. Most of the precious stones used for jewelry were still imported pre-cut from Europe. Gradually more women were employed in the industry and there were factories that had as many as several hundred employees. Increased consumption of luxury items by the expanding middle class and newly rich urbanites gave rise to more jewelry firms that offered customized work as well as mass-produced jewelry. For example, in 1855 Baldwin & Co. provided a watchcase studded with diamonds and valued at $1,800 on special request. In 1859 journeymen jewelers formed a union, apparently the first of its kind in the United States.[101]

While about 60% of the work-force in Newark's jewelry industry was American born, about a quarter were of German origin, and there was also a small percentage of Irish workers. Jewelry companies actively sought skilled workers in Germany as well as France. Newark also attracted jewelers who had learned or practised their trade in other areas of the United States. David C. Keep, a native of Massachusetts, had worked in Providence prior to moving to Newark where he formed a partnership with Moses Field.[102] In 1860 their firm had thirty-four workers and steam machinery. Keep had a $40,000 capital investment in the business. By 1860 there were 777 men and women working in the jewelry industry in Newark.[103]

Most of the jewelry produced in Newark was bought by firms in New York, Philadelphia and Boston, which in turn supplied jewelers throughout the United

99. Rainwater, *AJM*, p. 200.
100. *Newark Sentinel*, 25 Feb. 1851. Hirsch, p. 25.
101. Hirsch, pp. 26-32.
102. *Providence Directory* 1832, 1841-2; *Newark Directory* 1850-51.
103. Hirsch, pp. 25, 47-62. For information on individual firms see Rainwater, *AJM*, pp. 8-9 and throughout.

States, the West Indies and even abroad.[104] About one third of the Newark jewelry firms had showrooms in New York where they processed orders from abroad. If jewelry remained unsold and became out of fashion, it was melted down and sent to the U.S. Mint to be used for coinage.[105]

Newark continued to be noted for its production of good gold jewelry, as opposed to the cheaper products manufactured in Providence and Attleboro that were made of filled gold or plated metals. While many of the Newark firms specialized in making one or two kinds of jewelry, others made a diverse range of jewelry. Among the latter was Enos Richardson & Co., founded in 1841 under the name of Daggett, Richardson & Co. (Plate 202). Enos Richardson was born in Attleboro and served his apprenticeship in the jewelry trade in Philadelphia. In 1849, he became a co-partner of John B. Palmer, a jewelry manufacturer from Warren, Rhode Island. Their factory was in Newark and their mercantile business was at 23 Maiden Lane in New York. Palmer retired in 1865 and the firm continued as Enos Richardson & Co. into the twentieth century.[106]

Newark jewelers were somewhat slow to take advantage of registering designs at the United States Patent Office. Elihu Bliss was one of the first, patenting a finger ring that converted into a watch key in 1857.[107] The following year Charles W. Dickinson received a patent for an improved method of making loop chains for jewelry.[108] William Riker, whose firm was founded in 1846 as Riker, Tay & Searing, gained in stature throughout the century and received several patents. One was for an improved method of embossing designs on metal jewelry by means of a die-roll and a softer metal.[109]

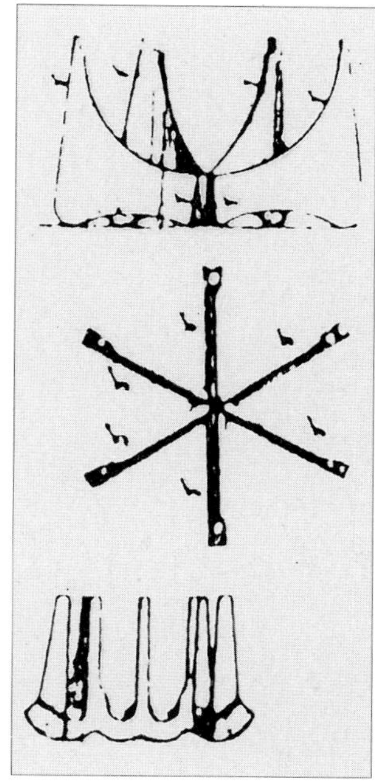

Plate 203. U.S. Patent 131,058, 3 September 1872. Ferdinand J. Herpers, Newark, N.J. Diamond setting.

A large portion of Newark patents pertained to bracelets, particularly to safeguarding their closures. Ball & Barnard equipped the bracelet with a spring blade secured by a cross bar.[110] William C. Edge, who had come from England in 1865, received several patents for making bracelets from chain fabric. One patent was for a machine used to manufacture the chain fabric and another for the method of applying the metal fabric on to a metallic band by turning the chain work down over the edges of the band.[111] Edge is reputed to have introduced the satin finish while working for Chattelier & Spence when he first arrived in New York. He also worked for Durand & Co. in Newark before starting his own business.[112]

Ferdinand J. Herpers specialized in manufacturing settings for stones. In 1872 he received a patent on a diamond setting that had the prongs radiating from a common centre (Plate 203).[113]

The firm established by George Krementz in 1866 continues today. In 1873, Krementz received patents concerning rings. One was for a die to make plain finger rings and the other was a die to enlarge and size rings.[114] Krementz (1837-1918) had served his apprenticeship with Alling, Hall & Dodd in Newark and worked for Smith & Ford in New York prior to establishing his own firm in Newark (see Colour Plate 241).[115]

Most famous among Newark jewelers' patents was the one invented by the Hyatts, I. Smith and John W., for making celluloid, the first plastic material used for jewelry. In 1874 they patented their formula and method of moulding it and immediately assigned the patent to The Celluloid Manufacturing Co. of Newark. The same year the Hyatts also patented what they called 'Factitious Ivory' and turned it over to the same company.[116] The invention of man-made materials for use in jewelry opened the door to a whole new concept of non-precious adornments.

104. *Newark Sentinel,* 25 Feb. 1851.
105. Ibid.
106. Bagnall.
107. #18,033.
108. #19,497.
109. #27,474. His other patents concerned ornamenting jewelry as well. #199,580; #202,588.
110. #107,325.
111. #125,940 and #133,146. Another patent was obtained in 1880, #228,746. Fourteen karat gold woven-wire fabric was still one of the major productions of the Edge Co. in the 1890s.
112. Rainwater, *AJM,* p. 81.
113. #131,058. Noted as a proficient piercer and die-cutter, Ferdinand Herpers and his sons concentrated on jewelers' findings. Herpers Brothers was established in 1865. The Newark Museum has a small collection of stone-set jewelry made by this firm about 1870-90 and given to the museum by Ferdinand J. Herpers. See also Rainwater, *AJM,* p. 121.
114. #140,423; #140,422.
115. Rainwater, *AJM,* pp. 146-7. Krementz became known in the 1880s for the one-piece gold collar button which he invented and patented in 1884.
116. #152,232 and #156,353.

Providence Jewelers

Building on the foundations established early in the nineteenth century in Providence by Nehemiah Dodge and others, the jewelry industry began to assume a major role in the city. With an estimated hundred workmen manufacturing jewelry there in 1810, the industry expanded during the mid-nineteenth century to almost 2,000 men and women working at that trade.[117]

For several decades Jabez Gorham produced jewelry such as gold beads, brooches, earrings and rings, before shifting his attention exclusively to the making of silverware. Gorham had served his apprenticeship with Nehemiah Dodge. In the 1820s he made filigree jewelry rivalling imported French filigree and he designed a gold chain that became known as Gorham or Gadroon chain. He also took his products on the road, travelling to Massachusetts, Connecticut, Vermont and New York. At first he met with little success, but eventually he prospered, establishing ties with jewelers in Boston and more rural areas that would serve him well in the years to come.[118]

In 1836 there were 143 jewelers, watchmakers, goldsmiths and refiners in Providence, excluding employees and allied craftsmen. In 1856 the annual product of Providence jewelry manufacturers had reached $2,771,600. The financial panic of 1857 caused employment in this volatile industry to plummet from nearly 1,500 employees to only 346. Fortunately the recovery was equally swift and in 1860 an all-time high of eighty-six jewelry manufacturing firms were located in Providence and there were over eight hundred jewelers listed as well.[119]

Among the supporting workers in 1860 were eighteen lapidaries and ten gold-plating firms. Isaac Burlingame, F.S. Eddy and Louis Leveck specialized in chasing jewelry. James Wood devoted himself to making tools for jewelers. John S. Sherman, who was a blacksmith by trade, offered his services in die-making, forging and tool repair work. Christopher Burr specialized in the engraving of precious metals. There were four specialists in enamelling. Thomas Quayle and Nathaniel Grant performed the processes of colouring gold jewelry. H. Griesrimer was a polisher of jewelry, while Thomas Taylor polished bloodstones. Others made jewelers' findings. Potter & Knight and George A. Sagendorph were manufacturers of lockets. In addition there were a large number of watchmakers, several optician/jewelers, refiners, assayers, comb makers, pattern makers, machinists, moulders and box makers. Aside from all these workers, there were hundreds of men who were silversmiths and produced vast quantities of silver and plated wares.[120]

Sackett, Davis & Co. was the largest jewelry firm in Providence in the mid-nineteenth century.[121] Adnah Sackett (1796-1860) was the founder of the firm, one of the first jewelry manufacturing firms in that city, and inventor of the machinery for making what was called Adelaide chain. The company had various partners, becoming Sackett, Davis & Co. in 1857 when Thomas Davis joined the firm. They prospered and continued until 1879. They also formed a branch in Philadelphia in 1874. A patent for an improvement in making chains from sheet metal was turned over to Sackett, Davis by its inventor James Lancelott.[122] Lauriston Towne, who was a partner of the firm about 1859 to 1861, also received a patent for making ornamental chain in 1864.[123]

John S. Palmer was another long-time manufacturer of jewelry in Providence. Born

117. Gere, *A.& E J.*, p. 45.
118. Carpenter, pp. 21-27. Proddow, p. 15, says Gorham was the first major manufacturer to wholesale gold and silver jewelry throughout America.
119. Boston *Transcript* quoting Providence *Journal*, 13 and 17 Jan. 1856; *Providence City Directories*, 1824, 1842, 1850, 1856, 1860.
120. *Providence City Directory*, 1860.
121. Rainwater, *AJM*, p. 207; *Providence Plantations* (1886).
122. #20,183. Lancelott of South Providence and Cranston, R.I. patented two other improvements for making ornamental chains in 1859: #23,303 and #25,837. See S. Bury, I, 366.
123. #44,899.

in 1824, he went to work for George and Smith Owen, local manufacturing jewelers, in 1840. Five years later Palmer joined forces with Christian C. Stave to form their own business. They made a general line of jewelry at first.[124] Palmer received patents pertaining to the construction of bracelets and the manufacture of jewelry.[125] An improvement in manufacturing plated metal finger rings came in 1870 and a machine for making the rolling stock for finger rings was patented by Palmer in 1872.[126] Palmer had taken his brother-in-law Charles S. Capron for his partner in 1852 and the firm of Palmer & Capron began to specialize in making gold rings (solid, rolled plate, and gold filled) as well as silver rings.[127] Capron took charge of the New York retail branch of the business.

Thomas H. Lowe came to Providence in 1848 from Birmingham, England, where he had trained and worked in the gold jewelry trade for twenty-one years. At the firm of Lutwich & Green in Birmingham he had learned the methods of making rolled plate and he brought these techniques with him to Providence. Very little had been done there in the way of gold plating before his arrival. Sayles Irons had developed a method of soldering a layer of gold to a layer of silver that was not very efficient or economical. The English method was to clamp a bar of gold on to a heavier bar of alloyed metal and then under high heat to sweat out the silver in the gold alloy while joining the two bars together with the help of borax. The bar was then rolled out to the required thickness. Lowe worked for G. & S. Owen at first, and then for two years with Munroe & Eddy before establishing his own business in 1850. One of his most active customers was Sackett, Davis.[128]

A number of Providence firms specialized in making watch and locket cases. Charles W. Field invented a machine for engraving ornament on these cases in 1857. In 1866 he was granted patents for the manufacture of watch rims and backs.[129] Henry A. Phillips also received a patent on his method of making rims for the same items in 1857. Daniel B. Waite got a patent on rims in 1861 as did Charles W. Clewley in 1862.[130] Designs for making lockets were patented by Charles G. Bloomer of Wickford, R.I. and Henry A. Church of Providence.[131] Potter & Knight were listed as locket manufacturers in the 1860 Providence Directory, as was George A. Sagendorph.

Bracelets were the speciality of Albert O. Baker. In 1872, Baker received a patent on a bracelet design and over the next few years was either the patentee or assignee of several other designs for bracelets. One group concerned various designs for forming different patterns of woven chain and were patented with two other Providence jewelers, Sanford W. Grant and James B. Black in 1874. The other group was assigned to Baker by Samuel S. Grant and involved chain fabric made of links of spiral-twisted metal wire for use in bracelets.[132] Other Providence manufacturers of bracelet patents were Joseph W. Grant, Charles H. Cook and Edward F. Presbrey.[133]

One of Presbrey's designs concerned japanned or enamelled bracelets, as did a patent of Charles A. Gamwell which was later assigned to the American Enamel Co. of Providence.[134] As enamelling became more widely used for decorating jewelry and as the techniques became improved, the number of enamellers working in the jewelry trade increased. Among the early enamelling firms were S.S. Wild & Son who began in 1864, James G. Whitehouse, R.F.J. Skuce, John H. Collingwood, John Marshall, Henry C. Spooner and James Taylor. Collingwood came from Birmingham and formed his company in Providence in 1861, making enamel as well as enamelled jewelry.[135]

124. Rainwater, *AJM,* p. 185. *Providence Directory* 1842, 1856, 1860.
125. #31,735 (1861); #72,224 (1867).
126. #110,587; #124,971.
127. Rainwater, *AJM,* p. 185.
128. Lowe's son Edwin continued the business after Thomas Lowe retired in 1883. Rainwater, *AJM,* p. 159. The firm continued until about 1915.
129. #17,416; #54,136-7.
130. #17,515; #32,159; 334,564.
131. #17,137 (1857); #151,843-4. The firm of Henry A. Church and G. M. Church had been established in 1826 by Peter Church and Whiting Metcalf. Rainwater, *AJM,* p. 62 and *Providence Directories.*
132. #133,291 (1872); #139,888 (1873); #139,361 (1873); #149,823-4-5 (1874).
133. #139,311 (1873); #156,858 (1874) and #159,214 (1875).
134. #150,754 (1874).
135. Rainwater, *AJM,* pp. 15, 66; *Providence Directory,* 1860.

Several Providence jewelers received patents for gem set jewelry. Isaac Lindsley had an inventive mind and an interest in mass-producing good jewelry. In 1857 he patented a setting for diamonds (Plate 204). In addition he patented a stone dressing machine and lamp.[136] Thomas J. Linton registered an improved method of mounting precious stones in 1859. In 1874 Robert B. Hubbard patented a setting for stones as did Thomas W. Fry in 1875.[137] In addition to making machines for stamping out parts for jewelry, Providence jewelers patented a jeweler's hand press and a jeweler's screw press.[138]

Attleboro Jewelers

Attleboro, a Massachusetts town settled in 1644, was situated on a branch of the Pawtucket River which provided water power for a manufacturing community. By 1837 jewelry was the fifth largest product here, following cotton goods, leather goods, metal buttons and combs.[139] Jewelry production was materially aided by the transmission of trade secrets for making filled and plated goods. Nehemiah Dodge of Providence claimed that 'the persons who first established themselves at Attleboro' purloined the secret from him under pretence of buying for country cousins'.[140]

J.F. Sturdy & Co. is credited with bringing the process of manufacturing rolled, gold plated stock for jewelry to Attleboro when the brothers J.F. and James H. Sturdy came from Providence in 1849. Experienced in the making of dies as well as jewelry, they developed a method of making rolled or stock plate. Furthermore, they shared their process with some of the other Attleboro jewelers. In 1861 they began producing rolled plate curb chains.[141] During the Civil War, they produced military badges of rolled plate as well as of gold and silver. Post-war factory workers increased from forty to eighty employees and sales increased to about $100,000 annually.

Draper, Tifft & Co., formed in 1821, was the first important jewelry firm in Attleboro. During the mid-nineteenth century, it became one of the largest in the country.[142] Their annual production in 1850 amounted to about $15,000 to $20,000 and they employed fifteen men and women.

One of the original members of Draper, Tifft & Co., Ira Richards, left the firm in 1834 and joined the company started by his son and a nephew under the name of Ira Richards & Co.[143] This company was the first to introduce steam power to Attleboro's jewelry manufacture in 1842.[144] Ira Richards & Co. produced a general line of rolled, plated jewelry. It became one of the largest companies in town in the mid-nineteenth century and employed between 200-250 workers. The company established a reputation for superior quality and variety of goods that was never surpassed by later Attleboro manufacturers. The town historian predicted in 1894 that 'so long as jewelry is connected with the name of Attleborough, so long will the fame' of this firm be remembered.[145]

Many of the firms in Attleboro began on a modest scale in small quarters. Some manufactured their jewelry in shops located in the Steam Power Company which was destroyed by fire in 1859 and immediately rebuilt. Others leased space in buildings owned by more successful firms. One was the building erected by Stephen Richardson in 1848. When it burned down in 1870, Richardson rebuilt the factory on the same site. Stephen Richardson had started his business in 1836 in partnership with Abiel Codding, employing only ten workers. By 1870 they were able to employ 135 workers in the manufacture of chains and novelties in gold and other metals. The

136. #18,288; #29,503 (1860); #124,837 (1872).
137. #26,371; #157,332; #165,722.
138. J. McWilliams, #143,023 (1873) and James E. Potter, #167,019.
139. John Hayward, *The New England Gazetteer* (Boston, 1839), n.p.
140. Quoted by Bagnall, p. 22.
141. John Daggett, *A Sketch of the History of Attleborough*, pp. 373, 378-9.
142. Ibid., pp. 368-9. The present account of the jewelry business in Attleboro relies heavily on the work of Daggett.
143. In 1836 Virgil Draper and George Morse joined the company and in 1841 they were replaced by Abiel Codding.
144. *A Sketch of Attleboro*, pamphlet in Genealogy File at Attleboro Public Library, no author given, no pagination.
145. Daggett, p. 371; Rainwater, *AJM*, p. 198, E. Ira Richards & Co.

firm established a rewarding trade with Europe and Cuba and, in the 1880s, were the only Attleboro company to ship their goods to Japan.[146]

It had been customary for Attleboro firms to exhibit their wares at the Western Hotel in New York, but by 1850 more and more companies were opening offices in the major cities. Draper, Tifft & Co. sold most of their production in New York and Philadelphia. Ira Richards & Co. opened branches in New York, Philadelphia and San Francisco.

Ornamental chain was one of the major items produced in Attleboro. It was in demand for jewelry, especially for holding watches and fobs or pendants and lockets. Chain fabric was also widely used for bracelets. B.S. Freeman & Co., established in 1847, specialized in vest chains and bracelets and was one of the first in Attleboro to produce rolled plated goods. One of the partners, Joseph J. Freeman, by studying a length of imported curb chain, was able to construct a machine that could turn out rolled plated curb chain. The first to be machine-manufactured in Attleboro, it became known as 'Freeman's curb chains'. A patent for manufacturing flat ornamental chain, obtained in 1872, was assigned by Joseph J. Freeman to Freeman & Co.[147] For the duration of the Civil War the firm converted production to military badges and buttons. At the height of their business, they employed sixty workers and had a New York office.

Henry F. Barrows & Co. was another local firm that specialized in making chains and was one of the first to make rolled plate. Nerney & Short, organized in 1862, concentrated on stock plated chains and producing electroplated metal.[148]

Several methods of making jewelry chains were patented by Egbert S. Richards in 1863, including one that incorporated an ornamental stone or glass inside the openwork of the metal link.[149] In 1865, Virgil Draper assigned his patented device for swaging chain links to Oscar M. Draper whose company had been established in 1862. Virgil Draper assigned three more patents for chain links to the same firm in 1871 and another in 1874.[150] Peter S. Bishop developed a machine for stamping chain links in 1866, and William F. Davis secured a patent on his machine for connecting links of ornamental chain in 1874.[151] W. & S. Blackinton manufactured plated chains exclusively. Established about 1866, the firm employed as many as 130 workers.

Bracelets were another speciality of Attleboro jewelers. Codding & Smith who started business together on the eve of the Civil War, produced mostly bracelets, along with a few small items such as charms and pins. Their firm grew from fifty to one hundred workers.[152] In 1870, David D. Codding received a patent for making bracelets formed of two pieces of wood. The same year his partner, Theron I. Smith, obtained a design patent for bracelets made of a raised central band with edge mouldings of contrasting colour. Smith obtained two more design patents for bracelets in 1871.[153]

Joseph M. Bates, who had learned the trade in Providence, and was a partner in the firm of Bates & Bacon started in 1857, made rolled gold plated bracelets. They employed up to two hundred workers in good years.[154]

The firm of Hayward & Briggs was organized in 1855. Charles E. Hayward, who had been apprenticed to Tifft & Whiting in Attleboro, managed the manufacturing of the jewelry, while Jonathan Briggs was in charge of their New York office. Their partnership lasted for thirty years and established a reputation for excellence. They employed about 125 workers and trained more than a generation of manufacturing jewelers. The gold used for their plated jewelry was always 18 karat gold.[155]

For many years, there were no assayers or refiners in Attleboro. There used to be a

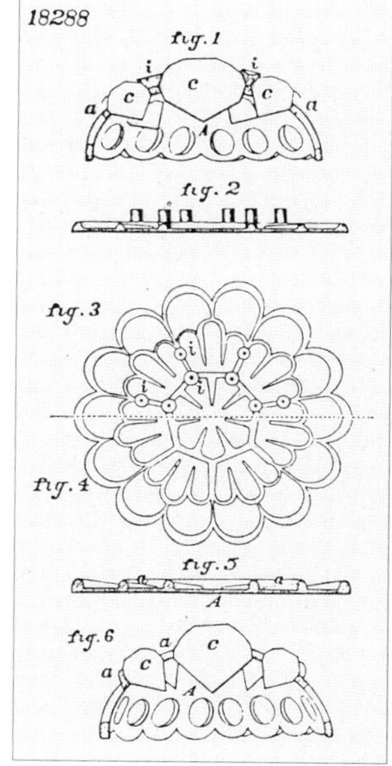

Plate 204. An improvement in pre-formed diamond settings was patented on 29 September 1857 by Isaac Lindsley of Providence, Rhode Island.

146. Daggett, p. 371.
147. #122,184. Daggett, p. 373.
148. In 1884, Peter Nerney patented the 'Nerney Patent Swivel' which proved a very popular item. The firm also made jewelry out of horn. Daggett, p. 379.
149. #38,842; design patent #1757 and #1761.
150. #50,200; design patents #4,723, #4,749, #4,857; #154,026.
151. #54,101; #151,362.
152. Daggett, p. 380.
153. #100,504; #4,546; #4,643; #4,644. Other patents for the manufacture of bracelets were issued to John Barclay, Abiel Codding, Jr., Isaac B. Staples, Moses H. Mason, Avery Fobes, John N. Thomson, Edward E. Barrows, Charles Wills and Charles Hayward.
154. In 1882, they were the first to manufacture watchcases in Attleboro. The cases were either 14 karat gold or filled gold. About 150 cases were produced in a day. Daggett, pp. 380, 377.
155. Daggett, pp. 372-3; Rainwater, *AJM*, pp. 116-7.

Frenchman who would stop in North Attleboro, calling at each shop to collect the shop sweepings, on his way to the assayers in Boston or New York. However, in 1854, George K. Davis & Co. established a refining and assaying business in Attleboro, to which they added smelting. By the 1880s they were processing about $60,000 worth of gold every year.[156]

In 1865, a company devoted to lapidary work was formed by the brothers James W. and John W. Luther. They cut and polished gemstones and also made imitation stones especially for the jewelry trade. They were considered to be very skilled at their work. They employed twenty workers in good times and their payroll amounted to about $500 monthly.[157] A patent for a mass-produced setting that would imitate cluster-set jewelry was obtained in 1868 by William O. Draper, Albert C. Sweetland & George Draper. Another patent was obtained for setting gems in 1875 by Herbert G. Mackinney who moved his business to Providence the following year. Robinson & Co. was noted for scarf pins, studs, and drops set with foiled stones.[158]

Because Attleboro was a town, and not a city like Providence or Newark, its production of jewelry was on a more limited scale. On the other hand, there was no other town in the country that produced more jewelry. It has been estimated that in 1879 there were at least fifty-three firms in Attleboro employing 2,081 workers with a monthly payroll of $101,461, roughly $48.75 a month per worker. The value of the monthly production shipped out of Attleboro was nearly $400,000.[159] The Attleboro Directory of 1879-80 included listings for seventy-five jewelry manufacturing companies. There were five firms that together employed 525 workers, the largest number of employees for any one shop being 125. Women worked in the offices, attached jewelry to cards and packed it for shipment. Some made chains in their homes.

While a few firms were known for high quality jewelry of 14-karat gold or even plated with 18-karat gold, Attleboro became known for its cheap, but appealing, plated jewelry. Some firms such as Sadler Bros. and White & Shaw made brass jewelry as well as ladies' hat and dress ornaments.[160] However, most of the Attleboro jewelers were producing a middling line of rolled, filled or plated jewelry of the sort we would call costume jewelry today. White & Shaw was one of the first to capitalize on the market for inexpensive jewelry and later specialized in jewelers' findings.[161] Their product was ideally suited to a town where labour and overheads were cheap and the cost of the jewelry could also be kept down by the use of base metals.

South and West

Cities and towns throughout the southern and western parts of the United States were supplied with both jewelers and jewelry by the centres of the trade in the north-east. For example, Philadelphia jeweler Felix Thibault moved to the District of Columbia about 1827, bringing with him $20,000 worth of fashionable jewelry and two full sets of silver. As the District grew in stature, it attracted artisans from nearby Alexandria, Virginia. James Galt was a watchmaker in Alexandria who moved to Washington about 1802. By the time of his death in 1847, his sons M.W. and William inherited a thriving business selling watches, jewelry and silverware. M.W. Galt & Brother enjoyed the prestige of patronage by Presidents, including both Abraham Lincoln and Jefferson Davis. When Mrs. Lincoln wore a seed pearl parure from Tiffany's to her husband's inauguration in 1861 (see Plate 140), Galt was soon able to sell a creditable copy to his customers.

156. Daggett, pp. 375-6.
157. Ibid., p. 380.
158. United States Patent Office #75,393 and ibid., p. 372.
159. There were several firms that did not provide statistics and this was estimated to add another 372 workers with a payroll of $19,750 and goods valued at $83,000. Daggett, pp. 396-7.
160. Daggett pp. 374-5, 383; Rainwater, *AJM,* p. 208.
161. Daggett, pp. 374-5.

Edward A. Tyler of Boston, who had been apprenticed in the watch and jewelry trade there, moved to New Orleans in 1838 where he established a very successful business in making and selling jewelry (Colour Plate 166). His exhibit at the Louisiana State Fair in 1866 won him 'a gold medal and a diploma for his chaste and elegant designs of home-made jewelry, manufactured in his own establishment', according to *The Daily Picayune*. The newspaper also noted that 'Mr. Tyler has an enviable reputation in our city, and throughout the Southwest, for manufacturing and selling nothing but the best'.[162] Tyler was credited with elevating public taste with his beautiful cameos 'of exquisite shades and richly set, but more artistically and delicately carved than anything we have seen'.[163]

More typical in the south was the firm of Hyde & Goodrich, established in New Orleans in 1824 as a branch of James N. Hyde & Co. of New York. Charles W. Goodrich came from New York too. As Hyde & Goodrich, they advertised in 1857 as the 'largest importers of jewelry, watches, plated ware, guns and pistols, and the only manufacturers of gold and silver wares in the south-west'.[164] The firm was dissolved soon after the bombardment of Fort Sumter in 1861. By the end of the war, the firm had emerged as A.B. Griswold & Co. No longer manufacturers of their wares, they advertised in 1873 as 'Importers of and Dealers in Watches, Diamonds and Fine Jewelry'. In addition, they were southern agents for Gorham silver and Howard watches, 'The Best American watch made'.[165]

Charleston, South Carolina, which had been so supportive of its jewelers in the past, fell prey to the ravages of war, economic disasters and fire in the mid-nineteenth century. For the most part, the jewelry firms imported the bulk of their goods from northern manufactories or from England. The firm of Hayden, Gregg & Co. became quite successful this way during the 1830s and '40s. At one point they enjoyed the services of J.W. Suley who had the reputation of being 'at the head of his profession as an ornamental worker of the precious metals'. George E. Atwell advertised in 1830 that he made all kinds of jewelry, but four years later was touting recently received shipments of American made jewelry as well as French and English jewelry.[166]

Jewelers, metalworkers and watchmakers joined in the rush of settlers coming to Chicago in the mid-century. Incorporated as a city in 1860, Chicago had attracted fifty-four workers in these trades that year. Most of them came from New England, but some came from abroad. Frederick Juergens (1796-1871) and his son Paul (1834-1909), and Sebastian Andersen from Germany were among the latter. Elijah Peacock (1818-1889) and his brother Joseph came from England where several generations of their family had been engaged in the jewelry business. Isaac Speer (1809-1879), who came from New Jersey, was one of the first to manufacture his own jewelry and silverware, and was apparently the first to mechanize these crafts in Chicago. He made insignia for fraternal organizations such as the Masons and Odd Fellows. Most of the jewelers were supplied by manufacturers in the east. By the 1850s Gorham was selling their silverware through the best jewelry stores in Chicago.

Matson & Hoes advertised in 1864 that they manufactured rich jewelry and silverware, and by that time had become the leading producers of these goods in the city. More and more people working at these trades were foreign immigrants, some of whom were already skilled artisans. After the Great Fire of 1871, large-scale production of jewelry and watches developed to meet the demands of the rapidly increasing settlers of the West who were connected to Chicago by the expanding railroads.[167]

162. 9 Dec. 1866, courtesy of the Historic New Orleans Collection.
163. *Daily Picayune*, 6 Nov. 1870.
164. H. Parrott Bacot, Carey T. and Charles L. Mackie., *Crescent City Silver*, pp. 4, 5.
165. Ibid., pp. 56-57.
166. Burton, pp. 70-71, 85-86 and 17-18.
167. Sharon S. Darling, *Chicago Metalsmiths*, pp. 10-16.

Among the most important products were watches and watchcases. The National Watch Co. of Chicago, established in 1864 by Benjamin Raymond, employed men who had worked for the well-known Waltham Watch Co. In 1866 Raymond's company built a factory in Elgin, not far from Chicago, where they were equipped to produce watches on an assembly line, utilizing interchangeable parts. This became the Elgin National Watch Co. in 1874. It gained a reputation for accuracy and Elgin watches became essential to railroad conductors, station agents and other employees requiring punctuality. At first, Elgin made only the movements and their cases were supplied by local jewelers. Fred Blauer was one of the first case makers in the city. C.H. Collins made watches and jewelry of oreide, an alloy of copper and zinc, which looked like gold. To distinguish it from his imitators' products, he called it Collins Metal. He offered rings, lockets, bracelets, earrings and pins of this metal in the latest style.[168] Soon a number of watchcase manufacturers made Chicago the centre of this industry in the West. Among the most successful producers were the Illinois Springfield Watch Co. (1869), the Rock Island Watch Co. (1871) and the Aurora Watch Co. (1883).[169]

Giles Bros. & Co., established in 1861, advertised themselves as agents for the Elgin and United States watches, and sold Jurgensen watches imported from Switzerland as well. They began manufacturing their own jewelry and in 1868 carried a 'splendid stock of DIAMONDS, BYZANTINE AND CORAL JEWELRY'.[170] Giles became one of the largest manufacturers of jewelry for wholesale and retail outside the east coast. They had outlets in Europe and conducted wholesale business in Canada and by 1882 in Hawaii. Their factory was equipped with a diamond-cutting machine and the firm gained the title of 'the Tiffany of the West'.[171]

Juergens & Andersen also became wholesale manufacturers after the Great Fire. While they too made gold and silver watches, they did a brisk business in precious stones and good jewelry.

To the production of jewelry in the east and the west was added the output of California jewelers as a result of the Gold Rush in 1848 (see pages 262-266). It becomes evident that the American jewelry industry had expanded dramatically in the mid-nineteenth century. In 1870 there were estimated to be 681 jewelry manufactories employing more than 10,000 workers of whom 1,500 were women. The total annual wages paid to the workers was about $4,500,000 and their yearly production amounted to $22,104,000.[172] By comparison, the city of Paris, the leading centre of jewelry production, alone supported 900 manufacturers with an annual production of about $12,000,000 in 1876.[173] In Birmingham, English manufactories employed 7,500 workers in 1866 and 14,000 in 1886.[174]

American manufacturers had a distinct advantage in having access to seemingly unlimited supplies of gold and silver discovered during this period in the western part of the country. The development of steam power, drop presses and other aids to mechanization allowed American production to become competitive with the traditional suppliers in England and France. In fact, by 1875 America was able to challenge Birmingham in the production of inexpensive mass-produced jewelry, exporting to England and other countries ever increasing quantities of jewelry. This in turn caused Birmingham to increase its own mechanization of the jewelry industry. [175]

Nevertheless in the area of fine, carefully crafted jewelry, England and France still held pre-eminence. Only Tiffany and a few other superior firms could satisfy the pretensions of wealthy Americans.

168. *Chicago Tribune,* 17 Dec. 1868.
169. S. Darling, pp. 18-19. *Wholesale Jeweler* 1889, p. 55.
170. *Chicago Tribune,* 17 Dec. 1868.
171. S. Darling, p. 22.
172. Benson L. Lossing, *The American centenary: a history of the progress of the republic of the United States,* p. 263.
173. Bagnall, p. 8.
174. Gere, *A.& E.J.,* p. 45.
175. Ibid., p. 45.

PART IV

LATE 19TH CENTURY 1875-1900

Introduction 1875-1900

With a backward look and high hope for the future, the United States began the last quarter of the nineteenth century in a mammoth celebration of the nation's centennial. The documentation and relics of past glories were put on display for latter generations to honour. Styles of the revolutionary period were revived. Through the exhibitions at the international exposition in Philadelphia in 1876, Americans sought to summarize the state of their arts and industries, in comparison with other nations, and to ascertain the direction of their future. While the centennial exhibition spawned a colonial revival, it also provided a remarkable showcase for industrial, agricultural and artistic achievements. 'The culture obtained by the millions of our people who have found in the fair a mine of information and suggestion, must have a beneficial effect upon the national character', said James D. McCabe, expressing the hopes of many in his *History of the Centennial Exhibition*.

The exhibits interested Americans in the products of their own artisans as well as the exotic goods shown by other countries. Nearly ten million visitors saw 30,864 exhibits sponsored by fifty different countries. A wealth of new ideas, rarely if ever encountered before in America, stimulated the imagination. Interest in the exotic was stirred by colourful presentations of Japanese, Chinese, Egyptian, Russian, Turkish and South American decorative arts, in a Disney Epcot Center milieu. These foreign designs served as inspiration to American artists and manufacturers who would spend the rest of the century, it seemed, reinterpreting every style that had ever been devised.

For the first time, millions of Americans were transported from their own little part of the world to a cosmopolitan vantage point. They were confronted by ingenious inventions and the latest improvements in each of their various occupations. Many of the visitors returned home with a determination to better their production and their country. They were eager to compete with the world.

The fair also stimulated a widespread desire to travel to foreign countries and to patronize foreign markets. The representative of Boucheron, the distinguished Parisian jewelry firm, noted that some wealthy Americans were holding back on their purchases from him at the Philadelphia fair, preferring to go to the Paris Exposition two years later. They reasoned that what they saved in duties by buying in France could pay for their trip abroad.[1] Boucheron received a medal in Philadelphia as well as favourable publicity. In the future, Americans abroad would remember the firm's participation in their centennial celebration and would make a visit to his shop in Paris a necessity during their European tours.

Travel was becoming ever easier at home and abroad. Steamship lines connected continents with regularly scheduled vessels. Railroads were expanding and consolidating. Communication systems were vastly improved with the development of the telegraph, telephone and more reliable mail service. The automobile was in its infancy and, by the end of the century, the aeroplane had been born.

From 1878 to 1893, with only occasional economic dips, the United States enjoyed an ever increasing abundance of productivity and wealth. More gold was found in Black Hills, South Dakota, in 1875 and in Coeur d'Alene, Idaho, in 1883. Silver was discovered in the Bunker Hill and Sullivan mines in Idaho in 1885. Spurred on by

1. Gilles Néret, *Boucheron Four Generations of a World-Renowned Jeweler*, pp. 42-4.

mineralogists and treasure hunters, diggers found precious stones, most notably in North Carolina, Maine and Montana.

In 1889, in celebration of the 100th anniversary of the federally constituted United States and the inauguration of the first President of the United States, the nation had another celebration. 'The ball of the century' was held in New York at the Metropolitan Opera House on 29 April under the creative direction of Ward McAllister. Gridlocked carriages delayed the arrival of more than 6,000 guests including President and Mrs. Harrison. Four rooms of the Opera House were set aside for the display of over two hundred portraits and hundreds of associated objects from the period of Washington's inauguration. In addition to the Washington March and the scheduled quadrilles, news reports made it clear, the lavish gowns and the richness of the jewels were the evening's main attraction.

During the month of April, Tiffany & Co. had been displaying the collection of native American minerals and precious stones that was soon to be sent to Paris for the international exposition in France. The collection, part of it on loan from private owners, had been amassed by Tiffany's gemmologist, George F. Kunz. The variety and beauty of the gems assembled from all over the United States was breathtaking. 'It will be a satisfaction', said one viewer, 'to have something besides bed quilts and photographs to represent the standard of high art' in this country, since 'at all previous Expositions, both in London and Paris, this continent has been very imperfectly represented'.[2] The exhibit included a stunning array of jewels. Pride was taken in the fact that many of the materials and designs were of American origin, but also that all of the work had been done by Tiffany's in house.[3] When the collection appeared at the Exposition, it received universal acclaim and Tiffany & Co. received gold medals for jewelry, the collection of gems and the Grand Prize for silverware.

Extravagances spread quickly after such public adulation. Diamond jewelry became almost commonplace. The most costly gifts imaginable were given with abandon to brides and bridal parties. Furthermore, jewelry of all sorts was mass-produced in prodigious quantity for all those who could earn a decent living. The democratization of diamond jewelry was exemplified by the purchases of the sybaritic, self-made millionaire called Diamond Jim Brady. Not only did he have complete sets of men's jewelry made of diamonds, emeralds, rubies, sapphires or pearls, but he showered his many friends and business associates with literally thousands of jewels.[4]

Novelty jewelry expanded on all levels, with rapid-fire innovations compelling one and all to continue to buy the latest in fashionable baubles. Designs were purloined from archaeological digs, the Renaissance, and Egyptian, Mogul and Japanese sources, to name only a few. Silver jewelry came into its own at last as the mining of the metal increased and the burgeoning jewelry industry perfected its machinery and technology. New materials, including plastic, rubber and imitation gems, were introduced to factory production. Regional tastes added to the richness of American jewelry design.

In the 1890s, some restraint returned to the scene. Significant financial failures and uncertainty over the gold standard impressed upon sensible people the reality of bursting bubbles. People began to appreciate that the most expensive jewels were not necessarily the most beautiful. Fewer jewels were worn and designs became more refined. Disenchantment with the industrial revolution's separation of the processes of creation had been building for several decades. Now it gave rise to two new artistic styles. Art Nouveau and the Arts and Crafts movement, while manifested in different

2. NY *Sun*, 17 Mar. 1889.
3. *Sun*, 4–17 Mar. 1889.
4. Parker Morell, *Diamond Jim*.

ways, shared the belief that hand work was better than machine work and that inexpensive materials found in nature were among the most beautiful.

The Tiffany display at the Paris Exposition in 1900 returned to the chauvinistic theme struck in 1889. 'It is intentionally and distinctive American', commented one observer. 'The whole continent seems to have been explored to obtain the materials, while every race indigenous to the soil has been made to offer tribute in the form of models or decoration schemes'.[5]

With the advent of Art Nouveau and Arts and Crafts, American jewelers were urged to return to the workshop of earlier centuries in which the process of creation was carried out under the direction of one person, albeit with the assistance of shop workers. They were urged to move on from the traditional designs that had been worked and reworked, to initiate new styles of their own. Their greatest contributions were yet to come.

The Centennial Exhibition

The last quarter of the nineteenth century was ushered in with a mighty celebration of the nation's birthday. The Centennial Exhibition was designed to display the progress of the United States in arts, industry, science and commerce in comparison with the achievements of the rest of the world. Philadelphia, the birthplace of the nation, was chosen as the logical location. The rapid growth of the railroads made possible the transportation of visitors from all parts of the country. Steady rain for several days before the opening of the Exhibition mercifully gave way to clearing skies. On 10 May 1876, the United States Centennial Exhibition was officially opened. Richard Wagner composed the *Centennial Inauguration March,* John Greenleaf Whittier wrote the *Centennial Hymn* sung by a thousand voices assisted by the orchestra and the great organ. Sidney Lanier wrote the *Centennial Cantata,* and the President of the United States and the Emperor of Brazil finally turned the wheels of the giant Corliss Engine, thereby setting the Great Exhibition in motion.

Located above the Schuylkill River in Fairmount Park were 249 buildings supporting and containing the exhibitions of countless countries. The largest building in the world, the Main Building, held the exhibits of American manufacturers. In the middle of the building, visitors looking for jewelry first encountered the display of Bailey & Co., Philadelphia's premier firm, in a pavilion with 'a large and beautiful collection of jewelry and precious stones'.[6] Nearby, a crescent-shaped Moorish pavilion, thought by many to be the most beautiful structure at the fair, contained the richest and dearest displays of Tiffany, Starr & Marcus, Gorham, and J.E. Caldwell.

The cameos of Starr & Marcus caused quite a stir. There were examples of '"modern school engraving" which are fully equal, and in some respects superior to the best efforts of the ancients', in the opinion of the special correspondent to one of the newspapers.[7] There was a head of Minerva cut by Rega of Naples, a carcanet of the thirteen Caesars with Mars and Venus in the centre, and a cameo head of Narcisse cut by Pistrucci. The portraits of Longfellow and Bryant were outstanding. 'Both are remarkably true to nature, the treatment of the hair and beard in the Longfellow cameo being particularly worthy of high praise', a critic reported.[8] Among the outstanding gem specimens were a diamond, a ruby and a sapphire, all of fine quality. Starr & Marcus also exhibited diamond and pearl jewelry, as well as coral brooches of note.[9]

The diamond jewelry exhibited by Tiffany was stunning. A large peacock feather

5. Harriet Edwards, 'The Goldsmith's Art at Paris' in *The Home Journal 55,* No. 29 (20 Sept. 1900), pp. 6–7.
6. McCabe, p. 367.
7. 13 June 1876, unidentified clipping, TA.
8. Ibid.
9. Proddow, p. 21.

studded with more than six hundred diamonds was set with a thirty-carat straw coloured diamond formerly in the collection of Charles, Duke of Brunswick (Plate 205). The diamonds encircling the eye were set in yellow gold and the next ring of diamonds was set in red gold, giving a very interesting effect to the colours reflected by the diamonds. The aigrette was constructed in sections that were joined in places with little springs, permitting the feather to quiver, a feature of the finest eighteenth century diamond jewelry. At the same time, the aigrette incorporated advanced techniques, such as the use of platinum rather than silver in some of the delicate areas of the design. The gold framework of the aigrette supported open-back settings so that light could penetrate from many angles.

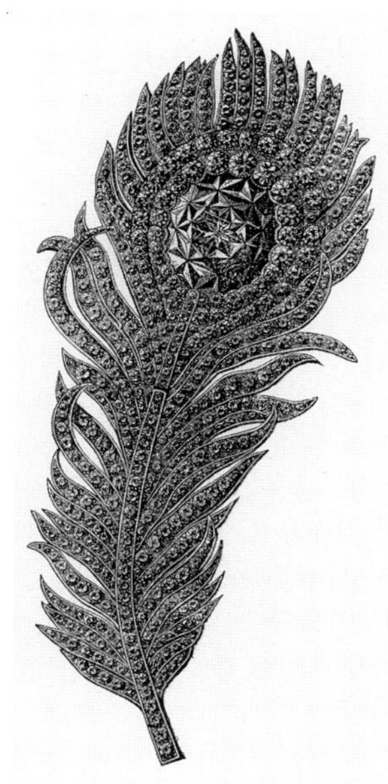

Plate 205. Illustration of the Brunswick diamond peacock feather brooch made for the Centennial Exhibition in Philadelphia in 1876 by Tiffany & Co., which appeared in James D. McCabe, The Illustrated History of the Centennial Exhibition *(Philadelphia 1876), p. 367. There were more than six hundred diamonds in addition to the large pale yellow diamond in the eye of the feather which had once been owned by the Duke of Brunswick.*

Valued at $15,000, the Brunswick feather pin was not the only significant piece of jewelry in Tiffany's display, the total of which was estimated to be $300,000. A necklace made of thirteen matched pairs of old East India diamonds had an enormous diamond in the middle. There was a pair of diamond earrings with a matching bracelet and a pair of solitaire diamond earrings.

'One of the most remarkable specimens of diamond setting in existence', one reporter said, was 'a perfect imitation of a full-blown rose, every leaf is detached and encrusted – I can use no other word – with small white diamonds of the very purest water. One large and peculiarly brilliant stone forms the centre and, as the light strikes it, it flashes out sparks of fire which are caught up and reflected back a thousand times by hundreds of gems around it, until the whole jewel looks more like some fairy thing than the result of a man's handiwork. The rose was made by an American workman in the Tiffany factory.[10]

A diamond brooch was made in the shape of three leaves on which were pearls of three different hues: white, pink and black. Pearls of the finest quality competed with the diamond jewelry. There was a four strand necklace of Oriental pearls and a set composed of a pearl necklace, brooch and earrings. Four perfectly shaped pear-shaped pearls were suspended from the two earrings. Colour was added to the Tiffany display by opals firing red and green flashes over the surface of pendants. Cat's eyes shimmered in a brooch and earrings, and rubies and sapphires shot thunderbolts of bold colours at the viewer. More easily obtained jewelry was displayed in a neighbouring case, notably conch shell jewelry, a fashion recently imported from Paris.

Among the 150 firms exhibiting in the category of jewelry, watches, silverware and bronzes, twenty-six were American. Tiffany took the honours for jewelry, jewelled watches and silver work. Robbins & Appleton of New York received a medal for their gold and silver watchcases. The Celluloid Manufacturing Co. was similarly recognized for its jewelry. J.H. Adams & Co. of Providence was honoured for its shell jewelry and combs, as were O.S. Spaulding of Mansfield, Massachusetts, and Milo Hildreth of Northborough, Massachusetts, for their tortoiseshell goods. Hamilton & Hunt and W.K. Potter of Providence won medals for rolled plate vest chains. The American Watch Co. of Waltham, Massachusetts, was honoured for their watches, their watchmaking machinery and their system of watchmaking. The Dennison Co. of Boston wrapped it all up by receiving notice for their production of jeweler's boxes, tags, labels and seals.

While Americans were pleased that their jewelry displays were superior to those of other nations, their pride was tempered by the fact that the foreign firms had been reluctant to subject their best work to the real dangers in shipment and so endured

10. Unidentified clipping dated 13 June 1876, TA.

Plate 206. Parure made of a variety of Brazilian beetle casings collected by Secretary of the Navy Robeson and set in a necklace, a pair of earrings, a pair of brooches and two pins, and displayed at the Philadelphia Centennial exhibition in 1876. Made by Ernest Kretzmar of Philadelphia. Length 19½in. (necklace). Smithsonian Institution.

Fig. 1.

B

A A

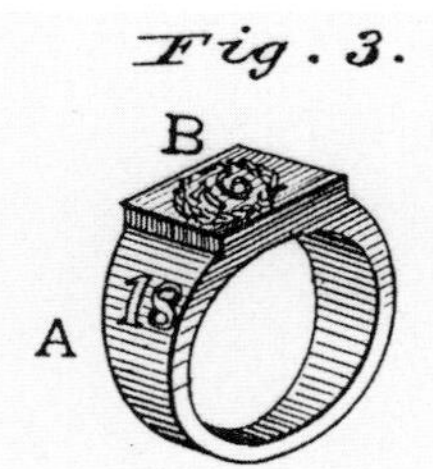

Plate 207. Patented ring designs of A.R. Lender of Washington in 1875. United States Patent Office, Design No. 8577.

the embarassment of their relatively poor showing. Some Americans felt that the foreign firms might have tried harder had they known how serious the competition would be. The hope that America's best would be compared firsthand with the finest jewelry of other nations was thereby thwarted.

The French display attracted attention because of its imitation jewelry, some made of diamond and ruby pastes, an area in which that nation had long excelled. They had a collection of paste reproductions of the world's greatest diamonds. Also noted was the gold jewelry set with the heads of humming birds or with Brazilian beetles. Among the most prestigious French jewelers, only Boucheron sent a small group of high quality jewelry. They displayed a beautiful diamond necklace worth $40,000 and a ruby and diamond coronet of equal value.[11]

Italy sent the most costly display which included a case of jewels provided by Bellezza, jeweler to King Victor Emmanuel. Fine cameos came from Francatti & Santamaria and Pio Siotto of Rome; mosaic jewelry from Florence; filigree and gold from Salvo & Sons of Genoa; and beautiful corals from Olivieri of Venice.[12]

Germany sent mostly imitation jewelry and genuine articles of the sort one

Colour Plate 167. American flag brooch. Made of 147 rubies, 135 sapphires and 307 diamonds mounted in gold and platinum. There are thirteen diamond-studded stars representing the original states. The flagstaff is ornamented with two diamond tassels. Tiffany & Co. stamped on plaque applied to back. Length 3¼in., width 3¼in. Tiffany & Co. Permanent Collection.

observer said 'no second-class jeweler in New York, London or Paris, would give…a place in his showcase'. While the German jewelry was considered ponderous and less graceful than that of the United States, Italy and France, there was still considerable interest in the exceptional cameo sets from Hanau and Pforzheim. Also noted were the painted and enamelled lockets, and the abundance of rich violet amethysts from this area.[13] The Austrian-Hungarian display featured beautiful garnets from Prague, mother-of-pearl jewelry from Vienna, and opals, one of which weighed 202 carats and was thought to be the world's largest.[14]

Representing the local jewelry of Great Britain were the displays of Whitby jet, Scottish pebble jewelry from James Aitchison of Edinburgh, and the well-cut Irish bog-oak jewelry from William Gibson of Belfast.[15] Norway sent remarkable filigree jewelry from Christiana, and Sweden exhibited filigree jewelry as well.[16] Russia sent jewelry made of lapis lazuli and malachite.[17] From South America came feather flowers and garlands made from the plumage of Brazilian birds and brooches made of bugs and beetles (Plate 206).[18] The Japanese exhibited rock crystal jewelry and the Chinese Cantonese carved ivory jewelry as well as jade, tortoiseshell and cameos.[19]

Inexpensive souvenir jewelry was made especially for the Centennial. In anticipation of the demand of the moment, jewelers began designing mementos for the Philadelphia Exhibition in 1875. A.R. Lender of Washington, D.C., created a wide banded finger ring with the number 17 on one side and 18 on the other (Plate 207). On top the bezel bore the figures 76 within a laurel wreath.[20] Another ring designed by A.V. Moore had four stars on each side, 1776 on one shoulder and 1876 on the other (Plate 208). The bezel could have been set with a faceted stone or with 1776 set off from 1876 by two stars embossed on each side with a thirteenth star in the centre.[21]

Several kinds of jewelry were set with photographic representations of buildings at the Centennial Exhibition. Simon Pfaelzer's breastpin could be set with views of the Main

11. Ingram, pp. 460-1.
12. McCabe, p. 419.
13. Ingram, pp. 433-4.
14. McCabe, p. 418; Ingram, p. 518.
15. McCabe, p. 389.
16. Ingram, p. 529; McCabe, p. 432.
17. Ingram, p. 474.
18. Ibid., p. 501.
19. Ibid., pp. 563, 573, and 585.
20. Design Pat. #8577 (1875).
21. Design Pat. #9,436 (1876).

Plate 208. Patented ring design of A.V. Moore in 1876. United States Patent Office, Design No. 9436.

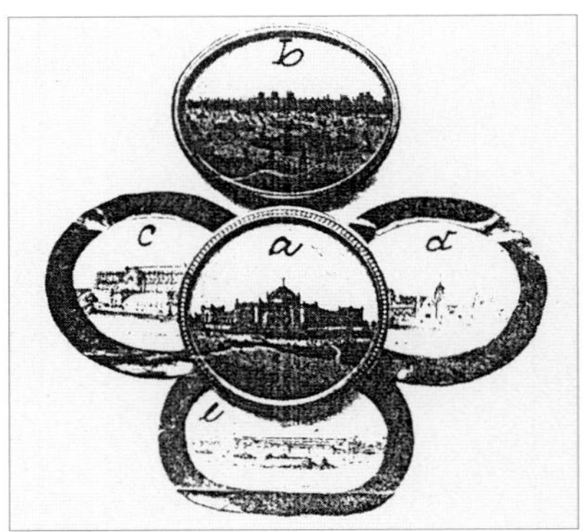

Plate 209. Above. Breast pin designs by S. Pfaelzer of Philadelphia, 28 December 1875. United States Patent Office, Design No. 8878.

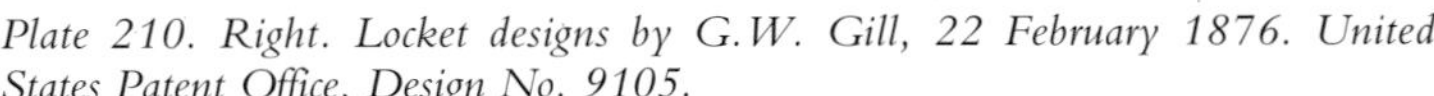

Plate 210. Right. Locket designs by G.W. Gill, 22 February 1876. United States Patent Office, Design No. 9105.

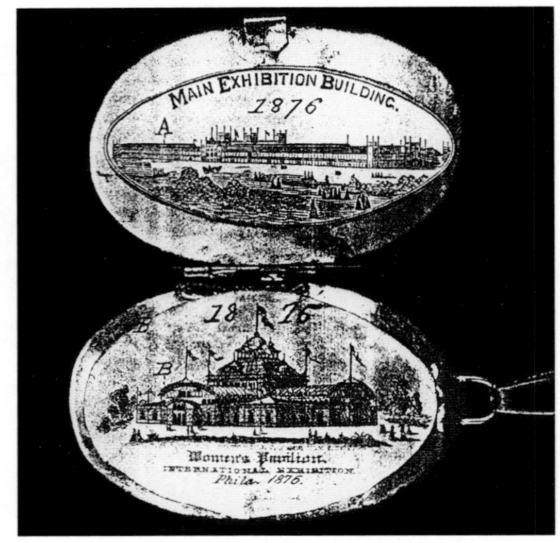

Building, Horticulture Hall, Agriculture Hall, Machinery Hall or Memorial Hall (Plate 209).[22] George W. Gill designed a locket set with views of the Main Building or the Women's Pavilion (Plate 210).[23] The Liberty Bell was featured in several designs. A jewelry pendant was made with a three-dimensional bell suspended inside a thirteen-pointed flat, cut-out star (Plate 211).[24] Earrings were made with the Liberty Bell suspended from a wreath of thirteen stars.[25] In both cases the bell bore its distinctive crack.

The exhibition designs included slightly better sorts of costume jewelry. During the centennial year, earrings dangling little silver bells became the latest fashion.[26] 'Miniature Copies of the Old Liberty Bell' were offered by Bigelow, Kennard in Boston, in the form of brooches, earrings and charms.[27]

The displays of jewelry at the Centennial celebration, ranging from the most extravagant bejewelled ornament to the tackiest geegaw, provided a panoramic view of the kinds of designs available in the United States at the beginning of the last quarter of the nineteenth century. There were grumblings that some of the finest work was done by foreign artists employed in America, but the truth was that America had completed its apprenticeship in shops and manufactories and was now ready to take a place among the master jewelers of the world.

Colonial Revival

The Centennial prompted nostalgic appreciation of the relics of the past. At last the country had accumulated a history. Out of the attics came the family links to important people and events surrounding the birth of the nation. If the competition to find connections to George Washington had been keen during his lifetime, it was insignificant compared with the devious and often fraudulent claims that were made during the Centennial years.

Salem, Massachusetts, took the lead in displaying relics of the past by staging its own Centennial Exhibition at the end of 1875. Among the diverse items on display in Plummer Hall was 'the last piece of jewelry worn by Louis XVI'. The history stated that the king had given it to his jailer to buy files, but he had been executed before he was able to use the files to escape.[28] The Salem exhibit was the first significant display ever staged of antique jewelry owned in America. Among the oldest items were a pair of early eighteenth-century diamond earrings, a seventeenth-century emerald pin and a diamond ring.[29] There were more than fifty examples of jewelry ranging from mourning rings and shoe buckles to a George Washington pin and a gold ring containing a likeness of Louis XVIII.

22. Design Pat. #8,878 (1875).
23. Design Pat. #9,105 and #8,937 (1876).
24. Philip C. Masi, Design Pat. #9,244 (1876).
25. J.I. Knight, Design Pat. 9,342 (1876).
26. Boston *S.E. Gazette*, 26 Mar. 1876.
27. Boston *Transcript*, 23 Jan. 1876.
28. *Catalogue of Antique Articles on Exhibition at Plummer Hall* (now PEM), #666, p. 3.
29. Ibid., #404, 401, 402, p. 13.

In addition to exhibitions and Centennial Balls, masquerades and Martha Washington tea parties sprang up everywhere. Old clothes lovingly preserved with lavender for four or five generations were unpacked, refurbished and proudly worn with ancestral jewels on the least provocation. Just as many of the colonial dresses were remade or refitted to be worn at the Centennial Balls, so family jewelry was remade at this time (see Colour Plate 55). 'At the Lady Washington tea-parties given in fashionable society, our belles delight to appear in the dress and jewels worn by their grandmothers at the receptions of Washington and Lafayette', wrote H. Hudson Holly.[30]

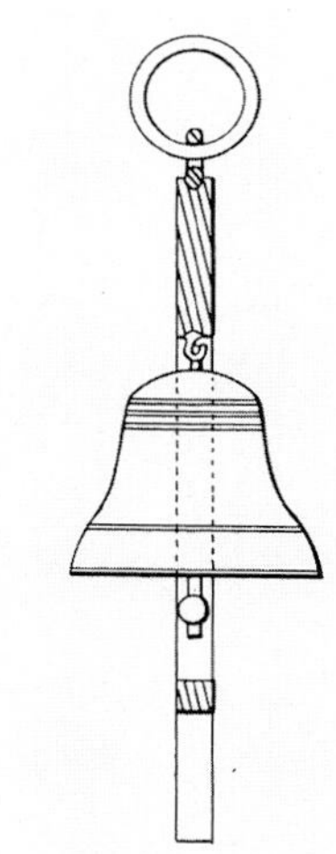

Plate 211. Designs for Liberty Bell jewelry pendants, by Philip C. Masi, 25 April 1876. United States Patent Office, Design No. 9244.

As early as 1868, American newspapers had carried reports of the French revival of eighteenth century fashions. 'Ornaments in the Louis XVI style are all the rage', one columnist wrote, 'Brooches in the form of bows, and enamelled lockets incrusted with precious stones of divers hues; ornaments of pink enamel, with Cupids painted in grisaille, or two shades of gray – such are the favorite ornaments this season'.[31]

A New York newspaper pointed out that the fancy dress of choice during 1876 was for Centennial costumes. For those who did not know what this meant, the reader was referred to Huntington's picture of the 'Republican Courts'. *Harper's Weekly* and other publications had columns devoted to the subject. These sources were not to be copied exactly but were meant to provide a basis for selection. The recommended hair style called for 'strings of pearls looped in the back hair', with the front hair drawn smoothly back from the face.[32] The *Boston Evening Transcript* went so far as to comment 'how like the old Copley portraits of the belles' of Boston, the young women looked at the Grand Centennial Ball held there in February 1876.[33] Powdering the hair was another affectation of the past that was part of the colonial revival. If the dress worn was only seventy years old, then the proper coiffure was *à la Josephine.* For the Boston ball in Music Hall, Mrs. A. Silsbee powdered her hair and dressed it with a pink aigrette and roses. Her jewels were set with topazes and amethysts which accented her rich brocade corsage and the train of her Marie Antoinette dress. Other 'quaint gowns' were complemented by strings of pearls and paste shoe buckles or, in the case of an empire dress made of embroidered India muslin, with a 'tiara of old cameos in front and golden chains in the coil'.[34]

The wedding attire of a Providence bride of a century earlier was worn by Mrs. Gregg at the centennial party held in Braintree, Massachusetts. Her gown was silk brocade trimmed with lace over a quilted blue satin petticoat. Her slippers were white satin with rose paste buckles. There were white flowers in her hair and she wore a necklace and earrings that belonged to the colonial bride. It was thought to be the most handsome outfit that had been seen at any centennial celebration. Then the report came in from the Salem Centennial Ball. One well-clad woman wore her family jewels – a necklace and hair comb set with eighty-five topazes. Another wore the emeralds once owned by the Governor's wife in Halifax, Nova Scotia. 'All this array of powdered hair, flowery brocades, high-heeled shoes, laces and diamonds, made such a brilliant impression on the usually quiet society of Salem, that its aristocratic members will probably indulge in another "centennial" before 1876 has passed out of the calendar into history', predicted the Boston newspaper.[35]

In the enthusiasm, it appears that more jewelry was worn during the celebration than had ever been owned in all the colonies. At the New York Centennial Ball 'there was a strong representation of the stately riches of one hundred years ago. Jewels flashed everywhere'.[36]

Among the Washington relics displayed at Centennial events was a paste shoe

30. *Modern Dwellings in Town and Country Adapted to American Wants and Climates* (NY 1878), pp. 194-5.
31. Boston *Transcript,* 27 Jan. 1868.
32. NY *Sun,* 12 Mar. 1876.
33. 25 Feb. 1876.
34. Boston *Transcript,* 25 Feb. 1876.
35. *Saturday Evening Gazette,* 23, 26 April 1876.
36. *Sun,* 26 Apr. 1876.

Plate 212 Portrait of Ann Pamela Cunningham by Stolle. Miss Cunningham organised the Mount Vernon Ladies Association which effectively rescued Mount Vernon and preserved it for the nation. She wears earrings and a brooch bearing the cameo likeness of George Washington. Courtesy, Senate Office Chambers, South Carolina.

Colour Plate 168. The uniformity of these gold beads confirms that they are Colonial revival in origin. The two beads nearest the clasp are engraved with the name of Florence M^c^Caulley on one and the date 1880 on the other. There are also gold ring spacers between the beads, strung on a silver chain. Owned by a Connecticut family. Length 15½in. Photograph by Peter J. Theriault. Private Collection.

buckle he once wore and a necklace made of carved bone said to have been given to Mrs. Washington by Lafayette.[37] Martha Washington parties had been started as a means of creating interest and raising funds for the preservation of Mount Vernon. Miss Ann Pamela Cunningham of South Carolina had led the efforts to save the Washington home in 1853. Formal possession took place in 1860. The Mount Vernon Ladies' Association held parties in their home states. Unfortunately Miss Cunningham died the year before the Centennial took place. In her portrait painted by Stolle (Plate 212), she wore a brooch and earrings set with cameos carved with the profile of the nation's first president.[38] During the Centennial year visitors to Mount Vernon numbered up to 1200 a day.[39]

The simple hollow gold beads so treasured by colonial women had almost gone out of fashion when the colonial revival rescued them. They were larger in size to suit a more affluent society (Colour Plate 168). 'Necklaces of gold beads are much worn for ball toilettes, and generally worn without locket', the Boston *Transcript* reported on 3 February 1876.[40]

The Colonial Revival set the stage for a series of new revivals and created a more widespread interest on the part of Americans in all kinds of jewelry from diamonds to innovative mass-produced novelties.

37. Displayed at Martha Washington party held in Boston, *Transcript,* 11 April 1876.
38. Paul Wilstach, *Mount Vernon,* between pp. 256-7.
39. *Sun,* 10 Nov. 1876.
40. Twenty years later, solid gold, hollow beads were offered wholesale in eight or five pennyweights, with either a Roman or polished finish. Bead necklaces made of rolled gold plate were available as well in extra, regular or second quality. S.F. Myers catalogue, New York, Hinks pp. 196-77.

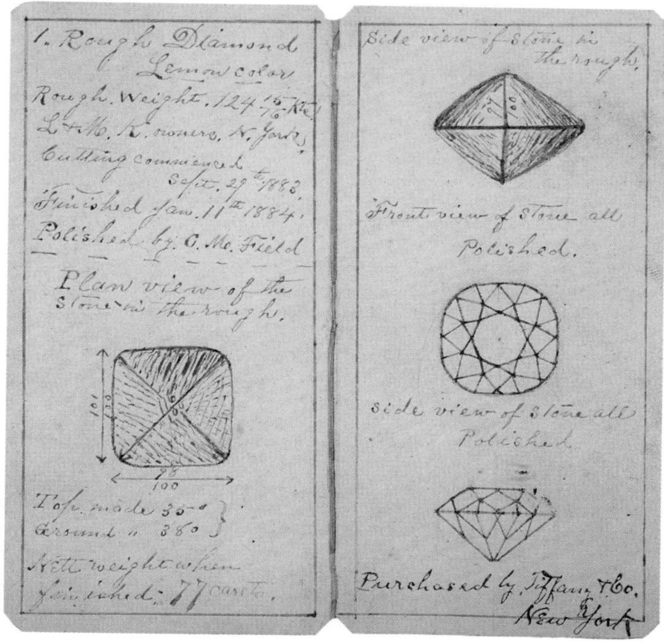

1. Rough Diamond
Lemon color
Rough Weight 124 15/16 Kts
Cutting commenced
Sept. 29th 1883.
Finished Jan. 11th 1884.
Polished by C. M. Field

Plan view of the
stone in the rough.

100

Top made 35°
Ground " 38°

Nett weight when
finished: 77 carats.

Side view of stone in
the rough.

Front view of stone all
Polished.

side view of stone all
Polished

Purchased by Tiffany & Co.
New York

Colour Plate 169. *Pages from the personal scrapbook of Charles M. Field who, with Henry D. Morse of Boston, developed the American-cut for diamonds, inventing the machine for precision cutting based on scientific principles. The sketches were made for the cutting of a lemon yellow diamond weighing 125 carat rough in 1883-4 and 77 carats after cutting. Tiffany & Co. purchased the stone and it is known as Tiffany Diamond No. 2. ©Christie's 1987.*

Ablaze with Diamonds

With the enormous explosion of diamonds emanating from the South African deposits discovered in 1869, jewelry of unprecedented richness bedazzled Americans as never before. It became commonplace in the last quarter of the nineteenth century for newspapers in major cities to describe the extravagant jewels worn to cultural and social events. Unlike some of their European counterparts who restricted the use of diamonds to the married and the middle-aged of social standing, a New York newspaper complained, Gothamites from cradle to grave seemed to be sprinkled with glittering stones. 'Diamonds flash from the buttons of a baby's layette, gleam on the dimpled hands of the tiniest child, sparkle on a young girl's fingers, and blaze from the neck and ears and wrists of the society belle, who pins her bonnet, buckles her shoe, clasps her garter, and fastens her girdle with their flashing splendor'.[1]

During the daytime it was customary to wear diamonds only if they served a useful purpose such as buttoning cuffs and securing hats. For evening dress diamonds were 'worn indiscriminately, here, there, and everywhere'. Little wonder that the first tier of the Metropolitan Opera House, opened in 1883, was referred to as the Diamond Circle in honour of the ornaments of its occupants. Few Americans had grown up with such luxury, but now their purchasing power coincided with increased supply and the sky seemed to be the limit.

Sources

Historically diamonds had come to the United States from India, and later from Brazil, by way of Holland and London where they had been cut. After 1870 the source shifted to South Africa where unprecedented rich diamond fields were discovered along the Vaal. By 1888 Sir Cecil Rhodes had established the De Beers Consolidated Mines which would control the supply and distribution of diamonds for the next century.

At first Americans were sceptical of the new supply, but by 1876 the New York

1. *Sun*, 7 Apr. 1889.

Commercial Advertiser reported that 'The prejudice against the African diamond...has been wholly overcome...The diamonds now seen in New York are mostly African'.[2] As evidence of this, the newspaper cited the great diamond for which Tammany Boss Tweed had paid $15,000 and the eighty-carat diamond that Colonel J.H. Wood of Philadelphia had recently purchased. The latter stone had come from a river near Port Natal and was valued at $50,000.

In 1868 a million dollars' worth of cut diamonds had been imported. In 1888 there were eleven million dollars' worth entering the country. One firm alone sold more diamonds in 1892 than the total importation in 1867.[3] Previously, most United States diamond buyers purchased their stones through importers or brokers, but by the 1880s some of the large retail firms were buying directly on the European markets and several established branches abroad for this purpose.[4] Casperfield & Cleveland, retail jewelers in the Bowery in New York, advertised holiday presents in December 1889, noting that the price of diamonds had increased thirty percent in the past year; but, because of the magnitude of their stock, they did not have to raise prices. They were prepared to 'undersell all the diamond dealers of the world'.[5]

America's first important diamond cutter, Henry D. Morse of Boston, advertised in 1876 that he was 'constantly in receipt of parcels of Rough Diamonds direct from the Mines which are cut and polished in my own workshop'.[6] He, and subsequently others, offered to recut misshapen or poorly cut diamonds for customers. The Boston *Transcript* reported as early as 1870 that 'jewellers in the principal cities are constantly sending their damaged and ill-cut stones here for repair'.[7]

Another source of diamonds came from the crown jewels that European royalty were obliged to sell during periods of political unrest. Tiffany & Co. alone purchased more than half-a-million dollars' worth of French royal jewels in 1887 for resale. Included were several famous Mazarin diamonds. The 'huge briolette of diamonds' in the group was resold by Tiffany to Andrew Jackson's son-in-law, Colonel James D. Safford. Mrs. Joseph Pulitzer was seen soon after the sale of the royal jewels wearing Eugénie's great necklace consisting of 222 big diamonds which Tiffany had bought for 183,000 francs.[8] By the 1890s, Americans had become serious buyers of the world's supply of good diamonds. They had also gained a reputation for buying carefully and seeking perfection in the diamond as well as in its faceting.

Facets

Relatively few Americans had been brought up in the nineteenth century with old-fashioned family jewelry set with stones of varying degrees of clarity and cut. However, their increasing interest in acquiring diamond jewelry coincided with the development by an American of new techniques for improving the quality and precision of faceting the stones.

In 1870 the Boston *Transcript* announced that Henry D. Morse, of the firm of Crosby, Morse & Foss, had perfected and been using for several years a cutting machine far more accurate and far less cumbersome than any of the old world contraptions.[9] Several patents were taken out in the name of Charles M. Field, Morse's shop foreman, in 1874 and 1876 in the United States, England, France and Belgium, for cutting machinery that revolutionized the art of diamond cutting.[10] These patents predate European patents on bruting machines by sixteen years.[11]

Not only did these improved machines reduce the time involved in cutting to one-

2. Quoted by Boston *Transcript*, 2 Feb. 1876.
3. Kunz, *Gems*, p. 313.
4. Ibid., p. 317.
5. *Sun*, 14 Dec. 1889.
6. *Transcript*, 14 Dec. 1876.
7. 20 Jan. 1870.
8. Purtell, p. 102.
9. 20 Jan. 1870.
10. 5 Oct. 1874.
11. David Federman, 'American Diamond Cutting: The Untold Heritage', *Modern Jeweler 84*, No. 1, 33-43. (January 1985), p. 37.

quarter, but they allowed the gems to be held firmly in steel arms, rather than held by hand, and accurately placed the gems at geometrically established angles to maximize their brilliance. Both the machine and a large brilliant diamond that had been cut by it were displayed at the Boston Mechanic Exposition in the autumn of 1874. The stone weighed, before cutting, 58 carats and was probably the largest and most costly diamond ever cut in this country, not to mention the most valuable, the Boston *Transcript* speculated (Colour Plate 169).

Previously, stones had been cut so that the maximum amount of material would be retained. By Morse's method the stones were cut according to principles of refraction and judicious choice of the type of cut most suitable to bring out the best qualities of the stone. Morse's brilliant cut, which became known as the American cut, had a higher crown and smaller table than the various brilliant cuts developed in the eighteenth century, such as the Perruzzi and the triple or old-mine cut, or the rounder Victorian cut of the nineteenth century. The crown facets of the American cut were at 34 to 34¼ degrees from the plane of the table of the stone. It was not until 1914 that Morse's discoveries would be developed and articulated by Marcel Tolkowsky in a treatise.[12]

Increased perfection in diamonds through cutting encouraged Americans to be more particular in selecting their stones and encouraged jewelers to be more adventuresome in selecting different cuts. One jeweler got so carried away that he designed a single pendant in the Turkish style with a rain of diamond drops illustrating various types of cuts 'such as rondelle, briolette, with lozenge facets; pear-shaped, table diamonds, etc.'[13]

Settings

In the past, settings had been constructed for maximum security. Circular collets were shaped in a continuous band that was worked over the girdle of the stone to ensure that the precious gem could not escape. When the desire for greater brilliancy became more widespread, the transparent setting became increasingly popular in the nineteenth century. The transparent setting discarded foil and metal backings and opened up the back of the collet so that the gem could receive light from below as well as above, thereby producing greater brilliance. The metal showing on top of the stone was cut down and concentrated at the widest parts of the stone and formed into supporting ribs.

By the mid-nineteenth century the ribs were translated into claws that stood up from structural supports. At the same time, mass-produced stamped settings were devised in which the claws were formed by engrailing the upper edge of the collets. By the 1870s the closed-back setting was used more often for traditional jewelry and for small background stones, while open-claw settings were used for featured stones and solitaires. Dieulafait, author of *Diamonds and Precious Stones* published in New York in 1874, recommended the open setting because it 'leaves the edge [girdle] of the stone clear...with beautiful effect for diamonds'.[14]

At first the claws, which projected inward over the top of the stone, travelled outwards as they passed the culet on the way to being joined to the circular base of the setting. With this open-claw style, both the tips and the hollows of the claws were exposed to view. A less visible type of claw setting was developed in which the claws tapered inward from the tips, following the inward slant of the pavilion. This was called an invisible setting because the inward taper of the claws below the girdle

12. For diagrams and a discussion of the history of cuts see Eric Bruton, *Diamonds*, pp. 210-234.
13. *Jewelers Review, 22* #14, 28 Aug. 1893.
14. p. 282. He called this modification of the open setting 'the knife-edge setting'. This term now refers to setting the mounted diamond on the thin edge of a wire or flat piece of metal.

15. Wigley, p. 105.
16. 15 Oct. 1876. The term invisible setting came to be used for 20th century square cut stones set so close together that it appeared no metal was present.
17. 15 Jan. 1882.
18. 22 July 1883.
19. p.281.
20. See patents 1878 (#202,402) and 1880; and Bury II, 560.
21. 2 Apr.

permitted only the tips of the claws to be seen from above.[15] In 1876 the New York *Sun* announced '"Invisible setting" is now preferred for all jewels and gems'.[16]

Tiffany, probably with the guidance of Morse, developed the American setting to be used with American-cut diamonds some time during the 1870s. The American setting had six (and later four) prongs that tapered inwards to an open circular base. The prongs were long and held the stone high for maximum sparkle and effect. By 1882 the *Sun* declared 'Engagement rings are solitaire diamonds set with as little gold showing around the stone as possible'.[17] The shift from visible to invisible claw settings can be documented in U.S. Patent Records of the 1870s with the changeover occurring about 1881. In 1883 the New York *Times* announced, 'The old high "gallery" setting has gone into disuse'.[18]

For centuries silver had been the metal of choice for diamond settings, even when the backs of the mounts were made of gold. Dieulafait noted in 1874 that gold was now almost always used for both colourless and coloured gems. He decried the change, saying that silver was more artistic and preserved the brilliancy and limpidity of the diamonds, adding to their splendour.[19] The best American jewelry still made use of gold for the understructure. Platinum, or rarely iridium, was sometimes used with gold or silver due to its greater strength and non-tarnishing nature. It was especially desirable for the prongs or at least for the tips of the claws. William A. Bates of Boston in 1878 favoured platinum tips since the diamond could still be set in a silver-coloured metal. Anthony Hessels of New York devised earring settings with platinum reinforcing the length of the claw.[20]

Toward the end of the nineteenth century other innovations in settings were devised. In 1876 the New York *Sun* noticed that 'some of the new diamond rings have the diamond deeply set in a heavy circlet of gold'.[21] This referred to what was soon known as the gypsy setting. Tiffany's 1878 catalogue described these as plain gold rounded bands with the stones 'buried in the gold, showing only the surface'. These could be mounted with diamonds or coloured stones and might be set with a diamond on each side. A variation of the gypsy ring was the Belcher setting which had claws cut out of the top of the bezel around the sunken stone.

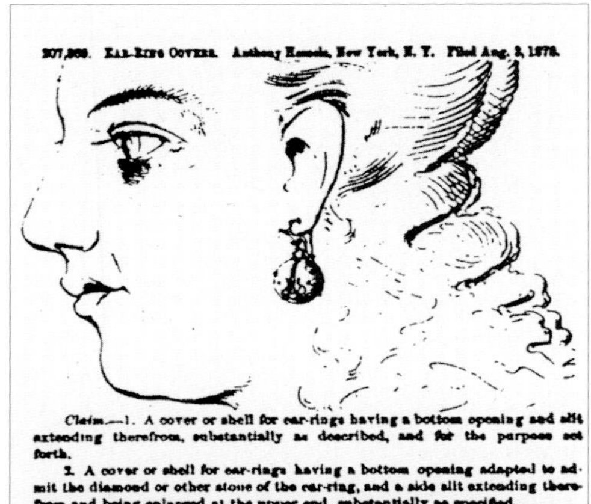

207,869. Ear-Ring Covers. Anthony Hessels, New York, N. Y. Filed Aug. 3, 1878.

Claim.—1. A cover or shell for ear-rings having a bottom opening and slit extending therefrom, substantially as described, and for the purpose set forth.

2. A cover or shell for ear-rings having a bottom opening adapted to admit the diamond or other stone of the ear-ring, and a side slit extending therefrom and being enlarged at the upper end, substantially as specified.

3. A cover or shell for ear-rings having a bottom opening and extension-slit for inserting the diamond or other stone of the ring, in combination with an interior gravity drop-plate for closing the bottom opening, substantially as shown and described.

Plate 213. Earring cover patent awarded to Anthony Hessels, New York, 10 September 1878, with 'A cover or shell for earrings having a bottom opening and slit extending there from'. United States Patent Office, No. 207,869.

Pavé settings in which the whole surface was covered or paved with stones became more and more widespread. The diamonds were held in position by the metal raised up as a result of drilling placement holes in the metal backing. Marquise cut diamonds were oval with pointed ends. These were sometimes imitated by covering a boat-shaped mount with pavé diamonds.

New Fashions for Diamond Earrings

Along with the American cut and the American setting, there were innovations in designs for diamonds which set the fashion for the mounting of other gems. The long pendant, and in fact the drop itself, vanished from earrings in the last decades of the nineteenth century, leaving only the top. They were often set with a single stone, a cluster, or sometimes took the shape of a flower. Earrings set with solitaires became exceedingly popular. Mrs. John Jacob Astor had a pair of solitaire earrings set with pure white diamonds the size of a thumbnail that were said to be worth a Broadway

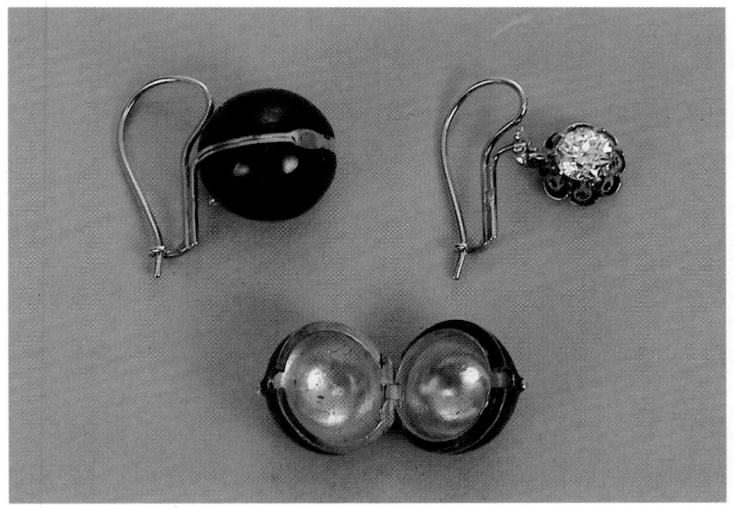

Colour Plate 170. Snap-on covers to protect diamonds were made by American jewelers for use with earrings in the 1870s and '80s. The gold covers were often enamelled black to make them more inconspicuous. This pair was made in New York about 1882 to 1885 in 14 karat gold and is similar to a design of George W. Washburn of West New Brighton, New York, patented on 11 July 1882, and improved in a patent of 30 June 1885. Length ⅞in. (fastener overall). Photograph by Peter J. Theriault. Private Collection.

Colour Plate 171. Covers to snap over pendent diamond earrings were an American innovation in jewelry in the 1870s. The covers could be plain black enamel or could be decorative with gold repoussé work as seen here. Edith Weber & Associates, New York.

house and lot.[22] It was reported that in the city 'every third lady you meet in the street and more than half the ladies at the theatre wear the brilliant jewels in their ears'.[23] To prevent the stones from being lost, a catch was added at the bottom to secure the lower end of the ear wire after it had passed through the pierced ear lobe.

Another means of protecting valuable diamond earrings was created by Anthony Hessels in 1878. This was a spherical cover that could be snapped over the stone, turning the solitaire into an ordinary ball drop (Plate 213). The cover had a hinge at one end joining the two halves and an opening in the other end so that the semispheres could close below the pendant loop. The covers could be plain or mildly ornamented gold, or ornamented with black enamel (Colour Plates 170 and 171). Providence designer Wellington P. Dolloff received a patent on earring covers in 1878, as did George W. Washburn of New York in 1882 and 1885. An earring shield made of either hard rubber or celluloid was patented by Richard Oliver in 1881.[24] By the mid-1880s, Heller & Bardel advertised fifteen different designs that would provide security for those who feared their precious gems would be lost or stolen *en route* to engagements.[25]

While the fashion for earring covers originated in New York, they could be found in other areas of the country as well. Henry Morse sold a pair of diamond earrings and a pair of covers for them packaged in a two-storey, fitted, purple velvet box.[26] Marsh & Bigney, wholesale jewelers in Attleboro, sold 'Roman Gold Cover Balls for [diamond ear] Drops' costing $10.50 to $15.00 a pair.[27]

An alternate fashion for securing earrings was developed at the end of the century. This was the ear stud which dispensed with the curved ear wire. Instead a short, straight threaded post was soldered to the back of the mount so that an ornamental nut could be attached to hold it securely in place. Earring studs were patented in 1879 by Louis Heckman of Wrentham, Massachusetts.[28]

Diamond Lace

In addition to the innovations in cutting and setting diamonds, there were new concepts in designs for diamond jewelry. At the Paris Exposition in 1878, French jeweler Oscar Massin exhibited novel costume ornamentation in the form of

22. TA, 'They have Gems Galore', c. 1889.
23. *Sun*, 7 Apr. 1889.
24. US Pat. Off. #208,968; 261,108; 321,407; 249,202.
25. Rainwater, *AJM*, p. 275.
26. PEM #132,903.
27. Catalogue, 1883, p. 160 B.
28. #216,954, 1 July, 1879.

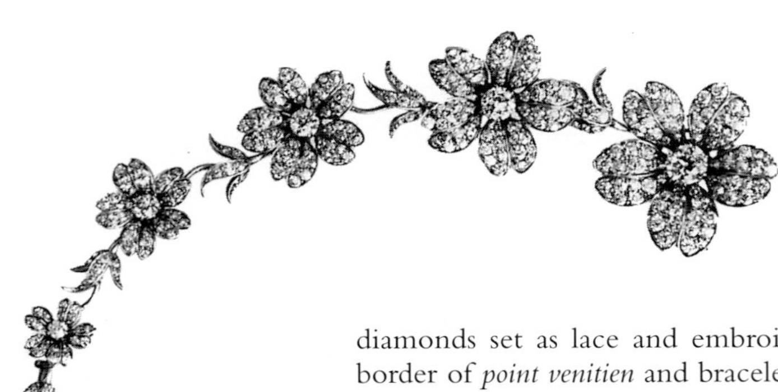

Plate 214. Diamond corsage piece made by Tiffany & Co., c.1880-1900, and owned by Susan Dwight Bliss, well-known New York benefactress of the Metropolitan Museum. She enjoyed jewelry in the 18th century style and owned books on jewelry and costume, including the original account of Marie Antoinette's diamond necklace. Gift of Susan Dwight Bliss, 1941. The Metropolitan Museum of Art.

diamonds set as lace and embroidery. There was a collar simulating *point genois,* a border of *point venitien* and bracelets in *dentelle* patterns. The diamond lace was priced by the meter. Massin is also credited with originating the illusion setting, and these lacy designs displayed diamonds with as little weight and supporting metal imaginable.[29] One particularly enchanting design was in the form of a loosely tied bowknot of lace-like ribbon with a simulated tulle background.

A decade later, in 1889, Tiffany exhibited a lacy diamond corsage ornament. This extravagantly large piece of ornamentation was fastened with a rosette, and then looped down to the opposite side where it was held by a another big rosette. The lace was scalloped on the lower edges and was airy and incredibly delicate. It was estimated that there were between 2,000 and 2,500 diamonds in it and that the whole affair was about three feet in length, varying from three to seven inches in width. One critic praised it as 'probably the best piece of diamond work of the size that has ever been executed'.[30]

Because it was so glittery, diamond lace proved a very eye-catching display, and in 1893 Paulding Farnham designed another confection for Tiffany in the form of an antique Spanish lace epaulette. It too was meant to be worn on one shoulder, in an asymmetrical style fashionable at the time, and was fixed to the shoulder with a large rosette. Other bow-like rosettes were scattered over the lower borders of the drapery. In addition to the diamonds, there were emeralds and yellow sapphires studding the lace.

Stomachers

Stomachers, a revival of mid-eighteenth century design, were worn by very few American women (Plate 214). Mrs. William Astor's stomacher had diamonds 'twelve rows deep, pendant from the corsage'.[31] It is little wonder that she was described as being 'absolutely ablaze with diamonds.[32] When American ladies were presented at Court in England in 1889, Mrs. Bradley Martin 'astonished ordinary folk with a display of diamonds which included a superb stomacher, one aigrette, and one sun'.[33] One hopes that she felt at least a little overdressed when Queen Victoria appeared in mourning black, her only jewelry made of jet.[33] Back in New York at the Patriarchs' Ball in December, Mrs. Martin received better press. Her stomacher was 'an agreeable novelty' forming a sort of latticework over her bodice.[34]

Related to the stomacher was the garland of diamonds worn on the corsage with loops of pearls swagged across the lower part of the bodice. This was a distinctly American fashion worn from the end of the nineteenth century into the first decade of the twentieth century.[35]

Necklaces

There were a number of ways diamonds could be set in necklaces. One of the most timeless was the single strand of graduated, matched, individually set diamonds in unadorned mounts. Called a rivière, this single row of diamonds had been fashionable a century earlier. In the Victorian era this was not enough for some socialites. Mrs. William K. Vanderbilt wore 'a double row of solitaires clasped round her slender throat', which even the New York *Sun* hesitated to assess.[36] Mrs. William Astor momentarily eclipsed Mrs. Vanderbilt when she appeared in a triple necklace of diamonds at the Charity Ball in New York in 1889.[37] Soon afterwards Mrs. Vanderbilt

29. Vever III, p. 475-80.
30. J. Zapata, 'The Rediscovery of Paulding Farnham....', *Antiques* (Mar. 1991), pp. 558-560.
31. *Sun*, 9 Jan. 1889.
32. Ibid., 26 Feb. 1882.
33. Ibid., 27 Feb. 1889.
34. Ibid., 22 Dec. 1889.
35. Rainwater, *AJM*, p.274.
36. 15 Jan. 1882.
37. 9 Jan. 1889.

returned from Europe with an extraordinary necklace two and a half yards long that had diamonds faceted into beads that were strung like a row of pearls. These 'large and very brilliant diamonds...are absolutely without any setting', the press reported, and the cost because of the waste in cutting and piercing them was so great, it was doubtful that the style would be widespread even among royalty abroad or millionaires in the United States.[38] The Princess of Wales had received a similar necklace as a wedding present and Mrs. Vanderbilt bought one for her own little princess, as her daughter was called, on the occasion of her marriage to the Earl of Fife.

Plate 215. Diamond and platinum dog collar owned by Mrs. Potter Palmer of Chicago, c.1890. Width 2¼in.-2⅜in. Chicago Historical Society.

While Americans desired novelty in their lesser jewelry, in general they wanted their diamond jewelry to look like the antique jewelry that they had not inherited from their Revolutionary ancestors. They wanted it to seem old, respectable and traditional. Many necklaces and sets of diamond jewelry were made in the floral style of the eighteenth century rococo taste. Clusters of diamond flower heads were joined together in graceful festoons with naturalistic leafage and scrolls.

It was not until the Tiffany exhibit at the Paris Exposition in 1889 that an American jeweler introduced an American theme into the design of a diamond necklace (Colour Plate 172). Designed by Paulding Farnham, the necklace alternated large cushion-cut diamonds with equally large round stones that were interspersed with quatrefoils in the shape of American hazelnut leaves and blossoms, in a manner espoused by Christopher Dresser.[39] The pendant also resembled a larger hazelnut leaf which had as its centrepiece a diamond valued at $45,000 and weighing over 25 carats.[40]

Necklaces wrapped closely around the neck were referred to as dog collars. Alexandra, Princess of Wales, was said to have favoured them because of an unsightly scar on her rather long neck. In the early 1880s, diamond dog collars were backed by a ribbon, often of black velvet, which set off the stones and the pattern, at the same time increasing the comfort in wearing them. Designs for ribbon-backed dog collars were made in the Louis Seize style with festoons of flowers and trophies of Cupid's bow and arrows and Hymen's torch crossed with a quiver of arrows, appropriate for a wedding gift (Colour Plate 173). By 1900 the collars had become much wider and consisted of multiple strands and much lattice work (Plate 215). Carrying this form of necklace to its logical conclusion, Mrs. Frank Leslie's dog had several collars set with diamonds.[41]

George Kunz reported in 1892 that 'A number of [diamond] necklaces worth over $100,000 each are owned in the United States, and one necklace, worth $320,000 was recently sold at the death of its owner'.[42]

Tiaras

Tiaras were worn by only a few women in the major cities of the United States. There was still a latent prejudice against royal pretensions. Mrs. William Astor had no hesitation, however, in adding a diamond tiara to her jewelry collection. Mrs. Bradley Martin was not shy either. On one occasion her tiara was likened to the Eiffel Tower and was said to have totally 'eclipsed Mrs. Delancy Kane's time-honored tiara, and

38. *Sun*, 4 Aug. 1889.
39. Christopher Dresser, *The Art of Decorative Design* (London, 1862, reprint NY 1977), Fig. 60, p. 73.
40. Zapata, *Antiques*, March 1991, pp. 558, 560.
41. Purtell, p. 106.
42. Kunz, *Gems*, p. 311.

Colour Plate 172. Diamond necklace designed for the exhibition at the Paris Exposition Universelle in 1889 by Paulding Farnham, Tiffany's artistic director. Inspired by the American hazelnut, the necklace had alternate hazelnut leaves and blossoms and a leaf-shaped pendant. The central diamond weighed 25 3/32 carats and was appraised at $45,000 and the necklace at $150,000. Used with the permission of Tiffany & Co. All rights reserved.

probably all the others that have been worn on this side of the Atlantic'.[43] Mrs. George Gould's diamond and pearl tiara (Plate 216) was called 'her splendid diamond crown, a mass of large white stones set in an open circle, and forming a series of inverted V's. This is said to be valued at $50,000'.[44]

Kunz told a reporter in 1889 that a single tiara had been made by Tiffany for a cost of $100,000.[45] Tiffany provided tiaras in the Louis Seize style that were set with diamonds and occasionally featured a single large coloured gem in the centre. These tiaras were heavily encrusted and substantial in design. By contrast, in 1893, Tiffany exhibited at the Columbian Exhibition in Chicago a light, ethereal, knife-edge tiara with a totally new aesthetic comprising minimal mounts and sinuous lines.[46]

Aigrettes

Aigrettes were more frequently worn as hair ornaments than were tiaras. A revival of mid-eighteenth century fashion, the aigrette was often studded with diamonds and held a spray of real feathers. The Brunswick diamond feather pin displayed at the Centennial Exhibition (see Plate 205) was an aigrette in the form of a peacock feather, the eye set with a thirty-carat diamond. Tiny springs joined sections of the feather so that the pin trembled as though a breeze were ruffling it.

The motion, and occasionally the height, of feather aigrettes could be annoying, especially to men when they sat behind them. With the help of the Audubon Society and other like-minded people, feathered aigrettes and stuffed song birds were finally given up, but not before this 'pernicious' fashion had 'ornamented many thousands of brainless heads and caused needless cruelty to countless harmless birds'.[47]

Another revived eighteenth century conceit, arrows were a rare ornament for the American coiffure. Arranged with a sheath, the arrow could be separated to pierce through the hair and then reinserted into the sheath to hold the jewel in place. With its obvious symbolism, it was especially appropriate for a wedding jewel. Mrs. Lorillard Spencer's arrow was used to fasten her bridal veil in 1882 (see Colour Plate 174).

Heavenly Bodies

Diamond suns were also uncommon. Mrs. William K. Astor was said to have introduced the first great diamond sun to New York society. One reporter felt that it was so big it looked too much like stage jewelry to be refined.[48] Mrs. John L. Gardner, Jr., of Boston wore her diamond sun on the back of her head which made it look like a brilliant setting sun.

A galaxy of star-shaped brooches of all sizes were often acquired in sets so that they could be worn in the hair and used to hold a clutch of orange blossoms in a bride's veil or in a row on a frame as a tiara. Princess Alexandra had made these stars famous. They were equally versatile decorating the costume here or there, fastening scarves, or suspended as a pendant. On one occasion Mrs. William Astor wore a dozen diamond stars in addition to her tiara. At the same ball Mrs. Cornelius Vanderbilt wore two

43. *Sun,* 22 Dec. 1889.
44. *JC 30,* no. 25 (24 July 1895), 38.
45. *Sun,* 7 Apr. 1889.
46. Zapata, *Antiques,* March 1991, p.558, Plate III.
47. H.C. Brown, ed., *Valentine's Manual of Old New York,* No. 11, p. 278.
48. *Sun,* 13 Oct. 89.

Colour Plate 173. Late 19th century Tiffany & Co. designs for diamond necklets in a revival of Louis XV motifs. Festoons of flowers or swags of floral clusters interspersed with trophies of Cupid's bow and arrow or Hymen's torch, suitable for a wedding present. Backed by a black velvet ribbon which not only added drama to the diamonds but also protected the wearer's neck. John Loring's Tiffany's 150 Years *(New York: Doubleday, 1987).*

diamond stars and a crescent in her hair.[49] Before long, everybody's grandmother was sporting a star set with diamonds, sapphires or pearls (Plate 217).

Diamond-encrusted crescents could be worn as hair ornaments or brooches, and were often purchased in sets of different sizes. Juliette Gordon Low, founder of the Girl Scouts, owned a big crescent as well as a small one. Crescent pins set with graduated diamonds often appeared with a star nestled in the curvature. These were

49. Ibid., 9 Jan. 1889.

Plate 216. Far left. Actress Edith Kingdon was married to George Gould, son of financier Jay Gould, in 1886. She revelled in pearls and knew how to wear them well. Her diamond tiara was boldly punctuated by large inverted pear-shaped pearls. An intricate diamond dog collar is scarcely noticed amid swags of multiple pearl necklaces. Her diamond stomacher dripped with pearls. Photograph from Kunz and Stevenson, The Book of the Pearl, *1908. Courtesy Gemological Institute of America.*

Plate 217. Left. Portrait of Mildred McLean Hazen Dewey (c.1850-1931), wife of Admiral George Dewey, painted by Theobold Chartran (1849-1907), in 1900. Mrs. Dewey wears her set of diamond stars suspended from her rivière of diamonds, in addition to a large corsage brooch and sizeable diamond ring. Length 50⅛in., width 35in. National Portrait Gallery, Smithsonian Institution.

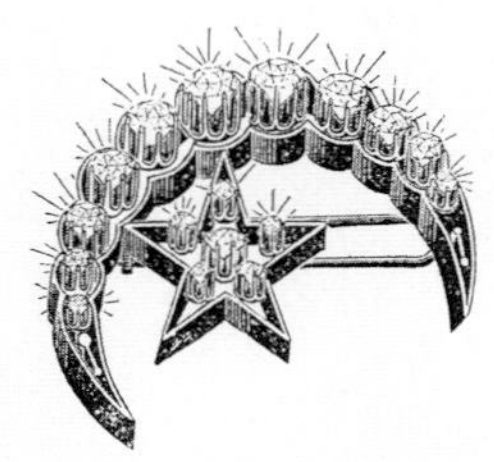

No. 1.	16 Diamonds.	Each,	$375.00.
No. 2.	Smaller "	"	225.00.
No. 3.	" "	"	150.00.
No. 4.	" Size.	"	112.50.

Plate 218. Crescent and star diamond jewelry was made available to the general public in 1883 through catalogues by such wholesale firms as Marsh & Bigney.

also available wholesale, either made of solid gold set with real diamonds or made of rolled gold set with stones called Congo diamonds (Plate 218).

The American preference for star and crescent pins was noticed by French jeweler and critic Henri Vever. At the Chicago Exposition in 1893, he saw thirty crescents and seventeen stars in various sizes, all of the same model, in the United States display. This led him to generalize that Americans bought jewels primarily for the diamonds, without bothering much about the design of the mounting.[50]

Swallows

Another type of brooch that could be purchased in sets was a swoop of swallows. In 1886, Juliette Gordon of Savannah, Georgia, was wed to the wealthy William Mackay Low of England. The groom presented her with a set of five diamond-studded swallow brooches (Plate 219). They could be worn in a variety of ways: singly, paired, in clusters, or altogether in flight, in the hair or on the corsage. Juliette wore three of them on the bodice of her dress in the portrait painted in London about 1887 by Edward Hughes.[51]

The concept of a suite of swallows as brooches is attributed to the genius of René Lalique (1860-1945) who came to Paris when he was sixteen and eventually provided designs for such famous houses as Cartier and Boucheron, both of whom had shops in London as well as Paris.[52] Jewelry historian Henri Vever dates Lalique's design to 1887 and assigns it to the Boucheron workshop. However, in the spring of 1882, the New York *Sun* reported that among Parisian novelties in lace pins were 'groups of birds, such as half a dozen diamond swallows in full flight'.[53] This innovative concept gave perspective and dimension to jewelry design and met with immediate success. Quickly the swallows migrated to England, where Juliette Low's bridegroom probably purchased her suite, and then to the United States where they proved equally prolific. Eventually they perched on mass-produced jewelry such as scarf pins and were stamped out in a single static flight pattern made of base metal and rhinestones.

Plate 219. Right. Photograph of Juliette Gordon Low wearing several brooches from her set of five diamond-studded swallows given to her in 1886 as a wedding present by her husband William Mackay Low, a wealthy Englishman. The set could have been purchased at Cartier's in London or in New York at Tiffany's where Mrs. Low later purchased jewelry for herself and as gifts. Courtesy of The Juliette Gordon Low Girl Scout National Center, Savannah, Georgia.

Bracelets

Diamonds enhanced bracelets in several new ways in the 1880s and '90s. Fashionable wide-band bracelets had medallions set with diamonds. Following the French style, Louis Seize designs of flowers were revived and set with diamonds against a deep blue enamelled background. Monograms were formed of a single line of graduated diamonds curving and twisting to shape the letters in an effective design.

The wide band bracelet was superseded by a thin bangle that had a jewel or a line of jewels set in knife-edge mounts in the centre. Some were only as thick as a wedding band. A tiny diamond butterfly perched on top of a plain bangle was a feature of fashion in 1890.[54]

An Embarrassment of Riches

Garters were an unexpected vehicle for showering actresses and other lovely ladies with more diamonds. Five hundred pairs were sold by Tiffany's in December 1880. One pair, with large emerald spiders with diamond and ruby legs, adorned the shapely legs of actress Lillian Russell.[55]

Diamonds were even worn at the beach. During the summer of 1889, the *Sun* reported that the bathing beauties at Long Branch

Plate 220. Still life portrait of Mrs. Leland Stanford's jewel collection, painted by Ashley David Montague Cooper (1856-1924) in 1898. Mrs. Stanford assembled one of the outstanding collections of jewels in the United States. In anticipation of her gift of the collection to Stanford University to be sold to benefit the University she and her husband founded in memory of their son, Mrs. Stanford commissioned Cooper to record her favourite pieces. Length 60in., width 84in. Gift of Jane Lathrop Stanford. Stanford University Museum.

wore their jewels at the beach where they paraded back and forth and struck poses on the sand. The ladies reasoned that this was the only sensible thing to do since there had been robberies there in recent years. It was safer to have their diamonds on their ears or around their necks and wrists than to risk leaving them in bath houses. Of course, they did not dare to venture into the surf for fear a breaker might rob them instead.[56]

Mrs. John Jacob Astor took no chances when she wore her diamonds in the city at night. The evening that she was bedecked with a reported $800,000 worth of jewels, she was accompanied by ten city policemen on horses to guard her as she made her way to the ball.[57]

Three American women, Mrs. John Jacob Astor, Mrs. Clarence Mackay, and Mrs. Leland Stanford, were each said to own more fine diamonds than any of the European royal families with the exception of the Queen of England and the Empress of Russia. Of the three collections, Mrs. Stanford's was unequalled. Her husband was the millionaire builder of railroads, Governor of California and United States Senator. Among her hoard of jewelry valued at two million dollars was a necklace worth $74,000. While others might like the latest fashion, Mrs. Stanford preferred historic jewels. Many of the finest pieces she bought from Tiffany's had belonged originally to Isabella II, former queen of Spain. Other pieces were acquired from dealers in Paris as well as New York. The collection included sixty pairs of earrings and enough diamonds to fill a quart cup. It was said that Mrs. Stanford wore all her jewels at one time to a private dinner party once, fastening them to her black tulle dress, and no doubt being very careful when she sat down.[58]

At the end of the century Jane Stanford gave her jewels to the University founded in 1885 and endowed by her husband in memory of their son Leland Stanford, Jr. Before the jewels were transferred to be sold for the benefit of the University library, she took the extraordinary step of commissioning a still life portrait of her favourite jewels painted by A.D.M. Cooper (Plate 220). The University Library bookplate depicted the donor, on her knees before Minerva, goddess of wisdom, offering her casket of jewels.

50. *Rapport*, p. 56.
51. Portait at National Portrait Gallery, Washington, D.C.
52. Vever III, 706.
53. *Sun*, 2 April 1882.
54. Ibid., 19 Jan. 1890.
55. Purtell, p. 107.
56. *Sun*, 11 Aug. 1889.
57. TA, unidentified clipping, *Gems Galore*, c.1889.
58. Ibid.; Purtell, pp. 121-22.

Plate 221. Painting of 'The Wedding Presents' by James Wells Champney in 1880, illustrating the widespread custom of exhibiting bridal gifts, including jewelry. Museum of the City of New York.

BRIDAL JEWELRY

While royalty had long enjoyed the luxury of extravagant wedding gifts, it was not until the 1880s that the custom of presenting lavish and numerous presents came to uppercrust American brides. The press eagerly described not only what was given, but also by whom, thereby contributing to the eye-popping presents sent by free spending or socially ambitious friends and relatives. The publicity of weddings of Queen Victoria's relatives served as a catalyst to the increasing pretensions of nouveau riche and old families alike. So did memories of the Diamond Wedding in 1858 in New York (see pages 197-201).

It became fashionable to display wedding gifts for all to see, with name cards of the donors. A painting of 'The Wedding Presents', by James Wells Champney (1843-1903) of Massachusetts, captures the scene and notes among the modest gifts of jewelry a Florentine piece, a demi-parure and a solitaire diamond ring (Plate 221). 'It is usually the custom to have one of Tiffany's men arrange on one long table or a series of smaller tables the rare and costly gifts of jewels and laces, silver and china, linen and bric-a-brac presented by wedding guests', reported the New York *Sun,* 'and an inconspicuous man in plain clothes and with alert keen eyes stands near to guard them'.[1]

Wealthy relatives provided the most stunning gifts of jewelry. When Lilia Osgood Vanderbilt, the daughter of William H. Vanderbilt, was married in New York on 20 December 1881 to Dr. William Seward Webb, her parents gave her a pearl and diamond necklace. Commodore Vanderbilt's wife gave her a set of diamonds. The Frederic Vanderbilts gave her a diamond and ruby ring 'of great value', while the

1. 20/28 April 1889.

Plate 222. Diamond daisy pin, one of ten made for presentation by William Mackay Low to the bridesmaids at his wedding to Juliette Gordon Low on 21 December 1886. The daisy had several levels of meaning. In the language of flowers, the daisy signified beauty and innocence, appropriate for young maidens. In addition Daisy was the nickname of the bride. The year of the marriage was written out in the leaves of the daisy. Length about 3in. Courtesy, The Juliette Gordon Low Girl Scout National Center, Savannah, Georgia.

Cornelius Vanderbilts presented the magnificent diamond necklace which Lilia chose to wear for her wedding. Her silver satin wedding gown made by Worth had a point lace veil that was secured by diamond clasps.[2]

Miss Bessie Hamilton Morgan received a pendant with two hearts united, set with diamonds, that the reporter thought were almost as large as the Koh-i-nur, with a large pendent pear-shaped pearl. It was the gift of Baron de Rothschild on the occasion of her marriage to August Belmont, Jr.[3]

The bridegroom carried his share of the burden. One commentator on the modern wedding noted sarcastically that the young man was expected to spend half his fortune on an engagement ring, either a diamond solitaire or, more recently, a set of three rings mounted with a diamond, sapphire and emerald respectively for the third finger of the left hand. The cynic felt this obligation was preventing men from marrying at all. Solitaire rings were set with as little gold showing around the stone as possible and could feature a ruby instead of a diamond.[4] So ubiquitous was the diamond solitaire engagement ring that the New York *Sun* noted, 'Solitaire diamonds in ordinary nineteenth century settings have already become monotonous as pledges of love and fidelity from a lover to his betrothed'. Instead the fiancé of Miss Annette Wetmore gave her an antique ring thought to be more than three hundred years old. It was set with 'a diamond of rare brilliancy and of the purest water, and is said to have once belonged to the crown jewels of Austria'.[5]

In addition, the groom was expected to give gifts, usually jewelry, to each of the bridesmaids (Plate 222). Lilia Vanderbilt's four nieces were each given a diamond pansy pin by Dr. Webb.[6] 'Bridesmaids' lockets, designed with reference to individuals, are prepared on request', Tiffany's informed their patrons.[7] The bride usually gave her attendants the flowers they carried and a locket, pin or bangle bracelet as a souvenir of the occasion. Likewise the groom's ushers were given mementos, usually scarfpins.[8]

Finally, the groom was obliged to purchase the simple band of gold engraved with the date of the wedding and perhaps a sentimental message or initials. Tiffany's said that 22-karat gold was standard for their wedding rings and that great care was taken by their jewelers in shaping and finishing their rings.[9]

As if this were not enough, the wealthiest grooms gave their brides additional jewelry, such as diamond earrings, crescent and star pins or a pearl necklace. Mary Alice Townsend's groom Charles Sackett gave her a 'superb necklace of solitaire diamonds'. Her veil was held by a diamond ornament on one side and an orange blossom spray on the other side.[10] The diamond necklace given to one bride by the groom was assessed at $25,000.[11]

When Caroline Berryman married Lorillard Spencer in October 1882, he gave her a large diamond arrow (Colour Plate 174). She used it to fasten the folds of her point lace veil on one side. The other side was held by a ruby-crested, diamond peacock 'whose starry tail fell gracefully over the lace'. Her solitaire necklace had a diamond and sapphire pendant and was sent by the groom's parents 'from over the sea'. Princess Cenci (formerly Miss Lorillard Spencer) gave the bride a diamond brooch so large that it almost covered the front of her corsage. 'These costly trifles formed but a small part of the wedding presents', the *Sun* reported, 'among which diamonds and precious stones played so conspicuous a part that it might almost have been called "a diamond wedding"'.[12]

Tiffany's catered to the marriage trade. They gave special attention to the designing

2. *Sun*, 21 Dec. 1881.
3. Ibid., 13 and 20 Nov. 1881.
4. Ibid., 5 Jan. 1882.
5. Ibid., 25 Dec. 1881.
6. Ibid., 21 Dec. 1881.
7. Tiffany & Co., *Catalogue*, NY, 1881/2.
8. *Sun*, 9 Oct. 1881.
9. Tiffany & Co., *Catalogue*, NY, 1881/2.
10. *Sun*, 22 Jan. 1882.
11. Ibid., 30 Oct. 1881.
12. 8 Oct. 1882.

Plate 223. Wedding jewelry worn by Consuelo Vanderbilt, who became the Duchess of Marlborough in 1895 upon her marriage, and subsequently worn when she attended the 1902 coronation of Queen Alexandra. Her husband's gift was a diamond belt which served as a stomacher. Her tiara set with large diamonds was the gift of her father William K. Vanderbilt. Behind the tiara she wore a coronet. Pearls once owned by Catherine the Great and the Empress Eugénie were a present from her mother. Her neck-brace of pearls with diamonds clasps, purchased in Paris on her wedding trip, she found painful to wear, and her tiara caused her head to ache. Photograph from Kunz & Stevenson, The Book of the Pearl, *1908. Courtesy, Gemological Institute of America.*

of bridal jewelry. They kept on hand a large selection of especially fine diamonds and purchased rare and beautiful gems from all over the world for this use.[13]

At least one bride already had her jewels. Cornelia Baylies wore the diamond necklace, stomacher and earrings that were heirlooms of her grandmother Mrs. Robert Ray of New York.[14]

Incredibly, by 1889 weddings had become even richer. Tiaras were added to the bride's splendour. One of the most fashionable New York weddings of the autumn season was that of Elizabeth Drexel and John Vinton Dahlgren. The daughter of millionaire banker Joseph Drexel wore a diamond tiara given to her by her mother. It was secured by orange blossoms held with diamond pins. Appropriate to her Roman Catholic wedding, the bride carried a prayer book, the gift of the groom's mother. The covers of the book were decorated with a cross, anchor and crown set with large brilliant sapphires, rubies and diamonds. Among the wedding presents on display at the bride's home was a ring believed to have been the engagement ring that Martin Luther gave to Catharine von Bora, the gift of the groom. It had been owned by the Dahlgren family since 1625, it was said. There was a ruby set in this large silver ring.[15]

Edyth Ward Newcom, bride of Reginald Henshaw Ward of New York in 1889, not only had the requisite diamond sunburst and solitaire necklace with pendant, but also an orchid made of diamonds for her corsage, a gift from her brother, and a diamond and moonstone brooch from her newly acquired mother-in-law. The wedding took place at home in the drawing room and upstairs there were three

13. Tiffany & Co., *Catalogue,* NY, 1881/2, p. 11.
14. *Sun,* Oct. 1882.
15. Ibid., 30 June 1889.

Colour Plate 174. Diamond arrow mounted in silver and gold, given by Lorillard Spencer to his bride Caroline Berryman of New York when they were married in October 1882. She used Cupid's arrow to gather the folds of her lace veil on one side. Set with more than a hundred old-mine and rose cut diamonds, the arrow was also worn by Mrs. Spencer when she posed for her portrait painted by Benjamin Potter prior to 1886 when the portrait was displayed at the Paris exhibition. ©Sotheby's Inc.

rooms *en suite* devoted to the wedding presents.[16] Commenting on this wedding, the *Sun* remarked that the scale of magnificence was such that it seemed more appropriate for a golden or diamond wedding after fifty or seventy-five years of married life. 'Indeed', the *New York Sun* said, 'the brides of the present day seem to start with all the gold and jewels that on rare occasions came to their grandmothers [only] after half a century'. The bride was so covered with diamonds that 'her dainty little figure was almost hidden'.[17]

When William H. Vanderbilt's granddaughter Florence Adele Sloane was married in 1894, she was deluged with presents arriving at the rate of thirty a day as the wedding approached. 'A gorgeous diamond sun, the largest one I have ever seen' was given to her by her father. A necklace made of diamonds and emeralds, worn a few times by her mother ('and therefore all the dearer to me') was passed on to the bride. Her uncle Cornelius Vanderbilt sent Florence a wondrous diamond stomacher and an enormous single pearl. She was so excited about it that she got her fiancé James Burden to take her in a hansom cab to their house so that she could thank them in person. Afterwards they went to the Burdens' house where she received the bridegroom's present 'in the hansom in the glare of the street lamp. It is the loveliest diamond collar, a tiara, or a pin. It is too dear of him to have given it to me', she wrote in her diary, 'that and my engagement ring in one year are certainly enough to turn my head and quite spoil me'.[18]

The apogee in extravagant bridal jewelry was reached when millionaire mothers began marrying off their American daughters to titled Europeans and Englishmen. Consuelo Vanderbilt could hardly hold her head up, so heavy was the diamond tiara given her by her father William K. Vanderbilt when she married the Duke of Marlborough in 1895 (Plate 223). It gave her a terrific headache every time she wore it. Her mother gave Consuelo the famous pearls once owned by Catherine the Great and the Empress Eugénie. The Duke gave his bride a diamond belt which she wore like a stomacher well above her waist. While on their wedding trip in Paris, the bride acquired more jewelry, including a very wide dog-collar made with nineteen rows of pearls. The diamond clasps on it only added to her discomfort since they chafed her neck. Conspicuous consumption to the point of pain was the price brides paid for wedding jewelry by the end of the nineteenth century.[19]

16. Ibid., 27 Nov. 1889.
17. Ibid., 27 Nov. and 1 Dec. 1889.
18. Quoted by Loring, p. 21.
19. Bury, II, 229, 236. See Néret, p. 9 for description of wedding gifts to Anna Gould, daughter of Jay Gould, who married Count Boniface de Castellone in 1895.

Imitations

Increased interest in diamonds and coloured stones used in making jewelry induced inventive minds to search for ways to make imitations that would fool the eye but cost a fraction of the real thing. There were various methods for achieving this end. The simplest and oldest solution was to substitute an inexpensive material for the genuine article. Glass was an early imitator of gems, but was soft and did not wear well. Using less expensive gem stones that resembled the rare and costly jewels was another common practice. These substitutes exhibited many of the same qualities, such as hardness or brilliance, and could fool almost all but the expert. Crystals, quartz and other colourless gems such as zircons, white topazes and white sapphires had long been passed off as diamonds.

In the last quarter of the nineteenth century, these substitutes were called by such names as 'Alaska stones', 'Australian pebbles', and 'Congo brilliants'.[1] George Howard & Co., New York, about 1880, advertised 'We also set in fine gold the fashionable Australian Pebble, so much worn now, which equals in brilliancy the real Diamond, and which the best judges cannot distinguish without applying a test'.[2]

S.F. Myers of New York offered 'Fine White Stone Brilliants (Congo Diamonds)' set in solid gold and lace pins, along with imitation diamonds and real diamonds.[3] The Golconda Gem was advertised by R.L. Griffith & Son in Providence as the 'nearest approach to a genuine diamond ever produced', with a warning, 'Don't be deceived by imitations'.[4]

Perhaps the finest of the look-alikes were quartz rhinestones extolled by a wholesale jewelry dealer in Detroit in 1889 as 'A SENSATION! The GEM of all Imitation Diamond goods ever produced. Our ⋆ Genuine ⋆ Rhinestones. The *lustre, life* and *fire* of this great Wonder of the 19th Century surprises diamond experts'.[5]

Another kind of imitation involved cutting the table and crown from a genuine gem and cementing it on to a glass pavilion of the desired colour. These reconstructed stones were called doublets. Garnet doublets were especially popular and were often set in fine gold mounts. The Boston *Courier* reported on 24 March 1889, 'The rage for jewels of all descriptions has brought the doublet stones to the fore again and many are worn by persons who not only wear these deceptive gems because of their cheapness, but because they feel safer than in wearing real jewels'.

The triplet was formed from a stone such as quartz with little colour that had a thin layer of richly coloured glass inserted at the girdle of the stone. Triplets made of opal had a thin layer of fiery opal sandwiched between crystal and matrix or some other base. This may have been the method used for the counterfeited opals the Boston *Courier* warned against on 24 March 1889.

About 1877, Fremy & Feil, French chemists, were able to produce rubies and sapphires by fusing imperfect gems, small stones, and gems with a colouring oxide such as chromium, and then cutting and polishing them. Kunz described these and other attempts to create new artificial rubies in an article published in the *Transactions of the New York Academy of Sciences* in 1886[6] Rudolph Oblatt of New York produced reconstructed rubies which reportedly caused prices for genuine rubies to drop considerably.[7] In 1889 Max Freund & Co. of New York advertised as sole agents for

1. Marsh & Bigney advertised in 1883 Alaska diamonds for women's sets of brooch and earrings mounted in the finest rolled gold plate and a line of solid gold Alaska diamond jewelry. pp. 247, 272-3.
2. Broadside, courtesy J. M. Cohen, Rare Books.
3. Hinks, p.207.
4. *JC*, 31 July 1895, *30*, No. 26.
5. Adolph Enggass in *The Wholesale Jeweler*, 1889, p. 89.
6. 4 Oct. pp. 3-10.
7. Wodiska, pp. 218-19.

Plate 224. Brooch made by Ferdinand J. Herpers, Newark, New Jersey, 1872, for Mrs. Herpers. Imitation diamonds set in gold. Width 1¹⁵⁄₁₆in. Photograph by Armen. The Newark Museum.

Plate 225. Complementary earrings to the brooch in Plate 224. Imitation diamonds set in gold with black enamelling on earring drops. Length 1¾in. Photograph by Armen. The Newark Museum.

reconstructed rubies in the United States.[8] Another reputable New York dealer in gems and gem minerals, A.H. Peteriet, made sapphires and rubies.

Numerous patents were granted for methods of making diamonds and other gems in the last decades of the nineteenth century. Several were granted to Frenchmen Samuel and Jules A. Grossiard and E.C. Clement.[9] Ernest E. Kipling of New York, importer and advertiser of a wide variety of genuine precious stones, was assigned Jules A. Grossiard's patent on the manufacture of imitation diamonds and gems, using a reflective coating for increased brilliance.[10] Richard A. Kipling of Paris was assigned Samuel Grossiard's patent for making artificial stones by fusing a piece of strass (paste) with enamel.[11] Ernest E. Kipling received a patent in his own right for 'a new article of manufacture, an artificial rose diamond, either with or without reflector coating'.[12] Auguste Victor Verneil, another French chemist, exhibited apparatus for flame-fusion in Paris in 1900. His method of producing sapphire 'evolved for the New York firm of Lazarus Heller & Son, was patented in America in 1910 and 1911'.[13]

In addition to enamels and reflective coatings, thermal treatment was utilized to increase the colour and brilliance of lack-lustre stones. Heat treatment had been employed for hundreds of years.

Imitation pearls had been made for centuries as well, and in the nineteenth century were often made of glass beads coated inside with a mixture of fish scales called pearl essence. A more effective method of pearl production had been developed by the Chinese. They introduced foreign objects into fresh-water molluscs so that a coating of nacre would form over them in the same way that true pearls were formed. About 1900 in Japan Mikimoto started the first commercial farming of round cultured pearls by introducing seed pearls into pearl oysters. It was not long afterward that man-made pearls began to affect the price of real pearls dramatically, as Mrs. Morton Plant discovered. She traded her house on Fifth Avenue at 52nd Street to Cartier for a string of fifty-five matched pearls. The property increased in value, but the pearls were soon worth only a fraction of their former value due to the production of commercial pearls.

Imitation gems were not always chosen because they were inexpensive. They could serve an artistic purpose as well, when matching stones or pearls were required by the design. A necklace made by Marcus & Co. used imitation rubies side by side with the real gems to provide a perfect match in colour (see Colour Plate 247).

8. *The Wholesale Jeweler*, p. 133.
9. Grossiard 28 Feb. 1882; 29 Apr. 1884; 2 Apr. 1889. Clement 2 Jan. 1883.
10. 28 Feb. 1882.
11. 2 Apr. 1882, #400,450.
12. 30 June 1885, #321,302.
13. Bury I 372-4 and footnote 86.

Colour Plate 176. Portrait of Mrs. John L. Gardner, Jr., by John Singer Sargent, c.1888, illustrates the dramatic way in which she wore her beautiful rubies, one as a pendant to a choker of pearls and two as pendants on the two loops of pearls around her waist. Sargent painted her portrait over a period of time. It is likely that he added the rubies after the portrait was exhibited at St. Botolph's Club in Boston in April 1888 and after her purchase of the three rubies in 1892. Sargent painted her portrait over a period of time. It is likely that he added the rubies after the portrait was exhibited at St. Botolph's Club in Boston in April 1888 and after her purchase of the three rubies in 1892. Length about 75in., width about 32in. Photograph by David Bohl, Boston. Courtesy, Isabella Stewart Gardner Museum, Boston.

Coloured Gems

Colour Plate 175. Diamond brooch made by Thomas Kirkpatrick, New York, c.1865-85. Courtesy, Skinner Inc.

While diamond jewelry was most coveted, a very strong wave of enthusiasm developed for coloured stones in the last quarter of the nineteenth century. Interest in coloured stones was precipitated by several recent developments. The return to naturalism, and the desire for novelty were prominent factors. The fashion for Japanese art was another. The oriental concept of reverence for humble materials of little monetary value added respect for stones that were not necessarily perfect, rare or costly, if they were beautiful to contemplate. There was also a desire for relief from the flood of colourless diamonds that pervaded the market. At the same time there had been a growing professionalism in the science of mineralogy which led to a search for gems of all kinds, in America as well as elsewhere.

It was in this climate that George F. Kunz (1856-1932) made his entrance. In 1879, he was hired as Tiffany's first professional gemmologist. In this position he was able to broaden the horizons and develop the taste of Americans interested in jewelry. Born in New York city, he studied at Cooper Union and began collecting minerals. When he was only fourteen,

Colour Plate 177. Left. Portrait of Mrs. Larz Anderson wearing the emerald brooch she chose for her presentation to King Edward VII and Queen Alexandra at the British Court in the Diplomatic Circle in 1904, in addition to her diamond tiara. Mrs. Anderson mentioned her jewels in one of her travel books entitled Odd Corners, *published in 1917. The Andersons had homes in Brookline, Massachusetts and Washington, D.C. The portrait was painted by Cecilia Beaux, c.1900. Length 82in., width 39½in. Museum of the Society of the Cincinnati, Anderson House, Washington, D.C.*

Colour Plate 178. Above. The hexagonal Indian emerald, once the featured ornament in the turban of a maharaja, was given to Isabel Anderson, wife of Captain Larz Anderson. She had it mounted in gold, bordered with diamonds, topped with a briolette emerald accented by diamond-studded foliage, and below set with a smooth, pear-shaped, detachable briolette. The brooch appears in her portrait precariously perched on the corsage of her diaphanous gown. Hexagonal emerald about 1¼in. x 1in. x 1¼in. ©Sotheby's Inc.

he corresponded with collectors in the United States and abroad. At the age of twenty he had provided the first of a number of mineral collections to colleges and museums. Travelling throughout America and Mexico, as well as to Australia, Asia and Russia, he was able to put together two major collections of gems, one given by J.P. Morgan to the American Museum of Natural History in New York. Kunz encouraged Americans to look beyond the obvious white diamond market to the wonderful world of colour.

Kunz located and then introduced Tiffany's customers to beautiful coloured stones that had been ignored by other jewelers. On one occasion, when he showed some of the gems to Oscar Wilde, the Irish playwright and wit exclaimed, 'I see a renaissance of art, a new vogue in jewelry in this idea of yours. Bah! who cares for the conservatives! Give them their costly jewels and conventional settings. Let me have these broken lights – these harmonies and dissonances of color'.[1]

Coloured gems included diamonds in a variety of colours. While they had often been regarded as second-class stones compared with white diamonds, they now were enjoyed for their divergent hues. Called 'fancies' today, coloured diamonds ranged from pink and lavender, yellow and green, blue and red, to brown and black. Thomas Kirkpatrick, New York jeweler, combined a brown and a black diamond with a colourless and a yellow diamond, and centred it with a ruby and some smaller diamonds to make a very effective brooch (Colour Plate 175).

In 1881 fashion critics noticed that coloured stones set with diamonds were becoming popular and that it was 'more fashionable this season to set diamonds in combination with coloured stones than by themselves'. Earrings set with large rubies, sapphires, or emeralds encircled with diamonds were more fashionable than diamond solitaires.[2] Diamonds reversed their position and assumed the secondary role of surrounding coloured stones.

The most important coloured stones continued to be rubies, emeralds and sapphires. Previously they had appeared in American jewelry less frequently than diamonds and were usually modest in size. Often they were combined with other gems in small ornaments such as rings. Now large, more important gems were selected and they were used in more prominent pieces of jewelry such as necklaces.

One of the most famous rubies owned in America was the ruby that had been given to Lola Montez by Louis of Bavaria. An Irish actress, dancer and darling of the gold diggers, Lola Montez (1818-61) found happiness on many continents and left a string of admirers as she travelled from Europe to California and Australia.[3] Her ruby, said to be worth $10,000, passed to Mrs. J.B. Hagan, wife of a California millionaire.[4]

Mrs. John Lowell Gardner, Jr., purchased her finest rubies from Boucheron whom she and her husband met in London where the famous French jeweler had a shop. In May 1892, they purchased a five-carat ruby ring and a pear-shaped ruby pendant weighing over twenty-three carats. A few weeks later they purchased a third ruby of nine carats which Boucheron had obtained from owners in the interior of India. He boasted that 'This magnificent ruby is one of the finest I have ever seen, and I do not think there is a better one'.[5] It was this ruby that one of Mrs. Gardner's friends called 'her crown jewel, the great ruby'.[6] In her portrait painted by John Singer Sargent Mrs. Gardner wore three ruby pendants in an unconventional way, suspended from her ropes of pearls, one at the neck and the other two from the loops across her waist (Colour Plate 176).

1. Quoted by Misiorowski & Dirham, 'Art Nouveau; Jewels and Jewelers', *Gems & Gemology, XXII* (Winter 1986) 225.
2. *Sun,* 11 Dec. 1881.
3. Schofield & Fahy, pp. 34-36.
4. *Sun,* 13 Oct. 1889. Mrs. Ogden Mills was noted for her rubies as well as her diamonds. *JC,* 24 July 1895, *30,* No. 25, p. 38.
5. Gardner Family Papers, Archives of American Art, Boston. The ring cost 55,000 francs; the pendant with its platinum and diamond chain cost 25,000 francs; and the India ruby cost £11,000.
6. Thomas Russell Sullivan, quoted by Tharp, p. 187.

World traveller Mrs. Larz Anderson of Brookline, Massachusetts and Washington, D.C., favoured emeralds. When she was presented to Edward VII and Alexandra in 1904, she wore 'an emerald and diamond tiara and on my corsage a big Indian emerald which a maharaja had once worn on the front of his turban' (Colour Plates 177 and 178 and also see page 357).[7] She had it reset in western style with diamonds surrounding the emerald. Mrs. William Astor took first prize for the most costly emerald and diamond necklace in the country.[8]

Mrs. Clarence Mackay purchased a necklace featuring very large sapphires from Boucheron at the Paris Exposition in 1878. The sapphires were mounted in silver ribbons and foliage studded with diamonds and were of a particularly beautiful blue colour. The central stone was over 159 carats. Jules Debut created the design for the necklace and a matching pair of cluster earrings.[9]

A spectacular set of twenty-three cushion-cut Kashmir sapphires were surrounded by diamonds and linked together by square-set diamonds in a necklace made by Cartier for Mrs. Mary Scott Townsend (Colour Plate 179). The necklace was detachable in several places. Mrs. Townsend used part of the necklace as a chain to fasten the rose silk stole she was wearing in a miniature portrait painted in 1894 by Amalia Kussner.[10]

The finest collection of sapphires in the United States was that of Mrs. August Belmont. However, the finest single sapphire belonged to Mrs. William Astor.[11] She wore it as a pendant 'with such quantities of diamonds that...the sapphire shines out among them as if it were indeed the stone that brought everlasting happiness'.[12]

All three of the major coloured gemstones had been discovered in the United States in recent years. North Carolina could boast of emeralds, rubies and varicoloured sapphires as well as diamonds.[13] In 1881 the New York *Sun* called attention to the 'Pink, blue, and vari-colored sapphires' coming from the mineral rich area of North Carolina.[14] Green rutile was found there in addition to true emeralds. The quantity of gems did not prove sufficient to make a fashion statement in the world of jewelry. However, North Carolina rubies were combined with diamonds and sapphires to form the stars and stripes of the navy flag for a scarfpin simulating a yacht flag in 1893.[15] Among the many gems exhibited at the 1893 Chicago World's Fair were sapphires of all colours, which prompted Henri Vever to remark on 'the richness of the American jeweler's palette'.

The best sapphires in the United States came from the area along the Missouri River near Helena, Montana, where corundum was first discovered about 1865. These gems appeared in fancy colours and occasionally in deep colours of red to blue. Their discovery was a byproduct of the search for gold in the area. Some of the stones were shipped for cutting to the New York firms of Tiffany and M. Fox & Co., and to a diamond cutter in Amsterdam.[16] In 1883 Tiffany's made a crescent set with Montana sapphires ranging in daylight colour from red at one end to bluish-red and then to blue at the other end. When seen in artificial light, the stones all looked red. The estimated production of sapphires sold to be cut into gems dwindled from $2,000 in 1883 to $60 in 1886.[17] However, in 1889, 'Sapphires deeply, darkly, beautifully blue from Montana' were set in California gold and exhibited by Tiffany at the Paris Exposition.[18]

In 1890, English jewelers Edwin W. Streeter and Horatio Stewart visited the area

7. Isabel Perkins Anderson, *Odd Corners* (1917).
8 TA, *Gems Galore*.
9. Néret, p. 44, Plate 42. Mrs. Clarence Mackay was the daughter-in-law of John Mackay of Comstock Lode fame.
10. The necklace was remodelled by a subsequent owner.
11. TA, *Gems Galore*.
12. *Sun*, 13 Oct. 1889.
13. Kunz, *Gems*, 42-48.
14. *Sun*, 11 Dec. 1881.
15. *Jewelers Review 22*, No. 14, 28 Aug. 1893, p. 36. See FN 20 and 40.
16. Stephen M. Voynick, *The Great American Sapphire*, p. 7.
17. Kunz, *Gems*, p. 49.
18. *Sun*, 17 Mar. 1889.

Colour Plate 179. Platinum mounted, sapphire and diamond necklace, late 19th century, made for Mary Scott Townsend, daughter of William Lawrence Scott, railroad and coal industrialist of Erie, Pennsylvania. Set with Kashmir cushion-shaped sapphires surrounded by old mine diamonds, the necklace was housed in a box imprinted with the name of Cartier. In a miniature of Mary Scott Townsend, painted by Amalia Kussner in 1894, she wears a detachable part of the necklace like a chain to secure a loosely draped stole across her shoulders. Over the years the necklace was remodelled and the square-shaped, diamond-set links were probably added, as they do not appear in the miniature portrait. Length about 22½in. (overall). ©1991 Sotheby's Inc.

Colour Plate 180. Left. Iris corsage ornament made by Tiffany & Co. and designed by Paulding Farnham, artistic director of the company, and exhibited in 1900 at the Paris Exposition Universelle. The iris blossom is set in oxidized silver with 120 faceted blue Montana sapphires. Diamond outlines and citrine bearding and an etched gold stem with demantoid garnet leaflets add naturalistic details. Marked TCO. Length 9½in. (including stem). Courtesy, Walters Art Gallery, Baltimore, Maryland.

Colour Plate 181. Below. Two crescents and a circle pin, set with Montana sapphires and pearls, made about 1910 and marked respectively by Krementz, Newark; Ehrlich & Sinnock, Newark; and D. De W. Brokaw, New York. Diameter ⅞in. (circle pin). Photograph by Peter J. Theriault. Private Collection.

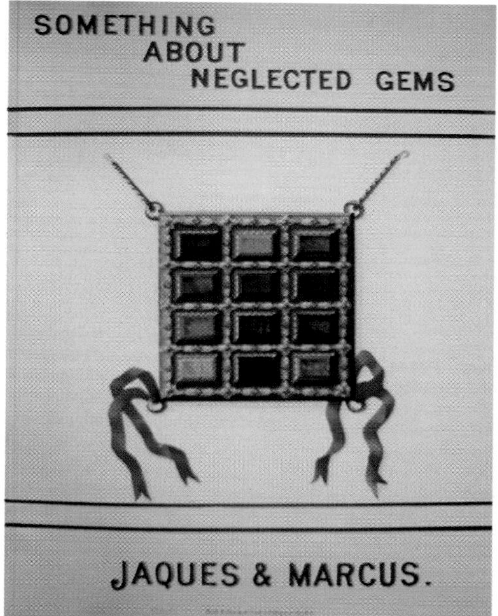

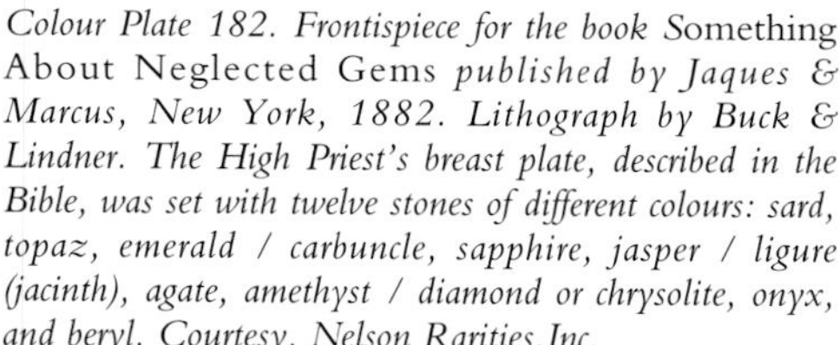

Colour Plate 182. Frontispiece for the book Something About Neglected Gems *published by Jaques & Marcus, New York, 1882. Lithograph by Buck & Lindner. The High Priest's breast plate, described in the Bible, was set with twelve stones of different colours: sard, topaz, emerald / carbuncle, sapphire, jasper / ligure (jacinth), agate, amethyst / diamond or chrysolite, onyx, and beryl. Courtesy, Nelson Rarities, Inc.*

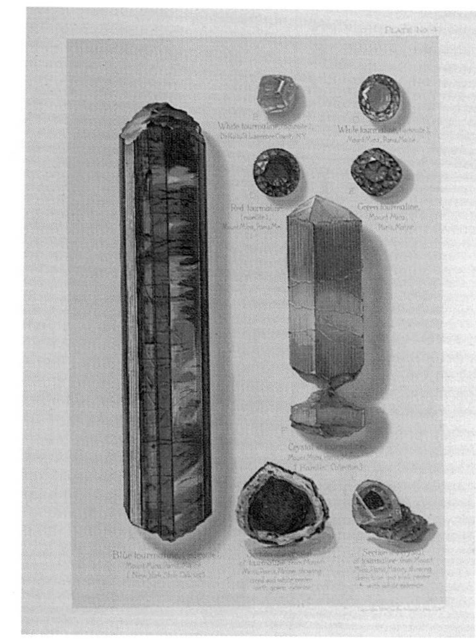

Colour Plate 183. Illustration of tourmalines of various colours which appeared as Plate 4 in George F. Kunz's book, Gems and Precious Stones of North America, *published in New York in 1890. All, except the white tourmaline (B) from New York State, were found at Mt. Mica in Maine. Length 8¾in., width 5½in. Photograph by Peter J. Theriault.*

Colour Plate 184. A butterfly brooch was designed to feature two slices of 'watermelon' tourmaline in its wings, a rutilated quartz body, a diamond mid-section, a garnet head, and demantoid garnet in its antennae. The brooch came from the shop of Knowlton, in business from 1879 to 1898 in Boston. Wing span: 2in. Courtesy, James Robinson Inc., New York.

and bought an interest in the small sapphire mining operations of the Spratt Brothers. The *Helena Herald* suggested that:

> in order to make the business of mining these Montana sapphires profitable, the public taste must be educated to appreciate their unusual colors, and this the English company will set about doing. Very beautiful effects in jewelry can be produced by combining the gems of different colors in rings, bracelets or necklaces. It is reported that a necklace of Montana gems was recently worn by a duchess at a ball given by the Prince of Wales and that it attracted much notice from connoisseurs.[19]

---

19. Voynick, pp. 16-17.

Appeals to patriotism also helped to promote Montana sapphires. These gems were used in what was billed as a truly American ring: a bald-headed eagle's claw clutching an American sapphire in a cluster of diamonds.[20]

The Sapphire and Ruby Mining Company of Montana, as the firm was grandly called, hoped to pay the expenses of their mining operations from gold and make their profits from sapphires. Edwin Streeter announced that, other than the discovery of diamonds in South Africa, there was nothing more important than the Sapphire & Ruby Mines of Montana. Nevertheless, their initial efforts failed because of underfinancing.

In 1895 Jake Hoover found more blue pebbles in his gold gleanings about a hundred miles away along Yogo Gulch, samples of which were sent to Kunz for an appraisal. Not only were these gems of the most desirable shade of rich blue, ruby and amethyst, but they were, Kunz said, the finest of any gemstones ever found in the United States.[21] The stones had fewer inclusions and the colour was more evenly distributed than it was in oriental sapphires. In addition they were radiant by day or by artificial light.

One hundred and twenty Yogo mine sapphires were chosen to create the wondrous iris corsage ornament that Tiffany sent to the Paris Exposition Universelle in 1900 (Colour Plate 180). The variation in their colour and size was artfully employed by designer Paulding Farnham to simulate nature. Diamonds set in platinum were used only to form the falls of the petals which were bearded with citrines set in gold. The stem was fashioned of textured gold and the little leaves were set with grassy green demantoid garnets. In this one magnificent jewel the reputation of the Yogo sapphires was secured. A silver medal was awarded for the Yogo sapphires at the Exposition.

In 1897 one quarter of the interest in the Yogo mine was sold to the London jewelry firm of Johnson, Walker & Tolhurst which also obtained shares in the New Mine Sapphire Syndicate, as Streeter's company was newly designated. In 1899, 125,000 gem sapphires were sent to England for cutting and setting, and in 1903 the production was worth over $250,000.[22] They became the most valuable gem resource of the United States.[23] Johnson, Walker & Tolhurst featured Yogo Sapphire jewelry in their catalogues and eventually some of the English-made jewelry made its way back to the American market.

One of the most appealing designs for Yogo sapphires produced by American jewelers was the slender crescent pin set alternately with sapphires and pearls. These were produced by a number of different firms, including Krementz and Ehrlick & Sinnock, both of Newark. D. De W. Brokaw of New York used the same combination for circle pins (Colour Plate 181).

In 1882 jewelers Jaques & Marcus published a little book called *Something About Neglected Gems.* The title page was illustrated with a coloured representation of the ancient High Priest's breast plate, bearing twelve different gems, each engraved with the name of the tribe to which it was consecrated (Colour Plate 182).[24] The authors discussed the various gems that had until recently been overlooked in jewelry, encouraging the public to develop 'a national taste both daring and original'. To this end, they enumerated the various attributes of coloured stones from alexandrites to zircons. It seems strange, they mused 'that people have been content with a colorless stone, while beautiful gems that have colors of wonderful richness and purity have been comparatively neglected. By the use of color the work of the jeweler is raised to a fine art'. Choosing from a variety of colours, the jeweler is like a painter who forms

20. *Jewelers Review, 22,* No. 13, 21 Aug. 1893.
21. Voynick, pp. 31-3.
22. Ibid., pp. 40 and 70.
23. M.N. Smith, p. 60.
24. *Exodus* 28: 17-20.

his own palette. If colourless diamonds are used, it should be as a complement to enhance the coloured stones, they said, in the same way that a florist adds white roses to violets and carnations to create an artistic bouquet.[25] The fashion reporter of the New York *Sun* read the book and summarized for its followers, 'Color in jewelry is at present studied as a fine art. It takes an artist to blend colored stones to advantage in fine ornaments'.[26]

Tiffany's catalogue for 1881-2 recommended 'among colored semi-precious stones: tourmalines, pink and blue topazes, peridots, Arizona garnets, moonstones, quartz cats eyes, and hyacinths [zircons]. Not only handsome but uncommon, usually set as solitaires, they cost from $15-$65'.

Kunz's book *Gems and Precious Stones of North America* published in 1890 was the first of its kind. It provided a guidebook for collectors and an enormous boost to the coloured gem market. 'Public interest in semi-precious stones has increased greatly during the last ten years', Kunz wrote. 'Formerly jewelers sold only diamonds, rubies, sapphires, emeralds, pearls, garnets, and agates, but at present it is not unusual to have almost any of the mineralogical gems, such as zircon, asteria or star sapphire or star ruby, tourmaline, spinel, or titanite, called for, not only by collectors, but by the public, whose taste has advanced in the matter of precious stones as well as in the fine arts'.[27]

Kunz estimated the value of stones produced in the United States and sold to be cut into gems from 1883 to 1888. In this six-year period, the dollar value of production was $5,500 sapphires, $200 emeralds, $1,100 amethysts, $10,000 beryls including aquamarines, $1,150 topazes, $2,800 tourmalines, $15,000 garnets, $8,500 moss agates, $8,000 turquoises, $8,650 quartzes, $33,500 smoky quartzes, and $430,000 gold quartz.[28]

Of all the coloured gems found in North America, tourmalines were most appealing for jewelry. This dichroitic gem was not appreciated until about 1700 when it was discovered among precious stones brought back from Ceylon on Dutch ships. Its name was taken from the Sinhalese word *turamali.* Tourmalines were found in Brazil, Siberia, and in Maine and California in the United States as well. Their beauty rests in the variety of their colours which often occur in combination within a single crystal (see Colour Plate 185). Shades of red (rubelite), blue (indicolite), green (elbaite), in addition to colourless (achroite) and black (schorl) were all discovered in Oxford County, Maine, in the nineteenth century.

Two schoolboys, Elijah L. Hamlin and Ezekiel Holmes, found the first examples on Mt. Mica. They had been looking for minerals late in the autumn and late in the day when the last rays of sunset were slanting across the earth. The green transparent crystal was clinging to the root of an overturned tree. Members of the Hamlin family periodically collected modest amounts of tourmaline from the area over the next half-century. It was not until the 1870s that Dr. Augustus Choate Hamlin began mining the deposits seriously.[29] The Mount Mica Tin & Mica Company was organized in 1881. Kunz believed that their tourmalines rivalled any found anywhere in the world (Colour Plate 183).[30] By 1890 about $50,000 worth of marketable gem tourmalines had been taken from Mt. Mica (Colour Plate 184). Today mines in nearby Newry still yield substantial quantities of gem tourmalines.

A splendid compendium of the Maine jewels was designed as a necklace by A.C. Hamlin. It had detachable pendants set with large tourmalines ranging from three to thirty-four carats, each a pretty piece of jewelry in itself. These could be fastened to

25. New York, 1882, p. 22-6.
26. 14 May 1882.
27. Kunz, *Gems,* p. 311.
28. Ibid., pp. 320-21.
29. Augustus Choate Hamlin, *The Tourmaline.*
30. Kunz, *Gems.* p. 71.

Colour Plate 185. The most important piece of jewelry made of Maine tourmalines in the latter part of the 19th century is the Hamlin necklace. Set with multicoloured tourmalines from Oxford County, the necklace was made from designs of Dr. Augustus C. Hamlin, whose father discovered Mt. Mica's tourmalines and who began serious mining of tourmalines in the 1870s. The central stone of the necklace is a luscious green tourmaline weighing 34.25 carats, surrounded by eight colourless beryls. These nine gems were cut by a lapidarist named Fox and were set by Samuel Reynolds of Boston. The rich pink rubellite (left of centre) Hamlin recorded as 'a seven carat rose tourmaline...changed by heat from a smoky brown'. [Perham, Maine's Treasure Chest, *pp. 240-242.] In total, there are seventy gems in the necklace. The yellow gold, archaeological style chain has a large number of pendant loops allowing for stones to be added or rearranged. At Hamlin's request, the necklace became the property of Harvard University upon the death of his granddaughter. ©1990 Tino Hammid. All rights reserved.*

Colour Plate 186. 18 karat gold and platinum brooch set with Montana sapphires, fresh water pearls and over 100 diamonds, accented with enamel. Marked with the special feather mark on the back of the brooch behind the large central pearl, indicating that it was exhibited by Tiffany & Co. at the Paris Exposition Universelle. Length 2¼in., width 2⅛in. Tiffany & Co. Permanent Collection.

Colour Plate 187. Tiara-shaped ring, 18 karat gold and platinum, set with seven sapphires of various colours, held in diamond-studded scrolls mounted with twenty-three old European diamonds, nineteen rose cut diamonds and two faceted rubies. Marked with the Tiffany 'World's Columbianum Exhibition' stamp. The exhibition was held in Chicago in 1893. Length 1⅛in., width 15/16in. Tiffany & Co. Permanent Collection.

Colour Plate 189. Above. Moonstone brooch surrounded by pearls, American, c.1890-1910. Marked on top of pin hook 14 Y by W.F. Cory & Bro., Newark, N.J. Length 1¼in. Photograph by Peter J. Theriault. Private Collection

Colour Plate 188. Left. Renaissance revival gold brooch set with a large peridot, diamonds, and pearls, with green enamel accents. Made by Marcus & Co., New York, c.1900, and marked M & Co on back. Oval pearl at top appears to have been lightly chased in two bands around its surface. Pin fastener can be removed and is held in place by a screw with a scrolled handle so that it can be worn comfortably as a pendant. Length 2½in. (overall). Photograph by Dennis Griggs. Private Collection.

the gold chain in various combinations (Colour Plate 185). The necklace was worn by Hamlin's wife. It was inherited by his granddaughter who also had two earrings set with pink and green tourmalines and beryls, and a cross set with six of the best tourmalines ever found in Maine.[31]

In 1889 Tiffany & Co. astonished visitors to the Paris Exposition with its breathtaking exhibit of tourmalines and many other choice native coloured gems, in both cut and natural forms (Colour Plate 186). The unique collection was put on display at Tiffany's in New York for several weeks prior to its shipment to the exposition, generating a great deal of interest.[32] In the 1890-91 Tiffany catalogue, tourmalines from Maine were included among the recommended gems of their Precious Stone department.

Some of the best amethysts and aquamarines found in the United States were also found in Maine. One handsome brooch was set in the twentieth century with a fifty carat amethyst surrounded by twelve local fresh-water pearls and mounted in gold found along the Swift River in the Eustis area of Maine. Kunz thought that the colour of this amethyst, and others like it found at Pleasant Mountain in Oxford County, was equal to the best deep purple Siberian amethysts. Other native sources of amethysts included Haywood County, North Carolina; Delaware County, Pennsylvania; New Hampshire and Rhode Island. In 1893, *Jewelers' Review* advised 'The old-fashioned amethyst earring, worn years ago, is reappearing'.[33] Imported amethysts from the Ural Mountains and Auvergne, France, were offered in Tiffany's catalogue of 1893.

The same catalogue offered aquamarines from Maine and North Carolina, as well as Brazil, Ural Mountains, and Siberia. Paulding Farnham of Tiffany's designed an aquamarine and diamond pendant brooch for the Chicago Exposition in 1893.[34] An outstanding specimen of aquamarine cut from a crystal mined in Stoneham, Maine, in the 1880s was displayed there too. The oval cut gem was over 133 carats. Together the two exhibits contributed to special interest in this stone.[35] Aquamarines of gem quality were also found in Massachusetts, Vermont and Pennsylvania.

Red garnets were still popular for jewelry and the market was deluged with mass-produced garnet jewelry from Bohemia. Philip Bissinger of New York city advertised as an importer of Bohemian garnet goods.[36] Bohemian garnets reached their height of popularity in the 1880s in pavé-set jewelry with very little of their silver mounts showing. By the end of the nineteenth century, production was served by about 400 stone gatherers, 3,000 cutters and drillers, 500 gold and silver smiths and 3,500 manufacturing jewelers, for a total of 9 to 10,000 workers in Bohemia's garnet industry.[37]

Very good garnets were found in Arizona, New Mexico and southern Colorado. They were referred to as American rubies. However, it was the green demantoid garnet that became highly fashionable in the late nineteenth century. Found in Russia, demantoids are clear and very sparky, with a rich fresh green colour. It was these garnets that were so desirable for the naturalistic animals, insects and leaves that abounded in jewelry at that time.

Peridot was often used instead of demantoids. It was less costly, and had a more yellow tint to its grass green colour. Kunz said that many of the peridots used in jewelry about 1890 were being taken out of jewelry that had been made two hundred years ago (Colour Plate 188).[38] The peridots found in the United States, particularly in Arizona, were abundant but small sized and not as desirable.

31. *Kennebec Journal,* 16 Dec. 1907; Jane Perham Stevens, *Maine's Treasure Chest Gems and Minerals of Oxford County,* pp. 205-6.
32. *Sun,* 2 April 1889.
33. *22,* No. 24, 6 Nov. p. 28.
34. Illustrated color plate VIII in Zapata, *Antiques,* March 1991, p. 564.
35. Jane Perham Stevens, *Gems & Minerals,* p. 29.
36. Located at 13 John Street. *Wilson's Business Directory of New York City,* 1875, p. 344.
37. *Gems & Gemology,* Fall 1991, pp. 168-69, citing an 1896 publication of Max Bauer, *Edelsteinkunde* (Leipzig).
38. Kunz, *Gems,* p 101.

Plate 226. Pyramidal moonstone pendant containing a bit of the hair of Robert Browning, sent to Isabella Stewart Gardner by a mutual friend after the poet's death in 1889. Diameter ⅝in. Photograph by David Bohl, Boston. Courtesy, Isabella Stewart Gardner Museum, Boston.

Opals, a quartz like silica, offer a kaleidoscope of colours as the light strikes them at different angles, adding intrigue as the change takes place (see Colour Plate 112) The traditional white or milky opals had come from Hungary (now Czechoslovakia) and a variety called fire opal came from Mexico and parts of the western United States. Opals were first discovered in South Australia in 1849 and in the 1870s throughout Queensland. Some specimens of Queensland opal were exhibited in Philadelphia at the centennial celebration.[39] Recovery of precious opal began in earnest in 1890 at White Cliffs in New South Wales. In 1893 Tiffany's offered opals from Queensland, as well as from Mexico and the state of Washington in the United States. Opal sales were greater than ever that year and earrings made of opals surrounded by diamonds were especially fashionable.[40]

Spectacular black opals were discovered at Lightning Ridge in New South Wales about 1887 and again in 1902 and 1905. These opals were particularly well suited for the artistic jewelry designed at the turn of the twentieth century. Bailey, Banks & Biddle in Philadelphia and Marcus & Co. in New York, as well as Tiffany, were very successful in using these gems to best advantage, picking out their inherent colours with touches of coloured enamel on the mounts.

A variety of feldspar, moonstone exhibits adularescence, a blue-white opalescence that steals across the cabochon giving it a ghostly fleeting quality. A pyramidal-cut moonstone was chosen by Isabella Stewart Gardner to cover the lock of Robert Browning's hair given to her by a mutual friend at the time of his death in 1889 (Plate 226). Because of the moving light exhibited by moonstones, some believed that there was a living spirit within these stones.

It was said in 1881 that Americans liked to use moonstones for pavé settings.[41] They were also widely used for brooches surrounded by pearls or diamonds (Colour Plate 189). Both Arts & Crafts and Art Nouveau jewelers appreciated the lively and mystic qualities of these stones (Colour Plate 190). They were carved into cameos (Colour Plate 191), sometimes with a cherub's head or with a man in the moon. Tiffany recommended moonstones for lacepins, along with cat's eyes, in their 1881-2 catalogue. Most of the moonstones used by American jewelers came from Ceylon, although some were native gems.[42] At the end of the century, moonstones were also fashioned into beads to be used like pearls. They were thought to bring good luck.

Labradorite, a feldspar like moonstone, shows a play of tints in shades of blue and green, a phenomenon known as labradorescence. It was found in Maine as well as the land for which it was named. It too appeared in jewelry around 1900 and was on occasion carved into cameos.

Less well known among gems of changeable colour were alexandrites from Ceylon and Takawaja, Asiatic Russia. This unusual gem had only been discovered in 1830 in

39. Augustus Choate Hamlin, *Leisure Hours Among the Gems,* p. 346.
40. *Jewelers Review, 22,* No. 10, 31 July 1893 and No. 11, 7 Aug. 1893.
41. Bury, II, 714.
42. M.D. Rothschild, *A Handbook of Precious Stones,* pp. 88-90.

Colour Plate 190. Moonstone parure, American, c.1900, set in white gold. Length 14½in. (necklace). Photograph courtesy of The Charleston Museum, Charleston, S.C. Private Collection.

Russia and given the name of Alexander II who had come of age that year. 'The lady who is so fortunate as to possess an Alexandrite this Winter will be the envy of her admiring friends', said the New York *Sun,* 'and possibly the destruction of her husband's balance at the bank: for ownership of such a trinket implies the disbursement of $5,000 at least'.[43] Alexandrites have the remarkable ability to change from green in daylight to a rich red in candlelight. It was this phenomenon that no doubt appealed to Mrs. John L. Gardner, Jr., who bought a brooch from Tiffany's in 1886 that was set with an alexandrite in combination with a ruby.[44]

Asterism is another phenomenon that adds mystery to its image. Cut in cabochons or convex, rubies and sapphires sometimes flash a six-pointed star, caused by foreign particles lying in various directions. 'One of the finest star sapphires known is owned

43. 27 Nov. 1881.
44. GFP, bill dated 13 Jan. 1886. It cost $1500.

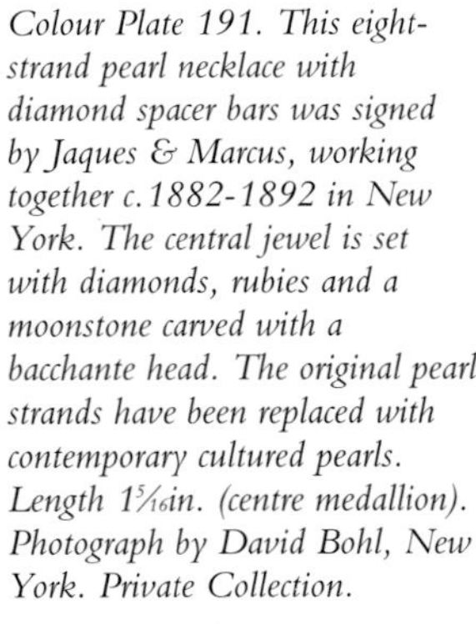

Colour Plate 191. This eight-strand pearl necklace with diamond spacer bars was signed by Jaques & Marcus, working together c.1882-1892 in New York. The central jewel is set with diamonds, rubies and a moonstone carved with a bacchante head. The original pearl strands have been replaced with contemporary cultured pearls. Length $1\frac{5}{16}$in. (centre medallion). Photograph by David Bohl, New York. Private Collection.

Colour Plate 192. Turquoise and pearl bracelet, American, c.1890. Length 6½in. Photograph by Peter J. Theriault. Private Collection.

Colour Plate 193. Right. A caged piece of Arizona turquoise becomes a sort of scarab with demantoid garnet eyes in a gold pendant marked by Marcus & Co. It is engraved on the back LB / 1891-1902. Length 1in. (excluding pendant loop). Photograph by Peter J. Theriault. Private Collection.

by a well-known gentleman' in New York, the *Sun* reported on 30 October 1881. Star-ruby rings were especially popular with gentlemen.[45]

Vever noticed the labradorite and cat's eyes in Tiffany's 1893 jewelry display, and pointed out that not only were these stones rarely used in jewelry, they had scarcely ever been seen in mineral collections until very recently.[46] Cat's eyes were so called because their changeable, undulating lustre resembled the slit eye of a cat. Chrysoberyl cat's eyes are the most desirable stones, but the same characteristic is exhibited by quartzes and other stones as well. Tiger eye became popular for cutting cameos and intaglios in the United States from 1880 to 1890. The chatoyancy gave these gems a mysterious quality that led to its use in warding off evil spirits.

Among other American gems exhibited at Chicago in 1893 were topazes from Colorado, Maine and New Hampshire, and beryls from Pike's Peak. Tiffany also displayed petrified wood from Arizona and turquoise from New Mexico. Unlike the other gems, these were not transparent. Turquoise was used extensively by western American Indians, working mines that had been developed by their ancestors and exploited by Spanish conquistadors (see pages 380-381). Often combined with ropes of tiny pearls in a bracelet (Colour Plate 192) or necklace, they could also be carved into a scarab and set in a pendant (Colour Plate 193).

Surprisingly, gentlemen enjoyed these fancy stones as much as women. 'Ten years ago you could hardly find an American gentleman of taste that would wear rings and studs of fancy stones', reported a jewelry salesman in New York, 'but now the outfit of a man of fashion is not perfect without them'.[47]

45. *Sun*, 15 Jan. 1882.
46. Henri Vever, Joaillier, 'Rapport', Rapports, *Exposition Internationale de Chicago en 1893...*, p. 62.
47. *Sun*, 30 Oct. 1881.

Plate 227. The portrait of Mrs. Isabella Stewart Gardner in Venice, by Anders Zorn, 1894, illustrates the exuberant way she wore her lengthy string of natural pearls. About 36in. x 26in. Courtesy, the Isabella Stewart Gardner Museum, Boston.

Pearls

Wealthy Americans provided the best market for the finest pearls in the last decades of the nineteenth century, according to New York jeweler Julius Wodiska.[1] The finest pearls were the largest, roundest and most lustrous products of the pearl oyster that were harvested from the sea, primarily from the Persian Gulf and the area around Ceylon, and from the Pacific, the Gulf of Mexico, and California waters. There were also small and irregular fresh-water pearls produced by the Unio mussels, but they lacked the iridescence or orient of the large salt-water pearls. Conchs also produced pink pearls occasionally and they enjoyed a brief period of popularity in the 1880s as a novelty.

However, it was the rope of large matched pearls that appealed to fashionable Americans. Those who travelled abroad bought these pearl necklaces from the leading jewelers in London or Paris. Others purchased their pearls from Tiffany's or their local jewelers. Mrs. William K. Vanderbilt acquired two 'second-hand' strings of pearls abroad, one of which had belonged to Catherine the Great and the other to the Empress Eugénie. In 1883, Mrs. Vanderbilt appeared at her fancy dress ball wearing the Russian empress's pearl necklace with her costume in the style of a Venetian Renaissance princess.[2]

It was not uncommon for even the wealthy to acquire their long ropes of pearls one length at a time. With interchangeable clasps, they were able to put them together in a variety of ways. Mrs. Frederick W. Stevens of New York acquired her pearls in this way. The *Sun* disclosed 'They have been collected with great care, and at long intervals, of course, regardless of cost, and each pearl is said to be absolutely perfect as to shape and color'.[3]

Mrs. John L. Gardner, Jr. bought her first section of forty-four fine white pearls in 1874 from Hancock & Co. in London. Her next five necklaces were purchased at two year intervals between 1884 and 1892 from Boucheron of Paris. The pearls gradually increased in size from sixteen grains on average to eighteen grains. The central pearl

1. *A Book of Precious Stones*, p. 77.
2. *JC*, 22 Nov. 1899, p. 50.
3. 3 Sept. 1882.

of the last string weighed 30 grains. In all there were 231 pearls that had cost 247,463 francs plus £925 for the Hancock strand.[4]

In her portraits by Anders Zorn in 1894 (Plate 227), after she had completed her collection, and by Ludovick Passini in 1892, Mrs. Gardner wore her pearls in all their stunning length, wrapped several times around her neck to form a sort of dog collar and then plummeting down to fingertip length. Her friend Henry James bedecked his fictional Milly Theale, American heiress, in his 1902 tale *The Wings of the Dove* in much the same way. He described the pearls as circling her neck twice and then 'hung, heavy and pure, down the front of the wearer's breast'.[5] When Mrs. Gardner had an audience with the Pope, she wore her pearls with a black dress specially designed for the occasion. He was said to have admired them greatly.[6] Before she died in 1924, Mrs. Gardner cut seven necklaces out of the original six and presented them to her nieces, her nephews' wives, and her two goddaughters. Her executor estimated their value altogether at $200,000.[7]

Edith Kingdon, the amply endowed actress who married Jay Gould's son George in 1886, exuberantly posed for photographs wearing her ropes of pearls from Tiffany's, a dog collar and a pendant pear-shaped pearl on her corsage. In a more restrained and thoughtful pose about 1900, she wore her pearls with a necklace-like stomacher made of pendant pearls and diamonds, a chain of pearls, a diamond dog collar and a pearl and diamond tiara (see Plate 216).

Pearl dog collars were popular with row upon row of small pearls held in place by vertical spacer bars, which were often set with diamonds, and a central jeweled plaque.

In 1881 fresh-water Unio pearls enjoyed a boom. They had been found in the mid-1800s in a number of areas in the United States: Texas, Ohio, Illinois and Tennessee. However, the molluscs found near Salem, New Jersey produced the largest pearls. One of the latter which was almost an inch wide brought $2,000 in Paris.[8] The less perfect, small pearls were used extensively for borders and accents in American-made jewelry and were often set in onyx jewelry.

Mississippi River Valley pearls also were widely used in jewelry of this period. Tiffany's designed a spectacular chrysanthemum (Colour Plate 194). Dogtooth pearls varying in length were arranged in a cluster characteristic of chrysanthemum morifolium and were given a diamond studded stem and leaves. The design was produced in several sizes. The irregular nature of the Mississippi River pearls was very well suited to such artistic jewelry.

Coloured pearls, like coloured gems, enjoyed a vogue. They ranged from cream to rose pink to grey black. In addition to traditional sources in the Pacific and Indian Oceans, the seas of Lower California were yielding pearl oysters. The Pearl Shell Company of San Francisco was enfranchised to fish these waters by the Mexican government in the 1880s. Some of the best black pearls were produced in this area, which also gave up variously shaped pearls tinted blue, green, and grey, as well as white pearls. Approximately 5,000 carats of pearls worth $200,000 were marketed through San Francisco in a single year.[9]

The abalone found off the California coast from Catalina to San Diego also produced a limited number of pearls. A group of the finest quality abalone pearls was made into a necklace valued at over $2,000. Another abalone pearl more than half an inch long was used to form the body of a fly for a pin.[10]

The shells of all these pearl-producing oysters could be used in jewelry as mother-of-

4. GFP.
5. Tharp, p. 162.
6. Tharp citing Thomas Russell Sullivan, the writer, who was in Rome at the same time, p. 183.
7. GFP.
8. Kunz, *Gems*, p. 240.
9. Ibid., p. 218-25.
10. Ibid., p. 236.

Colour Plate 194. Freshwater Unio pearls from the Mississippi River basin were admirably suited to create the blossom of a chrysanthemum set in gold and platinum with a diamond stem and leaves, by Tiffany & Co., c.1904. Unios were iridescent and varied in delicate tints. These American dog tooth pearls were highly recommended for jewelry by George F. Kunz, Tiffany's gemmologist. Designed by Paulding Farnham. Engraved L.R. Dec. 04, for Lillian Russell 1904, comic opera star. Length 5½in. John Loring's Tiffany's 150 Years *(New York: Doubleday, 1987).*

Colour Plate 195. Pearl pendant purchased by Henry Walters of Baltimore from George F. Kunz at Tiffany & Co. where it was made about 1900 to 1910. This pink pearl produced by a common conch (Strombus gigas) *weighs 4.71 grams and is housed in a diamond-set platinum cage, hinged at the base so that it can be opened. The 20in. long trace chain has a tiny diamond in every thirtieth link. Mark: eagle's head, restricted warranty. Walters Art Gallery, Baltimore.*

pearl. Large quantities of iridescent shell lining were used annually, much of it for fancy pearl button sets currently fashionable. An English worker of mother-of-pearl had visited San Francisco about 1870. Appreciating the potential of the abalone shell, he started making ornamental objects from the opalescent material. Soon these became sought-after souvenirs of California for eastern American and European tourists.[11] The most desirable colour, a peacock green, was used for small pieces of jewelry.

Jewelry made of conch shell was exhibited at the Philadelphia Exhibition in 1876 and was said to have been fashionable in Paris at the time. Pink pearls or conch pearls, from the common conch indigenous to the Caribbean and Bermuda, enjoyed popularity in United States jewelry, especially with Art Nouveau designers, at the turn of the century. The pearls rarely appeared in perfectly regular round shapes. If the colour was good they had considerable value. A silky moiré-like surface gave life to their soft pink colour. A large, 4.71 grams, ovoid conch pearl caged in diamond-set platinum was purchased by Henry Walters of Baltimore from George Kunz at Tiffany's and was subsequently given by him to his niece Laura Delano (Colour Plate 195). Kunz noted in 1892 that 'the taste for pink pearls is on the increase...A necklace of these pearls valued at $4,000 has been collected, which is worthy of mention' (see Colour Plate 232).[12]

11. Ibid., p. 238-9.
12. Ibid., p. 236.

Colour Plate 196. Above. 18 karat gold ship pendant in the style of Renaissance examples, suspended by three chains which suggest the ship's rigging. The hull of the galleon is shaped in citrine, the furled sails are enamelled white. the balustrades are blue and the rudder dark red. American, c.1890. Length 1½in. (overall). Photograph by Peter J. Theriault. Private Collection.

Colour Plate 197. Above right. Portrait brooch in the Renaissance style, made by Tiffany & Co., after the portrait of Maria de' Medici by Frans II Pourbus le Jeune in the Louvre Museum. The head is carved chalcedony, foil backed in pink. The figure wears a diamond-studded lace collar, rose diamond and opal earrings, gold crown, pearl necklace and a gown embellished with sapphires, emeralds and more diamonds, representing her coronation costume when she became Regent of France as a result of her marriage to King Henry IV of France in 1600. The fitted box containing the portrait brooch is stamped on silk Tiffany & Co., New York; Avenue de l'Opera 36 Bis, Paris. Tiffany established their Paris branch in 1868. ©1991 Sotheby's Inc.

Revival Styles

Renaissance Revival

The glorious products of the Renaissance jewelers were appreciated by those culling the beauties of the past. As early as 1869, the designs of Hans Holbein the younger (1497-1543) who worked in England from 1530 on, were published in London. The original drawings had been given to the British Museum in 1753. George William Reid, keeper of prints and drawings, selected a group of these designs to be published for the use of goldsmiths and jewelers. This contribution to the revival in the 1870s can be seen in a literal translation of the design for a neck pendant, number 6 in Plate XV, made by Tiffany & Co. It was described by Reid as 'Two ribbons, upon which is engraved or enamelled an inscription DARE MVLTO BEATIVS QVAM ACCIPERE; the centre composed of foliage ornamented with one jewel, the whole surmounted by a mask'. Tiffany chose to execute the design in enamel in colours of turquoise, white and red, and used a pearl for the central jewel in the foliage as well as in the pendent drop.[1]

Benvenuto Cellini (1500-1570) was a name well known in the United States. Art critics called upon his memory, citing his work as the model of excellence, and his century as the best in the history of artistic achievement. Eugène Plon's biography of Cellini was published in Paris in 1883. Cellini's pompous autobiography, first published in 1558, was published in a translation by John Addington Symonds in 1887. Cellini's treatises on goldsmithing and sculpture were translated and published by C.R. Ashbee in 1888.

1. Design in TA.

Ashbee's purpose in translating Cellini's treatises was to provide European and American craftsmen with information concerning the methods used by Renaissance goldsmiths to improve the quality of craftsmanship and artistry of modern jewelers and goldsmiths in an industrial world. The treatises became useful to the Renaissance revival as well as to the Arts and Crafts movement. Ashbee offered criticism of Cellini's work seen through eyes of the late nineteenth century. He thought that Cellini was a first rate craftsman and a second rate artist.

No documented jewelry by Cellini has been positively identified. His first treaty discussed techniques of niello, filigree, enamelling, setting jewels, cutting diamonds, punch work, seal cutting, die cutting as well as the methods of working and finishing gold and silver. The second treatise discussed sculpture.

Features of Cellini's work that were appropriated for the Renaissance revival included cameos, in jeweled and scrolled frames, full of mythology and classical figures and scenes. Pendants suspended from a ring by three jeweled chains, and decorated with complicated enamelled scenes; elaborate borders, strapwork and cartouches; caryatids or sculptural figures, and pendent baroque pearls were especially favoured. Dragons, sea horses, sirens, nude figures, profile portraits and masks, were joined by heraldic devices and architectural motifs.

Other pendant designs made use of interlaced strap or ribbon work and coloured stones set in contrasting shapes. Pendants displaying the favoured Renaissance design of St. George and the dragon were especially popular during the revival. Austro-Hungarian jewelers produced quantities of these pendants for Americans as well as Europeans (see Colour Plate 88). Cabochon garnets, with their rich red colour, were most satisfactory substitutes for rubies in the revival jewelry. The Columbian Exposition in 1893 gave added impetus to revival pendants imitating Spanish galleon designs (Colour Plate 196).

In England, Carlo Giuliano did much to popularize enamelled jewelry in the Renaissance revival style. He took the delicate enamelled designs that had been used during the Renaissance period to decorate the back side of jewelry and featured them on the front instead.[2] One example of jewelry in this style, displayed at the Exposition Universelle in 1867, could have been inspired by an Italian Order of the Golden Fleece of the sixteenth century. Giuliano's type of delicately enamelled jewelry did not seem to catch on in the United States. Whether it was due to lack of skilled enamellers there or whether the style lacked the substantial qualities that appealed to Americans, little if any of this jewelry seems to have been made or owned in America.

It was the front side of Renaissance jewelry that inspired American Renaissance revival designs. Elaborate open-work designs were set with richly coloured stones of different shapes, pearls and both large and small diamonds. Enamelling often appeared on the front as well but consisted of boldly coloured underlining that accentuated and bound the variously coloured stones into a unified whole. The capped pendent pearl lent a final Renaissance punctuation (see Colour Plate 188).

An elaborate brooch exhibited at the Pan-American Exposition in Buffalo in 1901 was designed by Paulding Farnham of Tiffany's in the style of the Italian Renaissance with a few Edwardian flourishes (Plate 228). Made of American baroque pearls as well as faceted emeralds and diamonds, the brooch had a cross in the centre, and upper terminals of lions with a diamond in each mouth. Winged cherubs lolled like bookends above the cross, while below were two playful nude females supporting the whole design.

2. Geoffrey Munn, *Castellani and Giuliano, Revivalist Jewellers of the Nineteenth Century*, pp. 119-20.

Plate 228. Photograph of a brooch exhibited at the Pan-American Exposition in Buffalo, New York, in 1901. The design created by Paulding Farnham reflects the Italian Renaissance style. Putti are sheltered at the top of the scrolls and pearls, while below two females, exhibiting a touch of art nouveau curves, serve as supporters. On each side and at the top, lions' heads are set with diamonds in their mouths. Emeralds provide occasional accents. Used with the permission of Tiffany & Co. All rights reserved.

Nowhere is the debt to the Renaissance more manifest than in an extraordinary little jeweled portrait brooch made by Tiffany (Colour Plate 197). Maria de' Medici, the wife of Henry IV of France, was portrayed in all her finery, carved from a lively piece of hardstone, and bedecked with the jewels and lace she was known to have loved. From the gold crown on top of her head, her diamond-set lace collar, diamond and opal earrings and pearl necklace, to her coronation dress ornamented with sapphires, diamonds and emeralds, the Regent of France still dazzles. The portrait brooch had its source in the painting of Maria by Frans II Pourbus le Jeune in the Louvre Museum.[3]

Cameos in jeweled symmetrical frames also were popular in the Renaissance revival style (see Plate 160). Mrs. August Belmont owned a beautiful French example (see Colour Plate 112). In an elegant mount set with diamonds, emeralds and pearls was an oval cameo carved from a stone with three layers of colour. The design was a chariot drawn by horses in a horizontal oval with a detachable vertical oval carved with a profile portrait of a man in a matching frame. The miniature portrait pendant or brooch in Renaissance-style frames set with pearls or diamonds, sometimes alternating, enjoyed a revival in the 1880s and 1890s too.

Rings participated in the revival in both form and motif. Tiffany drawings of the late nineteenth century show elaborate, carved gold shanks with sculptural figures or with skulls typical of the reliquary, *memento mori* jewelry of the Renaissance period. The fede ring with its clasped hands and heart was revived. More esoteric was the double ring made to fit over two fingers at once, known in Roman days. An example made by Marcus & Co. of New York (Colour Plate 198) had a faceted diamond set in each ring, one round and one oval with a deliberate desire to have them unmatched. In the space between the two fingers was set a rectangular sugar loaf cut emerald. The gold shanks and the deep collets holding the stones were richly carved. An awkward

3. Sotheby's *Newsletter 20,* Oct. 1991, NY.

Colour Plate 198. Above. A yellow gold double ring to be worn on two adjacent fingers was made by Marcus & Co., New York, c.1895. Marked M & Co. inside band. Two sugar-loaf diamonds are set in the conjoined rings with an emerald cabochon mounted in the space between the two rings. The shanks are deeply carved with Renaissance style scroll work. An intriguing revival of 4th century A.D. Roman double rings. Length 1½in. (overall). Photograph by Peter J. Theriault. Private Collection.

Colour Plate 199. Right. This illustration of 'The Necklace of Galatea' served as the frontispiece for William Arnold Buffum's Tears of the Heliades, *in which the author attempted to describe the great beauty of the multicoloured Sicilian amber. The book appeared in three editions in England printed in 1896, 1897 and 1898. The last edition was published in New York in 1900. Courtesy, Gemological Institute of America.*

sort of ring to wear – sometimes there were three rings conjoined – this form may have been used solely at funerals.

Engraving of gems enjoyed renewed attention. The art was widely practised in the Renaissance and during the revival the design was often enhanced by an encrustation of diamonds.

The Renaissance style penetrated mass-produced jewelry. William Kerr was one of a number of firms that turned out stamped silver jewelry with Celliniesque designs. Sculptural and figural designs with florid scrolls were widely favoured.

Niello work was simulated on the wide hinged band bracelets so much in demand in the 1870s and 1880s. Strapwork and floral borders were engraved and chased into the metal and certain recessed areas were filled with black enamel to bring out the design. By the 1880s these bracelets, often with patented hinges and clicks, were available in a variety of patterns. They could be purchased in solid gold or rolled plate, enamelled or simply chased, with raised gold ornaments or without, and for children as well as women.[4]

4. Marsh & Bigney cat., 1883.

Archaeological Jewelry

The fashion for what is now called the archaeological style of jewelry had its origins in the continual excavations of Pompeii and Herculaneum. The discovery in the 1830s near Rome of Etruscan tombs filled with gold finely worked with filigree and granulation led to the mid-nineteenth century proliferation of Etruscan and Roman gold jewelry (see pages 266-268). Characterized by large circular medallions and

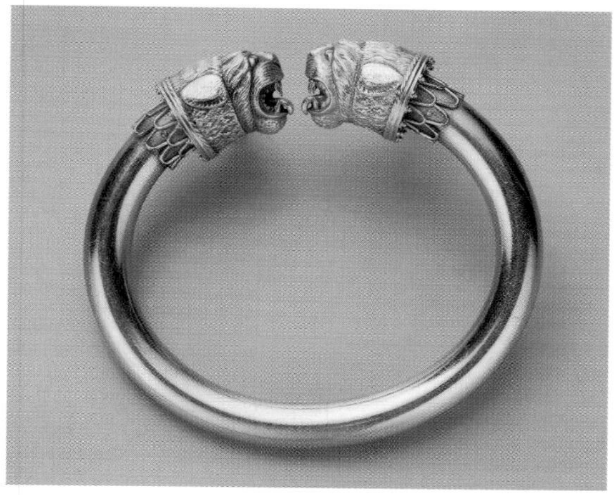

Colour Plate 200. Tiffany & Co. reproduction, c.1878, of an ancient Cypriot armlet found in the excavation of the Curium Treasure by General di Cesnola. Made of 18 karat gold, the tubular bracelet has lions' head terminals with chased work on the heads and manes, and decorative wire and bead work. Tiffany added an invisible spring hinge in the centre of the armlet which allows the armlet to open. Marked Tiffany & Co. /18 [K], stamped behind the lion's head on collar. 3⅝in. x 3in. Tiffany & Co. Permanent Collection.

bullae; settings of hardstones, mosaics and coins; substantial chains made of alternating sections; and pendants of tapering urns and fringe, the archaeological style permeated every form of jewelry.

The firm of Castellani, first in Rome and later in London, did more than any other to study and develop the innate possibilities of the technical achievements of the Etruscan gold workers. Castellani's shop in Rome was visited by Harriet Beecher Stowe and her Boston friend Annie Fields in 1856, a few years after the publication of Mrs. Stowe's incendiary novel, *Uncle Tom's Cabin.* The Castellanis were known to these American women as 'the world-famous workers in gold'. They were shown the Castellani collection of antique gems and reproductions. 'Mrs. Stowe was full of enthusiasm', her friend reported, 'and we lingered long over the wonderful things which the brothers [Alessandro and Augusto, sons of Fortunato Pio Castellani] brought forth to show'. When Mrs. Stowe admired a carved black onyx head of an Egyptian slave, the brothers offered it to her 'as a slight recognition for what you have done'.[1]

The collection of classical and medieval antiquities formed by Alessandro Castellani included gems and jewelry from Etruria, Phoenicia and Greece. Castellani hoped that the British Museum would acquire the entire collection. When this had not

1. Judy Rudoe, 'Alessandro Castellani's Letters to Henry Layard: Extracts concerning the 1862 International Exhibition in London and the Revival of Granulation' in *Jewellery Studies 5* (1991) 107, quoting Annie Fields, *Authors and Friends* (Boston 1896) p. 171.

Colour Plate 201. Hollow gold bracelet with lion's head terminals, derived from the Curium bracelet, probably made by Charles F. Mason of Attleboro, Massachusetts, in 1881. Mason Draper & Co. was an Attleboro jewelry firm with an office in New York at 176 Broadway. 2⅛in. x 2⁵⁄₁₆in. Photograph by Peter J. Theriault. Private Collection.

Colour Plate 202. Woven gold snake, flexible bracelet with ruby eyes. Owned by Fay Witte Ball (1868-1971). Length 29in. (overall). Photograph courtesy of The Charleston Museum, Charleston, South Carolina. Private Collection.

materialized, Alessandro, hoping to find an American buyer who could pay the £40,000 price he asked, brought the collection to the Philadelphia Centennial where it occupied a prominent place in the Art Gallery. The Boston *Transcript* praised the Castellani collection as well as the firm's great skill in reproducing antique jewelry, and feared that it was not appreciated 'by the crowd of visitors who surround the cheap jewelry stands near it'.[2]

When no one stepped forward to buy the collection, it was suggested that joint purchase be made by the museums of Boston, New York, Philadelphia and Washington, and that the collection be circulated among the four institutions. 'Who can say', queried the Boston *Transcript,* 'that, if we keep them [i.e. the Castellani collection] in our museums, our goldsmiths will not so profit by this study of their technical and artistic perfection, as to be able eventually to make works of their own worthy to be classed with those now made at Rome by the first goldsmith of his time?'[3] Castellani's proposal failed. While Alessandro Castellani was in the United States for the Exhibition, he read his paper on *Antique Jewellery and its Revival* to audiences at the Archaeological Association in Buffalo, and at the Pennsylvania Museum and the School of Industrial Art in Philadelphia. This paper was published in the Centennial city in 1877.[4] Castellani's exhibit and lectures created a revival of interest in ancient jewelry forms and techniques. The ancient simple borders of twisted wire and designs of gold beading became more complex in their revival. The repertoire for which the Castellani firm became renowned included granulation, filigree and enamel.

Further interest in archaeological jewelry was stirred up by Henry Layard, the archaeologist whose discoveries at the site of Nineveh excited great interest in the 1850s and 60s. So too did the ornaments brought to light by the excavations of Dr. Heinrich Schliemann at Mycenae and Hissarlik (thought to be the site of ancient Troy) completed in 1873.[5]

American jewelers were unable to attain the degree of technological skill achieved by the Etruscans or by Castellani, but they strove to produce a similar effect. There were a number of pieces of jewelry said by their American owners to have been made by Castellani although they bear no marks. A pair of gold earrings featured cherubs riding on the backs of birds (Plate 229). A parure with vase-shaped pendants of polished Sicilian amber, set so that the amber could be readily removed, was purchased by William Arnold Buffum (Plate 230). Buffum was the author of a book on amber, *The Tears of the Heliades* published in London in 1896. He was especially interested in Sicilian amber and used what appears to be a very similar necklace for the colour frontispiece for the book (Colour Plate 199). He called it 'the Necklace of Galatea'.

A second parure, also set with removable amber pendants, was purchased by Buffum from Pierret of Rome.[6] Ernesto Pierret (w.1845-98) was considered one of the best jewelers in Rome, 'second only to Castellani, whose copies of antique jewellery are of the highest order', according to John Murray's 1869 guide to Rome.[7] Buffum spent many years in Europe where he assembled one of the world's finest collections of amber. It was bequeathed to the Museum of Fine Arts, Boston in 1901. The colour tones of this Sicilian amber were distinguished from other ambers by its fluorescence and were thought by Buffum to be even more vivacious than those of opal.[8]

In the post-centennial period, the design sources of archaeological

2. 16 Oct. 1876.
3. 28 June 1876. A catalogue of the exhibition was published in 1877. Tait, *I*, p. 192.
4. It was first published in 1862 in London.
5. Bagnall, p. 6.
6. Geoffrey C. Munn attributes the parure shown here to Pierret and the second amber set given to the MFA at the same time to Castellani.
7. Quoted by Munn, p. 159.
8. William Arnold Buffum, *The Tears of the Heliades*, pp. xix, 11.

Plate 229. Pair of gold earrings in the form of cherubs riding on the backs of birds, unmarked, but attributed by the donor to the firm of Castellani, Rome, c.1873. Minute granulation to give texture to the appearance of tightly curled hair on the heads of the cherubs and filigree for details of the cherubs' wings, the reins and the feathers of the birds are techniques Castellani derived from 3rd century B.C. Etruscan jewels in the Campana Collection. Length ¾in. Gift of Edward Jackson Holmes. Courtesy, Museum of Fine Arts, Boston.

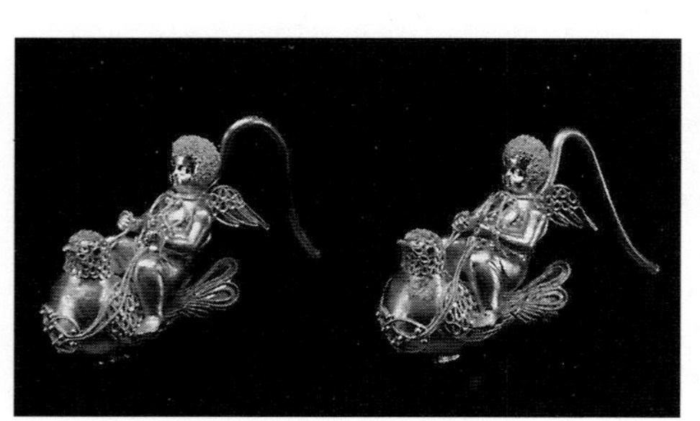

Plate 230. One of two sets of gold and Sicilian amber jewelry, made in Italy about 1870, in the collection of William Arnold Buffum. This set and another similar set were made especially for Buffum, one by Castellani and the other by Pierret, according to information provided at the time of Buffum's bequest in 1901 to the Museum of Fine Arts in Boston. Buffum, a Bostonian collector and connoisseur, made amber his speciality and was praised for his contributions on behalf of this gem. In sunlight, Sicilian amber flashes colours from light blue and rose to deep azure and ruby red, much like opal. Buffum described the hues as being 'of the primeval world, the imprisoned color shades of an earlier and more exuberant clime'. [The Tears of the Heliades or amber as a gem *(London, 1896.)] Length 20½in. (necklace). Bequest of William Arnold Buffum. Courtesy, Museum of Fine Arts, Boston.*

jewelry were extended to the discoveries made by General Luigi Palma di Cesnola who, in 1876, returned to the United States with a collection of more than 10,000 objects of antiquity which he had dug up during his six years as consul to Cyprus. The Curium treasures, as they were called, were of Greek, Phoenician, Assyrian and Egyptian origin. Di Cesnola offered his collection to the Metropolitan Museum of Art and soon became director of the museum.

With admirable foresight, di Cesnola commissioned Tiffany to make copies of certain objects in this collection that could be purchased by museums abroad. One of these reproductions was an armlet with lion heads at each end of a hollow tube which Tiffany equipped with a concealed spring hinge (Colour Plate 200). The terminals were cast and then chased. Beading and delicate wire appliqués filled the area between the bracelet tubing and the terminals. So accurately did the copy reproduce the appearance of the original, that di Cesnola told Tiffany that if the piece had not been marked with the firm's name, he might not have been able to tell them apart. There were technical differences in addition to the hinge however. The Curium armlet was made of gold-plated bronze with gold embossed terminals, and the fangs were applied (Plate 231). On the Tiffany version, the chased texture of fur covered the front

Plate 231. Original Curium gold plated armlet excavated by General di Cesnola in 1875. The Cesnola Collection, purchased by subscription 1874-1876 (74.51.3559). The Metropolitan Museum of Art.

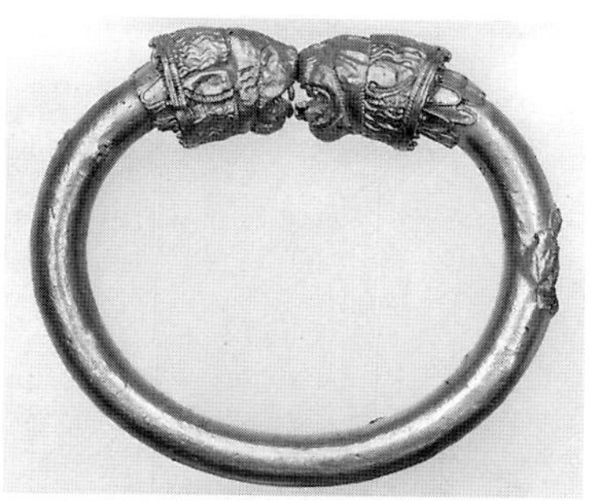

Colour Plate 203. Above. Gold brooch and earrings set with glass micromosaics of flamboyant polychrome birds, marked with appliqué tag bearing the name of INNOCENTI on back of brooch on top. Italian,c.1870-1890. Elaborate scroll grape with grape-vine border which is open at the top. Length about 3⅛in. Bequest of Miss C.L.W. French. Gold pendant set with glass micromosaic of polychrome beetle on white ground and red border. Italian, c.1870-1890. Roman hallmark inside locket on back. Also on the back are the letters AEI in relief which means 'for ever' in Greek. Length about 1½in. (overall). Bequest of Maxim Karolik. Courtesy, Museum of Fine Arts, Boston.

Colour Plate 204. Left. Cleopatra's head adorns this gold enamelled brooch, with entwined snakes on each side of a sun disc. Probably made in Newark, c.1880. Length 1 9/16in. Photograph by Peter J. Theriault. Private Collection.

Colour Plate 205. Gold locket and pearl bracelet, made in India, presented to Edward D. Ropes by Hindu merchant Taria Topan at Zanzibar, c.1880. Length 1¾in. (locket). Gold bracelet (lower left), presented by the wife of Taria Topan to the wife of Captain Nathan B. Batchelder, Length 2¼in. Photograph by Mark Sexton. Peabody Essex Museum.

of the head.[9] In 1887, the original armlet and other treasures were stolen from the Museum. Fortunately Tiffany, a Trustee of the Museum, still had one of the reproductions of the armlet which he gave to the Metropolitan. The original was never recovered.

Tiffany had exhibited his copies of the Curium treasures at the Paris Exposition in 1878 and received a gold medal for jewelry in addition to much favourable publicity for the excellence of workmanship. 'The copies of the gold ornaments of the Cesnola collection were wonderful specimens of elaborate and almost deceptive imitation of the antique originals, even to their defects and imperfections', according to the *American Fine Arts Commission Reports.*[10] George Augustus Sala, an English journalist, thought that the Curium treasures outshone the discoveries of Schliemann and

9. Tait, I, 155; II, 257, #978 and Fig. 84; Purtell, p. 91.
10. Quoted by Tait, I, 155.

Colour Plate 206. Mogul armlets and aigrette, set with emeralds and other gems that correspond with the signs of the Zodiac, India, mid-18th century, owned by the Maharani and Maharaja of Delhi respectively, and purchased by Mrs. John L. Gardner, Jr., of Boston in 1884. Length 5in. (aigrette). Photograph by David Bohl, Boston. Courtesy of the Isabella Stewart Gardner Museum, Boston.

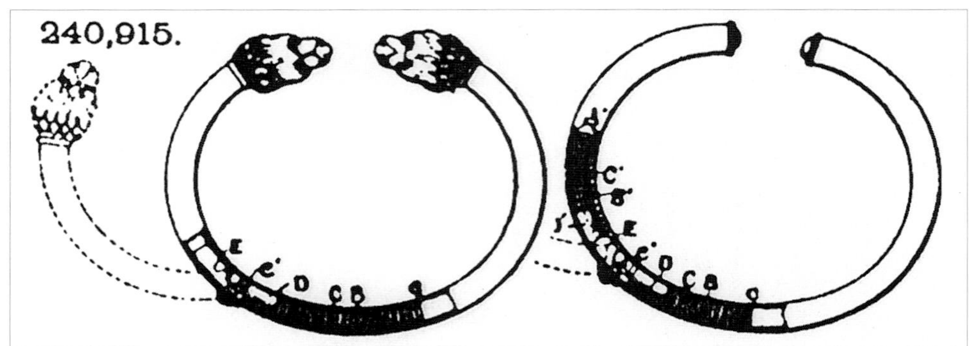

Plate 232. Bracelet derived from the Curium armlet and made with a hinge so that it was self-closing, a feature patented by Charles E. Mason of Attleboro, Massachusetts, on 3 May 1881. United States Patent Office, No. 240,915.

Castellani. 'Too much praise cannot be bestowed on Messrs Tiffany', he said, 'they are indeed triumphs of imitative goldsmith's art'.[11] The *Artisan Reports by the Society of Arts* pointed out that the copies were suitable for study or a museum, implying that they were not suitable for wearing.[12] Hoop earrings 'with heads of animals at the terminations, not unlike those found by Gen. Cesnola at Cyprus, will be much worn', predicted Tiffany's in 1881.[13]

An American jewelry firm soon produced a more useful version of the animal-headed armlet. Charles E. Mason of the Attleboro firm of Mason, Draper & Co., known for its patent bracelets, received a patent on 3 May 1881 for a hinged bracelet with lion's head terminals clearly derived from the Curium armlet copied by Tiffany (Plate 232). The patent, however, was not on the artistic design of the bracelet. It was on its hinge which provided a spiral spring with a stop to make the bracelet self-closing. The lion's head bracelets were made of hollow tubes, with cast and chased heads, and had ruby-coloured glass cabochons set in the eyes facing outward (Colour Plate 201). The patent tag applied inside the bracelet near the hinge bore the date Nov. 12. 78.

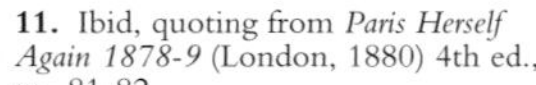

11. Ibid, quoting from *Paris Herself Again 1878-9* (London, 1880) 4th ed., pp. 81-82.
12. Ibid., I, 155.
13. Tiffany & Co., *Catalogue* 1881-2, p. 30.
14. 11 Dec. 1881.
15. Pat.#239,890, 5 April 1881.
16. Pat.#108,863; #229,276.

Mason, Draper & Co. had a New York Office at 176 Broadway, and this office apparently supplied Tiffany's with their lion-head bracelets. The Tiffany Catalogue for 1881-2 stated, 'A very popular bracelet is a patent "spring bracelet" that obviates the necessity for clasps and requires no guard chains, as it cannot slip from the arm. They are made of one or two tubes of gold, either plain or adorned with Etruscan tracery. Some of them terminate with fleur de lis, lions heads, or other devices; and lace pins and earrings are made to match many of the patterns'. The price range at Tiffany's for the plain bracelets was $9.50 to $56. If they were set with jewels they could cost from $30 to $200. In 1881 the New York *Sun* reported that bracelets were the favourite jewelry item and made a most acceptable Christmas present. The newspaper also noted the current revival of Etruscan gold jewelry.[14]

Plate 233. Herman Unger of Newark, New Jersey, patented a method of hinging bracelets on 5 April 1881. The dragon's head terminals were not patented but were shown with the description of the hinge. United States Patent Office, No. 239,890.

A somewhat similar type of bracelet was designed by Herman Unger of Newark, New Jersey (Plate 233). The ends of Unger's bracelet overlapped and the sections of the bracelet could be pivoted laterally. The terminals were ornamented with dragon's heads.[15] Other bracelets were made with dog or wolf's head terminals at one end of the bracelet, with diamonds set in the eyes and in the snarling mouths of the animals. The other end of the bracelet was flattened, shaped and ornamented like a spoon handle. These bracelets often bore an applied tab stamped with the patent dates 'Oct.25, 70/June 29, 80'. The first date referred to a patent on the spring for the joint of a bracelet, issued to Henry Carlisle, Jr. of Philadelphia. The second date indicated a patent on a bracelet formed of two curved pieces with a spring in the joint that would leave a space between the terminals at all times. The second patent was issued to John A. Riley and Charles S. Freer of New York city.[16]

The same tag with the double patent dates appeared on one of the most elaborate bracelets of the animal-head variety (Plate 234). One terminal had a shackled ring. The other end had the upper part of a

Plate 234. Cerberus bracelet made of burnished gold, in original box imprinted and sold by Theodore B. Starr of New York, c.1880. One end had a shackled ring and the other featured the three-headed Cerberus with diamonds set in the eyes and jaws. Two patent stamps dated 25 October 1870 and 29 June 1880 relate to the spring hinge. The surface is ornamented with granulation and delicate twisted wire designs. Courtesy of Christie's, New York.

triple-headed dog set with diamonds in the eyes and jaws. The heads were held in one leashed collar. The detailed finishing included carving and applied granulation and twisted wire ornamentation. Cerberus, the three-headed dog of Roman mythology that guarded the entrance to Hades, was known to many Americans of the period through Orpheus and Cerberus, the first major sculpture executed by Thomas Crawford (1813-1857). The sculpture was exhibited at the Boston Athenaeum from 1844 to 1872, when it was moved to the Museum of Fine Arts in Boston.

Carlo Giuliano, who had worked for Alessandro Castellani, made significant contributions to the archaeological style in jewelry. In addition to fringed necklaces and jewelry set with intaglios, Giuliano incorporated antique coins in his designs. During a visit to London in July 1886, Isabella Stewart Gardner of Boston bought 'a gold Roman ring' set with an intaglio from Carlo Giuliano for £4.10.0 (Plate 235).[17] A set of gold jewelry, mounted with gold coins in the style of Giuliano, is said to have been owned by a member of the Adams family of Boston, possibly by Mrs. Henry Adams. An 1883 publication attributed the set to Boucheron.[18]

The archaeological style persisted into the twentieth century. In 1903, Henry Walters bought a number of interesting necklaces and a bracelet from Giacinto Melillo, who had learned his skills from Alessandro Castellani in Naples. Melillo continued to produce archaeological jewelry and was awarded the Grand Prix and the Legion of Honour at the Exposition Universelle in 1900.[19] Walters' selections favoured scarab set necklaces, one of which resembled an Etruscan necklace in the Castellani collection at the British Museum. It had been excavated at Canino. Another reflected the Egyptian Revival style.

17. GFP.
18. German periodical *Gewerbehalle,* cited and illus. by Bury II, 713, plate 202.
19. WAG, pp. 237-39, Plate 670.

Plate 235. Gold ring purchased from Carlo Giuliano in 1886 by Mrs. John L. Gardner, Jr., of Boston, when she was in London. The bezel contains an intaglio and is supported by musicians playing the flute on each side. Length 1¹⁄₁₆in., width ¹⁵⁄₁₆in. Photograph by David Bohl, Boston. Courtesy of the Isabella Stewart Gardner Museum, Boston.

Egyptian Revival

Periodic contact with Egyptian culture brought the art of the Nile, with its pictorial language and colourful palette, to Europe and eventually to jewelry designs in America. The Napoleonic conquest of Egypt and the discovery of the Rosetta Stone early in the nineteenth century had an impact on the arts, as is evident in the drawings of Percier and Fontaine in France. Another wave of enthusiasm resulted from the opening of the Suez Canal in 1869 and the thundering success of Verdi's *Aida,* performed in New York in 1873. Continuing archaeological discoveries in tombs such as those of Queen Ah Hotpe in 1859, Queen Mereret in 1894 and Tutankhamen in 1923, kept the

Colour Plate 207. Drawing of an aigrette designed by Paulding Farnham for Tiffany's exhibition at the Columbian Exposition in Chicago in 1893. The tapering emerald nestles into a pierced sea urchin shaped cushion. Diamonds form a band around the emerald and are mounted on delicate wands to form the feathery spray. Dimensions of drawing, 6½in. x 6½in. (overall). Used with the permission of Tiffany & Co.

Colour Plate 208. Hand ornament marked by Tiffany & Co., probably designed by Paulding Farnham, New York, c.1900. Set with turquoise, garnets, sapphires, peridot, zircons, hessonite, beryls, tourmalines, chrysoberyls and pearls. Private Collection.

Egyptian revival alive for well over a century.

The most obvious manifestation of the Egyptian style in jewelry was the use of scarabs as gems. For centuries scarabs were worshipped as symbols of the sun god. They were carved out of stones and glazed steatite or made of what is now called Egyptian faience. They were made in the form of the sacred beetle with hieroglyphs on the back, and were used as seals or worn as amulets. In the early 1860s in London, Carlo Giuliano made a gold pendant in the Etruscan manner embellished with filigree and granulation, and set with a scarab carved from cornelian.[1] Giuliano made a collection of original scarabs, some of which he set into brooches.

A popular substitute for authentic scarabs in nineteenth-century revival jewelry was the skeleton of the South American beetle. The shells of this species were less fragile than other beetle shells and yet had brilliant iridescent colours of blue-green. At the Philadelphia Centennial Exhibition, a parure set with a variety of South American beetles, collected by Secretary of the Navy George M. Robeson, was displayed. This exotic ensemble was executed by a Philadelphia jeweler, Ernest Kretzmar, and like Giuliano's pendant relied heavily upon the Etruscan style for its design (see Plate 206).[2] Several decades later a scarab-set parure was made by Marcus & Co. and is now at the Smithsonian Institution. The design was quite simplified with a double row of beetles. The length of the lower central scarabs was increased by the addition of tiny charms some of which had coiled snake motifs.

1. Fig. 90, Munn, pp. 84-85; 129; based on an example in the Campana collection.
2. Rainwater, *A.J.M.*, p. 147. Kretzmar was listed in Philadelphia *Directories* between 1867 and 1896.

Colour Plate 209. Brooch made of tiger's claws by Tiffany & Co., New York, c.1885. Courtesy of Primavera Gallery.

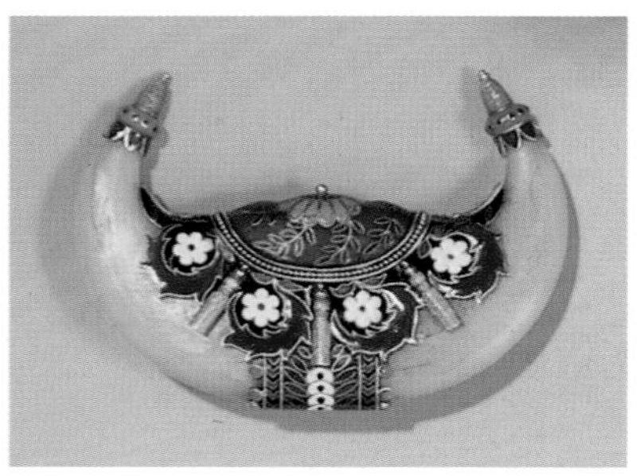

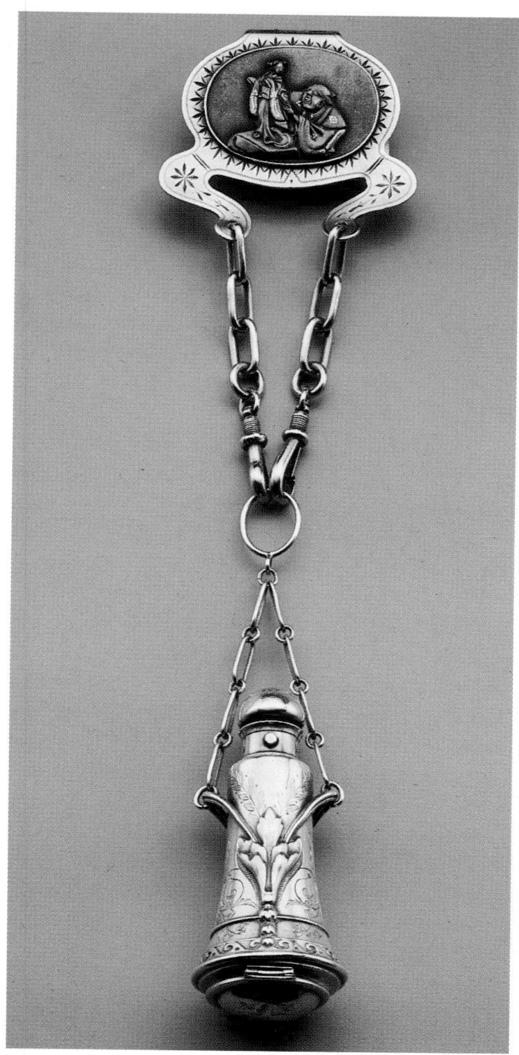

Colour Plate 210. Chatelaine hook made of silver, copper and gold, with a perfume bottle suspended by two chains. The central medallion at the top depicts a Japanese man and woman. Marked on back TIFFANY & CO. / 3037 / STERLING / M / 1268 / UNION-SQUARE. Tiffany & Co. Permanent Collection.

Colour Plate 211. Japanese bar pin made of a black copper alloy inlaid with gold and silver (shakudo) with motifs of fans, flowers, birds and featuring a ship and a stork, made for the western market about 1875-1890. Length 2⅝in. Photograph by Mark Sexton. Peabody Essex Museum.

Colour Plate 212. Pair of gold bracelets with applied floral branches in the Japanese style with two colours of gold and platinum buds. Engraved S F L; Sarah Lindley Fox 1873; and Fanny A. Logan June 20, 1882. Marked inside the band TIFFANY & C[o] New York. Length about 2¼in. (overall). Courtesy, The British Museum.

Some time prior to 1903, Henry Walters purchased five different gold necklaces with pendent scarabs cut from steatite, cornelian, lapis lazuli and other stones, attributed to Giacinto Melillo (1845-1915) of Naples.[3] Melillo also made copies of antique jewelry and won honours for his exhibits at the Paris Exposition in 1900. Louis Comfort Tiffany, fascinated by the iridescence of beetles, made a modernized version of the scarab necklace with beetles created by his innovative enamelling techniques.[4]

Tiffany & Co. produced a number of successful Egyptian designs. Most famous was a three-piece mantel set made of marble and ormolu about 1885. The sphinx-topped tomb bearing the clock on its facade and the two flanking obelisks were decorated with all the motifs popularly associated with the kingdom on the Nile.[5] Drawings in the Tiffany Archives make use of Egyptian shapes and motifs in jewelry. Brooches, rings, shirt pins, earrings and charms were made of scarabs. Finger rings were made from tightly coiled sacred cobras with round faceted gems set in their heads. The

3. WAG, Fig. 679, pp. 238, 240.
4. Plate Loring, pp. 140-41.
5. MMA, *19th-Century America*, #232.

6. #240,096, 21 April 1881.
7. *Jewelers Review, 23,* 41, No. 21, Fig. 46.
8. Ibid., *21,* No. 10, 31 July 1893, 'Novelties in Jewelry'.
9. Ibid., *22,* #14, 28 Aug. 1893, p. 36.
10. Becker, *Antique and 20th C. J.,* pp. 167-174.
11. *22,* 30, No. 14, 19 June 1893.
12. WAG, #702, pp. 244-5. See also J. Anderson Black, *A History of Jewelry,* pp. 44, 48.

cobra signified power. Recumbent and sejeant sphinxes formed fobs. The spread-winged vulture, the emblem of Nekhebet, formed the centrepiece of a beaded necklace that had lotus finials as clasps. The lotus symbolized resurrection. The eye of Horus was another significant symbol for the Egyptians who believed it would protect them from the evil eye.

The snake, representing eternity, had been popular as a motif in jewelry for centuries. It had been given new prestige in the nineteenth century when Queen Victoria received an engagement ring in this design from Prince Albert. Snakes formed frames for lockets and brooches, and were very fashionable for bracelets. *Godey's Lady's Book* supplied directions and the materials for making these serpentine bracelets out of woven hair and other pliant materials (see Colour Plate 127 and page 215). Sometimes the snake was given a gold head set with turquoises and pearls, with a red jewel for the eye, and a gold tip to its tail. By the end of the century, snake bracelets were made of articulated gold sections and were wrapped around the upper arm, in the manner of Cleopatra as performed by Sarah Bernhardt (Colour Plate 202). A Newark patent for a snake bracelet was issued to Augustus S. Crane in 1881.[6]

A twisting silver cobra formed the handle of a jeweled hand-mirror in the Egyptian style that was exhibited at the Columbian Exposition in 1893. The face of the mirror was cut out of rock crystal from North Carolina and mounted with green gold and lapis lazuli. The cobra was inlaid with gold and encircled one of the eight scarabs on the back of the mirror.[7] The same year, hat pins made with diamond-studded snakes coiled around sizeable freshwater pearls were the latest fashion.[8] Snakes were used for cuff-link buttons, key rings, bracelets, lace pins, and chatelaines with the watch hanging from the serpent's mouth. There were scarf rings with the end of the snake twisted in the shape of the owner's initials, and finger rings with from two to four coils. In 1893 a ring made of four bands of gold and platinum was referred to as an 'Egyptian ring'.[9]

Characteristic Egyptian colours were red, turquoise, blue and occasionally green. In jewelry these colours were supplied by cornelians, turquoises, lapis lazuli and green feldspar, or by coloured inlays of glass and ceramic.[10] For Egyptian revival jewelry, glass mosaics were often used to supply the colour (Colour Plate 203). Enamels also could be used to good effect, especially against a coloured gold ground (Colour Plate 204). A typical American example featured the head of Cleopatra in profile, ornamented with red and green enamel. The pair of snakes, entwined to form the frame, had ruby eyes. In 1893, *The Jewelers' Review* reported, 'The newest production in Egyptian jewelry represents the Goddess Isis with out-stretched wings. The latter are of transparent enamel and the figure of gold. The entirety is finished in the most artistic style of true Egyptian'.[11]

Mogul Jewelry

With Queen Victoria's ascendancy as Empress of India in 1876 came greater interest on the part of westerners in the arts of India. American ships had been engaged in the trade with India since the early days of United States independence. In 1802 there were no less than six ships from Salem, Massachusetts, in the harbour at Calcutta on a single day. Ports such as Calcutta, Bombay, and Madras were well known to American captains, as were the merchants there who supplied them with textiles, china, furniture, spices, coffee, tea and indigo. Tortoiseshell and filigree jewelry also provided a good commodity for trade back home. Occasionally Mogul jewelry was acquired for personal use, often as a gift from one of the merchants or local potentates, as a gesture of friendship. This distinctive type of jewelry had been made during the Mogul Empire in the sixteenth and seventeenth centuries and continued to be made during the next two centuries.

Extravagant, exotic and colourful, Mogul jewelry featured seed pearls and bright red and green gems, with an abundance of pendants and tassels. Translucent enamel work added to the richness of the floral designs on the reverse side. Aigrettes; armlets; rings for toes as well as fingers; anklets; and ear, nose and forehead ornaments were among the Mogul ornaments that surprised and fascinated the western world.

The American Consul in Zanzibar, Edward D. Ropes of Salem, received a bracelet as a gift from the Hindu merchant Taria Topan (Colour Plate 205, left). Another prize brought back from India to the United States was a double bracelet made with three double rows of seed pearls and set with emeralds (Colour Plate 205, centre). A cast gold locket made by a goldsmith in India found its way to Massachusetts in the same manner (Colour Plate 205, right).

In 1883 and 1884, the colourful Mrs. John L. Gardner, Jr. of Boston travelled to the Far East. With her love of the exotic, Mrs. Gardner was intrigued by the jewelry she and her husband saw at the shop of A.N. Jacob while they were in Calcutta (Colour Plate 206). There was a pair of armlets that had belonged to the Maharani of Delhi.[1] They were set with twelve different stones which corresponded to the signs of the Zodiac: coral, pearl, zircon, turquoise, cat's eye, spinel, emerald, ruby, diamond, sapphire, yellow ruby or topaz and beryl. As Jacob explained to the Gardners, 'the natives...believe that the stars and their abode have something to do with our sistem and therefore, each man and woman has own charm in one of the Gems and as they dont know which is it, they were [wear] 12 charms, 9 charms or 7 charms that one of the number might be theirs'.

There was also a *kalgi,* the ornament worn on the front of the turban to hold a feather plume. It had been owned by the Maharaja of Delhi and was set with nine charm gems. The plume was mounted with shaped flat diamonds. A large flat, square emerald was centred below. The feather holder was carved from white jade. It is possible that Mrs. Gardner had seen the account in a Boston newspaper some years before that had described Mogul style jewelry. The description was memorable: a jeweled aigrette with its 'delicate plume...formed of the sprays of the feathers of the ostrich, so tender as to look rather like fine hair than any quantity of plumage', and 'the massive armlets...well calculated to make an imposing effect on occasions of native gatherings'.[2] With her well-known penchant for startling the natives in Boston, Mrs. Gardner thought it over and then acquired both the *kalgi* and the armlets.[3]

Isabel Anderson was given a turban brooch by an Indian maharaja shortly after her marriage to Ambassador Larz Anderson in 1897 (see Colour Plate 178). The luscious hexagonal emerald was remounted in western fashion with a border of old-mine diamonds and foliated scroll work at the top, crowned by a briolette emerald. A detachable pear-shaped emerald, capped with rose-cut diamonds and a briolette diamond, could be suspended from the brooch. Mrs. Anderson later described wearing the jewel when she was presented at the British Court in the Diplomatic Circle in 1904: 'on my corsage a big Indian emerald which a maharaja had worn in the front of his turban'.[4] Her portrait, still on view at their former home on Massachusetts Avenue in Washington, D.C., includes this jewel precariously pinned to her tulle-draped corsage (see Colour Plate 177).

1. These armlets were taken from the Palace by British soldiers at the time of the Sepoy mutiny of native troops in 1857. The armlets were auctioned off with other plunder and were bought by an officer whose widow later sold them to A.N. Jacob. GFP, c. 31 Jan. 1884, microfilm.

2. Boston *Transcript*, 26 Jan. 1870. The jewelry described was exhibited in London that winter, 'the first important gifts of British manufacture... officially presented to the Indian princes and dignitaries'.

3. Letter from A.N. Jacob to J.L. Gardner Jr., in Calcutta; JLG pencil memo of purchase on 31 Jan. 1884. GFP, microfilm.

4. Quoted from Mrs. Anderson's travel book *Odd Corners*, published in 1917, quoted in Sotheby catalogue 16 Apr. 19[illegible] sale.

Colour Plate 213. Group of jewelry made about 1880 in the Japanese style. The hammered gold brooch in the shape of a fan; the pair of studs set with reverse crystal intaglios of Japanese figures; the triangular stud with cut-corners and an applied heron are all marked on back by TIFFANY & C°. The half set, made in four colours of gold with a shell and heron motif, and the three-colour gold necklace with openwork plaques in the form of bird cages are all attributed to Tiffany & Co. on the basis of similar marked examples. Width about 2½in. (bar pin). Courtesy, The British Museum.

An unusual aigrette was designed by Paulding Farnham and made by Tiffany's for the 1893 Columbian Exposition (Colour Plate 207). The preliminary drawing showed a large pear-shaped emerald resting on a gold openwork cushion of floral reticulation. From the top of the Peruvian emerald a spray of diamonds shot skyward, mounted on the thinnest of shafts of various lengths. The finished aigrette had a rounder, inverted pear-shaped emerald, which tapered as it settled into the top of a pierced gold sea urchin. The spray held ostrich feathers.[5]

While the Mogul style of jewelry played a minor role in the history of jewelry in America, it played a dramatic one which continued to surface from time to time. A necklace made early in the twentieth century by Tiffany & Co. adapted the floral patterns and colours of Mogul jewelry to a gold necklace studded with sapphires, rubies and a pendent emerald.[6] Suspended from triple cords of woven silk, the necklace had a jeweled clasp and two plaques that served as spreaders which provided variations on the design of the central pendant.[7]

Colour Plate 214. Pendant locket in the Japanese style, gold, with a compartment in the back for a lock of hair or a picture. Marked by Tiffany & Co., New York, c.1880. Length 2⅜in. (overall). Courtesy, Janet Zapata.

---

5. TA drawing and photograph (present location of aigrette unknown).
6. Proddow #30, p. 56.
7. Janet Zapata, 'The Islamic Influence in European and American Jewelry', *Antiques*, September 1992, p. 265.

The Japanese Style

Elements of the radically different Japanese style of design and ornament reached the United States in a variety of ways. While there had been a few earlier contacts, it was not until 1854 that Japan was opened to trade with the United States after Commodore Matthew C. Perry signed the Treaty of Kanagawa. The first significant display of Japanese art was seen in the western world in 1862 at the London Exposition, but it went unnoticed by Americans engaged in the Civil War. Japan itself became embroiled in a civil war in 1868 that resulted in the end of feudalism there and an enormous change to the country.[1]

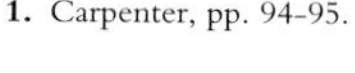

1. Carpenter, pp. 94-95.

Colour Plate 215. 18 karat gold bangle bracelet, incorporating three colours of gold, attributed to Carrow, Bishop & Co., New York and Philadelphia, c.1880-1885. Two patent stamps are located on each end of the bracelet. One dated 11 May 1880 was granted to Clement B. Bishop, New York, who assigned the patent to himself and John S. and William D. Carrow, New York (see Plate 236). The patent concerned the projecting ribbed edges which served to protect the applied ornament on the bracelet's band. United States Patent No. 227,476. The second patent was granted to Charles Heim, Corona, New York, on 14 October 1879, and reassigned to Hale and Mulford, New York, and concerned projecting rims of bracelet edges as well (see Colour Plate 242). United States Patent No. 8928. Photograph by Peter J. Theriault. Private Collection.

227,476. BRACELET. Clement B. Bishop, New York, N. Y. assignor to himself, John S. Carrow, Philadelphia, Pa., and William D. Carrow, New York, N. Y. Filed Aug. 18, 1879.

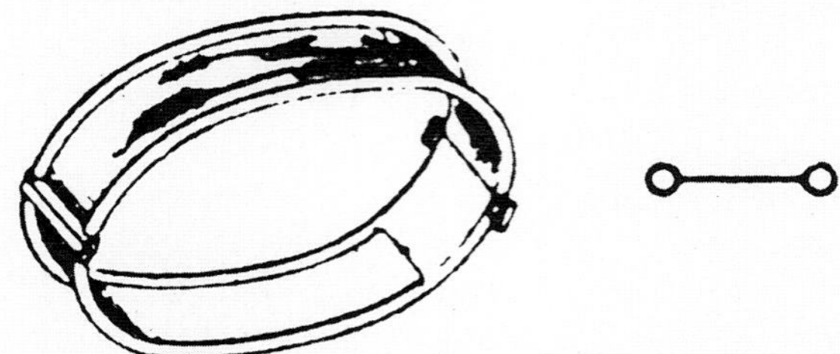

Claim.—A single-plate bracelet, each half of which consists of a plate having on each edge a rib projecting equally from both sides of the said plate and forming part of the plate itself, as set forth.

Plate 236. United States Patent No. 227,476 dated 11 May 1880 granted to Clement B. Bishop, New York, who assigned the patent to himself and John S. and William D. Carrow, New York. The patent concerned the projecting ribbed edges which served to protect the applied ornament on the bracelet's band. A second patent was granted to Charles Heim, Corona, New York, on 14 October 1879, and reassigned to Hale and Mulford, New York, and concerned projecting rims of bracelet edges as well (see Colour Plates 242 and 243) United States Patent No. 8928. Photograph by Peter J. Theriault. Private Collection.

Japanese metalwork had not been appreciated in the west before its appearance at the Exposition Universelle in 1867. The high degree of technical skill exhibited by these wares created quite a stir. By 1869 Tiffany was advertising choice Japanese bronze vases for their customers. At the same time, Japanese wood block prints, illustrations in books, and paintings made their way to this country. These influential objects also circulated in France and England where they added an intriguing new element to the work of artists such as Whistler, Manet and Degas in Europe, and artists in America such as John Singer Sargent, William Merritt Chase and John LaFarge, the latter having begun to collect Japanese art in the early 1860s.

Books concerned with Japanese design and related decorative arts were available to designers at both Tiffany's and Gorham. *The Keramic Art of Japan* by Audsley & Bowes was published in 1875 and soon became part of the Tiffany & Co. library.[2] Gorham's company library included printed volumes of engravings such as *Manga* and *Kacho Gaden* by Hokusai, architectural details and pattern books, as well as albums containing photographs and watercolours of Japanese birds and flowers.[3] Among the pertinent French books was Louis Gonse's *L'Art Japonaise* published in Paris in 1883. Tiffany's Edward C. Moore began collecting Japanese art. His collection grew to include about nine hundred items, not only metalwork but pottery, textiles and swords.

The Japanese exhibit was one of the highlights of the Philadelphia Centennial Exhibition in 1876. It surprised and enchanted visitors because it represented an 'utterly new and different way of dealing with a familiar topic'.[4] Bewildering, curious, wonderful, grotesque and bizarre were some of the adjectives used to describe the Japanese display of arts and crafts. The extraordinary bronze work and combination of contrasting metals that were used for embossing and inlaying captured special attention.

Christopher Dresser, whose books on design were very influential in promoting the aesthetic movement in England, found lessons in the guiding principles of nature that were quite in accord with the Japanese reverence for all things. In the winter of 1876, Dresser travelled to Japan where he bought art objects for Tiffany's, some of which were sold at auction in New York in June 1877 and some of which were kept for study purposes.[5] The sale increased interest in Japanese art. Tiffany had introduced the

2. George A. Audsley and James Lord Bowes (London 1875). Carpenter, *Tiffany*, p. 230.
3. Carpenter, p. 95.
4. Ingram, pp. 559-6.
5. Part of his purchases were for Londros & Co. in England. Carpenter, *Tiffany*, p. 184.

Japanese style in its silver flatware line in 1871 and gradually extended it to other forms of metalwork.

At first Japanese ornament was applied to the surface of current western forms of jewelry. By 1874 chatelaines in the Japanese taste were available (Colour Plate 210). Early patterns were characterized by the use of birds, branches and twigs, along with flowers in the oriental mode. Increasingly, metals such as copper and different colours of gold and silver were mixed to provide interesting colour effects. Gold and copper metalwork was known as *shakudo* while silver and copper work was called *shibuichi*. The combined metals were hand-hammered, unplanished, or given a matt finish.

An alloy of silver, copper, lead and sulphur was used to fill areas of chased or engraved designs in metalwork to achieve the type of decoration known as *niello*. The combined metals were fired at a low temperature to form a kind of inlay similar in effect to the vitreous glassy material used in enamelling. *Niello* became associated with the Japanese taste. In March 1877, *Godey's Lady's Book Advertiser* reported, 'For lovers of odd things, is silver jewelry inlaid with color in niello work; the designs are mostly Japanese, and this chromatic decoration is very effective in long brooches for shawls, fan-shaped buttons for the sleeves, large buckles for belts, etc.' (Colour Plate 211).[6] The technique allowed an exceptional amount of detail in complicated designs on a reduced scale.

Although the Japanese preferred silver to gold, Tiffany employed Japanese techniques to great effect in a pair of bracelets made of two colours of gold and accented with platinum flowers (Colour Plate 212). The sides of the bracelets were subtly convex, the borders were beaded and the branches of flowers were applied in single stalks with angles decidedly oriental. A Tiffany necklace combined the Japanese elements with an archaeological style of pendent plaques affixed to a chain with decorated pendent rings and spacers (Colour Plate 213). The panels had a background of vertical filigree wires, representing bird cages, which contained alternate designs of birds or flowers. The designs were reversed on one side to give balance to the overall effect. The bird panels showed a variety of poses, from perched to swooping and wings spread or folded. The three colours of gold added to the intrigue of the detail.

The Japanese fan motif and the effectiveness of a hammered gold background can be seen in a small brooch made of eighteen karat gold, featuring the ubiquitous butterfly (Colour Plate 213). Cranes against bullrushes framed in scallop shells were featured in a half-set of gold with the addition of white gold for the decorative motifs.

Good jewelry presented a studied, erudite distillation of Japanese designs that created something new. However, commercial jewelry tended to present a view seen through western eyes. Japanese figures in imagined every-day poses decorated a pair of studs set with reversed crystal intaglios that were colourfully painted. A figure, more 'oriental' than truly Japanese or Chinese, appeared on a multicoloured, 22 karat gold marquise-shaped locket held in a bamboo wishbone bail (Colour Plate 214). The flower that the figure pointed to was made of platinum. In the back was a glazed locket to hold a photograph or a lock of hair, a feature unknown in Japanese jewelry. A breastpin was made in 1893 in the form of a Japanese wooden sandal with polished gold buckles and straps, and coloured gold soles, an idea that would never have occurred to a Japanese designer.[7]

6. p.294.
7. *Jewelers Review, 22* #9, 24 July 1893.

Colour Plate 216. Spray pin in two colours of gold with turquoise forget-me-not flowers and a bird with brilliant hummingbird feathers, a feature popular with some Americans during the last half of the 19th century. This example may be of American origin, c.1860. Length about 3⅞in. The British Museum.

Novelties

In the middle of the Centennial year, Mrs. Peter Ronalds of New York gave a fancy ball. To the amazement of her guests she appeared before them as the goddess of music wearing a diadem made of burning gas jets. Not only was her rig novel, it was positively breathtaking. More remarkable perhaps was that she managed to keep her hair from going up in flames at the same time. 'Ever since the Centennial in 1876', commented *The New York Times,* 'the practice for getting up novelties in the various trades has had a steady and widespread growth'.[1]

While novelties in American jewelry had been introduced in the eighteenth century on a very modest scale, it was more than a century later that they proliferated in response to an insatiable public demand. Novelties could be made of precious or common materials. They could be beautiful or grotesque, whimsical or fearful. Above all, they were of a fleeting, transient nature, momentary and tricky. Often the designer of a successful gimmick patented his idea to buy himself protection for the few years his invention was in demand.

Most of the novelty jewelry was related directly to innovations in science, industry and leisure activities. Increased interest in natural history drew attention to the insects,

1. 22 July 1882.

Colour Plate 217. Pair of gold and feathered salmon flies made as pins to be worn rather than for piscatorial purposes. American, late 19th century. Length 2in. Photograph by Peter J. Theriault. Private Collection.

Colour Plate 218. This wingless insect has a single large natural pearl for its body, ten demantoid garnets in the upper body, and ruby eyes. Marked on hook J & M for Jaques & Marcus who were working in partnership in New York about 1882 to 1892. Length 1⅛in. Photograph by Peter J. Theriault. Private Collection.t

birds and animals that inhabited previously unexplored areas of the world, as well as those encountered in everyday life. Hunting, fishing and hiking, no longer necessities for survival, were now pursued as game sports. Pleasant outdoor activities were enjoyed by those with free time. The development of the bicycle, games such as lawn tennis, golf and baseball, horse racing and other games of chance, introduced new motifs that revealed a person's preferences. Mechanical inventions not only allowed quick mass-production of new designs, but also provided ways to give the jewelry moving parts. Young American women travelling abroad in 1875 were reported to be wearing novel earrings bought in Chicago or Washington, D.C. that featured steamers, steam engines and omnibuses.[2]

The element of surprise was usually present, as when it was reported in 1882 that 'There is now an odd fancy about earrings. Two of a kind are no longer scrupulously held to be a pair, but odd stones are worn as a pair. You will see a pink pearl on one ear and a black one on the other, or you will see a diamond one in one ear and a clear white pearl on the other'.[3]

Among the novelties featured by Tiffany's in 1878 were fads that had just appeared in Paris or London and others that came from less frequently culled areas such as Russia, Denmark and Spain. In addition they offered their own special productions made in their own workshops which could not be purchased anywhere else. They urged their patrons to consult with them about having jewelry made in any particular symbols of their own devising.[4]

Bracelets

Bracelets were especially adaptable as fads. They were reasonably priced and yet quite noticeable. 'Spring' bracelets were the newest fashion in the last quarter of the nineteenth century. The spring placed in the joint of a two-part bracelet allowed it to close automatically without clasps or guard chains.[5] As a result, bangle bracelets that were big enough to go over the hand in one piece went out of fashion. Band bracelets were also made to look like belts and were adjustable to any size by means of their buckles and eyelets.

Gold band bracelets were given a new twist by the addition of a padlock for fastening the loops or eyes on the ends of the band. Tiffany's suggested that 'The bracelet may be placed on a lady's arm by a gentleman, who retains the key, perhaps

2. *Englishwoman's Domestic Magazine,* 1875, quoted by Bury II, 567.
3. *Sun,* 9 July 1882.
4. Tiffany & Co., *Catalogue,* NY, 1878, p.2.
5. Henry Carlisle, Jr., of Philadelphia, Pa., patented his bracelet spring joint in 1870 and it continued to be used by other jewelers in the 1880s.

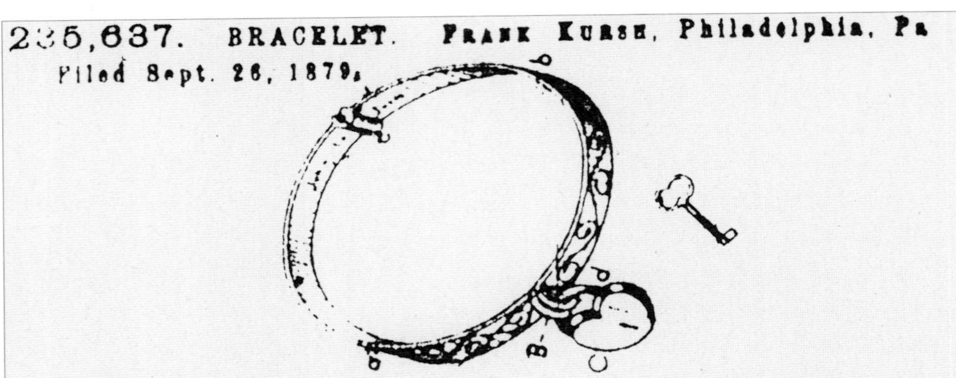

235,637. BRACELET. FRANK KURSH, Philadelphia, Pa. Filed Sept. 26, 1879.

Claim.—1. As a new article of manufacture, a bracelet having the sections *a b*, provided with an eye or eyes, B, in combination with the suspended lock C, substantially as stated.

2. The sections *a b*, with eyes B, and the collar or tube D, combined and arranged substantially as and for the purpose set forth.

Plate 237. Design for a bracelet with lock and key clasp, patented 21 December 1880 by Frank Kursh of Philadelphia, Pennsylvania. The bracelet had one or two eyes through which the hasp of the padlock was fitted. United States Patent Office, No. 235,637.

wearing it as a charm on his watch-chain'.[6] Frank Kursh of Philadelphia and Newark had received a design patent in 1880 for this type of bracelet (Plate 237). In 1888, the band was changed to a chain, giving it a more enslaving appearance, and was patented in this form by Louis P. Juvet of Glen Falls, New York.[7] Another variation on this theme was the bracelet fitted with a combination lock that opened to letters.[8] A few dandies were wearing these bangles on their left wrist, usually hidden beneath the cuff. Their sweethearts were said to keep the key to the bangle's lock 'where a woman always hides her jewels and carries her treasures'.[9]

Other novel bracelets available in American jewelry shops were those made of three gold circles joined together by stones the initials of which spelled out a name or a wish, harking back to the 'regard' rings earlier in the century. The same design was used for dog-collar necklaces as well.[10] Arthur von Briesen, a New York jeweler, patented a design for a bracelet that had a coin-box built into it.[11] Bracelets especially for shopping were equipped with a pencil attached. A swivel eye attached to a bracelet allowed for the suspension of numerous other objects such as gloves, pocketbooks and umbrellas, serving as a wrist-bound chatelaine.[12]

William Edge made a bracelet of 'lazy tong' construction so that it could be expanded and contracted to make it fit any wrist.[13] The 'Hellene' bracelet was made of Etruscan gold, coiled, and set with jewels. Another flexible bracelet was woven of gold wire and wrapped around the wrist three times. It had jewels or tracery decorating its ball terminals. Most popular of all were the flexible serpent bracelets that conformed to the wrist or arm and were set with gems for eyes or with jeweled heads. They could be extended for use as necklaces as well.

Scarf Pins

Nowhere was novelty more diverse than in scarf and lace pins decorated with

> emblems for nearly every trade and profession. There are tiny locomotives and lanterns for railroad men, steam-boats and ships for navigators, and swords and guns for military men. Then there are pins for polo-players, croquet pins, lawn-tennis pins, and archery pins. Ladies lace pins are made of gold and diamonds to imitate a half-opened pea pod, the diamonds taking the place of the peas. There are also facsimiles, in gold and silver of guitars, mandolins and banjos, quivers filled with arrows, and bows fully strung.[14]

6. Tiffany, *Catalogue,* 1881/2.
7. Design Patent #11,893, 3 August 1880 and #18,189, 20 March 1888.
8. Tiffany, *Catalogue,* 1881/2, p. 25.
9. *Sun,* 16 June 1889.
10. *Sun,* 10 Sept. 1882.
11. #334,844, 26 Jan. 1886.
12. #452,830, 26 May 1891.
13. 20 Jan. 1880.
14. 'Unique Things in Trade', NY *Times,* 10 Sept. 1882.
15. Tiffany, *Catalogue,* 1881/2.
16. 2 April 1882.
17. *Sun,* 27 Dec. 1881.
18. Ibid., 26 Feb. 1882.
19. Ibid., 5 Nov. 1882.
20. #225,820, 23 Mar. 1880. In 1865 English jeweler Harry Emanuel had patented a method of using feathers and plumage, using shellac to glue them to their mounts. (Bury I, 361).
21. Plate D, opp. p. 71, #30. The Jock Scott had originated in England.
22. Bury II, 292B, p. 558.
23. Tait I, 118, #808. *Jewelers Review, 22,* #7, 10 July 1893.

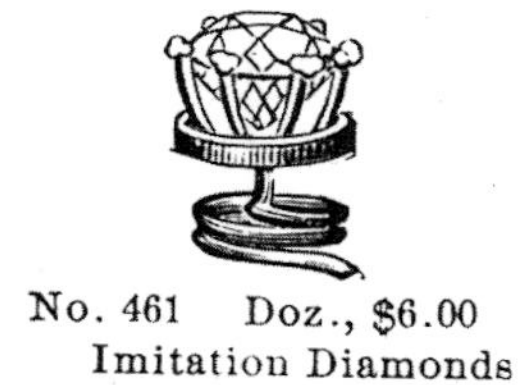

No. 461 Doz., $6.00
Imitation Diamonds

No. 1214. Doz., $10.12.
Foil Set.

Tiffany's offered horse devices (whips, stirrups and horseshoes), sporting motifs ('gunning, yachting, polo, archery, cricket, tennis') and frogs, animals and birds 'in comical attitudes'.[15] They also turned baroque pearls into a variety of creatures and mounted them on the tops of scarf pins. The American lace pins were more eccentric than even the Paris designs, the New York *Sun* reported. Particular attention was drawn to a diamond poodle jumping through a sapphire and ruby hoop, and three pearl-bodied mice chasing each other across a gold bar of music. These were thought to be suitable as Christmas, Easter or bridal presents.[16] Tadpoles were especially popular with the ladies in California, as were bulls and bears for stock brokers.[17]

Birds of a Feather

Whole hummingbirds were worn in ladies' hair, nestled in flowers, lace and ribbons. It was the increased skill of the taxidermist rather than that of a jeweler which made this possible. Women wore hummingbirds perched upon their shoulders.[18] Most spectacular of all was the young lady who wore a coronet of hummingbirds on her head.[19] Hummingbirds were one of the notable attractions in Central and South America that enticed American tourists in the last quarter of the nineteenth century. Artists like Frederic Church and Martin Johnson Heade were attracted by the brilliance of colours, lushness of nature and exotic birds and flowers in the tropics. Heade studied and drew both hummingbirds and orchids. The luminist paintings he painted from his studies in the last few decades of the nineteenth century had an effect on the public and the jewelry of the period (Colour Plate 216).

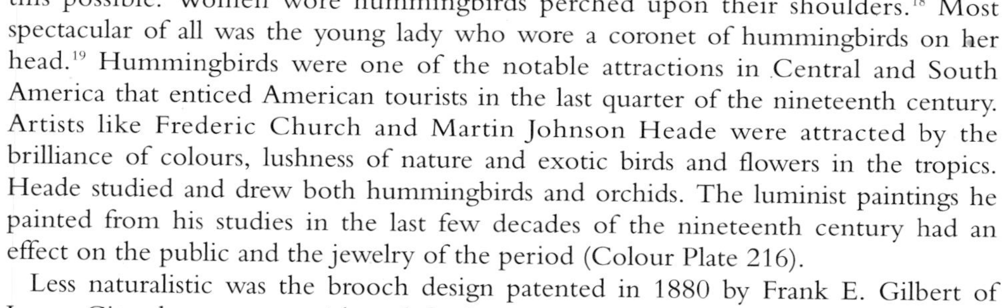

No. 617. Doz., $10.50.
Foil Back.

Less naturalistic was the brooch design patented in 1880 by Frank E. Gilbert of Jersey City that was set with real feather ornaments. In a conventional elongated frame the feathers were laid within a recess with the quill ends pointed toward each other. An ornamental shield was placed over the centre to cover the quills and hold the feathers in place.[20]

No. 89. Doz., $11.25.
Pearl Horseshoe.

Hunting and Fishing

Exotic materials and real feathers were used for tying flies and for pins made to look like the fly-fishing lures used for sport fishing during the height of the Victorian era (Colour Plate 217). Feathers of the jungle cock of South America were combined with those of the wood duck, kingfisher and pheasant. Different patterns were given their own peculiar names and became popular in different areas of the country. Mary Orvis Maybury's *Favorite Flies and Their History* was published in Vermont in 1892. It illustrated in colour the fishing flies most favoured by American anglers. Among them was the Jock Scott, one of the best of salmon flies, still valued for its combination of colours and patterns as well as its success in North Atlantic salmon fishing.[21] It was turned into a gold pin that could have been worn by a man or woman, angler or otherwise. A stick pin, with a salmon fly executed in reverse intaglio by the Pradiers (Ernest William and his son Ernest Marius) in England, was set by Tiffany & Co. in a circular mount wrapped with fishing line.[22] The rod, reel and creel also made suitable motifs for sporting jewelry. For trout fishermen there was a scarf pin with a ruby-eyed trout of coloured gold.[23]

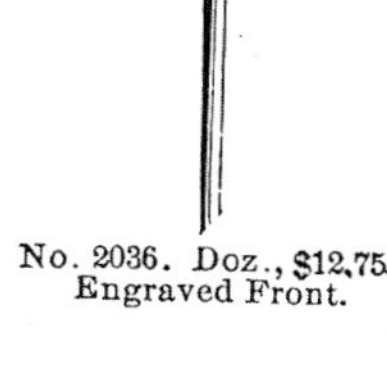

No. 2036. Doz., $12.75.
Engraved Front.

Plate 238. Group of stickpins advertised by Marsh & Bigney of Attleboro, Massachusetts, in 1883 catalogue, showing the appeal to the various interests of their customers.

The sport of hunting made its mark on jewelry too. 'The latest novelty in ornaments are *bijoux de chasse*', the New York *Times* confirmed in 1882, 'consisting of

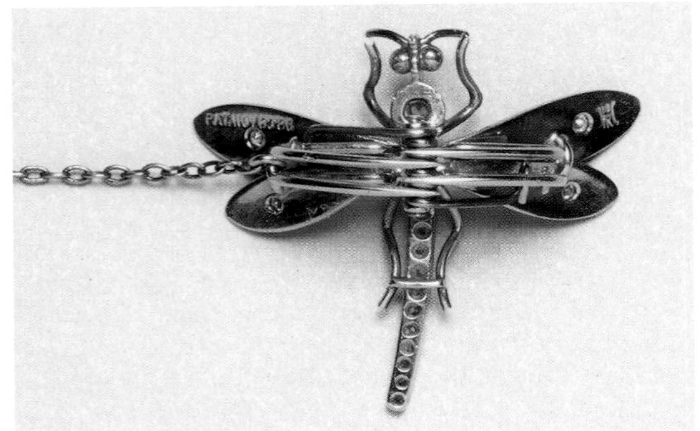

Colour Plate 219. Above left. Dragonfly pin with folding wings, set with green peridots on the body and diamonds on the wings. Stamped with patent date Nov. 30, 1886. The patent was obtained by Jethro C. Cottle of New York, for a mechanism allowing a claw on the back to open when the wings of the dragonfly are pinched together to secure the pin to fabric (#353,482, 30 November 1886). See Plate 140. Courtesy of Janet Mavec.

Colour Plate 219A. Above right. Reverse of the dragonfly pin illustrated in Colour Plate 219.

brooches made of the tip of a stag's horn ornamented with light foliage of silver surrounding the head of a horse or stag, also in silver; from the brooch hangs a chain of pieces of horn, linked with silver, to the end of which are suspended all sorts of sporting emblems...in horn and silver'.[24]

Not only tiger's claws were worn (see Colour Plates 155 and 209, and Plate 180), but other game animal parts were displayed in jewelry. Rabbit's feet were made into pendants and worn as good-luck charms. Scottish jewelry, which had been popular in the mid-century, took a new lease on life with its incorporation of hunting trophies in fancy articles made of horns and hoofs.[25]

Members of the Society of Elks wore the teeth of their mascot set in gold or silver badges and buttons. An article in the *Saturday Evening Post* in 1901 charged that a man in Montana had cornered the market in elk teeth with a cache worth $200,000, and that the American elk was being threatened with extinction.[26] The Indians had long prized elk teeth and believed that they held magical powers. The *New York Times* remarked in 1882 that silver-tipped boar's teeth were popular as pins for the ladies as well.[27] Alligator teeth were carved and set in American jewelry in 1891.[28]

As for domesticated animals, Marsh & Bigney illustrated horse's heads with bloodstone seals set in the neck in their 1883 catalogue. There were also horseshoes, jockeys, hunting dogs and deer in a choice of items, particularly pins and fobs. A pin decorated with the scene of a jockey astride his horse was patented in 1883, coinciding with the increased interest in horse racing in America.[29]

Creepy-Crawlies

Especially popular were the creeping creatures, particularly if they were somewhat frightening. Caterpillars cleverly reproduced in gold were so life-like that they seemed to crawl. This was effectively true of one species made with ruby eyes and stripes formed of emeralds with topazes running down each side. It seemed to move with every step or turn of its wearer. A guest at the Vanderbilt reception in 1881 told an uptown jeweler that he had seen 'a jeweled lizard circling a coil of hair on the head of a leader of fashion'.[30] Lizards studded with peridots, or better yet with demantoid garnets, and snakes masquerading as bracelets, necklaces and rings, slithered across the arms and necks of fashionable ladies and wrapped around their fingers. Serpent rings

24. 9 July 1882.
25. *Jewelers Review, 22,* #6, 3 July 1893.
26. 30 Mar. 1901, quoted in *Antiques,* Mar. 1984, pp. 664-5.
27. 10 Sept. 1882.
28. Bury I, 249.
29. #13,730, 13 Mar. 1883, H. Untermeyer.
30. *Sun,* 27 Dec. 1881

Colour Plate 220 A message of good luck spelled out in 18 karat gold discs dangling from a bar pin, popular in the 1880s. Skinner, Inc.

Colour Plate 221. Ivory monocular and binocular Stanhopes, American, c.1880, fitted with tiny images such as the Lord's Prayer and a letter headed with the Confederate flag. Length ⅝in. Photograph by Terry Richardson. Courtesy, The Charleston Museum, Charleston, South Carolina.

were priced according to the number of coils they made around the finger, from one to four and $8.50 to $500.[31] One young man ordered an enamelled green snake with emerald eyes as a present for his fiancée. He had it equipped with fangs of sharp curved needles to protect her from unwanted suitors.[32]

Crustaceans and other creatures of the sea emerged to delight landlubbers in search of a design no one else had seen. One year it was the lobster, next year a crab, and then a flotilla of octopi washed ashore.

All kinds of insects lighted upon the costumes of the well-dressed, in the form of scarf and lace pins, brooches and hair ornaments (Colour Plate 218). S.F. Myers offered gold scarf-pin insects with moonstone wings, ruby bodies and emerald heads or coloured with enamel and inlaid with pearl.[33] In addition to the Brazilian beetles set in jewels to look like antique scarabs (see Plate 206), single beetles were made of precious materials. In 1893 one could purchase an iridescent brown beetle with a dark opal body striped with diamonds, rubies and emeralds. For others the ordinary potato bug whose body was formed of an inch-long rose-cut diamond with tiny diamonds delineating its crooked legs was even more desirable. Houseflies trapped in spiders' webs became the featured decoration of a brooch and dress studs.

In a related eccentricity, living fireflies were worn in the hair of young ladies on the west coast, 'their living jewels flashed and gleamed and glowed as never diamonds did'. The news of this inspired a New York jeweler to make fireflies that would last indefinitely. He fashioned them from dark rubies with diamond wings into earrings and a necklace from which one firefly was suspended from an almost invisible wire.[34]

Butterflies and Dragonflies

Butterflies of infinite variety were most beautiful. 'Simultaneously with the movement for the revival of gay colors in apparel comes a reproduction in jewelry of the most brilliant objects to be found – tropical butterflies', the *Jewelers' Review* announced in 1893 (see Colour Plate 184). While butterflies had appeared before in jewelry, they were not the precisely executed Brazilian species that were now seen in all their intricate shades of colours.[35] They could be gem set, enamelled, engraved, sawn out or made of filigree.[36] Rubies and turquoises decorated the commonplace rolled gold plate butterfly scarf pins.[37] Scarf, lace and hair pins and brooches alike were suitable perches for these lovely gifts of nature.

The dragonfly was considered especially beautiful for jewelry. 'Its long posterior

31. Tiffany, *Catalogue*, 1881/2.
32. 'Animals in Jewelry', *Sun*, 27 Dec. 1881.
33. Catalogue 1896, p. 223 in Hinks.
34. *Sun*, 27 Dec. 1881.
35. 22, #5, 1893.
36. Myers, *Catalogue*, Hinks, *Victorian Jewelry*, p. 210.
37. Ibid. p. 224.

Plate 239. Selection of fine solid gold charms offered by Marsh & Bigney, Attleboro, Mass., 1883, displaying a variety of personal interests.

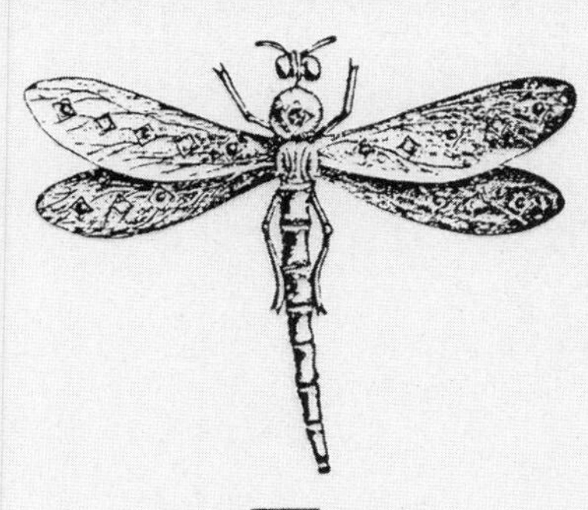

Plate 240. A.J. Hedges & Co. of Newark, New Jersey, advertised this veil pin with articulated wings on 17 July 1895 in the Jewelers' Circular & Horological Review 30, *27 (see Colour Plate 219). Courtesy of Janet Zapata.*

extremity, outstretched wings and solid body give it peculiarly valuable properties for the setting of precious stones' (Colour Plate 219 and Plate 240).[38]

Flowers

In their catalogue for 1881-2, Tiffany's introduced 'an exclusive novelty' in a series of lace pins featuring flowers that represented different sentiments:

Woodbine	Bond of love
Fern	Sincerity
Snowdrop	Consolation
Primrose	Early Youth
Ivy	Friendship
Periwinkle	Sweet Remembrance
Pansy	Thought (Pensée)

Little books were published that helped to explain the language of flowers. Pansies were most favoured, but there were orchids, roses, and other flowers to consider (Plate 241). Lilies of the valley were used for mourning jewelry. Their sentiment was appropriate for a grieving heart. When made of gold and set with pearls they looked very handsome applied to a rectangular bar of black onyx. In 1879 Herman Unger of

38. *Jewelers Review*, 22, #23, 30 Oct. 1893.

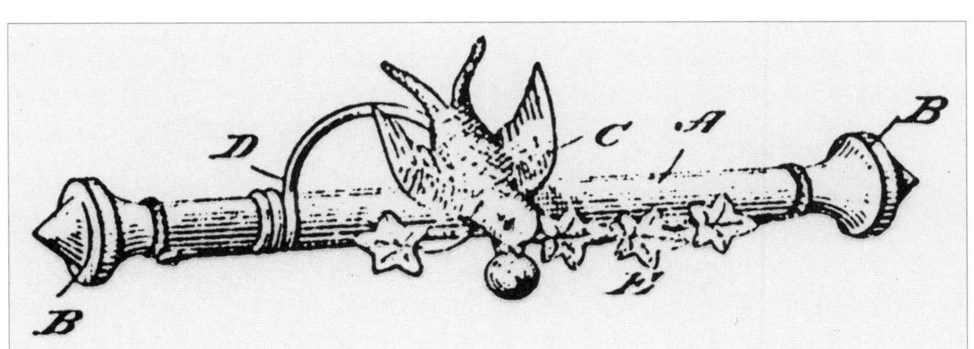

Plate 241. Top. Design for a bar pin featuring a bird with part of an ivy vine in its beak, patented by Adolph Vester of Attleboro, Mass., 13 April 1880. United States Patent Office, No. 11,735.

Plate 242. 'Jet onyx' bar pins were advertised by Marsh & Bigney of Attleboro, Mass., in their catalogue of 1883.

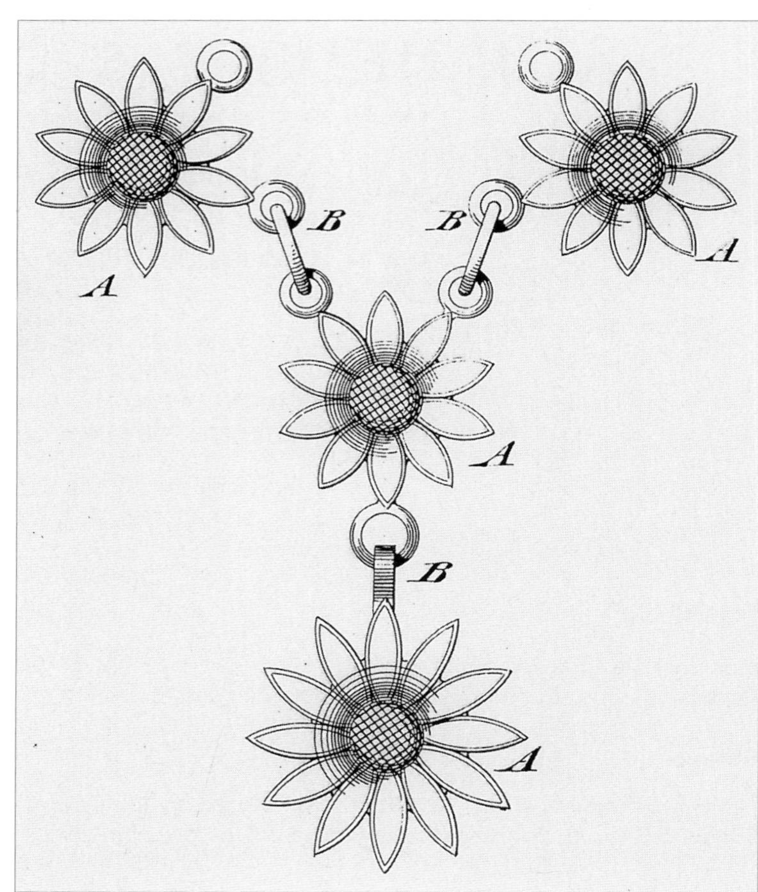

Plate 243. Daisy necklace design patented by H.W. Woods on 1 May 1877, appropriate for young ladies engaged in May Day and Daisy Chain festivities. United States Patent Office, No. 9,955.

Newark patented this design for a bracelet.[39] It proved very popular. Jewelry made in this style was sold wholesale and retail by Marsh & Bigney in 1883 (Plate 242) and was still being sold in 1896 by S.F. Myers & Co. Single onyx flower heads were used as lace pins and brooches, and crapestone renditions were widely sold.

Daisies, representing beauty and innocence, were considered especially appropriate for young ladies to wear. The New York *Sun* described a daisy-chain necklace made of silver filigree daisies which had gold centres (Plate 243). Topazes and pearls were used to make gem-set daisies. The orange blossom, worn on the veil of brides, signified chastity or purity. It also represented an important crop of the state of California. In 1887 an orange blossom branch was the source of inspiration for a brooch designed by Simeon H. Lucas of San Bernardino (Plate 244). The complementary earrings featured a single orange of textured 'orange peel' gold. [40]

39. #11,237, 10 June 1879.
40. #17,916, 29 Nov. 1887.
41. NY *Times*, 25 Dec. 1881, 'Modern Uses of Old Coins'.
42. Marsh & Bigney, *Catalogue*, p.210.
43. NY *Times*, 11 Feb. 1990.
44. Flower, p. 45.

Plate 244. Simeon H. Lucas of San Bernardino, California, patented a design of an orange branch and fruit for a brooch and oranges for earrings, 29 November 1887. United States Patent Office, No. 17,916.

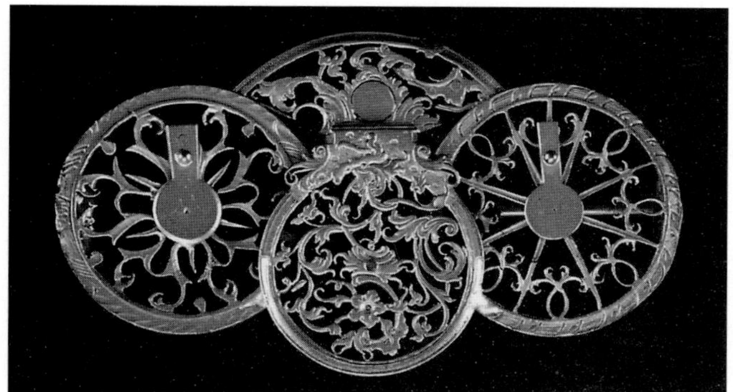

Plate 246. Brooch composed of watch cocks taken from the works of old watches, a brief fashion in America about 1880. Photograph by David Bohl, Boston. Courtesy, Society for the Preservation of New England Antiquities.

Plate 245. Silver vest chain, with art nouveau plaques and medallion, suspended from each other, with a clasp to attach a watch. Marked with superimposed initials of UB inside a circle with STERLING above and 925 FINE below, for Unger Bros. of Newark, New Jersey, working from 1872-1914. Length 6¼in. (overall). Photograph by Dennis Griggs. Private Collection.

Coins and Watchcocks

The fad for jewelry made from ancient coins became so widespread in the 1880s that it was impossible to supply enough authentic antique coins to meet the demand. Jewelers in New York reproduced thousands, setting them in rings, earrings, scarf pins, sleeve buttons, bracelets, necklaces and watch cases. Some jewelers took the time to make the setting suitable to the style of Greek coins. If the coin was truly ancient and in good condition, a scarf pin could cost as much as $600. This form of antique mania originated in France where the aureus, a Roman coin, was particularly desirable for ladies. It was France that supplied American jewelers with quantities of antique Italian and Greek coins, but there were simply not enough to go around.[41]

It soon became fashionable to substitute American gold and silver coins, some of which were rare and valuable. The silver half-dime of 1802, with its bust of Liberty and large eagle, was especially prized. Scarf pins made of these and other coins cost between ten and thirty dollars and were highly recommended for Christmas presents in 1881. The Liberty Head half-dollar of 1827 was used as the terminus for a vest chain made of linked half-dimes some of which were polished smooth on one side to receive an initial or monogram (Plate 245). The other two silver discs of the same half-dime size were engraved with floral sprays. Eventually silver and gold discs were made to look like American coins with a laurel wreath and date on one side, and an appealing motif on the other side, such as a bird, a lighthouse or an Indian head.[42]

It was a German custom for the groom to present a gold or silver coin to his bride as a token of his worldly goods. The German immigrants of the mid-nineteenth century brought this tradition with them to the United States. With the interest in coin jewelry after the Centennial Exhibition, silver coins used as love tokens were often polished off on one side and engraved with the initials or first name of the beloved. Less frequently, they were set with a gem, embellished with gold wire or were enamelled. Due to the excessive use of coins for such things as jewelry, Congress enacted a law in 1901 prohibiting the mutilation of United States coins. This brought the fancy for coin jewelry under control, but it has never totally extinguished the custom.[43]

Somewhat related was watchcock jewelry which enjoyed a brief vogue about 1885. It was made from the beautifully engraved caps that covered the escapement wheels of old watches. Usually made of heavily gilded brass, these caps were joined together with links and turned into bracelets or necklaces (Plate 246). Singly they could be used for the bezels of rings. Especially popular in England, they were condemned even there because so many old watches were being scavenged to be put to this use which was likened to the despicable use of furry feet in brooches.[44] While not nearly as widely acclaimed in America, watchcock jewelry occasionally turns up in nineteenth century collections.

Hands

The carved likeness of a human hand and wrist had been worn as an amulet since the sixteenth century, especially in Spanish speaking countries, to ward off the evil eye. The fingers could be held in various positions to express different meanings. Often there was a neatly decorated cuff and a ring or a bracelet. Carved from crystal and ivory, wood or jet, these amulets could be worn as pendants. Although their meaning was different, they bore a certain resemblance to the hand-in-hand, fede rings of Roman times.

In the nineteenth century the fashion developed for carving the graceful hand and wrist of a beautiful woman to be given to a lover or friend as a souvenir. The left hand of Princess Pauline Bonaparte was carved by Canova from Carrara marble and displayed at the Exhibition in Vienna in 1873. On her hand was a wedding ring with a black enamel guard ring set with a diamond solitaire, and on her wrist was a black enamelled bracelet, giving the sculpture a very realistic appearance.[45]

Brooches carved from ivory and coral displayed delicately modelled hands lightly grasping a bouquet of flowers (see Colour Plate 126). Examples from Switzerland, Italy, Germany and England indicate the widespread acceptance of this design. Coral hand fobs from Italy found their way to the watch chains of Americans as well. One Charleston lady owned a link bracelet of coral to which was attached a coral hand with a gold bracelet and ring studded with turquoise beads. The hand held a clutch of coral fobs, including one in the shape of a fish, another a dog and several dog-teeth of different colours of coral (see Colour Plate 137).

By the 1880s, American-made hands were fashioned from ivory and coral (Plate 247). Marsh & Bigney's wholesale catalogue of 1883 illustrated a right hand of mother-of-pearl clenching a short baton, with a wide gold fancy cuff, and a left hand with an ornamental gold cuff holding a gold key.[46] There were scarf pins with hands holding an imitation diamond between the thumb and index finger (see Plate 218). These were made of rolled silver or gold plate.[47] Hands with ruffled cuffs held a bunch of strawberries with coloured leaves and fruit set with stones. Others held flowers

45. *Sun*, 9 July 1882.
46. p. 205, #6,7. They cost $3.75 and $6.00 a piece.
47. *Catalogue*, Hinks, *Victorian Jewelry*, p.218.

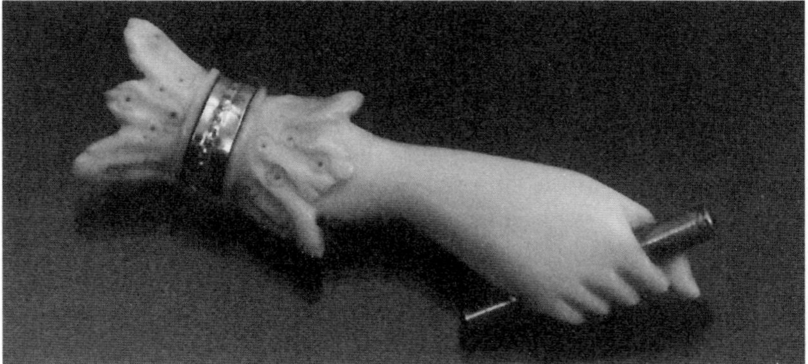

Plate 247. Carved ivory pin, American, c.1870-90, with hand holding a gold baton and a gold bracelet around the lace cuff on the lower part of the forearm. Owned in Wiscasset, Maine. Length 1¹⁵⁄₁₆in. (See Plate 239, bottom, second from left.) Photograph by Peter J. Theriault. Private Collection.

with enamelled petals, with an imitation diamond in the centre.[48] Cuff-links were made of chased or plain silver in the form of a clasped hand with the index finger pointing as was often used to draw attention in newspaper advertisements.[49] By 1896 the hand held a miniature telescope with a microscopic view inside.[50]

Stanhopes and Graphiscopes

Tiny fobs made in the form of binoculars or monoculars through which a print or photograph could be seen were introduced about 1875. They were given the name 'Stanhope' because it was Charles, Earl Stanhope (1753-1816) who created the convex lens that made it possible to see very small images. The lens was made from a glass rod about one-tenth of an inch in diameter with one convex end. The other end was flat with a microphotographic image on it. Stanhope's invention was combined with the microscopic photograph developed by a French chemist named René Dagron (1819-1900) about 1860 and the use of collodion film invented in 1851 by Frederick Scott Archer. Altogether, these miniature viewers proved very popular novelties appropriate as souvenirs.[51]

In addition to watch fobs, there were Stanhopes incorporated in bracelet charms, pins, crosses and rosary beads as well as needle cases and mechanical pencils. They were usually made of ivory, although the barrel fob from Niagara Falls was made of wood. While Stanhopes were very well suited for girlie pictures and nudes, many of the pictures were religious, scenic or commemorated significant events.

One monocular Stanhope revealed a Confederate flag at the top of a typed letter pertaining to events of the Civil War (Colour Plate 221). Another held a miniature photograph of loved ones. 'View brooches' were considered very pretty, particularly when they held scenes of buildings in Washington such as the White House, Washington Monument and the Capitol – or even the Philadelphia Mint.[52] These made most appropriate accessories to wear on the 4th of July.

In New Hampshire, Stanhopes in the form of telescopes held pictures of the Old Man of the Mountain at Franconia Notch, one of the most famous scenic sites in the state. Another showed a child kneeling with the Lord's Prayer printed below.[53] Yet another contained the Apostles' Creed. The 1883 wholesale catalogue of Marsh & Bigney illustrated miniature binoculars made of mother-of-pearl and gold with views for $6.[54] Fobs and charms with views of the 1893 World's Fair in Chicago were available in 14 karat, gold-fill or sterling.

A related form of jewelry incorporating a photograph was the locket which contained a graphiscope (Plate 248). The locket opened and a lens fastened inside the base could be pivoted up and used to see the photograph embedded inside the top. There were also little gold lockets in the form of tiny books or albums to contain photographs of your own choice, some made for two pictures and some for four.[55] John B. Newman of Milford, Pennsylvania, patented a ring in 1888 that had an inner ring with either pictures or ornaments on its face so that a variety of designs could be displayed one at a time beneath a transparent cover.[56]

48. Ibid., p. 215.
49. *Jewelers Review, 22,* #18, 25 Sept. 1893, p. 22.
50. *Catalogue,* Hinks, *Victorian Jewelry,* p.238.
51. Bruce Bank, 'Stanhopes', *Mass. Bay Antiques,* Mar. 1985, pp. 8, 36.
52. *Jewelers Review, 22,* #6, 3 July 1893.
53. Example at New Hampshire Historical Society.
54. Marsh & Bigney, *Catalogue,* p.204, #34.
55. Ibid., p. 204, #15, #16.
56. #392,357, 6 Nov. 1888.

Plate 248. Graphiscope lockets made of the 'Finest rolled plate Roman gold', advertised by Marsh & Bigney, Attleboro, Mass., in their catalogue of 1883.

Combination Jewelry

The idea of making jewelry so that it could be used for more than just decorative purposes or more than one purpose had been around for a long time. However, in the last quarter of the nineteenth century the concept found great appeal. In 1880 two jewelers in New Jersey designed a cross that could be worn as a pendant, but which had detachable parts that could be worn as earrings or lace pins.[57] Another ingenious design was constructed so that a flexible ornament could be clasped together to be worn as a finger ring or unfolded for use as a bracelet. It could even be attached to a back plate with fittings so that it served as a lace pin.[58]

There were rings that held perfume or a toothpick, lace pins that doubled as flower holders, and lockets in which chewing gum could be stashed.[59] There were brooches and bracelets which were hinged so that they opened out into button hooks. An ornamental chain had a cigar cutter concealed in one of its sections. One particularly useful locket contained a letter and coin scale.[60]

Most absurd of all was the bar pin made in the form of a button hook that was only decorative and did not work. A bracelet was made to look as if it harboured a real watch in its elaborate basket-work band, but it too was a fraud.[61] An ornamented table knife, reduced in scale, was turned into a bar brooch, its handle ornamented in a simplified Japanese design. There were earrings to go with it that were shaped like dinner plates on which rested a knife, fork or spoon.[62]

Automated Jewelry

Under the title 'Philosophical Jewelry', an editorial appeared in the journal of the Franklin Institute in Philadelphia concerning the invention of jewelry motivated by electricity. A French clock maker named Trouvé used little galvanic batteries and springs to make brooches move. The wings of diamond-set birds flapped, grenadiers and rabbits beat drums or chimed bells, monkeys played violins, and a skull's eyes rolled and its mouth opened and closed. The battery pack was concealed in the wearer's pocket and was tipped over on its side or upside down to set the mechanism in action, thereby mystifying all who saw the jewelry move.[63]

Pneumatic and automatic jewelry, patented in 1881 by Curt W. Meyer of New York, had figures animated by means of a pneumatic tube and bulb hidden in a pocket. Electric jewelry that lit up was made by Alfred Haid of Rahway, New Jersey in 1885. His patented method consisted of two parallel pins insulated from each other, supporting a cage in which was an incandescent lamp, with circuit connections between the lamp and the pins.[64]

Galvanic finger rings, with electronegative magnetic metal inserted into an electropositive metal band, were patented in the United States in 1878 by Eugène A. Osselin of Paris and Abraham Meyer of Syracuse, New York.[65] Curative properties were attributed to these electric rings which were worn to relieve the pain of rheumatism.[66]

Lockets, earrings and other kinds of jewelry were made to pivot so that sections could be rotated and spheres turned into demispheres.[67] Imported steam engine brooches had wheels that turned because of a small movement placed behind it. In a similar fashion the tail of a peacock was made to move and two stars in a brooch moved back and forth.[68]

57. #235,683, 21 Dec. 1880.
58. #257,732, 9 May 1882.
59. #292,963, 5 Feb. 1884; #272,985, 27 Feb. 1883; #314,502, 24 Mar. 1885; #395,515, 1 Jan. 1889.
60. #465,468, 21 Dec. 1891; #393,239, 20 Nov. 1888; #324,281, 11 Aug. 1885; #324,465, 18 Aug. 1885.
61. #20,298, 11 Nov. 1890, Edw. L. Logee, Providence.
62. #15,532, 11 Nov. 1884.
63. Report, c. 1870.
64. #240,441, 19 April 1881; #818,726, 10 Mar. 1885.
65. #204,502.
66. Rainwater, *AJM*, p. 275.
67. #368,894, 30 Aug. 1887.
68. *Jewelers Review, 22,* #8, 17 July 1893.

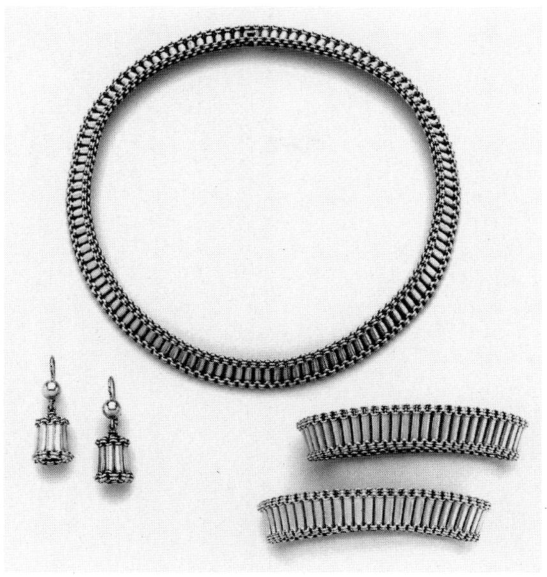

Plate 249. Set of silver jewelry in a very modern style for 1875-1885, marked by Gorham & Co., Union Square, New York, probably at the small shop Gorham operated in New York at that time. The earrings have gold ear wires. Length 7½in. (bracelets). Photograph by Witt McKay. Courtesy of Proctor Collection.

The Silver Bonanza

The discovery of the Comstock Lode of silver near Virginia City in Nevada in 1859 had an enormous impact on the arts and the economy of the United States. There, and in Colorado and other parts of the Western Territories, was an incredibly rich supply of the metal that American colonists had been seeking three centuries earlier. The gold rush was waning, but the silver age was beginning. It was nourished by a number of factors such as demonetization of silver by the Coinage Act of 1873 and devaluation of the metal due to increased supply. New methods were developed for mining and refining ore. New techniques of manufacturing were invented for commercial production.

Lower prices for silver permitted greater use of domestic silver wares by the ever-increasing upper and middle classes. John Mackay, the 'silver king', was one of the first and most conspicuous consumers. A disappointed gold-rusher, Mackay became one of the partners of the Comstock mines. Half a ton of silver was sent directly from his mine to Tiffany's in New York to be fashioned into the most extravagant silver service ever made in America. All 1,250 pieces were shipped to Paris for display at the Paris Exposition in 1878 where the service won a grand prize.

Silver jewelry enjoyed great popularity. Interest in ethnic ornaments had been growing and peasant jewelry had traditionally been made of silver. Italy produced a great deal of silver jewelry, as Mark Twain confirmed when he wrote, 'These filagree *[sic]* things are Genoa's speciality. Her smiths take silver ingots and work them up into all manner of graceful and beautiful forms. They make bunches of flowers, from flakes of wire of silver that counterfeit the delicate creations the frost weaves upon a window pane...'[1] In 1876 A. Stowell & Co. of Boston advertised that a box of 300 ounces of silver jewelry from Genoa had just been received. The Centennial celebration in 1876 provided a silver opportunity for the sale of baubles made of this metal. Silver brooches, earrings and charms were offered by Bigelow, Kennard in Boston.[2]

The Gorham Company, which had given up the production of jewelry several decades earlier, began producing jewelry again. They advertised in 1877 that they made sterling necklaces, brooches, bracelets and earrings, as well as crosses, lockets and charms (Plate 249). In addition there were scarf pins and scarf rings for the

1. Bury, II, 558, Plate 292A. 260 workers in twenty workshops in 1862 were estimated to be producing silver filigree jewelry in Genoa.
2. *Transcript,* 23 June 1876.

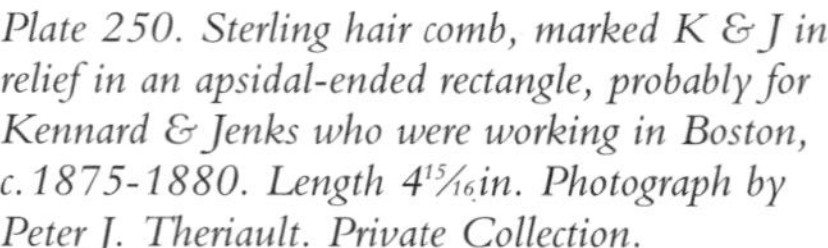

Plate 250. Sterling hair comb, marked K & J in relief in an apsidal-ended rectangle, probably for Kennard & Jenks who were working in Boston, c.1875-1880. Length $4\frac{15}{16}$in. Photograph by Peter J. Theriault. Private Collection.

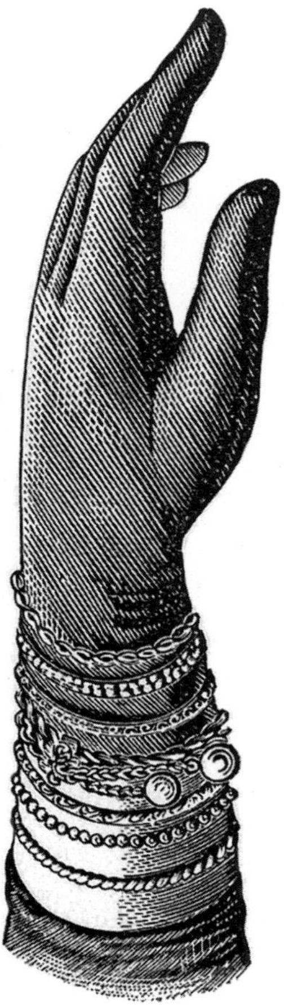

Plate 251. Henry Read of Providence, Rhode Island, advertised in The Wholesale Jeweler *in 1889 a variety of sterling silver bangle bracelets and 'Old Medallion Lace Pins'. Etched work and oxidizing received careful attention.*

gentlemen and hair bands and belt clasps for the ladies.[3] Ornamental hair combs were made of silver by a number of American firms such as Tiffany during the 1870s (Plate 250). Some were plain (see Plate 221) while others were elaborately pierced and engraved.

The rage for Japanese art and objects also played a part in the increasing popularity of silver jewelry. By 1870, Tiffany was producing both silver wares and silver jewelry in the Japanese style.[4] Decorative motifs included fans, cranes, birds executed with hand hammering, matt finishes, mixed metals and oxidation.

Serpent bracelets made of silver or silver gilt were very popular.[5] Bangle bracelets were among the most desirable forms of silver jewelry. One variety was called the 'porte bonheur' (see Colour Plate 220) and was a good-luck bangle. Narrow bands dangled circular pendants, each with a different letter embossed on the side. Together they spelled out 'BONHEUR'. The New York *Sun* pointed out in the fall of 1881 that this type of bracelet had been 'so long jingling in scores from ladies' wrists', but was on its way out of fashion.[6] Bracelets and bangles made of silver cost from $1.50 to $30 at Tiffany's according to their catalogue in 1881-2. Oxidized silver bracelets were made with letters spelling the receiver's name on one side of the bangles and the giver's name on the other side.[7]

Collections of these bracelets, as well as the thin twisted or plain silver bangles, were worn together on the arm (Plate 251). In 1889 the latest fashion in silver bangles was the 'Shakespeare' bracelet. The narrow band was embossed with a sentimental quotation selected from the bard's works.[8]

A silver bracelet called a Charity bangle had a small round box attached to it. The box was meant to contain a coin, to make it easy for its wearer to perform her acts of charity. These were $5.50. A bracelet with a coin box embedded in its band was patented in 1886 by Arthur von Briesen of New York.[9] Other silver bracelets had pencils attached to them and were worn by shoppers. Patents were taken out by other jewelers on bracelets made with a miniature padlock for the clasp. The key to open it could be held by the one who had locked it on his loved one's wrist. By 1893, the *Jewelers Review* reported that 'oxidized silver Bangle bracelets', which had only flagged in fashion a decade earlier, 'are once more in demand'.[10]

Chatelaines, which had declined in the mid-nineteenth century, were revived at the time of the Centennial, at first for masquerade parties and then in earnest. When they first reappeared at colonial costume parties, they were ridiculed in Boston. The

Plate 252. Chatelaine made by Tiffany & Co., New York, c.1888. Hook marked TIFFANY & C° / 9504 M. STERLING, with six chains attached to pin case (marked by Gorham), memorandum case, sheath for tiny letter opener (marked by Tiffany), card case, whistle (marked by Tiffany), cross, spectacle case and scent bottle. The hook plaque and whistle are lettered CAMP ISOLA. Length 16⅛in. (overall). Photograph by Dennis Griggs. Private Collection.

oversized watches hung too far below the waist and the chatelaine ornaments of enormous proportions were deemed a burlesque.[11] A different sort of chatelaine was worn for Renaissance-revival or Medici dress which was popular at the same time. It consisted of a long string of large beads made of silver, amber, jet or wax, wound around the waist several times, the ends looped over and hanging down from the left side.[12]

Silver chatelaines of the late nineteenth century featured hookplate designs that followed the style of silver brooches of the period and represented all the various revival patterns from rococo to neo-Greek and Renaissance revival. A repoussé hookplate in the rococo style needed two belt hooks to support the weight of the long chains and ornaments (Plate 252). The accoutrements consisted of a memorandum case with ivory or celluloid leaves, a card case, a shagreen spectacle

3. Reprinted from *JC* in *Silver,* May-June 1990.
4. Carpenter, *Tiffany,* pp.180-201.
5. *Sun,* 11 Dec. 1881.
6. 16 Oct. 1881.
7. *NY Times,* 10 Sept. 1882.
8. *Sun,* 9 June 1889.
9. #334,844, 26 Jan. 1886.
10. #16. XXI, 11 Sept. 1893, p. 22.
11. Boston *E Transcript,* 8 Feb. 1874.
12. Ibid.

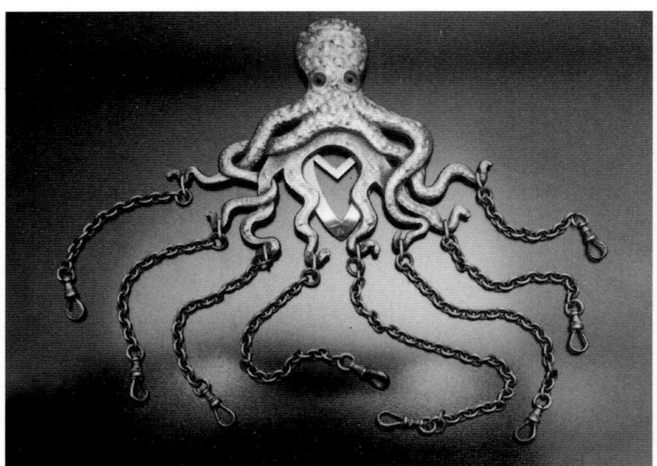

Plate 253. Chatelaine in the form of an octopus, marked STERLING and with pseudo hallmarks of Gorham Co., Providence, Rhode Island, 1887. Clasps on chains to hold attachments marked COIN. Red glass eyes of octopus have black beads in the middle for the pupils. Width 4¾in. (hook plate). Photograph by Peter J. Theriault. Private Collection.

Plate 254. Medallion brooch made by Unger Brothers, Newark, New Jersey, c.1895. Classical head with dragon on top of helmet and set with a small faceted amethyst. Diameter 1¾in. Marked on back with superimposed UB and STERLING 925 FINE. Buckle stamped with rococo repoussé decoration marked by GORDON CLASP CO. PAT[ENT]. DEC. 22-96. Length 4¼in. (clasped). Photograph by Peter J. Theriault. Private Collection.

case, a scent bottle, a pin holder, a sheathed letter opener and a whistle. Bouquet holders were also hung on chatelaines.[13] These items could be purchased all at once and in the same style or collected from different sources as the fancy pleased. In stark contrast to the old styles, an octopus served as a chatelaine, being equipped by nature to hold eight objects in its tentacles at once (Plate 253). Made by Gorham, the octopus was given red glass eyes with black-beaded pupils.

Fans, small purses and even umbrellas were suspended from these chatelaines. Tiffany offered them in silver 'plain and variously enriched', for $6 to $100.[14] In the 1890s, chatelaine trappings had themes. There were chatelaines with sewing equipment, chatelaines with religious pendants and chatelaines for the literary sort of person.[15]

Fashion notes for New Yorkers in the autumn of 1882 announced that 'Buckles of all kinds, antique, modern, medieval, metallic, and jewelled, will be very fashionable'.[16] As the belts widened in the last decades of the century, the buckles became ever larger and more important to the dress. There were gold jeweled buckles for evening wear, but for everyday dress the silver buckle was essential (Plate 254). Described by one reporter, the most popular buckle was 'hammered and twisted into most grotesque designs, chased, etched and enamelled to varying degrees of elegance and expense'.[17] Often the silver was oxidized to accentuate the design. The greater the weight of the silver, and the more massive the design the tinier seemed the waist upon which it appeared.

In America the latest fashion was apt to appear first in humble objects. Some of the most interesting art nouveau designs made their début in this way. Unger Brothers of Newark made colonial-revival, repoussé buckles and brooches, as well as art nouveau designs, in the form of flora and females, created for the firm by Philemon O. Dickinson. Unger used stamping machines to turn sheet metal into repoussé designs without the traditional time-consuming method of hand-hammering (Plate 245). Many of the patterns were copied from French examples and other European jewelry illustrated in trade journals. The dies for producing Unger's jewelry were saved and in recent years were purchased and are once again in production. Restrikes are available without the backplates and with ordinary cheap fasteners.

Newark's William B. Kerr & Co. popularized French art nouveau motifs in their

13. *Sun*, 17 Dec. 1876.
14. Tiffany, *Catalogue*, 1881/2, p.49.
15. Katharine Morrison McClinton, *Collecting American 19th Century Silver*, pp. 242-245.
16. *Sun*, 17 Sept. 1882.
17. Undated clipping from the New York *Sun*, c. 1880-90.

Plate 255. Silver 'antique' coin bracelet, made by George W. Shiebler & Company, New York, c.1880. Four overlapped and graduated coins with classical heads on each side, linked together at the back to increase comfort and flexibility. Marked on back of clasp S in middle of spread wings / 1179 and STERLING/S. Diameter 1in. (clasp medallion). Photograph by Dennis Griggs. Private Collection.

mass-produced silver jewelry, turning out a prodigious number of brooches embossed with tousled women's heads. Though stamped out of sheets of metal, these pieces of jewelry had backplates and so appeared substantial, but were light to wear.

Theodore W. Foster & Bro. and Ostby & Barton of Providence produced their share of art nouveau designs in silver jewelry. Averbeck introduced American designs in the form of 'Flor-a-Dora', after a popular musical of the day, and the 'Gibson Girl' after illustrations of Charles Dana Gibson.[18] Robert S. Gatter's trade catalogue of 1903 illustrates pins, lockets, scarf pins, bodice and sash pins, slides and fobs in art nouveau patterns similar to those of Unger.[19]

George W. Shiebler, of New York, well known for his creative designs in flatware, expanded his silver productions to jewelry (Plate 255). Most successful was his introduction of medallion designs on coins and other archaeological designs. His use of Greek letters and mottoes in relief and with oxidation added to the antique appearance of his brooches and bangles. He is thought to have been the first to take up Renaissance openwork in jewelry.[20] His Homeric medallion designs were used for both brooches and flatware.[21]

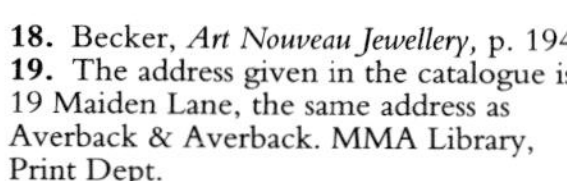

18. Becker, *Art Nouveau Jewellery*, p. 194.
19. The address given in the catalogue is 19 Maiden Lane, the same address as Averback & Averback. MMA Library, Print Dept.
20. Rainwater, *AJM*, p. 215.
21. *Silver*, Sept.-Oct. 1990.

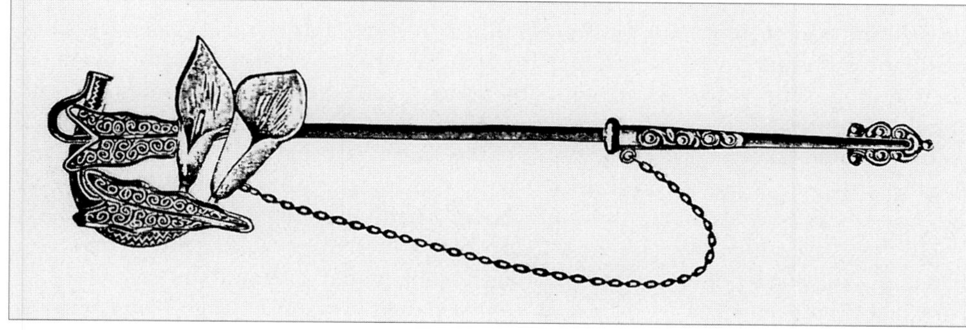

Plate 256. S.F. Myers of New York, one of the largest jewelry firms in the United States, sold solid silver scabbard lace pins of all sorts as illustrated in their catalogue of 1896.

Plate 257. Silver bracelets, c.1870s, acquired by George F. Kunz from Indian scout 'Charley', purchased by Tiffany & Co., New York, for the World's Columbian Exposition of 1893. The bracelets reveal the transfer of designs between Navajo or Zunis and the Plains Indians. All are made from sheet metal and have rocker-engraved designs. Smithsonian Institution.

REGIONAL

Because the United States was continuously settled by such a variety of the world's people, there is a great richness of jewelry design. The immigrants brought with them their own cultural traditions, craft techniques, motifs and preferences for colour, texture and materials. A random look at some of the distinctive regional strains in widely separated areas provides an indication of the cultural diversity and the wealth of forms and motifs circulating within the United States at the end of the nineteenth century.

Southwestern Indians

In the mid-nineteenth century, the Navajo in New Mexico and Arizona began to learn the techniques of silvermaking from the Pueblos and Spanish who inhabited their region. They made head stalls for horse bridles and belts ornamented with simple silver *conchas* for their own use (Colour Plate 222). The conchas were large round or oval brooch-like ornaments. As the territory became safer, American and Mexican traders began to travel to the area. Among the immigrant Mexicans were blacksmiths and silversmiths who contributed to the growth of jewelry production. Soon the Navajo, the Pueblo, Zuni and other tribes were making silver bracelets, earrings, rings and conchas. Different tribes contributed different designs which in turn had been influenced by European designs passed to them through Plains Indians. The rocker-engraving (Plate 257) or zig-zag borders, which had entered Indian jewelry through the silver ornaments given them by English and French colonists, were gradually replaced by stamped designs and repoussé work. American coins circulating in the area contributed a source of a better grade of silver than they had been able to use previously.

Bracelets were penannular, flat bands with engraved designs or were ridged. Others were made of narrow, rounded, twisted wire. The American Indians who inhabited the California coast up to Alaska, and the Zuni, Pueblo and Navajo Indians traditionally used the abalone shell for charms and appliqué ornament on silver jewelry.[1] About 1890 the Navajo began setting rings with turquoise. The Navajo also made heavy silver necklaces of round silver beads that were often interspersed with

1. Kunz, *Gems*, 238.

the so-called 'squash blossom' terminals, their version of the much used Spanish pomegranate motif that appeared as ornaments on Mexican jackets and trousers (Colour Plate 222). Pendants attached to the necklaces were often *naja* or crescent-shaped ornaments, with either open or closed tips ending with little buttons or hands (Plate 258). This design was a form of amulet brought from Europe and used on horse bridles to protect against the evil eye.[2] Many of these designs and forms appeared in the jewelry of other Western, Central and South Plains tribes and passed between them and the American and Mexican traders in a manner of cross-pollination.

In the 1880s, native jewelers began incorporating other materials in their jewelry. The Zuni especially developed their lapidary and mosaic work. Trade items such as beads, glass and marble were used for setting jewelry as was turquoise which the Indians valued greatly. Turquoise had been mined in New Mexico in prehistoric times and in Arizona, and now these mines were reopened. Glass substitutes for turquoise were sometimes used after 1900.

George Kunz remarked in 1892 that the American Indians in New Mexico had revived their jewelry skills in 'a very desultory manner'. They sold their ornaments in Santa Fé and along the route of the railroad that passed near their mines. They carried the beads, he said, in their mouths and sold them for twenty-five cents a mouthful. The beaded necklaces and ornaments made nice souvenirs and cabinet specimens, but Kunz doubted that many of them were ever worn back home.[3]

As the nineteenth century ended, the Navajo had acquired renown as makers of jewelry. As the sales to tourists increased, the Indian's technique and tools improved. New designs were created for the non-native market. An original style of jewelry found its place in American design. Eventually the Indians began wearing the tourist jewelry themselves.[4]

Plate 258. George F. Kunz purchased this necklace from Indian scout 'Charley'. It was strung with old stamped silver buttons and has a naja pendant with stamped button terminals. Purchased and exhibited by Tiffany & Co., New York at the Columbian Exposition in Chicago in 1893. Smithsonian Institution.

California

The jewelry made in California was both ingenious and distinctive. Unbound by, but not immune to, English and French prototypes, California jewelers also took advantage of their Spanish connections and their local resources. They were influenced too by the considerable Chinese influx that accompanied the Burlingame Treaty of 1868 and allowed unlimited immigration from that country to the United States.

The gold quartz jewelry that Robert Sherwood claimed to have originated continued to grow more and more popular (see pages 262-264). 'Every California tourist feels in duty bound to bring away something to remind him of his trip to the Golden Gate', the *Jewelers' Circular* pointed out in May 1885, 'Visitors to California are importuned at all points in that State to purchase specimens of the native productions of precious metals, decorative stones, etc.' California jewelers created seal rings, scarf pins, cuff buttons and watch charms from native stones, and were hoping 'to supply the entire Pacific coast with jewelry made in San Francisco'.[5]

Most of this jewelry was made with white quartz showing veins or spots of fine gold which, depending on the attractiveness of its appearance, was worth from three

2. Arthur Woodward, *Navajo Silver*.
3. Kunz, *Gems*, pp. 56-57.
4. Lawrence P. Frank, Jr., *Indian Silver of the Southwest 1868-1930*, pp. 3-9.
5. p.105. Photocopy courtesy of Edgar W. Morse.

to forty dollars an ounce. George Kunz estimated that in 1890 the value of the rough material used for jewelry was $40,000 to $50,000 annually. 'One lapidary at Oakland, California, where most of the cutting of this material is done', said Kunz, 'bought nearly $10,000 worth within a year, and a large jewelry firm in San Francisco, during the same time, purchased nearly $15,000 worth'.[6] Kunz probably was referring to Levison Bros.' California Jewelry Co. in the first instance since they were the largest establishment of its kind on the west coast and had their own lapidaries. They also had their own diamond setters and could offer both native stone and diamond work.[7]

As the demand increased, the gold quartz jewelry changed from simple designs to a variety of more elaborate settings in every possible kind of jewelry and decorative objects, including bracelets and watch chains, lace pins and perfume bottles.[8] Kunz felt that the designs were not as tasteful or as well mounted as they might have been (Colour Plate 223). Black gold quartz from Calaveras and Amador Counties was used in California too. Rose gold quartz was a combination of translucent quartz laid over a carmine-coloured paste. It appeared in conjunction with the white and black gold quartz for half sets, rings and scarf pins that sold for two to ten dollars apiece.[9] Imitation gold quartz was devised by Le Duc, Connor and Laine of San Francisco, using electricity, but they soon gave it up because it was unprofitable.

Jewelry made of abalone shell also became a speciality of California. While a great deal of this handsome iridescent material was sold to buttonmakers in New York and to jewelers in France, England and Germany, abalone mother-of-pearl jewelry came to be considered by tourists 'as distinctively Californian as a piece of big-tree [giant sequoia] bark'.[10]

Another distinctive material used by jewelers in California was jade. In small shops in Chinatown in San Francisco, oriental jewelers made pins, rings and bracelets of jade and fine gold. Far eastern designs were executed in repoussé and ciselé, utilizing fantastic animals, butterflies and other Chinese motifs. Ornaments were sometimes embellished with enamel, pearls, natural feathers and very fine filigree. The French jewelry historian Henri Vever visited California when he was in the United States for the Chicago World Fair in 1893 and was very interested in the shops and productions of Chinese jewelers in San Francisco. He described their methods of working and mentioned the shops of Lai-Shang and Gim-Hi as being of a certain importance.[11]

New Orleans

The ethnic mixture in the United States was nowhere richer than in New Orleans, Louisiana. To the native population of Cherokee were added layers of French and Spanish (Creole), African, German and other Europeans, in addition to migrant Americans from the East, Kentucky and Tennessee. All had their own set of beliefs and symbols, whether they were Catholic or Protestant or believed in voodooism.

In New Orleans Mardi Gras took root. An outgrowth of the Lenten season established by the Catholic Church between Ash Wednesday and Easter, Mardi Gras refers to 'Fat Tuesday' or Shrove Tuesday, the last day before the restrictions of Lent and fasting begin. The celebrative carnival that marks the last day of revelry was brought to New Orleans by the French settlers in the seventeenth century. In spite of bans when the celebrations began to get out of hand in the late eighteenth century, the French creoles continued to enjoy parties and private balls during Carnival season.

6. Kunz, *Gems*, pp. 117-18.
7. p. 141. Courtesy of Edgar W. Morse. See also Paul Evans, pp. 8-10.
8. Kunz, *Gems*, pp. 118-19.
9. Ibid., p. 118.
10. Ibid., p. 239.
11. *Rapports* (Paris, 1894) p.75.

Plate 260. Silver Carnival Rex pin made by Maurice Scooler as a 'krewe favor' for the Mardi Gras celebration in New Orleans on 14 February 1888. 'The Realm of Flowers' was the theme for the parade that year, and the butterfly silhouette of the pin provided inspiration for the Rex invitation. Scooler, born in Bavaria in 1827, came to New Orleans about 1842 where he was employed for several years by a jeweler in the Third District. About 1848 he started his own business and was active until he died in 1900. 1¼in. x 1½in. Gift of the Friends of the Museum. Louisiana State University Museum of Art, Baton Rouge, Louisiana.

Plate 259. The Queen's regalia, made for the Phunny Phorty Phellows for the New Orleans Mardi Gras, 18 February 1898. The crown, sceptre, gauntlets and girdle are made of gold washed base metal with imitation stones. This set was worn by Queen Henryetta Kahn, the gift of her 'King' William M. Levy. While Mardi Gras jewelry came from France originally, it was made in the United States by the latter part of the 19th century. Length 7¾in. (gauntlets). The Historic New Orleans Collection 1984.210.1,2,3,5.

Costume parties resumed in the 1820s and masks were worn while celebrants travelled to and fro. In 1857, The Mystick Krewe of Comus, a secret society formed by a few Creoles and a group of American men, initiated a parade followed by a private ball. Suspended during the Civil War, the parades returned with peace and Carnival took on a new life. Additional Krewes were formed, Mardis Gras was declared a legal holiday, and official colours of purple, green and gold were decreed.[12]

Part of the extravagance that developed along with Mardi Gras was the elaborate costume jewelry manufactured for the King and Queen of the Carnival and the pins and badges distributed to the court officials. The regalia included crowns, stomachers or girdles, bracelets and necklaces (Plate 259). At first the jewelry was made in France, but as this became more costly some of the regalia was American made. The mounts were made of base metal and the stones were rhinestones or glass.

Pins and badges were made by Frantz & Opitz, Maurice Scooler, Theresa Hausmann & Sons, and other New Orleans silversmiths. The custom of giving out these silver favours was initiated by the Mystick Krewe of Comus on the occasion of the 25th anniversary ball in 1882. Other krewes followed suit. The pins were designed in accordance with the parade or ball theme of the year (Plate 260). In 1888 the theme was 'The Realm of Flowers'. The lithographic invitation of the Krewe of

12. Maud Lyon, 'A Brief Introduction to Carnival in New Orleans'.

Plate 261. The Rex invitation to the reception at the Royal Opera House during the Mardi Gras celebration on 14 February 1888 was cut in the shape of a butterfly with outspread wings. When the wings were folded, the silhouetted butterfly resembled the design of the Rex silver pin. 8⅞in. x 11⅛in. The Historic New Orleans Collection 1960.14,80.

Rex displayed a garden of beauties both floral and female (Plate 261). Its silhouette was that of a butterfly and this motif appeared perched on the side of the crown-shaped pin.[13]

Scandinavian Jewelry

While Swedish immigrants had come to Delaware in the seventeenth century, it was not until the mid-nineteenth century that Scandinavian settlers arrived in America in substantial numbers. Settlements, mainly in Wisconsin and Minnesota, reached their peak from 1868 to 1883, with over 100,000 immigrants in 1882 alone. With them came their Nordic customs and traditions, among which were their distinctive sets of bridal jewelry and filigree work.

The bridal crown was the centrepiece of a wedding set (Plate 262). Its usage was probably derived from the Catholic custom of placing crowns on the sculptured images of the Madonna that adorned churches. The crowns symbolized virginity and were worn by brides for their elaborate marriage services. The body of the crown was pierced and outlined with beading. The points and sides of the crown were hung with long spangles. Flat birds perched on and between the points and held concave discs in their beaks to add to the glitter. In addition, the crown was set with jewels, real gems or for the less affluent coloured glass gems. While many were made of gold and silver, the jewelry was also made of gilt brass. Bridal sets remained in the family and were worn at weddings generation after generation. The family of Olaf Skaar brought their crown with them when they emigrated from Norway to La Crosse, Wisconsin. It had been made in the mid-eighteenth century, probably in Bergen.

Most, if not all, of the bridal jewelry was brought from the old country. There are no known examples today that were made in the United States. It is doubtful that in the rural areas settled by Scandinavians the trade of the goldsmith could have been supported. In some cases the church owned the jewelry and provided it for wedding services. In an article in the *Boston Evening Transcript* on 17 July 1856, concerning 'Swedish Bridal Crowns', the reporter noted, 'It is quite regal in appearance, gilt, and frequently costs as much as four pounds sterling – a large outlay for a Swedish bride', explaining that the parish priest often bought a crown and then rented it to his parishioners. This custom resulted from a synod decision in 1584 recommending the

13. Bacot, pp. 90-91.

melting of unused church silver and making of crowns from the metal so that they might be lent to brides for the ceremony.

Earrings and brooches with elaborate swinging concave-disc drops were made to match the crown. The nineteenth century bridal sets became smaller and lighter and made greater use of filigree work, a technique in which Norwegian and Swedish goldsmiths excelled. Tourists travelling in Scandinavia brought back examples, as they still can do today (Colour Plate 225). Often the open heart with a crown above was a featured element.

Plate 262. Norwegian traditional wedding jewelry featuring a mid-18th century wedding crown brought from Norway to Iowa by the Skaar family in the 19th century and worn by brides in the community. Photograph by Charles Langton. Courtesy of the Vesterheim Norwegian-American Museum, Decorah, Iowa.

Local Jewelry

Local materials were used for jewelry in scattered areas throughout the United States and gave a special flavour to each region which appealed to tourists, whether they were proud Americans or foreign travellers looking for novelty. Certain areas gained a measure of fame from their inventiveness in producing trinkets made of unusual substances that could not be found elsewhere. For example, in 1879, a Savannah, Georgia, newspaper advertised that they could supply Florida jewelry that was made to order.[14] This may have referred to jewelry made of shells which Florida continued making for the tourist trade in the twentieth century.

Indigenous agates, while no threat to the centuries old Idar-Oberstein production, were appealing because of their strong colours and sentimental value. Agate Bay on Lake Superior yielded rich red banded agates that were cut or left natural, polished, drilled at one end and turned into charms. Agates found along the Connecticut River from Amherst, Massachusetts, to Guilford, Connecticut, were called 'chalcedonic balls of Torringford' and resembled cornelian in their layers of colour. These made handsome cut seals.[15] Local agates were combined with pyrite, rhodonite, moonstone and other minerals to form an American version of Scotch pebble jewelry in the 1890s. Pins were designed as 'crowns, knots, thistles, shepherd's crooks, nails, horseshoes, crescents, daggers...and many like shapes', according to mineralogist George Kunz.[16]

Along the east coast, quartz pebbles were found in large quantity and cut into gems and seals for tourists. The local material was often augmented by imported cut stones and the buyer was none the wiser. Shops on Narragansett Pier in Rhode Island gained a reputation for this deceptive trade. The smoky quartz found at Pike's Peak in Colorado was actually sent abroad to be cut and sent back to be made into tourist jewelry. Perhaps the most famous transparent quartz was found in Herkimer County, New York, at Lake

14. A.L. Des Bouillons, *Savannah Morning News*, 1 Jan. 1879.
15. Kunz, *Gems*, pp. 329-30.
16. Ibid., pp. 329-30.

Colour Plate 222. Navajo jewelry of the early period, 1860-1910. Squash blossom necklace and pendant set with a round flat turquoise in the centre. Stamped decoration on terminals. Length 19⅛in. Concha belt, leather with rectangular buckle and seven elliptical conchas with repoussé centres. Two bracelets (left) set with thirteen small Nevada turquoises, (right) hammered band, set with single cabochon turquoise. Ketoh, worn on wrist to protect from the sting of the bowstring when hunting, elliptical turquoise in centre, repoussé and stamped decoration. Length 3¼in. Pair of earrings, wire hoop with spherical beads. Length 1⅝in. The Minneapolis Institute of Arts.

George. Because of its brilliance, it was sold as 'Lake George' or 'Herkimer diamonds'.[17]

In eastern Pennsylvania, anthracite coal was turned into the tourist's jet jewelry and was sold along the route of the railway. Beads, scarf and lace pins, bracelets and charms were all popular items. This trade totalled $2,500 to $3,000 in cost a year. Anchors, boots and hearts were favourite designs.[18] Trilobite fossils were used for the same purposes in various parts of the United States, especially near Cincinnati, Ohio, and Covington, Kentucky. The fossilized limestone sparkled brightly because it was covered with tiny calcite crystals and so made very pretty pins and charms.[19] Fossil coral, found along the shores of Little Traverse Bay in Michigan, was cut and polished by lapidaries there and set in charms, seals and cuff buttons. In 1900, between four and five thousand dollars' worth of these items were sold. Other sources of fossil coral jewelry were Dubuque and Iowa City, Iowa.[20]

Together these souvenirs represented a small part of the continuing search for what was truly American in jewelry.

17. Ibid., pp. 109-11.
18. Ibid., p. 204.
19. Ibid., p. 330.
20. Ibid., p. 198.

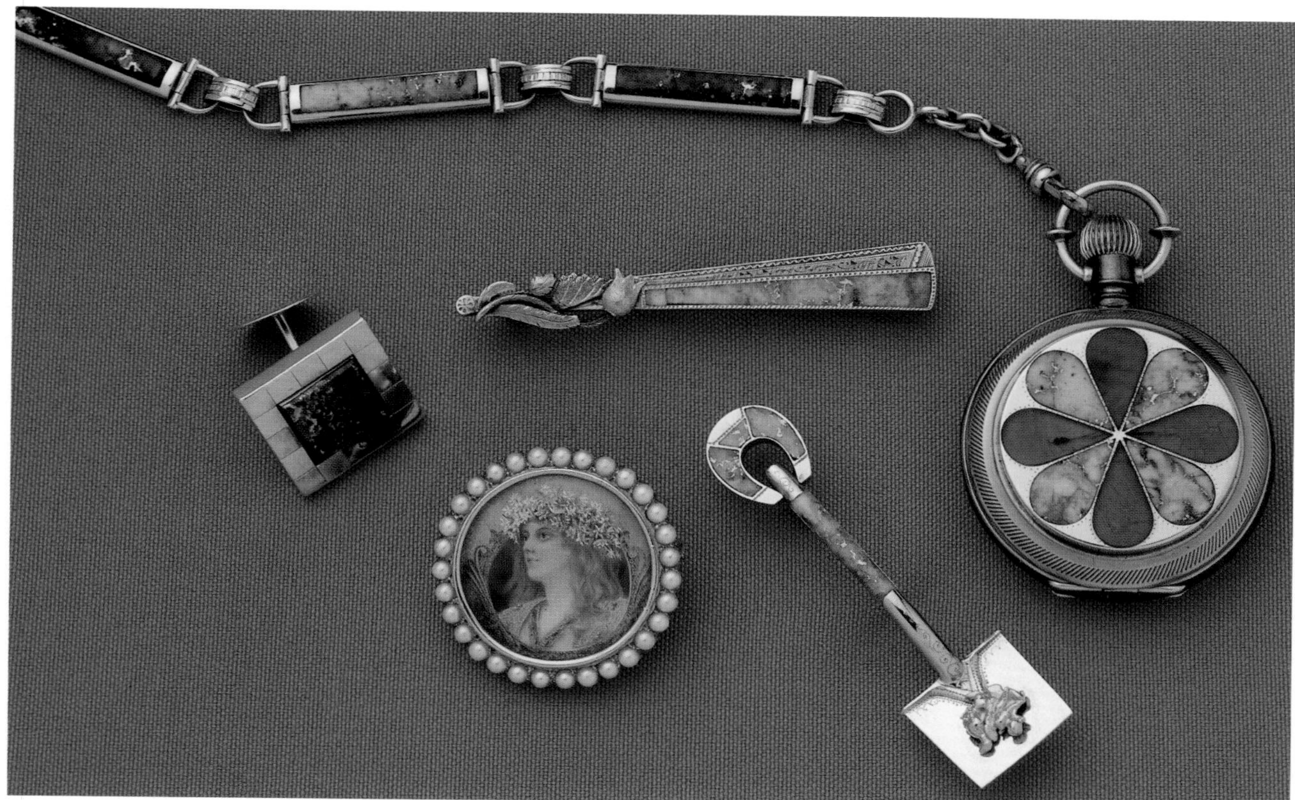

Colour Plate 223. Gold quartz jewelry, California. Square cufflink (one of a pair) stamped G.C.S. & CO. for George C. Shreve and Company of San Francisco. Engraved J.L. de F. /Sept. 14 / 1882. Private Collection. Brooch in form of miner's shovel holding gold nuggets and with a good-luck horse shoe handle. Length 2⁷⁄₁₆in. Collection of Don Ritchie, as are the rest of the pieces. The circular brooch is stamped on back Shreve & Co. Its miniature painting on ivory is unsigned. Diameter 1¼in. Pin in the shape of a closed fan with a single lily-of-the-valley handle, in the art nouveau style of the turn of the 19th century. The watch, made by the American Watch Co. in Waltham, Mass., was set in a case made of California gold and inlaid with varicoloured gold quartz as was its matching chain. The case is stamped with a star in an octagonal punch. Engraved inside front case Jane Kelly / Kelso, Wash. Diameter 1⅝in. (case of watch).

Colour Plate 224. Gold ring, made by Black Hills Jewelry Manufacturing Co., located in Dead City and Lead, South Dakota, c.1900, made with three colours of gold, with a characteristic grape vine and grape motif. Still operating as Landstrom's Jewelry.

Colour Plate 225. 18th century Norwegian wedding jewelry, silver gilt, said to have been made of silver from the Kongsberg mines. Belt clasps, breast pins, rings and pendants were traditional forms of Scandinavian wedding jewelry. Length 5⅝in. (heart-shaped pendant). Photograph by Mark Sexton. Peabody Essex Museum.

New Styles

Art Nouveau Jewelry

The seeds of a new artistic style of jewelry were sown in the latter part of the nineteenth century in reaction to the sterility of design fostered by the industrial revolution. The new art turned to nature, simplicity and asymmetry, all of which were to be found in the recently discovered art of Japan. There was also a renewed interest in flowing, sinuous lines and the graceful energy of the human form in controlled motion. The ornate burden of Victorian designs was spurned, and the freshness and vitality of life was explored instead.

First called 'artistic', the style was later christened L'Art Nouveau, in tribute to the name of the gallery established in Paris in 1895 by Samuel Bing. Bing was an oriental art dealer who exhibited the work of international artists, including Lalique and Louis Comfort Tiffany, creators of original designs and techniques in jewelry in the art nouveau style.

Jewelers became enchanted by the new ideals. On one hand, they created incredibly realistic flowers, insects and birds, calling upon the finest enamellers and gem-setters to imbue them with the subtle colours of nature. On the other hand, they gave vent to a dream world of mythical beasts and fantasies that could tickle the fancy or mildly terrify. Reduced to a single line, their art was the sinuous, sensual, even erotic, subtly smooth, moving line of life.

To achieve their goals, the artistic jewelers turned to a variety of materials provided by nature, commonplace as well as precious, to enhance their designs. Polished and stained ivory and horn were effective canvases on which to work their art. Enamels and glass gave great latitude to the range of colours that could be combined in a single piece. Jewelry could be painted with multicoloured enamels, creating shading and texture in a new exciting way. It could also incorporate areas of transparent coloured enamels in a new technique called *plique-à-jour.* By this method, the design was formed of metal outlines filled with coloured enamels, with no backing so that the enamels were open to the light like tiny stained glass windows.

Gems became secondary materials. Perfectly clear, flawless diamonds were considered less interesting than coloured stones with unusual effects, such as moonstones, opals and baroque pearls. Opals, with their individuality, changing flashes of colour and their hidden imagery, were especially pleasing to jewelers, as were the newly discovered tourmalines of Maine and California, with their unending variations of colour, often within a single crystal. Two green stones became newly popular, no doubt because of the pervasiveness of green in nature which appealed to art nouveau jewelers. One was the demantoid garnet, with a very rich green colour and great brilliance, that had been discovered in Siberia in the 1860s. The other was the peridot, popular in antiquity, which had become very rare.

The new art made its appearance in American jewelry in the designs of Paulding Farnham of Tiffany & Co. displayed at the 1889 Exposition Universelle in Paris (Colour Plate 226). These jewels took the form of exotic orchids. Realistically modelled and subtly enamelled in distinctive colours, they had a diamond dew drop here and a glistening stamen there. The stems were pavé set with diamonds or rubies. Occasionally, contrasting petals were diamond-set with gold to give them texture. In March of 1889, the orchid jewels were displayed at Tiffany's before their shipment to Paris. They attracted more attention in New York 'than any flower show, display of orchids, or any other of nature's beauties ever brought together in this city' (Colour Plate 227).[1]

Like coloured stones in their endless variety and beauty, orchids were the object of great attention in the 1870s and '80s. Greenhouses made possible their propagation in the United States, and interest was stimulated by such artistic renderings as the paintings of Martin Johnson Heade (1819-1904).[2] Among the wealthy Americans who cultivated orchids were Mrs. Mary Jane Morgan and Jay Gould, both patrons of Tiffany & Co. as well. In fact, Gould was so impressed with the display of the orchid jewelry destined for the Exposition that he bought a number of them for himself.

Theodore Child, reporting from the Paris Exposition for the *New York Sun,* compared the Tiffany display of jewelry and silver with the French exhibits. He felt that, in spite of the excellence in technique of the French entries, the work of Boucheron, Bapst and Falize lacked invention and freshness of design. It was Tiffany's, Child felt, that exhibited taste, technical skill and inventiveness. 'One thing that particularly strikes the European is the variety of materials employed by Tiffany, the strange sorts of horn, the careful toning of ivory mounts'.[3] For those who thought the display so outstanding that it must have been produced by Frenchmen working for Tiffany, Child stated emphatically that it was 'composed exclusively of objects made in America by American workmen and with American materials'.

It was not until the time of the 1889 Exposition and the Tiffany exhibit that René Lalique (1860-1945) turned his attention to the techniques of enamelling. Still a young man, this imaginative designer began making flowers, butterflies and bows enamelled in vibrant colours.[4] In the 1890s he experimented with sculptural designs in gold with naturalistic motifs. He became especially interested in the potential of glass and combined it with his highly developed skills in the nuances of enamelling. Soon he had assumed a primary position in the development and expression of the new artistic movement in France.

Lalique is often said, perhaps erroneously, to be the first art nouveau jeweler to use horn as a material for jewelry.[5] Horn had been used for ornamental hair combs in the eighteenth century and throughout the nineteenth century for jewelry, although it had been used as a substitute for tortoiseshell more often than for its own qualities and appearance. However, it was not until 1896, seven years after Tiffany had exhibited striking horn objects at the 1889 exposition, that Lalique exhibited his first piece of horn jewelry.[6]

Louis Comfort Tiffany (1848-1933), son of the founder of Tiffany & Co., was well aware of Lalique's work just as Lalique was aware of Tiffany's. Samuel Bing undoubtedly provided a link between these two artists. Bing featured Lalique's work in 1895 and the French jeweler was becoming ever more widely known and imitated. More artist than businessman, Louis Tiffany had studied in Paris in 1868 and 1869 and travelled in North Africa and Spain where he was influenced by Moorish and oriental designs and colour. His first success came as a painter. In 1878, with Candace Wheeler and Samuel Colman, he established Louis C. Tiffany & Associates, providing decorative furnishings for theatres, clubs and private homes, and for renovations in

1. *Sun,* 17 March 1889. 'One of the most interesting features of the jewelry display is a large number of orchids, which are made of enamelled gold, set with sapphires to resemble the color of the plant'.
2. Penny Proddow and Debra Healy, 'Tiffany's orchids of 1889' in *Antiques,* April 1989, pp. 900-905.
3. *Sun,* 7 July 1889.
4. Becker, *ANJ,* p. 48.
5. Misiorowski and Dirham, *Gems & Gemology,* XXII, 217.
6. Becker, *ANJ,* pp. 64-6. *Sun,* 7 July 1889.

Colour Plate 226. Exotic orchid brooches designed by Paulding Farnham (1859-1927) were introduced by Tiffany & Co. for the Exposition Universelle in Paris in 1889. As a preview, the collection of enamelled gold brooches were displayed before shipment to France. Jay Gould, who raised orchids in his greenhouse, bought a number of these ever blooming brooches from the collection. The mottling of the enamel and the glistening of the diamond stem created a remarkably naturalistic effect. Length 3⅛in. Private Collection.

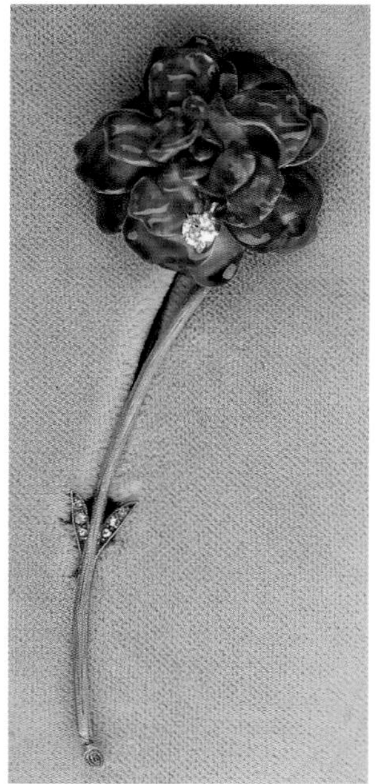

Colour Plate 227. Small purplish flower pin with diamond dew drop, derived from the larger flower designs of Tiffany & Co., c.1890. Length about 2½in. (overall). Photograph by Dennis Griggs. Private Collection.

several areas of the White House. He became especially interested in experimenting with glass, particularly for stained glass windows, a medium in which he met with considerable success. By 1889 he was named Director of Design at Tiffany & Co. where he had his own floor for creating a variety of work from mixed metals to enamels and eventually jewelry. During the same year he also arranged for Samuel Bing to be his agent in Paris.

Tiffany continued his experiments with glass, attempting to find a way to reproduce the iridescent sheen found on glass shards dug up at ancient sites such as Troy and Cyprus. The result was the rainbow glass he called Favrile which he first exhibited to the public in 1896. Favrile glass suddenly became much in demand to represent all kinds of shimmering brilliant colours in nature, from butterfly wings to beetle backs, in vases, table services, boxes, lampshades and every conceivable whimsy. Louis Tiffany collaborated with Paulding Farnham on several pieces exhibited at the Paris Exposition Universelle of 1900. A jeweled scent bottle made of Favrile glass and mounted with Mexican fire opals, diamonds and rubies set in gold was enamelled *en guilloche* in colours reiterating the iridescent colours of Favrile and opals, so that the whole object took on the appearance of a living creature emerging from the earth.

Louis C. Tiffany's experiments and creations continued to exemplify the Art Nouveau style, drawing inspiration from Oriental, Byzantine, Egyptian, Medieval and Celtic sources to create new and daring designs in the twentieth century. In 1902 he

Colour Plate 228. Orchid comb made by René Lalique, French, c.1903-04. Bought by Henry Walters of Baltimore, Maryland, at the St. Louis World's Fair in 1904 where it was exhibited as a diadem valued at $1,000. The orchid is carved from a single piece of ivory and is enamelled with brown striping. The three leaves in plique-à-jour *are highlighted with veins of diamonds. Marked on upper edge of one leaf LALIQUE. Length 7in. (including horn comb). Walters Art Gallery, Baltimore.*

founded his own department of Tiffany & Co. which became known as the Tiffany Studio and began making jewelry.[7]. George Kunz kept him supplied with an impressive selection of coloured stones. Opals, turquoises, and baroque pearls were among the favourite gems on his palette.

While Americans were still patronizing well-known firms such as Boucheron in France and Tiffany in New York at the turn of the century, a few purchased jewelry from Lalique. Henry Walters, who, with his father, formed one of the most significant collections of jewelry in America, was so impressed with the exhibit of glass jewelry displayed by Lalique at the 1904 World's Fair in St. Louis that he purchased the entire display. An orchid comb was carved out of a single piece of ivory and set off by three penetrating *plique-à-jour* leaves with spines of diamonds (Colour Plate 228).[8] The pansy brooch Walters bought had a large simulated sapphire in the centre of overlapping layers of pale blue moulded glass, blossoms and *plique-à-jour* leaves.[9] Translucent glass berries and enamelled leaves centred with a champagne-coloured citrine took on the unsettling form of a multiwinged, single-eyed flying insect (Colour Plate 234). Most prescient in design of all the Lalique jewelry acquired by Walters was the necklace made of claw-

7. Zapata, 'The Opal', *Antiques*, Sept. 1993, pp. 318-27.
8. WAG, Fig. #708.
9. Ibid., Fig. #707.

Plate 263. Tiara, set with diamonds and American turquoise, exhibited by Tiffany & Co. at the Paris Exposition in 1900. The tentacular, moving nature of the base of the tiara and the inverted pyramidal shape of the central ornament reveal the influence of the art nouveau movement. Used with the permission of Tiffany & Co. All rights reserved.

tipped relief panels carved from horn into prowling tigers and interspersed with large tortoiseshell incisors, set in sculptured gold mounts (Colour Plate 235).

While Tiffany & Co. continued to produce the formal, conservative diamond jewelry for which the firm had become famous, even here art nouveau insinuated itself. The turquoise and diamond tiara, exhibited along with the Favrile scent bottle at the 1900 Paris Exposition, possessed the tell-tale, inverted triangular shape in the centre and was anchored by wide-spreading animated tentacles (Plate 263). A gold bracelet was given real substance by the forcefulness of the waving lines flowing over it and ending in external swirls (Colour Plate 231).[10]

Marcus & Co. in New York followed a similar path, selecting from the art nouveau repertoire and adapting it to their own style. Like Tiffany, Marcus & Co. turned orchids into jewelry, but their orchids had the crushable fragile petals and leaves of nature formed in *plique-à-jour.*[11] One of their orchid pendants hung from a twisted stem of pavé diamonds with conch-pearl berries dangling below (Colour Plate 229, left). More lifelike without the diamonds, an iris brooch in the round was formed entirely of *plique-à-jour,* except for its bunchy stems enamelled to match (Colour Plate 229, right).[12] The cellular appearance of the network holding the transparent glass gave the effect of the microscopic nature of the plant.

Herman Marcus died in 1899, but his sons George Elder and William continued the business.[13] Marcus & Co. designs developed a characteristic sinuous line often given outline by a slender enamelled tracery. Seen in an other-worldly brooch made of a blister pearl verging on a face with cabochon emerald eyes, the enamelled line gave life and motion, and capped the calyx of the pendant pearl below (Colour Plate 233).[14] Marcus diamond jewelry also reflected the art nouveau style and appeared at its best when combined with rich black opals and enamelling in the same colours found flickering in the south-east Australian stones.[15]

10. Proddow, Fig. #18.
11. Ibid., Fig. #24, p. 53.
12. *ANJ* #281, N. Bloom.
13. Proddow, p. 52, repeats the story that a member of their firm studied the technique of *plique-à-jour* enamelling in Paris with Lalique.
14. Proddow, Fig. #22, p. 50.
15. Becker, *ANJ*, #292.

Plate 264. Necklace and pendant drawings, c.1898, by Edward Colonna (1862-1948) who came to work in the United States in 1882, and whose work in jewelry is best known through drawings given by him to the Newark Public Library in 1923. Courtesy, The Fine Print Collection, The Newark Public Library.

Plate 265. A dark red plique-à-jour *background silhouettes a gold stork in the reeds in this watch pin made by William Riker & Sons of Newark, New Jersey, c.1900. Riker worked with Taylor & Baldwin before 1846 when he began his own business, continuing until 1892 when he was succeeded by his sons. The company mark on the back of the watch pin is an R above a scimitar. Skinner Inc., Boston.*

There was a pronounced similarity between the Marcus blister-pearl brooch and a pendant made about 1900 by Edward Colonna (1862-1948), a German artist who studied in Belgium before coming to the United States in 1882. He worked from 1883 to 1884 for Louis Comfort Tiffany Associates and then for the New York architect Bruce Price. Just how much effect he had on American jewelers, or whether they instead influenced Colonna's work, has yet to be determined. Colonna moved about, working as a designer in Ohio, going to Montreal in 1890, and stopping in New York briefly before returning to Europe in 1893.[16] Some of his drawings/designs are at the Newark Public Library in New Jersey (Plate 264).[17] A comparison of the Marcus and Colonna pieces shows the Marcus version to be more pleasing. It is less squashed looking and more whimsical, less angular and more sinuous.

American *plique-à-jour* jewelry did not enjoy the popularity that the French did. Tiffany made occasional use of *plique-à-jour* to form borders and accents.[18] A blue and green, scrolled border was used effectively to enhance a blue and green black-opal teardrop pendant. The pendant loop had the same decorative motif enamelled, but not transparent, making the transition to its matching chain which had decorative links in a coordinated design without either the enamelling or *plique-à-jour.* Small watch pins were popular when made of gold with a *plique-à-jour* enamel background and an openwork design of a stork, heron or swans (Plate 265 and Colour Plate 232). These designs were simplified

16. He was associated with Samuel Bing from 1898 to 1903 and his work was well received at the Paris Exposition in 1900. Although he returned to Canada in 1903 and to New York in 1913, he spent his time in France after 1923 in relative obscurity.
17. Vever III, 650.
18. Becker, *ANJ*, p. 289.

Colour Plate 229. Marcus & Co. of New York achieved naturalism in flower jewelry by indicating the structural aspects of the plant using plique-à-jour *enamelling, and in the pendant (left) diamonds, conch pearls and platinum. The iris brooch relies effectively on a gold framework for the* plique-à-jour *enamel cells. Length 4½in. (orchid), 4¼in. (iris). Photograph by David Behl, New York. Private Collection.*

Colour Plate 230. Inset. Natural pink pearls form the luscious buds on this floral spray that can be worn as a brooch or a pendant. Made by Marcus & Co. in New York about 1900, combining gold, green plique-à-jour *leaves, translucent enamelling on the flowers which have diamond centres, and diamonds on the central ridge of leaves. Length 2¾in. Courtesy, N. Bloom & Son, London.*

Colour Plate 231. Both of these pieces marked by Tiffany & Co. in the late 19th century use swirling lines to achieve the art nouveau idea of motion. The scent bottle is carved from rock crystal and set in yellow gold with diamonds and a large amethyst. The gold bangle bracelet is set with amethysts, garnets, zircons and brown peridot now called sinhalite). Length 5in. (scent bottle). Photograph by David Behl, New York. Private Collection.

Colour Plate 232. Yellow gold watch pin with a heron amid lily pads and reeds. Plique-à-jour *plaques of red, blue, green and yellow. Lily pads studded with two small diamonds and a whole pearl. Heron's eye set with tiny cabochon ruby. Marked on back with R and scimitar for William Riker & Sons, Newark, New Jersey, c.1900, and 14K. Diameter 1in. Photograph by Dennis Griggs. Private Collection.*

Colour Plate 233. Indian-inspired brooch, early 20th century and art nouveau brooch, c.1900, made and marked by Marcus & Co., in yellow gold settings with emeralds enhanced by green enamelling. The mogul style brooch features a carved emerald behind a spray of flowers, diamonds and a baroque pearl. The art nouveau brooch has a blister pearl and is similar to a design attributed to Edward Colonna by Henri Vever in his history of La Bijouterie Française. *Length 1⅞in. (left), 2¼in (right). Photograph by David Behl, New York. Private Collection.*

19. Vever III, 708.

and made suitable for mass-production by William Riker of Newark. They were derived from French pendants that were much more intricate and subtly designed and made by French jewelers such as Lalique.[19] Lalique's pendant was framed by the outline of the two conjoined swans, their heads forming volutes at the top. There were two swans on a rippling pond with blades of greenery in the background as well as in the foreground.

For the most part, Americans appear to have been wary of the exaggerations of the art nouveau style. In general, they were conservative and preferred their good jewelry to look like traditional good jewelry. Conversely they liked the art nouveau designs for their costume jewelry. Mass-produced silver jewelry in this style enjoyed a landslide popularity, as did the creepy-crawling creatures of the insect and animal kingdoms (see pages 366-367). The female face or form, so much in demand for French art nouveau jewelry, appeared in American jewelry more often in the mass-produced designs made of silver. It might be chic for Sarah Bernhardt to wear the far out art nouveau designs in her plays, but it was too much for well-heeled Americans, and was left for the parvenues and novelty jewelers.

Arts and Crafts Jewelry

The Arts and Crafts movement rose from the same roots as the art nouveau style. While they shared many ideals, the two developed into complementary but differing styles. The Arts and Crafts method was more substantial, rational and constrained, while art nouveau was more imaginative and free-spirited. Arts and Crafts was weightier and more intellectual, whereas art nouveau was lighter and more emotional.

The Aesthetic Movement in England, born in reaction to the mechanical, mass-produced objects displayed at the Crystal Palace exhibition in 1851, was led by John Ruskin (1819-1900) and William Morris (1834-1896). Not only did they denounce the factory and its products, they mourned the loss of individuality and artistic values. They protested the alienation of workers from the creative processes and the subsequent loss of pride in their work. They hoped to revive the old craft system before it was too late. Through their writings and lectures, Ruskin and Morris laid down the principles on which they hoped to build the future of artists and craftsmen. With the establishment of art schools and guilds, they proposed to educate and encourage future generations.

Ruskin organized the Guild of St. George in 1871, the first of several such guilds, and the Arts and Crafts Exhibition Society was founded in 1888. The message expounded by these organizations was not only to practise time-honoured methods in workshops, but also to teach members of the trade and the public in order to raise the appreciation of artistic expression in all areas of life. Apprentices, art students and amateurs were encouraged as well as professional workers. Mass-production and separation of tasks were targets for disdain, although collaboration of specialists had been an accepted part of artistic work for centuries. Arts and Crafts advocates shared with art nouveau proponents a desire for artistic freedom, and an appreciation of materials for their colour and natural qualities, rather than for their rarity or high cost. While art nouveau jewelers often worked in gold, Arts and Crafts jewelers preferred silver and lesser metals such as copper and aluminum.

Evidence of hand craftsmanship was often allowed to remain, proclaiming to all the rejection of machine production. Not only were the hammer marks often retained, but sometimes they were actually hammered on to a planished surface with a steel die. Both Tiffany and Gorham were using these techniques in their silverware by 1876. Theodore Child noted that 'Tiffany introduced Europe to the charms of hammered or *martelé* silver in 1878, almost twenty years before William Codman named his new line of Gorham's art nouveau silver 'martelé'.[1]

Coloured stones, more often cabochon than faceted, were preferred to diamonds. Mother-of-pearl, moonstones and opals were prized for their natural shimmering lights. Irregularities in the material chosen added interest as in turquoise matrix and baroque pearls.

The Arts and Crafts movement in America manifested itself first in the establishment of schools of design and annual exhibitions. The Rhode Island School of Design was founded in Providence in 1877 and was committed to the improvement of jewelry design, silversmithing and shop work. Prizes were offered annually to this school's best students by the New England Jewelers and Silversmiths' Association.[2] The first Art Workers Guild in the United States was organized in Providence in the mid-1880s. In Boston, the Lowell School of Practical Design was established and the School of Drawing and Painting was started at the Museum of Fine Arts. Charles Eliot Norton, who had been Harvard's Professor of Fine Arts since 1874, was an old friend and admirer of John Ruskin. Norton sought to improve the arts through education and played a key role in bringing the Arts and Crafts movement to America.

Boston, still acknowledged as the cultural centre of the United States and the defender of good taste, became the first city to form a Society of Arts and Crafts. Henry Lewis Johnson, a craftsman who had attended craft exhibitions in England for almost a decade, organized a similar exhibition in Boston in April 1897 that received national attention. On 28 June 1897, the Boston Society of Arts and Crafts was incorporated for the sole purpose of developing and encouraging higher standards in the handcrafts, leaving other worthy reformations of social, economic and political concerns to the Arts and Crafts guilds in England and other countries.

Arthur J. Stone, an Englishman who had studied at the National School of Design as well as at the Ruskin Museum in Sheffield, and who had been working as a silversmith and chaser-designer in the United States since 1884, became an active member and prize-winner in the Boston Society. A necklace made by Stone for his wife Elizabeth soon after their marriage in 1896 shows the influence of Christopher Dresser, one of the leading exponents of the philosophy of the Aesthetic Movement in England (Colour Plate 236). Dresser's book, *The Art of Decorative Design* published in London in 1862 was owned by Arthur Stone. The design of the pendant owes a great deal to Fig. 60 and Dresser's way of looking up to a branch from below. Stone filled out and softened the basic design, adding life to it by a judicious use of tendrils loosely binding the design together, giving it a sense of growing.[3]

Frank Gardner Hale (1876-1945) was one of the best of the early Arts and Crafts jewelers in Boston. Hale studied in England, first with C.R. Ashbee (1863-1943), designer and architect, at the Guild and School of Handicraft in Chipping Campden.[4] Ashbee was well known as a proponent of the Arts and Crafts movement. Subsequently Hale studied with Frederick Partridge (1877-1942) in London. Partridge worked in the French style and had been associated with Ashbee when the Guild of Handicraft moved in 1902 to Chipping Campden in Gloucestershire. Hale came back from England in

1. *Sun,* 7 July 1889. It was not until 1897 that Gorham called their art nouveau wares 'martelé'.
2. Wodiska, p. 278.
3. The design is said to have been inspired by one of the border elements of Ghiberti's Baptistry doors.
4. Edith Alpers, 'F.G. Hale: U.S. Pioneer in Arts & Crafts', *Heritage,* August 1989, pp. 192-5.

Colour Plate 234. Brooch made by Lalique, French, c.1903, bought by Henry Walters of Baltimore in 1904 at the St. Louis World's Fair where it was exhibited as a 'corsage ornament representing snowballs' and valued at $700. The central gem is a cushion-shaped, champagne coloured, faceted citrine. The snowball berries are made of translucent glass. Marked at top edge of central section LALIQUE. Length 2⅝in. Walters Art Gallery, Baltimore.

Colour Plate 235. Detail of a gold necklace made by Lalique, c.1903-04, and purchased by Henry Walters at the St. Louis World's Fair, 1904. Plaques of carved horn strident tigers alternate with tortoiseshell incisors. Claws extend downward on each side of the plaques. Marked on clasp LALIQUE. Length 2⅜in. (teeth). Walters Art Gallery, Baltimore.

Colour Plate 236. In contrast to the Art Nouveau designs of Lalique (Colour Plates 234 and 235, opposite page), the Arts and Crafts style can be seen in this gold and diamond necklace and pendant made by Arthur J. Stone (1847-1938), Gardner, Massachusetts, 1914, for his wife Elizabeth. Length 20in. (chain), 1⅞in. (bar). Photograph by Geoffrey Stein, Boston. Private Collection.

1907 and established his Copley Square Studio. He met with immediate success. By 1909, he was considered to be 'the most all-around jeweler in the country', according to a Boston newspaper.[5] Less prejudiced perhaps was the opinion of Julius Wodiska, author of *A Book of Precious Stones* published in New York and London in 1909, and a manufacturing jeweler and importer of gems for thirty years in New York. Wodiska called Hale's display at a recent Society of Arts and Crafts exhibition in Boston 'a valuable and most interesting...collection of exquisitely designed, excellently drawn, and well executed pieces'. Not only were Hale's jewels definite in design, but 'the construction of his mountings of gems is practical and would satisfy the mechanical requirements of manufacturers of jewelry commercial *[sic]*, which a good deal of the work of exponents of arts and crafts jewelry would not'.[6] Hale's work was also exhibited in New York at the Clausen Galleries.

Hale's English training strongly marked his early work. Soon his own style emerged in brooches and pendants of harmonious design, set with coloured stones in both silver and gold, with motifs derived from nature, sometimes studded with gold beads. Hale combined moonstones with Montana sapphires in controlled, swirling, open-work frames. Montana sapphires were coupled with blue and lavender zircons and green tourmalines with peridots in an Arts and Crafts version of a Renaissance-style brooch

5. Alpers, FGH, p. 194.
6. Wodiska, p. 276.

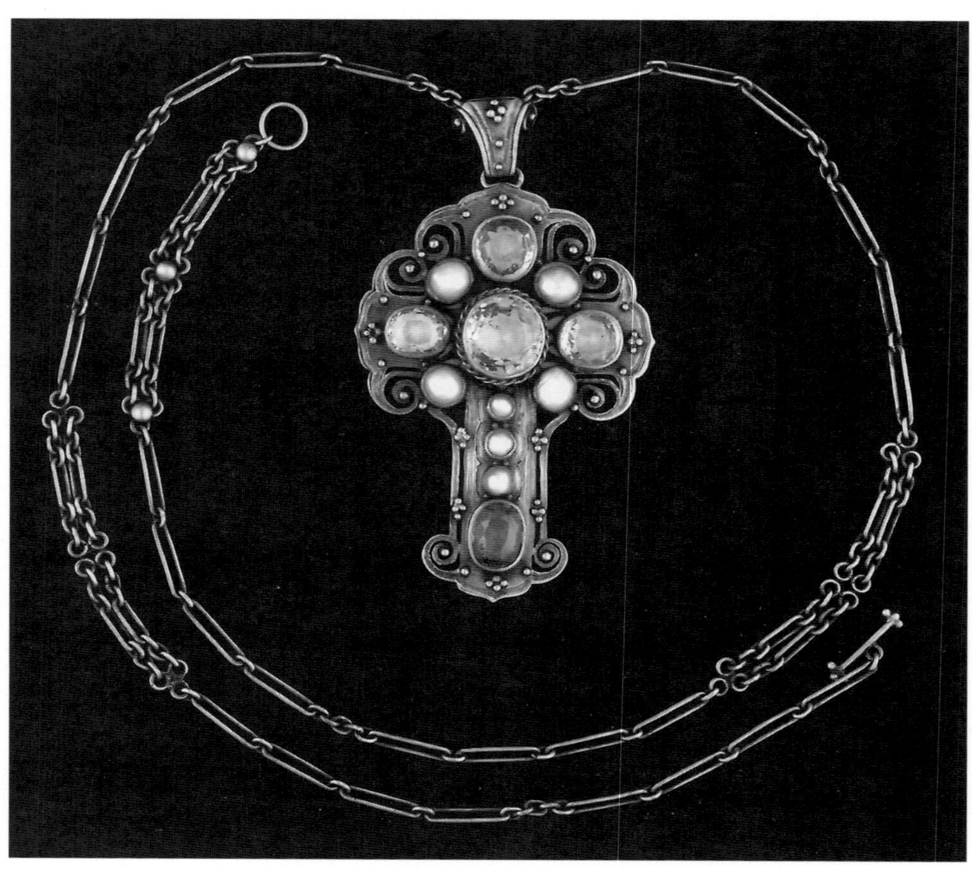

Plate 266. Green gold cross which takes the form of a fruitful tree. Pierced work and applied pellets add to the strength of the design. Amethysts and other faceted stones in shades of violet and salmon are set off by baroque pearls. The original chain has long and short lengths of a fetter and knot pattern. The necklace was made and marked by Josephine Hartwell Shaw. Bequest of the maker in memory of her husband, Frederick A. Shaw, in 1914. Courtesy, Museum of Fine Arts, Boston.

(Colour Plate 237). Hale's work had a widespread effect. His jewelry was shown in exhibits and he lectured across the country on the Arts and Crafts approach to art. He was instrumental in the establishment of the Jewelers Guild of the Boston Society of Arts and Crafts.

Hale's first assistant was Edward Everett Oakes (1891-1960). In 1914 Oakes became affiliated with Josephine Hartwell Shaw (1865-1941), another of the Arts and Crafts jewelers who had studied at the Pratt Institute in New York (Plate 266). Established in 1883, the Pratt Institute in Brooklyn played a significant role in the development of the movement. The Director of the Department of Fine and Applied Arts was Walter Scott Perry. The first class in jewelry, enamelling and hammered metal was organized in 1900 and taught by Joseph Aranyi who had worked for Tiffany & Co.

Oakes joined the Boston Society in 1916 and the following year established his own shop. He exhibited his work in the Chicago Art Institute Annual Exhibitions and at the Detroit Society of Arts and Crafts. His designs were naturalistic, asymmetrical and conservative.[7] Among his earliest jewelry was a gold necklace made for Arthur Stone's wife Elizabeth (Colour Plate 238). Its elegance emanated from the simplicity of its design. The necklace was made of triple rows of chains with gradually diminishing rectangular open-work

7. Edith Alpers, 'Edward Everett Oakes (1891-1960), a master craftsman from Boston, Massachusetts', *Jewellery Studies* 3, pp. 73-9.

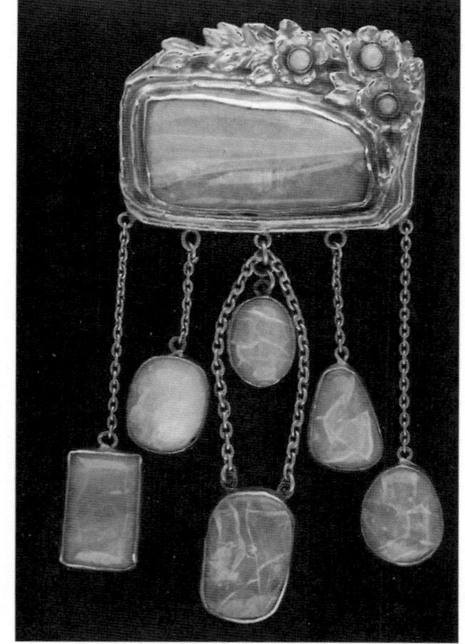

Plate 267. Gold brooch with variously shaped opals, made by A. Fogliati in Chicago, c.1905. Fogliati was associated with the Hull-House metalworkers where he lectured and where the Chicago Arts and Crafts Society held its meetings. The brooch was made for Mrs. John J. Glessner (Frances), one of his students. Length 2¼in. Chicago Historical Society. 1983.131.3.

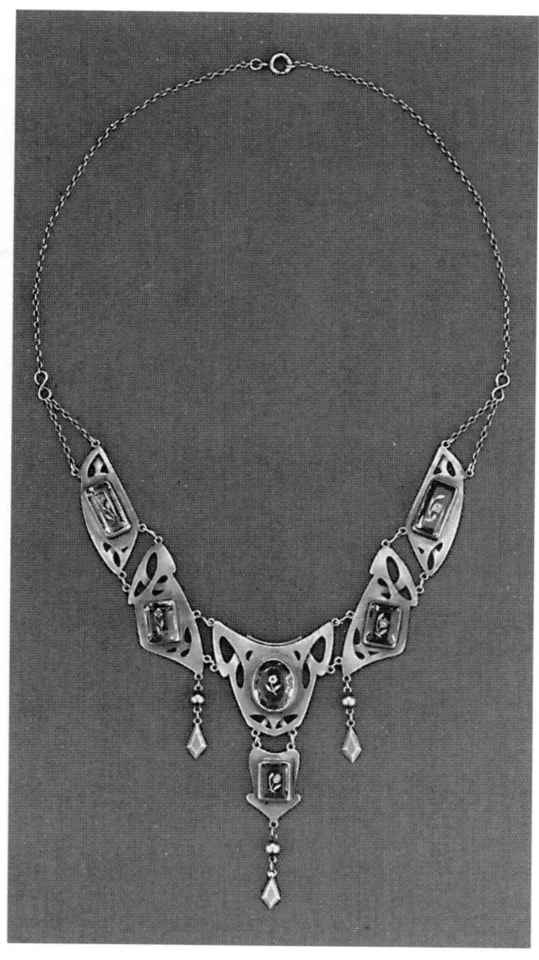

Plate 268. Jewelry made by Florence Koehler (1861-1944), Chicago and New York, early 20th century. Pin-pendant with sapphires, pearls, emeralds and enamel on gold. Length 2¼in. Necklace, pearls and enamel on gold. Length 14in. Comb, pearls and enamel on gold. Width 4¾in. Gift of Emily Crane Chadbourne, 1952 (52.43.1-.3). Metropolitan Museum of Art.

Plate 269. Necklace, Kalo Shop, Park Ridge, Illinois, silver gilt with amethysts, diamond chips, and gold leaf, 1905-14. Length 18¾in. Americana Fund, 1989.448.1. Photograph by Robert Hashimoto, ©1993 The Art Institute of Chicago, all rights reserved.

settings of natural fresh-water pearls. The clasp became an integral part of the design (Colour Plate 239, below).

Among other Boston jewelers who exhibited at the Society of Arts and Crafts, Mountford Hill Smith was singled out by Wodiska for the numerous excellent silver crucifixes he made that were set with both precious and semi-precious stones. H. Gustave Rogers represented the Marblehead handicraft shop on Boston's North Shore. A number of women were cited for their noteworthy contributions, including Jane Carson, Theodora Walcott, Laura H. Martin, Elizabeth E. Copeland, Martha Rogers, Florence H. Richmond and Jessie Lane Burbank.[8] In 1914 Josephine Hartwell Shaw received the Boston Society's bronze medal for most distinguished craftsman (Plate 266).

Boston led the Arts and Crafts movement in the United States and served as its centre. The Boston Society accepted distinguished craftsmen from other cities, and some of its members joined a few of the other twenty-four societies that were eventually formed throughout the country.

In addition to the Pratt Institute where Mrs. Shaw had studied, New York City was blessed with the Cooper Union established in 1897 with impressive museum holdings. Their collection of scrapbooks included one devoted to jewelry, providing a sourcebook for every imaginable form of jewelry. Their course on jewelry designing was directed by Edward Ehrle and prizes were awarded by the trade journal, *The Jewellers' Circular Weekly.*[9] New York also had the New York Society Library, founded in the eighteenth century, the best collection of source books for jewelry in the city.

8. Wodiska, p. 277. Designs by Richmond and Hale illustrated opposite p. 274.
9. Ibid., pp. 273-4. The 1908 prize went to Frederick E. Bauer.

Colour Plate 237. Zircons, diamonds, sapphires, tourmalines and peridot provide an unusual colour combination in this gold brooch made by Frank Gardner Hale (1876-1945) of Boston who was awarded the Medal of that city's Society of Arts and Crafts in 1915. Length 2½in. Photograph by Witt McKay. Private Collection.

Colour Plate 238. Necklace made of gold and freshwater pearls by Edward Everett Oakes (1891-1960) for Arthur J. Stone's wife Elizabeth, early 20th century. Length 16in. Photograph by Witt McKay. Private Collection.

Colour Plate 239. Citrine and pearl brooch (top), c.1900, flanked by a spray of flowers circled by vines and leaves. Marked BELL and 14 K, for a Boston jeweler. Small citrine oval clasp below marked on top of snap OAKES in an oak leaf for Edward Everett Oakes (1891-1960), Boston, c.1915. Length ¾in. (clasp overall). Photograph by Peter J. Theriault. Private Collection.

Exhibitions were sponsored by the National Art Club with the National Society of Craftsmen in New York and included the work of the jewelry class taught by Miss Grace Hazen of Gloucester, Massachusetts.

Chicago, the second largest city in the United States in 1890, was the site of the second Society of Arts and Crafts established in this country. Because of its democratic nature and social conscience, Chicago was most receptive to the ideals of the British movement. Not only did Chicago's members travel to England but proponents such as C.R. Ashbee visited and lectured in Chicago, first in 1900, where he visited his friend, social reformer Jane Addams who had founded Hull-House after seeing Ashbee's Toynbee Hall in London. Hull-House became the headquarters for Chicago's new Arts and Crafts Society (Plate 267). The School of the Art Institute of Chicago disseminated their principles, particularly under the tutelage of Louis J. Millet, who taught decorative design and architecture from 1891-1918.[10] In 1902 a major exhibition of student work took place at the Art Institute and continued annually until 1921. Jewelers exhibiting at these events included James H. Winn (1866-c.1940), Jessie M. Preston and Essie Myers.

10. S. Darling, pp. 34-43.

Colour Plate 240. Early 20th century gold jewelry designed by Louis Comfort Tiffany in the Egyptian revival style. The necklace is hung with favrile glass beetles, a technique in glassmaking created by Tiffany, and advertised in the Tiffany & Co. Blue Book *from 1909 to 1914. The brooches exhibit the painterly accomplishments in enamelling of Louis C. Tiffany which form a sympathetic setting for precious gems. John Loring's* Tiffany's 150 Years. *(New York: Doubleday, 1987).*

In 1905 the Kalo Art-Craft Community was established in Chicago by Clara P. Barck and her husband George S. Wells. It became a workshop and school for metalwork and jewelry and exerted an important influence over the Arts and Crafts movement in Chicago for several generations (Plate 269).[11]

The Arts and Crafts movement appealed to Americans who associated handcrafts with their glorious past. While the movement itself lost momentum after the First World War, it has never died out in America where there is still a continuous resurgence of arts and crafts principles, practitioners and handmade jewelry.

11. Ibid., pp. 43-75.

Jewelers

Designations among jewelers changed over the centuries. In 1700, there were jewelers and goldsmiths; in 1800, there were manufacturing jewelers and retail jewelers. By the last quarter of the nineteenth century, there were all of these, backed up by skilled ancillary craftsmen, but in addition there were wholesale jewelers and jobbers as well as artistic and commercial jewelers. Industrialization had caused an explosion that fractured the jeweler's trade into its component parts. Organizations and publications arose to help solve the common problems that resulted from the new more complex system. International exhibitions were staged to promote, stimulate and improve production.

The artistic jeweler, who shunned mass-production and worked in the time honoured way, continued either in his own workshop or in the workshop of large exclusive jewelry firms such as Tiffany & Co. Tiffany prided itself on its quality and the fact that every aspect of the jewelry trade could be carried on in its own workrooms, including repair and remodelling tasks. In each area of the United States outstanding jewelry firms appeared. Some were new and others were firms that had been in business for several generations. New York became the undisputed centre of the fine jewelry trade. Providence rivalled Newark and surpassed Attleboro in the commercial production of jewelry. Chicago and St. Louis served the midwest and San Francisco the west.

The usual pattern for the jewelry trade was to prepare, beginning in August, for the mid-December holiday trade. There was a lull and then by mid-January new orders began to come in from jewelers who had cleared out their old stock. These orders continued to come in until about June when another slump occurred until the August production began.

Recession, fire and theft were serious concerns for the jewelry trade. While times were generally good during the last quarter of the nineteenth century, there were three years – 1882, 1893 and 1897 – when the industry faltered. If customers declined to purchase, as they did in the spring of 1882, retailers and jobbers found themselves overstocked. As a result, many jewelers lost their jobs or were reduced to working half or three-quarters of a day. Large manufacturers and wholesale houses, as well as small jewelry firms, failed if they did not have the means to wait until the economy recovered. In 1882 it was reported that 'In Providence where more jewelry, both good and bad, is made than in any other American city, many shops have entirely stopped, and their workmen come trooping back here [to New York city] looking for employment which they certainly cannot find in New York this season. The same thing has happened over in Newark'.[1]

One of the problems was the ever-decreasing profit of the manufacturer of jewelry. When the ledger was tallied during the 1882 recession, the manufacturer received between 5 and 15% of the profit, while the jobber received 20 to 33%. The prestigious jewelry store, with its own workshop, could still earn 50 to 100%, or at

1. *NY Sun*, 13 Dec. 1882.

Tiffany's 300 to 400%, but the ordinary store might be fortunate to make 33%.[2] Increased competition demanded lower prices. Reduction of production costs was achieved primarily by development of machinery or by lowering the quality of the raw materials.

A variety of other steps were taken to offset losses. During one dull period in the 1890s George Howard & Co. undertook a 'Grand Gift Sale by the Popular Method of One Price for all articles'. They charged $5 for every item listed on their broadside, a price that was a quarter of the regular retail price.[3] The jewelry ranged from sets of pearl, garnet, amethyst, ruby, diamond and onyx mounted in 18 karat gold. Rings, scarf pins, bracelets, lockets, vest chains, studs and buttons were all only $5 per item. The jewelry made in their own manufactory they were able to sell for much less than the wholesalers who had to buy from other manufacturers. Eager to keep the customers they garnered from their $5 sale, George Howard & Co. said 'We deal in nothing but first-class goods, excluding entirely all galvanized or plated trash which has been so extensively sold to country dealers within the past few years'.

The danger of fire was particularly worrisome for a trade that required such valuable material. One night early in March 1877, fire broke out in the centre of the New York jewelry trade in the Waltham building at Nos. 1, 3 and 5 Bond Street. The Fire Department arrived promptly, but they faced unusual obstacles that were inherent in the jewelry business. The iron-clad doors and shutters, as well as the strongest of locks, intended to protect the very valuable materials of the trade, made it impossible for the firemen to rescue them. The many flues and carrier tubes provided conduits through which the heat and flames were able to spread to all parts of the building and out of the range of the hoses. The elevator shaft served as 'a gigantic chimney'. Finally the iron front of the building, twisted and bent, collapsed carrying the contents of the floors above into the raging cauldron.[4]

It took weeks to work through the debris to locate surviving safes and valuables, and to assess the losses. Dozens of firms housed in the building were seriously affected by the fire. The Gorham Manufacturing Company of Providence occupied the ground floor of Nos. 1 and 3 Bond Street and had only recently been extensively renovated. The firm estimated that they lost $275,000 worth of solid silver and Gorham plate; only about $10,000 in solid silver was salvaged. Furthermore, the rest of their merchandise was kept in show cases and not in safes and, because it was on the ground floor, it had been buried under all the other debris.[5]

The Whiting Manufacturing Company announced the morning after the fire that the Whiting Building at Broadway and Fourth Street would be available to any of the stricken firms that needed the space. The jewelry firm of Hale & Mulford quickly accepted. They had occupied a part of the ground floor for their office and salesroom and all of the fifth floor for their factory. They urgently needed space for both operations. In addition to the loss of about $60,000 worth of stock, they had lost expensive tools and machinery amassed over a fifteen-year period. Carter, Howkins & Sloan, a manufacturing jewelry firm established in Newark in 1841, accepted the offer as well. However, because their factory was in New Jersey, their New York losses were minimized and production was uninterrupted. In addition, their jewelry and their books had been secured in several safes, thereby saving their enamel and chain work.

Some of the smaller firms found quarters nearby or at Maiden Lane and Broadway.

2. Ibid.
3. Broadside, Courtesy, J.M. Cohen Rare Books.
4. *JC*, March 1877, unpaginated.
5. Ibid., April 1877.

Colour Plate 241. Enamelled gold brooch made by Krementz & Co., Newark, N.J., c.1900, set with diamonds and pearl. Collection of The Newark Museum. Purchase 1992 Dr. and Mrs. Earl LeRoy Wood Bequest Fund.

Colour Plate 242. Pair of bracelets, coloured gold, with twisted wire decoration, New York, 1879. Made by Charles Heim, Corona, New York or Hale & Mulford, New York City. Heim patented the projecting flange on the edge of the bracelet which is stamped Feb. 25, 1879 [U.S. Patent No. 212,692]. Reissued on Oct. 14, 1879 to Hale & Mulford. Width 1⅞in. Photograph by Leland Cook by courtesy of the Magazine Antiques. *The Charleston Museum, Charleston, SC.*

Robbins & Appleton, who had built the Waltham Building in 1871, specialized in the manufacture of gold watch cases. Their factory was on the top floor of the building. The watch movements were stored in safes, but because of their delicacy and the need for precision, they were worthless, as were the machines. At least the gold could be melted down and reworked. The estimated loss was $250,000 in addition to the building which was valued at $215,000. Their case factory was moved across the street to Nos. 7 and 9 Bond Street and quickly put into production. The factory in Waltham, Massachusetts, was at full tilt trying to fill orders. In the meantime orders were being supplied from surplus in their Boston and Chicago stores.

Colour Plate 243. Above. Coloured gold bangle bracelet fashioned in the Etruscan style, New York, c.1880. Twisted wire decoration around one half of band. Marked inside PAT'D FEB. 25 / 1870 / Oct. 14 79 / MAY 18.80. This patent [No. 212,692] was issued to Charles Heim, Corona, N.Y. and reissued to Hale & Mulford, New York City. Width 1⅞in. Photograph by Peter J. Theriault. Private Collection.

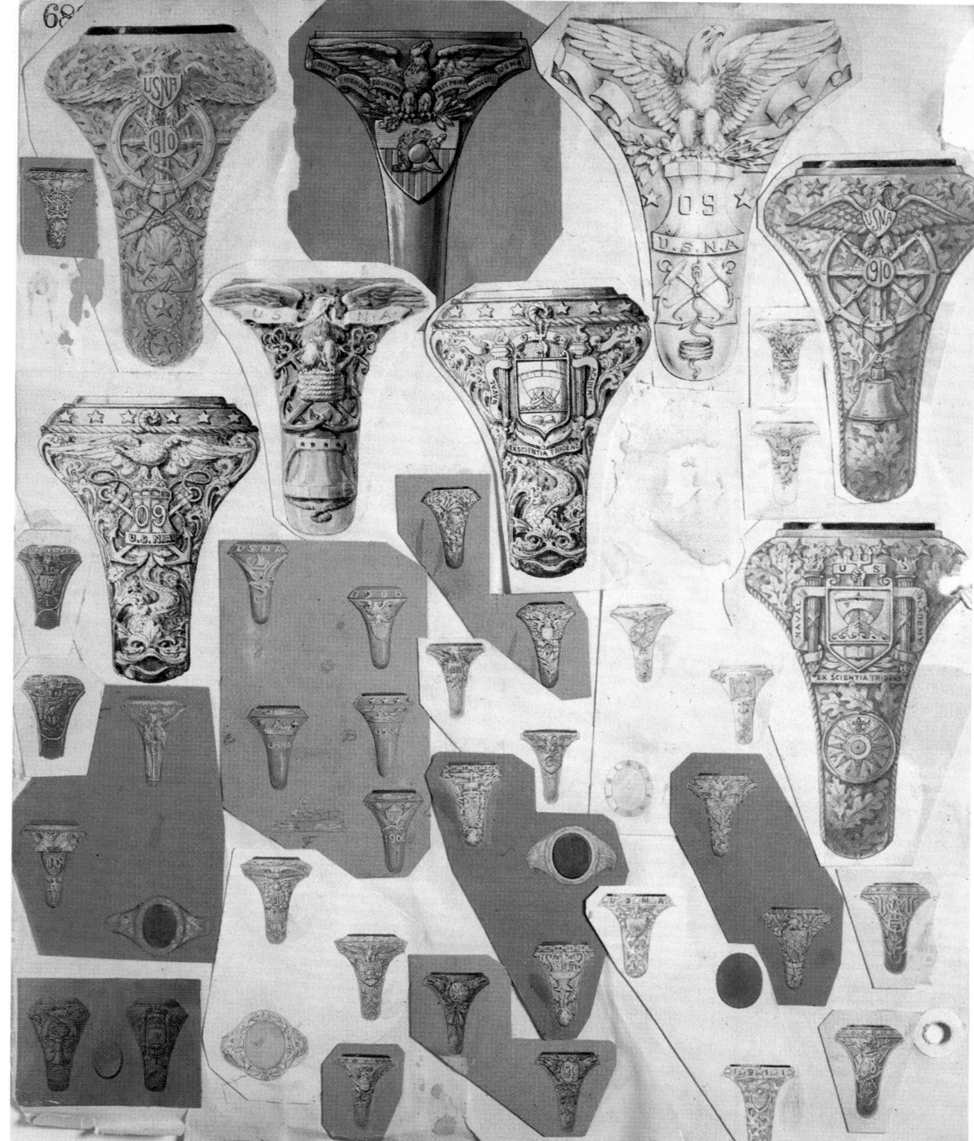

Colour Plate 244. Right. Class rings were made by Tiffany & Co. for the United States Naval Academy. These drawings show the diversity of symbolic designs made in the early 20th century. The ring in the lower right corner was designed in 1898. John Loring's Tiffany's 150 Years. *(New York: Doubleday, 1987).*

Some lessons were to be learned by jewelers everywhere. Comparison was made between brands of safes. Valentine & Butler's safe did the job, as did the Herring safe. Safes by Marvin, Hendrickson and Terwilliger also passed muster. Others failed. If the safe fell with the door up, there was far less damage than if the doors landed face down and allowed water to get to the contents. It was also learned that jewelry with a bright finish survived in good condition, while coloured jewelry was rendered useless because of severe tarnishing.

Many of the companies were insured and obtained agreeable settlements promptly. Nevertheless, as the *Jewelers Circular* was quick to point out, 'this building contained more valuable contents than any other of its size in the city, and the damage will be proportionately large. The materials stored therein consisted of precious gems, valuable metals and machinery, which last can never be replaced'.[6]

Increased losses by theft and deceit were another great concern of jewelers everywhere. In 1883, robberies throughout the country caused retail jewelers in New

6. Ibid., March 1877.

York, Philadelphia and other eastern cities to form a national protective union similar to the wholesale dealers' Jewelers League that was established in New York in 1877. They wanted to increase protection of their stores. Because of the debts run up at New York firms by out of state dealers, robberies of jewelers in other cities were also inflicting serious losses on the New York jewelers. Almost $100,000 worth of jewelry had been stolen in the six months prior to March 1883, and the robbers were still at large. The new organization hoped to track down and convict jewelry thieves. The New York Union had been able to catch the culprit in every case during its five years of existence.[7]

The Jewelers League of New York City was established in 1877 for the mutual benefit and protection of workers in the jewelry and allied trades. This organization provided families of deceased members with financial assistance. By 1880, their membership had increased from 560 to 1,040.[8] The same year New York journeymen jewelers organized a trade union to improve the conditions of workers in the jewelry trade. Founding members were particularly concerned because some jewelry manufacturers were employing often inexperienced people to make silver, base metal or thinly plated gold jewelry in tenement houses for very low wages.[9] In 1874, the *Jewelers' Circular* began publication in New York, subsequently advertising as 'a compendium of news, technical instruction and valuable suggestions for the conducting of a jewelry business'.[10]

One of the new specialty groups to be organized within the jewelry trade was that of the diamond cutters. In 1877, the New York *Sun* had reported, all the cutting and polishing of rough diamonds that came into New York was being processed by two diamond cutters. The development of superior American methods of cutting and polishing increased the demand for American diamond cutters. By 1882 an additional five or six cutters were operating in New York and altogether they dressed and polished about a twentieth of the diamonds sold in that city, amounting to about 5,000 carats of rough. Labour was paid two to three times as much as in Europe for the same work.[11]

Henry D. Morse, who was responsible for revolutionizing the diamond cutting industry, employed about thirty workers in his Boston establishment and had twenty-four steam driven polishing wheels. At first his workers were brought from abroad, but Morse soon began to train the men and women he employed himself. By 1884 it could be said, 'Now the atelier of Mr. Morse may be considered as essentially American both in its artists and its arrangements'. That year when Morse's abilities were at their peak, he was asked by Tiffany & Co. to cut the largest stone ever cut in the United States. This was the South African, Tiffany Diamond No. 2 which Morse successfully reduced from 125 carats to 77 carats.[12]

At his death in 1888, the skills Morse had perfected had been introduced into about a dozen shops in the United States, among which were Tiffany's own cutting room and Isaac Hermann's shop in New York. By 1890, it was apparent that New York would be the diamond capital of the United States. The census for that year listed sixteen cutting firms in New York City and only three in Boston. In 1895 several new foreign firms had established shops in Brooklyn and Lower Manhattan, no doubt prompted by the Dingley Tariff passed in 1894 to encourage domestic trade. The Dingley Tariff imposed a 25% duty on cut stones and a 10% duty on uncut stones. In 1896 the duty was lifted causing a recession in the cutting trade until it was reinstated in 1897.[13]

Following the precedent of the diamond cutters union formed in Amsterdam in 1894, American diamond cutters set up their first trade union in 1895. It was not

7. *NY Times,* 27 Mar. 1883.
8. Ibid., 22 Jan. 1881 (8-2).
9. Ibid., 30 May 1880.
10. 31 July 1895, p. 32.
11. *NY Sun,* 19 Feb. 1882.
12. Hamlin, *Leisure Hours*, pp. 247-50.
13. Federman, *Modern Jewelry,* pp. 38-40 and *Minerals Yearbook* 1883-84, p. 691 and 1895-96.

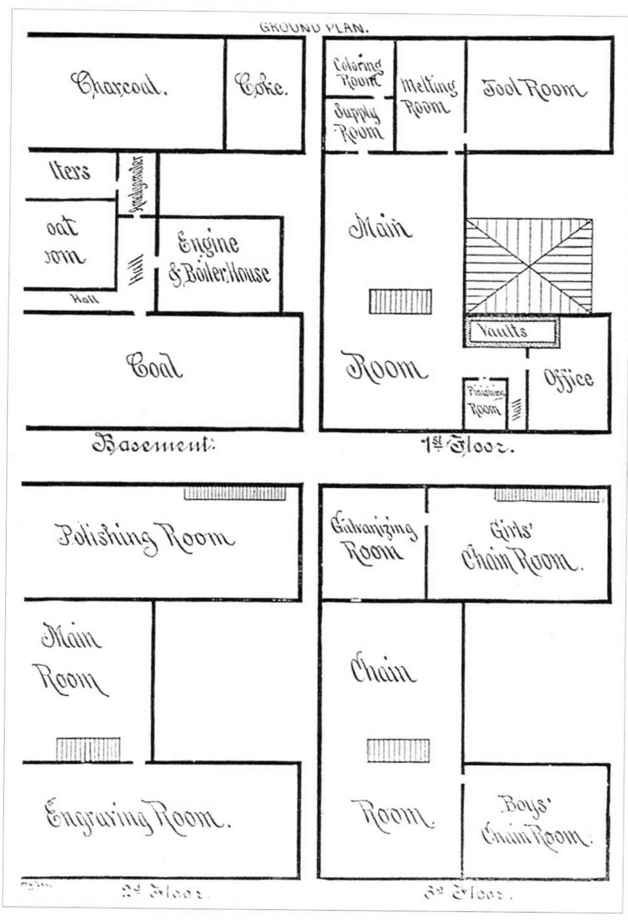

until 1902 that the well organized effective Diamond Workers Protective Union was put into operation. Among the 375 members of this union, most were natives of Amsterdam and some were from Belgium and other European countries, with only a few American-born cutters. Most of the diamond workers were located in New York City, Boston, Chicago or Cincinnati.[14]

From 1875 to 1900, immigrant jewelers continued to refresh the American jewelry trade. Most came to the centres in New York, Boston, Providence, Newark, and Philadelphia, and to a lesser extent to Attleboro. In 1860 in Newark more than half the workers had been foreign born. 44.6% were American born, while 21.2% were Irish, 26.2% German and 8.1% were other.[15] Providence at the same time was largely supplied by workers of British stock and lesser numbers of German, Irish, French and Italian jewelers. In 1889, Gorham employed workmen from Russia and Germany, as well as English, French and American.[16] By the turn of the century, William C. Codman reported that 70% of the Gorham Co. workers under his direction were English and the rest were primarily Scandinavian. Graduates of the National Art Training School in London, who once found good jobs there, increasingly found jobs in the United States and Australia more attractive. Among prominent Englishmen who achieved success in the precious metals industry in Providence were Codman, head of design, and George Wilkinson, managing director, of Gorham.[17] In contrast, in 1893 one-sixth of the 120 workers employed by Shreve & Co. in San Francisco were Frenchmen and there were a number of Chinese jewelers working on their own in that city.[18]

Plate 270. Floor plans indicate the location of the various operations involved in the manufacture of gold jewelry as illustrated in William R. Bagnall's booklet, The Manufacture of Gold Jewelry *(New York, 1882), describing the history of Enos Richardson & Co. of Newark.*

By 1876, Providence maintained a leading position among the successful commercial jewelry producing centres in the United States. There were almost two hundred firms in operation there in 1886, and this number continued to rise to 250 in 1899. The industry employed about 2,700 manufacturing jewelers in 1875 and about 8,750 in 1899.[19]

Newark, while smaller in scale, maintained a reputation for good gold jewelry, as opposed to filled or plated gold goods (Colour Plate 241). In his short history of *The Manufacture of Gold Jewelry* published in 1882, William R. Bagnall described the industry as it existed then at Enos Richardson & Co. in Newark. His description of the plant and the processes provided an excellent picture of the state of the art at that time. The company had been formed in 1849 at the corner of Columbia and Green Street (see Plate 202), and its brick factory had been enlarged to a building 70ft by 100ft. It comprised four storeys including the basement, which provided areas for storing coal and a separate engine and boiler house. Two rooms were used for retrieving sweepings and filings of gold produced during the process of making the jewelry. These were collected from the workrooms every day. The gold was ground to dust and then treated in an amalgamator, saving the company thousands of dollars (Plate 270).

14. Wodiska, pp. 255-8.
15. Hirsch, p. 47.
16. Proddow, p. 42.
17. Bury II, 610-11.
18. Vever, *Rapport.*
19. Alfred M. Weisberg, *Why Providence?* (Providence 1988).

Plate 271. Main room on the second floor of the Enos Richardson Company in Newark.

Plate 272. In a corner of the second floor the colouring of jewelry took place. The Roman finish, for example, was achieved by boiling the jewelry in an acid solution.

On the first floor, the offices and vaults were located near the finishing room (Plate 271). The work produced was carefully examined by skilled workers for flaws or omissions. Each day the necessary materials were picked up by the workmen and the manufactured goods were returned to the supply room on the first floor. Another room was given over to the process of colouring gold by treating it in an acid solution (Plate 272). An area was provided for melting gold, silver and copper, and alloying it to the proper proportions. The first floor also housed the tool room where machines, dies and tools were made. Finally, there was an area occupied by rolling machines used to flatten the metal and drop-presses used for forming the metal, and where soldering was done.

The upper floors were devoted to the other manufacturing processes (Plates 192 and 193) and the assembling of the various parts of the design. There was a boys' chain room and also a girls' chain room. The jewelry was then engraved, enamelled,

Colour Plate 245. Gold fob watch set into the enamelled flower from a wild rose bush, with diamond studded bezel around the dial and in the foliage of the stem. A similar lapel watch was exhibited by Tiffany & Co. at the Exposition Universelle of 1889 in Paris. Marked Tiffany & Co. / New York on back of pin near branch. 3¼in. x 1½in. Tiffany & Co. Permanent Collection.

filed, ground down, polished and marked. There were about fifty polishing lathes in constant use and some sixty engravers. The total number of employees was around four hundred.

By the end of the century, marks signifying the quality of the gold and the maker were frequently placed on the jewelry. There were no regulatory agencies such as the government or guild halls requiring this to be done in the United States, as was the case in some countries. Trade marks began to be registered through the United States Patent Office in 1870. Tiffany & Co. did not register their trade mark until 1893, although they had frequently marked their silver wares in the same way since 1868.[20] In the 1880s and '90s, trade marks appeared on a variety of goods. Joseph Muhr of Philadelphia had a trade mark for his alloy for jewelry. Artificial gems were the subject

20. #23,572, 5 Sept. 1893.

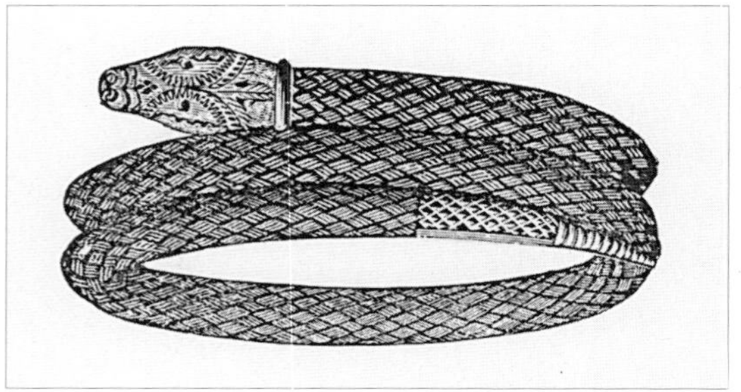

Plate 274. *'Roman Gold Color Woven Bracelets' were in great demand with customers of Marsh & Bigney of Attleboro in their 1883 catalogue.*

of the G.H. Cahoone & Co. trade mark.[21] Other trade marks were used on specific forms of jewelry such as rings, bracelets, scarf pins and earrings.

In 1896, the first listing of American jewelry manufacturers' marks was published by *Jewelers' Circular* and included 1,800 marks. This guide has been reissued in intermittent editions to the present day.[22] In 1906, the United States National Stamping Law was passed, requiring jewelry manufacturers to mark their goods with the quality of the metal, i.e. 14K, 18K, 22K. It was not until 1961 that the maker's mark was required. In 1988, Dorothy T. Rainwater published the first comprehensive listing of trade marks and jewelers in *American Jewelry Manufacturers.*

Wholesale Jewelers

During the last quarter of the nineteenth century, the wholesaler assumed an important role in the jewelry trade. With greater quantities of jewelry on the market came the need for greater salesmanship, wider distribution, and better methods of advertising, all of which caused an increase in sales staff, stock, and overheads. The rise of jobbers and wholesale distributors not only increased the overall cost of each piece of jewelry sold, but it also widened the growing gap between customer and creator. In the old days, when the customer bought directly from the jeweler, the only costs were for materials and workmanship. Now these two items represented only a small fraction of the price charged. Mass-production and cheaper materials helped to offset the increased expense of middlemen.

Wholesale jewelers issued catalogues detailing the goods that they could supply to other jewelers, illustrating the designs and specifying the costs.[23] In 1883 Marsh & Bigney of Attleboro called themselves 'The Busiest House in America' and jobbers in diamonds, watches, jewelry, silverware, clocks, spectacles, tools and materials. The firm was able to supply almost all of a jeweler's requirements, no matter where he might be located.

The Marsh & Bigney catalogue for 1883 offered promptness, square dealing and low prices. They guaranteed the quality of the goods as described. In return, they urged customers to date their letters, sign their names and include the state as well as the town in their address. The goods were sent C.O.D. to any place in the country. If the customer was not located near a railroad line, he could receive his order through the nearest post or express office. Customers enclosed with each order enough money to guarantee the express charges. If they sent references, Marsh & Bigney would open accounts with responsible merchants for orders amounting to more than $25. Cheques drawn on Chicago or New York banks were most acceptable. Small orders had to be prepaid or else they were sent C.O.D.

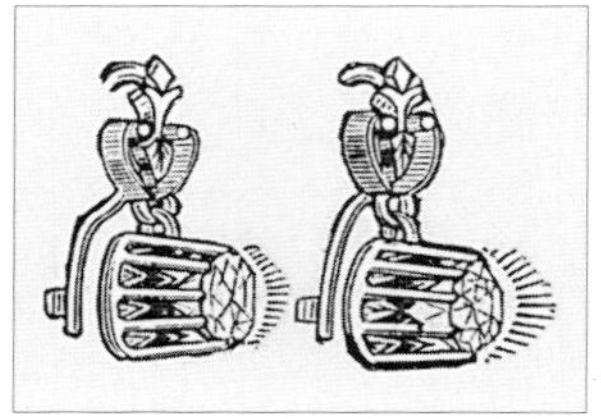

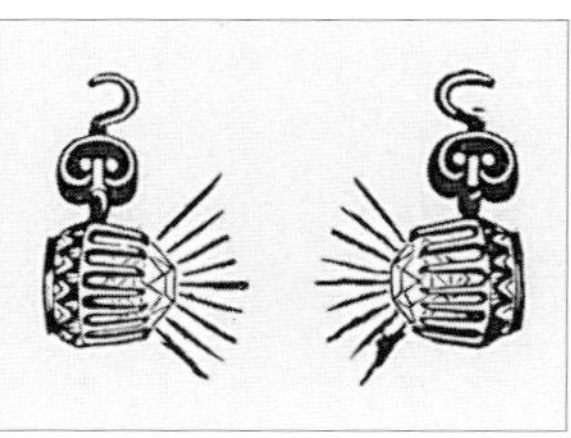

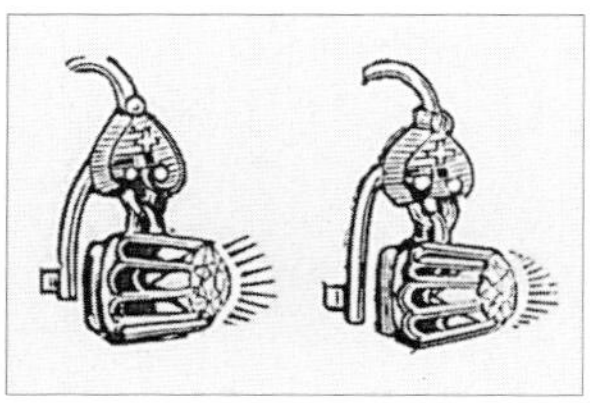

Plate 273. *In their catalogue for 1883, Marsh & Bigney of Attleboro offered diamond ear drops with 'Roman Gold Cover Balls', to make diamond earrings less conspicuous when travelling.*

Marsh & Bigney's catalogue contained 287 pages of illustrations of the goods they carried, seventy-seven of which were items of jewelry (Plates 273 to 275). An additional two pages inserted in the centre were printed with silver diamonds on a

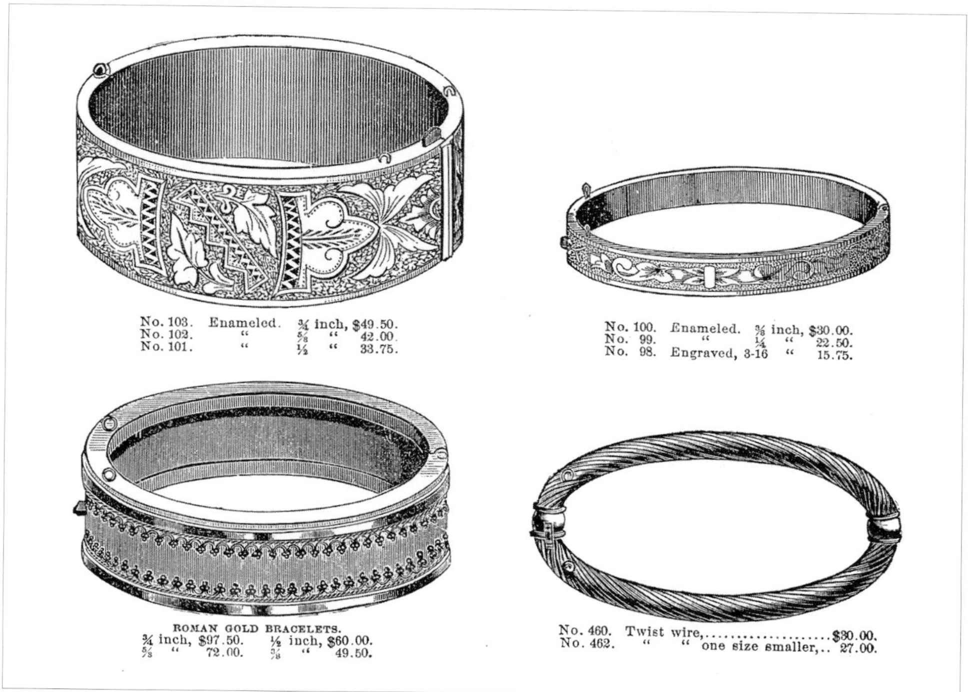

Plate 275. Solid gold bracelets were also available to Marsh & Bigney's catalogue customers in 1883, including the bracelet (lower left) patented by Charles Heim. (See Colour Plate 242).

light green background to enhance their latest designs in diamond jewelry. Prices ranged from $18 to $450 according to the size of the 'good quality of White Diamonds' they used and the weight of the 18K mountings.

Rings were ordered according to sizes measured by the recently patented Allen's Standard Gauge. Most of the rings were plain and polished, but some had hammered finishes or engraved bands. Marsh & Bigney prided themselves on selling solid gold rings, stating 'no Filled Heads sold by us'. However, they also offered jewelry, including rings, that was made of filled gold or rolled gold plate, or with gold fronts and backs. Silver rings and novelty jewelry were also available. Described as 'new and pretty' were rolled plate pins made of white metal and set with rhinestones. Some of the jewelry was set with real rubies, sapphires, amethysts, turquoises, coral, pearls, garnets, onyx and agates. Other examples were set with ruby, sapphire or emerald doublets or Alaska diamonds.

Less expensive items such as rolled plate charms, little lockets and crosses, or hard-solder gold rings, and some of the earrings, studs and stick pins were sold by the dozen. Bracelets were still being sold in pairs. Half sets, consisting of a brooch or bar pin and matching earrings, were available from Marsh & Bigney in all the current designs ranging from Roman gold revival styles to Japanese enamelled and engraved patterns. 'We have over fifty patterns of these fast selling pins in stock at all times', the catalogue advised, and 'The proper way is to order them assorted'.

For gentlemen, there were scarf pins, studs, sleeve and collar buttons, rings, charms, lockets, watches, chains and fobs. There was even one style of gold earring suitable for men. In addition to all the forms of jewelry for ladies, there were also half sets designed for young misses, and cuff pins for babies. Patented items such as ball-back ear knobs and lever-back buttons were available as well.

Decorative chains required thirty-five pages to illustrate the variety of forms and designs for both men and women. Some of the guard and matinée chains were produced by another Attleboro firm, William and Sumner Blackinton. Fire gilt vest

21. #15,658, 3 July 1888; #19,876, 14 July 1891.
22. The 1909 edition included the text of the Trade-mark Law of the United States, 20 February 1905, and its amendment of 4 May 1906; the National Stamping Law, 13 June 1907; the Stamping Law of Massachusetts, 28 May 1907; and the Gold Law for New York, 1 January 1906. Also included were two brief articles: 'Historical Sketch of Makers' Marks' by J.H. Buck and 'Marks of Gold and Silver Smiths' by F.W. Fairholt.
23. Lawrence B. Romaine, *A Guide to American Trade Catalogs 1744-1900.* Lists 66 jewelry catalogs, pp. 221-224, and their current availability in U.S. public institutions.

Colour Plate 246. Three cameo brooches from Tiffany & Co., late 19th century, with classical scenes cut in agate, set with diamond borders in yellow gold. The top scene is the Triumph of Aphrodite. The central brooch has a pastoral scene and is engraved Apr. 30, 1884. The cameo below is cut with revelling eroti. *Length 2⁷⁄₁₆in. (top brooch). Photograph by David Behl, New York. Private Collection.*

chains were manufactured locally by Oscar M. Draper.[24] Marsh & Bigney also carried imported red garnet jewelry in such a variety of designs that they were able to show only a few samples of the styles to give some idea of the cost and design. Special orders were encouraged for a few kinds of jewelry. They offered to make anything the customer might want in diamond jewelry. Lockets and rings could be engraved with initials or emblems for a small charge and on a week's notice.

While a number of jewelry directories were already being issued, these publications lumped manufacturers together with jobbers. It was now felt that a listing of jewelry jobbers alone would be welcome. In 1889, the first edition of *The Wholesale Jeweler* was published in Providence.[25] The goal was to provide retail jewelers with a list of wholesale dealers, including their addresses and what they had to offer. The list would also be of use to other jobbers and to manufacturers who sold to jobbers. Many advertisers announced that they sold only to jobbers. Included in the directory were jobbers, buyers and importers throughout the United States, from Maine to California and from Minnesota to Texas, as well as from Canada. There were also a

24. Both firms were established in the Attleboro area in the 1860s. Rainwater, *AJM,* pp. 45 and 79. Blackinton later moved to Providence.
25. The directory was organized by the publishers of *The Manufacturing Jeweler,* also located in Providence.

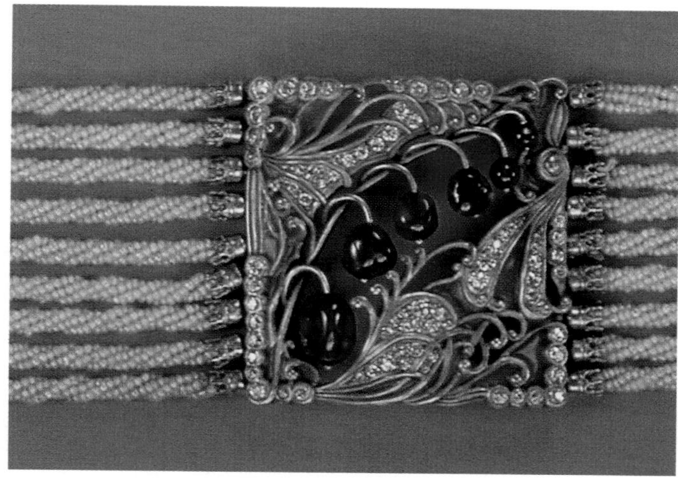

Colour Plate 247. In this art nouveau dog-collar necklace, Marcus & Co. made use of both genuine and synthetic rubies to achieve the precise proportion desired. Twisted ropes of pearls provided a greater degree of comfort than did the metal mounts. Diamonds highlight the central plaque and small plique-à-jour *panels accent the design. Courtesy of Christie, Manson & Woods. Photograph courtesy of Gemological Institute of America.*

large number of advertisements of the jewelry trade, identifying specialities and illustrating their products.

The advertisements shed light on the extent of the wholesale business. G.W. Cheever & Co. of North Attleboro illustrated their patented 'Lorimer Combined Bracelet & Glove Buttoner' which was available in gold, silver and plate. Fowler Bros. of New York specialized in 'English Crape Stone Jewelry' and quoted *Appleton's Cyclopedia* published in 1885: 'Crape Stone is an article used for Jewelry to be worn in Mourning'. Flint, Blood & Co. manufactured gold filled and rolled plate rings, 'Including fancy set rings with real and imitation stones, bands, half round, imitation diamond, and double rings in a great variety of styles'. They solicited the export trade. Odenheimer & Zimmern manufactured 'the celebrated O. & Z. interchangeable initial rings, lockets and buttons' in New York. Henry C. Haskell illustrated his 'Razzle Dazzle Puzzle Ring'. J.E. Draper & Co. of North Attleboro and Henry Read of Providence advertised as makers of sterling silver novelty jewelry.

Stanley Bros. of Attleboro Falls were the only makers of 'Standard' chains. 'Volunteer' cable chain was also their speciality among 1,500 different patterns of chain. B.A. Ballou & Co. of Providence supplied the trade with pin stems with seamless joints, catches and ear wires. R.L. Griffith & Son, also of Providence,

Colour Plate 248. Celtic buckle marked by Theodore B. Starr, early 20th century, richly wrought in yellow gold and set with diamonds, sapphires, emeralds and a large cabochon Mexican fire opal. Length 2¼in. Photograph by David Behl, New York. Private Collection.

26. Myers *Catalogue* 1894; Hinks, *Victorian Jewelry*, pp. 192-256.

featured their new line of brooches. They had over 700 different designs of scarf pins. They also hawked their wares at the Astor House in New York (Plate 276) at the start of every season and at the Palmer House in Chicago once a month. Charles F. Irons was also represented at the Astor House showings. His company specialized in emblem pins and charms.

Hancock, Becker & Co. boasted that it made 'the only complete line of Imitation Diamond Jewelry for the wholesale trade, in original designs, guaranteed as represented in quality'. E.E. Ripley, an importer of precious stones, advertised his gems in a few lines at the bottom of almost every spread. R.A. Kipling advertised the firm's Paris office and advised customers that 'Commission orders for Parisian fancy articles should be sent direct to the Paris Office'. Kipling also noted his manufactory in Oberstein, Germany, and recommended 'the new Proserpine stone, made for the mourning goods trade'.

Manufacturing jewelers Kallmeyer Bros. advertised as importers, jobbers and designers. Their factory was in Providence, but they had what they called western salesrooms in Detroit. They also would send 'Selection Packages' to creditable customers at no charge. In addition, they employed seven travelling salesmen.

H.F. Carpenter and George M. Baker, both of Providence, advertised as a gold and silver refiner, sweep smelter and assayer, providing prompt returns. Carpenter also produced his own 'Chemically Pure Gold' for colouring jewelry uniformly and his own oxidizing fluid for producing a permanent black oxidization on silver. Schneider & Betz in Buffalo, New York, served as gold and silver platers, enamellers and engravers to the trade. The Seery Manufacturing Co. of Providence was the only fire-gilt chain manufacturer and supplied jobbers with nothing else. They made 'only the nobbiest patterns and finest styles of work'.

Plate 276. Many jewelers who did not have offices in New York came to Astor House where they hired rooms and conducted business, as seen in this advertisement in The Wholesale Jeweler *for 1889 published in Providence, Rhode Island.*

Some of the advertisements were concerned with watches, both imported and domestic, and watch cases. In Pittsburgh, I. Ollendorff was the special agent for the Dueber Watch Case Co. and for the Aurora, Hampden and Paillard watch companies. Members of the National Association of Jobbers in American Watches were listed by location in the back of *The Wholesale Jeweler.* The Aurora Watch Co. and Blauer Watch Case Co., both in Illinois, advertised movements and watch cases respectively. Optical goods and pen and pencil cases were included among the notices. Silverware was advertised by both Towle and Whiting.

S.F. Myers & Co., manufacturing and wholesale jewelers in New York, had 'everything pertaining to the trade', according to his advertisement in *The Wholesale Jeweler* of 1889. In the triangular block between Maiden Lane and Liberty Street, Myers had four buildings consisting of twenty-three departments (Plates 277 and 278). There were entrances on both streets. Sales were conducted in the rooms on the ground floor. Offices were located on the second floor. The other three floors were occupied by the workshops. The company had trade mark specialities on four different American watches known by the names of The Globe, Century, Crown and Crescent. They carried clocks, silverware, optical goods, tools, diamonds and jewelry. In 1894, Myers offered the most complete line of goods for the 'home and export' trade through catalogues sent to potential customers.[26]

The jewelry illustrated in the Myers catalogue featured many of the

Plates 277 and 278. *The establishment of S.F. Myers & Co., wholesale jewelers in New York, boasted that theirs was the largest company of its kind in the United States in 1894. Courtesy of Diana Cramer and* Silver Magazine.

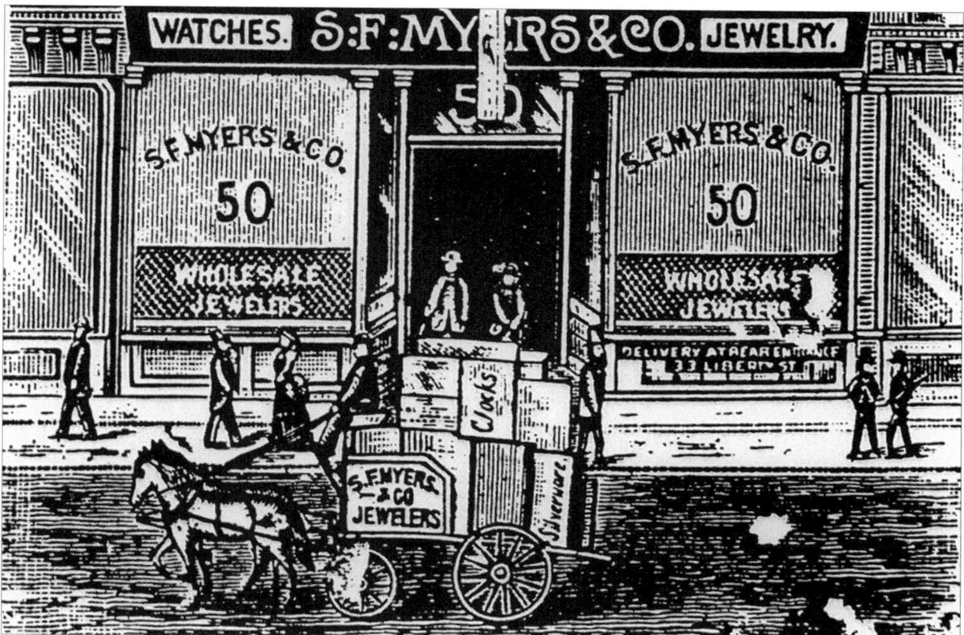

very same designs that had appeared in the Marsh & Bigney catalogue a decade earlier. When new designs appeared, they were decidedly lighter, more feminine and consisted largely of bowknots, scrolls, flowers and coils. Rings with marquise mountings, and mountings at right angles to the shank of the ring had appeared in the Marsh & Bigney catalogue too, as had crossover rings and bracelets. Myers' examples were less substantial and made of a minimum of metal. Among small brooches, Myers included several flower heads that were coloured with fancy enamelling and centred with a tiny diamond, no doubt as a result of Tiffany's exhibit

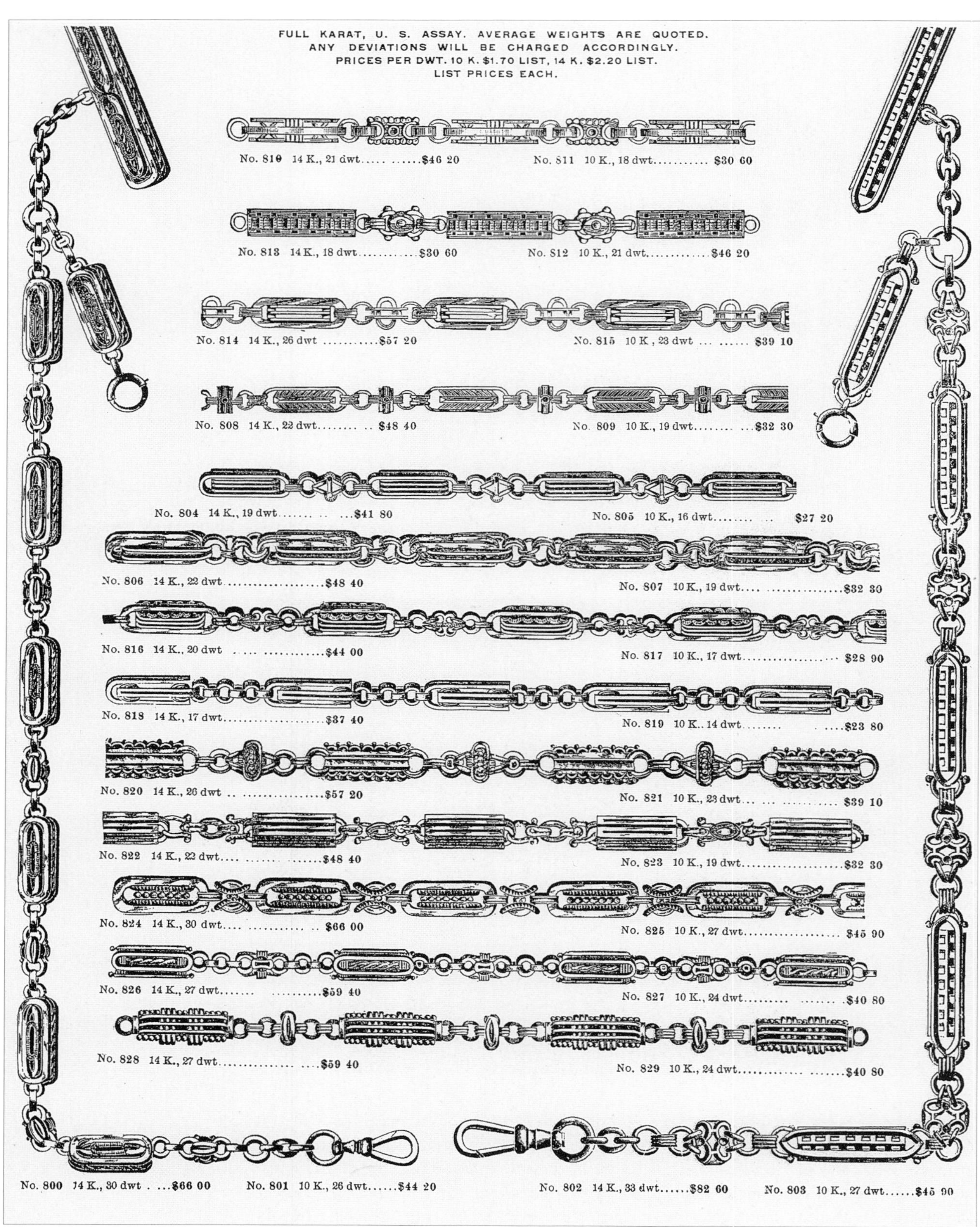

Plate 279. S.F. Myers sold an enormous quantity of gold chains in a variety of patterns as seen in their catalogue published in New York in 1894.

Plate 280. Moore & Evans of Chicago illustrated ladies' rolled gold pins in their catalogue of 1898. Many were set with pearls, spar balls, shells, or coral, and some were enamelled.

of enamelled flowers at the 1889 Paris Exposition. Filigree in silver was in greater abundance, especially for belts and buckles. The brooches were often accompanied by straight pins connected to the brooch by means of a safety chain. 'Jersey Pins' had come into fashion and consisted of two stick pins with matched or compatible ornamental heads and joined by a chain (see Plate 256). Hair pins and hat pins were added to the Myers line, as were chatelettes, a reduced form of the chatelaine, which had a decorative brooch with a short chain suspended from it to hold a small, decorative watch and fobs. Chains had become more delicate. Victoria vest chains had sprouted an extra branch of chain to hold more charms (Plate 279). Myers added the colonial style of hollow gold beads in solid 14 karat gold or in rolled gold plate, polished or Roman finish.

Moore & Evans of Chicago issued a catalogue in 1898 which revealed the further refinement of jewelry designs at the end of the nineteenth century.[27] Genuine diamond pins set in 14 karat gold mountings were included, along with rolled or gold filled pins set with brilliants (Plate 280). Enamelled jewelry included a greater variety

27. Ibid., pp. 265-328.

of colours. A new kind of Jersey pin appeared with a bangle suspended from the centre of the connecting chain. Earrings, which were becoming ever less conspicuous at the end of the century, now were often set with a solitaire or small cluster and had a screw or stud back for fastening. Lockets also were much reduced in size. A greater variety of men's vest chains were offered including the Dickens, Pony, Bicycle and Marlborough styles. Added to the usual selection of American watches, this mid-western firm offered a choice of pocket knives and revolvers.

By the end of the nineteenth century, wholesale jewelry catalogues were produced by specialized manufacturers as well as general line suppliers. Herpers Bros. of Newark featured mass-produced settings (crown, spread base, oval, circlet, flush and pearl), galleries, safety catches, pins, fasteners, and ring blanks.[28] H. Muhr's Sons of New York, Philadelphia and Chicago specialized in making rings and promoted the 'Violane du Cap The Wonderful Transformation Gem Stone A Delicate Violet Color Ruby by Night'.[29] John Robbins Manufacturing Co. of Boston issued a catalogue devoted to the badges and medals they produced.

Outstanding Jewelry Firms of the Late Nineteenth Century

Among the thousands of American jewelry firms prospering during the last quarter of the nineteenth century, there were some that attained great renown both in that country and abroad. International exhibitions played an important role in bringing celebrity to individual firms as well as in the promotion of jewelry as an art form. The effect of the Philadelphia Centennial Exhibition in 1876 has already been illustrated (see pages 302-306). The Paris Exposition Universelle of 1889 further stimulated the production of splendid pieces of jewelry as well as special exhibits. The award winning display of native American minerals and precious stones, some in their natural form and some cut, was assembled by George F. Kunz for Tiffany & Co. The society editor of the New York *Sun* predicted that 'The Paris Exposition will, of course, be the great attraction this summer, and hundreds [of Americans] will run over for a few weeks just to see the wonders that it has to show'.[30]

Not only did the Exposition provide an opportunity for potential customers to see what was being produced in other countries, it allowed American jewelers to see what the foreign competition was doing. Theodore Child reported in the New York *Sun* that of all the French jewelry exhibited the best was made by Boucheron, Bapst and Falize. Child noted the perfection of their craftsmanship, but he observed that their designs lacked inspiration and inventiveness. On the other hand, he believed that Tiffany's display was a testament 'to the taste and inventiveness of the manufacturers and to the wealth and luxury of the people by whose patronage they lived.[31] 'In execution and dainty finish, Tiffany is equal to the French, and in certain details he surpasses them', Child concluded. Certainly the exquisitely enamelled exotic orchid jewels contributed heavily to his glowing review (see Colour Plate 226). French jewelers acknowledged that 'they owed a debt to their Transatlantic brethren' for certain aspects of their craft that were worthy of study in these remarkable orchids.[32]

Paulding Farnham (1859-1927), who had joined Tiffany's about 1885, was in large part responsible for the firm's outstanding success at the Exposition and for the gold medal won by the jewelry made under his direction (Colour Plate 245). Not only were native gem stones featured, but some of the designs were based on native

28. The MMA in New York has a very good collection of jewelry catalogues and advertisements of the late 19th and early 20th century in its research library.
29. Rainwater, *AJM*, pp. 121 and 176.
30. 17 March 1889.
31. 7 July 1889.
32. Proddow, p. 42, citing *JC*, 19 Jan. 1927, p. 47.

American sources. A stunning necklace, for instance, took its inspiration from the American hazelnut leaves and blossoms (see Colour Plate 172).[33]

The Chicago World's Exposition, celebrating Columbus' discovery of America, took place in 1893. In addition to American gems and designs, Farnham explored variations on the centuries old designs of European, Turkish, Egyptian and Japanese jewelry. French jeweler and historian Henri Vever reviewed Tiffany's exhibit favourably overall, paying the ultimate Gallic compliment by saying that the work must have been executed by craftsmen 'of Parisian blood', although this was not the case.[34] He also felt that many of the pieces were based on French prototypes, and this is borne out by illustrations published in his history of French jewelry. To cite a single example, the diamond lace epaulette designed by Farnham for this exhibit took its inspiration from the work of O. Massin.[35] However, some designs were inspired by foreign cultures of such variety it seems that Farnham was trying to gain the experience of centuries by reinterpreting the outstanding designs of a whole world of cultures.

What Tiffany did was an inspiration to other American jewelers. An article in *The Jewelers' Circular* in 1877 explained that even though Tiffany & Co. 'as manufacturing jewelers [had] no direct business relation with the readers of this Journal, yet their large and choice production for twenty-five years past belongs to the trade no less, of course, than if it had been distributed through a hundred retail stores instead of one'.[36] The influence that Tiffany's had on the progress of the trade was immense. 'For in any line of luxury', the *Circular* pointed out, 'the higher development in the few precedes and draws after it the popular movement'. Progress in the jewelry trade was measured by the *Circular* in terms of 'growth of expenditure, taste and exclusiveness'. Without Tiffany's leadership, the trade would have been more imitative and provincial. Instead it had been educated and elevated to a high standard of excellence.

While it is impossible to discuss all the outstanding firms during this final period of our study, it seems appropriate to mention the jewelers that Henri Vever noticed at that time. Vever expressed regret that other American jewelers beside Tiffany's had not exhibited their jewelry at the Chicago Fair so that they too could be honoured. While in the United States for the Fair, he took the time to visit the establishments of Theodore Starr, Jaques & Marcus, Howard, Reiman, all of New York, as well as Spaulding in Chicago, Mermod & Jaccard in St. Louis, and Shreve in San Francisco. In these firms he saw interesting and 'even very remarkable' jewelry.[37]

Among the outstanding jewelers Vever found in New York, Herman Marcus was one of the most noteworthy. It was Marcus who may well have inspired Charles L. Tiffany to feature fine jewelry. Born in Germany on 25 December 1828, Marcus worked for Ellemeyer, the Court jeweler in Dresden. In 1850 he came to New York where he worked for Tiffany for a few years, and then for Tiffany's rival Ball, Black & Co. It is likely that he was the designer of some of the Oviedo wedding jewelry in 1859 (see Plates 134 to 137). Marcus joined, as a junior partner, with Theodore B. Starr in the firm of Starr & Marcus on John Street in October 1864. Their exhibition at the Philadelphia Centennial received favourable notice. In 1877 Tiffany persuaded Marcus to return to his company as a co-partner and in 1878 Marcus represented Tiffany's at the Paris Exposition. The New York *Times* noted that 'Mr. Marcus has exercised a strong and healthy influence on his trade during his long connection with it, and he has done much in the development of public taste. The display of jewels

33. Zapata, *Antiques*, March 1991, pp. 558-60.
34. Quoted by Zapata, ibid., p. 563.
35. Vever, *III*, 473-5.
36. *Silver*, May-June 1990, p. 12.
37. Vever, *Rapport*, p. 73.

which he prepared for the Philadelphia Exhibition is well remembered'.[38]

Herman Marcus' son William E. Marcus established a jewelry firm in partnership with George B. Jaques. In 1882 they published an artful little book entitled *Something About Neglected Gems* which encouraged readers to make greater use of gems other than diamonds, rubies, sapphires and emeralds (see Colour Plate 182).[39] At some point, Herman Marcus left Tiffany and joined his son's firm. Jaques was bought out in 1892 and the firm became Marcus & Co. (Colour Plate 247), joined also by George Elder Marcus, another son of Herman.[40]

At the time of his death in 1899, Herman Marcus was revered as one of the best men ever to work at the jeweler's trade in New York. His knowledge of both the business and the art were unsurpassed. He was especially interested in mythology and no one knew more about cameos than he did.[41]

Theodore B. Starr (1837-1907), with whom Marcus had been in business from 1864 to 1877, had come from New Rochelle, New York, to the city where he worked first for Read & Taylor, importers of jewelry and watches at 12 Maiden Lane, and then for Peckham, Merrill, Fitch & Co. at 19 John Street. During Starr's partnership with Marcus, the firm was located at 22 John Street. In 1876 Starr & Marcus exhibited cameos at the Philadelphia Exhibition that 'were among the most exquisite in the world, and were selected with skill and taste'.[42] Some were enhanced by enamelled settings. Necklaces made of diamonds and pink pearls and brooches made of coral also attracted attention.[43]

While other jewelers moved uptown, Starr continued downtown. In 1882 his jewelry store extended from 206 Fifth Avenue through to 1126 Broadway. His show window became newsworthy when an attempted robbery was foiled because of the three separate panes of glass spaced three inches apart one in front of the other.[44] During the 1895 recession, Starr advertised modest items such as 'Gold & Jeweled Veil Pins, Hat Pins, Hair Pins, Combs, Gold Belt Buckles'.[45] However, the firm continued making fine jewelry into the first two decades of the twentieth century (Colour Plate 248).

Less well known today of the jewelers Vever visited, Howard & Co. was established in 1866 in New York and was considered a competitor of Tiffany's. The firm was located at 264 Fifth Avenue in 1886. A cast brooch bearing their mark was made in 18 karat gold of four colours with floral festoons very much in the French style (Plate 281). Howard & Co. advertised in 1898, only seventeen shopping days before Christmas, recommending diamonds, emeralds, rubies, sapphires and pearls for the public's inspection.[46] They had a branch in Paris at 37 Avenue de l'Opéra at the turn of the century.

The Reiman, mentioned by Vever, was probably William Rieman who was listed among jewelers in the 1886 New York City Directory at 7 Astor House and in 1897 at 1255 Broadway. A pearl and diamond dog collar by Rieman was illustrated by Wodiska in his *Book of Precious Stones* published in 1909.

In Chicago, Vever mentioned Spaulding & Co. This firm was begun in 1852 by Samuel H. Hoard and was purchased by Henry A. Spaulding in 1889.[47] Previously Spaulding had managed the Paris branch of Tiffany & Co.[48] In the 1890s the firm was located on State Street where they produced both jewelry and watches.

At the Chicago World's Fair in 1893, Mermod and Jaccard of St. Louis installed a very grand pavilion on the edge of the main avenue of the Palace of Manufacturers

38. 16 Sept. 1877.
39. They were located at 41 Union Square, at the corner of 17th Street in 1882. In 1891 they were listed in *Phillips' Business Directory of New York City* at 857 Broadway at East 17th Street. See Proddow, p. 20.
40. The firm continued at 857 Broadway and 17th, according to the *Trow Business Directory of New York City*, 1897.
41. His obituary appeared in *JC* on 25 Oct. 1899.
42. McCabe, p. 368.
43. Proddow, p. 21.
44. NY *Sun*, 29 Sept. 1882.
45. NY *Times*, 6 Dec. 1895.
46. Ibid., 6 Dec. 1898.
47. In between, the firm was known as Hoard & Avery, Hoard & Hoes, James H. Hoes & Co., Matson & Hoes, and N. Matson & Co. S. Darling, p. 10.
48. S. Darling, p. 23 and Rainwater, *AJM*, p. 224.

Plate 281. Four-colour gold brooch, cast and chased with a grotesque mask above festoons of flowers and bowknots in the French style, c.1880. Marked on back HOWARD & C^{O}. 18 K. for Howard & Company, a New York firm in business from 1866-1922. Length about 2in. Hull Grundy Gift. The British Museum.

which caught the eye of Henri Vever. The display of beautiful jewelry, Vever thought, was very carefully made. There were diadems, necklaces, brooches and a large assortment of rings. Most noteworthy was a strand of spherical opals, strung like pearls, with a diamond rondelle between each pearl.[49] Vever visited their manufactory which employed between thirty and thirty-five workers, several of whom were French.

The most interesting firm of all, from M. Vever's point of view, was that of Shreve & Co. in San Francisco. It was possible here for a piece of jewelry to pass through all the phases of manufacturing, from rough mineral, transformed into bullion, and then into a jewel. Vever thought that French apprentices could learn a great deal in this situation. Because of the great abundance of precious metals in California, Shreve & Co. was able to use native rough gold and silver which they processed themselves. When the firm was founded in 1852, communication with the rest of the country was difficult. It was therefore necessary for Shreve & Co. to organize its workshops so that they were capable of being self-sufficient. As a result, by 1893 when Vever wrote his Report, the firm did their own lapidary work, die cutting, engraving, stamping, enamelling, gilding, horology and box making. They employed forty jewelers and twenty engravers, who were paid between $3 and $7 a day. Repoussé workers earned $3.50 to $6. Gemsetters were paid about $200 a month. A day's work was nine hours long with half an hour for lunch, monitored by a time clock.[50]

The nineteenth century ended with another Exposition in Paris in 1900. Tiffany & Co. won seventeen medals including a grand prize for jewelry. 'It is, indeed, a triumph for the nation at large, and for the Tiffany artists in particular', extolled Harriet Edwards in *The Home Journal*.[51] The success, she believed, came from the collaboration of outstanding designers and artisans. Paulding Farnham, artistic director

49. *Rapport*, p. 72-73.
50. Vever, *Rapport*, pp. 73-74.
51. 55, #29 (20 Sept. 1900): 6-7.

of the firm, and George F. Kunz, gemmologist, both received two gold medals, and artisans and foremen in the manufacturing departments garnered silver medals. 'Does not that designation of co-laborers tell the tale of the success both commercial and artistic of American art?' asked Harriet Edwards, 'Here each one himself impresses his individuality upon his works, and to his is given the credit, no matter how insignificant the task'.

Tiffany & Co. encouraged artistic ability probably more than any other establishment in the country. Apprentices were encouraged to develop their talents and make use of the company's own art library and collection of art objects. Farnham himself had been trained in the 'Tiffany School' under Edward C. Moore whose position as Secretary of the board of Tiffany & Co. Farnham assumed upon Moore's death in 1891.[52] A measure of Farnham's success was the iris brooch made of Montana sapphires (see Colour Plate 180) which was not only a piece of jewelry, but also a work of art, a collector's item and a grand collaboration. As *The Art Exchange* pointed out, 'At once it proclaims the artist taking pleasure in his work and lovingly fashioning his own fancies through sheer delight in his craftsmanship...There is no thought of the machine and of articles being turned out by the dozen, whether we regard the brooch or a vase'.[53]

Charles L. Tiffany's son Louis Comfort (1848-1933) was also a collaborator in the Paris Exposition exhibit of 1900. After studying abroad in the 1860s and '70s, Louis began experimenting with glass. In 1888 he developed his distinctive Favrile glass. For the Exposition, working with Farnham, he created a scent bottle of Favrile that mimicked and accentuated the fiery Mexican opals set in its enamelled stopper. The design as well as the technique was original and stunning. Harriet Edwards concluded 'This exhibit emphasizes once more the rapid growth of American art within the last twenty-five years, and it is gratifying that American artists receiving American education and training are now acknowledged to be the peers of that nation [France] which for so long has been considered to be without an equal in matters pertaining to art'.

For three centuries, Americans had been making, importing, buying and enjoying jewelry. Some Americans had too much jewelry, many had too little. Some sought to impress, while others sought jewelry that embodied sentiments and ceremonies reflecting their innermost thoughts. Jewelers and their patrons came from many different countries. The jewelry they made and wore provided endless variety and amazingly rich sources of information about the American people.

The quest for originality of design and flawless workmanship compelled all but the most crass commercial manufacturer to continue along the path of their predecessors. Americans historically have prided themselves on their ingenuity and the quality of their work. They have also wanted their jewelry to mean something to them, whether it was made of precious materials or not. By the end of the nineteenth century, jewelers found inspiration in the artistic movement and the creative designs that would propel them and their patrons into the limitless possibilities of the twentieth century.

52. Zapata, *Antiques,* 3/91, p. 558.
53. May 1900, *44,* No. 5, p. 112.

Bibliography

ORIGINAL SOURCES

Barrell, Joseph (1739-1804), Letter Book, Barrell Collection, Massachusetts Historical Society, Boston, Mass.

Brigden, Zachariah (1734-1787), Account Book, Beinecke Library, Yale University, New Haven, Conn.

Clapp, Henry W., and Palmer, James, Design / Account Book, New York, 1829-1833. William Lanford.

Curwen Family Manuscripts, Peabody Essex Museum Library, Salem, Mass.

Dyckman, States, Papers, Boscobel, Garrison-on-Hudson, New York.

Faneuil, Peter, Letter Book, New England Historic Genealogical Society, Boston, Mass.

Fenno, William, Account Book, 1824-1827, Worcester, Mass., American Antiquarian Society.

Gardner, Mr. and Mrs. John L., Jr., Papers, Archives of American Art, Boston, Mass.

Lang, Edward (1742-1830), Account Book, Peabody Essex Museum Library, Salem, Mass.

Lyon, Maud, 'A Brief Introduction to Carnival in New Orleans', November, 1984, Louisiana State Museum.

Monfredo, Rachel Jean, 'American Finger Rings / Representing Bonds of Relationships', M.A. Thesis, Early American Culture, University of Delaware, 1990.

Mott, James S., Account book, 1833-1844, New-York Historical Society Library.

Oakes, Edward E. (1891-1960), Papers, Archives of American Art, Boston, Mass.

Preble, Edward, Memorandum Book, 1802-1805, Maine Historical Society, Portland, Me.

Revere, Paul (1735-1818), Account Books, Massachusetts Historical Society Library.

Richardson, Francis (1681-1729), Account Book; Richardson, Joseph (1711-1784), Account of Philip Hulbeart Estate, Downs Manuscript and Microfilm Collection, Winterthur Museum Library, Winterthur, Del.

Richardson, Joseph (1711-1784), Account Books, Historical Society of Pennsylvania Library, Philadelphia, Pa.

Richardson, Joseph, Jr. (1752-1831), Account Book, 1796-1801, Historical Society of Pennsylvania Library, Philadelphia, Pa.

Richmond Island Trove, Maine Historical Society, Portland, Me.

Rogers, Daniel (1735-1816), Account Book, Peabody Essex Museum Library, Salem, Mass.

Salem and Essex County Miscellaneous Manuscripts, Peabody Essex Museum Library, Salem, Mass.

Salisbury Family Papers, American Antiquarian Society, Worcester, Mass.

Society of the Cincinnati, Papers, Washington, D.C.

Tiffany & Co., Archives, scrapbooks of clippings and original designs, Parsippany, N.J.

Washington, George (1732-1799), Invoices & Letters, 1755-1766, and Ledgers, A, B, C (1750-1799), Library of Congress, Washington, D.C.

Washington, George, Household Account Book, 1793-1797, Historical Society of Pennsylvania Library, Philadelphia, Pa.

Waters, Deborah Dependahl, 'The Workmanship of an American Artist: Philadelphia's Precious Metals Trades and Craftsmen, 1788-1832', University of Delaware, Ph.D. thesis, 1981.

Probate Records

Essex County, Massachusetts, Probate Court Records, Salem, Mass.
Suffolk County, Massachusetts, Probate Court Records, Boston, Mass.
Virginia, Accomack, Wills, 1692-1715, Research Library Files, Museum of Early Southern Decorative Arts, Winston-Salem, North Carolina.

BOOKS

Abbott, Henry G., *Antique Watches and How to Establish Their Age,* Chicago, 1897.
A Sketch of Attleboro, pamphlet in Genealogy File, Attleboro Public Library, Mass.
Bacot, H. Parrott; Mackie, Carey T. and Charles L., *Crescent City Silver,* New Orleans, La., 1980.
Bagnall, William R., *The Manufacture of Gold Jewelry,* New York, 1882.
Barr, Elaine, *George Wickes,* New York, 1980.
Barret, Richard Carter, *Bennington Pottery and Porcelain,* New York, 1958.
Becker, Vivienne, *Antique and 20th Century Jewellery,* New York, 1982.
Becker, Vivienne, *Art Nouveau Jewelry,* New York, 1985.
Becker, Vivienne, *Fabulous Fakes The History of Fantasy and Fashion Jewellery,* London, 1988.
Beckman, Elizabeth D., *Cincinnati Silversmiths, Jewelers, Watch and Clockmakers,* Cincinnati, Ohio, 1975.
Beecher, Charles, *Harriet Beecher Stowe in Europe,* Hartford, Conn., 1896.
Belden, Bauman L., *Indian Peace Medals Issued in the United States 1789-1889,* New Milford, Conn., 1966.
Belden, Louise Conway, *Marks of American Silversmiths in the Ineson-Bissell Collection,* Charlottesville, Va., 1980.
The Diary of William Bentley, D.D., 4 vols., Salem, Mass., 1905-1914.
Bilodeau, Francis W., *Art in South Carolina 1670-1970,* Charleston, S.C., 1970.
Bishop, J. Leander, *A History of American Manufactures from 1608-1860,* Philadelphia, 1868.
Black, J. Anderson, *A History of Jewelry,* New York, 1974.
Boultinghouse, Marquis, *Silversmiths, Jewelers, Clock and Watch Makers of Kentucky 1785-1900,* Privately printed, 1980.
Bowen, Abel, *Bowen's Picture of Boston,* 3rd ed., Boston, 1838.
Britten's Old Clocks and Watches and their Makers, New York, 1956; Antique Collectors' Club edition, Woodbridge, England, 1977.
Brown, H.C. ed., *Valentine's Manual of Old New York,* No. 11, New York, 1926.
Brix, Maurice, *List of Philadelphia Silversmiths and Allied Artificers from 1682 to 1850,* Philadelphia, 1920.
Buffum, William Arnold, *The Tears of the Heliades* (Sicilian amber), London, 1896.
Buhler, Kathryn C., *Mount Vernon Silver,* Mount Vernon, Va., 1957.
Buhler, Kathryn C., *American Silver 1655-1825 in the Museum of Fine Arts Boston,* 2 vols., Boston, 1972.
Buhler, Kathryn C. and Hood, Graham, *American Silver Garvan and other Collections in the Yale University Art Gallery,* New Haven and London, 1970.
Burton, E. Milby, *South Carolina Silversmiths 1690-1860,* Charleston, S.C., 1941; revised and edited by Warren Ripley, 1991.
Bruton, Eric, *Diamonds,* Radnor, Pa., 1978.
Bury, Shirley, *Jewellery,* 2 vols., Woodbridge, England, 1991.
Bury, Shirley, *Jewellery Gallery Summary Catalogue,* London, 1982.

Bury, Shirley, *An Introduction to Rings,* London, 1984.
Bury, Shirley, *An Introduction to Sentimental Jewellery,* London, 1985.
Butterfield, Lyman H., ed., *The Book of Abigail and John* [Adams], Boston, 1975.
Carlisle, Lilian Baker, *Vermont Clock and Watchmakers Silversmiths and Jewelers 1778-1878,* Burlington, Vt., 1970.
Carpenter, Charles H., Jr., *Gorham Silver 1831-1981,* New York, 1982.
Carpenter, Charles H., Jr., and Mary Grace, *Tiffany Silver,* New York, 1978.
Carrick, Alice van Leer, *Shades of Our Ancesters,* Boston, 1928.
Carter, Alison J., *The Hull Grundy Gift to Cheltenham Art Gallery and Museums,* Part I and II, Cheltenham, 1986.
Catelle, W.R., *Precious Stones,* Philadelphia and London, 1903.
Chapman, George, and Marston, John, *Eastward Ho,* 1605.
Chickering, Elenita C., *Arthur J. Stone 1847-1938,* Boston, 1994.
Clarke, Hermann Frederick, *John Coney, Silversmith (1655-1722),* Boston and New York, 1932.
Clifford, Anne, *Cut-Steel and Berlin Iron Jewellery,* Bath, 1971.
Clutton, Cecil, and Daniels, George, *Watches,* New York, 1965.
Cook, Clarence, *A Girl's Life Eighty Years Ago* [Eliza Southgate Bowne], New York, 1888.
Crossman, Carl L., *The China Trade,* Princeton, N.J., 1972. Antique Collectors' Club edition, Woodbridge, England, 1991.
Culme, John, *The Directory of Gold and Silversmiths, Jewellers and Allied Traders 1838-1914,* 2 vols., Woodbridge,1987.
Curtis, George Munson, *Early Silver of Connecticut and Its Makers,* Meriden, Conn., 1913.
Cutten, George B., *The Silversmiths of Georgia, together with Watchmakers & Jewelers,* Savannah, Ga., 1958.
Cutten, George B., *Silversmiths, Watchmakers and Jewelers of the States of New York outside New York City,* Hamilton, N.Y., 1939.
Cutten, George B., *The Silversmiths of Virginia,* Richmond, Va., 1952.
Cutten, George B., *The Silversmiths of North Carolina,* Raleigh, N.C., 1948.
Curwen, George Rea, *Funeral Customs,* Salem, Mass., 1893.
D'Allemagne, H.R., *Les Accessoires du Costume et du Mobilier,* 2 vols., Paris, 1928.
Daggett, John, *A Sketch of the History of Attleborough,* Boston, 1894.
Darling, Sharon S., *Chicago Metalsmiths,* Chicago, 1977.
Darling Foundation, *New York State Silversmiths,* New York, 1964.
Dieulafait, Louis, translated by Fanchon Sanford, *Diamonds and Precious Stones,* New York, 1874.
Dow, George Francis, *Every Day Life in the Massachusetts Bay Colony,* Boston, 1935.
Doyle, Bernard W., *Comb-Making in America,* Boston, 1925.
Dresser, Christopher, *The Art of Decorative Design,* London, 1862, reprint New York, 1977.
Dunlap, William, *A History of the Rise and Progress of the Arts of Design in the United States,* 2 vols., bound as 3, New York, 1969, reprint of original edition of 1834.
Earle, Alice Morse, Two Centuries of Costume in America, 2 vols., New York, 1898.
Edwards, Charles, *The History and Poetry of Finger-Rings,* New York, 1855.
Edgarton, Miss S.C., *The Flower Vase; containing the Language of Flowers and Their Poetic Sentiments,* Lowell, Mass., 1844.
Ellsworth, Henry, *A Digest of Patents,* Washington, D.C., 1840.
Emanuel, Harry, *Diamonds and Precious Stones,* 2nd ed., London, 1867.

Evans, Joan, *A History of Jewellery 1100-1870,* Boston, 1970.
Evans, Joan, *English Jewellery from the Fifth Century A.D. to 1800,* London, 1921.
Evans, Joan, *English Posies and Posy Rings,* London, 1931.
Fales, Martha Gandy, *Early American Silver,* New York, 1973.
Fales, Martha Gandy, *Joseph Richardson & Family, Philadelphia Silversmiths,* Philadelphia, 1974.
Fales, Martha Gandy, *American Silver in the Henry Francis du Pont Winterthur Museum,* Winterthur, Del., 1958.
Fitzpatrick, John C., ed., *The Writings of Washington from the Original Manuscript Sources 1745-1799,* Washington, D.C., 1931-44.
Flower, Margaret, *Victorian Jewellery,* London, 1951.
Flynt, Henry N., and Fales, Martha Gandy, *The Heritage Foundation Collection of Silver and New England Silversmiths,* Old Deerfield, Mass., 1968.
Forbes, H.A. Crosby; Kernan, John D.; Wilkins, Ruth S., *Chinese Export Silver 1785 to 1885,* Milton, Mass., 1975.
Ford, W.C., ed., *Correspondence and Journals of Samuel Blatchley Webb,* 3 vols., New York, 1893.
Foster, Joshua James, *British Miniature Painters and their Works,* London, 1898.
Frank, Lawrence P., Jr., *Indian Silver of the Southwest 1868-1930,* West Chester, Pa., 1990.
Freedley, Edwin T., *Philadelphia & its Manufactures,* Philadelphia, 1858.
Funck-Brentano, Franz, translated by H. Sutherland Edwards, *The Diamond Necklace,* London, n.d.
Gee, George E., *The Silversmith's Handbook,* London, 1885.
Gere, Charlotte, *Victorian Jewellery Design,* London, 1972.
Gere, Charlotte, *European and American Jewellery,* London, 1975.
Gillingham, Harrold E., *Indian Ornaments Made by Philadelphia Silversmiths,* New York, 1936.
Goldsborough, Jennifer Faulds, *Silver in Maryland,* Baltimore, 1983.
Goodwin, Maud Wilder, *Dolley Madison,* New York, 1896.
Greeley, Horace, et al., *The Great Industries of the United States,* Hartford, Conn., 1872.
Grimwade, Arthur G., *London Goldsmiths 1697-1837,* London, 1976.
Groce, George C., and Wallace, David H., *The New-York Historical Society's Dictionary of Artists in America 1564-1860,* New Haven and London, 1957.
Hackett, Fred H., ed., *The Industries of San Francisco,* 1884.
Hamlin, Augustus Choate, *The Tourmaline,* Boston, 1873.
Hamlin, Augustus Choate, *Leisure Hours Among the Gems,* Boston, and New York, 1891.
Hamlin, Augustus Choate, *The History of Mount Mica of Maine,* Bangor, Me., 1895.
Hastings, William T., *The Insignia of Phi Beta Kappa,* Washington, D.C., 1964 and 1968.
Hayward, John, *The New England Gazetteer,* Boston, 1839.
Heal, Sir Ambrose, *The London Goldsmiths,* Cambridge, 1935.
Hinks, Peter, *19th Century Jewellery,* London, 1975.
Hinks, Peter, *Victorian Jewellery*, New York, 1991.
Hirsch, Susan E., *Roots of the American Working Class: The Industrialization of Crafts in Newark, 1800-1860,* Philadelphia, 1978.
Hoopes, Penrose R., *Shop Records of Daniel Burnap, Clockmaker,* Hartford, Conn., 1958.
Hoyle, Pamela, *The Boston Ambience,* Boston, 1981.
Hume, Ivor Noel, *Here Lies Virginia,* New York, 1963.
Ingram, J.S., *The Centennial Exposition,* Philadelphia, 1876.
James, C.L.R., *The Black Jacobins,* New York, 1963.

Jaques, George B., and Marcus, William E., *Something About Neglected Gems,* New York, 1882.

Jewelers' Circular-Keystone, *The Jeweler's Dictionary,* 2nd ed., New York, 1950.

Johnson, Dale T., *American Portrait Miniatures in the Manney Collection,* Metropolitan Museum of Art, New York, 1990.

Kaplan, Arthur Guy, *Official Identification and Price Guide to Antique Jewelry,* 6th ed., New York, 1990.

Kunz, George F., *Gems and Precious Stones,* New York, 1892.

Kunz, George F., *The Curious Lore of Precious Stones,* Philadelphia and London, 1913.

Kunz, George F., *Rings for the Finger,* Dover publication, New York, 1973, originally published 1917.

Kunz, George F., and Stevenson, Charles, *The Book of the Pearl,* New York, 1908.

Lavender, David, *California,* New York, 1976.

Lewis, M.D.S., *Antique Paste Jewellery,* Boston, 1970.

Longacre, James B., and Herring, James, *The National Portrait Gallery of Distinguished Americans,* Philadelphia, 1868.

Loring, John, *Tiffany's 150 Years,* New York, 1987.

Lossing, Benson J., *The Home of Washington,* Hartford, Conn., 1870.

Lossing, Benson J., *The American centenary: a history of the progress of the republic of the United States,* Philadelphia, 1876.

McCabe, James D., *The Illustrated History of the Centennial Exhibition,* Philadelphia, 1876.

McClellan, Elizabeth, *Historic Dress in America,* Philadelphia, 1904.

McClinton, Katharine Morrison, *Collecting American 19th Century Silver,* New York, 1968.

Mack, John, ed., *Ethnic Jewelry,* New York, 1988.

Mackay, Donald C., *Silversmiths and Related Craftsmen of the Atlantic Provinces,* Halifax, N.S., 1973.

Mason, Anita, and Packer, Diane, *An Illustrated Dictionary of Jewelry,* New York and London, 1974.

Mason, Frances Norton, ed., *John Norton & Sons, Merchants of London and Virginia,* Richmond, Va., 1937.

Miller, Lillian B., 'The Puritan Portrait', *Seventeenth Century New England,* Boston, Mass., 1984.

Morell, Parker, *Diamond Jim* [Brady], London, 1935.

Morse, Edgar W., ed., *Silver in the Golden State,* Oakland, Cal., 1986.

Morse, Jedidiah, *The American Universal Geography,* Boston, 1819.

Muller, Helen, *Jet Jewellery and Ornaments,* Bletchley, England, 1980.

Munn, Geoffrey, *Castellani and Guiliano, Revivalist Jewellers of the Nineteenth Century,* London, 1984.

Murdoch, Tessa, comp., *Treasures and Trinkets* Jewellery in London from pre-Roman times to the 1930s, The Museum of London, 1991.

National Museum of Canada, *The Covenant Chain Indian Ceremonial and Trade Silver,* essay 'The Covenant Chain' by N. Jaye Fredrickson, Canada, 1930.

Néret, Gilles, *Boucheron Four Generations of a World-Renowned Jeweler,* New York, 1989.

Nevins, Allan, and Thomas, Milton Halsey, ed., *The Diary of George Templeton Strong,* 4 vols., New York, 1952.

Oliver, Andrew, *Portraits of John Quincy Adams and His Wife,* Cambridge, Mass., 1970.

Park, Lawrence, *Gilbert Stuart, an Illustrated Descriptive List of His Works,* ed. by William Sawitzky, New York, 1926.

Parsons, Charles S., *New Hampshire Silver,* Warner, N.H., 1983.
Peterson, Harold L., *The American Sword 1775-1945,* Philadelphia, 1965.
Phillips, John Marshall, *American Silver,* New York, 1949.
Pickford, Ian, ed., *Jackson's Silver and Gold Marks,* Woodbridge, England, 1989.
Pleasants, J. Hall, and Sill, Howard, *Maryland Silver 1715-1830,* Baltimore, Md., 1930.
Poesch, Jessie, *The Art of the Old South,* New York, 1989.
Proddow, Penny, and Healy, Debra, *American Jewelry, Glamour and Tradition,* New York, 1987.
Prown, Jules David, *John Singleton Copley,* 2 vols., Cambridge, Mass., 1966.
Purtell, Joseph, *The Tiffany Touch,* New York, 1971.
Rainwater, Dorothy T., *American Jewelry Manufacturers,* West Chester, Pa., 1988.
Rainwater, Dorothy T., *Encyclopedia of American Silver Manufacturers,* New York, 1975; third revised ed., West Chester, Pa., 1986.
Ravenel, Harriott H., *Eliza Pinckney,* New York, 1896.
Rifkin, Blume J., *Silhouettes in America 1790-1840,* Burlington, Vt., 1987.
Riis, Thale, and Boe, Alf, *Om Filigran,* Oslo, 1959.
Rolt, *A New Dictionary of Trade & Commerce,* London, 1761.
Rothschild, M.D., *A Hand-Book of Precious Stones,* New York and London, 1901.
Sargent, William Mitchell, comp. and ed., *Maine Wills 1640-1760,* Portland, Me., 1887.
Sataloff, *Art Nouveau Jewelry,* Bryn Mawr, Pa., 1984.
Schofield, Anne, and Fahy, Kevin, *Australian Jewellery,* Woodbridge, England, 1991.
Schwartz, Jeri, *Tussie Mussies: Victorian Posey Holders,* New York, 1987.
Scottish Rite Masonic Museum of our National Heritage, *Masonic Symbols in American Decorative Arts,* Lexington, Mass., 1976.
Sellers, Charles Coleman, *Portraits and Miniatures by Charles Willson Peale,* Philadelphia, 1952.
Sellers, Charles Coleman, *Charles Willson Peale,* New York, 1969.
Sheffield, John Lord, *Observations on the Commerce of the American States,* London,1784.
Shreve, Crump & Low, *Selling Quality Jewels Since 1800: A History of Shreve, Crump & Low Co,* Boston, 1974.
Shugart, Cooksey, and Gilbert, Richard E., *Complete Price Guide to Watches,* Cleveland, Tenn., 1994, 14th ed.
Sinkankas, John, *Gemstones of North America,* New York, 1959 (vol. I), 1976 (vol. 2).
Smith, Captain John, *The Travels, Adventures and Observations of Capt. John Smith,* Richmond, Va., 1819.
Smith, Marcell N., *Diamonds, Pearls & Precious Stones,* Boston, 1913.
Snowman, A. Kenneth, *The Master Jewelers,* New York, 1990.
Souvenir of the Centennial Exhibition: Connecticut's Representation at Philadelphia, 1876, Hartford, Conn., 1877.
Speight, A., *The Lock of Hair,* London, 1871. Reprinted by Jesse Haney & Co. as *Hair Ornaments for Souvenirs and Jewelry,* New York, c.1871/2.
Steele, J. Parish, *The American Watchmaker & Jeweler,* New York, 1868, supplement, 1873.
Stevens, Jane Perham, *Gems and Minerals,* Freeport, Maine, 1983.
Stevens, Jane Perham, *Maine's Treasure Chest Gems and Minerals of Oxford County,* West Paris, Me., 1972.
Strickler, Susan E., assisted by Marianne E. Gibson, *American Portrait Miniatures The Worcester Art Museum Collection,* Worcester, Mass., 1989.
Stronge, Susan; Smith, Nima; and Harle, J.C., *A Golden Treasury, Jewellery from the Indian Subcontinent,* London, 1988.

Stuart, Isaac William, *Life of Jonathan Trumbull, sen.,* Boston, 1859.
Supplement to the Second Edition of Trade-Marks of the Jewelry and Kindred Trades, published by The Jewelers' Circular Publishing Co., N.Y., 1909.
Swan, Bradford F., 'Prints of the American Indians, 1670-1775', in *Publications of the Colonial Society of Massachusetts Boston Prints and Printmakers 1670-1775,* Boston, 1973.
Tait, Hugh, ed., *Jewelry 7000 Years,* New York, 1987.
Tait, Hugh, ed., *The Art of the Jeweller,* 2 vols., London, 1984.
Tharp, Louise Hall, *Mrs. Jack* [Gardner], Boston, 1965.
Tharp, Louise Hall, *Saint Gaudens and the Gilded Era,* Boston, 1969.
Thomas, M. Halsey, ed., *The Diary of Samuel Sewall 1674-1729,* 2 vols., New York, 1793.
Thompson, Francis M., *The History of Greenfield, Massachusetts,* Greenfield, Mass., 1904.
Tracy, Berry B., et al., *19th Century America, Furniture and other Decorative Arts,* New York, 1970.
United States Patent Office Records, 1790-1900.
United States Patent Office, Design Records, 1870-1900.
Untracht, Oppi, *Jewelry Concepts and Technology,* New York, 1982.
Vever, Henri, *La Bijouterie Française au XIXe Siècle,* 3 vols., Paris, 1906-1908; reproduced Firenze, n.d.
von Khrum, Paul, *Silversmiths of New York City 1684-1850,* New York, 1978.
Voynick, Stephen M., *The Great American Sapphire,* Missoula, Montana, 1985.
Walters Art Gallery, Jewelry Ancient and Modern, New York, 1979.
Ward, Anne; Cherry, John; Gere, Charlotte; and Cartlidge, Barbara, *Rings Through the Ages,* New York, 1981.
Warwick, Edward, and Pitz, Henry, *Early American Costume,* London and New York, 1929.
Weeden, William B., *Economic and Social History of New England,* 2 vols., Boston and New York, 1890-91.
Wehle, Harry B., *American Miniatures,* New York, 1937.
Wharton, Anne Hollingsworth, *Heirlooms in Miniatures,* Philadelphia and London, 1898.
The Wholesale Jeweler, Providence, R.I., 1889.
Wigley, Thomas B., *The Art of the Goldsmith and Jeweller,* London, 1898.
Williams, Carl M., *Silversmiths of New Jersey (1700-1825),* Philadelphia, 1949.
Willich, A.F.M., *The Domestic Encyclopedia,* 3 vols., Philadelphia, 1826.
Wills, Garry, *Cincinnatus* George Washington and the Enlightenment, New York, 1984.
Wilson, Forest, *Crusader in Crinoline* [Harriet Beecher Stowe], Philadelphia, London, New York, 1941.
Wilson, H., *Silverwork and Jewellery,* London, 1903; reprinted 1951.
Wilstach, Paul, *Mount Vernon,* New York, 1916.
Wodiska, Julius, *A Book of Precious Stones,* New York and London, 1909.
Woodward, Arthur, *Navajo Silver,* Flagstaff, Arizona, 1971.
Wroth, Lawrence C., *Abel Buell of Connecticut,* Middletown, Conn., 1958.
Zapata, Janet, *The Jewelry and Enamels of Louis Comfort Tiffany,* New York, 1993.

ARTICLES

Alpers, Edith, 'Edward Everett Oakes (1891-1960), a master craftsman from Boston, Massachusetts', *Jewellery Studies* 3, pp. 73-79.
Alpers, Edith, 'F.G. Hale: U.S. Pioneer in Arts & Crafts', *Heritage,* August 1989, pp. 192-195.

Berry, Michael, 'Drawn Upon Sattin and Ivory: Mourning Designs of Samuel Folwell 1793-1813', *Twenty-eighth Annual Washington Antiques Show (1983),* Washington, D.C., 1982, p. 74-75.

Biggs, Ann A.; Hummel, Charles F.; Lanier, Sterling E., 'Some Sidelights on Early Boston Silver and Silversmiths', *Winterthur Newsletter,* 24 October 1958.

Carroll, Diane Lee, 'European and American Jewelry of the Nineteenth Century', *The Museum,* New Series, Spring 1967, The Newark Museum, Newark, N.J.

Connecticut Historical Society *Bulletin, 25,* January 1960, pp. 24-31.

Crowningshield, Robert, 'American Freshwater Natural Pearls', *Gems & Gemology, XXV,* No. 1, Spring 1989, p. 37.

Dallett, Francis James, 'The Thibaults, Philadelphia Silversmiths', The Magazine *Antiques,* April 1969, pp. 547-49.

Deutsch, Davida T., 'Washington memorial prints', The Magazine *Antiques,* March 1989, pp. 742-753.

Dirham, Dona M.; Misiorowski, Elise B.; Thomas, Sally A., 'Pearl Fashion Through the Ages', *Gems & Gemology,* 21, No. 2 (Summer 1985), pp. 63-78.

Edwards, Harriet, 'The Goldsmith's Art at Paris', *Home Journal 55,* No. 29 (20 September 1900), pp. 6-7.

Evans, Paul, 'Gold Quartz: The Jewelry of San Francisco', *Spinning Wheel,* May 1977, pp. 8-10.

Fales, Martha Gandy, 'The Early American Way of Death', Essex Institute *Historical Collections,* April 1964, pp. 75-84.

Fales, Martha Gandy, 'The Case of the Double Identity' [Daniel Rogers], Essex Institute *Historical Collections,* January 1965, pp. 40-49.

Fales, Martha Gandy, 'Federal Bostonians and their London jeweler, Stephen Twycross', The Magazine *Antiques,* March 1987, pp. 642-49.

Fales, Martha Gandy, 'The jewelry [at Mount Vernon]', The Magazine *Antiques,* February 1989, pp. 512-17.

Fales, Martha Gandy, 'Jewelry in Charleston', The Magazine *Antiques,* December 1990, pp. 1217-27.

Fales, Martha Gandy, 'Stephen Twycross, London Jeweller, and his American Patrons', *Jewellery Studies 6,* 3741, Society of Jewellery Historians, London, 1994.

Federman, David, 'American Diamond Cutting: The Untold Heritage', *Modern Jeweler 84,* No. 1, 33-43. (January 1985).

'Forty Years Ago', *Jewelers' Circular XXIV,* No. 1 (3 February 1892).

Gibbs, M.J., 'Precious Artifacts: Women's Jewelry in the Chesapeaks, 1750-1799', *Journal of Early Southern Decorative Arts,* May 1987, pp. 52-103.

Given, Lois, 'The Great and Stately Palace', *The Pennsylvania Magazine of History and Biography LXXXIII* (July 1959), p. 269.

Gowans, Alan, 'Freemasonry and the neoclassic style in America', The Magazine *Antiques,* February 1960, pp. 172-75.

Hull Grundy, Ann, *Apollo,* October 1959.

Hume, Edgar Erskine, 'General George Washington's Eagle of the Society of the Cincinnati', *The Numismatist XLVI,* No. 12, December 1933, pp. 749-59.

Johnson, J. Stewart, 'Silver in Newark', *The Museum,* New Series, *18,* Nos. 3 and 4, Newark, N.J., 1966.

Kemp, Doris E., 'Whitby Jet', *Lapidary Journal, 40,* May 1968, No. 2, p. 38.

Kunz, George F., *Transactions of the New York Academy of Sciences,* 4 October 1886, New York.

Massachusetts Historical Society *Collections, Series 5, IV,* 502-03; *Proceedings* 72, 436.

Misiorowski, Elise B., and Dirham, Dona M., 'Art Nouveau; Jewels and Jewelers', *Gems & Gemology XXII* (Winter 1986), No. 4, pp. 209-228.

Misiorowski, Elise B., and Hays, Nancy K., 'Jewels of the Edwardians', *Gems & Gemology, 29* (Fall 1993), No. 3, pp. 152-171.

Mount Vernon Ladies' Association of the Union *Annual Report,* Mount Vernon, Virginia, 1980.

Palmer, Arlene M., 'American Heroes in Glass: The Bakewell Sulphide Portraits', *American Art Journal, XI,* No. 1 (January 1979), pp. 4-26.

Proddow, Penny, and Healy, Debra, 'Tiffany's orchids of 1889', The Magazine *Antiques,* April 1988, pp. 900-905.

Robinson, Eric H., 'Problems in the Mechanization and Organization of the Birmingham Jewelry and Silver Trades', *Winterthur Portfolio* 1973, pp. 65-101.

Rudoe, Judy, 'Alessandro Castellani's Letters to Henry Layard: Extracts concerning the 1862 International Exhibition in London and the Revival of Granulation', *Jewellery Studies 5* (1991).

Schluter, Jochen, and Weitschat, Wolfgang, 'Bohemian Garnet – Today', *Gems & Gemology* (Fall 1991), pp. 168-173.

Schofield, Anne, 'Australian Jewellery in the 19th and early 20th century', *The Australian Antique Collector,* Darlinghurst, Australia, 1983.

Suzawa, Gilbert S., 'Seril Dodge: Real Jewelry Industry Pioneer?', *University of Rhode Island Quarterly,* Summer 1979.

Tolman, Ruel P., 'A Document on Hair Painting', The Magazine *Antiques,* March 1930, p. 231.

Tolman, Ruel P., 'Human Hair as a Pigment', The Magazine *Antiques,* December 1925, p. 353.

Trent, Robert F., 'The Charter Oak Artifacts', Connecticut Historical Society *Bulletin 49* (Summer 1984), No. 3, pp. 125-57.

Watson, F.J.B., 'French 18th Century Art in Boston', *Apollo,* December 1969, p. 179.

Wilmerding, John, 'White House Collection of American Paintings', The Magazine *Antiques,* July 1979, p. 137.

Wood, Elizabeth Ingerman, 'Thomas Fletcher, A Philadelphia Entrepreneur of Presentation Silver', *Winterthur Portfolio* 3, Winterthur, Delaware, 1967.

Young, Linda, 'Golden toil / Westralian Digger Brooches', *The Australian Antique Collector,* January-June 1986, Darlinghurst, Australia.

Zapata, Janet, 'The Rediscovery of Paulding Farnham, Tiffany's designer extraordinaire', Part I: Jewelry, The Magazine *Antiques,* March 1991, pp. 556-567.

Zapata, Janet, 'The Islamic Influence in European and American Jewelry', The Magazine *Antiques,* September 1992, pp. 360-369.

Zapata, Janet, 'The Opal', The Magazine *Antiques,* September 1993, pp. 318-327.

MAGAZINES

The Magazine *Antiques,* 1922-1994.

Frank Leslie's Illustrated Newspaper, New York, 1859-1862.

Gleason's Pictorial Drawing Room Companion, 1852-1853.

Godey's Lady's Book and Ladies' American Magazine, Philadelphia, 1840-1870.

Jewellery Studies, Society of Jewellery Historians, London, vols. 1-6, 1983-1993.

The Jeweler's Circular and Horological Review, New York, 1869-1900.

Mme. Demorest's *Monthly Magazine,* 1867.

Revue de la Bijouterie, Joaillerie, Orfèvrerie I, No. 6, October 1900.

Silver, Whittier, California, 1968-1994.

NEWSPAPERS

Boston Gazette, 1738-1772.
Boston News-Letter, 1771-1772.
Columbian Centinel, Boston, 1804-1823.
Federal Gazette, Philadelphia, 1793-1816.
Independent Journal: or the General Advertiser, Philadelphia, 1779-1785.
New-York Gazette & the Weekly Mercury, 1763-1776.
Pennsylvania Gazette, Philadelphia, 1755-1765.
Pennsylvania Journal & Weekly Advertiser, Philadelphia, 1758-1784.
Pennsylvania Packet, Philadelphia, 1785-1799.
Saturday Evening Gazette, Boston, 1876.
Sentinel, Newark, N.J., 1822-1851.
South Carolina Gazette, Charleston, 1741-1794.
Sun, New York, 1875-1889.
Times, New York, 1852-1898.
Transcript [also *Daily Evening Transcript*], Boston, 1840-1881.

COMPILATIONS OF NEWSPAPER ADVERTISEMENTS

Belknap, Henry Wyckoff, *Artists and Craftsmen of Essex County, Massachusette,* Salem, Mass., 1927.
Craig, James H., *The Arts and Crafts in North Carolina 1699-1840,* Winston-Salem, N.C., 1965.
Dow, George Francis, *The Arts and Crafts in New England,* Topsfield, Mass., 1927.
Gottesman, Rita Susswein, *The Arts and Crafts in New York, I* (1726-1776), New York, 1938; *II* (1777-1799), 1954; *III* (1800-1804), 1965.
Prime, Alfred Coxe, *The Arts & Crafts in Philadelphia, Maryland and South Carolina,* First Series, 1721-1785 (The Walpole Society, 1929); Second Series, 1786-1800 (Topsfield, Mass., 1932).
Prime cards, Winterthur Library, Winterthur, Delaware.
Research files, Museum of Early Southern Decorative Arts, Winston-Salem, N.C.

CITY DIRECTORIES

Bibliography of American Directories Through 1860, compiled by Dorothea N. Spear, Worcester, Mass., 1961.
Boston Directory, 1789-1893.
Boston [Almanac & Business] Directory, 1838-1893.
Boyd's Philadelphia City Business Directory, 1876, 1885.
Directory of the City of Newark, 1836-1856.
Johnston's Business and Professional Directory, Philadelphia, 1900.
Maine Register, Portland, Me., 1855-90.
McElroy's Philadelphia City Directory, 1860.
Phillips' Business Directory of New York City, 1891.
Providence Directory, 1824-1900.
San Francisco Directory, 1852-1860.
Trow's New York City Directory, 1861, 1863.
The Trow Business Directory of New York City, 1897.
Wilson's Business Directory of New York City, 1875, 1886.

EXHIBITION CATALOGUES

Benes, Peter, *Charles Delin Port Painter of Maastricht and Amsterdam,* Historical Society of Old Newbury, 1987.

Benes, Peter, *Old-Town and the Waterside,* Two Hundred Years of Tradition and Change in Newbury, Newburyport, and West Newbury, 1635-1835, Newburyport, Mass., 1986.

Bohan, Peter J., *American Gold,* Yale University Art Gallery, 1963.

Bragg, Lillian Chaplin, and Wilder, Cornelia, *Savannah's Antique Hair and Mourning Jewelry,* Savannah, 1945.

Christie's jewelry auction catalogues.

Duval, Cynthia, *Infinite Riches: Jewelry Through the Centuries,* St. Petersburg, Florida, 1889.

Eidelberg, Dr. Martin, *E. Colonna,* essay, The Dayton Art Institute, Dayton, Ohio, 1983.

Essex Institute, *Catalogue of Antique Articles on Exhibition at Plummer Hall,* Salem, Mass., 1875.

Heydt, George Frederic, 'A Glimpse of the Tiffany Exhibit' at the Columbian Exposition, Chicago, *Godey's Magazine,* August 1893, pp. 1-14.

Kaplan, Wendy, *'The Art that is Life': The Arts & Crafts Movement in America, 1875-1920,* Museum of Fine Arts, Boston, Mass., 1987.

Levine, Gilbert, *The Jeweler's Eye,* The Hudson River Museum, New York, 1986.

Lincoln, Louise, *Southwest Indian Silver from the Doneghy Collection,* The Minneapolis Institute of Arts, 1982.

Massachusetts Historical Society Staff, *Witness to America's Past: Two Centuries of Collecting by the Massachusetts Historical Society,* 1991.

Metropolitan Museum of Art, *19th-Century America,* New York, 1970.

Parker, Barbara Neville, ed., comp., *New England Miniatures 1750-1850,* Museum of Fine Arts, Boston, 1957.

Peterson, Harold L., *American Silver Mounted Swords 1700-1815* A Catalog of an Exhibition at the Corcoran Gallery of Art, Washington, D.C., 1955.

Philadelphia Museum of Art, Philadelphia: *Three Centuries of American Art,* Philadelphia, 1976.

Smith, Julia B., 'The Jewelry Industry in Newark', brief survey prepared for an exhibit of Newark-made jewelry at the Newark Museum, 1929.

Sotheby's jewelry auction catalogues.

Sotheby Parke Bernet Inc., 100 *Years of Collecting in America The Story of Sotheby Parke Bernet,* New York, 1984.

Sprague, Laura F., et al., *Agreeable Situations Society, Commerce and Art in Southern Maine, 1780-1830,* The Brick Store Museum, Kennebunk, Me., 1987.

'The Tiffany Display at Paris', *The Art Interchange 44,* No. 5 (May 1900), pp. 112-113.

Vever, M. Henri, Joaillier, 'Rapport', Rapports, *Exposition Internationale de Chicago en 1893,* Comité 24, Bijouterie, Joaillerie, Orfèvrerie; Etats-Unis, pp. 47-76, Paris, 1894.

Walters Art Gallery, *Objects of Adornment* Five Thousand Years of Jewelry from the Walters Art Gallery, Baltimore, New York, 1984.

Warren, David B., Howe, Katherine S., and Brown, Michael K., *Marks of Achievement Four Centuries of American Presentation Silver,* New York, 1987.

TRADE CATALOGUES

Iron & Russell, Providence, R.I., c.1900.

Marsh & Bigney, Illustrated Wholesale Price List, Attleboro, Mass., 1883.

Mermod & Jaccard, St. Louis, Missouri, 1899.

Moore & Evans, Catalogue, Chicago, 1898.
Myers, S.F., New York, N.Y., 1885, 1894.
Romaine, Lawrence B., *A Guide to American Trade Catalogues 1774-1900,* New York, 1990. (Dover Publications Inc. reprint of R.R. Bowker Co., NY 1960 edition).
Steinau, Joseph, & Co., Cincinnati, Ohio, c.1873.
Tiffany, Young & Ellis, *Catalogue of Useful and Fancy Articles,* New York, 1845, reprinted by Tiffany & Co., 1983.
Tiffany & Co., Catalogues, New York, 1878; 1881-2; 1890-91.

ABBREVIATIONS

AAS	American Antiquarian Society
DMMC	Downs Memorial Manuscript Collection
EIHC	Essex Institute *Historical Collections*
GFP	Gardner Family Papers
GIA	Gemological Institute of America
GW	George Washington
JC	*The Jeweler's Circular and Horological Review*
MCNY	Museum of the City of New York
MESDA	Museum of Early Southern Decorative Art
MFA	Museum of Fine Art, Boston
MHS	Massachusetts Historical Society
MMA	Metropolitan Museum of Art
NEHGS	New England Historic Genealogical Society
N-YHS	New York Historical Society
P&C	Palmer & Clapp Design Book
PEM	Peabody Essex Museum
PMA	Philadelphia Museum of Art
PR	Paul Revere Ledgers
SFP	Salisbury Family Papers
SPNEA	Society for the Preservation of New England Antiquities
TA	Tiffany Archives
USMA	United States Military Academy
V & A	Victoria and Albert Museum
WAG	Walters Art Gallery
WM	Winterthur Museum

INDEX

Page references in bold type refer to captions or illustrations

Index